COMPARATIVE LAW CASEBOOK

Stefan Albrecht Riesenfeld

COMPARATIVE LAW CASEBOOK

Professor Stefan A. Riesenfeld
and
Dr. Walter J. Pakter

Transnational Publishers, Inc.
Ardsley, New York

Published and distributed by Transnational Publishers, Inc.
410 Saw Mill River Road
Ardsley, NY 10502, USA

Phone: 914-693-5100
Fax: 914-693-4430
E-mail: info@transnationalpubs.com
Web: www.transnationalpubs.com

Library of Congress Cataloging-in-Publication Data

Riesenfeld, Stefan Albrecht, 1908–
Casebook on comparative law / by Stefan A. Riesenfeld and Walter J. Pakter.
p. cm.
Includes index.
ISBN 1-57105-220-8
1. Comparative law—Cases. I. Pakter, Walter. II. Title

K558 .R54 2001
340'.2—dc21 2001052028

Manufactured in the United States of America

Table of Contents

PART IV: ACQUISITION OF PROPERTY RIGHTS IN MOVABLES OTHER THAN BY TRANSFER FROM THE OWNER: BONA FIDE PURCHASE AND ACQUISITIVE PRESCRIPTION

Preface

Professor Stefan Albrecht Riesenfeld (1908–1999), one of the great jurists of the twentieth century, was at home *inter alia* in bankruptcy, commercial law, international law, legal history and property law, not only from the United States perspective, but from that of Western Europe and South America. His name evokes universal admiration and affection for his up-to-date erudition, his pointed wit and the humanitarian ideals which he instilled in his pupils in many lands. From 1986 until shortly before his death, February 17, 1999, the undersigned assisted Professor Riesenfeld in teaching the Comparative Law Seminar at the School of Law of the University of California, Berkeley (Boalt Hall) and in preparing the materials presented therein.

This Casebook reflects the increasing role of comparative law in modern practice. Despite vast differences in the approaches of various civil law countries, considerable convergence has occurred through legislation and creative decision-making (cf. *infra* p. 249). Part II, *Constitutionalization and Internationalization of Private Rights* and Part III, *Transactions Securing Performance* illustrate this trend. In areas where convergence has been less pronounced, as seen in Part I, *Judicial Organization* and Part IV, *Bona Fide Purchase and Acquisitive Prescription,* courts still reveal a profound interest in foreign law. The study of comparative legal institutions not only places our own law in broader perspective, it facilitates communications with foreign scholars and practitioners worldwide.

Case notes indicate sources for further study. All translations are by the authors. Translations preserve the highly stylized drafting techniques of the original legislation and decisional law. Omissions are indicated by three asterisks (* * *). Footnotes have been renumbered consecutively for each chapter. Internal page numbers have been provided for some lengthy decisions in order to facilitate examination of the original text.

The authors are indebted to Thomas H. Reynolds, Librarian for Civil law and the entire staff of the Boalt Hall Law Library for their indefatigable assistance over the years in locating materials, and to Transnational Publishers for its skill in preparing this volume.

Walter J. Pakter, PhD., D.Phil. (Oxon.), LL.M. (Berk.)
Attorney at Law

PART I

Judicial Organization and Sources of Law

1/Judicial Organization

A. FRANCE

1. The French Constitution

The French Constitution of 1958 was amended four times between 1992 and 1995. The first of these amendments occurred with the enactment of Constitutional Law No. 92-554 of June 25, 1992,[1] passed to permit the ratification of the Treaty of Maastricht. It amended Articles 2, 54 and 74 of the Constitution and added a new Title XIV, consisting of Arts. 88-1, 88-2, 88-3 and 88-4, entitled 'Of the European Communities and the European Union.'

The next amendment was by way of Constitutional Law No. 93952 of March 27, 1994, modifying Titles VIII, IX, X and XVI of the Constitution. It contained a reform of the *Conseil Supérieur de la Magistrature* (Superior Council of the Court Officers) and the creation of the *Cour de Justice de la République*. Its objective was to strengthen the independence of the judiciary and the other officials charged with the administration of justice and to institute a judicial body with jurisdiction over criminal offenses committed by members of the Government in the exercise of their functions.[2] This Constitutional Law was the result and the remnant of a major constitutional revision that had been initiated in 1992.

On November 10, 1991, President Mitterand announced that before his term of office ended, he would submit to Parliament and the French people the modifications of the public institutions he deemed to be necessary. In pursuance of this intent, on November 30, 1992, he published the text of his proposals for a revision of the Constitution declaring it to be their aim 'to assure a better balance of the powers of Gov-

---

1. 66 La Semaine Juridique [JCP] (éd. G.) 1992 III 65559.

2. See Nguyen Van Tuong, *La reforme du Conseil supérieur de la magistrature et la création de la Cour de justice de la République*, 67 JCP (éd. G.) I 3703 (1993).

ernment, to improve the guarantees of the independence of the judicial officials, and to reinforce the rights of citizens.'

To examine the desirability and sufficiency of his proposals, he appointed a Committee of consultants under the chairmanship of Dean George Vedel which was to and did render its report on February 15, 1993. The report of the Consultative Committee on the revision of the Constitution was published in the Journal Officiel of February 16, 1993. It was deliberated by the Council of Ministers on March 10, 1993. The Council approved of the majority of the amendments recommended by the Vedel Committee and organized them into two proposals of constitutional laws, numbered Nos. 231 and 232 which were introduced in the Senate on the following day. The first dealt with the guarantees and rights of the citizens and the organs protecting them; the second was concerned with the organization and functions of and the balance between the governmental institutions. The intervening elections shifted the powers between the political parties, initiating the so-called cohabitation period. The new Baladur Government informed the Parliament, sitting as constitutional congress (Const. Art. 89), that for the time being, it endorsed only the first of the two bills. It passed on July 27, 1993 by a large majority, but not without being truncated considerably. Eliminated were the proposals for post-promulgation review of the constitutionality of laws — which was quickly done by the two assemblies with the blessing of the Government[3] — and the proposal to insert in Art. 1 of the Constitution an express provision to the effect that 'everyone has a right to respect for his private life and his personal dignity.'[4]

The third Constitutional amendment was enacted on November 13, 1993 to modify the constitutional provisions on the law of asylum.[5] As a result, many French authors have deplored that France still falls short of being an *État de Droit.*[6]

The fourth constitutional amendment was enacted, after the election of the new president, in the form of the Constitutional Law Nr. 95-880 of August 4, 1985 'extending the scope of the applicability of the referendum, instituting a single ordinary parliamentary session, modifying the regime of the immunity of members of parliament and abolishing the provision relating to the French Community (reprinted in D. lég. 403 (1995)). The new provision on the referendum (Const. Art. 11) added '*projects of laws relating to the economic or social policy of the nation and the public services associated therewith*' to the original subjects and mandated opportunity of input by each of the two houses of Parliament in the organization of a referendum proposed by the government. On the political and legal implications of this reform, see the

3. see Nguyen Van Tuong, op. cit. at ftn. 2.

4. Th. S. Renoux, *Si le grain ne meurt...* in *La Révision de la Constitution de 1958,* [1993] Revue française de Droit constitutionnel No. 14, 271 at 283.

5. see Luchaire, *Le droit d'asil et la révision de la Constitution,* [1994] Revue de droit public 5-43.

6. M. Arneller, *Le Comité consultatif pour la révision de la Constitution et le Parlement* [1993], Revue française de droit constitutionnel Nr. 14, p. 258, at 261; E. Desmons, *Révision Constitutionnelle, Justice constitutionnelle et État de droit,* Les Petites Affiches No. 143, p. 21. (1994).

comments by M. Viviano, *La révision constitutionnelle de 1995: Nouveau renforcement de l'exécutif*, Les Petites Affiches No. 123 p. 4 (1995).

2. The French Judicial System

The basic features of the French judicial organization were established by Napoleon I. It distinguished between jurisdiction in civil, criminal and commercial matters and jurisdiction over administrative disputes. Jurisdiction over civil, criminal and commercial matters was attributed to various types of lower courts and to a highest court, called *Cour de Cassation* (Court of Cassation). Jurisdiction over administrative controversies was attributed to a central governmental body called the *Conseil d'État* (Council of State), which gradually developed a special division in charge of adjudication of legal controversies involving administrative actions claimed to be illegal.[7]

a. Organization of French courts, other than administrative courts.

The organization and jurisdiction of the courts for civil, commercial and criminal matters is governed by the Code of Judicial Organization.[8] The Code is merely a consolidation of legislative and executive texts and therefore is divided in legislative (*L*) and regulatory (*R*) provisions. Procedures in these courts is governed by separate codes or statutes, in particular the New Code of Civil Procedure[9] and the Code of Criminal Procedure.[10]

1) Courts of First Instance.

The courts of first instance are (i) the *tribunaux de grande instance* (ii) *tribunaux d'instance* and (iii) specialized tribunals. By far the most important court of first instance is the *tribunal de grande instance,* which has general jurisdiction of first in-

7. See S. Riesenfeld, *The French System of Administrative Justice,* 18 Boston University L. R. 48 *et seq.*, 400 *et seq.*, 715 *et seq.* (1938).

8. *Code de l'organisation judiciaire* [*C. org. jud.*], promulgated by Decrees 78-329 and 78- 330, March 16, 1978 as amended.

9. The Code of Civil Procedure was completely revised by a series of decrees, in particular Decree Nr. 75-1123 of December 5, 1975, establishing a New Code of Civil Procedure [Nouv. C. pr. civ.], and Decree Nr. 81-500 of May 12, 1981, establishing the provisions of Books III and IV of the New Code and amending certain provisions of the Code.

Other amendments were made from time to time, such as Art. 1031-1 Nouv. C. pr. civ. introducing a procedure for the exercise by the Cour de Cassation of its new jurisdiction to render advisory opinions. [Decree Nr. 92-228 of March 12, 1992].) *See* infra n. 18.

One of the most recent revisions concerns the enforcement of judgments. Bk. 5 of the old Code (entitled *Of the execution of judgments*) was replaced by a new law enacted in 1991, Law Nr. 91-650 of July 9, 1991, reforming the civil procedures of execution. It was implemented by Decree Nr. 92-755 of July 31, 1992 and went into force on January 1, 1993.

10. Art. 398-1 Code of Criminal Procedure (*Code de Procédure pénale [C.PR.PÉN.]*).

stance (C.org.jud. Arts. L.311-1 to L.311-15 and R.311-1 to R.311-38.) There are 181 *tribunaux de grande instance,* some of which are composed of a large number of judges. Ordinarily, judgments are rendered by panels of 3 judges, with the result that each tribunal has at least 3 judges. The *tribunaux d'instance* have jurisdiction over controversies below a monetary ceiling. Among the specialized tribunals, the commercial tribunals are of general interest.

Criminal jurisdiction is exercised by *tribunaux de police* (Arts. 521-523 *C.PR.PÉN.*), *tribunaux correctionnels* (Arts. 496 et seq. C.PR. PÉN.) and *cours d'assises* (Arts. 231 et seq. C.PR.PÉN.). Criminal courts normally consist of three judges, but since 1995 certain minor infractions punishable by up to 5 years of imprisonment are heard by a single judge.[11]

2) *Appellate Courts*

The principal courts of appeal dealing with civil, commercial and criminal matters are the *Cours d'Appel.* Their organization and functions are governed by the Code of Judicial Organization, Arts. L. 211-1, 212-1, 212-2 and 213-1 *et seq.*, and Art. R. 211-1, R. 212-1 *et s.* and the New Code of Civil Procedure (*Nouveau Code de procédure civile* [*Nouv.C.pr.civ.*] Art. 496.) The court is divided into a number of chambers. It is composed of the first president, presidents of the chambers, and councillors. A panel must comprise at least 3 judges to render a judgment.

There are 35 courts of appeal, of which 30 have their seat in metropolitan France including Corsica. Details are regulated by decrees of the Council of State.

3) *The Court of Last Resort: Court of Cassation (*Cour de Cassation*)*

(a) *History*

The history of the Court of Cassation spans 200 years. It was established under the name Tribunal de Cassation by a statute of November 27 and December 1, 1790. It was composed of 42 judges. It was renamed *Cour de Cassation* by a senatus consultum of 28 floréal of the year XII (May 18, 1804), establishing the Empire. Its organization and functioning varied in the course of time.

A major reorganization occurred in 1947 by the decree of July 23, 1947[12] which eliminated the preliminary examination by a panel called the *Chambre des Requêtes* and established additional civil 'chambers' and a super-panel called an *assemblée plénière* (full bench).

---

11. Art. 398-1 *C.PR.PÉN.* N. Stolowy, *Un juge unique pour le tribunal correctionnel, Les Petites Affiches* October 13, 1995 No. 123 p. 9. Pre-1995 cases are collected in Jean Pradel & André Varinard, *Les Grands arrêts du droit criminel II Le Procès* (1994).

12. D. 275 (1947).

(b) Present Organization

The present organization and types of adjudicatory composition of the Court of Cassation is governed by the Code of Judicial Organization.[13] It is composed of:

The First President (*Le premier président*)
Chamber presidents (*présidents de chambre*),
Councillors (*conseillers*),
Adjunct Councillors (*conseillers référendaires*),
The Attorney General (*procureur général*),
The First Advocate General (*Le premier avocat général*),
Advocates General (*avocats généraux*),
The Chief Clerk,
Clerk of the Chambers.

The total number of councillors (in addition to the First President and the Chamber Presidents) varies from time to time. At present the court is composed of 1 First President, 6 Chamber Presidents, 85 Councillors, 2 Councilors in Extraordinary service, 16 Adjunct Councillors belonging to the second group of the first grade and 27 Adjunct Councillors belonging to the second grade. In addition there are 1 Attorney General, 1 First Advocate General and 22 Advocates General.[14]

(c) Plenary Sessions

The Court of Cassation is divided into 6 chambers. It adjudicates recourses sitting as one of the six chambers, or forming a 'mixed chamber' (*chambre mixte*), or as the 'full bench' (*assemblée plénière*). At present, the Court is composed of one criminal chamber and five civil chambers which are in turn specialized: 3 chambers dealing with civil controversies, 1 dealing with commercial and financial matters and 1 dealing with social matters, such as labor, social security, workers compensation and family allowances.

Because the Court of Cassation had no control over its docket, the five Civil Chambers and the Criminal Chambers of the Court were hopelessly overburdened. Various reforms to alleviate the situations were discussed. Ultimately Parliament enacted Law nr. 97-395 of April 23, 1997 relating to the examination of petitions for review by the Court of Cassation.[15] This Statute reduced the number of judges normally required for the adjudication of a case.

While prior to that legislation ordinarily a minimum of five judges belonging to one of the five civil chambers was required for the adjudication of a petition and a

---

13. C. org. jud. Arts. L.111-1 to 111-4, Arts. L.121-1 to 121-6, Arts. L.131-1 to 131-7 and Arts. R.121-1 to R.121-7 and R.131-1 to R.131-20.

14. Decree 96-482, of May 31, 1996, *D. lég.* 260 (1996).

15. 117 Gazette du Palais 318 (1997).

minimum of three judges sufficed only by way of exception in simple cases, with the consent of the parties, the new law reversed the situation. According to Articles 2 and 3 of the new statute, the Code of Judicial Organization, Art. L. 131-6 is amended and supplemented by a new Article L. 131-6-1 providing that petitions for review are passed upon by a panel of three judges, if the case presents no difficulties and that panels composed of a minimum of five judges are required only if the three-judge panel refers the cases to chamber or if the President of the Court or the Chamber president orders such disposition ex officio or upon request of the Attorney General or one of the parties.

In addition, the new Statute Art. 1 reduced the number of judges constituting the Full Assembly (*l'assemblée plénière*) of the Court by amending Art. L. 121-6 of the Code of Judicial Organization.

The *Mixed Chamber* has jurisdiction over controversies which are allocated to several civil chambers and which may lead to disagreement among chambers or when there is no majority vote in a chamber. The mixed chamber is composed of judges belonging to at least 3 chambers, viz. of the First President, the presidents and deans (most senior judge) of each chamber and two councillors of each chamber, i.e., at least 10 judges. (Art. L.121-5 C. org. jud.).

The *Assemblée Plénière* is convoked if a matter poses an issue of principle, especially if there is a conflict between the lower courts and the Court of Cassation or if a court of appeal to which a controversy was remanded renders a judgment which is again attacked for the same reasons. The *assemblée plénière* comprises the First President, the presidents and most senior judge of the chambers and one councillor of each chamber, i.e., 19 judges.[16]

(d) Decisions on the Merits

Until 1979 the Court of Cassation was a court of error, without jurisdiction over the merits. In other words, the court could not render a judgment on the merits; it could only vacate the judgment of the court of appeal and remand the case either to another court of appeal or to other judges of the court below.

Since that time, however, it may dismiss a case for lack of jurisdiction of the French courts or dismiss the case on the merits if the facts found by the court below permit such disposition. (Art. L.131-5 C. org. jud.; Art. 627 Nouv.C.pr.civ.).

The jurisdiction of the Court of Cassation is invoked by means of a pleading called '*pourvoi*' (writ of error) or more specifically '*pourvoi en cassation*' (recourse for vacating). The request must contain assignments of errors (*moyens*), the drafting of which is actually a special art. These assignments may be subdivided into branches. The court disposes of each assignment submitted unless it deems such response un-

---

16. A. Perdriau, *La Chambre mixte et l'assemblée plénière de la Cour de Cassation*, 68 J.C.P. I 3798 (p. 465) (1994).

necessary.[17] As a result, the judgments of the court are both terse and highly structured.

(e) Advisory jurisdiction.

By an amendment of the *Code of Judicial Organization* of May 15, 1991[18] the Court of Cassation was vested with jurisdiction to render advisory opinions upon a question submitted to it by a court of ordinary jurisdiction in non-criminal cases raising a novel question of serious difficulty arising in a number of controversies. The opinion of the Court of Cassation, which is called an advice (*avis,*) rather than a judgment (*arrêt*), is not binding on the court which formulates the question.

In exercising this jurisdiction, the Court is composed of the First President, the chamber presidents and 2 councillors designated by each chamber especially concerned.[19] The Attorney General (*procureur général*) or an advocate general represents the view of the government.[20]

The advisory opinions of the Court, along with the judgments of the full assemblies, the *chambres mixtes* and of the five civil chambers are published in the *Bulletin des arrêts de la Cour de Cassation, Chambres Civiles.*

(f) Deliberations of the Court of Cassation

In the Court of Cassation, deliberations are prepared by the report of a designated member of the bench, the '*juge rapporteur*' (Art. 1012 Nouv.C.pr.civ.), which is delivered at a meeting of the judges (Art. 1017 Nouv.C.pr.civ.). In addition, the bench hears the submission of the advocate general, who in important cases may be the attorney general him- or herself. The redaction of a judgment is stylized and succinct. In some cases the text of the reports of the *juge rapporteur* or of the submissions of the advocates general is published and reveals the precedents and literature upon which the judgment was actually based.

(g) Cassation under the New Code of Civil Procedure

In addition to provisions on the operation of the Court of Cassation contained in the Code of Judicial Organization, Art. L. 111-1 to L. 153-3, and R. 121-1 to R. 151-1, the jurisdiction of the Court of Cassation and the procedures to engage the jurisdiction of the Court are governed by the New Code of Civil Procedure, in particular,

---

17. For details see Boré, *La Cassation en Matière Civile* sec. 3309-18 (1988).

18. Art. 1031-1 Nouv. C. pr. civ. Law no. 91-491 of May 15, 1991 modifying the Code of Judicial Organization and instituting the request to the Court of Cassation for advice, implemented by Decree no. 92-228 of March 12, 1992.

19. Code of Judicial Organization, new title V Arts. L.151-1 to 151.3.

20. The new law is discussed in A.- M. Morgan de Rivery-Guillaud, *La saisine pour avis de la Cour de cassation,* 66 J.C.P. Doctrine, Nr. 3576 (1992).

Arts. 527, 604-639, 1031-1 to 1031-7 and 1032 to 1037. Generally speaking, Art. 605 Nouv.C. pr. Civ. provides that the petition for annulment is available only against the judgments of last resort. It does not matter whether the judgment disposes of all or some part of the controversy.

Ordinarily, the petition for annulment concerns defects of a particular judgment, but according to New Code of Civil Procedure Art. 617 and 618, the inconsistency of a junior judgment with a senior judgment may also be a ground for annulment if the judge below ignored the plea of res judicata or neither of the two inconsistent judgments was subject to appeal, though not rendered in last resort.

An example of the applicability of Art. 617 is the case of *Laurent v. Bolcioni*, Court of Cassation (Comm. Ch.), Judgment of November 19, 1996, *Petites Affiches*, July 7, 1997 p. 16. In that case, the Tribunal of Commerce of Paris, by Judgment of April 28, 1988, dismissed a petition for opening insolvency proceedings against the Société G.E.T.E. for the reason that its cessation of payments had not been proven. Subsequently, on October 17, 1988, the Tribunal opened insolvency proceedings against Société G.E.T.E. and fixed the date of cessation of payments as April 17, 1988.

By Judgment of October 13, 1992, the Court of Appeal of Paris pronounced the personal bankruptcy of the manager and director of G.E.T.E., M. Laurent, for the reason that he had failed to declare the cessation of payments of G.E.T.E. as required by law, on the basis of the French Insolvency Act of 1985, Art. 189(5). M. Laurent claimed that the imposition of personal bankruptcy because of his failure to declare the cessation of payments within 15 days after April 17, 1988, although the tribunal by Judgment of April 28, 1988 had found that G.E.T.E. was not in the state of cessation of payments at that date, entitled him to an annulment of the Judgment of the Court of Appeal of Paris pursuant to Article 617 of the N.C.C.P.

The Court of Cassation (Comm. Ch.) rejected the petition holding that the Court of Appeal, in considering April 17, 1987 as the date of the cessation of payments was not bound by the last judgment of the Tribunal and that therefore there existed no inconsistency of judgments within the meaning of Art. 617.

A case involving Art. 618 is set out in full *infra*.

b. Constitutional Council (Conseil Constitutionnel).

The Court of Cassation is not empowered to declare a statute which has been enacted and promulgated to be unconstitutional. A special judicial body, called the Constitutional Council (*Conseil constitutionnel*), is charged with review of the constitutionality of legislation before its promulgation.

The composition and jurisdiction of the Conseil constitutionnel is governed by the French Constitution of 1958.[21] The Council consists of nine members appointed

---

21. French Constitution of 1958 Arts. 56-63, as amended by Constitutional Law 74-904 of Oct. 20, 1974, and implemented by Ordonnance nr. 58-1067 of Nov. 7, 1958, enacting the organic law of the Council.

for a term of nine years of whom three are appointed by the President of the Republic, three by the President of the National Assembly, and three by the President of the Senate. In addition, the former presidents of the Republic are life members. The president of the Council is nominated by the President of the Republic. His vote prevails if the vote is split equally.

The Constitutional Council must pass on the constitutionality of so-called organic laws and the parliamentary rules of procedure and may be called upon to review of the constitutionality of simple laws, including laws approving the ratification of treaties, if such review is requested by the President of the Republic, the Prime Minister, the President of the Assembly, the President of the Senate or sixty deputies or sixty senators.

In its decision of July 16, 1996 (N.º 96-377), D. Jur. 69 (1997), the Constitutional Council was asked by the requisite number of legislators (senators or deputies) to pass on the constitutionality of the not yet promulgated law aiming at the strengthening of the repression of terrorism and of attacks on persons vested with public authority. The new law amended Art. 421-1 of the Penal Code by adding to the list of acts of terrorism acts with the aim of gravely disturbing the public order by aiding the irregular entry, circulation or stay of an alien as defined in Article 21 of the Ordinance Nº. 45-2658 of November 2, 1945. The request of the legislators asserted many grounds for the unconstitutionality of the new legislation but also questioned the constitutionality of Art. 21 of the Ordinance of 1945 itself.

In that respect, the Constitutional Council found the constitutional challenges to be groundless, but before reaching that conclusion the Constitutional Council noted:

> "10. — Considering in the first place, that the conformity of a law already promulgated may effectively be contested on the occasion of a submission to the Constitutional Council of legislative provisions which modify, complete or alter the scope of the same; that the law submitted to the Council has the object in its Art. 25 to limit the scope of the applicability of Art. 21 of the Ordinance of November 2, of 1945; that therefore the Council has to examine the constitutionality of that provision and to pass on the objections analyzed below:"

c. *Administrative Courts*

1) *History*

Judicial control of administrative acts was withdrawn from the regular courts during the French Revolution and entrusted to the *Conseil d' Etat* (Council of State), a body created by the constitution of November 15, 1799 (22 Frimaire An VIII), art. 52 by decree of June 11, 1806, which established a special litigation commission (*commission du contentieux*) within the Council. The Council of State remained the principal body charged with the adjudication of controversies involving administrative acts for a century and a half. A statute of May 24, 1872 reconfirmed this role.[22]

A reorganization of administrative justice in 1953 (Decree nr. 53-934 of September 30, 1953) created administrative tribunals in metropolitan France, Corsica and the overseas territories of various types. Because of the unmanageable case load of the Council of State, Law nr. 87-1127 of December 31, 1987 created 5 intermediate courts of appeal, having cognizance of appeals from the judgments of the administrative tribunals falling within their jurisdiction.[23]

2) Present Organization

In 1997, Decree nr. 97-457 of May 9, 1997 created a sixth administrative court of appeal in Marseille, in addition to the other administrative courts of appeal, with seats in Bordeaux, Lyon, Nancy, Nantes and Paris and vested each of them with appellate jurisdiction over specified administrative tribunals operating in metropolitan France (26), Corsica (1) and the overseas territories of various types (8).

The composition and procedure before these courts is governed by the *Code des Tribunaux administratifs et Cours administratives d'appel* of 1989[24], as amended. As all modern French codifications, the Code consists of a legislative and regulatory portion, the latter dealing primarily with the procedure before these bodies. The legislative portion of the Code is based on the law of 87-1127 of December 31, 1987 on the reform of administrative litigation[25], as most recently amended by the Law nr. 97-276 of March 25, 1997;[26] the regulatory part codifies the decrees governing the procedure before the administrative tribunals and administrative courts of appeal,[27] as last amended by Decree nr. 97-563 of May 29, 1997, concerning the functioning of the administrative tribunals and administrative courts of appeal and the procedure before these jurisdictions and amending the Code of the administrative tribunals and courts of appeal.[28]

Although the administrative judges are not members of the judiciary, their independence is guaranteed by a number of legislative enactments, in particular by the Law nr. 86-114 of January 6, 1986, establishing the rules guaranteeing the indepen-

22. Important presentations of the history of the *Conseil d' Etat* are *Le Conseil d' Etat, Livre jubilaire, publié pour commémorer son cent cinquantième anniversaire, 4 nivôse an VIII/24 December 1799 (1952)* and *Le Conseil d' Etat, son histoire à travers les documents d'époque* 1799-1974 (1974)

23. See J. Rivero & J. Waline, Droit Administratif (14 ed. 1992) pp. 156-175.

24. Cf C. Gabolde, *Le nouveau code des tribunaux administratifs et des cours administratives d'appel,* D.chron. 11 (1990).

25. Cit. supra at n. 23.

26. Law Containing status rules relating to the staffs of the administrative tribunals and administrative courts of appeal. Articles 9 and 10 D. Lég.207 (1997).

27. Codified by Decree nr. 89-641 of September 7, 1989 reproduced in Ch. Huglo & C. Lepage-Jessua, *Codes des procédures administratives contentieuses* (Paris: Litec 1989) 709.

28. 71 JCP III Nr. 68470 (p.61) (1997).

dence of the members of the administrative tribunals,[29] as last amended by the Law Nr. 97-276 of March 25, 1997, enacting status rules with respect to the staff of administrative tribunals and administrative courts of appeal,[30] implemented by Decree nr. 97-859 of November 18, 1997 on the status of the members of the administrative tribunals and the administrative courts of appeal.[31]

3) The Council of State: Composition and Functions

The organization of the Council of State and its membership have undergone many changes during its long history. At present the *Conseil d'Etat* is composed of five administrative sections, one of which is called the Section of the Report and Studies, and one adjudicatory or litigation section (*section du contentieux*). The four administrative sections, other than the Section of the Report and Studies, are designated as Section for the Interior, Section for Finance, Section for Public Works and Social Section. Matters falling within the jurisdiction of the various ministries are distributed among these four sections according to an order issued by the prime Minister upon proposal by the Keeper of the Seals, Minister of Justice, Decree nr. 63-766 of July 30, 1963 on the organization and functioning of the Council of State, Art. 9. For a recent order of that kind, see Order (*arrêté*) of May 22, 1997 distributing the affairs among the administrative sections of the Council of State.[32]

The Council of State is a large organization. Its formal head is the Prime Minister and in his or her absence the Minister of Justice. Its actual head is the vice-president. The personnel of the Council of State constitutes a hierarchal system composed of (i) the vice-president, (ii) the section presidents, (iii) councilors of State in regular service and councilors of State in extra-ordinary service, (iv) masters of petitions (*maîtres des requêtes*), (v) auditors of the first class and (vi) auditors of the second class, recruited from high-ranking graduates of the national school of administration.

The number of councilors of State, masters of petitions and auditors has varied over the years. Currently, the number of officials attached to the Council of State is approximately 275, depending upon recruitment, promotion, compulsory retirement, death and resignations. In 1988, e.g. the Council of State included the vice-president, six section presidents, one hundred and one councilors of State in regular service, twelve councilors of State in extra-ordinary service, one hundred and thirteen masters of petitions, and twenty-four auditors (263 officials).[33]

---

29. D. Lég. 167, implemented by Decree nr. 87-554 of July 17, 1987 on the Superior Council of the administrative tribunals.
30. 117 Gazette du Palais Lég. 267 (1997); D. Lég. 207 (1997).
31. 71 JCP Part III nr. 68546 (1997).
32. 117 Gaz. du Palais, Lég. p. 500 (1997).
33. G. Braibant, Le droit administratif français, 2d. ed 1988, p. 462.

4) The Litigation Section

The Litigation Section of the Council of State performs the role of the highest French administrative court. It functions primarily, but not exclusively, as court of cassation. It is the most numerous section of the Council of State, but some of its members serve at the same time in one or more of the sections of the Council. The Litigation Section is comprised of the president of the section, three adjunct presidents, ten councilors of State in regular service, serving as presidents of the section's ten subsections, twenty councilors of State in regular service, serving as associate judges of the subsection, and additional councilors of State in regular service, masters of petitions and auditors, all in all more than one hundred officials.

The whole of the Litigation Section never sits as a bench. The adjudicatory functions are performed by a single subsection, two or more united subsections, the litigation section sitting as an adjudicatory panel, or the adjudicatory or litigation assembly (*assemblée du contentieux*).

The Litigation (or Adjudicatory) section sitting as a judicial panel is composed of the president of the section, its three adjunct presidents, the presidents of its ten subsections, the reporting judge and two councilors of State in regular service primarily attached to administrative sections, a total of 17 judges.

The Litigation Assembly which constitutes the most authoritative judicial formation consists of the vice-president of the Council of State, the president and the three adjunct presidents of the Litigation Section, the president of the sub-section in charge of the controversy, the reporting judge and the presidents of the five administrative sections, i.e. a twelve-member bench.

Judgments of the adjudicatory (litigation) assembly and of the litigation section sitting as panel are exceptions. Most cases are handled by united subsections.

The procedure employed by the adjudicatory formations is governed by the Decree nr. 63-766 of July 30, 1963 on the organization and functioning of the Council of State, as amended in particular by the Decrees nr. 88-905 of Sept. 2, 1988 and nr. 97-177 of December 24, 1997 (D. 1988, lég. p. 414 and D. 1997 lég. p. 26). In addition to the arguments of the parties, the bench is advised by the reporting judge and a commissioner of the government (*commissaire du gouvernment*) who represents the public interest similar to the *avocat général* in the Court of Cassation. The commissioner of the government is usually selected from the masters of petitions.

In addition to its adjudicatory jurisdiction, the Litigation Section, since 1988, is vested with advisory jurisdiction over questions of a seriously difficult and repetitive nature arising in controversies pending before the lower administrative tribunals or courts.[34]

Although the members of the administrative tribunals and administrative courts of appeal are not members of the judiciary in the constitutional sense their independence is assured by the Law nr. 86-14 of January 6, 1986, establishing the rules guar-

34. Law nr. 87-1127 of December 31, 1987, Art. 12.

anteeing the independence of the members of the administrative tribunals and the administrative courts of appeal, as amended by the law nr. 97-226 of March 25, 1997 on the status of the membership of the administrative tribunals and administrative courts of appeal. Similar rules tend to assure the independence of the members of the Council of State[35]

The judgments of the adjudicatory sections of the Council of State and occasionally the opinions of the commissioners of the government or the reports of the reporting judges are published in the professional periodicals. A special collection of the decisions of the Council of State, the Recueil Lebon (1821–1996) ceased to appear in 1996.

d. The Court for the Resolution of Jurisdictional Conflicts (Tribunal des Conflits)

The bifurcation of jurisdiction over controversies into two branches, (i) civil and criminal on the one hand and (ii) administrative on the other, necessitated the creation, in 1872, of a special court for the resolution of jurisdictional conflicts between the two branches, called *Tribunal des conflits.* It consists of three councilors of the Court of Cassation and three councilors of State in regular service together with Minister of Justice as president plus two further judges, usually one from the Council of State and one from the Court of Cassation, selected by the other seven judges.

The Court only resolves jurisdictional disputes. It may not settle substantive differences of opinion between the Court of Cassation and the Council of State on other issues, thus leaving important questions *in limbo,* often for decades.

3. Legislation.

a. **Code of Judicial Organization (*Code de l'organisation judiciaire* [*C. org. jud.*])**

Art. L. 121-4. C. org. jud.

The judgments of the Court of Cassation are rendered either by one of the chambers or by a mixed chamber or by the full assembly.

* * *

Art. L. 121-5. C. org. jud.

If a mixed chamber is constituted pursuant to Arts. L. 131-2 and 131-3, it is composed of judges belonging to at least three chambers of the court. The mixed chamber is presided over by the First President or if he is unavailable by the most senior chamber president. In addition, it comprises the presidents and deans of the chambers which compose the same and two councillors of each of these chambers.

35. Cf. J. Rivero & J. Waline, Droit administratif (14 ed. 1992) p. 165, nr. 196.

Art. L. 121-6 C. org. jud.

The full assembly is presided over by the first president or if he is unavailable by the most senior chamber president. In addition, it comprises the presidents and deans of each chamber as well as two councillors of each chamber.

Art. L. 131-2 C. org. jud.

A transfer to a mixed chamber may be ordered when the controversy involves an issue which normally belongs to the subjects attributed to several chambers either if the issue has received or is apt to receive divergent solutions by the chambers; it must be transferred if the votes are split equally.

The referral to the full assembly may be ordered when the controversy poses an issue of principle particularly if there exist different solutions among the lower courts or between the lower courts and the Court of Cassation. It must be so referred if, after a first judgment or order was vacated, the judgment of the court of remand is attacked for the same reasons. * * *

Art. L. 132-1 C. org. jud.

The Attorney General delivers his speech at the hearings of the mixed chambers and the full assembly as well as at the general meetings of the Court. He also states his opinion before the chambers and the formation of the Court for the delivery of advisory opinions when he deems it to be appropriate.

Art. L. 132-2 C. org. jud.

If the Attorney General is prevented from appearing, he is replaced in the exercise of his functions by the First Advocate General or, if unavailable, by an Advocate General designated by the Attorney General.

Art. L. 132-3 C. org. jud.

The Advocates General deliver their opinions in the name of the Attorney General, before the chambers to which they are attached.

They may be designated by the Attorney General to appear also before the other formations of the Court.

Art. L. 151-1. C. org. jud.

Before ruling on a complaint raising a new question of law, presenting a serious difficulty and occurring in numerous cases, courts of the judicial system may, by a decision not subject to review, seek an opinion from the Court of Cassation, which shall announce its opinion within three months of the petition.

Any further decision on the merits of the case shall be suspended until the opinion of the Court of Cassation, or, in the absence of one, until the expiration of the abovementioned period. However, emergency or conservatory measures may be taken.

The opinion rendered does not bind the court which submitted the request. It shall be communicated to the parties.

The provisions of the present article are not applicable in criminal matters.

b. New Code of Civil Procedure (*Nouveau Code de procédure civile* [*N.C.pr.civ.*])

Art. 1012 N.C.pr.civ

The president of the panel to which the controversy is assigned designates a councillor or adjunct councillor of that panel to act as Reporting Judge.

Art. 1019 N.C.pr.civ

The Court of Cassation renders its decision following the opinion of the office of the public attorney (*ministère public*).

4. Cases and Notes

THE FRENCH COURTS IN OPERATION

a. The Chaumet Jewels

Court of Cassation (Full Assembly)
Judgment of November 29, 1996
Sté Chaumet et al. c. S.A. Béhar
71 *La Semaine Juridique* [=J.C.P.] (Gen. ed.), 1997, Nr. 22807.

The Court — Upon the Motion to reject the petition for review interposed by the defendant and upon the only assignment of error:

On the basis of Art. 4 of the Civil Code;

Considering that the petition for review directed against two decisions of which one emanates from a criminal law court and the other from a civil law court, is admissible because, although not rendered in the last instance, both of them are not susceptible to an ordinary remedy, are irreconcilable and entail a denial of justice;

Considering that by Order of July 17, 1990, which has become final, the delegate judge in the judicial reorganization of the Société Chaumet pending in the Commercial Court of Paris has rejected the action for restitution of a set of jewels instituted by the Société Claude Béhar; that by a Judgment of May 26, 1995, which has become final, the correctional chamber of the Court of Appeal of Paris has ordered the restitution to the Société Claude Béhar of this set of jewels which had been seized by the investigating judge;

That these two irreconcilable judgments must be annulled to permit remand to a court to issue a new decision.

For these reasons:

Declares the petition for review admissible;

Annuls the Order of the judge delegate of July 17, 1990 and the Judgment of the Court of Appeal of May 26, 1993 in its holding ordering the restitution to the Société Claude Béhar of the set of Jewels placed under seal Nr. 8 and for a new adjudication remands the parties to the Correctional Chamber of the Court of Appeal of Paris in another composition.

Messrs. Truche, First President; Le Gunehec, Bézard, Beauvois, Zakine, Lemontey, Gélineau-Larrivet, Pres., Mme Aubert, Cons. Rapp., Mr. Monnet, Av. Gén.

Appendix

France, Civil Code Art. 4

The judge who refuses to deliver a judgment under the pretext of the silence, the obscurity or the inadequacy of the law may be prosecuted as guilty of the denial of justice.

France, New Code of Civil Procedure Art. 618

The inconsistency of judgments may, in derogation of Art. 605, also be invoked, if two decisions, even if not rendered by courts of last instance, are irreconcilable and none of them are subject to an ordinary remedy; the petition for review is admissible even if one of them was already subject to a petition for review and the same was rejected.

NOTE

The judgment is commented upon by Professor Thierry Le Bars in 71 *La Semaine Juridique* [J.C.P.] II 22807 (March 19, 1997). The annotation relates further details of the facts and comments on the legal basis of the Judgment of the Assemblée plénière. We learn that the jewels were originally deposited in May 1986 by the Société Claude Béhar with the Société Chaumet, Geneva. They were "sold" by letter to the Société Chaumet, Brussels, which in turn ceded them to the Parisian parent corporation, Société Chaumet et Cie. In 1987, the brothers Chaumet and their partnership were placed in judicial insolvency proceedings. In addition, the brothers Chaumet were accused of certain economic crimes, but not of offenses relating to the jewels. The Société Claude Béhar tried to obtain restitution of the jewels, an attempt which failed in the insolvency proceedings because of a lack of proof of ownership, but succeeded in the criminal proceedings.

The Société Béhar petitioned for review of both decisions pursuant to the New

Code of Civil Procedure, Art. 618. The Commercial Chamber of the Court of Cassation which was first seized with that petition, referred the same to the Assemblée plénière which annulled both decisions below.

b. Case of Dominique N.

Introduction

The following materials present the final judgment, the report of the Reporting Judge, and the opinion of the Advocate General in a case involving the right of a person to an official certification of his or her sex change.

Court of Cassation, First Civil Chamber
Judgment of May 21, 1990
Case of Dominique N.
(with Report of the Reporting Judge and
Opinion of the Advocate General.)
64 JCP (éd. G.) no. 21588 (1990).

A.

Judgment

The Court, upon two joint assignments of error:

Considering, that, according to the judges on the merits, Dominique N., born on June 18, 1948, was on the register of personal statistics listed as belonging to the female sex; that since an early age she considered herself as a boy and engaged in games of boys; that, after having submitted herself to various medical treatments and having undergone several surgical operations, she has brought an action in the Tribunal de grande instance for the substitution in her birth certificate of the words 'male sex' for the words 'female sex'; that the judgment under attack (Court of Appeal, Bordeaux, 1st Ch., March 5, 1987), after having found, following the experts, that Dominique N. was a true transsexual, dismissed her action for the reason that the psychological or psychosocial sex alone could not have priority over the biological, anatomical or genetic sex, that sex is an objectively determined and immutable element for which the best criterium is drawn from the chromosomic structure; considering that Dominique N. with the first assignment of error contends that the Court of Appeal in refusing to recognize her male sexual identity as it results from her modified morphology and her psychic attitude has violated Art. 8, par. 1 of the European Convention on Human Rights and Fundamental Liberties; that in a second assignment of error, she blames the court for having failed to modify her civil status although the principle of indisposability of the civil status of persons does not bar the alteration of the sex in the case of true transsexuality, i.e. if the divergence of psychological and genetic sex is independent of the role of the subject, irresistible, predominant and irremediably acquired; but considering that transsexuality even if it is medically recognized cannot be analyzed as a true sex change, since the transsexual although having lost some of the characteristics of her original sex has not acquired those of the opposite sex — and considering that Art. 8, par. 1 of the European Convention on Human Rights, by providing that each person has a right to the respect of his private and family life, does not mandate the attribution to a transsexual of a sex which in reality is not his — wherefrom it follows that the assignment of errors cannot be accepted, rejects the petition.

[M. Jouhaud, Pres.; M. Massip, Reporting Judge; Mme Flipo, Advocate General; S.C.P. Urtin Petit and Rouseau-Van Troeyen, Attorney]

B.

Report of Councillor Massip

Dominique N. was born in Viet Nam. Her father was a military physician, her mother a nurse. Since her childhood days she was convinced that she belonged to the male sex, a conviction which was still strengthened when she reached puberty and entailed difficulties and a breach with her family.

Dominique absolved successfully the study of medicine and obtained a diploma in psychiatry.

Affected by depressive spells, she underwent in 1971 psychotherapy which resulted in failure. In 1972 she received a hormone treatment for masculinization, in 1975 a mastectomy (removal of the breasts), and in 1979 a total hysterectomy (removal of the ovaries and the uterus). Since that date the taking of testosterone maintains her, in the absence of all female hormone secretion, in a male hormonal state.

She still possesses a vulva and vagina, but a still more complete transformation of her morphology may be achieved through a transplant of a penis (creation of a neopenis, though not operational, resulting in a closing off of the vulva). This operation is presently contemplated.

In this condition, Dominique, in July 1983, instituted an action in the Tribunal de Grande Instance of Bordeaux demanding that in her birth certificate the words 'female sex' be replaced by the words 'male sex.'

The Tribunal of Grande Instance ordered the examination of experts. Doctor Y submitted his report of September 3, 1984. He expressed the opinion that although the genetic sex of Dominique was female the sexual behavior and appearance was male and that her demand for a change in civil status was justified by the concern to prevent the risk of a definitive marginalization of her existence with its train of depressions and the risk of a suicidal epilogue. On the other side, Doctor Z and Doctor W, in their report of November 20, 1984, concluded that there existed a state of transsexuality characterized by the physical female sex of an individual who wants and considers herself to be male. They indicated that the transformations undergone had a beneficial effect on the depressive and suicidal behavior of Dominique and that the only way to dissipate the actual conflict situation was the legal recognition of the male sex of a subject genetically female. In a Judgment of September 16, 1985 the Tribunal of Grande Instance of Bordeaux rejected the demand of Dominique N., holding that no true sex change had occurred and that the issue was not to bring the civil status into conformity with the true situation, i.e. the true sexual identity of the interested party, but with the notion which she formed about her personality and identity.

The Court of Appeal of Bordeaux, by Judgment of March 5, 1987, affirmed the judgment below. It admitted — with the experts — that a case of true transsexuality was present. But it considered that the psychological or psychosocial sex alone could not override the biological, anatomical, and genetic sex and that Dominique, despite the castrations suffered by her, was still of the female sex. For the Court of Appeal, sex is an objectively determined and unalterable element the best criterium of which is its chromosomic formula.

Dominique N. has interposed a petition for cassation. She assigns two errors.

In the first assignment, she contends that in refusing to recognize in respect to Dominique N. her male sexual identity such as results from her modified morphology, her psychic state and her socio-professional role the court has violated Art. 8, par. 1 of the European Convention on Human Rights and Fundamental Liberties.

According to the second assignment, the principle of the compulsory nature of the civil status does not preclude a sex change in the case of a true transsexuality, i.e. when a divergence between the psychological and the genetic sex is independent of the will of the subject, irresistible, preponderant and irremediably acquired. This is the situation in the case at hand as the Court of Appeal moreover has recognized in a manner that it should not have rejected the demand of a change of the sex. * * *

In order to assess the merits of these two assignments of error, it is helpful to specify briefly the nature of transsexuality, to recall the precedents in this matter and the positions taken on that issue by the European Court of Justice for Human Rights, and, finally, to say a word on the legislative problem posed by transsexuality.

I. *Transsexuality*

[Under this heading the Reporting Judge engages in a brief presentation of the character of sex and transsexuality and the current medical treatment thereof.]

II. *The Position of Jurists*

The traditional position, both of theory and practice relied on the sex as it was determined genetically and morphologically and refused to take into account transformations obtained by hormonal and surgical treatments (principle of the non-disposability of the personal status).

But an evolution took place both in the theory and in the jurisprudence of the courts on the merits.

Since 1980 a certain number of decisions have been rendered which have admitted the change of the sex of transsexuals. The idea was formed that the principle of the non-disposability of the civil status, although it opposed the law taking account of a change voluntarily obtained by an interested party, did not imply the immutability of the status of persons. It is therefore possible to alter the sex of a person if an evolution is produced in him which is not voluntary but appears to be compelled by factors — even if of purely psychic character — against which he was unable to resist.

Such a case would be that of transsexuals. In the case of a conflict between the physical sex on the one hand and the psychological sex on the other, it is the latter which ought to prevail in order to permit the social integration of the subject.

One could cite in that sense a considerable number of judgments by tribunals of grande instance or of courts of appeal which became final because they gave satisfaction to the applicant and the public ministers usually failed to make use of means of review.

But there are also judgments and orders which reached the opposite result. They are those which have been submitted to the Court of Cassation, which has been prompted to render seven judgments on the subject.

In the two Judgments of December 16, 1975 (Bull. Civ. I, nos. 374 and 376) we have said that it was impossible to take a modification of the sexual attributes by way of hormonal or surgical treatment into consideration if the interested party had undergone it voluntarily (Judgment No. 1) but have let it be understood that account could be taken of an involuntary morphological change following a treatment imposed in a concentration camp (Judgment No. 2).

In a Judgment of November 30, 1983 (Bull. Civ. I, no. 284) we have rejected a petition against a judgment which refused to admit a sex change despite a favorable medical report, for the reason that 'the court of appeal had found that despite the operations undergone by her, Nadine V. was not of the male sex,' a somewhat sibylline formulation which could have been interpreted as expressing on our part the intention to consider the notion of sex change as a question of fact, left to the appreciation of the courts on the merits. But one could also see in it the notion, expressed by implication, that only the objective sex, the physical sex, be counted.

The formulation could also be explained by an embarrassment, by the caution not to adopt too rigid a formula which could entail the submission of proposed legislation or an action before the European Court of Human Rights.

In two further Judgments of May 3, and 31, 1987 (Bull. Civ. I., Nos. 79 and 116), the First Chamber reverted to the approach of 1975. In the first judgment (which is the only judgment of cassation) the Chamber vacated the judgment below by stating that it did not follow from that judgment that a change of sex existed by virtue of a cause outside the will of the applicant. In the second judgment it rejected the petition by stating that the court of appeal had shown that the actual condition of the applicant was not the result of elements which existed prior to the operation undergone by the applicant but of the deliberate will of him.

But there still existed an ambiguity because it is possible to attribute two meanings to the notion of foreign cause:

— a narrower meaning: modification imposed by an accident or external force;
— a broader meaning: One could consider as a 'cause external to the will' an evolution undergone by virtue of psychic constraints. One should not adhere to the criterion of 'exteriority to the individual' but to the criterion of irresistibility.

It is the broader conception to which the decisions of the courts on the merits adhere, which are favorable to the thesis of transsexuality (See, very clearly, the Court of Appeal of Paris, October 21, 1987, D. 1987, *Inf. rap.* 231).

The last two judgments were rendered by our Chamber on June 7, 1988 (Bull. Civ. I, no. 176) and May 10, 1989 (Bull. Civ. I, n. 189). In both of these judgments, we rejected the petition against two judgments rejecting a petition for sex change by pronouncing that the judges below could have found that the psychological and social considerations invoked were insufficient to justify a sex change.

This formulation is again susceptible to different interpretations: insufficient in the particular case, thus leaving the supposition that in other instances, more characteristic, the sex change could be admitted; insufficient as a general proposition, which would outlaw any sex change because of transsexuality.

It is the latter interpretation which logically ought to prevail because in both of these cases the courts of appeal had held that one must rely on the anatomical and genetic characteristics and that the consciousness of belonging to the opposite sex could not militate against the objective factors.

The detailed analysis of the decisions rendered leads therefore to the admission that the First Civil Chamber of the Court of Cassation has, in the matter of transsexuality, adopted a negative position. This has not escaped jurists as alert as Mrs. Michelle Gobert in her remarkable chronicle which she devotes to transsexuality (62 JCP I 3361 (1988)) or Mrs. Jacqueline Rubellin Devichi (Rev. Trim. Dr. Civ. p. 721 *et seq.* (1989).)

III. *The Position of the European Court of Human Rights*

The European Court of Human Rights was twice called upon to express itself on the problem of transsexuality. Transsexuals in fact have brought their case before the Court with the claim that a violation of Arts. 8 and 12 of the European Convention on Human Rights and Fundamental Liberties had occurred.

A priori their thesis appears to be unfounded. Art. 8 par. 1 is limited to the affirmation of the right of anyone to the respect of his private life, and par. 2 to the prohibition of any interference with the exercise of this right by public authorities.

Nevertheless the European Commission on Human Rights has expressed the opinion that a state which refuses the new sex to a transsexual following a medical treatment does not respect his private life [quoting at length from *Van Oosterwijck against Belgium*, Ser. A no. 40, and *Matter of Rees*, Ser. A. no. 106].

The Court itself, however, has been much more prudent and, properly speaking, has not taken a position.

In *Van Oosterwijck* it dismissed the case because the legal remedies were not exhausted in Belgium.

In *Rees* it also dismissed the case resting its decision on certain particularities of British law: right to a free change of the Christian name, right to choose the appellation Mr. or Mrs., rarity of resort to the birth certificate. But it also noted that the text did not compel the acceptance of the thesis of the transsexuals and that it involved a subject matter where there existed no common view among the States Parties and where they enjoyed a broad area of discretion.

IV. *The Legislative Problem*

Is there a need for legislation with respect to transsexuality?

Although theoretically legislation is conceivable in both senses and may assume either a prohibitive or permissive character, in practice the problem boils down to the question whether in the case of transsexuality the law should recognize the existence of a sex change which can be noted on the registers of the civil status.

Certain states have done so, among them Sweden (Law of April 21, 1972), the Federal Republic of Germany (Law of September 10, 1980); Italy (Law of April 14, 1982), and The Netherlands (Law of April 24, 1985). In France a bill proposed by Mr. Caillavet was submitted to the Senate. The European Parliament, in its session of September 11, 1989, adopted a resolution favorable to transsexuals.

But the public authorities and the physicians do not favor a legislative measure. They fear that, as it has been found in Italy, a permissive legislation will unleash and multiply the demands for a sex change. They are alarmed by the confrontation with the difficult problems engendered by the recognition of transsexuality. * * *

These are the factual ramifications of the problem which we must resolve. * * *

One must choose: Either to adopt the position of the Court of Appeal of Bordeaux which indicates that for it the sex is the physical sex and nothing else; or, conversely, to admit that the psychological elements can take precedence over the physical elements and lead to the recognition of a sex change. * * *

It is appropriate to observe that the solution consistent with a refusal to admit that transsexuality entails a true alteration of the sex which must be noted in the civil register does not lead denying the transsexual syndrome and depriving it of any effect.

* * *

If your reporter has thought it appropriate to devote such an extensive discussion to a question which the Chamber is familiar with, since it has debated the same on numerous occasions, it is because it seemed to him that the moment has come to reflect anew about the delicate and painful problem of transsexuality.

* * *

C.

Conclusion of Mrs. Françoise Flipo,
Advocate General at the Court of Cassation

You have today to pass on four cases of transsexuality; four women who want to change their sex in order to become men. A situation which occurs more rarely than the reverse according to medical statistics and to judicial decisions rendered as much by yourselves as by judges on the merits.

Between 1975 and 1989 you have rendered seven consistent judgments (two in 1975, two in 1983, 2 in 1987, one in 1988, and one in 1989) which have rejected applications for an alteration of the civil status based on a sex change, interposed by transsexuals who had undergone hormonal treatments followed by surgical operations.

One can speak therefore already of a 'constant jurisprudence' in the technical sense attributed to that term. We will return to that shortly.

The new cases arise under analogous conditions as the old ones and one could therefore reasonably think that they did not raise special contentions before you and would be resolved in conformity with the principles already laid down by yourselves.

But one finds oneself relying on a legal situation which is somewhat paradoxical: your judgments span a certain period of time (14 years), lower courts have been addressed during that interval; some of them have accepted the thesis of the transsexuals and ordered an alteration of their sex in the registers of civil status with the approval of certain authors who are favorably inclined. The state attorneys, with rare exceptions have not interposed a petition for cassation in these cases.

This explains why while numerous appellate courts have rejected the applications of the transsexuals and continued to do so in conformity with the doctrine expressed by your judgments or changed their jurisprudence to be in conformity with yours, some have pursued an inverse path (notably Paris, two recent judgments: October 21, 1987 and April 19, 1988, D. 1987, *inf. rap.* 231 and D. 1988, *inf. rap.* 137).

Today, aided by the amplifying echo of certain journals and media and aided also, to be sure, by the compassion which their status understandably inspires, transsexuals again try to make you recognize that, following castrations or plastic surgery, men ought to be considered to have become women or women to have become men, which you should translate into a reversal of your jurisprudence.

Before entering into the merits of the problem it is necessary to reach an understanding on the meaning of the words and the nature of the issue. [A lengthy discussion of sex and transsexuality follows.] * * *

The fundamental question which is posed by transsexuality is the following: if an individual does not recognize himself in the physical or genetic sex which is his and under which he is listed in the civil register, is it necessary to give precedence over that sex to the opposite sex of psychosocial or cerebral nature, is it necessary to give effect to the voluntary transformations of the individual and to alter the sex in the acts of civil status in order to draw therefrom all the legal consequences?

A redoubtable question, even if the phenomenon is marginal. A redoubtable question because an affirmative answer would be of a nature to shake the basis on which our society rests.

You have through your decisions given a negative reply. [A lengthy discussion of the seven judgments follows.] * * *

In sum: on the one hand you conclude that the psychological sex (or psychosocial, behavioral, or cerebral) cannot prevail over the anatomical, genetic, or biological sex, that cannot be modified by anything, let us repeat, in the present state of science; on the other hand you believe that no account can be taken of the treatments or operations which result from a deliberate will of the subject and which do not result from a cause outside his will.

Your decisional law thus appears to be clear, consistent, and, as we said before, constant. Therefore one is a little surprised to read in the recent report of the interministerial working group on Bioethics and Law [a number of statements are criticized by Mrs. Flipo].

* * *

[The next segment discusses the difficulties flowing from a recognition of transsexuality and a right to a sex change.]

How many other difficulties would the judge encounter on his route: marriage, divorce, parenthood, parental authority, adoption, to mention only a few.

* * *

Such problems cannot be resolved by judicial decisions. They can be resolved only by legislation. If the judge is the guarantor of the law, if he has to interpret it, he cannot make it.

What one asks of you today, as too often, is to transgress your role as a regulatory court and to usurp the place of the legislator.

* * *

The transsexuals enjoy today the possibility without exposure to the rigors of the criminal law to find some relief in treatments and operations. The relaxation of the social constraints leaves them the ability to live de facto if not de jure with the person of their choice without shocking public opinion.

The present state of the legal texts does not permit to go further. You have traced by your judgments the limits of your power. * * * We will add that in your last two judgments you have already rejected complaints of a violation of Art. 8 of the European Convention on Human Rights. * * *

In the four cases which are submitted to you today we can only suggest a dismissal of the petitions.

NOTES

1. *Sequels.* The four judgments of May 21, 1990 of the First Civil Chamber of the Court of Cassation, of course, were disappointing to the petitioners in these cases. A similar disappointment had been suffered previously by a number of other parties who after a surgical sex change sought a modification of their official civil status. One of them was a certain Norbert Antoine B. who, after a surgical change of his bodily characteristics, sought a change of her first names and recognition of her new sex in the official records. She lost in all three instances, the First Civil Chamber of the Court of Cassation rejecting her petition by Judgment of March 31, 1987.

Not discouraged, Miss B. sought relief under the European Convention of Human Rights, especially Art. 8 thereof, which entitles everyone 'to respect for his private and family life, his home and his correspondence'. The European Court of Human Rights, by judgment of the plenary Court of March 25, 1992 (*B. v. France*)[36] held that complainant by virtue of French law was placed into a situation which in its totality was incompatible with the due respect of her private life. As a result the Court condemned France to pay the complainant FF 100,000 for non-pecuniary damages.

In view of this judgment, the Court of Cassation sitting in Full Assembly reconsidered the relief available in cases of transsexualism in its two judgments of December 11, 1992.[37] In those cases, two former males, after a surgical sex change, sought a modification of their civil status registration. The rejection of their claims by the courts of appeal was overturned by the Court of Cassation. In one of these judgments (*In the Matter of René X,* translated infra), the Court explicitly referred to the European Convention on Human Rights as the legal source and, relying on Art. 627 par. 2 of the New Code of Civil Procedure, granted the appropriate relief without remand. In the second case the Court remanded it to another court of appeal because the original court had failed to call for expert medical testimony.

2. For annotations to the judgment of the European Court of Human Rights, see the notes by Prof. J.-P. Marguénaud, D. Jur. 101 (1993) and by Th. Garé, 66 JCP (éd.

36. Eur. Court H.R., Series A no. 232-C (1992); 16 European Human Rights Reports 1 (1993).

37. For the French texts of these judgments, see 67 J.C.P. 1993 II 21991, p. 46. The report of the judgments is accompanied by the opinion of the First Advocate General, Mr. Michel Jéol (p. 41), and by an annotation of Mr. G. Mémeteau, (p. 47).

G.) II 21955 (1992). For an annotation of the 2 recent judgments of the Court of Cassation see annotation of G. Mémeteau.[38]

c. In the Matter of René X.

Court of Cassation, Full Assembly,
Judgment of December 11, 1992
In the Matter of René X.
67 J.C.P. II 21991 (1993).

The Court — Upon the one assignment of error — On the basis of Art. 8 of the European Convention for the Protection of Human Rights and Fundamental Freedoms, Articles 9 and 57 of the Civil Code [C.C.] and the principle of the indisposability of the status of persons;

Considering that, because, following a medico-surgical treatment undergone for therapeutic reasons, a person presenting the syndrome of transsexualism no longer possesses all characteristics of his original sex and has taken on physical appearance resembling the other sex to which his behavior corresponds, the principle of respect for the private life warrants that his civil status now indicate the sex of which he has the appearance; that the principle of the indisposability of the status of persons does not prevent such a modification,

Considering further that Mr. René X, born on March 3, 1957, was registered in the civil status records as being of the male sex; that, considering himself from his childhood as a girl, he underwent a hormonal treatment since his 20th year and, at age 30, underwent the removal of his external sexual organs with the creation of a neovagina; that following his operation, he filed with the Tribunal de Grande Instance the request for the substitution on his birth-certificate of the words 'female sex' for the words 'male sex', as well as for the change of his first name; that the tribunal decided that Mr. X could assume the first name Renée but rejected his other claims; that the judgment under attack confirmed the judgment of the first judges for the reasons that the intimate conviction of the interested party of belonging to the female sex and his wish to behave like that did not suffice for a recognition that he had become a woman and that the principle of the indisposability of the status of persons prohibited taking account of transformations obtained with the help of voluntarily prompted operations;

Considering, however, that the court of appeal, adopting the conclusions of a court-appointed psychiatric expert, found that Mr. X showed all the characteristics of transsexualism and that the medico-surgical treatment which he had undergone gave

38. *Ibid.*

him a physical appearance which now resembled more that of the female sex than that of the male sex; that consequently it found that the social life of the interested party conformed to the sex which he appeared to have; wherefrom it follows that in deciding as it did, the court below failed to draw from its findings the legal consequences flowing therefrom;

And considering that, pursuant to Art. 627 par. 2, Nouv. C. pr. civ. it is proper to terminate the litigation by applying the appropriate legal rule;

For these reasons: Rescinds and annuls between the parties the judgment rendered by the Court of Appeal of Aix-en-Provence of November 15, 1990; — orders that no remand be made; — orders that Renée X, born on March 3, 1957, be designated in the civil status records as being of the female sex; — Orders that the present judgment be noted in the margin of her birth certificate.

[Messrs. Drai, First Pres., Le Gunhec, Dutheillet-Lamonthézie, Bézard, de Bouillane de Lacoste, Kuhnmunch, Beauvois, Presidents, Gélineau-Larrivet, Judge-reporter, Jéol, First adv. gen.]

NOTES

1. The rights of transsexuals have been much debated in France and elsewhere in the light of comparative law, not only by the reporting judge and the First Advocate General in the 1992 cases, but also elsewhere, e.g. the report of Senior Councillor Jacques Massip about a conference on *Transsexualism, Medicine and Law,* held at the Free University of Amsterdam, April 14-16, 1993, Les Petites Affiches, No. 64 p. 13 (1993); Margaret Otlowski, *Legal Status of a Sexually Reassigned Transsexual,* 64 Austr. L.J. 67 (1990).

2. *Germany.* See *Transsexuellengesetz of September 10, 1980 BGBl I 1980, 1654ff. Comment Alfred Schneider, Zur Feststellung der Geschlechtszugehörigkeit nach dem Transsexuellengesetz* 45 NEUE JURISTISCHE WOCHENSCHRIFT [NJW] 2940 (1992). Judgment of January 26, 1993, German Federal Constitutional Court, relating to limitations on the change of first name of transsexuals. (46 NJW 1517 (1993).)

3. France. In France, the further question exists whether a transsexual is entitled to a change of his or her first name. The issue arises now under the Law Nr. 93-22 of January 8, 1993, amending the Civil Code with respect to the civil status, the family and the rights of the child and establishing a judge for family matters (D. Lég. 179 (1993)) which, inter alia, revised the provisions of the Civil Code relating to the naming of children and changes of first names.

While, in general, French courts are reluctant to find the requisite legitimate interest for the change of a family name or first name (Arts. 60 and 61 CC as added), the case of a transsexual constitutes an exception. See Jacques Massip, Note to Trib. gr. inst. of Agen, Judgment of June 19, 1992 (*Mlle X.*), Les Petites Affiches, No. 62, p. 20 (1994). Note by P. Nicoleau to same Judgment, D. Jur. 86 (1994); Isabelle Corpart-

Oulerich, *Transsexualism et Prénom,* Les Petites Affiches, 1993, No. 90, p. 45; see, in general, J. Rubellin-Devichi, *Une importante réforme en droit de la famille,* 67 J.C.P., éd. G. Nr. 3659 (1993).

4. *International Treaties.* As has been pointed out before, the Constitutional Council may only review the compatibility with the Constitution of statutes before they are promulgated. Promulgated statutes are not subject to be declared unconstitutional by either the Constitutional Council or the Court of Cassation. This applies also to statutes which authorize the ratification of a treaty.

Under Art. 55 of the French Constitution, a self-executing treaty prevails over a prior or subsequent statute. However, only the Court of Cassation is authorized to determine the consistency of a statute with a treaty ratified by France. The Constitutional Council has no jurisdiction over that issue. Hence only the Council of State or the Court of Cassation can find a statute to be violative of the European Convention for the Protection of Human Rights and Fundamental Freedoms and inapplicable to the extent of the inconsistency. This has given the ECHR practically a quasi-constitutional status. The text case is a good illustration of this development.

According to Art. 760 of the French Civil Code, illegitimate children, conceived as a result of adultery committed by their father or mother, who are also parents of legitimate children, may inherit in competition with the legitimate children of their parent, but their share is only one half of the share which they would have inherited had they been legitimate. The other half accrues to the shares of the heirs not affected by the adultery.

In the case of *M.M. c. M.R.*, the Court of Cassation (First Civ. Ch.) Judgment of June 25, 1996, 71 JCP (gén.) II 22834, held that Art. 760 violated neither Arts. 8 and 14 of the ECHR, nor the New York Convention on the Rights of the Child, because the latter applied only to the rights of minors and Arts. 8 and 14 of the former did not deal with inheritance rights.

In a series of recent cases involving the effect of the New York Convention on the Rights of the Child of Nov. 20, 1989, the Court of Cassation held that the superiority of treaties applied only to treaties which are directly applicable, a character which the Convention on the Rights of the Child did not have because of the indefinite nature of its provisions and the expressed intent of its framers. (See Court of Cassation, (i) Judgment of March 10, 1993 (Bull. Civ. III 1 Nr. 103, p. 69); (ii) Judgment of June 2, 1993 (Bull. Civ. 1993 VI 1 Nr. 195, p. 135); (iii) and (iv) Judgment of July 15, 1993 (I) and Judgment of July 15, 1993 (II) (Bull. Civ. VII, 1 Nr. 259(1) and (2), p. 178, annotated by Councillor Massip, D. 1993 J. 361 and D. 1994 J. 191.)

The Council of State (*Conseil d'État*) now follows the approach of the Court of Cassation: C.E. *assemblée du contentieux* [C.E. ass.] Judgment October 20, 1989 (*Nicolo*), Receuil de décisions du Conseil d'Etat [Rec. C.E.] (1989) 190; C.E. ass. June 29, 1990, (*G.I.S.T.I.*), Rec. C.E. 171 (1990). In *G.I.S.T.I.* the Council of State reaffirmed that a normative act violating an international convention is invalid and held that the administrative judiciary has the power to interpret an international convention.

This rule applies only if the international convention has not been terminated or suspended by the government, C.E. ass. December 18, 1992 (*Préfet de la Gironde c. Mahmedi*), Rec. C.E. 446 (1992). This case involved an appeal from the judgment of an administrative tribunal, reversing an expulsion order issued by the Prefect of the Gironde against Mr. Mahmedi, a Moroccan national, on the ground that the expellee had entered France without a valid French visa in his passport claimed to have been lost. Mr. Mahmedi had come to France in 1989 after the French government had suspended an agreement between France and Morocco concluded in 1983, exempting Moroccan nationals from the visa requirement. The suspension was due to recent terrorist activities by Moroccans in France. It was communicated by the French Minister of Foreign Affairs in the name of the French government through a letter addressed to the Moroccan embassy in Paris on October 11, 1986. The suspension was notified to the public by a notice in the Official Journal.

The letter to the Moroccan embassy referred to the well-known fact of recent terrorist activities of Moroccans in France and based the suspension on the fundamental change of circumstances resulting therefrom. In view of these facts, the Council of State did not question the validity of the suspension of the 1983 agreement and concluded that the action of the Prefect rested on a valid legal basis and that the order of the Administrative Tribunal was to be annulled.

The Council of State did not discuss whether it had the power to question the validity of the suspension or whether it constituted a political act not subject to review by the Council of State. The latter approach was urged by Mr. Lamy, the Commissioner of the Government (performing a function similar to that of the *avocat général* in the Court of Cassation) and apparently followed by the 'High Assembly.' In his opinion (published in Rec. C.E. (1992) 447-453), Mr. Lamy discussed at length whether a judicial body had the power to determine independently whether a treaty was terminated or suspended or whether it was bound by the view of the executive. See also note by F. Julien-Laferrière, D. J. 1 (1994).

If the Council of State declares an administrative regulation to be illegal because it violates a basic principle of law, that holding binds the ordinary courts even if the decision of the administrative court was rendered in a controversy involving different parties. *Cie nationale Air France c. Mme Rabussier,* Cass. Soc. December 7, 1993, 68 JCP Nr. 22245 (p. 158) (1994) (involving an internal regulation providing an earlier retirement age for female pilots than for males). It is not clear whether this rule can be extended to cases involving statutes held to be invalid because they are inconsistent with treaties.

5. *Portugal.* In Portugal the Constitutional Court has held that it itself could determine whether a treaty has ceased to be binding because of a fundamental change of circumstances, Judgment Nr. 145/89 of January 26, 1989, Boletim do Ministerio da

Justica, Vol. 383, p. 20 (involving Art. 48 of the Geneva Convention on a Uniform Law for Bills of Exchange and Promissory Notes of June 7, 1930).

d. The Case of Farhat Saïdi

Court of Cassation (Crim.)
Judgment of May 4, 1994
66 J.C.P. Jur. 22349 (1994); D. Jur. 80 (1995).

The Court,

Upon the second assignment of error based on the violation of the general principles of criminal procedure and Article 6 § 1 and 3 d) of the European Convention on Human Rights and Fundamental Freedoms; allegedly committed by reason:

> 'that the Judgment of August 12, 1993 (of the Court of Appeal of Aix-en-Provence) under attack declared Farhat Saïdi guilty of frustration of the execution of exclusion from the French territory; despite the fact that the Judgment of the European Court for Human Rights of September 20, 1993 — holding that there was a violation of Articles 6 § 1 and 3, *d*) of the European Convention for the Protection of Human Rights and Fundamental Freedoms in the criminal proceedings instituted against Farhat Saïdi which terminated in the Judgment of October 1, 1987 condemning him to 8 years imprisonment and permanent exclusion from the French territory — necessarily deprived the Judgment of October 1, 1987 as well as the Judgment of August 12, 1993 under attack, which is its consequence, of any legal basis.'

Considering that this assignment of error which is based on a judgment of the European Court of Human Rights is inoperative, that actually the decisions rendered by that Court under the conditions specified in Articles 19 and 50-54 of the European Convention for the Protection of Human Rights and Fundamental Freedoms have no direct effect in internal law upon the decisions of the national courts;

Upon the first assignment of error, based on a violation of Article 27 of the Decree 1945/593 of November 2, 1945; of the Code of Criminal Procedure, lack of reasons and failure of a legal basis, because the Judgment of August 12, 1993 which is under attack declared Farhat Saïdi guilty of 'frustration of the execution of a measure of exclusion from French territory,' although, on the one hand, the judgment under attack, which did not establish that Farhat Saïdi, who was subject to exclusion from French territory reentered the national territory, failed to characterize the substantive element of the offense charged; and although, on the other hand and in any case, the defendant could legitimately believe that the Decision of the European Commission for the protection of human rights of May 14, 1992 suspended the enforcement of the

Judgment of November 1, 1987 which had particularly imposed a definite exclusion from French territory; and that this legitimate belief deprived, in any state of the matter, the charged offense of its intentional element.

Considering that the judgment, which the judgment under attack confirms, announces that on May 6, 1993 Farhat Saïdi has frustrated the execution of a measure of escort to the frontier resulting from the Judgment of the Court of Appeal of October 1, 1987 condemning him to a definite exclusion from national territory and that already in 1991 he disregarded the obligation thus imposed upon him,

Considering that in the state of these pronouncements the appellate court has justified its opinion without incurring the grievances alleged,

That the assignment of errors, therefore, must be discarded.

Rejects the petition.

NOTES

1. Noted by P. Chambon, loc. cit.

2. See note by R.-R. Renucci on Judgment of February 3, 1993 in D. Jur. 515 (1993).

3. The European Court on Human Rights Judgment of September 20, 1993 (*Saïdi v. France*) is published in Eur. Court H.R., Series A no. 261-C.

4. In 1994 the European Convention for the Protection of Human Rights and Fundamental Freedoms was amended to replace the existing European Commission and Court of Human Rights with a new permanent Court. Protocol no. 11 (English, French and German text available in 1995 Bundesgesetzblatt II 578.)

5. See Council of State, Judgment of May 26, 1995, 384 Petites Affiches No. 95. p.11.

e. The Extradition of Mrs. Aylor

France, Council of State
Adjudicatory Assembly
Judgment of November 15, 1993
Case Nr. 144590: Mrs. Aylor
Recueil des Décisions du Conseil d'Etat 283 (1993)

(With the conclusions of the government commissioner Vigouroux.)

Petition by Mrs. Joy Davis Aylor to the Council of State for annulment of the decree of January 1, 1993 according her extradition to the American authorities and stay of its execution.

Having examined the French-American Convention on Extradition of January 6, 1909; the Law of March 10, 1927; the European Convention on the Protection of Human Rights and Fundamental Freedoms of November 4, 1950, together with its 6th additional protocol; the International Covenant on Civil and Political Rights; the Law of October 9, 1981; the Order Nr. 45-1708 of July 31, 1945; the Decree no. 53-934 of September 30, 1953 and the Law no. 87-1127 of December 31, 1987;

Considering that by virtue of the Law of October 9, 1981 the death penalty was abolished in France; that according to the terms of Art. 1 of the protocol no. 6 to the European Convention for the Protection of Human Rights and Fundamental Freedoms, introduced into the French internal legal order following its ratification authorized by the Law of December 31, 1985 and its promulgation ordered by the Decree of February 28, 1986: 'The death penalty is abolished; nobody may be condemned to such penalty nor executed', that the infliction of the death penalty upon a person who has been made the object of an extradition granted by the French Government would be contrary to the French *ordre public*; that consequently, if one of the offenses for which extradition is demanded from the French authorities is subject to capital punishment according to the law of the requesting party, the extradition can legally be granted because of that offense only upon the condition that the requesting party gives sufficient assurances that the death penalty incurred shall not be imposed or will not be executed.

Considering that the request for extradition presented by the American Government against Mrs.Aylor is based upon a crime punishable with the death penalty, conspiracy to commit a capital crime and incitement to commit such a crime; that pursuant to the criminal law of Texas, the State whose courts have jurisdiction in the case, an accused found guilty of a capital crime incurs the death penalty;

Considering that according to Art. 16 of the Law of March 10, 1927 cited above, the advice of the Chambre of Accusation is adverse if the Court is of the opinion that the legal conditions have not been met; that the Chambre of Accusation of the Court of Appeal of Aix-en-Provence, by issuing, on July 3, 1991, a favorable advice regarding the extradition upon the condition that the death penalty, if imposed would not be executed, has neither misconstrued the provisions of Article 16 cited above, nor rendered its advice self-contradictory;

Considering that by the decree under attack and in conformity with this advice, the French Government has granted extradition of the petitioner to the American authorities 'under the condition that if the petitioner is condemned to the death penalty by the State of Texas, the sentence will not be executed'; that on the one hand, by notes of September 27, 1991 and April 1, 1992 the U.S. Embassy communicated the assurance given by the American Government to the French Government that if Mrs.Aylor were condemned to the death penalty by the State of Texas, the sentence would not be executed; that on the other hand, the American authorities have transmitted to the French authorities the promise, given in the name of Texas by the chief prosecutor for the county of Dallas where Mrs.Aylor would be tried, that the public prosecutor in charge of the case would not seek the death penalty against the petitioner; that by virtue of section 1 of Art. 37-071 of the Texas Code of Criminal Procedure such a penalty cannot be imposed unless it is requested by the public prosecutor; that under these conditions petitioner's contention that the decree under attack is not supported by sufficient guaranties and that her extradition is violative of the French *ordre public* is unfounded;

Considering that it does not follow from the record that the extradition of Mrs. Aylor exposes her to treatments in contravention of Art. 3 of the European Convention for the Protection of Human Rights and Civil Liberties, nor that it threatens to deprive her in disregard of the provision of Art. 6(1) of the Convention, of her right to a fair trial.

Rejects.

NOTES

1. The judgment has been criticized for ignoring 'beautiful questions of international law' posed by the commentator (Professor Denis Alland of the University of Caen) in 98 *Revue Générale de droit international public* 1011 (1994). In particular, the commentator wonders how the performance of a treaty concluded between a European and a non-European Power in 1909 may be affected by France's ratification of the ECHR and the creation of a European *ordre public.* Moreover, he questions the binding force of the promise of the United States and the Texas public prosecutor, a doubt which prompted the commissioner of the government, M. Vigouroux, to consider these guarantees to be insufficient.

2. This judgment authorizing the extradition from France to Texas represents an episode in the prosecution and ultimate conviction of Joy Davis Aylor of Dallas (Tex.) charged with the murder of Rozanne Gailiunas, the girlfriend of Mr. Aylor, the estranged husband of Joy. Joy's father, now deceased, was a wealthy contractor. The killing of Rozanne occurred in 1983 and was actually performed by a hired gunman George 'Andy' Hopper who was contacted by a pest-control contractor Bill Garland, the brother-in-law of Joy. Mrs.Aylor claimed that she wanted only to 'rough up' her husband and that the idea to kill Rozanne originated with Bill Garland and 'Andy'. Nevertheless, Joy paid money to Andy as a reward for his assistance, a sum which was delivered by way of an automechanic named Brian Kreafle.

Evidence of Mrs. Aylor's role in the killing of Rozanne was not obtained until 1988 when the police got a tip from Joy's sister Carol Garland. Between the murder and that time Joy had been hidden by her lover named Jodi Packer who was actually connected with the prosecution. In 1990, before the trial, Joy escaped to France by way of Canada with the help of Packer and a man named Wilson. In France Joy was joined by Packer. She was arrested in 1991 and her extradition was upheld by the Conseil d'État on November 15, 1994. The story is recounted in The Orlando Sentinel, August 19, 1994 p. A16. 'Socialite Who Fled U.S. Found Guilty in Murder Plot' and more fully in The Dallas Morning News, May 29, 1995 p. 19A.

3. The same result was reached in the *Cox v. Canada,* U.N. Human Rights Committee (Geneva/New York) October 31, 1994, 7 *Revue Universelle de droits de l'homme* 13 (1995).

4. For a case decided by the *Assemblée du contentieux* see Conseil d'État, Judgment of February 14, 1996, limiting a lawyer's right to a public hearing where this would disclose secrets protected by the law. 70 J.C.P. 22669 (p. 294) 1996.

B. ITALY

1. The Italian Judicial System

a. Ordinary Courts

Italy, like France, separates courts with jurisdiction over civil and criminal matters from courts or judicial bodies with jurisdiction over administrative controversies. The Italian Constitution of December 27, 1947 allocates ordinary judicial functions to courts established by the Law on the Organization of Justice[39] of January 30, 1941 as amended, and the exercise of administrative justice to the Council of State and other administrative tribunals, established by statute. (Const. Arts. 102 and 103.) The Italian legislature created regional administrative tribunals of first instance by Law n. 1034, December 6, 1971.

The organization of the administration of justice is governed by statute. (Const. Art. 108.) The organization of the ordinary courts is still governed by the Law on Organization of Justice of 1941 as amended. The principal courts of first instance, depending on the nature and the amount of the controversy, are (i) the *giudici di pace* (justices of the peace), (ii) the *preture circondariali* (District Magistrates Courts) or (iii) the *tribunali ordinari.*[40] There are 166 *tribunali ordinari,* 166 *preture circondariali* and more than four and one half thousand justices of the peace. The *preture circondariali* replaced the existing *preture* and the latter were converted into separate sections of the appropriate *pretura circondariale.*[41]

The chief intermediate courts are the 26 courts of appeal. At the top of the hierarchy is the *Corte suprema di cassazione*. The style of the Italian courts is not as formalized as that of the French judiciary.

The Court of Cassation

As in France, the *Corte suprema di cassazione* is a mega-court. It is composed of three civil sections, one section for labor controversies and six penal sections. The Court's membership consists of a First President, an Adjunct President, Section Presidents and Councillors. The three civil sections have special categories of controver-

39. *Ordinamento giudiziario* [Ord. Giud.] R.D. of January 30, 1941 nr. 12, as amended.

40. Ord. Giud., Art. 1 (1) as amended by Law of November 21, 1991 nr. 374, on the estabishment of the Justice of the Peace, Art 45.

41. Law of February 1, 1989 Nr. 30, as amended by Law of July 26, 1991 nr. 246, Laws of February 11, 1995, Nrs. 125, 126 and 127.

sies allocated to them. Ordinarily matters are adjudicated by the section to which the case is attributed, sitting as a panel of five judges, one of whom is the president.

In some cases the controversy must be or may be adjudicated by 'united sections.' In civil matters these cases involve issues of jurisdiction or issues in which the single sections have ruled differently or which the First President considers to be of particular importance. (Art. 374 New Code of Civil Procedure, *Codice di procedura civile* [*C.P.C.*]). The united sections may consist of united civil sections or united criminal sections (Art. 67 *Ord. giud.*) In any case in which the Court sits as united sections, the bench consists of a president and eight judges from the civil or criminal sections as the case may require.

The 'recourse for cassation' in civil matters requests that the Court vacate the judgment for lack of jurisdiction, errors of law, and other reasons specified by statute (Art. 360 C.P.C.) In cases other than those lacking jurisdiction, the case is remanded to another judge of the same judicial level, unless no further findings of fact are required.[42] If the Court vacates the judgment for erroneous application of the law, it pronounces the rule which binds the judge below. If the court below reached the correct result but gave an erroneous reason, the Court corrects the reason without vacating the judgment of the court below (C.P.C. Art. 384 par. 2).

In each case a member of the bench acts as reporting judge (*relatore*). The hearing of the cases is opened with a summary of the case by the reporting judge. Following the pleadings of the parties the public attorney (*pubblico ministero*) presents his or her reasoned conclusions (C.P.C. Art. 379).

The Supreme Court of Cassation maintains a special office which extracts and registers the principles of law applied by the Court in its decisions (*Ufficio del massimario e del ruolo,* Art. 68 Ord. giud.). The same office also cooperates with the electronic retrieval system (*CED*).[43]

b. Administrative Courts

The highest Italian administrative court is the *Consiglio di Stato* (Council of State). It is both an administrative and a judicial body (Constitution, Arts. 100 and 103). Its existence reaches back to the establishment of Italian unity in 1861. It did not exercise judicial functions until 1889.

Today the composition of the body is governed by the Law n. 186 of April 27, 1982.[44] The Council of State is divided into six sections of which the first three exercise consultative functions, while Sections IV, V and VI exercise judicial functions.

---

42. Arts. 383 and 384 par. 1 C.P.C., as amended by Art. 66 of the Law of November 26, 1990, effective on January 1, 1993).

43. See E.Giannantonio, Italian Legal Information Service (1984). For a historical-comparative study of judgment writing see G. Gorla, *Sulla via dei 'motivi' delle 'sentenze': lacune e trappole,* 101 FORO ITALIANO 201 (1980).

44. *Le Leggi* 1982 I 740.

Each adjudicatory section consists of 2 Section presidents, of which one is a titular officer, and at least 12 councillors. The consultative sections have at least 9 councillors each in addition to 2 Section presidents.

The judicial sections sit in panels composed of one of the presidents and four councillors. In some instances cases are adjudicated by the judicial sections, sitting as full bench (*adunanza plenaria.*[45]) In that case the President of the Council presides and the bench is composed of in addition 12 judges, viz. 4 from each of the three judicial sections.

All in all the personnel of the Council consists of the President of the Council, 15 Section Presidents and 72 Councillors of State.[46]

c. *Constitutional Court*

Italy, in its Constitution of December 27, 1947 established a separate Constitutional Court to pass on the constitutionality of statutes.[47] (Arts. 134-137 Constitution of the Republic of Italy.) It is composed of 15 judges of whom one third are nominated by the president, one third by the Parliament and one third by the members of the supreme ordinary and administrative judiciaries. The judges are chosen for a period of 9 years from members of the higher ordinary or administrative judiciary, full professors of law or lawyers after 20 years of practice.

Details concerning the submission of proceedings regarding constitutionality and of the guaranties of the independence of the judges of the court are governed by a constitutional law of February 9, 1948.[48] The other rules necessary for the composition and operation of the court are contained in an ordinary law of March 11, 1953.[49]

It is a very busy court. Apart from the cases involving the applicability of Community law, the jurisdiction of the Court consists of so-called 'concrete' norm-control, i.e. the question of constitutionality must arise within the framework of a litigation pending in the ordinary courts.

'Abstract' norm control, i.e. the review of the constitutionality of legislation outside a pending controversy, can be sought by specified governmental authorities only in cases involving the legislative powers of the regions. In that connection the question has arisen whether the Constitutional Court has jurisdiction.

Accordingly, Italy adopted the so-called 'concentrated' form of review of the constitutionality of statutes or acts having the force of law, the question of constitutionality to be submitted by a judge either on his or her motion, or if raised by the parties and not held by the judge to be obviously unfounded. The statutory rules are imple-

45. Law nr. 186 of April 27, 1982, Art. 5

46. Table A of the Law nr.186 of April 27, 1982.

47. *Le Leggi* 849 (1947).

48. See infra p.42. See also Italian Constitution, Arts. 137(1) and 138.

49. March 11, 1953 Law n. 87, *Le Leggi* I 261 (1953), enacted pursuant to Italian Constitution, Arts. 137(2) and 64(3) .

mented by Rules of Court of March 24, 1958. The case-law of the Court is reported, inter alia, in *Giurisprudenza Costituzionale* (1956–), a periodical published by Giuffrè, Milan.

The Constitutional Court and Community Law

The Court has had to pass several times on the status of European Community law in the Italian judicial system. In contrast to the French *Conseil Constitutionnel,* it can declare laws already promulgated to be unconstitutional and invalid. (Art. 136. Const.) Until then, a judge must apply an Italian statute, unless it is formally repealed. The only exception to that rule is constituted by statutes which are in conflict with primary or secondary Community law.

Although Italy does not follow the French rule that a subsequent statute cannot be inconsistent with a prior treaty provision so long as it is internationally binding, the Italian Constitutional Court has held that by reason of the Italian Constitution (Art. 11), an Italian judge must 'disapply' a national statute to the extent that it conflicts with Community law.[50]

In particular the question has arisen whether the Constitutional Court has jurisdiction to invalidate a regional law because of a conflict with Community law. The Court has given an affirmative answer.

In the Judgment of November 10, 1994, n. 384, involving proposed legislation of the Region of Umbria regarding the replanting of grape vines, the Constitutional Court held that it possessed jurisdiction *via principale* (abstract norm control) with respect to proposed regional legislation upon a recourse submitted by the national governments.[51] The Region challenged the recourse as inadmissible, primarily because a conflict between Community law and the law of a member state, escapes the control of the Constitutional Court, as recognized by the judgment of the Italian Constitution Court in Case 1984 No. 170 (*Granital*) and later cases.

The Court held the contention to be unacceptable. Because of the liability of the Italian state for legislative violation of its own duties, even if emanating from the regions, it was necessary and proper to admit a recourse by the national government against a regional law not yet in force that is suspected of being violative of Community law.

As a matter of caution, the Court added that the converse did not follow. A region may only attack a national law already in force. Moreover, a conflict between a national law and Community law is to be within the jurisdiction of the ordinary

50. Italian Constitutional Court, Judgment of June 8, 1984 (*S.p.a. Granital c. Amministrazione delle Finanze*), nr. 170, 29 Giur. Cost., I, 1098 (1984); Italian Const. Ct., Judgment of April 21, 1989 (*S.p.a. Fragd c. Amministrazione delle Finanze*), 34 Giur. Cost., I 1001 (1989)).

51. 147 *Giur. Italiana* I col. 334 (1995). The Court's holding was reiterated in several subsequent cases, e.g. Corte Cost. Judgment of March 30, 1995, n. 94, 147 *Giur. Italiana* I, 74 (1996), with ann. M. Galdi (Violation of EC Treaty, Art. 93); 147 *Giur. Italiana* I, 185 (1996) (*Pres. Cons. Ministri c. Reg. Sicilia*).

courts. The Court also rejected other challenges to the admissibility and held that the recourse succeeded on the merits.

The Judgment of November 10, 1994 is commented upon by A. Celotto, *Dalla 'non applicazion' alla 'disapplicazione' del diritto interno incompatible con il diritto comunitario,* 147 Giur. It. I col. 341 (1995) and M. Ruotolo, *Competenza della Corte costituzionale in materia di contrasto tra norme comunitarie e leggi regionali impugnate dal governo in via principale.* 147 Giur. It. I col. 333 (1995). This decision is followed by the Constitutional Court's Judgment of March 30, 1995 n. 95, 57 *Riv. di diritto internazionale* 444 (1995).

The text-cases *infra* before deal with the role of international law in Italian law. In general, Italy follows the U.S. rule that so far as the internal effects are concerned, a later statute primes a prior treaty. Recently, however, the Italian Constitutional Court appears to have afforded a higher status to the European Convention for the Protection of Human Rights and Fundamental Freedoms (November 4, 1950). *In re Mujanovic and Hakimi* illustrates this new trend.

The *Corte Costituzionale*'s Judgment of April 28, 1994 No. 168 (*In re Potenziani*) concerned the failure of the Italian Penal Code to exclude minors from the penalty of confinement in a penitentiary. The Court held, *inter alia,* that the relevant provisions of the Penal Code were not automatically corrected by a rule of customary international law, because there was no consensus on the issue.

2. Legislation on Review of Constitutionality

a. Constitutional Law of February 9, 1948, enacting norms relating to proceedings concerning constitutionality and the independence of the Constitutional Court. Reprinted in Codice di diritto amministrativo II p. 3175 (¶330) ed. F. Falletti *et al.* (Milan 1989)

Sec. 1

The question of the constitutionality of a statute or an Act having the force of a statute of the Republic (Const. Art. 134) which is raised ex offico or urged by one of the parties in the course of a litigation and not deemed to be manifestly unfounded by the judge is referred to the Court for its decision.

Sec. 2

When a region is of the opinion that a statute or an act having the force of a statute of the Republic invades the sphere of competence allocated to it by the Constitution, it may upon deliberation of the regional government, institute an action for the determination of constitutionality before the Court within 30 days following the publication of the statute or the act having the force of a statute. (Const. Art. 127).

A statute of a region may be attacked because of unconstitutionality not only in the cases and forms specified in the preceding paragraph and Art. 127 of the Constitution, but additionally, by another region which is of the opinion that its own competence is infringed. The action is initiated upon deliberation of the government of the region within 60 days after the publication of the law.

b. Law of March 11, 1953, N. 87 (Le Leggi 261 (1953))

Norms concerning the establishment and the functioning of the Constitutional Court.

Sec. 23

In the course of a litigation pending before a judicial authority, one of the parties or the public attorney may raise the question of constitutionality by means of a proper pleading, indicating

a) the provisions of the statute or an act having the force of a statute of the State or region which are affected by unconstitutionality.
b) the provisions of the Constitution or of constitutional laws that are assumed to be infringed.

The judicial authority, if the controversy cannot be determined independently of the question of unconstitutionality and it does not consider the question to be manifestly unfounded, issues an order which, referring to the terms and reasons of the pleading raising the question, provides for the immediate transmission of the papers to the Constitutional Court and suspends the pending controversy (C.p.c. Art. 295).

The question of the constitutionality may be raised ex officio by the judicial authority before whom the controversy is pending by an order containing the information specified in letter a) and b) of the first paragraph and the preceding paragraph.

* * *

Sec. 31

The question of the constitutionality of the law of a region may, in accordance with the last paragraph of Art. 127 of the Constitution, be raised within the period of 15 days after the date on which the president of the Council of Ministers had received the communication from the president of the government of the region that the law has been approved the second time by the council of the region.

The question is raised, after a prior deliberation of the council of Ministers, by the President of the Council by means of a direct recourse to the Constitutional Court and notified within the period provided in the preceding paragraph to the president of the government of the region.

The recourse must be deposited in the office of the Clerk of the Court within ten days after the notification.

3. Cases and Notes

a. *In re Mujanovic and Hakimi*

Italy, Corte Costituzionale
Judgment of January 19, 1993, No. 10
38 Giurisprudenza Costituzionale, 52 (1993).

Proceedings concerning the constitutionality of Articles 555(3), 456(2) and 458(1) of the Code of Criminal Procedure [C.P.P.], instituted by the following orders:

1) order issued on March 2, 1992 by the Pretor of Turin, Separate District of Moncalieri, in the criminal proceedings against Mujanovic, Kasim, registered as n. 207 in the Register of Orders, 1992;

2) order issued on February 27, 1992 by the Tribunal of Milan in the criminal proceedings against Hakimi, Noureddin, registered as n. 233 in the Register of Orders, 1992.

Having noted the intervention of the President of the Council of Ministers and having heard, on November 19, 1992, the reporting Judge A. Baldassarre, the Court, presided over by Casavola, renders the following judgment.

FACTS

* * *

LAW

1. The Pretor of Turin, separate District of Moncalieri, — in the course of a criminal proceeding, in which an accused alien declared during the hearing, through an interpreter, appointed by the judge at the beginning of the interrogation, that he had been ignorant until that moment of the content of the accusation served upon him by reason of his absolute ignorance of the Italian language, — raised the question of the constitutionality, in respect to Articles 3(1), 24(2) and 76 of the Constitution, of Article 555(3), Code of Penal Procedure, (C.P.P.) in that part in which it fails to provide that the summons must be served on an accused alien who does not know the Italian language also in translation into the language which he knows.

The Tribunal of Milan, during the hearings in a proceeding against an accused alien who did not know the Italian language -after the rejection by the judge in charge of the preliminary investigation of the request for an abbreviated proceeding because of its untimeliness, and after the Tribunal's own rejection of the request for postponement in terms presented by the accused's defender, — has raised the question of the constitutionality, in reference to Art. 24(2) of the Constitution, of the combined rule of Art. 456(2) C.P.P. and Art. 458(1) C.P.P., in the part in which it fails to provide that the advice, — envisaged by Art. 456(2) C.P.P. which contains the period within which an abbreviated proceeding may be requested, — must be translated into the language known to the accused alien, who is ignorant of the Italian language. In a subordinated way, the judge below has raised the question of the constitutionality — likewise with reference to Art. 24(2) of the Constitution — of Art. 458(1) C.P.P. in that part in which it provides that the commencement of the seven days period, governing the request for abbreviated proceedings, runs from the date of the service of the order on the accused, rather than, in the case of an accused alien who does not know the Italian language, of the service of the advice on the defender if it is perfected subsequently.

Although the question of constitutionality raised by the Pretor of Turin and that raised by the Tribunal of Milan are aimed at different provisions, and although the parameters invoked in one and the other coincide only partially, the respective proceedings are joined to be decided in one judgment in consideration of the fact that in both instances the judges below seek additional pronouncements having an analogous content. More precisely, both judges suggest that, in order to safeguard the constitutional principles involved, and in particular the right of defense, it is necessary to introduce into the law governing criminal procedure, a specific provision mandating that an accused alien, who is ignorant of the Italian language, be served, *together with* a translation into a language known to him, with all documents of the criminal proceedings, upon which depend a timely and detailed knowledge of the accusation (the summons to appear before the Pretor) or alternatively, the exercise of significant rights guaranteed to the accused by the norms of criminal procedure (advice, contained in the summons to an immediate trial, of the choice of the accused to request an abbreviated proceedings within seven days of the service of the order).

2. Both questions are not well-founded within the meaning indicated in the opinion.

Upon the premise that the exception of inadmissibility by reason of irrelevance, raised by the State Advocate, must be rejected once the judge submitting the question has not unreasonably identified the provision which applies to the controversy pending before him, and that it is not within the powers conferred upon this court when reexamining the relevancy to substitute itself to the judge *a quo* by indicating different norms which in its opinion would resolve the case involved or at any rate be influential upon its decision (see e.g. the Judgments nrs. 89 of 1984, 189 of 1986, and 125 of 1987), it is appropriate to observe that the judges *a quibus* request from this Court additional norms, the substantive content of which is already present in the current system.

The interpretive presupposition which is the starting point of the judges below consists in the conviction that the actual rule of Art. 143(1) C.P.P. concerning the right of the accused to receive assistance of an interpreter free of charge applies strictly to oral acts and, therefore, can be extended to written acts only in cases expressly provided as exceptions to that rule: i.e., the request by an Italian citizen belonging to a recognized linguistic minority to receive a translation in his mother tongue, of procedural acts addressed to him (Art. 109(2) C.P.P.) and the invitation to declare or elect domicile within the state directed to an accused alien, which invitation must be composed in the language of the accused when it appears from the file that the latter does not know the Italian language (Art. 169(2) C.P.P.). Nevertheless, upon a comprehensive examination of our legal order, the interpretative presupposition set forth above cannot be shared.

The Convention for the Protection of Human Rights and Fundamental Freedoms, signed at Rome on November 4, 1950, and put into effect in Italy by the Law of August 4, 1955, nr. 848, establishes in Art. 6(3)(a) that 'everyone charged with a criminal offense has the * * * right * * * to be informed promptly in a language which he understands and in detail, of the nature and cause of the accusation against him.'

A provision which is totally identical is also contained in Art. 14(3)(a) of the International Covenant on Civil and Political Rights, signed in New York on December 19, 1966 and put into effect in Italy by the Law of November 25, 1977 nr. 881. The international norms just mentioned were introduced into the Italian legal system with the force of law possessed by the acts containing the mandate of execution (cf. judgments nrs. 188 of 1980, 153 of 1987 and 323 of 1989) and are today in effect. Certainly, they cannot be considered abrogated by the subsequent provisions of the Code of Penal Procedure, not so much because the latter are limited by the directive contained in Art. 2 of the Delegation Law of February 16, 1987 nr. 81 ('the Code of Penal Procedure must be * * * conformed to the rules of the international conventions, ratified by Italy and relating to personal rights and criminal proceedings') as rather because it involves norms derived from a source resulting from an atypical competence and as such not susceptible to abrogation or modification by the provisions of an ordinary law.

Owing to the tie between norms just referred to and Art. 143 C.P.P. which assures to them the guaranty of efficacy and applicability *in concreto,* the right of the accused to be informed promptly and in detail, in a language which he understands, of the nature and cause of the accusation served upon must be considered a perfect subjective right which is directly actionable (see, by analogy the judgment nr. 62 of 1992). And because it involves a right whose guarantee, though also expressed in acts with the rank of ordinary legislation, expresses a content with a value implicit in the constitutional recognition, for the benefit of a person (citizen or alien) of the inviolable right of defense (Art. 24(2) of the Constitution), it follows that by reason of its nature as fundamental principle within the meaning of Art. 2 of the Constitution, the judge is subject to the interpretative obligation to confer upon the norms which contain the guarantees of the rights of defense, for the purpose of an exact comprehension of the accusation, an expansive meaning, directed to make the above indicated right of the accused as concrete and effective as possible.

3. In enacting a norm of general character to regulate the right of the accused to be assisted free of charge by an interpreter, Art. 143 c.c.p. has produced within the system of criminal procedure a significant innovation in comparison with the regulation of the procedure governed by the previous code. In fact, while in the latter one, Art. 326 C.P.P. fashioned the figure of the interpreter so as to include it without surplus within the category of the aids of the judiciary-anchoring the characteristic function of that institution in the need to assure the objective intelligibility of all procedural acts by means of the homogeneity of the language used and without distinction between declarations and depositions emanating from the accused-Art. 143 of the new code, conversely, while retaining for the interpreter the typical function as collaborator with the judiciary (subs. 2), distinctly marks the difference with the previous system by assigning to interpreter primarily a function and role which characterizes institutions destined for the protection of the defense as well as by shaping the resort to the interpreter as the object of a specific right of the accused by defining his relative function as 'assistance' (subs. 1).

This innovation which underscores the value of the right of defense as an instrument of a real participation of the accused in the proceedings through an effective comprehension of the various acts and separate moments in the development thereof, places the new system of criminal procedure in harmony with the principles contained in the human rights conventions ratified by Italy (cf. Art. 14(3)(f) of the International Covenant on Civil and Political Rights of which Art. 143(1) C.P.P. is almost a literal reproduction). Because of this relation with these principles, heightened by the necessary connection with the constitutional values belonging to the rights of defense (Const. Art. 24(2)), Art. 143(1) C.P.P. possesses a particular expansive force which the criminal judge may not ignore when faced with interpretation.

In consequence of these considerations, it is evident that we cannot share the interpretive presupposition which prompted the judges below, viz. that the norm of Art. 143(1) C.P.P. has to be viewed as a norm subject to strict interpretation which permits as sole exception from the rule that the interpreter can be used only with respect to oral acts, those which are expressly specified in the Code of Penal Procedure (cf. Articles 109(2) and 169(3)).

* * *

6. The interpretation, in the terms just set forth, of the right to the aid of an interpreter free of charge, based on Art. 143 C.P.P., dispels the constitutional doubts voiced by the Pretor of Turin and the Tribunal of Milan in the orders set forth above, and responds to the proper limits of relevance of the questions submitted to this court by the judges below. Under this aspect it is specified, in fact, that in both cases, the lack of knowledge of the Italian language on the part of the accused alien must be ascertained from the beginning of the preliminary investigation at the moment of the respective arrests and the related hearings of confirmation. Therefore, it is of evident

relevance to make an announcement signifying the actualization of the right of the accused to a notification, translated in the language known to him, of the summons to appear before the pretor in one case and of the summons to an immediate proceeding before the competent tribunal in the other case.

In view of our decision the question of the constitutionality of Art. 458(1) C.P.P. raised subordinately by the Tribunal of Milan with the second order indicated above loses any materiality.

For these reasons the Constitutional Court, through its assembled judges,

— declares unfounded, within the meaning specified in the opinion, the question of constitutionality raised by the Pretor of Turin in his order set forth above. * * *

— declares unfounded, within the meaning specified in the opinion, the question of constitutionality, raised by Tribunal of Milan in its order set forth above. * * *

NOTES

1. Art. 3(1) of the Italian Constitution guarantees the equality before the law of all citizens without distinction according to sex, race, language, religion, political opinion or personal or social condition. Art. 24(1) provides that defense is an inviolable right in any state or instance of the proceeding. Art. 76 deals with the limitations on the delegation of legislative power to the government.

2. The case illustrates the difficulties resulting for the judiciary from the entry into force on October 24, 1989 of the new Code of Criminal Procedure [C.P.P.] bringing many innovations. A particularly important procedural novelty consists in the *giudizio immediato* (immediate trial) which dispenses with the need of a preliminary interrogation. (Art. 453-458 C.P.P.). This type of procedure is apposite when the proof appears evident. Immediate trial can, however, take place only if the accused has been notified by the order of that type of the procedure, together with the instruction that he may choose either that procedure or an immediate alleviated sentence (Art. 444-448 C.P.P.). In the case before the Milan Tribunal, the accused, a Tunisian alleged drug dealer, was faced with that choice.

3. The judgement is translated and reproduced to familiarize the reader with the style of the Italian Constitutional Court and, above all, with the new quasi-constitutional status attributed to the Human Rights Convention.

In particular, the ECHR has been considered to constitute a source of general European fundamental rights, binding also the European Union. (Treaty of Maastricht, Article F). See also J. F. Flauss, *Les Droits de l'Homme, Comme Elément d'une Constitution et de l'Ordre Européen,* Les Petites Affiches 1993 nr. 52, pp. 8-15.

4. In connection with the judgment of the Italian Constitutional Court, it may be mentioned that Italy thus joined the ranks of the European countries which have attributed to the European Human Rights Convention a rank higher than that of do-

mestic statutes, especially Austria, Belgium, Cyprus, France, Luxembourg, Netherlands, Portugal and Spain.

5. In other European countries, the Convention is self-executing or converted into domestic law, but has only the status of a statute, e.g. in Germany, Denmark, Switzerland and Turkey.

In Great Britain, Ireland, Norway and Sweden the Convention is not part of the domestic law, see A. Bleckmann, *Verfassungsrang der Europäischen Menschenrechtskonvention*? 21 EuGRZ 149 (1994).

b. In re Potenziani

Italy, Corte Costituzionale
Judgment of April 28, 1994 No. 168
In Re Potenziani
39 Giurisprudenza Costituzionale, 1254 (1994).

Proceedings concerning the constitutionality of Articles 17 and 22 of the Penal Code to the extent that they apply the penalty of the penitentiary to minors under eighteen submitted by the Minors' Court for the Marche di Ancona by decree issued on December 2, 1993.

Facts

1. In the course of a criminal prosecution involving a minor charged with a crime punishable with the penalty of penitentiary (intentional aggravated homicide of an ascendant) the Minors' Court for the Marche di Ancona has raised the question of the constitutionality of Art. 17 and 22 of the Penal Code in the part in which these provisions fail to exclude the applicability of the penalty of the penitentiary to minors with reference to Articles 10(1), 27(3) and 31(2) of the Constitution. These provisions mandate:

> Art. 10(1) The legal system of Italy conforms itself to the generally recognized norms of international law.
>
> Art. 27(3) Penalties may not consist of treatment contrary to the sense of humanity and must aim at the re-eduction of the condemned.
>
> Art. 31(2) The Republic protects motherhood, childhood and youth, favoring the institutions necessary for that purpose.

* * *

3. The referring Tribunal sees a contrast between the Constitutional provisions cited above and Articles 17 and 22 of the Penal Code in the part in which these articles fail to exclude the applicability of the penalty of the penitentiary vis-à-vis an accused minor, an omission which in the opinion of the judge *a quo* creates a conflict

a) with Art. 10(1) of the Constitution because thereby the Italian legal system 'does not adapt itself to numerous conventional norms of international law governing the subject' (not specified by the referring judge);

b) with Art. 27(3) of the Constitution, because of the mix-up between the requirement of re-education and pedagogical treatment of minors;

c) with Art. 31(2) of the Constitution because of the infringement of the mandate of protection of childhood and youth.

4. Under this aspect, the Judgment Nr. 140 of 1993 does not resolve the issue because the reliance of the judicial reality 'which indicates a substantial difference in the treatment of a minor in view of his condition also with respect to the imposition of the maximum punishment' as well as the fact that actually the judges for minors refrain from applying the perpetual punishment, does not eliminate the abstract possibility of such application.

* * *

6. The President of the Council of Ministers has intervened in the proceedings and was represented by the Legal Department of the State (*Avvocatura Generale dello Stato*).

In the brief, the Department referred to the considerations set forth in the above mentioned Judgment Nr. 140 of 1993 of this Court, deeming these considerations to be exhaustive, also with respect to the issue raised by the Minors' Court of the Marche and therefore has requested a declaration of the admissibility, or lack of foundation of the same question, reiterating this position in the oral argument.

* * *

Legal Reasons

1. The question has been raised as to the constitutionality of Articles 17 and 22 of the Penal Code in the part in which they fail to exclude the penalty of the penitentiary vis à vis minors less than 18 years old. * * *

2. Preliminarily, it is necessary to reject the exception of inadmissability invoked by the Legal Department of the State which claims that the question is identical with that held to be inadmissible by the Judgment Nr. 140 of 1993.

In that respect the Court observes that it reached its conclusion with reference to a question which was posed in different terms, since in the former proceedings unconstitutionality was claimed not only with respect to Art. 22 of the Penal Code, i.e. one of the norms challenged in these proceedings, but, in conjunction therewith, with respect to the whole body of norms which governs the mechanism of the concurrence of attenuating or aggravating circumstances. For that reason, the above mentioned judgment observed that the question stated in that fashion posed a request of legislative character, given that, by involving in its totality the resolution of the concurrence of circumstances, the pronouncement of this Court, being tied to the submission, would amount to an inadequate result, since, in the pursuit of the corrective aims then proposed 'a selective normative intervention might take place which defines the conditions in which the exemption from the balancing of circumstance may happen; and that might also be so in order to prevent the production of effects which go beyond that purpose of the question.' * * *

The decree which initiates the present proceedings * * * by virtue of the specificity of the pronouncement requested does not result in the exposure to a risk of effects exceeding the objective aimed at. * * *

3. On the merits, the question raised with reference to Art. 10(1) of the Constitution cannot be considered by virtue of the generality of the assumed non-conformity of the challenged norms with 'numerous conventional norms of international law governing the subject,' since the decree of reference does not permit it to identify either the provisions or least of all the normative content to which the judge *a quo* intends to refer.

On the other hand, in consequence of the case-law of the Court (Judgments Nr. 153 of 1987, Nr. 96 of 1982, Nr. 188 of 1980, Nr. 48 of 1979, Nr. 69 of 1976, Nr. 104 of 1969, Nr. 48 of 1967, Nr. 135 of 1963 and Nr. 32 of 1960) which, with respect to the article of the Constitution invoked, delineates the automatic adaptation to the generally recognized rules of international law, with reference to the general principles or norms of customary character, it must be emphasized that it is not possible to ascertain in this subject a general principle or custom because from the multi-faceted panorama of the legislation of other States close to that of our country, the existence of one of these generally recognized norms to which Art. 10(1) of the Constitution refers, does not emerge considering the extreme diversity of the provisions governing the regime of the severest punishment in the various countries.

Although such a general reference to 'conventional norms' is nót capable to serve in the determination of the constitutionality of the denounced norms, nevertheless the Court deems it opportune for the purpose of clarifying the meanings of the other constitutional parameters, to analyze and verify the conformity of our legislation with the obligations assumed on the international plane.

> [After listing and analyzing a large number of international instruments dealing with the protection of human rights in general and the protection of minors in particular, the Court concludes that Article 31 of the Constitution is the principal implementation of these agreement to which Italy is a party. Art. 27(3) of the Constitution, standing alone, does not serve as a basis for a declaration of the unconstitutionality of the subjection of minors to confinement in the penitentiary, because any punishment must have educational functions, as was already pointed out in the judgment of the Constitutional Court Nr. 264 of 1974. Moreover, confinement to a penitentiary is no longer for life.]

5.1 The question, however, is well-founded with reference to Art. 31 in connection Art. 27(3) of the Constitution. If Art. 27(3) does not per se expose the provision of the penalty of the penitentiary and the character of the perpetuity within the meaning of Articles 17 and 22 of the Penal Code to the charge of unconstitutionality, this provision requires a different reading when it is coupled with Article 31 of the Constitution which mandates a fundamental differentiation between the punitive treatment of minors and the general system of penalties.

From Article 31 of the Constitution, which provides a special protection for infants and youths, and from the institutions necessary for that purpose, flows the incompatibility of the imposition of the penalty of the penitentiary on minors under eighteen because it lumps together with respect to such particular institution of undubitable severity in the same primitive context all subjects, without taking account of the particular condition of minors.

This latter condition — as is already underscored in the Judgment Nr. 140 of 1993 in which an intervention of the legislator with respect to the imposition of the penalty of the penitentiary also on minors was derived — requires 'to differentiate as far as possible between the treatment of minors and the general system of criminal law.'

This differentiation mandated by Art. 31, of the Constitution, read also in the light of the obligations specified in the light of the international conventions mentioned above, which obligate the states to accord a special protection to minors, gives to Art. 27(3) of the Constitution in regard to the latter a significance distinct from that which applies to the generality of subjects with respect to the re-educative function of punishment. This function -given the particular attention which must be reserved, in obedience to Art. 31 of the Constitution, to the education problems of the young — must be considered for minors to be, if not exclusive, at least predominant which manifest an incurable contrast between it and the norms denounced, i.e. Art. 17 of the Penal Code which lists, among the penalties for crimes that of the penitentiary and Art. 22 of the Penal Code which characterizes this penalty as perpetual — both relating to the generality of subjects, without excluding minors.

6. As a consequence of the principal declaration of unconstitutionality it is also necessary, by virtue of Art. 27 of the Law of March 11, 1953 Nr. 87, to declare the partial unconstitutionality of the other mentioned provisions of the Penal Code, so as to make there the necessary adjustments apt to prevent the declaration of the unconstitutionality of Art. 17 and 22 of the Penal Code in the aforementioned sense from becoming inoperative, considering the inseparable nexus which, as has been seen, exists between the provisions in issue for the purpose of determining the penalty applicable to minors. The consequential character of the declaration of unconstitutionality which affects Art. 69 of the Penal Code thus impacts on the mechanism of the comparison of circumstances for the limited effects of the principal issue and cannot entail, as had been discussed already before, those effects exceeding the purpose of the question spelled out in the Judgment Nr. 140 of 1993.

Art. 69 of the Penal Code, as has been shown in the illustration of the mechanisms provided thereby in the case of a concurrence of heterogenous circumstances, determines the applicability of the penalty of the penitentiary also to a minor, either when the process of comparison produces a finding of a prevalence of aggravating circumstances, entailing a life sentence (as it is the case in the proceedings *a quo*), or in other instances of a finding of prevalence or merely of equivalence between the attenuating and aggravating circumstances, in the case of a crime punishable with the penitentiary, as contrasted with a situation in both of these cases indicating the applicability to the minor of the attenuation provided in Art. 98 of the Penal Code. The consequential declaration of the unconstitutionality, pursuant to Art. 27 of the Law of March 11, 1953 Nr. 87, of Art. 69 of the Penal Code, instead would permit the application also in these cases of the above mentioned diminution of punishment.

The consequential declaration of unconstitutionality can operate therefore only so as to eliminate from the system the unconstitutional part of the discipline, by way of the exclusion of the provisions regarding the process of balancing with respect — and limited — to the situations specified above.

Vice versa, it would not be a solution consistent with the limits flowing from a declaration pursuant to Art. 27 of the Law Nr. 87 of 1953, nor, more generally with the requirement of a proportionality between the actual crime and punishment if the Court would render a pronouncement which would arrive at a confirmation of the prevalence of the circumstance provided by Art.98 of the Penal Code in the cases in which the abstract possibility of the applicability of the penalty of the penitentiary to minors comes into play. * * *

7. In order to render the principal declaration of unconstitutionality fully effective it is also necessary to declare the consequential unconstitutionality of Art. 73(2), given the incompatibility with the Constitution of the substitute mechanism there provided in the case of a convicted criminally responsible minor. Obviously, because of the declaration of consequential unconstitutionality of Art. 73. cit. the penal judge is charged with the task of determining the penalty which is applicable in lieu of the penitentiary in the case — different from that of the proceedings *a quo* — in which there is a concourse of several crimes committed by the minor each of which is subject to confinement of not less than 24 years.

FOR THAT REASON

The Constitutional Court declares the unconstitutionality of Articles 17 and 22 of the Penal Code in the part in which they fail to exclude the applicability of the penalty of the penitentiary to a criminally responsible minor; it also declares, in application of Art. 27 of the Law of March 11, 1963 Nr. 87

a) the unconstitutionality of Art. 69(4) of the Penal Code in that part in which it provides that in respect to a criminally responsible minor the provision of Art. 69(1) is applicable in the case of a concurrence between the attenuating circumstances specified in Art. 98 of the Penal Code and one or more aggravating circumstances which call for the penalty of the penitentiary, as well as in the part in which it provides that with respect to such a minor the provisions of Art. 69(1) and (3), of the Penal Code are applicable in the case of a concurrence between the attenuating circumstances accompanying the commission of a crime punishable with the penalty of the penitentiary;

b) the unconstitutionality of Art. 73(2) of the Penal Code in the part in which it provides the penalty of the penitentiary in the case of a concurrence of several crimes committed by a criminally responsible minor, each of which is punishable with confinement of not less than 24 years.

NOTES

1. The text case illustrates the difficulties confronting the Court in reaching the apposite result without technically overruling a prior judgment involving the same substantive issue.

2. Observe that the Court refused to find a rule of customary international law banning the penalty of the penitentiary for minors under eighteen years, despite the numerous international declarations and agreements for the treatment of minors, but that the Court nevertheless resorts to these instruments in order to read Art. 31 of the Constitution in the light of the obligations specified therein.

3. The text case is commented upon by M. Ruotolo, *L'illegittimità costituzionale della pena dell'ergostolo nei confronti del minore: un segno di civiltà giuridica* 147 Giurisprudenza italiana 358 (1995) and by President E. Gallo, *Pena dell'ergastolo per i minori: davvero incostituzionale?* 39 Giurisprudenza costituzionale 1267 (1994).

c. Samo Pahor: Constitutionality of Italian C.P.C. Art. 122

Italy, Corte Costituzionale
Judgment of January 29, 1996, No. 15 (*Samo Pahor*)
148 Giurisprudenza Italiana I, 254 (1996).

1. The question of constitutionality submitted by the Pretor of Triest to examination of this Court is whether Art. 122(1) of the Code of Civil Procedure [C.P.C.] is in conformity with Articles 6 and 10 of the Constitution and Article 3 of the Constitutional Law of January 31, 1963 n.1 (Special Charter of the Region Friuli-Venezia Giulia) to the extent that by establishing in general that '*in the entire proceeding the use of the Italian language is prescribed*', it does not permit an Italian citizen belonging to the Slovenian linguistic minority in an execution proceeding before a judge having jurisdiction in a territory where such minority resides, to use, upon his request, his native language in the acts executed by him, utilizing in reference to them an Italian

translation and also to receive the acts of the judicial authority or the opposing party in translation into his language.

For reasons of relevance, the scope of the question submitted is restricted to the use of the language in civil enforcement procedures, consisting in the case at bar of garnishment proceedings as explained in the statement of facts. It is moreover evident — since there are no reasons to differentiate in the protection of minority languages and in the present case of the Slovenian language between this and that phase of civil proceedings, whether cognition or execution — that the arguments upon which the decision rests are destined to have a broader scope with respect to the right of the Slovenian minority to use their native language in general in controversies before a judge in which Art. 122(1) C.P.C. applies.

2. The protection of the linguistic minorities is one of the cardinal principles of the current order which the Constitution establishes by virtue of Art. 6, mandating that the Republic render it effective 'with apposite norms'. This principle, which represents the overcoming of the idea of the closed national state of the eighteenth century and a departure of great political and cultural significance with respect to the nationalistic notions manifested by fascism, has been evaluated many times by the jurisprudence of this Court, also because it encounters other principles — sometimes defined as supreme — which qualify inevitably and necessarily the current system (Judgments Nrs. 62 of 1992, No. 768 of 1988, No. 289 of 1987 and No. 312 of 1983), the pluralistic principle recognized by Art. 2 * * * and the principle of equality recognized by Art. 3 of the Constitution. * * *

With these provisions the Italian Constitution participates in the actual supranational movement in favor of the coexistence of human groups with diverse identity within the same political organizations of statehood, a movement pregnant with possible effects upon internal public law and which finds expression in the International Covenant of Civil and Political Rights, adopted on December 16, 1966 by the General Assembly of the U.N. and ratified by Italy with the Law of October 25, 1977 Nr. 881. After having proclaimed the principle of equality, without distinction by reason of language, national origin and birth, in the enjoyment of the rights recognized in the Covenant itself and the obligation of the states to render them effective according to their respective constitutional procedures, Art. 27 establishes that '*in those states in which ethnic, religious or linguistic minorities exist, persons belonging to such minorities shall not be denied the right, in community with other members of their group, to enjoy their own culture, to profess and practice their own religion, or to use their own language.*'

Nevertheless, the reference which the order of submission, by way of Art. 10(1) of the Constitution, makes to this norm, does not attribute to it constitutional legitimacy for the purposes of the present question.

In the first place, by virtue of formal reasons, one cannot say that in this case, as in other cases of the same type, one encounters a rule of generally recognized international law to which Art. 10 of the Constitution refers to incorporate the same into the Italian legal order, attributing thereto the effect of constitutional norms, as well as excluding the possibility to derogate therefrom by reason of fundamental principles of our order (Judgment Nr. 48 of 1979). Additionally, it rests on a resolution of the U.N. General Assembly, attached to a text which expresses an international agreement which has meanwhile found numerous adhesions and therefore is effective as a multilateral agreement, and, even if the principles there proclaimed have universal scope because of their intrinsic nature, the adhesion to this covenant by and it validity in Italy derives from an act of the sovereign individual will of the State expressed in the form of legislation. And that — while it does not prevent the attribution of great importance to these norms in the interpretation of the corresponding, but not always identical norms in the Constitution — bars the reliance on them as parameters in the judgment of the constitutionality of laws. * * *

In the second place, the reference contained in the order of submission to Art. 27 of the Covenant is irrelevant, if not outright counterproductive, in view of the content thereof, which

> guarantees the use of the native language in communications among members of the same minority as a way of existing and instrument of their cultural identity, but does not guarantee the external use of the language in relations with individuals or authorities not belonging to the same minority, which, instead, is the core of the question under consideration.

3. The Slovenian linguistic minority is the beneficiary, in addition to the general protection of Art. 6 of the Constitution, of that provided by other norms.

* * *

5. On the basis of the preceding considerations and the reconstruction of the norms governing the case under examination, the intent of the submitting judge, which favors the protection of the Slovenian language in the proceedings pending before him, appears to be fully justified. But this does not signify also that the question posed by him must be declared well-founded. In fact, the censured Art. 122(1) C.P.C. is not actually opposed to a translation of that intent into reality. It contains a provision with which the norms for the protection of the linguistic minority — such as they are specified in the group consisting of Arts. 6 of the Constitution, 3 of the Special Charter of the Region Friuli-Venezia Giulia and 8 of the Treaty of Osimo — may be combined; is not an incompatible norm which must be removed.

The official language of the proceedings continues to be one and the same, but an interested party may demand to use his native language, with the result that his own acts, expressed in Slovenian, are translated into the Italian language, and the acts of others, expressed in Italian, are translated into the Slovenian language. One language -Italian- is by virtue of Art. 122 the language in which the acts of the proceedings are composed and expressed. The other — in this case Slovenian — is the language which is added to the first as a means of the protection of the linguistic identify of the individual belonging to a linguistic minority. * * *

7. * * *

The Law of July 14, 1967 Nr. 568 has provided for the creation of functions as translator and interpreter in the districts of the Courts of Appeal where the necessity of such services exist and subsequent laws have determined the measure of the respective expenditures. It is not within the jurisdiction of this Court to evaluate the sufficiency of those provisions for the purpose of effectuating the rights in question.

* * *

For these reasons,

The Constitutional Court declares that the question of the constitutional validity of Art. 122(1) C.P.C., raised with reference to Arts. 6 and 10 of the Constitution and Art. 3 of the Constitutional Law of January 31, 1963 by the Pretor of Triest in the order indicated herein is not well-founded.

d. Judgment of January 23, 1974

Italy, Corte Costituzionale
Judgment of January 23, 1974, NR. 13 (*Regional Government of Bolzano*)

In the case of the *Regional Government of the Province of Bolzano v. The President of the Council of Ministers,* Constitutional Court, Judgment of January 23, 1974 nr. 13, 19 *Giurisprudenza Costituzionale* 47 (1974), the president of the regional council of the province of Bolzano instituted proceedings in the Constitutional Court, asking for a declaration of the unconstitutionality of the state Law of April 24, 1935 nr. 740 establishing the National Park of Stelvio, asserting that the act in question contravened Art. 5 of the Constitutional Law of November 10, 1971 nr. 1 as well as Art. 13 of the Constitutional Law of February 26, 1948 nr. 5 relating to the powers of the provinces in which the park was located (including Bolzano). The President of the Council of Ministers, as defendant, contended that the recourse was inadmissible because, if justified on the merits, it would involve a question of abrogation rather than unconstitutionality and therefore not be within the jurisdiction of the Constitutional Court. In addition, the defendant raised the issue of the time bar specified in Art. 32 par. 2 of the Law of March 11, 1953 nr. 87 on the composition and function of the Constitutional Court.

The Court dismissed the recourse as inadmissible. It held that although in general a subsequent law inconsistent with a prior law abrogates the same pursuant to Art. 15 of the introductory provisions of the Civil Code, this rule is inapplicable if it is intended to keep the prior law operative. This is the case in particular with respect to the state laws antedating the attribution of special status to the regions and provinces by the constitutional laws of 1971. This view is confirmed by the specification of time limits for the direct recourse (*ricorso in via principale*) by regions or provinces against state legislation, Law of March 11, 1953 nr. 87 Art. 32(2).

NOTE

1. Note that the norm control in the present case is an instance of *abstract* norm control rather than *concrete* norm control which is governed by Art. 23-30 of the Law of March 11, 1953 nr. 87.

C. GERMANY

1. INTRODUCTION

In Germany, the organization and functions of the judiciary are governed by Articles 92-104 of the Basic Law of May 22, 1949, as last amended by law of March 26, 1998 (BGBl 1998 I 610).[52]

According to the Basic Law, judicial power is vested in the Constitutional Court, the federal courts established pursuant to the Basic Law and the Courts of the *Länder* (states) (Basic Law, Art. 92). The federal courts provided by the Basic Law are the Supreme Courts for civil and criminal matters, for administrative matters, for finance matters, for labor controversies, and for social security controversies (Basic Law, Art. 95).

Accordingly, Germany divides controversies into five categories: (i) civil and penal; (ii) administrative; (iii) finance matters; (iv) labor and (v) social security.

---

52. The term Basic Law rather than Constitution was chosen because of the division of Germany into two German states. The term Constitution was to be reserved to Germany's Magna Carta after reunification. Actually reunification was accomplished by the accession of the new *Länder* to the western federation. As a result, Art. 146 was modified in Art. 4 of the Reunification Treaty of August 31, 1990 providing for the retention of the designation Basic Law until the adoption of a new constitution.

The term Basic Law was by no means coined in 1949. It had been used in the preliminary sketch of the short-lived constitution of March 28, 1949, which had been proposed under the title *Draft of the Basic Law of the German Empire* by the so-called Committee of Seventeen of the provisional parliament. Even before that time, the constitution of Hanover of September 26, 1833 had the title Basic Law of the State. Its abrogation by the king led to the protest and dismissal of the famous Seven of Göttingen. See F.S. Schnapp, *Wilhelm Eduard Albrecht*, 51 NJW 1541 (1998). Cf. D. Kühne, *150 Jahre Revolution von 1848/49-ihre Bedeutung für den deutschen Verfassungsstaat*. 51 NJW 1513, 1518 (1998). H.-J. Vogel, *Das Vermächtnis der Paulskirche* 51 NJW 1534. B.F. Kern, *Georg Besseler*, 51 NJW 1549 (1998).

2. German Court System

a. Ordinary Courts

Each category of controversies is within the jurisdiction of a separate hierarchy of tribunals with a federal supreme court on the top level. The German names for these 5 supreme courts are:

(i) *Bundesgerichtshof* (*BGH*), the Federal Court for Ordinary Jurisdiction, the highest court for civil and criminal matters, sitting in Karlsruhe;
(ii) *Bundesverwaltungsgericht (BVerwG)*, Federal Administrative Court, the highest court for administrative controversies, sitting Leipzig (BGBl 1997 I 2742 (1997));
(iii) *Bundesfinanzhof* (*BFH*), Federal Finance Court, the highest court for tax matters, sitting in Munich;
(iv) *Bundesarbeitsgericht* (*BAG*), Federal Labor Court, the highest court for labor controversies, formerly sitting in Kassel, now moved to Erlangen; and
(v) *Bundessozialgericht (BSG)*, Federal Social Security Court, highest court for social security controversies, sitting in Kassel.

The organization and jurisdiction of the ordinary courts of justice is governed by the Law on the Organization of Courts (*Gerichtsverfassungsgesetz* [GVG]), as revised in 1975,[53] with subsequent amendments.[54] The ordinary courts are the courts of first instance consisting of district and circuit courts (*Amtsgerichte* or *Landgerichte*)[55], intermediate courts of appeal, (*Oberlandesgerichte*)[56] and the highest court in that branch of jurisdiction, the Federal Court for Civil and Penal Matters, the *Bundesgerichtshof* (*BGH*).

The BGH, comprising 122 judges, is divided into panels called Senates, in numbers determined by the Ministry of Justice.[57] Currently it consists of 12 Senates for civil matters, 5 Senates for criminal matters and 8 Special Senates (*Spezialsenate*), consisting of 1 Senate for anti-trust matters, 1 Senate for agricultural matters and 6 Senates for disciplinary matters. The categories of cases allocated to them are[58]:

---

53. BGBl 1975 I 1077.
54. Law of October 28, 1996
55. GVG §§ 23, 23a, 23b, 71.
56. GVG § 119 (jurisdiction in civil matters).
57. GVG § 130.
58. Plans of the distribution of affairs among the different senates of the federal courts, *Bundesanzeiger* 1998 Nr. 35a of February 2, 1998. Up-to-date information is available on the website, www.unikarlsruhe.de/~BGH/index.html.

Ist Senate: Copyright, unfair competition, trademarks, shipping and freight;

II^{d} Senate: Maritime matters, including maritime insurance, business organizations, movable property;

IIIrd Senate: Damage claims against the state and public officials, claims based on the Convention on Human Rights;

IVth Senate: Probate and insurance litigation;

Vth Senate: Real property issues;

VIth Senate: Torts and medical malpractice;

VIIth Senate: Construction contracts;

VIIIth Senate: Sale and exchange of chattels, leasing, landlord and tenant;

IXth Senate: Restitution, suretyship, execution against real property, bankruptcy and avoidance of fraudulent conveyances;

Xth Senate: Patents and protection of chips;

XIth Senate: Banking law, bank guarantees, securities;

XIIth Senate: Law of persons, family law, matrimonial property.

In order to preserve uniformity of adjudications among the various Senates within the Supreme Court for Civil and Criminal Matters and among the 5 Supreme Courts, special formations are provided, viz: the Large Senate of Civil Matters, the Large Senate for Criminal Matters, the United Large Senates and in cases of disagreement among supreme courts, the Common Senate of the Supreme Courts.

The convocation or and procedure before the Large Senate for Civil Matters, the Large Senate for Criminal Matters and the United Large Senates (VGS) are governed by §§ 132 and 138 of the GVG as amended by the Law for the Simplification of Judicial Administration of 1991.

The creation and functions of the Common Senate of the Supreme Courts are governed by Art. 95(3) of the Basic Law, as amended by Law of June 18, 1968 and the Law for the preservation of the uniformity of the adjudications of the supreme federal courts of June 19, 1968 (BGBl 1968 I 661).

Usually a senate for civil matters sits as a five judge panel. If a senate is composed of more than five judges, the allocation of cases belonging to the type of controversies assigned to that senate to the individual judges is subject to objective criteria, determined by the presiding judge before the commencement of the judicial year. The large Senate for Civil Matters consists of the president of the court and one member of each senate for civil matters, the large Senate of Criminal Matters consists of the president of the court and two members of each senate for criminal matters and the United Large Senates are composed of the president of the court and the members of the Large Senates (normally 22 judges in addition to the president), *GVG* §132V.

The Common Senate of the Supreme Courts, whose sole function is to resolve existing disagreements among supreme courts, normally is comprised of the presidents of the five supreme courts, the presiding judges of the senates involved and one additional member of the senates involved, hence a bench of at least nine judges,

RsprEinhG[59] §3. The procedure before the Common Senate is governed by the law June 19, 1968.

The organization and jurisdiction of the other four judicial branches are subject to comparable provisions in the relevant statutes. Thus the organization and functions of the administrative courts are governed by the Law on The Administrative Courts (*VerwGO*),[60] those of the finance courts by the Law on Finance Courts (*FGO*),[61] those of the labor courts by the Law on Labor Courts (*ArbGG*),[62] and those of the social security courts by the Law on Social Security Courts (*SGG*).[63]

All of the supreme courts of these four branches are divided into several senates and therefore may have to form a Large Senate to handle disagreements. According to the *Plans of the Distribution of Affairs among the Different Senates* of these courts for the year 1998[64] the following structural picture emerges:(i) *BVerwG*, composed of 11 senates for petitions of review, 2 senates for disciplinary matters, 2 senates relating to military service and a large senate; (ii) *BFH*, composed of 11 senates and a large senate; (iii) *BAG* composed of 10 senates and a large senate; (iv) *BSOCG*, composed of 14 senates and a large senate.

The *BGH* is not a court of error but a court of revision which, on petition for review, examines the whole record as to the correct application of the law. The petition for revision in civil matters and its admissibility is governed by the German Code of Civil Procedure (*Zivilprozessordnung* [*ZPO*] of 1877) §§545-566a. In pecuniary controversies in which the gravamen does not exceed the amount of DM 60,000 and in non-pecuniary controversies a petition for review is only admissible if the court of appeal has allowed it in its judgment. Such permission must be given if the issue involved is of fundamental significance or if the court departs from a precedent of the BGH or of the Common Senate of the Federal Supreme Courts. (ZPO §546).

b. Federal Constitutional Court (Bundesverfassungsgericht).

The Basic Law establishes a separate constitutional court[65] which, inter alia, is vested with exclusive jurisdiction of the constitutionality of normative acts, in partic-

---

59. Gesetz zur Wahrung der Einheitlichkeit der Rechtsprechung der obersten Gerichtshöfe des Bundes, June 19, 1968, or Rechtsprechungseinheitlichkeitsgesetz [RsprEinhG] BGBl I 661 (1968)

60. Law of January 21, 1960 as revised and republished on March 19, 1991 (BGBl 1991, I 686) as last amended by the Law of November 1, 1996, BGBl 1996 I 1126. For an annotated edition see Eyermann, Verwaltungerichtsordnung, Kommentar, 10th ed. (1998).

61. Law of October 6, 1965, BGBl 1965 I, 1477, as amended by the FGO — amendment law of November 21, 1992, BGBl 1992, I 2109

62. Law of July 2, 1979, BGBl 1979 I, 853, 1036.

63. Law of September 23, 1975, BGBl 1975 I , 2525.

64. Bundesanzeiger 1998, Nr. 35a of February 20, 1998.

65. Basic Law, Arts. 92, 93, 94, 100.

ular of legislation.[66] In that respect the Basic Law departed from the prior situation and chose to adopt the so-called Austrian model of *concentrated* judicial review. The Federal Constitutional Court is composed of 16 members, one half of whom are elected by the House of Deputies (*Bundestag*) and the other half by the Federal Council (*Bundesrat*).

A special statute, the law on the federal constitutional court,[67] governs the composition and procedures of the court and determines the cases in which its judgments have the force of law. According to that law the federal constitutional court consists of 2 senates of 8 members, one of whom is the president of the court and also serves as presiding judge of one of the senates.[68] Each senate adjudicates the controversies assigned to it pursuant to §14(1) to (3) of the BVerfGG. The full bench is convoked to resolve disagreements between the senates.[69]

Constitutional review is exercised in three types of proceedings, called concrete norms' control, abstract norms' control and constitutional complaints. Concrete norms' control takes place when in a pending litigation a court entertains serious doubts on the constitutionality of an applicable statute or other rule of law. In that case the court must suspend the proceedings and submit the issue to the BVerfG.[70] Abstract norms' control is exercised where it is requested by the federal government, a state government or one third of the members of the House of Deputies.[71] Federal legislation is subject to abstract norms' control even after its entry into force. Constitutional complaints may be lodged by any person who claims that a governmental act, including a final judicial decision, infringes on a fundamental right of his or a constitutional guarantee based on the Basic Law, Articles 20(4), 33, 38, 101, 103 and 109.[72] A constitutional complaint may be directed against a federal statute directly infringing claimants' constitutional rights[73] or against a final judicial decision, including a judgment of the BGH.

In the latter case, the federal constitutional court does not sit as a court of a super-revision. The supreme court has the constitutional power to err. It likewise may, by way of progressive development of the law, adapt the interpretation of existing statutes to new scientific insights and notions of fairness. The constitutional court

---

66. Basic Law, Act 93(2), 93(4a) and 100.

67. Bundesverfassungsgerichtsgesetz (*BVerfGG*) as most recently revised on August 11, 1993, BGBl 1993 I, 1474.

68. BVerfGG §§2, 5-10, and 15.

69. BVerfGG, §16.

70. BVerfGG, § 13 (11), §§ 80-85.

71. BVerfGG, §13 (6), §§76-79.

72. BVerfGG, §13 (8a) and §90.

73. An example of a statute purportedly directly infringing a complainant's constitutional rights was the law authorizing the ratification of the Unification Treaty, to the extent that it perpetuated expropriations by the occupation powers without compensation. The BVerfG (First Senate), by order of November 19, 1991 held that the constitutional complaint was admissible, but unfounded, 85 BVerfGE 117 (1992).

may only determine whether a judgment is arbitrary or violates a constitutional right of the complainant.[74]

An interesting case in point concerned the liability of physicians, one of whom had unsuccessfully performed a sterilization and thus caused the unwanted birth of a healthy fourth child and the other of whom had failed to recognize the medical indications of the likelihood that a pregnant patient would give birth to a mentally defective child and to inform the parents of the danger. The Supreme Court, on petition for review, in one of these cases, declared that both physicians were liable to the parents for the costs of the support of the child.[75]

Both physicians filed constitutional complaints against the respective judgments which were dismissed as unfounded by the BVerfG, First Senate.[76] In its reasons the court stated: "The interpretation of ordinary statutes, including the choice of the applicable methods, belongs to the regular courts. The constitutional court merely assures that the requirements of the Basic Law are complied with." In the particular case it was argued that the Second Senate had held that the birth of a child could never be deemed to be the cause of an injury. The First Senate concluded that the statement referred to did not amount to a holding and therefore did not necessitate the invocation of the full bench, despite the fact that the Second Senate during the pending of the case before the First Senate, had adopted a resolution declaring that the statement relied upon by complainants was a basis of its decision.[77]

Because of the staggering increase in constitutional complaints the BVerfGG was amended so as to provide some relief for the overburdened Senates. According to BVerfGG §15a (1) and (2) each Senate may establish several chambers, consisting of three members of the Senate to deal inter alia with constitutional complaints. A constitutional complaint must be admitted for decision either by the Senate itself or by a chamber. In certain in cases the admission is mandatory. In some cases the chamber may pass on the merits of the complaint.[78] Currently each Senate has established three chambers.[79]

The categories of the decisions of the BVerfG and their effect are governed by the BVerfGG[80] only cursorily, and the applicable law has been refined by the court signif-

74. BVerfG (First Senate), Order of November 12, 1997, 51 NJW 519 (1998).

75. Relying on prior judgments to that effect, BGH (VIth Senate for Civil Matters) Judgment of November 16, 1993), 124 BGHZ 128 (1994); 47 NJW 788 (1994) and authorities cited.

76. BVerfG (First Senate), Order of November 12, 1997 (1 BvR 479/92 and 1 BvR 307/94), 51 NJW 519 (1998).

77. BVerfG (Second Senate) Order of October 22, 1997, 51 NJW 523 (1998). For a case referred to and decided by the Full Bench, see BVerfG (Full Bench), Order of April 8, 1997; 95 BVerfGE 322 (1997) on the significance of Basic Law, Art. 101 I 2 for the selection of the panels of regular judges in divisions of courts with more than the required number of judges.

78. BVerfGG §§93a-93d.

79. Plan for the distribution of affairs for the BVerfG for the year 1998.

80. BVerfGG, §31(1) and (2).

icantly over the course of time. The decisions of the court are either orders (*Beschlüsse*) or judgments (*Urteile*).[81] A decision may either annul a statute or declare it to be incompatible with the Basic Law. Annulment of a statute usually has *ex tunc* and *erga omnes* effect. Since that result may create a legal vacuum, the effect of which would worsen the prior situation, the court has restricted the retroactive effect of some of its decisions and attributed to them only *ex nunc* or even *in futuro* effect, with the result that the incompatible statute is tolerated as to the past and for a limited period *in futuro*. In a famous instance[82] the Court even laid down rules governing in the interim between the date of its decision and the enactment of a new statute. The legal situation of the parties affected by the statute held to be incompatible with the basic Law remained unresolved until clarified by the new law.

Since according to the Basic Law[83] rules of customary international law prevail over domestic legislation, the BVerfG is vested with jurisdiction to determine whether a rule of international law is part of the federal law and generates directly rights and obligations of individuals.[84] It is an unresolved question whether the BVerfG is a court of last resort and under a duty of submitting preliminary questions under EC-Treaty Art. 177 to the ECJ which is a legal judge pursuant to Basic Law, Art. 101 I 2.

The so-called concrete control of norms (see supra note b(2)) and the concentration of it in the Federal Constitutional Court, applies only to the so-called post-constitutional laws; pre-constitutional legislation, to the extent that it conflicts with the Basic Law, is considered abrogated thereby. This issue is left to the jurisdiction of the ordinary courts (2 BVerfGE 124, 128 *et s.* (1953); constant case-law.)

An exception to the rule is recognized for those pre-constitutional laws which the legislator, after the Basic law had entered into force, 'received in its intent' (66 BVerfGE 248, 254 (1984) with further references). Whether such reception is or is not present depends on various factors. Mere lapse of time is not sufficient, but strengthens the conclusion that such acceptance has occurred, if the subject matter has been considered in post-constitutional legislation. (Cf 70 BVerfGE 126, 129 (1985).)

2. *TEXTS:* Excerpts from the German Basic Law and other relevent statutes:

a. *Basic Law* [GG],
b. *Law on the Federal Constitutional Court* [BVerfGG],
c. *Law on the Organization of Courts* [GVG],

d. *Law for the Preservation of the Uniformity of the Adjudications of the Supreme Courts of the Federal Republic* [RsprEinhG].

---

81. BVerfGG, §25 (2) decision based on oral argument is designated as a judgment, a decision without prior oral argument is designated an order.

82. BVerfG (First Senate), Order of March 5, 1991 (1BvL 83/86 and 24/88), 84 BVerfGE 9 (1992).

83. Basic Law, Art. 100 II.

84. BVerfGG, §13 (12), §14 (2), §31 (2), §§ 83 and 84.

a. GG

THE BASIC LAW (*GRUNDGESETZ* [*GG*])

Art. 93 GG
(Jurisdiction of the Federal Constitutional Court)

(1) The Federal Constitutional Court decides:

1. The interpretation of the Basic Law in controversies about the scope of the rights and duties of one of the supreme federal organs of the Federation or other participants which possess rights of their own either pursuant to the Basic Law or the internal order of a supreme organ of the Federation.

2. In cases of disagreements or doubts about the formal or substantive compatibility of federal or state legislation with the Basic Law or the compatibility of state legislation with other federal law upon the petition of the federal government, a state government or one third of the members of the House of Deputies.

3. and 4. * * *

4a. Constitutional complaints which can be brought by anyone who claims that a public authority has infringed one of his fundamental rights or one of his rights contained in Arts. 20(4), 33, 38, 101, 103, and 104.

4b. & 5. * * *

(2) The Federal Constitutional Court is competent also in other cases assigned to it by law.

Art. 94 GG
(Composition and Organization of the Federal Constitutional Court)

1. The Constitutional Court consists of Federal Judges and other members. The members of the Constitutional Court are elected one half by the House of Deputies and one half by the Federal Council. They may not be members of the House of Deputies, the Federal Council, the Federal Government or corresponding state organs.

2. A federal statute governs its constitution and procedure and determines in which cases its decisions may have the force of law. It may provide that constitutional complaints require the prior exhaustion of legal remedies and subject the admissibility to a special procedure.

Art. 100 GG
(Concrete control of norms,
International law as part of Federal law)

(1) If a court considers a statute, the validity of which is relevant for the decision to be unconstitutional, the proceedings must be suspended and * * *, if the Basic Law is involved, the decision of the Federal Constitutional Court be sought. This applies also if the infringement of the Basic Law by a state statute or the inconsistency of state law with law is in issue.

(2) If in a litigation a doubt arises whether a rule of customary international law forms a part of the law and whether it creates rights and duties for an individual (GG Art. 25), the court has to request a decision of the Federal Constitutional Court.

b. BVerfGG

LAW ON THE FEDERAL CONSTITUTIONAL COURT

(Gesetz über das Bundesverfassungsgericht [BVerfGG]
(Revised August 11, 1993, BGBl 1993 I 1474.)
Part I
§2 BVerfGG

(1) The Federal Constitutional Court consists of two panels (Senates).

(2) For each Senate 8 judges are elected.

(3) Three judges of each Senate are elected from judges of the Supreme Courts.

* * *

§13 BVerfGG

The Federal Constitutional Court decides the cases assigned to it by the Basic Law:

1. * * * (Art. 18 GG).
2. * * * (Art. 21, par. 2 GG).
3. * * * (Art. 41, par. 2 GG).
4. * * * (Art. 61 GG).
5. * * * (Art. 93, par. 1, nr. 1 GG).
6. In cases of disagreements or doubts about the formal or substantive compatibility of federal or state legislation with the Basic Law or the compatibility of state legislation with other law upon petition of the government, a state government or one third of the members of the Federal House of Deputies, (Art. 93, par. 1, nr. 2 GG).
7. * * * (Art. 93, par. 1, nr. 3 GG).
8. * * * (Art. 93, par. 1, nr. 4 GG).

8a. Constitutional complaints (Art. 93 par.1, nr.4a & 4b GG).

9. * * * (Arts. 98, par. 2 and 5 GG).

10. * * * (Arts. 98, par. 99 GG).

11. The compatibility with the Basic Law of a federal or state statute or the compatibility with federal law of a state statute or other state law upon request by a court (Art. 100, par. 1 GG).

12. * * * (Art. 100, par. 2 GG).

13. * * * (Art. 100, par. 3 GG).

14 * * * (Art. 126 GG).

15. * * * (Art. 93, par. 2 GG).

§14 BVerfGG

(1) The First Senate of the Federal Constitutional Court has jurisdiction with respect to the norms control proceedings (§13 nr. 6 and 11) in which primarily the incompatibility of a provision with the fundamental right or rights flowing from Articles 33, 101, 103 and 104 GG is asserted as well as with respect to constitutional complaints, except constitutional complaints pursuant to Art. 91 and Constitutional conflicts concerning election law.

* * *

§15a BVerfGG

(1) The Senates establish, for the duration of a business year, one or more chambers. Each chamber consists of 3 judges. The composition of a chamber shall not remain unaltered for more than three years.

(2) Prior to the beginning of each business year, the Senate determines for its duration the distribution among the reporting judges of the petitions pursuant to §80 and of the constitutional complaints pursuant to §§ 90 and 91, the number and composition of the chambers, as well as the substitutes for their members.

§16 BVerfGG

(1) If one Senate in a legal question wishes to depart in a legal question from the view thereof of the other Senate expressed in a decision, the full court must pass on it.

(2) * * *

Part II

* * *

§31 BVerfGG

(1) The decisions of the Federal Constitutional Court are binding upon all constitutional organs of the Federation and the States as well as upon courts and officials.

(2) In the cases of §13, nrs. 6, 11, 12 and 14, the decision of the Federal Constitutional Court has the force of law. This applies also in the cases of §13, nr. 8a if the Constitutional Court declares a statute to be compatible or incompatible with the Basic Law or to be void. To the extent that a law is declared to be compatible or incom-

patible with the Basic Law or other federal law or to be void, the holding is to be published by the Federal Minister of Justice in the Official Journal. A corresponding rule applies to the holdings in the cases of § 13 nrs. 12 and 14.

Division IX
Proceedings in the cases of §13, nr. 11.
§80 BVerfGG

(1) If the conditions of Art. 100, par. 1 of the Basic Law are met, the courts must immediately seek the decision of the Federal Constitutional Court.

(2) The reasons must specify to what extent the decision depends on the validity of the legal provision and with which superior legal norm it is incompatible. The files must be added.

(3) The request of the court is independent of an assertion of the invalidity of the legal provision by one of the parties.

§81a BVerfGG

The Chamber may establish the inadmissibility of a petition pursuant to §80 by a unanimous resolution. The decision is reserved to the Senate, if the petition is submitted by the constitutional court of a state or a Federal supreme court.

* * *

Division 15
Proceedings in the Cases of §13, nr. 8a.
§90 BVerfGG

(1) Anyone may institute a constitutional complaint in the Federal Constitutional Court with the assertion that a public authority has infringed one of his fundamental rights or one of his rights flowing from Articles 20(4), 33, 38, 101, 103 and 104 of the Basic Law.

(2) If the infringement can be redressed by judicial proceedings, the constitutional complaint is only admissible after exhaustion of the legal proceedings. The Federal Constitutional Court, however, may pass immediately on a constitutional complaint filed prior to the exhaustion of legal remedies if it is of general significance or if the complainant would suffer a grave and unavoidable injury if he has to resort first to a judicial remedy.

§93 BVerfGG

(1) The constitutional complaint must be filed and furnished with reasons within a month. The period starts with the service of the * * * decision.

(2) * * *

(3) If the constitutional complaint is directed against a statute or another act of a public authority against which no judicial remedy exists, the constitutional complaint

must be filed within one year after the entry into force of the statute or the issuance of the act.

(4) * * *

§93a BVerfGG

(1) The constitutional complaint must be accepted for decision.
(2) It must be accepted for decision
  a) to the extent that it has fundamental constitutional significance,
  b) if it is indicated for the enforcement of the rights listed in § 90, par. 1. This may also be the case if the complainant would suffer a specially grave injury by the denial of a decision on the merits.

§93b BVerfGG

The Chamber may deny the acceptance of a constitutional complaint or accept it in the case of §93c. Otherwise, the Senate passes on the acceptance.

§93c BVerfGG

(1) If the conditions of §93a(2)(b) are met and the Federal Constitutional Court has already passed on the relevant constitutional question, the Chamber may grant the constitutional complaint if it is manifestly justified. The decision is equivalent to a decision by the Senate. A decision which declares with the force of law that a statute is incompatible with the Basic Law or other law or void, is reserved to the Senate.

(2) * * *

§93d BVerfGG

(1) A decision pursuant to §93b and 93c is rendered without oral argument. It is not subject to review. A denial of the acceptance of a constitutional complaint needs no stated reasons.

(2) * * *.

(3) The decisions of the chamber are unanimous. An acceptance by the Senate is decided when at least 3 judges vote in its favor.

c. GVG

Law of the Organization of Courts
(*Gerichtsverfassungsgesetz* [GVG]).
§ 132 GVG

(As amended by Art. 2 Nr. 11 of the Law for the Simplification of the Administration of Justice [*RPflVereinfG*], Dec. 17, 1990.)

(1) At the Supreme Court for Civil and Criminal Matters there are established a Large Senate for Civil Matters and a Large Senate for Criminal Matters. The Large Senates form the United Large Senates.

(2) In the event a Senate, in a legal question, wishes to depart from the decision of another Senate, the Large Senate for Civil Matters renders the decision, if one Senate for Civil Matters wants to depart from another Senate for Civil Matters or the Large Senate for Civil Matters * * * the United Large Senates decide if a Senate for Civil Matters wants to depart from a Senate or the Large Senate in Criminal Matters. * * *

(3) A submission to the Large Senate * * * is only permitted if the Senate from whose decision a departure is sought declares upon inquiry by the Senate which wishes to depart, that it still adheres to its decision. * * *

(4) The Senate before which a case is pending may submit a legal question of fundamental significance to the Large Senate, if this is necessary to the development of the law (*Rechtsfortbildung*) or to the preservation of uniform adjudications.

(5) The Large Senate for Civil Matters consists of the President and one member of each Senate for Civil Matters. * * *

d. RsprEinhG

Law for the Preservation of the Uniformity of the Adjudications of the Supreme Courts of the Federal Republic. *(Gesetz zur Wahrung der Einheitlichkeit der Rechtsprechung der obersten Gerichtshöfe des Bundes).* June 19, 1968 (BGBl I 661 (1968)).

§1 *Establishment of the Common Senate.*

(1) For the preservation of the uniformity of the adjudications of the supreme courts listed in Art. 93(1) of the Basic Law, there is established a Common Senate of these supreme courts.

(2) The Common Senate has its seat in Karlsruhe.

§2 *Jurisdiction*

(1) The Common Senate decides when a supreme court in a question of law intends to depart from the decision of another supreme court or the common senate.

(2) If, according to the laws on the judicial organization or procedural laws, the large senate or the united large senates of a supreme court must be invoked, the common senate may pass on the question only if the large senate or the united senates wish to depart from the decision of another supreme court or the common senate.

§3 *Composition*

(1) The Common Senate is composed of:

1. the presidents of the supreme courts,

2. the presidents of the involved senates, and
3. an additional judge from each of the involved senates.

* * *

§11 *Submission Procedure*

(1) The procedure before the common senate is initiated by way of a submission order (*Vorlegungsbeschluss*). It must identify the decision of the supreme court from which the submitting senate wishes to depart. The resolution must give the reasons and must be served on the parties.

(2) The senates, the large senates or the united large senates of the supreme courts seek the decision of the common senate directly. At the same time, the proceedings before the submitting senate must be suspended.

* * *

§15 *Object of the Decision*

(1) The common senate, after oral proceedings, decides only the question of law.
* * *

§16 *Effect of the Decision*

The decision of the common senate binds the submitting senate with respect to the pending controversy.

4. Illustrative Cases: *Cases decided by a Large Senate for Civil Matters, the Common Senate for Civil Matters, the Common Senate of the Federal Supreme Courts or the Federal Constitutional Courts.*

a. Lost use-value case.

BGH Large Senate for Civil Matters,
Order of July 9, 1986. D. (Pl.) v. B. *et al.* (Def.)
98 BGHZ 212 (1987).

It may constitute a compensable economic loss if the owner of an object used by himself, at any rate of a house serving as his residence, is prevented temporarily from making use thereof as the result of a tortious interference with the property, although he does not incur any expenses or losses of income. (BGB §§ 249, 252)

I

Plaintiff is owner of a comfortably furnished residence which is her own home. Below her premises defendants constructed row-houses on a steeply declining building lot. The necessary excavations on the incline were not properly carried out and the stability of plaintiff's building was temporarily impaired. As a consequence the City prohibited the use of her dwelling by the plaintiff during the period from August 12 to August 16, 1981.

In addition to the costs of the repairs which are no longer in dispute, plaintiff demanded payment in the amount of DM 3,000 plus interest as compensation for the loss of the use of her residence. She alleges that during the period of the prohibition to make use of her building she and her husband lived in a camper which was placed in the vicinity of the premises. Defendants, however, claim that the spouses were daily in the house.

The district court and the court of appeal dismissed the complaint. With the admitted petition for revision plaintiff prosecutes her complaint. The Fifth Senate for Civil Matters shares the view of the appellate court that plaintiff, even assuming a total loss of the use of her residence during the period of the use prohibition, has not suffered an economic loss but merely a non-economic non-compensable injury and wishes therefore to dismiss the petition. In order to assure uniformity in the court's adjudications it submits, pursuant to § 137 [now § 132] GVG, the following questions to the Large Senate for Civil Matters:

1. Does it constitute a compensable economic loss if the owner of an object used by himself, in particular of a house occupied as his residence, is temporarily prevented from using the same by reason of an interference with his property even though he does not incur additional expenses or loss of income as a result of such prevention?

2. If compensable damages resulting from the loss of use are held to exist, how is the amount of these damages to be computed?

II

In the case law of the Supreme Court for Civil and Criminal Matters there is no uniform answer to the question of the compensability of use-losses, as is demonstrated in detail in the order of submission (published in VersR 189 (1986) = 40 WM 266 (1986) = 44 JZ 387 (1986)).

The III., VI., VII., and VIII. Senate for Civil Matters have, on principle, given an affirmative answer to that question, if the prevailing business practices (*Verkehrsauffassung*) attribute to the ability to make use of one's property for one's own purposes an independent economic value and the loss is felt by the owner, because, but for the injurious event, he could and would have made use of the property. On that basis the courts, since the decisions of the III. Senate for Civil Matters of September 30, 1963 (40 BGHZ 345, 349 et seq. (1964)) and III ZR. 186/61 (17 NJW 717 (1964) = VersR. 380 (1964)), have awarded to the owner of a motor vehicle used by himself compensation for a temporary loss of its use even if he does not rent another car to bridge the gap. The decisions dealing with the loss of the use of motor vehicles resulting from tort or relating thereto in other connections rest on the notion that it is precisely the usually uninterrupted disposability of objects of that kind which is purchased, with the result that the impairment of their use constitutes an impairment of the monetary equivalent of these expenditures (40 BGHZ 345, 348, 350 (1964); 63 BGHZ 393, 397 (1975); 74 BGHZ 231, 234 (1980); 76 BGHZ 179, 185 (1980); 86 BGHZ 128, 131,

133 (1983) * * * and that the tortfeasor should not be relieved if the victim assumes the deprivations resulting from his giving up the use (45 BGHZ 212, 216 (1966); 56 BGHZ 214, 215 (1971); 63 BGHZ 393, 396 (1975); 70 BGHZ 199, 204 (1978); 76 BGHZ 179, 186 (1980); 86 BGHZ 128, 132 (1983)). This type of use is contrasted with one which customarily is viewed as a hobby (76 BGHZ 179, 187 (1980) — pool), as a luxury (63 BGHZ 393, 398 (1975) — fur coat; 86 BGHZ 128, 133 (1983) — camper), or as mere means of leisure-enjoyment (89 BGHZ 60, 64 (1984) — motor sport boat) and which therefore is considered valuable only for an increased enjoyment of life but without independent economic value.

On this basis the VIII. Senate for Civil Matters, although with express limitation to contractual liability, awarded use-loss compensation to the owner of a house for its temporary inhabitability resulting from the post-contractual fault of the tenant (Judgment of June 14, 1967, 20 NJW 1803 (1967) (not fully reported).) The same analysis — although buttressed by a resort to the normative purpose of the statutory warranties for the affirmation of the independent monetary value of the opportunity of utilization — was adopted by the VII. Senate for Civil Matters as basis for its decision of October 10, 1985 (96 BGHZ 124 (1986)) which, likewise in the context of contractual liability, awarded damages to the owner against a construction company for the unusability of parking spaces in a garage during the contractually required elimination of defects.

In contrast to these precedents, the V. Senate for Civil Matters expressed doubts against the permissibility of awards of damages for use-losses 'outside a sharply defined area of typical mass risks' already in its Judgments of May 14, 1976 (66 BGHZ 277 (1977)) and of April 21, 1978 (71 BGHZ 134 (1978)), thereby anticipating its arguments in the resolution of submission. As to liability in tort, at any rate, the Senate took the position in its Judgment of November 30, 1979 (75 BGHZ 366 (1980)) that a mere impairment of the use of a lot which does not amount to a total loss of usability is not a compensable economic loss.

The prevailing view of the literature seems to reject the qualification of the temporary loss of the use of one's property as an economic damage and considers such loss only as the source of damage which in the case of the use of one's own property has merely the character of a non-compensable non-economic loss.

[Editors' note: Extensive discussion of the views of a lengthy list of commentators is omitted.]

III

The Large Senate takes the view that, apart from the cases of the use of one's motor vehicle, at any rate also in the cases of objects upon whose uninterrupted disposability to the owner the lifestyle of the owner depends, as in the case of a house serving as his residence, the temporary loss of its use by the owner due to a tortious interference with the property constitutes a compensable loss if the owner would have made such use at the time of the deprivation. At any rate, subject to this limitation, monetary compensation is barred neither by the law nor the need for legal security. Rather a just and complete compensation of economic damages requires that losses of this kind do not remain uncompensated.

1. The Civil Code [BGB] for purposes of the law governing compensation of damages, has not defined the concepts of assets and economic damages, but has left them to the elaboration by text-writers and the courts. In general the present Federal Supreme Court, as formerly the Imperial Supreme Court, determines economic damages to the subject-oriented totality of a person's assets by means of a comparison of the economic situation created by the injurious event with that which would have existed but for this event (27 BGHZ 181, 183 et seq. (1958); 40 BGHZ 345 (1964); 75 BGHZ 366, 371 (1980); 86 BGHZ 128, 130 (1983)).

The Senate proposing the question points out correctly that the computation of a difference, oriented on the value of existing assets, is incapable of showing diminutions incurred by the loss of a self-use of an object. In this type of computation, the depreciation of an object for its use, if no expenses are incurred for the acquisition of a surrogate, becomes manifest only if there is a loss of gain owing to the impossibility of commercial utilization or the avoidance of expenditure or debts by means of the exploitation of the object.

a. Nevertheless, the case-law of the Federal Supreme Court has affirmed the conclusion that the difference method as value-neutral computation method does not relieve the court from valuing the items inserted in the balance sheet on the basis of the purpose of liability for damages and the compensatory function of the reparation of damages. In this sense the difference method, which by the way is not spelled out in the Code, is a normative requirement (cf. 50 BGHZ 304, 306 (1969) — *GSZ*). To be sure in the balance sheet of the difference, economic damages are always expressed as decrease of activa or increase of passiva; but it is the task of legal valuation to determine the parameters of the balance sheet for the purpose of compensation for damages.

b. A difference computation, designed to compensate economic losses, cannot neglect that the essence and significance of the ownership of assets is not exhausted by its existence — the holding of it — but that it includes all the opportunities immanent in such ownership, to utilize it for the achievement of one's purposes (cf. already, Savigny, *System des heutigen Römischen Rechts,* 1840, Vol. I p. 339). This functional attribution is protected by the law relating to economic interests.

If in the case of a tortious invasion of such rights the compensation for impairment of exploitation — because expressed in monetary terms — were to comprise only losses in a commercial exploitation, it would neglect that ownership of assets not only enables this type of utilization but that self-use also constitutes a profitable activation of such assets the diminution of which may affect the economic sphere of the owner in a comparable way, although it is not expressed in a loss of income.

In the case of a motor vehicle its private use by the owner is often not only an important component of his assets but frequently serves as the economic basis of his living standard resting thereon, especially if his occupation depends on the motor vehicle. To an even greater extent does the decision to meet one's need for a place to live by way of home ownership depend primarily on economic considerations.

The market evaluates the aptitude of such economic goods to be utilized for private purposes in their price and registers their temporary loss as a temporary depreciation. If this depreciation corresponds to a noticeable impairment of the owner's living standard because he depended on the use of the property during the period of the loss thereof, this impairment is without relevance only for a caculation which rests entirely on an augmentation increase or diminution of the assets. Such an approach, however, is not mandated by the essence and destination of the ownership of assets.

2. Likewise it is also not required by § 252 BGB. In the case of a commercial productive exploitation of an object, the impairment of its use-value is usually expressible in terms of a loss of profits the compensation of which is expressly mandated by § 252 BGB. This provision underscores the significance which the legislator, in the law of damages, has attributed to losses in the commercial, profits producing utilization of economic goods; an analogous provision for the self-use of one's assets is lacking. But that does not permit to conclude, as the Senate proposing the question does, that the law has decided against compensation of losses in the self-use of these objects not entailing a loss of profits. Section 252 BGB was designed to clarify that — in contrast to prior codifications — the entire economic interest, independent of the degree of culpability, must be compensated (Mot. II 17f). To that extent this provision implements the principle of full reparation flowing from § 249 BGB. Into this conception fits also § 252 sentence 2 BGB, which the jurisprudence until now has considered only as an attenuation of the burden of proof designed to prevent that the injured owner is relegated to a minimum recovery in the case of damages that are difficult to demonstrate.

3. Without extension to impairments of the self-use of property the law of compensation for damages would entail unsatisfactory results especially in the case of assets which are of central significance for one's own mode of life.

* * *

4. It is, however, necessary that the indicated supplementation of the Code remains limited to such objects upon whose uninterrupted disposability the life-style by means of self-use is typically dependent.

* * *

IV

The elaboration of methods for quantifying such use-losses, the appositeness of which depend in large measure upon the class of things affected and the existing governing control mechanisms, must primarily be left to the practice. Legal limits are set only to the extent that the computation of damages must not run afoul of the purposes of indemnification, in particular of the application of objective criteria mandated by § 253 BGB, and not render a uniform way of compensation impossible.

Basically unsuitable as a measure of damages is the amount which the owner would have had to spend for renting a surrogate object to bridge the period of deprivation because in this case the compensation interest and not the reparation interest is in issue. The former does not depend on what the owner saves because he satisfies his needs with his own property but on what value is attributed to the availability of the object for self-use. Likewise the owner cannot demand to be placed in a position as if he had rented the property to the tortfeasor. A measure of damages of that kind may be appropriate in particular fields because of a special conflict of interests, but it does not correspond to the general principles governing compensation for damages. What is to be compensated is the loss of use within the framework of a planned exploitation through self-use, not lost gains based on a transfer of the use to a third party for rent, a use which the owner never intended.

It is possible, however, to resort to valuation methods which govern the commercial transfers of use for a price, to the extent that they can be realizable cleared of the value elements incident to the commercial utilization. Also, proportionate allocation of expenditures made for the lost use (such as interest on the capital expended for the acquisition of the object, current expenditures for the disposability of the object, age depreciation of the object during the period of its unusability apart from depreciation due to use) may be appropriate items in the computation of damages. In contrast to the view voiced by the Senate submitting the question, it would not seem to be impermissible in this connection, by means of a moderate addition to the common costs considered by the market as the floor of the use-value to take account of the fact that the radiations of the unavailability of such economic objects upon the total worth of the assets connected therewith are incapable of an exact determination in their particularity.

The methods of valuation here discussed do not, however, preclude other suitable methods.

NOTE

The text case is noted by T. Rauscher in 40 NJW 53 (1987).

b. Intervening Excessive Security Case

BGH Large Senate for Civil Matters,
Joined Cases 1 and 2/97,
Order of November 27, 1997
upon references by the IX. and XI. Senate
for Civil Matters.
— BGHZ —; 19 ZIP 235 (1998).

Holding

1. In cases of revolving global security interests granted by means of forms in the event of intervening over-security, the grantor is entitled to a non-discretionary

release even then when the security agreement contains no or only a discretionary release clause.

2. In cases of revolving global security interests granted by means of forms, neither an express release stipulation, nor a numerically defined coverage limit, nor a clause governing the valuation of the collateral are prerequisites for their validity.

3. If the grant of revolving global security interests by means of a form contains no or an inappropriate coverage limit, this limit (taking account of the costs of administration and enforcement of the collateral), with reference to the realizable value of the collateral, amounts to 110% of the secured claims.

4. Universally valid standards for the valuation of collateral in the event of the happening of the condition for the resort to the security cannot be laid down in advance for either a transfer of property as security or a global assignment.

5. The threshold for the generation of a right to a release of collateral is normally at 150% of the estimated value (BGB § 237, sentence 1).

REASONS

A. The parties of the two referrals which are joined for a common deliberation and decision are engaged in a contest with respect to the validity of pre-formulated global assignments and transfers as security of property in revolving stock-in-trade.

I.

1. The referral by the IXth Civil Senate of March 6, 1997 (IX ZR 74/95, 18 ZIP 632 (1997) = 13 EWiR 483 (1997) = 52 WM 750 (1997)) was based on the following facts:

Defendant Bank granted the debtor, whose trustee in bankruptcy is the plaintiff, loans in the amount of approximately DM 1,350,000. As security, the debtor, a manufacturer of furniture, transferred to defendant title to its inventory and assigned all its present and future accounts. The form containing the agreement of the transfer of the title as security of December 22, 1982, included in Nr. 12 the following release clause which referred to Nr. 2 of the agreement. These stipulations provided:

> "If the value of all security interests granted in this agreement exceeds substantially and not only temporarily the coverage limit fixed in Nr. 2 of this agreement, the Bank, upon request by the grantor of the security interest will release collateral of its choice."

***

The amounts to be filled in under Nr. 2 were left blank. In 1990, the Bank sold its claims and the security interests securing the same for DM 700,000. Plaintiff claims to be entitled to DM 500,000 by virtue of BGB § 816 par. 1 sentence 1, for the reason that defendant had disposed of the collateral without legal right. The transfer of title as security and the global assignment of accounts were claimed to be invalid because an adequate release clause was lacking.

The district court (*Landgericht*) and the circuit court of appeal (*Oberlandesgericht*) dismissed the complaint. With its petition for revision plaintiff pursued its claim:

2. The IXth Senate for Civil Matters is of the opinion that both security agreements are not invalid because they failed to include an adequate release clause.

a. The Senate conceded that the agreements did not meet the requirements laid down by existing case law of the VIIth, VIIIth and IXth Senates for Civil Matters.

b. But the IXth Senate is of the opinion that this case law can no longer be followed, without serious limitations. An absolute right to a release of the grantor in the case of a not only transient subsequent over-security is immanent in any fiduciary security transaction even without express stipulation. A discretionary release clause is invalid. An express numerically defined coverage ceiling and a clause governing the valuation of the collateral are in the opinion of the Senate not prerequisites for the effectiveness of revolving global securities. Such security interests according to the Senate are valid also without a numerically defined coverage ceiling or a clause for the valuation of the collateral. Coverage ceiling and standards for the valuation of the collateral could be ascertained by interpretation of the security agreement.

3. Since the VIIIth Senate for Civil Matters declared that it no longer adhered to its former view, the IXth Senate directed an inquiry to the VIIth Senate for Civil Matters pursuant to GVG § 132III. The VIIth Senate for Civil Matters responded that it adheres to its view that global assignments of accounts without express stipulation of a coverage ceiling are invalid pursuant to BGB §138 I only with respect to cases in which it is impossible by way of interpretation to fix that ceiling as the face amount of the assigned accounts, such as cases involving business branches with, according to experience, a high risk of shortfall.

4. The IXth Senate does not consider the prerequisites for a referral of a controversy to the Large Senate for Civil Matters because of divergent legal views pursuant to GVG § 132 par. 2 as being present. Nevertheless, it is of the opinion that a referral should be made to the Large Senate for the purpose of the development of the law and the assurance of uniform adjudications in view of the decisions of the XIth Senate for Civil Matters which consider a discretionary release clause without a numerically defined coverage limit as effective (133 BGHZ 25, 28 *et seq.* (1997) = 17 ZIP 1996, 1164 = WM 1996, 902, 903). Therefore, pursuant to GVG § 132 par. 4, it refers to it the following questions:

a) In the case of a transfer as security of inventory with revolving content or a global assignment of accounts by means of forms, is the grantor of the security interest if a subsequent excess security occurs entitled to a non-discretionary release even where the security agreement does not contain any or only a discretionary release clause?

b) Is the transfer of property in inventory with revolving content or a global assignment by means of forms effective only if an appropriate coverage limit or standards for the valuation of the collateral are fixed?

c) If the answer to question b) is affirmative, is it possible to supplement the security agreement which contains no or only a materially inappropriate coverage clause with a firm coverage ceiling with firm valuation standards and therefore to consider it as valid?

II

1. The referral order of the XIth Senate for Civil Matters of May 13, 1997 (XI ZR 234/95 = 51 WM 1195 (1997), 18 ZIP 1185 (1997)) is based on the following facts: Defendant bank granted an individual merchant an operation credit. The latter assigned as security all accounts the debtors of which had names commencing with the letters A-W. In the form utilized for the global assignment of August 20, 1974 it was provided:

> "6. . . . As soon as the assigned accounts exceed the amounts of the claims of the bank against the debtor by more than ... %, upon demand of the debtor, the bank, according to its choice will retransfer accounts up to the amount of the excess."

The figures for the percentage were not filled in.

***

In 1984, plaintiff levied upon one of the assigned accounts. He received DM 20,975.62 from the account debtor. He surrendered this amount to defendant in view of the global assignment. He demanded repayment of that sum because he contended that the global assignment was invalid due to the lack of an express stipulation of a coverage ceiling. The county court and the circuit court of appeal granted the complaint. The admitted petition for revision requested dismissal of the complaint.

2. The XIth Senate for Civil Matters would like to hold the global assignment to be valid, despite the absence of an express, numerically fixed coverage ceiling. Although the VIIIth and the IXth Senate for Civil Matters no longer consider an expressly stipulated coverage ceiling as necessary, the XIth Senate still feels prevented from deciding in that way because of the position of the VIIth Senate for Civil Matters. According to that position, global assignments without an express coverage ceiling are invalid pursuant to §138 I BGB (BGH, 12 ZIP 152 (1991). The VII Senate for Civil Matters, upon inquiry pursuant to GVG §132III has declared to still adhere to that view for cases in which the coverage ceiling, because of the high risk of a short-fall cannot be fixed by way of interpretation as the face value of the assigned accounts.

The XIth Senate therefore, pursuant to GVG § 132 II, has referred the following question:

> "Is a global assignment or transfer as security of revolving inventory effective even if an (appropriate) coverage ceiling or standard for the valuation of the collateral are not expressly agreed upon?"

The Large Senate for Civil Matters gives an affirmative answer to the question referred to it by the XIth Senate for Civil Matters and question a) referred to it by the IXth

Senate for Civil Matters. The questions b) and c) of the IXth Senate are answered as stated in the holding.

REASONS

I

The questions referred to the Large Senate for Civil Matters are admissible.

II

1. The Large Senate for Civil Matters responds affirmatively to the question a) submitted by the IXth Senate for Civil Matters. The grantor of a security interest, in the event of an over-security, has a right to a non-discretionary release even when the security agreement contains no or only a discretionary release clause.

a) Accounts assigned as security and property transferred as security constitute post-accessory fiduciary security interests. Every agreement granting security interests of that kind establishes a fiduciary relation even without an express clause to that effect. That applies regardless of whether a bargained or pre-formulated agreement is involved or whether a single object or global revolving collateral is in issue. (133 BGHZ 25, 40 (1996) = 17 ZIP 1164 (1996) ; 18 ZIP 632 (1997)). The fiduciary character of the security agreement has the result — except for transfers of security interests subject to conditions subsequent — that the secured party has the duty to restore the collateral to the extent that it is definitely no longer necessary even before the end of the agreement. This duty follows, according to BGB §157, from the fiduciary character of the security agreement and the balance of the interests of the parties (citations omitted). To the extent that security interests are not only temporarily no longer necessary, i.e. that definite over-security exists, their retention by the secured party is unjustified.

The decision whether collateral is to be released therefore does not depend on the discretion of the secured party.

Rather if and to the extent that a not only temporary supervening over-security of the secured party occurs, a partial release is mandatory. Room for the exercise of discretion by the secured party exists only in the decision which of several objects of security interests he will release. That follows from BGB § 262 and corresponds to the policy of BGB § 1230 first sentence. * * *

b) . . .

c) A limitation of the contractual right to a release by way of a stipulation which subjects the release to the discretion of the secured party is in the case of pre-formulated assignments and transfers as security ineffective, because it constitutes a violation § 9 AGBG (Law on General Terms of Agreements.) Such a stipulation, which is not only of a declaratory nature and therefore subject to judicial control (AGBG § 8) limits essential rights flowing from the character of security agreements (AGBG § 9 II(2)). * * *

The limitation of the grantor of the security interest to a right to an examination of the release claim normally endangers the accomplishment of the purpose of the agreement (AGBG §9 II 2). An agreement which predicates the right to a release upon the discretion provides the secured party with a room for discretion conflicting with its purpose, even though it is clear that the collateral is in part no longer needed. Although the decision of the secured party is subject to judicial control pursuant to BGB § 315 III, such control is limited to the question of whether it exceeds the limits of equity. Under these conditions, a right to the release of the grantor of the security interest would exist only if the scope of the discretion of the secured party were exceptionally reduced to zero.

* * *

d. The invalidity of discretionary release clauses does not entail the total invalidity of the grant of security interests by means of forms.

Rather, the invalid release clause is replaced also in the case of revolving global security interests by the right to a release independent of the discretion of the secured party (§ 6 II AGBG, 133 BGHZ 25, 32 *et s.* (1997)). The application of AGBG §6 II does not violate the constitutionally protected freedom of contract. The fiduciary character of a security agreement cannot be eliminated by subjecting the release of collateral to the discretion of the secured party. (133 BGHZ 25, 30 (1997). . . .)

The application of AGBG § 6 II is not barred by the prohibition against reductions for the purpose of upholding the validity of transactions (124 BGHZ 371, 375 *et s.* (1994)). This signifies that a single pre-formulated contractual clause which contravenes AGBG §9, may not be reduced to the barely permissible content and thereby validated (cf. 84 BGHZ 109, 114 *et s.* (1982) * * *); instead, the over-extensive clause is replaced by the governing legal provision. Exactly this consequence occurs in the case at issue. * * *

2. The Large Senate for Civil Matters responds affirmatively also to the question posed by the XIth Senate for Civil Matters.

a) The express stipulation of a numerically fixed appropriate coverage ceiling, i.e. a threshold to ascertain the existence of over-security is also in the case of security agreements, granted by use of a form, relating to revolving global security interests not a condition of their validity. The Large Senate does not share the view of the VIIth Senate for Civil Matters (50 NJW 651 (1997)) that global assignments without an expressly stipulated coverage limit are invalid pursuant to BGB § 138 par. 1 if they involve assets subject, according to experience, to a high short-fall risk.

aa) In the case of a not merely transitory over-security of the secured party, the grantor of the security has a right to a release. As the VIIth Senate for Civil Matters itself recognized in its older judgments, this right to a release bars the assumption that revolving global security interests, because of supervenient over-security, are unethical even when a numerically defined coverage ceiling is not stipulated in the security agreement. The right to a release which is immanent in any fiduciary grant of a security interest may be enforced without unconscionable burden also in branches with a high short-fall risk. It normally avoids therefore both the tying up of the debtor and the endangering of other creditors.

Under these circumstances, the application of BGB § 138 par. 1 is inappropriate. Otherwise it would have the result that even commercial enterprises in branches with a high short-fall risk would be prevented from validity agreeing with credit institutions upon bargained or pre-formulated global assignments without express stipulation of a coverage limit. No reason exists for such a general rule.

The view that global assignments without express stipulation of coverage ceilings are unethical would leave the secured party unprotected precisely in the cases where it needs legal protection most because they involve borrowers belonging to a business branch with a high short-fall risk. This result is particularly strange in a case where the debtor has become insolvent.

In such a case, the trustee in bankruptcy could successfully assert the invalidity of the entire global assignment pursuant to BGB §138 par. 1. This exceeds by far the interests of the debtor meriting protection because it would apply when there never existed excess security and therefore a right to release (BGH 18 ZIP 632 (1997) = 52 WM, 750, 757 (1997); BGH 18 ZIP 1185 (1997) = 52 WM, 1197, 1201 (1997).

bb) That does not mean that BGB §138 par. 1 has lost all significance for the determination of the validity of the pre-formulated grant of global security interests. Security agreements may be unethical because of a cumulation of different security interests or initial excessiveness (BGH (IXth for Civil Matters), Judgment of April 28, 1994, 15 ZIP 939 (1994)).

b) An express definition of the standards for a valuation of the collateral likewise is not in any case a prerequisite for the validity of revolving global security interests. To the extent that the VIIIth and the IXth Senate for Civil Matters required such a standard for the validity of a pre-formulated transfer as security of inventory with changing content, both Senates have abandoned their prior position. In the opinion of the Large Senate such a clause cannot be required, primarily for the reason that the principle of the freedom of contracts leaves it to the choice of the parties whether and in what detail they wish to determine the prerequisites for a release claim.

Moreover there exist no generally accepted standards for the determination of the value of unknown future accounts or collections of tangible assets with revolving content. The interests of the parties in the clarification of the conditions of claims are served by rebuttable rules of proof.

3. Question b) submitted by the IXth Senate for Civil Matters is answered by the Large Senate for Civil Matters as follows:

> In the case of pre-formulated security agreements which do not contain any or a materially inappropriate coverage clause, the coverage limit — relative to the realizable value of the collateral — amounts to 110% of the secured

claims. The limit for the arising of a release claim in normally located at 150% of the applicable estimated value (BGB §237 first sentence).

a. The affirmative answer to the question referred to by the XIth Senate for Civil Matters whether revolving global security interest granted by the use of form are valid even when an appropriate coverage ceiling and standards for the valuation of the collateral are not expressly stipulated, does not constitute a complete answer to the question b) submitted by the IXth Senate for Civil Matters, whether global security interests are only effective, if an adequate coverage ceiling and standards for the evaluation of the collateral are "fixed". The IXth Senate for Civil Matters considers it possible in such cases to supplement the agreement with a defined coverage ceiling with defined standards of valuation, and only because of this possibility considers also security agreements without an appropriate coverage ceiling clause to be valid (50 NJW 1570 (1997)). "Fixed" in question b) must be understood as expressly agreed upon or unambiguously determinable.

b. The coverage ceiling, the crossing of which signifies over-security as a prerequisite for the contractual right of release, flows from the fiduciary character of the security agreement, taking account of its purpose and the interests of the parties meriting protection, even where an express stipulation is lacking. Over-security is regularly present when the realizable value of the collateral, at the time it is resorted to, exceeds the secured claims by 10%, leaving the question of the valuation of the collateral to 3 c) of this opinion. * * *

bb.) (1.) The value of the collateral equals the amount of the proceeds which can be realized by way of disposition thereof. The view of the IXth Senate for Civil Matters (50 NJW 1570, 756 *et s.* (1997)) that in the absence of a stipulation to the contrary, the value of assigned accounts consists of their face amount and in the case of a transfer as security of stock-in-trade of the market price of the goods or, if such price does not exist, their purchase price or production costs is not shared by the Large Senate.

Security interests must prove their value when the debtor is incapable of performance, above all in the event of his insolvency. (26 BGHZ 181, 191 (1958)); *** The secured party may not be compelled by means of a right thereto to release collateral which may be needed in the case of the debtor's subsequent insolvency. The value of collateral is measured by the proceeds realizable in the case of the bankruptcy or of collective proceedings against the debtor. This, in the case of claims is according to experience not their face amount but a substantial lesser sum. * * *

(2) The normal purpose of a security agreement to secure the creditor is only achieved, if, in the event of an insolvency of the debtor, the realizable proceeds of the collateral cover the secured claims. This regularly is only accomplished by a coverage ceiling of 110%

* * *

c) The enforcement of the right to a release is in actual practice not unconscionably hampered by valuation difficulties;

aa) To be sure, there exist no generally applicable standards (independent of the respective business branch) for the determination of the realizable value of the collateral in the event of a resort thereto in the case of either assigned accounts or stock in trade transferred as security. The opinion of the IXth Senate for Civil Matters that an agreement without a valuation clause could be supplemented by way of interpretation with firmly established standards of valuation (50 NJW 1750 (1997)) is not shared by the Large Senate for Civil Matters.

* * *

bb) Nevertheless a mere establishment of the coverage limit at 110% of the secured claims without any guide for the valuation of the collateral is neither theoretically nor practically appropriate. Rather, prompt enforcement of the right to a release requires directions for the valuation process.

If it were possible to have contests about the valuation of the collateral in the event of the need of a resort thereto, without any framework and if any possible though improbable risk of the secured party had to be considered in the determination of the value of the collateral, the right to a release would have no practical significance. An appropriate regard of the justified interest of the debtor to dispose of excess collateral therefore renders it necessary to balance the particular difficulties of proving an over-security with simple presumptions and rule on the burden of proof.

(1) From BGB §§232 *et seq.* the rebuttable presumption may be deduced that the creditor's interest in the collateral is adequately protected by the subtraction of one third from the face value of the assigned accounts or the estimated value of the merchandise transferred as security. * * *

(2) The deduction of one third from the valuation of movable property (BGB §237 sentence 1) has the result that a right to a release is normally generated only when the market or respectively the purchase price or the production costs of the merchandise transferred as security to the extent that they have to be taken into account and other collateral is not available, amounts to 150% of the secured accounts. Analogous rules apply to the face value of the accounts that are capable of being taken into account. * * *

4. Since BGB §§232 *et seq.* are not designed to govern global assignments and transfers as security, and do not contain any rules which fit all cases, the addition of 50% constitutes only an orientation help. This, however, has the effect that the party which contends that a deduction of one third or a release threshold of 150% — with reference to the face amount of accounts or the market price or respectively the purchase price or production costs of merchandise is inappropriate in the case at issue, must make detailed allegations to that effect and furnish proof thereof. This applies also if the parties fixed the deduction or the coverage limit by use of contract forms differently without regard to the actual risks involved. (AGBG § 9).

Conversely, an appropriate advance determination of the value of the collateral in the light of the special situation of clearly defined business branches does not automatically disadvantage the debtor inappropriately.

The general allegation that the proceeds from a resort to collateral amount only to one half of its regular value is insufficient to be accepted. The experience was known to the legislator of BGB §§232 et seq. (*Motives*, Vol. I p. 390). Nevertheless he did not establish a coverage threshold of 200%.

NOTES

1. The text-case constitutes the climax to a tortuous sequence of consultations among the VII., VIII., IX., and XI. Senates for Civil Matters of the German Supreme Court for Civil and Criminal Matters, regarding the validity of adhesion contracts whereby the debtor granted security interests by way of global assignments as security of existing and future accounts or other intangibles or by way of transfers as security of ownership in revolving inventory or stock-in-trade. In cases of that type there was agreement among the four senates involved that such adhesion contracts were invalid in toto because of a violation of certain general clauses in the civil code or of the law prohibiting certain contract clauses (AGBG), unless they contained express stipulations protecting the debtor against supervening over-security of the secured party, cf. BGH (IX. Senate for Civil Matters), Judgment of January 31, 1994, 124 BGHZ 371 at 376-378.

In the course of time it was realized that the total invalidity of the security agreement in these cases overshot the mark and, in the event of a subsequent bankruptcy of the debtor, resulted not so much in a preservation of the economic freedom of the debtor, as in a windfall for his other creditors. Because of this dilemma the XI. Senate for Civil Matters of the BGH was inclined to abandon the existing approach in these cases and to find a more appropriate solution in reliance on the consequences of the fiduciary character of German security agreements relating the tangible personal property and intangibles as collateral. To accomplish this revolution the XI. Senate needed either the agreement of the other senates concerned, or, in the case of disagreement, its resolution by the Large Senate. As a result the XI. Senate had to make inquiries at the other senates to ascertain their position. By Order of January 23, 1996 (WM 1996, 476, ZIP 1996, 542), directed to the VIII. and IX. Senate, the XI. Senate asked whether the addressee adhered to their view that global assignments by use of forms are invalid in toto if they do not contain an express stipulation establishing a non-discretionary duty of the secured party to release excess collateral. This question was followed by a second inquiry of the XI. Senate, this time addressed to the VII. VIII., and IX. Senate by order of April 16, 1996 (ZIP 1996, 957), asking whether the senate adhered to the view that a global assignment without fixation of a coverage ceiling was either invalid pursuant to BGB §138 I (VII. Senate) or unenforceable pursuant to AGBG §9 I (VIII. and IX. Senate).

The VIII. Senate communicated informally that it no longer adhered to its former view. The IX. and VII. Senate declared that, while they agreed in many respects with the XI. Senate for Civil Matters, they entertained different views on a number of aspects. The IX. Senate in its order of reply of July 11, 1996 (ZIP 1996, 1426) stated that is no longer adhered to the view that a global assignment without express fixation of a coverage limit is unenforceable pursuant to AGBG §9 I, but that it did not agree on essential points with the reasons given by the XI. Senate in its order of inquiry of April 16, 1996. Finally, the VII. Senate for Civil Matters replied to the inquiry of the XI. Senate and to an inquiry of the IX. Senate of July 11, 1996 (ZIP 1996, 1429) that it still adhered to its former views with respect to cases where the respective business branches according to experience sustained a considerable shortfall in the event that a resort to the security is needed, Order of October 10, 1996 (ZIP 1997, 234, WM 1997, 311). Because of the uncertainties and disagreements which had surfaced, both the IX. Senate by order of March 6, 1997 (ZIP 1997, 632; WM 1997, 750) and the XI. Senate by order of May 13, 1997 (ZIP 1997, 1185; WM 1997, 1197) invoked the Large Senate for Civil Matters of the BGH, submitting the question set forth in the reply together with an exposition of their position thereon.

2. The text-case relates only to supervening over-security. In situations where the possibility of an initial unconscionable over-security exists, as in the case of a cumulation of global security interests, BGB §138 would still entail the invalidity of the entire respective security agreement, BGH (IX. Senate for Civil Matters), Judgment of March 12, 1998 (ZIP 1998, 684).

c. *Delay in the Composition of the Reasons for a Judgment after its Public Announcement.*

COMMON SENATE OF THE GERMAN FEDERAL SUPREME COURTS.
Order of April 27, 1993
46 NJW 2603 (1993).

FACTS

The controversy below focuses on the question of whether the license to operate the nuclear power plant in B. was validly issued. The Appellate Administrative Tribunal rejected the appeal after oral argument in a judgment announced on June 28, 1989. The judgment was written in its entirety, signed by all judges and transmitted to the clerk on January 11, 1990. The 7th Senate of the Federal Supreme Administrative Court would like to annul the judgment and remand the case to the court below for a new argument and decision. It is of the opinion that the judgment was not provided with reasons within the meaning of § 138(6) of the Law on the Procedure of the Administrative Courts (VwGO[85]) because it was not fully composed, and, signed by all judges, transmitted to the clerk until more than five months after its announcement. The Senate feels that a delay of that length fails to guarantee either the correspondence between the true and the given reasons or their correct documentation.

85. Verwaltungsgerichtsordnung, revised on January 1, 1991, BGBl I 686.

Because the 7th Senate considered itself impeded to decide accordingly, owing to the jurisprudence of other senates of the Federal Supreme Administrative Court (BVerwG), it decided on May 23, 1991 to submit to the Large Senate of the Federal Supreme Administrative Court the question whether a judgment that has been announced without reasons, is not furnished with reasons within the meaning of § 138(6) VwGO, if facts, reasons, and instructions about appeal are not reduced to writing, signed by the judges and delivered to the clerk within five months (10 NVwZ 1185 (1991)). The Large Senate would like to give an affirmative answer (11 NVwZ 1085 (1992)), it is, however, prevented from doing so because it would depart from the jurisprudence of other Federal Supreme Courts. The Large Senate noted that the Federal Supreme Finance Court, the Federal Supreme Labor Court and the Federal Supreme Social Court have construed provisions analogous to §138(6) VwGO as deeming judgments announced without reasons as not being furnished with reasons, if the delay between announcement and the composition of reasons or the transmission to the clerk exceeded one year.

* * *

The parties to the controversy below were given the opportunity to express their views. They waived a hearing.

The Common Senate of the Federal Supreme Courts holds:

> A judgment which at the time of its announcement is not yet fully written is not furnished with reasons within the meaning of §138(c) VwGO unless the facts and the reasons for the decision are reduced to writing, specially signed by the judges and delivered to the clerk within five months.

REASONS

1. The Common Senate of the Federal Supreme Courts has jurisdiction over the question submitted. It is composed of the presidents of the Federal Supreme Courts, two judges of the Large Senate of the Federal Supreme Administrative Court and two judges of the First Senate of the Federal Supreme Labor Court (§ 3 I nr. 1; §4 V RsprEinhG[86]). The Common Senate has decided that if the Senate which submits the question to the Common Senate wants to depart in a legal question from the decision of several other Federal Supreme Courts, only that Senate participates which of all the mentioned Supreme Courts was the last one to pass on the question (26 NJW 1273 (1973); 33 NJW 172 (1980).) This means the last preceding divergent decision of a Supreme Court antedating the order of reference (Common Senate, 105 BFHE 101, 104).

86. Law for the Uniformity of the Adjudications of the Supreme Courts (1968) (*supra* p. 68).

* * *

The senates of the Supreme Finance Court are no longer involved since they declared in the present proceedings that they agree with the Large Senate of the Federal Supreme Administrative Court (BVerwG). Accordingly, the last senate to disagree is the First Senate of the Supreme Labor Court (BAG) which held, in a judgment of April 7, 1992 (NZA 1992, 1144), that a decision is not furnished with reasons only if more than one year has expired between announcement and service.

2. The remaining divergences between the order of the Large Senate of the BVerwG and the decisions of the BAG, BSG and BGH mentioned therein concern 'the same legal question.'

* * *

3. The Common Senate of the Federal Supreme Courts answers the question submitted to it as set forth above. * * *

Pursuant to §108 I2 VwGO, a judgment of the court must indicate the reasons which have governed the judicial conviction. This mandate is only complied with, if the reasons which, according to §117 I2 VwGO, are given in the judgment (which must be reduced to writing and signed by the participating judges, §117 II5 VwGO) are the same as the reasons on which the judgment, following the arguments and deliberation, was based (§108 I1 VwGO). In order to assume this correspondence, it is necessary that the period between the deliberation and the announcement of a judgment not yet fully composed, and its completion, signature and delivery to the clerk, is not too long. §117 IV VwGO takes account of this in that it obliges the judges who participated in the decision to deliver a judgment that at the time of its announcement was incomplete within the indicated meaning, in completed form to the clerk within two weeks of the day of its announcement (§117 IV VwGO). If that cannot be done for exceptional reasons, the judgment signed by the judges must be delivered to the clerk within these two weeks without facts, reasons and instructions on further review. In that case, facts, reasons and instructions on further review must be reduced to writing 'soon thereafter,' signed by the judges and delivered to the clerk. * * * The expression 'soon thereafter' is an undefined legal term, which does not denote a fixed interval but an open period. Its concretization must be achieved in view of the documentary function of the reasons for the judgment which §117IV sentence 2 second half VwGO wants to assure. The danger that this function because of the dwindling judicial memory cannot be achieved in a particular case increases with the length of time between the oral argument and the deliberations on the one side and the composition of the reasons on the other. Therefore, it is necessary to concretize the concept 'soon thereafter' in a way that leaves to the practice sufficient flexibility as indicated by the indefinite expression 'soon thereafter,' but also marks a limit which is clear and recognizable for all affected. That purpose can be achieved best, as the Common Senate of the Federal Supreme Court following the opinion of the Large Senate of the Supreme Administrative Court, finds, by resort to the 5-month period of §552 ZPO. True, §552 ZPO does not apply to administrative controversies (§173 VwGO). This does not, however, prevent for the purpose of concretizing the term 'soon thereafter', resort to the legislative evaluation expressed in §552 ZPO and — as in civil proceedings — 'for the purpose of avoiding misrecollections' and for 'reasons of legal security', a limitation of the period for the subsequent composition, signature and delivery to the clerk of a judgment which was incomplete when announced to a maximum of 5 months (Cf. BGH, 40 NJW 2446 (1987).)

* * *

NOTES

1. Decisions of the Common Senate of the Federal Supreme Courts are *aves rarae*. Another instance is the decision of February 6, 1973 (26 NJW 1273 (1973)) mentioned in the text case.

2. An important recent instance in which the 2. Senate of the Federal Supreme Court decided to submit a question to the Common Senate of the Federal Supreme Courts concerned the question of the amount of the damages which a creditor may recover from a manager and majority owner of the shares of a GmbH because the defendant failed to file a timely petition in bankruptcy. The 2d Senate took the view that the defendant was not liable because his conduct was not dictated by self-interest but that responsibility for the full damages could possibly be based on BGB § 823 II and GmbHG §64I. In taking a negative position on both issues, the 2d Senate was in apparent conflict with decisions of other Senates of the BGH as well as with a decision of the Federal Supreme Labor Court (BAG). Invocation of the United Large Senates of the Federal Supreme Court for Civil and Criminal Matters was not required because the affected Senates informed the 2d Senate that they no longer adhered to their previous opinions.

Another Senate was no longer occupied with the judgment. As a result, only a Senate of the BAG still adhered to its divergent case-law. The detailed order to submit the question to the Common Senate is published in 46 NJW 2931 (1993). In the meantime, the BAG likewise abandoned its position.

As a result, the proceedings before the Common Senate were terminated and the 2d Senate rendered its judgment on June 6, 1994.[87] The judgment and its consequences are commented upon by Uhlenbruck, 15 ZIP 1153 (1994) and Eyber, 47 NJW 1622 (1994).

---

87. 15 ZIP 1103 (1994) = 48 ZEITSCHRIFT FÜR WIRTSCHAFTS - UND BANKRECHT [WM] 1428 (1994).

3. Another instance in which the Common Senate was invoked, but ultimately did not have to pass on the issue referred to it, concerned the effect of a foreign insolvency proceeding on pending proceedings by or against the insolvent. In 1997, the Senate of the BGH having jurisdiction over insolvency matters (IXth for Civil Matters) wished to hold that, by analogy to §240 ZPO, such proceedings should be suspended, but it considered itself prevented from holding so because of decisions of other senates of the Supreme Court for Civil Matters and the I. Senate of the Supreme Finance Court. After being informed by the other Senates of the BGH that they no longer adhered to their former views, the XIth Senate submitted the question to the Common Senate (Order of November 26, 1997, 51 NJW 928 (1998)).

Before the decision on the merits by the Common Senate, the Ist Senate of the Federal Finance Court decided to adhere to the view of the IXth Senate for Civil Matters (Order of January 21, 1998). Accordingly, the Common Senate dismissed the proceedings. (51 NJW 1543 (1998)). Subsequently, the parties settled the matter and the petition for reviewed was withdrawn.

d. *Equality of Sexes*

Federal Constitutional Court of Germany
Impact on Family Name of Spouses and Children
Order of March 3, 1991
in the Cases 1 BvL 83/86 and 24/88
Art. 3 Par. 2 GG
84 BVerfGE E (1992)

Holding

I. §1355 par. 2, sentence 2 BGB (Civil Code) as revised by the First Law for the Reformation of the Marriage and Family Law of June 14, 1976 (BGBl I 1421), conflicts with the Basic Law, Art. 3 par. 2.

Until a new statutory rule enters into force, §§1355 and 1616 BGB must be applied with the following modifications:

1. If after the date of the publication of this holding in the Official Journal of Federal Legislation (BGBl) the spouses do not make a determination pursuant to §1355, par. 2, sentence 2, BGB, each spouse retains provisionally the name used by him or her before the marriage.

2. If, accordingly, the spouses do not use a common family name, the name of a legitimate child is provisionally determined as follows:

The legal representatives may, prior to the certification of the child's birth, instruct the Status Official (*Standesbeamter*) that the child bears the family name of the father, the family name of the mother or a composite name formed out of these names in any chosen sequence. If they fail to make a determination, the child obtains a double-name formed from the names of both spouses. The sequence is determined by lot.

REASONS

A.

The certified questions ask whether it is consistent with Basic Law [GG], Art. 3, par. 2 that the family name of the husband becomes the family name of the couple, if at the time of the marriage celebration the spouses do not designate one of their family names as their common family name.

I.

According to the Civil Code [BGB] of August 18, 1896 (RGBl I 195), the wife obtained the name of her husband at the celebration of their marriage. This provision was changed by the Equality of Rights Law of June 18, 1957 (BGBl I 609) to the effect that the wife was entitled to add her maiden name to the common family name. In a decision of May 31, 1978 (48 BVerfGE 327 (1978)) the Federal Constitutional Court held that this provision conflicted with Art. 3, par. 2 GG.

2. Even before that date, §1355 BGB was modified by the First Law for the Reformation of the Marriage and Family Law of June 14, 1976 (BGBl I 1421).

The bill of the Government (BTD 7/650) provided that the betrothed shall be obligated to determine their common family name (marital name) at the celebration of their marriage. The official in charge was supposed to celebrate the marriage only after the requisite declaration. The betrothed had the option between the family name of the husband, the family name of the wife, and a composite name formed out of the names of both. The House of Representatives (*Bundestag*) accepted the proposal of making the official conclusion of the marriage contingent upon the prior declaration of the betrothed determining the marital name but eliminated the choice of a composite name. In addition, departing from the government proposal, it resolved to authorize the spouse whose name did not become the marital name to place his or her name before the marital name (BTD 7/3119 pp. 4 & 11).

The Federal Council (*Bundesrat*) raised doubts against obligating the betrothed to make a declaration on the marital name because that might limit the freedom of decision of the spouses. Even if it should be assumed that the exclusive designation of the husband's name as family name would contravene the principle of equality of sexes, it would suffice that a choice between the name of the husband or that of the wife is offered. The supplemental option needed to escape the compulsion of a declaration could properly be tied to the husband's name (BTD 7/3268 p. 2).

Ultimately, both houses assented to the proposal of the reconciliation committee (BTD 7/4992) which agreed largely with the Federal Council's proposals relating to the marital name, but accepted the resolution of the House of Representatives to the extent that the 'passed-over' spouse received the right to place his or her name ahead of the family name.

§1355 BGB accordingly received the following text:

(1) The spouses use a common family name (marital name).

(2) On the occasion of their marriage ceremony the spouses, by way of a declaration to the Status Official, may designate the family name of the husband or the wife as the marital name. If they do not make a designation to that effect, the family name of the husband is the marital name. Family name is the name which is entered in the birth certificate of the betrothed at the time of the celebration of the marriage.

(3) A spouse whose family does not become the marital name by declaration to the Status Official, may place his or her family name or the name used at the time of the celebration of the marriage ahead of the family name. The declaration requires public certification.

(4) * * *

The determination of the family name governs also the name of a child stemming from the marriage; a legitimate child receives the names of the parents, pursuant to §1616 BGB.

II

The proceedings in which the prelinary question arose concern requests of spouses who received the name of the husband as marital name, pursuant to §1355 par. 2, sentence 2 BGB, because they made no designation pursuant to §1355 par. 1, sentence 1 BGB.

1. Proceedings 1 BvL 83/86:

a. The applicants in the initial proceedings are German nationals who at the celebration of their marriage made a declaration to the Status Official to the effect that each of them wished to retain his or her family name during the marriage. The status official thereupon, pursuant to §1355 par. 2, sentence 2 BGB, entered the husband's name as marital name on the marriage certificate. The spouses applied for a correction of the marriage certificate to the effect that each of them continues to use his or her family name during the marriage.

b. The District Court (*Amtsgericht*) suspended the proceedings and submitted the question to the Federal Constitutional Court whether the provision of §1355 par. 2, sentence 2 BGB, is unconstitutional to the effect that the wife loses her family name and that the husband's family name becomes the marital name.

The District Court states that the decision upon the application for correction of the marriage certificate depends upon the provision submitted for examination. The application of the spouses must be characterized as separate applications by either spouse. The wife has lost her family name upon the marriage ceremony and received the husband's name as marital name solely because of §1355 par. 2, sentence 2 BGB. Therefore, according to the District Court, it depends upon the constitutionality of this provision whether the entry of the husband's name as applicant's marital name is correct. If the provision conflicts with the constitution, a gap in the statutory law results and the status official was not authorized to enter the husband's name as the common marital name.

The choice of the husband's name in the residual regulation causes a discrimination against the wife because her family name would only become the marital name if she were able to persuade her husband to make a declaration to that effect, while the husband is not forced to reach an agreement with his marital partner since in the case of disagreement his family name automatically becomes marital name. Biological or functional differences for this disparate treatment are not evident.

2. Proceedings 1 BvL 24/88:

a. Applicants in the initial proceedings are likewise German nationals. At the marriage ceremony, they declared that they were not able to designate a common family name according to §1355 par. 2, sentence 1 BGB; they also objected to the entry of the husband's family name as the marital name. The status official nevertheless took the view that according to §1355 par. 2, sentence 2 BGB, the husband's name had become the common marital name of the spouses and entered it in the marriage certificate.

The spouses filed separate applications in the District Court. The husband demanded that the marriage certificate should be corrected to indicate that his wife and he did not have his family name as the common marital name. The wife filed the same application and, alternatively, she asks to instruct the status official to indicate in the marriage certificate that the wife retained her former family name.

b. The District Court suspended the proceedings and submitted to the Federal Constitutional Court the same question as in the proceedings of 1 BvL 83/86. According to the court, the applications for correction of the marriage certificate or for instructions to the status official are admissible, but on the basis of current legal provisions without merit. Since the wife, however, lost her family name and acquired her husband's name as marital name only because of §1355 par. 2, sentence 2 BGB, the decision depends upon the question whether that provision is consistent with the Basic Law or unconstitutional and invalid. The unconstitutionality of the provision is evident in the light of the history of the mandate of equality. The legislator failed to perform the task, imposed by Art. 3 par. 2 of the Basic Law, to achieve the equality of the sexes, when he predicated his regulation upon the traditional disadvantages of the female sex. Other possibilities were open to him. Thus, as the Federal Constitutional Court stated in its order of March 8, 1988 (78 BVerfGE 38 (1989), he was under no duty to prescribe a common family name. If it were impossible to find a solution which prescribed a duty of having a common family name in conformity with Art. 3

par. 3 of the Basic Law, the legislator would be obliged by the Constitution to amend §1355 BGB by adding a provision which would enable the betrothed to retain their family names after their marriage.

III.

The Federal Minister of Justice in the name of the Federal Government, the senator for the administration of justice of the Land Berlin, and the President of the Council of Ministers of the Land Schleswig-Holstein entered opinions on the submitted question.

1. The Federal Minister of Justice considered §1355 par. 2, sentence 2 BGB to be constitutional. The legislator, who wanted to preserve the principle of a single marital name, which in itself raises no constitutional objections, had only limited possibilities for the determination of a common marital name. Denial of a marriage celebration in the cases where the prospective spouses cannot agree upon a common name would have been not only objectionable under the aspects of public policy but also constitutionally questionable because it would violate the liberty to marry and deprive the children of the status of legitimacy and the possibility to grow up in the legitimate family of their parents.

In enacting the thus-necessary residual solution, the legislator, for practical reasons, could tie this solution only to the name of one or the other of the spouses since other solutions would have been less appropriate and a double-name could not have resolved the problem because of the resulting need for a determination of the sequence of the names in that case. The legislator in enacting §1355 chose the least discriminatory solution because it gave the parties the choice to select one of the family names as the marital name and only the cases where a declaration was lacking relied on the choice of the husband's name in harmony with the German names tradition. The effect of the resulting inequality between husband and wife was attenuated by the provision which authorized the spouse whose name had not become the marital name to place his or her name before the marital name and to use it in daily affairs.

In addition, the difficulties of finding a sex-neutral solution would remain, even if the principle of a single marital name were abandoned. In that case, the regulation of the name of the children would have to contain a residual regulation for the situation where the parents could not reach an agreement for which an appropriate solution not tied to the name of one of the parents is not evident. The determination of the name of the child could not be delegated to a guardian when the welfare of the child offers no criteria for the choice between the names of the father or mother or the sequence of these names in the formation of the combined name.

2. The Senator for Justice of the Land Berlin expresses the opinion that §1355, par. 2, sentence 2 BGB incorporates unequal treatment by reason of sex, in conflict with Art. 3(2) of the Basic Law. * * *

3. The President of the Council of Ministers of the Land Schleswig-Holstein likewise is of the view that §1355 par. 2, sentence 2 BGB is unconstitutional. * * *

B.

The submitted resolutions are admissible.

The submitted resolutions make it sufficiently clear that at least the decision on the applications of the wives for correction of the marriage certificates depends on the constitutionality of the provision to be examined. Therefore, it is not necessary to pass on the question whether that issue is also relevant for decision on the applications of the husbands.

C.

§1355 par. 2, sentence 2 BGB conflicts with Art. 3, par. 2 of the Basic Law.

I.

Art. 3 par. 2 of the Basic Law prohibits relying on the difference in sex as a valid reason for unequal legal treatment. This rule does not interdict provisions which differentiate between men and women according to the nature of the respective relations in view of objective biological or functional differences (cf. 63 BVerfGE 181, 194 (1983) with further references). The traditional character of a particular relation by itself, however, does not suffice to justify an unequal treatment. The constitutional mandates would lose their function of achieving the equality of sexes in the future if the present social reality would have to be tolerated (57 BVerfGE 335, 344 (1981)). The principle of the equality of sexes requires strict application. This holds true in particular in cases where women are discriminated against; for Art. 3 par. 2 of the Basic Law has the principal purpose of serving the elimination of such discrimination (74 BVerfGE 163, 179 (1987)).

II.

According to §1355 par. 2, sentence 2 BGB the husband's name becomes the marital name unless the spouses select one of their family names as marital name. This provision therefore treats men and women unequally in respect to the determination of the family name. This unequal treatment is not justified because of objective differences of the sexes. It is also not constitutionally legitimized because of other reasons.

* * *

D.

It follows that §1355 par. 2, sentence 2 BGB conflicts with Art. 3, par. 2 of the Basic Law. The legislator must enact new provisions which observe the mandate of equal treatment and which include a transitional provision for prior cases. In the interest of clarity in the legal situation it is necessary to prescribe in the present decision a provisional regulation operative until the enactment of new legislative provisions.

I.

On principle a norm that conflicts with the Basic Law must be declared to be invalid (§ 82 par. 1 in conjunction with §78, first sentence). This rule, however, does not apply if, in cases where the general or special equal treatment principles are infringed, constitutionality can be achieved in various ways and the declaration of invalidity would anticipate legislative action or if the declaration of invalidity would produce a situation even less in conformity with the Constitution (61 BVerfGE 319, 356 (1983), and 83 BVerfGE 154 (1991)).

Therefore, the holding must be limited to a declaration that the unconstitutional provision conflicts with the Basic Law, because a declaration of its invalidity which on principle would apply for the whole time in which the provision was in force (1 BVerfGE 14, 37 (1952)) might result in a significant legal insecurity which would be intolerable in the law governing names. §79 par. 2 which limits materially the consequences of a declaration of invalidity with respect to legal relations created in the past and thus avoids legal insecurity is here not directly applicable because the legal effects of §1355 par. 2 BGB, sentence 2 occur without intervention of an official authority or court (37 BVerfGE 217, 362 (1974); 48 BVerfGE 327, 340 (1978)). The effects of the unconstitutionality for the marital name of spouses who celebrated their marriages in the past require therefore a special legislative regulation (37 BVerfGE 217, 263 (1974)).

II.

1. The legislator is obliged to enact a new legislative regulation governing the marital name at least for the cases in which the spouses do not designate the marital name pursuant to §1355 par. 2, sentence 1 BGB. He has a wide range of options at his disposal. He may decide to retain the system of a common family name with a sex-neutral residual solution. He, however, is also free to permit exceptions from the principle of the common name or to enact a comprehensive reform of the law governing the marital name.

2. If a provision is declared to be in conflict with the Basic Law, that provision on principle may no longer be applied by the courts or administrative authorities (37 BVerfGE 217, 261 (1974); 82 BVerfGE 126, 155 (1991)).

a. This, however, may not have the consequence that, until the enactment of an amendment, a marriage may be celebrated only if the betrothed make a declaration with respect to the common family name pursuant to §1355 par. 2, sentence 2 BGB. An interpretation to that effect of the remaining portion of §1355 BGB is out of the question on constitutional grounds, because it would lead to a bar to marriage, not provided by law. In that connection, we need not pass on the question whether it would be substantively reconcilable with Art. 6 par. 1 of the Basic Law to elevate a common designation of the marital name within the limits of §1355 par. 2, sentence 1 BGB to a requisite for the celebration of a marriage. At any rate the constitutional guarantee of the freedom to marry could be limited by the legislator only on the basis of a decision made after careful balancing of relevant factors. The legislator, however, wanted to avoid a restriction of freedom to marry by way of a compulsory declaration.

b. Until new legislation, therefore, rules catching the residual cases must be laid down. But this does not justify a provisional retention of the applicability of the unconstitutional rules. To be sure this would avoid the uncertainty about the name to be used by the spouses if they fail to make a declaration pursuant to §1355 par. 2, sentence 1 BGB, cf. 37 BVerfGE 217, 260 (1974); 61 BVerfGE 319, 356 (1983). The continued application, however, would result in new infringements of the Constitution which the subsequent new legislation could not remedy at all or only under renewed infringement of the right of personality.

The birth-name of a human being is an expression of his or her individuality and identity; an individual, therefore, is entitled, on principle, that the legal order respects and protects his or her name. A name change cannot be required without weighty grounds (78 BVerfGE 38, 49 (1989)). To be sure, these constitutional requirements are not violated by the duty of the spouses to have a common marital name. But the additional compulsion of the respective wives, pursuant to §1355 par. 2, sentence 2 BGB, to abandon their own name and assume their husbands' name as family name cannot be justified by reason of public interest because it is established that the rule of residual cases which relies on the husband's name is unconstitutional. Since the legislator, in enacting the required new provisions, must fashion another rule governing the marital name, the wives subject thereto could avail themselves of the new possibilities of determining the name only by way of a further name change and thus at the price of a further infringement of their right of personality.

c. The provisional rules must catch the cases in which the spouses made no declaration pursuant to §1355 par. 2, sentence 1 BGB. Otherwise, the existing law remains applicable. The status official therefore will first have to ask the betrothed pursuant to §13a of the Marriage Law whether they wish to make a declaration.

aa. In the cases in which the prospective spouses upon inquiry do not designate a family name within the framework of the available legal options, the least burdensome solution for the transitional period would be that the spouses retain their pre-marital names. This transitional solution does not preempt the legislator but facilitates a new system because it avoids a multiple name change. After the new law enters into force, it will have to be determined which name the spouses will use in the future.

bb. The provisional exception from the principle of a common family name in the cases mentioned makes it necessary to also prescribe a provisional rule for the name of the children. The starting point for this determination, on the basis of §1355 par. 2, sentence 1 BGB and Art. 220 par. 5 of the Introductory Law to the BGB, is the choice between the name of the father and that of the mother. At the same time account must be taken of the legislator's freedom of choice and of the limits resulting from the functions of the Federal Constitutional Court. Therefore, a solution must be selected which impairs the rights of the persons involved as little as possible and which does not render a new legislative arrangement more difficult.

To oblige the spouses to determine the name of the children already at the celebration of the marriage is out of the question because that would limit the freedom to marry. A tie to the name of only one parent is likewise not feasible because that would encounter constitutional doubts. Thus an enlargement of the parents' right of choice appears to be the least burdensome solution. The possibility of the choice of a composite name-with optional sequence-appears to be apt to diminish the cases where the parents fail to agree. In addition, this solution presents the least obstacles to a future regulation. In the case of a disagreement, it is appropriate to give the child provisionally a composite name and authorize the status official to determine the sequence by lot. This procedure does not disadvantage one of the parents as it would by an alphabetical sequence.

3. For spouses who were married before the publication of this decision without having made a declaration pursuant to §1355 par. 2, sentence 1 BGB, the rule of §1355 par. 2, sentence 2 BGB remains for the time being in force. The legislator, however, is obliged to enact a special rule for these cases. For reasons of legal certainty and peace he is not obliged to eliminate retroactively all consequences of that provision. He must take care, however, that it is possible to eliminate for the future the disadvantageous consequences of the former unconstitutional legal situation (37 BVerfGE 216, 262 (1974); 48 BVerfGE 327, 340 (1979)).

The requisite legislative transitional provisions must at any rate be available to all spouses whose marital name was determined pursuant to §1355 par. 2, sent. 2 BGB. They must have the possibility to have a name which flows from a regulation in conformity with the principle of non-discrimination by reason of sex. The details of the transitional rules depend on the content of the future law on the marital name. If the legislator departs from the principle of a common marital name or permits exceptions therefrom, he will have to examine whether the options granted by the new system must not be made available also to spouses who in the past made a declaration pursuant to §1355, par. 2, sent. 1 BGB.

A correction of the entries in the civil status registers with respect to spouses who were married prior to the publication of this decision is at present impossible because their family name, until the new legislation, is still determined pursuant to §1355 par. 2 sent. 2 BGB.

NOTES

1. The declaration of the *incompatibility with the constitution* of the existing provisions governing the marital name of spouses and of the children of such marriages compelled the German parliament to revise §§1355, 1616-1618, 1720, 1737, 1740 *et seq.* 1757 and 1765 BGB, dealing with the marital name, the name of children of the

marriage, and the name of children born out of wedlock, legitimized and adopted children, etc. *Law Governing the Law of the Family Name* December 16, 1993, [1993] BGBl I 2054. The new statute abandons the mandatory common family name and permits the spouses to retain their names used prior to the marriage.

Since the new law no longer requires a common family name for the parents, difficulties arise with respect to the name of the children if the parents cannot agree. In a case of that type, the name is ultimately determined by the court of guardianship. See St. Liermann, *Der 'Namensrichter' des Familiennamensrechtsgesetzes vom 16.12.1993*, 42 ZEITSCHRIFT FÜR DAS GESAMTE FAMILIENRECHT [Fam RZ] 199 (1995).

2. The judgment of the Constitutional Court did not invalidate the unconstitutional statute, either *ex tunc* or *ex nunc*, and confined the relief to the parties below to a suspension of the proceedings until the enactment of the new law. The question of the power of a court, declaring a statute to be unconstitutional to restrict its holding to the controversy before the court and subsequent cases, but leaving prior determinations on the basis of the unconstitutional statute unaffected, has been much discussed by courts and text-writers. It is related to, if not a special aspect of, the general problem of the legitimacy of prospective overruling. The leading case on the constitutionality of prospective overruling in the United States is *Great Northern Railway v. Sunburst Oil & Refining Co.*, 287 U.S. 358 (1932).

For a good comparative discussion, see C. Mouly, *Comment Limiter la Rétroactivité des Arrets de Principe et de Revirement?*, Les Petites Affiches, nr. 53 p. 10. (1994) and G. Engelbrecht, *"Barber" und die Folgen*, 7 EuZW 395 (1996).

The Court of Justice of the European Communities has rendered a number of judgments with prospective application, entitled to direct effect in the state courts. According to the Italian Constitutional Court such ruling must affect at least the parties to the controversy, *S.p.a. Fragd c. Amministrazione delle Finanze*, It. Const. Ct. Judgment of April 21, 1989 34 Giur. Cost., I 1001 (1989) see supra p. 40n.

3. Note that the German Constitutional Court itself fashioned a transitional rule applicable until the enactment of the the new statute. In the United States, the Supreme Court postponed the effect of its prospective ruling that the jurisdictional provisions of the Bankruptcy Reform Act of 1976 were unconstitutional several times to permit Congress to devise a new system, *Northern Pipeline Construction Co. v. Marathon Pipe Line Co.* 458 U.S. 50 (1982). See Riesenfeld, *Creditors' Remedies and Debtors' Protection*, (4th ed. 1987) 462.

e. *Legal Judge and Overstaffed Divisions of National Courts*

Introduction

A good example of the interplay of the jurisdiction of the Federal Constitution Court and the jurisdiction of the ordinary courts, including the jurisdiction of the

Common Senate of the Federal Supreme Courts, the United Large Senates and the Large Senates of the Federal Supreme Court for Civil and Criminal Matters, is furnished by a series of judgments and orders of these courts relating to the advance identification of the judges called upon to participate in a particular case when the division of the court charged with the respective class of controversies includes more than the needed number of judges (so-called over-staffed judicial divisions.)

In the years 1989, 1991 and 1992, the First Senate for Civil Matters of the Federal Supreme Court for Civil and Criminal Matters was in that situation, having seven judges instead of the minimum five. The presiding judge issued a plan for the participation of the individual judges in particular cases coming to the Senate pursuant to § 21gII of the Law on the Organization of the Judiciary (*GVG*) but the losing parties in some of these cases argued that the presiding judge had not observed the mandates of §21IIg and the standards of such assignment required by art. 101 I2 of the Basic Law. They petitioned the Tenth Civil Senate, which had jurisdiction over such petitions, to vacate the judgement of the First Civil Senate and order reinstatement of the prior status.

The Tenth Senate intended to grant the relief requested, but felt prevented from doing so because of holdings to the contrary by the First and Fourth Senate in Criminal Matters. Upon inquiry, both Senates declared to adhere to their prior position. The Tenth Senate decided therefore to refer the matter to the United Large Senates of the Supreme Court for Civil and Criminal Matters, pursuant to what is now § 132 II-V of the GVG relating to the development of the law and maintenance of uniform adjudications. (Order of March 30, 1993, 46 NJW 1596 (1993)). It asked the VGS the following questions:

1. Are principles laid down by the presiding judge of a Senate for Civil matters of the BGH with extra judges compatible with §21g II GVG, if they are established prior to the beginning of the judicial year but do not contain abstract rules prescribed in advance for the participation of the judges in the individual cases?
2. If the first question is answered in the negative, has that the consequence that, pursuant to § 579I of the Code of Civil Procedure, the judgment of a Senate for Civil Matters of the BGH is subject annulment with the limitation period of § 586 ZPO?

The United Large Senates answered the first question by distinguishing between new cases and cases already decided. With respect to pending cases it held that the participating judges had to be determined pursuant to abstract principles fixed in advance in writing.

For former cases it sufficed that the determination of the participating judges was not arbitrary but made in the exercise of proper judicial discretion for adequate reasons.

The new rules must be observed in the next business year.

An answer to the second question was therefore not called for.

The United Large Senates ruled that it was not necessary to submit the issue to the Common Senate of the Federal Supreme Courts because there was no conflict with the views of the Supreme Finance Court (BFH) with respect to the results reached for prior cases. Similar judgments of the Supreme Administrative Court, moreover, antedated the entry into force of the Law of June 19, 1968, establishing the proceedings before the Common Senate of the Supreme Courts.[88]

Apparently the United Large Senates of the BGH saw no need to refer the case to the Federal Constitutional Court, despite the involvement of Art. 101 I 2 of the Basic Law. Ultimately, however, the Full Bench of the Federal Constitutional Court did decide the relevant issues, reaching the same results as the VGS, BVerfG (Plenum), Judgment of April 8, 1997 (see *infra*.)

Composition of the Bench and Art. 101 I 2 GG
BVerfG (Plenum)
Judgment of April 8, 1997
95 BVerfGE 322, 50 NJW 1497 (1997)

The Significance of Basic Law, Art. 101 I 2 for the Determination of the groups of Professional Judges forming the Composition of the bench in the case of chambers or senates with more then the requisite number of Judges.

Regarding the facts. Subject to the procedure before the full court in question, which demands are made by Art. 101 I 2 GG (Basic Law) for the determination of the groups of professional judges forming the bench in the case of a chamber or senate composed of more than the requisite number of judges needed for a judgment.

In the case pending before the First Senate of the BVerfG (1 Bv R 1644/94), a decision must be made on the question whether the challenged judgment of the Second Senate of the BFH (Federal Supreme Finance Court) with respect to the composition of the bench rest on a violation of Art. 101 I 2 of the Basic Law. The senate of the BFH renders judgment in a composition of five judges pursuant to § 10 III FGO (Law of the Procedure of the Finance Courts). In the year 1994, the president of the Court allocated to the II. Senate, in addition to the presiding judge, five additional judges. It was accordingly over-staffed by one judge. The Order of the Presiding Judge of December 15, 1993 determined the participation of the members of the Senate pursuant to §4 FGO in conjunction with §21 g II first half-sentence I of the GVG (Law on Judicial Organization.)

"I. Within chambers or senates composed of several judges the presiding judge allocates the matters for which each judge is responsible.

---

88. Resolution of May 5, 1994 (United Large Senates of the Supreme Court for Civil and Criminal Matters) 15 ZIP 809 (1994) = 47 NJW 1735 (1994).

> II. The presiding judge determines prior to the commencement of the judicial year, for its duration, the principles governing the participation of the members; this order may only be changed when it is necessary because of over-commitment, inadequate relief, change or permanent disability of the individual members of the chamber or senate."

In the order of the presiding judge, each other judge was eliminated from different sittings according to a sequence thereof. The agenda of each sitting included all matters which had been received until Thursday of the preceding week with the votes of the reporter and co-reporter. The reporters were determined with regard to the need of speed and work burden. The final composition of the bench depended therefore on the respective agendas.

The First Senate is of the opinion that this system of participation is incompatible with Art. 101 of the Basic Law (cf. 48 NJW 2703 (1995)). Legal Judge within the meaning of Art. 101 I 2 of the Basic Law in its view is not only the court as organizational unit and the bench before which the arguments take place and which decides the case. Legal judges are also the judges who are called to decide the individual case. These should be identified as clearly and unambiguously as possible in the plans of the courts for the distribution of and participation in the cases. With respect to the chambers or senates with more than the judges needed to sit in a case it follows that the presiding judge must before the commencement of the business year determine according to abstract general criteria which members of a chamber or senate participate in the particular judicial acts. With the last-mentioned rule the First Senate wishes to depart from the view of the Second Senate of the Federal Constitutional Court expressed in the orders of February 3, 1965 (18 BVerfGE 344 = 38 NJW 1219 (1965)) and of January 15, 1985 (69 BVerfGE 112 = NVwZ 647 (1985).) True, in the order of February 3, 1965 it is also stated that legal judge within the meaning of Art. 101 I 2 of the Basic Law is not only the Court as organizational unit and as the adjudicatory body, but also the judges called for the decision of the individual case. It is also emphasized that the rules of the determination of the legal judge must from the outset establish as unambiguously as possible, which court, which chamber or senate and which judges are called for the adjudication of the individual case. (*Cf.* 18 BVerfGE 394, 399 = 18 NJW 1219 (1965).) On the other hand, however, it is deemed to be acceptable that the presiding judge of a chamber or senate with extra members calls the judicial members to participate in judicial action according to his discretion and not pursuant to an in advance determined plan. The constitutional requirement of the specification of the judge is met, if his power to decide a concrete case derives from general rules on jurisdiction in the codes of procedure, the distribution of matters and the designation by the presiding judge, cf. BVerfGE 18, 344, 351 et seq. = 18 NJW 1219 (1965). In the Order of January 15, 1985 (NvwZ 647 (1985), the Second Senate of the Federal Constitutional Court had reaffirmed this view. Which judges belonging to an adjudicatory body will participate in a particular case did not require an advance determination under Art. 101 I 2 of the Basic Law; pursuant to the constitutional provision it is only examined whether the presiding judge exercised his or her discretion without arbitrariness (69 BVerfGE 112, 120 et seq.)

The First Senate of the Federal Constitutional Court resolved in the case 1 BvR 1644/94, to ask the Second Senate according to §48 II GOBVerfG whether the latter retained its above-mentioned position. The Second Senate gave an on principle affirmative answer. Thereupon the First Senate submitted the issue to the full bench of the Federal Constitutional Court. 48 NJW 2705 (1995). The full bench held that Art. 101 I 2 of the Basic Law requires on principle that in the case of a chamber or senate with extra professional judges, the designation of the judges who participate in an individual case has to be made in advance pursuant to abstract criteria.

REASONS

I. . . . .

II. With the considerations set forth above the full bench of the Federal Constitutional Court takes account of the fact that the notions of the requirements of the legal judge have gradually been refined in the course of time and that, in consequence of this development, the demand for determination in advance as precise as possible of also the judges participating in an individual case has gained increasingly stronger emphasis (cf. 126 BGHZ 63, 85 = 47 NJW 1735 (1994).)

1. In the beginning, under the regime of §16 sentence 2 of the Law on the Organization of the Courts in its original text of January 27, 1877 (RGB1. p 41) and the equally worded Art. 105 sentence 2 of the Weimar Constitution, the demand for the advance determination on the basis of abstract-general criteria of the members of an adjudicatory body with extra members called upon to participate in particular cases may have been considered to be subject to waiver.

Related thereto is also that Art. 101 I sentence 2 of the Basic Law the wording of which is identical with these provisions is tied to the legal situation created by them (cf. 18 BVerfGE 344, 351 = 18 NJW 1291 (1965).) But also a legal tradition grown in decades does not prevent an evolution which takes account of changed perceptions. The plan for the distribution of business, which assigns the cases and the judges needed for disposition to specified chambers or senates, and the participation plan which in the case of chambers or senates with extra members governs the assignment of cases to individual judges, determine the legal judge only in their joint operation. It is only logical to subject also the participation plan to the constraints of Art. 101 I 2 of the Basic Law.

2. The BVerfG also formerly never expressed in its jurisprudence that, in a chamber or senate with extra members, the selection of the judges called upon to decide the concrete cases touches upon the guarantee of a legal judge and thus under this aspect may raise a constitutional problem. To be sure, it saw the constitutional resolution of that problem in constitutional barriers against extra members and deduced that from

the need for a legal judge (cf. 18 BVerfGE 394, 349 et seq. = 18 NJW 1219 (1965) 22 BVerfGE 283, 286). This approach to a resolution, however, was induced by the legislative situation then prevailing and did not take sufficient account of the independent significance of the constitutional guarantee of Art. 101 I 2 of the Basic Law.

3. With this decision the interpretation of Art. 101 I 2 of the Basic Law is clarified and further developed. It is therefore necessary to still tolerate the prior rules of participation in a chamber or senate with extra members for a transitional period, in order to give an opportunity to the ordinary courts to adapt their practice to the now clarified constitutional situation. The necessity of such transitional periods has been recognized by the BVerfG in cases of changed constitutional interpretation — which is particularly present in the case of a refinement of the existing case law by way of a decision of the full bench — on various occasions (cf. 84 BVerfGE 239, 284 et seq. = 44 NJW 2129 (1991); 58 BVerfGE 257, 280 = 35 NJW 921 (1982) with further references). The ordinary courts have the duty to assure compliance with the requirements mandated by Article 101 I 2 of the Basic Law beginning at the latest July 1, 1997 with respect to proceedings pending after that date.

NOTES

1. Article 101 of the Basic Law provides:

> "(1) Exceptional Courts are prohibited. Nobody may be deprived of his legal judge.
> (2) Courts for special subject-matters may only be created by legislation."

2. The German Federal Constitutional Court has construed the meaning or scope of Article 101 I 2 on several occasions. Particularly significant is the holding that the ECJ, and now the CFI, is a legal judge within the meaning of Art. 101 I 2d sentence, Decision of the Federal Constitutional Court (2d Senate) October 22, 1986, In the Procedure involving the Constitutional Complaint of the Firm *Wünsche*, 73 BVerfGE 339 at 366–370; Decision of the Federal Constitutional Court (2d Senate) of April 8, 1987, In the Procedure Involving the Constitutional Complaint of Frau Kloppenburg, 75 BVerfGE 223, [1988] C.M.L.R. 12.

In the *Wünsche* case, the BVerfG rejected the constitutional complaint of the complainant against a judgment of the Federal Finance Court because the Court had failed to resubmit under Article 177 EC-Treaty the question as to the validity of certain Commission regulations concerning the import of champignon preserves. The Constitutional Court held that the Federal Administrative Court had not violated complainant's constitutional right under Art. 101 I 2 by refusing to make a new referral to the ECJ. Such refusal was not arbitrary.

In the *Kloppenburg* case, which involved the vertical direct effect of untransposed directive, the Federal Finance Court denied the direct applicability of the Sixth VAT Directive, although the ECJ had affirmed this effect upon a preliminary question interposed by the court below, Judgment of February 22, 1984, Case 70/83, ECR 1075, 1087 (1984). The Federal Constitutional Court decided that the Federal Finance Court, by not resubmitting the question as to the direct effect of untransposed directives to the ECJ had committed an objectively arbitrary violation of Art. 101 I 2 and therefore vacated the Judgment.

3. A violation of Article 101 I 2 due to a failure to submit a preliminary question is committed only by a court or tribunal of a Member State against whose decisions there is no judicial remedy under national law. (EC Treaty, Art. 177 III).

An interesting application of that provision occurred in a recent case involving the constitutional complaint against a final judgment of an appellate labor court. The case involved a gardener who had been dismissed because his employer, the manager of apartment houses, decided to replace the gardening department with an independent contractor. The gardener brought an action for unlawful dismissal, arguing that the termination violated Art. 4 of the Council Directive 77/187. The appellate labor court dismissed the action without submitting the interpretation of the Directive to the ECJ. At the same time it denied a petition for review by the Federal Labor Court. The Second Chamber of the First Senate of the Federal Constitutional Court denied the admission of the constitutional complaint, Order of June 13, 1997, 8 EuZW 18 (1997). The chamber conceded that the appellate labor court had committed a serious violation of complainant's constitutional right under Art. 101 I 2 of the Basic Law. Nevertheless, the constitutional complaint was declared to be inadmissible because it involved neither a question of fundamental significance, nor necessary to the enforcement of complainant's rights. (BVerfGG §93a II lit.a and 93 a II lit. B), for the reasons that in the meantime the ECJ had clarified the interpretation of the Directive 77/187 in the case of Ayse Sűzen, 50 NJW 2039 (1997) and the merits of an action would not require a different result.

D. RUSSIAN FEDERATION (RF)

LAW OF JULY 23, 1994 ESTABLISHING THE CONSTITUTIONAL COURT OF THE RUSSIAN FEDERATION[89]

PART ONE
ORGANIZATION OF THE CONSTITUTIONAL COURT AND STATUS OF JUDGES

89. [1996] EuGRZ 219; [1995] WIRO 13.

Chapter I. General Provisions

Art. 1

The Constitutional Court —
The Judicial Organ of the Control of Constitutionality

The Constitutional Court is the judicial organ of the control of constitutionality; it exercises the judicial power independently and freely by means of constitutional adjudication.

Art. 2

Legislation Governing the Constitutional Court of the RF

Jurisdiction, formation and activity of the Constitutional Court are governed by the Constitution of the Russian Federation and the present federal constitutional law.

Art. 3

Competence of the Constitutional Court of the RF

(1) For the protection of the bases of the constitutional order, the fundamental rights and freedoms of men and citizens and for the security of the primacy and direct applicability of the Constitution of the RF in the entire territory of the RF, the Constitutional Court of the RF possesses the following competences:

1. It determines the constitutionality of
   a) Federal statutes and normative acts of the President of the RF, the Federal Council, the State Duma, and the Government of the RF,
   b) the constitutions of the Republics, charters, laws and the normative acts, of the constituents of the RF which have been issued in respect to questions appertaining to the jurisdiction of the organs of the governmental power of the RF and the organs of the governmental power of the constituents of the RF;
   c) of agreements between organs of the federal governmental power and organs of the governmental power of the constituents of the RF and of agreements between organs of the governmental power of constituents of the RF;
   d) of international treaties that have not yet entered into force.
2. The Constitutional Court of the RF decides controversies relating to their jurisdiction
   a) between federal organs of the governmental power;
   b) between federal organs of governmental power and organs of governmental power of constituents of the RF;
   c) between the highest state organs of governmental power of the constituents of the RF.
3. The Constitutional Court decides complaints based on the infringement of constitutional rights and freedoms of citizens and, upon referral by the

courts, examines the constitutionality of a statute which has been applied or is to be applied in a concrete case.

4. The Constitutional Court of the RF interprets the Constitution of the RF.
5. The Constitutional Court of the RF issues opinions on the observance of prescribed procedures of the impeachment of the President of the RF based on treason or another grave crime.
6. The Constitutional Court of the RF is entitled to introduce bills in questions which are within the scope of its competence.
7. The Constitutional Court of the RF exercises the additional functions which are vested in it by the Constitution of the RF, a treaty of the Federation or a Federal constitutional law; it may also exercise the rights which are conferred upon it by means of agreements, concluded pursuant to Art. 11 of the Constitution, relating to the delimitation of matters of jurisdiction or competence between the organs of the federal governmental power and the organs of governmental power of the constituents of the RF, if these rights do not conflict with the nature of the Constitutional Court of the RF as a judicial body and its function as a judicial body for the control of constitutionality.

(2) The Constitutional Court of the RF decides exclusively legal questions.

(3) The Constitutional Court of the RF, in the adjudication of constitutionality abstains from any determination and ascertainment of factual circumstances in all cases in which this is within the jurisdiction of other courts or organs.

(4) For questions relating to its internal operation the Constitutional Court of the RF enact a set of internal rules of the Constitutional Court of the RF.

Art. 4
Composition, Formation and Duration of the Competences of the Constitutional Court of the RF

(1) The Constitutional Court of the RF consists of 19 Judges who are appointed by the Federal Council upon a proposal by the President of the RF.

(2) The Constitutional Court of the RF can exercise its functions if at least three-quarters of these nineteen judges are holding office.

(3) The competences of the Constitutional Court of the RF are not subject to any durational limitation.

Art. 5
Basic Principles of the Activity of the Constitutional Court of the RF

The basic principles of the activity of the Constitutional Court of the RF are independence, collegiality, publicity, adversarial proceedings and equality of arms of the parties.

Art. 6

Binding Power of the Decisions of the Constitutional Court of the RF

The decisions of the Constitutional Court of the RF are binding in the entire territory of the RF for all representative, executive and judicial organs of governmental power, for the organs of local self-government, for enterprises, authorities, organizations, officials, citizens and their associations.

Art. 7

Guarantees of the Activity of the Constitutional Court of the RF

* * *

Chapter II

Status of the Judges of the Constitutional Court of the RF

Art. 8

Qualifications of the Candidate for the Office of Judge of the Constitutional Court of the RF

As judge of the Constitutional Court of the RF may be appointed any citizen of the RF who on the day of the appointment is at least 40 years of age, enjoys a blameless reputation, has received a high legal education, has at least 15 years experience in a legal occupation and possesses a recognized high qualification in the field of law.

Arts. 9-11

* * *

Art. 12

Duration of the Office of Judge of the Constitutional Court of the RF

(1) A Judge of the Constitutional Court is appointed for a 12 year term. The age limit for the exercise of the office of Judge of the Constitutional Court of the RF is 70 years.

(2) The appointment of a Judge of the Constitutional Court of the RF for a second term is not permitted.

(3) A Judge of the Constitutional Court of the RF commences his office at the time when he pronounces his oath of office. His office ends on the last day of the month in which his term of office ends, or in which he completes the 70th year of his life.

Art. 13

Guarantees of the Independence of the Judges of the Constitutional Court of the RF

* * *

Art. 14

Irremovability of the Judges of the Constitutional Court of the RF

(1) A Judge of the Constitutional Court of the RF is irremovable.

(2) The official functions of a Judge of the Constitutional Court of the RF cannot be terminated or suspended in another way or for other reason than as provided in this federal constitutional law.

* * *

CHAPTER III

Structure and Organization of the Activity of the Constitutional Court of the RF

Art. 20

Form of the Organization and Proceedings of the Constitutional Court

(1) The Constitutional Court of the RF conducts proceedings and renders decisions in sittings of the full bench or in sittings of the Senates of the Constitutional Court of the RF.

(2) The Constitutional Court of the RF consists of 2 senates consisting of 10 or 9 Judges of the Constitutional Court of the RF respectively. The personal composition of the senates is determined by lot, as provided in the rules for the internal organization of the court.

(3) Participants in sittings of the full bench are all Judges of the Constitutional Court of the RF, while the participants in the sittings of the senates are the Judges who are members of the respective senate.

(4) The President and the Vice-president of the Constitutional Court of the RF may not belong to the same senate.

(5) The personal composition of the senates may not remain unchanged for more than 3 consecutive years.

(6) The order in which the judges of a senate preside over its sitting is determined in a sitting of the senate.

Art. 21

Questions to be Determined by the Full Bench of the Constitutional Court of the RF

* * *

Art. 22

Questions to be Determined by the Senates of the Constitutional Court of the RF

* * *

PART TWO
GENERAL RULES GOVERNING PROCEEDINGS BEFORE THE CONSTITUTIONAL COURT OF THE RF

Chapters V-VIII

PART THREE
PARTICULAR FEATURES OF THE PROCEEDINGS BEFORE THE CONSTITUTIONAL COURT OF THE RF IN THE DIFFERENT CATEGORIES OF PROCEEDINGS

Chapter IX

Adjudication of questions relating to the constitutionality of normative acts of organs of governmental power or the constitutionality of agreements between them.

Art. 84
The Right to Invoke the Constitutional Court of the RF

The right to invoke the jurisdiction of the Constitutional Court of the RF to determine the constitutionality of the normative acts listed in Art. 125, par. 2 of the Constitution of the RF and of the agreements between the organs of the governmental power is granted to the President of the RF, the Federal Council, the State Duma, a fifth of the members of the Federal Council or Duma, the government of the RF, the Supreme Court of the RF, the Supreme Court of Arbitration and the Organs of the legislative or executive power of the components of the RF.

Art. 85
Admissibility of the Proceedings

(1) An invocation of the Constitutional Court of the RF to examine the constitutionality of a normative act of an organ of governmental power or of an agreement between organs of government power or of particular provisions thereof is admissible if the initiator of the proceedings believes that the normative act or the agreement is invalid because of its unconstitutionality or that it is valid, despite a contrary official decision by federal organs of governmental power, the highest governmental organ of the constituents of the RF or their officials to not apply such act or agreement because of unconstitutionality.

(2) The invocation of the Court to examine the constitutionality of a normative act of a constituent of the RF is admissible if the normative act is issued with reference to a question which is within the competence of the organs of the federal governmental power or within the common competence of the organs of the governmental power of the RF and the organs of the governmental power of the constituents of the RF.

* * *

Art. 86
Limits of the Examination

(1) The Constitutional Court of the RF examines the constitutionality of normative acts or organs of the governmental power and of agreements between them

1. in respect to the content of the norms;
2. in respect to the form of the act or agreement;
3. in respect to the procedure of the signing, the conclusion, the adoption, the promulgation or party in force;
4. under the aspect of the separation of powers into legislative, executive and judicial power fixed in the Constitution;
5. under the aspect of the delimitation, fixed by the Constitution of the RF, of the competencies of the federal organs of the governmental power;
6. under the aspect of the delimitation of the objects of the jurisdiction and competence between the organs of the federal governmental powers of the components of the RF, as they are fixed in the Constitution of the RF, in a covenant of federation or in other agreements on delimitation of competencies.

(2) The examination of the constitutionality of normative acts of organs of governmental powers and agreements between them which were made before the entry into force of the Constitution, is conducted by the Constitutional Court of the RF only in respect of the norms.

Art. 87
The Final Decision on the Merits

(1) The result of proceedings on the merits in the case of an examination of the constitutionality of a normative act of an organ of governmental power or of an agreement between organs of governmental power is expressed in one of the following decisions of the Constitutional Court of the RF:

1. that the normative act or agreement or particular provision thereof are constitutional;
2. that the normative act or agreement or particular provisions thereof are unconstitutional.

(2) The determination of the unconstitutionality of a normative act or agreement or particular provision thereof is ground for the repeal of provisions of other normative acts which rest on the normative act or agreement declared to be unconstitutional, repeat the same or contain identical provisions as were the object of the invocation. The provisions of these normative acts and agreements may not be applied by courts, other organs and officials.

Chapter X
Proceedings Relating to the Unconstitutionality of Treaties of the RF that have not yet Entered into Force

Art. 88
Right to Invoke the Constitutional Court of the RF

The right to invoke the Constitutional Court of the RF to examine the constitutionality of a treaty that has not yet entered into force is granted to the President of the RF, the Federal Council, the State Duma, a fifth of the members of the federal Council or of the representatives of the State Duma, the Government of the RF, the Supreme Court of the RF, the Supreme Court of Arbitration of the RF and the organs of the legislature and executive power of the constituents of the RF.

* * *

Chapter XI
Proceedings for the Resolution of Conflicts Relating to Competence

Art.5 92
The Right to invoke the Constitutional Court of the RF

The right to apply to the Constitutional Court of the RF for the decision of a conflict of competence belongs to each organ of governmental power taking part in the conflict that is listed in Article 125(3) of the Constitution of the RF and to the President in the case provided in Article 185(1) of the Constitutions of the RF.***

Chapter XII
Review of the Constitutionality of Laws by Reason of Complaints alleging infringement of the Rights and Liberties of Citizens

Art. 96
Right to invoke the Constitutional Court of the Russian Federation

The right to invoke the Constitutional Court of the RF by means of individual or collective complaints by reason of infringement of their constitutional rights and liabilities is open to citizens whose rights and liabilities are infringed by a statute that has been applied or is subject to application in a concrete litigation, or to associations of citizens or other organs and persons designated in a federal statute. The complaint, in addition to the documents listed in Art. 38 of this Federal Constitutional Law, must be accompanied by a copy of an official document which confirms the application or possible application of the challenged law in the decision of the concrete case. The issuance of a copy of that kind of document takes place, upon a request of the complainant, by the official or the organ which is in charge of the case.

Art. 97
Admissibility of the Complaint

A complaint by reason of an infringement of the constitutional rights and liberties is admissible if

1. A statute touches upon the constitutional rights and liberties of the citizens;
2. The statute has been applied or is subject to be applied in a concrete case, the examination of which has been concluded or which is pending before a court or body that applies the statute.

Art. 98

Consequences of the Acceptance of the Complaint for Review

Following the acceptance by the Constitutional Court of the RF of the complaint because of the infringement of the constitutional rights and liberties of the citizens by a statute, it notifies the court or other organ in charge of the matter in which the challenged statute has been applied or is going to be applied, of the acceptance. The notification does not entail a termination of the proceedings. The court or other body which is in charge of the matter in which the challenged statute has been applied or is subject to being applied, may suspend the proceedings until the decision of the Constitutional Court of the RF.

Art. 99

Limits of the Review

The limits of the review of a statute which has been challenged in a complaint because of infringement of the rights and liberties of the citizens with respect to its compatibility with the Constitution of the RF are defined by Art. 86 of this federal constitutional law.

Art. 100

Final Decision of the Case

Upon the basis of an examination of a complaint charging an infringement of the constitutional rights and liberties of the citizens, the Constitutional Court renders one of the following decisions:

1. Declaration that the statute or specified provisions of it are consistent with the Constitution of the RF;
2. Declaration that the statute or specified provisions of it are not consistent with the Constitution of the RF.

In the case that the Constitutional Court has declared that a statute which has been applied in a particular controversy is not consistent with the Constitution of the RF, that controversy is subject to a review by the competent authority according to the appropriate procedure. In the case of a declaration that a statute or specified provisions of it are inconsistent with the Constitution of the RF, the court costs of the citizens or their associations are subject to reimbursement in the established order.

***

Chapter XIII

Proceedings in Cases Relating to the Constitutionality of Statutes upon Reference by Courts

Art. 101

Invocation of the Constitutional Court of the RF

A court which in proceedings of whatever instance concludes that a statute which in the pending case was or had to be applied is unconstitutional submits this statute to the Constitutional Court of the RF to examine its constitutionality.

Art. 102

Admissibility of the Referral

The referral is admissible, if the statute was applied in the pending case or, in the opinion of the court, is to be applied.

Chapter XIV

Proceedings in Cases concerning the Interpretation of the Constitution of the RF

Art. 105

Right to invoke the Constitutional Court of the RF

The right to apply to the Constitutional Court for the interpretation of the Constitution belongs to the President of the RF, the Federal Council, the State Duma, the Governments of the RF, the Organs of the Legislative Powers of Constituents of the RF.

Art. 106

Binding Effect of the Interpretation of the Constitution of the RF

* * *

Chapter XV

Proceedings in a Case relating to the Rendition of an Opinion concerning the Observance of the Prescribed Procedure for the Impeachment of the President because of Treason or another Grave Crime.

a. Smirnov

Constitutional Court of The Russian F.R. Decision of December 20, 1995 (Nr 17-P)

Constitutional Complaint by V.A. Smirnov contesting the constitutionality of Art. 64 of the Russian Criminal Code.

Competence: Constitution, Art. 125 par. 4 and Constitutional Law on Constitutional Court, Art. 3 I 3(2) and (3), Art. 22 II 3, Arts. 36, 74, 96, 97, 99.

Facts. V.A. Smirnov was convicted by the Judgment of October 26, 1982 of the Criminal Chamber of the Moscow City Court of Treason, consisting of refusal to return from abroad, communication of state secrets to a foreign nation and assistance to hostile activities. Affirmed the Supreme Court in 1991.

The Constitutional Court *held* that the provisions of Criminal Code, Art. 64a were valid to the extent that they penalized the communication of state secrets to a foreign power or the assistance to the perpetration of hostile activities, but violative of Art. 27 par.2 and 55 par.3 of the Constitution to the extent that they penalized the flight abroad and the refusal to return.

Two of the nine participating judges filed dissenting opinions. German translation of the Judgment by M. Hartwig and T. Beknazar, 25 EuGRZ 144-146 (1998), comments by A. Nussberger, *Die Grundrechte in der Rechtsprechung des russischen Verfassungsgerichts, Ausgewählte Entscheidungen aus den Jahren 1995-97,* 25 EuGRZ 105, 113 (1998).

b. World War II Art Booty

An interesting illustration of the jurisprudence of the Constitutional Court of the Russian Federation is furnished by its decision of April 6, 1998 in a controversy between the Duma and the Federal Council on the one hand and the President of the F.R. on the other. The controversy arose as the result of the failure the President to sign an act, adopted by the Duma on February 5, 1997 and by the Federal Council on March 5, 1997, providing that the cultural objects seized by the U.S.S.R. during World War I should remain the property of the Russian F.R. President Yeltsin considered the act violated the rules of international law and conventions to which the Russian F.R. is a party and returned the bill to the two chambers. Thereupon the Duma on April 4, 1997 and the Federal Council on May 14, 1997 again voted for the adoption of the law without changes, acting with the requisite qualified majority. Nevertheless, the President again returned the law to the two chambers without his signature.

Both chambers decided to submit the law again to the President — the Duma on

June 10, 1997 and the Federal Council of June 14, 1997, — insisting that the President had the constitutional duty to sign it. Nevertheless, the President again returned the law to the two bodies. As a result, the Duma as well as the Federal Council invoked the Constitutional Court with the request to decide whether the President had the duty to sign the law in issue.

The Court joined both proceedings pursuant to Art. 48 of the Federal Law on the Constitutional Court. The President justified his continued refusal to sign the law with the contention that the renewed adoption of the law by the Federal Council by way of the circulation of a questionnaire pursuant to its rules of procedure rather than by vote in a session violated the Constitution and that the vote in the Duma failed to comply with its rules of procedure because the requisite quorum was not present.

The Court ruled that the President was not entitled to pass on the constitutionality of the rules of procedure of the Federal Council without submitting that question to the Constitutional Court by a petition to that effect. So far as the vote in the Duma was concerned, the Court pointed out that it was not empowered to exercise a preventive norms control and therefor could not pass on the constitutionality of legislation before it was signed by the president and published. As a consequence, the Court held that the President was under a duty to sign the act subject to his right to contest the constitutionality thereafter.

A German translation of that decision (nr. 11 of 1998) is published in 25 EuGRZ 378 (1998); for summary in French see 34 Revue française de droit constitutionnel 387 (1998) and M. Hartwig, *Beutekunst-Gesetz vor den Verfassungsgericht der Russischen Föderation; Die Entscheidung vom 6. April 1998*, 25 EuGRZ 369 (1998).

The law was signed by the President and promulgated on April 15, 1998. On the same day the President, on the basis of Art. 125 para. 2 of the Constitution of the Russian F.R. and Arts. 3 para. 1(1a), 22 para. 2(1a), 36, 84 and 85 of the Federal Law on the Constitutional Court, requested that Court to examine the constitutionality of certain provisions of the Law Concerning the Cultural Objects which as a result of the Second World War were brought to the U.S.S.R. and are now within the territory of the Russian F.R., as well as of the procedure whereby the law of April 15, 1998 was adopted, in particular the decisions of the Duma of April 4, 1997 and the Federal Council of May 14, 1997.

With respect to the merits, the application emphasized that the challenged law violated numerous provisions of the Constitution such as Articles 6(2), 8(2), 130(1), 10, 15(3), 35, 55(2) & (3), 112(1) and 114(1), and in particular its Art. 15(4), pursuant to which federal law may not contradict the generally recognized principles and norms of international law and the international treaties of the R.F. which constitute an integral part of its legal system.

For a German translation of the lengthy text of the petition see the translation by A. Nussberger, 25 EuGRZ 423 (1998).

Cf. also M. Hartwig, *Moskau locuta — causa non finita; Das Beutekunst-Gesetz vor den Verfassungsgericht der Russischen Föderation*, 25 EuGRZ, 369 (1998).

NOTE

1. See H. Hausmaniger, *Towards a "New" Russian Constitutional Court*, 28 CORNELL INT'L L.J. 349 (1995).

E. REPUBLIC OF HUNGARY

1. Introduction

1. In Hungary, the Constitution of 1949, as revised on several occasions, especially by Act XXXI of 1989, which initiated the transition to parliamentary democratic government, establishes in Chapter XII (Arts 54-70k) a catalogue of *Fundamental Rights and Duties* and in Chapter IV (Art. 32a) provides for the creation of a Constitutional Court.

Pursuant to this mandate, Parliament, by Act XXXII of 1989, defined the organization and jurisdiction of that body. In view of the hurried nature of that legislation, it suffered from many ambiguities and unresolved issues which had to be settled by the Court itself.[90]

The Court is composed of 15 members and vested with jurisdiction specified in Art. 1, viz., to (a) investigate ex ante cases of unconstitutionality of provisions of bills, acts of Parliament adopted but not yet promulgated, the Parliament's rules of procedure and international agreements; (b) investigate ex post cases of unconstitutionality of legislative provisions; ... (d) decide constitutional complaints lodged in cases of violations of constitutional rights; (e) terminate cases of unconstitutionality manifested in omission.

Procedures under Art. 1(e) may be initiated ex officio. Art. 26 authorizes separate opinions. Procedures relating to investigations ex post of unconstitutionality are governed by Act XXXII of 1989 Arts. 37-43. If the Court establishes the unconstitutionality of a provision of a national law, it shall annul that provision wholly or in part (Art. 40) and publish its decision in the Official Gazette, whereupon the provision shall lose effect (Arts. 41(1), 43(1) and (2).) Nevertheless, the Court, may set another date for the annulment of an unconstitutional provision of a law or its applicability to concrete cases other than those stated in Art. 42(1) and Art. 43(1) and (2), if that is warranted because of reasons of legal certainty or because of an important interest of the applicant for the procedure.

---

90. Cf Lázló Sólyom, *The First Year of the Constitutional Court*, 33 Acta Juridica Hungarica 5 (1991); A. Takács, *Dilemmas of Constitutionalism in the Decisions of the Hungarian Constitutional Court*, id. 217.

2. Texts

CONSTITUTION OF THE REPUBLIC OF HUNGARY

Chapter IV Constitutional Court
Art. 32/A

(1) The Constitutional Court shall review the constitutionality of legislation and shall perform such other functions as may be conferred upon it by law.

(2) In the case of establishing their unconstitutionality the Constitutional Court shall annul the laws and other enactments.

(3) In the cases defined by the law, anyone may initiate proceedings in the Constitutional Court.

(4) The fifteen members of the Constitutional Court shall be elected by Parliament. A nominating committee comprising one member from each of the parties represented in Parliament shall nominate the candidates for the Constitutional Court. Two thirds of the affirmative votes of the MPs shall be required for electing members of the Constitutional Court

(5) The members of the Constitutional Court shall not be affiliated with any party and shall not carry on any activities outside of those within the competence of the Constitutional Court.

(6) For the adoption of the law on the organization and operation of the Constitutional Court, two third of the votes of the MPs present shall be necessary.

Chapter XII Fundamental Rights and Duties

* * *

Art. 59

In the Republic of Hungary everyone is entitled to the protection of his or her reputation and to privacy, including the privacy of the home, of personal effects, particulars, papers, records and data, and to the privacy of personal affairs and secrets.

3. Illustrative Case

An important illustration of the operation of the Hungarian Constitutional Court is its Decision No. 60/1994 of December 22, 1994, involving the constitutionality of Act XXII of 1994, the so-called Lustration Law.[91]

The statute had the purpose of barring some former office holders, secret informers and members of the political police from occupying certain public offices and other key positions in public life. The Act mandated the preservation of secret files compiled by the preceding regime and authorized their use by specified author-

91. Translation in EAST EUROPEAN CASE REPORTER OF CONSTITUTIONAL LAW 159 (1996).

ities for the purpose of background checks on affected individuals. The constitutionality of the Act was challenged by several complainants for a variety of reasons, inter alia, the infringement of the constitutional right to informational self-determination protected by Art. 59 of the Constitution.

The Court, calling the case 'proceedings from petitions for review of the constitutionality of Act XXII of 1994 and on the official proceedings aimed at establishing the unconstitutionality of said Act on the basis of omission', declared numerous provisions of the Act to be unconstitutional. The declaration of unconstitutionality of portions of the Act and of a decree of the Interior Ministry for its implementation, however, had to be effective as of different dates, according to the provisions involved.

Certain subsections of Section 2, Section 4 and the second half of Section 8 were to lose force, and the Ministerial Decree to be considered repealed, on the date of the promulgation of the decision; other subsections of Section 2 were to lose force on the date the amendment of that Section goes into force.

In addition, the Court found that Parliament had created an unconstitutional situation by omitting the enactment of certain guarantees, in particular of the exercise of the right to informational self-determination by failing to provide for destruction of the records once the respective individuals have been investigated. The Court called upon Parliament to meet its legislative obligation by a specified date.

One judge wrote a concurring opinion, but expressed the view that the determination that omission had created an unconstitutional situation and the initiation by the Court of a procedure to resolve this issue, without the default meeting the criteria of Section 49 of the CC Act, exceeded the Court's jurisdiction.

F. THE UNITED KINGDOM, GREAT BRITAIN, ENGLAND AND WALES

1. Organization of the Courts

The organization of the courts and the administration of justice varies according to which component of the United Kingdom (i.e. Northern Ireland, Scotland or England and Wales) is involved. In England and Wales, the matter is governed by a large number of statutes. Case law based on older statutes,[92] though still relevant, has been fundamentally altered by the Civil Procedure Act 1997 (1997 c12) authorizing the Civil Procedure Rules 1998 (Statutory Instruments No. 2132 (L17) (p. 6791). The Civil Procedure Rules 1998 set out a new procedural code covering all proceedings in the High Court, Court of Appeal, Civil Division and the County Courts.

92. Primarily The Courts and Legal Services Act (1990 c 41); the Administration of Justice Act 1985 (1985 c 61); The County Courts Act 1984 (1984 c 28); The Supreme Court Act 1981 (1981 c 54). Details have been introduced by Statutory Instruments, e.g. County Courts Procedure (SI 1995 No. 2839 (L16) p. 8080)).

a. House of Lords

The supreme court of appeal in the United Kingdom[93] is the *House of Lords,* sitting as its Appeals Committee. It is composed of the ex officio members, i.e. the Lord Chancellor and the ex-Lord Chancellor and the Lords of Appeal in Ordinary, who are appointed by the Crown on the advice of the Prime Minister in consultation with the Lord Chancellor from barristers of at least 15 years' standing or judges with at least two years service.

The office of Lord of Appeal in Ordinary was created by the Appellate Jurisdiction Act 1876 (c59) s6. Originally the appointment of two such life-time peers was authorized. Their number was subsequently increased. At present there are 12 'Law Lords' in office. An appeal to the House of Lords requires a leave to appeal which may be granted either by the Court of Appeal or by the House itself.[94] The petition is heard by three Law Lords.[95]

b. Court of Appeal

The next lower court in the judicial hierarchy is the Court of Appeal. Its organization and functions are governed by The Supreme Court Act 1981.[96] The Court of Appeal is a component of the Supreme Court of England and Wales, the other components being the High Court of Justice and the Crown Court.

The Court of Appeal is composed of two divisions, the criminal division and the civil division. The Lord Chief Justice is the president of the former and the Master of the Rolls is president of the latter. The criminal division of the Court of Appeal also functions as the Courts Martial (Appeal) Court. The Court of Appeal is composed of ex officio judges, including the Lord Chancellor, former Lords Chancellor, the Lord Chief Justice, the Master of Rolls, the President of the Family Division, the Vice Chancellor, and the ordinary Lords Justices of Appeal. (Supreme Court Act 1981 s2). The maximum number of the ordinary Lords Justices of Appeal was originally fixed at eighteen, but it was provided that this number could be increased from time to time by Order-in-Council. In 1996 the number of ordinary Lords Justices of Appeal was increased to 35.[97]

---

93. In appropriate cases, decisions of the House of Lords may be appealed to the European Court of Justice and/or the European Court of Human Rights.

94. Administration of Justice (Appeals) Act (1934 c40) s1(1).

95. Administration of Justice (Appeals) Act (1934 c40) s1(2).

96. 1981 c54 s2(1).

97. Maximum Number of Judges Order 1996, SI 1996 Nr. 1142 (p. 3725).

c. *High Court of Justice*

The *High Court of Justice,* which is a component of the Supreme Court of Justice, is the superior trial court of England and Wales. It is divided into three divisions, namely: (i) the *Chancery Division,* (ii) the *Queen's Bench Division* and (iii) the *Family Division.*

The judges of the High Court are the Lord Chancellor and the Vice-Chancellor, who are the president and the vice-president of the Chancery Division, the Lord Chief Justice, who is the president of the Queen's Bench Division, the President of the Family Division and the puisne judges who are attached to the three divisions. Their maximum number is fixed at 85.[98]

Part of the Chancery Division is a Patents Court and parts of the Queen's Bench Division are an Admiralty Court and a Commercial Court. The puisne judges of the High Court attached thereto are nominated by the Lord Chancellor. The jurisdiction of the Commercial Court is specified in The Supreme Court Act 1981.[99]

d. *County Courts*

The jurisdiction of the County Courts is determined by The County Courts Act 1984 (1984 c. 28), as modified by The Courts and Legal Services Act 1990 (1990 c. 41). The latter Act attributes vast powers to the Lord Chancellor to allocate the judicial business between High Court and county courts. County courts are courts of record and have a seal. The county courts sit in about 270 districts into which England and Wales are divided. The county courts are courts for smaller or simple claims. The initial judgment usually is rendered by a registrar. In contested cases a judge will decide the controversy.

2. Case: *Regina v. Secretary of State for Employment*

HOUSE OF LORDS

Regina v. Secretary of State for Employment

Ex parte Equal Opportunities Commission and Another

92 Oct. 25, 26, 27, 28;
Nov. 1;
94 March 3

Lord Keith of Kinkel, Lord Jauncey of Tullichettle, Lord Lowry, Lord Browne-Wilkinson and Lord Slynn of Hadley

98. Maximum Number of Judges Order 1987, (SI 1987 No. 2059).

99. 1981 c54, s62(3).

APPEAL from the Court of Appeal.

This was an appeal by the applicants, the Equal Opportunities Commission and Mrs. Patricia Elizabeth Day, by leave of the House of Lords from the decision of the Court of Appeal (Dillon, Kennedy and Hirst L.JJ.) [1993] 1 W.L.R. 872 given on 6 November 1992 affirming by a majority (Dillon L.J. dissenting) in the case of the commission and unanimously in the case of Mrs. Day the decision of the Divisional Court of the Queen's Bench Division (Nolan L.J. and Judge J.) [1992] I.C.R. 341 given on 10 October in respect of the first of two applications for judicial review directed to the respondent, the Secretary of State for Employment.

The Court of Appeal refused the applicants leave to appeal from their decision, but on 25 February 1993 the Appeal Committee of the House of Lords (Lord Templeman, Lord Jauncey of Tullichettle and Lord Woolf) [1993] 1 W.L.R. 872, 908 allowed a petition by them in respect of the first application for leave to appeal.

The facts are stated in the opinion of Lord Keith of Kinkel.

Lord Lester of Herne Hill Q.C. and *Monica Carss-Frisk* for the applicants.
Michael Beloff Q.C. and *Stephen Richards* for the Secretary of State.

Their Lordships took time for consideration.

3 March 1994. LORD KEITH OF KINKEL. My Lords, article 119 of the E.E.C. Treaty (Cmnd. 5179-II) provides:

> "Each member state shall during the first stage ensure and subsequently maintain the application of the principle that men and women should receive equal pay for equal work. For the purpose of this article, 'pay' means the ordinary basic or minimum wage or salary and any other consideration, whether in cash or in kind, which the worker receives, directly or indirectly, in respect of his employment from his employer. Equal pay without discrimination based on sex means: (*a*) that pay for the same work at piece rates shall be calculated on the basis of the same unit of measurement; (*b*) that pay for work at time rates shall be the same for the same job."

The Council Directive of 10 February 1975 (75/117/E.E.C.) ("the Equal Pay Directive") spells out the right to equal pay in greater detail. Article 2(1) of the Council Directive of 9 February 1976 (76/207/E.E.C.) ("the Equal Treatment Directive") provides:

> "For the purposes of the following provisions, the principle of equal treatment shall mean that there shall be no discrimination whatsoever on grounds of sex either directly or indirectly by reference in particular to marital or family status."

Article 5(1) and (2) provide:

> "1. Application of the principle of equal treatment with regard to working conditions, including the conditions governing dismissal, means that men and women shall be guaranteed the same conditions without discrimination on grounds of sex. 2. To this end, member states shall take the measures necessary to ensure that: (*a*) any laws, regulations and administrative provisions contrary to the principle of equal treatment shall be abolished; . . ."

Section 2 of the European Communities Act 1972, so far as material for present purposes, provides:

> "(1) All such rights, powers, liabilities, obligations and restrictions from time to time created or arising by or under the Treaties [see section 1(2)], and all such remedies and procedures from time to time provided for by or under the Treaties, as in accordance with the Treaties are without further enactment to be given legal effect or used in the United Kingdom shall be recognised and available in law, and be enforced, allowed and followed accordingly; and the expression 'enforceable Community right' and similar expressions shall be read as referring to one to which this subsection applies. (2) . . . at any time after its passing Her Majesty may by Order in Council, and any designated minister or department may by regulations, make provision — (*a*) for the purpose of implementing any Community obligation of the United Kingdom, or enabling any such obligation to be implemented . . . or (*b*) for the purpose of dealing with matters arising out of or related to any such obligation or rights . . . or the operation from time to time, of subsection (1) above; and in the exercise of any statutory power or duty, including any power to give directions or to legislate by means of orders, rules, regulations or other subordinate instrument, the person entrusted with the power or duty may have regard to the objects of the Communities and to any such obligation or rights as aforesaid. In this subsection 'designated minister or department' means such minister of the Crown or government department as may from time to time be designated by Order in Council in relation to any matter or for any purpose, but subject to such restrictions or conditions (if any) as may be specified by the Order in Council. . . . (4) The provision that may be made under subsection (2) above includes . . . any such provision (of any such extent) as might be made by Act of Parliament, and any enactment passed or to be passed, other than one contained in this Part of this Act, shall be construed and have effect subject to the foregoing provisions of this section; . . ."

By the European Communities (Designation) (No. 3) Order 1982 (S. I. 1982 No. 1675) the Secretary of State for Employment was designated for purposes of section

2(2) of the Act of 1972 in relation to measures to prevent discrimination between men and women as regards terms and conditions of employment.

The United Kingdom legislation aimed at preventing such discrimination is to be found in the Equal Pay Act 1970 and the Sex Discrimination Act 1975, but nothing in the present case turns on any provision of either of these Acts. What is in issue is those provisions of the Employment Protection (Consolidation) Act 1978 which set out the conditions which govern the right not to be unfairly dismissed, the right to compensation for unfair dismissal and the right to statutory redundancy pay. These conditions require that an employee should have worked a specified number of hours a week during a specified period of continuous employment. In general, the qualifying periods for entitlement to each of the rights in question are (a) two years of continuous employment for employees who work for 16 or more hours per week, and (b) five years of continuous employment for employees who work between eight and 16 hours per week. Employees who work for fewer than eight hours per week do not qualify for any of the rights in question. The provisions of the Act which set out these conditions are to be found in sections 54, 64, 68, 71, 81 and 151, and Schedule 13, which need not be referred to in detail. It is common ground that the great majority of employees who work for more than 16 hours a week are men, and that the great majority of those who work for less than 16 hours a week are women, so that the provisions in question result in an indirect discrimination against women.

On 21 March 1990 the chief executive of the appellant Equal Opportunities Commission ("E.O.C.") wrote to the Secretary of State for Employment referring to the provisions of the Act of 1978 concerning redundancy pay and compensation for unfair dismissal and expressing the view that these constituted indirect discrimination against women employees, contrary to Community law. The Secretary of State was asked to give urgent consideration to that matter and to inform the E.O.C. whether the government would be willing to introduce the necessary legislation to remove the discrimination inherent in the Act of 1978, giving reasons for his decision if the reply was in the negative. The Secretary of State replied by letter dated 23 April 1990, stating, inter alia:

> "[We do not accept that] statutory redundancy pay and statutory compensation for unfair dismissal constitute 'pay' within the meaning of article 119 . . . or . . . that they fall within the Equal Treatment Directive . . . we believe that our current statutory thresholds are entirely justifiable. These thresholds have existed in one form or another ever since employment protection legislation was first introduced. Their purpose is to ensure that a fair balance is struck between the interests of employers and employees. We have no plans to change the thresholds."

On 6 June 1990 the E.O.C. obtained leave to move for judicial review, the matter in respect of which relief was sought being stated as:

> "The decision of the Secretary of State for Employment dated 23 April 1990 declining to accept that the United Kingdom is in breach of its obligations under Community law by providing less favourable treatment of part-time workers than of full-time workers in relation to the conditions for receipt of statutory redundancy pay and compensation for unfair dismissal."

The substantive relief sought was expressed in these terms:

> "1. A declaration that the United Kingdom is in breach of its obligations under article 119 of the [E.E.C. Treaty] and [Council] Directive (75/117/E.E.C.) by providing less favourable treatment of part-time workers (most of whom are women) than of full-time workers (most of whom are men) in relation to the conditions for receipt of statutory redundancy pay and compensation for unfair dismissal. 2. A declaration that the United Kingdom is in breach of its obligations under [Council] Directive (76/207/E.E.C.) by providing less favourable treatment of part-time workers (most of whom are women) than of full-time workers (most of whom are men) in relation to the conditions for receipt of statutory redundancy pay and compensation for unfair dismissal."

At a later stage the application was amended so as to bring in as second applicant Mrs. Day, who had been employed by Hertfordshire County Council as a cleaner for just under five years working 11 hours a week and had been made redundant, and so as to seek certain further declarations and also mandamus to compel the Secretary of State to introduce legislation to abolish the discriminatory provisions of the Act of 1978.

The application was heard by a Divisional Court consisting of Nolan L.J. and Judge J. [1992] I.C.R. 341 who on 10 October 1991 dismissed it. On appeal by the E.O.C. and Mrs. Day to the Court of Appeal [1993] 1 W.L.R. 872 the decision of the Divisional Court was by a majority affirmed (Kennedy and Hirst L.JJ., Dillon L.J. dissenting). The E.O.C. and Mrs. Day now appeal to your Lordships' House.

The principal issue of substance raised by the proceedings is whether the indirect discrimination against women involved in the relevant provisions of the Act of 1978 has been shown to be based upon objectively justified grounds, that being the test propounded by the European Court of Justice in *Bilka-Kaufhaus G.m.b.H. v. Weber von Hartz* (Case 170/84) [1987] I.C.R. 110 for determining whether or not measures involving indirect discrimination constitute an infringement of article 119 of the E.E.C. Treaty. A number of procedural points were, however, argued in the courts below and before this House.

It is convenient first to consider whether Mrs. Day is properly joined in the present proceedings against the Secretary of State. Redundancy pay is "pay" within the meaning of article 119 of the Treaty: *Barber v. Guardian Royal Exchange Assurance*

Group (Case C 262/88) [1991] 1 Q.B. 344. If the discriminatory measures in the Act of 1978 are not objectively justified, Mrs. Day has a good claim for redundancy pay against her employers, the Hertfordshire Area Health Authority, under article 119, which by virtue of section 2(1) of the Act of 1972 prevails over the discriminatory provisions of the Act of 1978. She would also have a good claim under the Equal Pay Directive and the Equal Treatment Directive, which are directly applicable against her employers as being an emanation of the state: *Marshall v. Southampton and South West Hampshire Area Health Authority (Teaching)* (Case 152/84) [1986] Q.B. 401. Mrs. Day's claim against her employers is a private law claim, and indeed she has already started proceedings to enforce it in the appropriate industrial tribunal, these having been adjourned to await the outcome of the present case. The industrial tribunal has jurisdiction to decide questions as to objective justification for discriminatory measures, and has done so on many occasions, in particular in the *Marshall* case. I see no good reason why a purely private law claim should be advanced in the Divisional Court against the Secretary of State, who is not the claimant's employer and is not liable to meet the claim, if sound. The determination of such claims has been entrusted by statute to the industrial tribunal, which is fully competent to deal with them. It is suggested that different industrial tribunals might reach different decisions on the facts in relation to objective justification, but a suitable test case upon the question of principle, supported by the E.O.C. under the power conferred upon it by section 75 of the Act of 1975, would be capable of settling the question definitively. I conclude that the Divisional Court was not the appropriate forum to adjudicate upon what so far as Mrs. Day is concerned is her private law claim, and would dismiss her appeal, but without costs.

Turning now to the position of the E.O.C., the procedural points taken by the Secretary of State are (1) that the E.O.C. has no locus standi to bring the present proceedings, (2) that the E.O.C.'s case does not involve any decision or justiciable issue susceptible of judicial review, (3) that the Divisional Court had no jurisdiction to declare that the United Kingdom or the Secretary of State was in breach of any obligations under European Community law, and (4) that the Divisional Court was not the appropriate forum to determine the substantive issues raised by the applicant.

Dealing first with the question of locus standi, R.S.C., Ord. 53, r. 3(7) provides that the court shall not grant leave to apply for judicial review "unless it considers that the applicant has a sufficient interest in the matter to which the application relates." Section 31(3) of the Supreme Court Act 1981 contains a provision in the same terms. The matter to which the E.O.C.'s application relates is essentially whether the relevant provisions of the Act of 1978 are compatible with European Community law regarding equal pay and equal treatment. Has the E.O.C. a sufficient interest in that matter? Under section 53(1) of the Act of 1975 the duties of the E.O.C. include:

> "(*a*) to work towards the elimination of discrimination, (*b*) to promote equality of opportunity between men and women generally . . ."

If the admittedly discriminatory provisions of the Act of 1978 as regards redundancy pay and compensation for unfair dismissal are not objectively justified, then steps taken by the E.O.C. towards securing that these provisions are changed may very reasonably be regarded as taken in the course of working towards the elimination of discrimination. The present proceedings are clearly such a step. In a number of cases the E.O.C. has been the initiating party to proceedings designed to secure the elimination of discrimination. The prime example is *Reg. v. Birmingham City Council, Ex parte Equal Opportunities Commission* [1989] A.C. 1155, where the E.O.C. successfully challenged the policy of the council as regards the relative availability of grammar school places for girls and for boys, in proceedings which reached this House and in which it was not suggested at any stage that the E.O.C. lacked locus standi. In *Reg. v. Secretary of State for Defence, Ex parte Equal Opportunities Commission* (unreported), 20 December 1991, it was common ground that the E.O.C. had locus standi. Another instance is *Reg. v. Secretary of State for Social Security, Ex parte Equal Opportunities Commission* (Case C 9/91) [1992] I.C.R. 782, which went to the European Court of Justice. In my opinion it would be a very retrograde step now to hold that the E.O.C. has no locus standi to agitate in judicial review proceedings questions related to sex discrimination which are of public importance and affect a large section of the population. The determination of this issue turns essentially upon a consideration of the statutory duties and public law role of the E.O.C. as regards which no helpful guidance is to be gathered from decided cases. I would hold that the E.O.C. has sufficient interest to bring these proceedings and hence the necessary locus standi.

The next question is whether there exists any decision or justiciable issue susceptible of judicial review. The E.O.C.'s application sets out the Secretary of State's letter of 23 April 1990 as being the reviewable decision. In my opinion that letter does not constitute a decision. It does no more than state the Secretary of State's view that the threshold provisions of the Act of 1978 regarding redundancy pay and compensation for unfair dismissal are justifiable and in conformity with European Community law. The real object of the E.O.C.'s attack is these provisions themselves. The question is whether judicial review is available for the purpose of securing a declaration that certain United Kingdom primary legislation is incompatible with European Community law. It is argued for the Secretary of State that Ord. 53, r. 1(2), which gives the court power to make declarations in judicial review proceedings, is only applicable where one of the prerogative orders would be available under rule 1(1), and that if there is no decision in respect of which one of these writs might be issued a declaration cannot be made. I consider that to be too narrow an interpretation of the court's powers. It would mean that while a declaration that a statutory instrument is incompatible with European Community law could be made, since such an instrument is capable of being set aside by certiorari, no such declaration could be made as regards primary legislation. However, in the *Factortame* series of cases (*Reg. v. Secretary of State for Transport, Ex parte Factortame Ltd.* [1990] 2 A.C. 85; *Reg. v. Secretary of State for Transport, Ex parte Factortame Ltd. (No. 2)* (Case C 213/89) [1991] 1 A.C. 603; *Reg. v.*

Secretary of State for Transport, Ex parte Factortame Ltd. (No. 3) (Case C 221/89) [1992] Q.B. 680) the applicants for judicial review sought a declaration that the provisions of Part II of the Merchant Shipping Act 1988 should not apply to them on the ground that such application would be contrary to Community law, in particular articles 7 and 52 of the E.E.C. Treaty (principle of non-discrimination on the ground of nationality and right of establishment). The applicants were companies incorporated in England which were controlled by Spanish nationals and owned fishing vessels which on account of such control were denied registration in the register of British vessels by virtue of the restrictive conditions contained in Part II of the Act of 1988. The Divisional Court (*Reg. v. Secretary of State for Transport, Ex parte Factortame Ltd.* [1989] 2 C.M.L.R. 353), under article 177 of the Treaty, referred to the European Court of Justice a number of questions, including the question whether these restrictive conditions were compatible with articles 7 and 52 of the Treaty. The European Court [1992] Q.B. 680 answered that question in the negative, and, although the final result is not reported, no doubt the Divisional Court in due course granted a declaration accordingly. The effect was that certain provisions of United Kingdom primary legislation were held to be invalid in their purported application to nationals of member states of the European Economic Community, but without any prerogative order being available to strike down the legislation in question, which of course remained valid as regards nationals of non-member states. At no stage in the course of the litigation, which included two visits to this House, was it suggested that judicial review was not available for the purpose of obtaining an adjudication upon the validity of the legislation in so far as it affected the applicants.

The *Factortame* case is thus a precedent in favour of the E.O.C's recourse to judicial review for the purpose of challenging as incompatible with European Community law the relevant provisions of the Act of 1978. It also provides an answer to the third procedural point taken by the Secretary of State, which maintains that the Divisional Court had no jurisdiction to declare that the United Kingdom or the Secretary of State is in breach of obligation under Community law. There is no need for any such declaration. A declaration that the threshold provisions of the Act of 1978 are incompatible with Community law would suffice for the purposes sought to be achieved by the E.O.C. and is capable of being granted consistently with the precedent afforded by *Factortame.* This does not involve, as contended for the Secretary of State, any attempt by the E.O.C. to enforce the international treaty obligations of the United Kingdom. The E.O.C. is concerned simply to obtain a ruling which reflects the primacy of European Community law enshrined in section 2 of the Act of 1972 and determines whether the relevant United Kingdom law is compatible with the Equal Pay Directive and the Equal Treatment Directive.

Similar considerations provide the answer to the Secretary of State's fourth procedural point by which it is maintained that the Divisional Court is not the appropriate forum to decide the substantive issues at stake. The issues at stake are similar in character to those which were raised in *Factortame.* The Divisional Court is the only

English forum in which the E.O.C., having the capacity and sufficient interest to do so, is in a position to secure the result which it desires. It is said that the incompatibility issue could be tested in proceedings before the European Court of Justice instituted by the European Commission against the United Kingdom under 169 of the E.E.C. Treaty. That may be true, but it affords no reason for concluding that the Divisional Court is an inappropriate forum for the application by the E.O.C. designed towards a similar end and, indeed, there are grounds for the view that the Divisional Court is the more appropriate forum, since the European Court of Justice has said that it is for the national court to determine whether an indirectly discriminatory pay practice is founded on objectively justified economic grounds: see *Bilka-Kaufhaus G.m.b.H. v. Weber von Hartz* (Case 170/84) [1987] I.C.R. 110, 126.

I turn now to the important substantive issue in the appeal, which is whether or not the threshold provisions in the Act of 1978 have been shown to be objectively justified, the onus of doing so being one which rests on the Secretary of State.

In *Bilka-Kaufhaus G.m.b.H. v. Weber von Hartz,* the European Court of Justice said, at p. 126:

> "36. It is for the national court, which has sole jurisdiction to make findings of fact, to determine whether and to what extent the grounds put forward by an employer to explain the adoption of a pay practice which applies independently of a worker's sex but in fact affects more women than men may be regarded as objectively justified economic grounds. If the national court finds that the measures chosen by Bilka correspond to a real need on the part of the undertaking, are appropriate with a view to achieving the objectives pursued and are necessary to that end, the fact that the measures affect a far greater number of women than men is not sufficient to show that they constitute an infringement of article 119."

Somewhat broader considerations apply where the discriminatory provisions are to be found in national legislation. In *Rinner-Kühn v. F.W.W. Spezial-Gebäudereinigung G.m.b.H. & Co. K.G.* (Case 171/88) [1989] E.C.R. 2743, the question at issue was whether German legislation which permitted restrictions on the right of part time workers to sick pay contravened article 119 of the E.E.C. Treaty, considering that a great majority of part-time workers were women. The court said, at pp. 2760–2761:

> "12. In such a situation, it must be concluded that a provision such as that in question results in discrimination against female workers in relation to male workers and must, in principle, be regarded as contrary to the aim of article 119 of the Treaty. The position would be different only if the distinction between the two categories of employees were justified by objective factors unrelated to any discrimination on grounds of sex (see the judgment of 13 May 1986 in *Bilka-Kaufhaus G.m.b.H. v. Weber von Hartz* (Case 170/84)

> [1986] E.C.R. 1607). 13. In the course of the procedure, the German Government stated, in response to a question put by the court, that workers whose period of work amounted to less than 10 hours a week or 45 hours a month were not as integrated in, or as dependent on, the undertaking employing them as other workers. 14. It should, however, be stated that those considerations, in so far as they are only generalisations about certain categories of workers, do not enable criteria which are both objective and unrelated to any discrimination on grounds of sex to be identified. However, if the member state can show that the means chosen meet a necessary aim of its social policy and that they are suitable and requisite for attaining that aim, the mere fact that the provision affects a much greater number of female workers than male workers cannot be regarded as constituting an infringement of article 119. 15. It is for the national court, which has sole jurisdiction to assess the facts and interpret the national legislation, to determine whether and to what extent a legislative provision, which, though applying independently of the sex of the worker, actually affects a greater number of women than men, is justified by reasons which are objective and unrelated to any discrimination on grounds of sex. 16. The reply to the question referred by the national court must therefore be that article 119 of the E.E.C. Treaty must be interpreted as precluding national legislation which permits employers to exclude employees whose normal working hours do not exceed 10 hours a week or 45 hours a month from the continued payment of wages in the event of illness, if that measure affects a far greater number of women than men, unless the member state shows that the legislation concerned is justified by objective factors unrelated to any discrimination on grounds of sex."

The original reason for the threshold provisions of the Act of 1978 appears to have been the view that part time workers were less committed than full-time workers to the undertaking which employed them. In his letter of 23 April 1990 the Secretary of State stated that their purpose was to ensure that a fair balance was struck between the interests of employers and employees. These grounds are not now founded on as objective justification for the thresholds. It is now claimed that the thresholds have the effect that more part-time employment is available than would be the case if employers were liable for redundancy pay and compensation for unfair dismissal to employees who worked for less than eight hours a week or between eight and 16 hours a week for under five years. It is contended that if employers were under that liability they would be inclined to employ less part-time workers and more full-time workers, to the disadvantage of the former.

The bringing about of an increase in the availability of part-time work is properly to be regarded as a beneficial social policy aim and it cannot be said that it is not a necessary aim. The question is whether the threshold provisions of the Act of 1978 have been shown, by reference to objective factors, to be suitable and requisite for achieving that aim. As regards suitability for achieving the aim in question, it is to be noted that the purpose of the thresholds is said to be to reduce the costs to employers of employing part-time workers. The same result, however, would follow from a situation where the basic rate of pay for part time workers was less than the basic rate for full-time workers. No distinction in principle can properly be made between direct and indirect labour costs. While in certain circumstances an employer might be justified in paying full-time workers a higher rate than part-time workers in order to secure the more efficient use of his machinery (see *Jenkins v. Kingsgate (Clothing Productions) Ltd.* [1981] 1 W.L.R. 1485) that would be a special and limited state of affairs. Legislation which permitted a differential of that kind nationwide would present a very different aspect and considering that the great majority of part-time workers are women would surely constitute a gross breach of the principle of equal pay and could not possibly be regarded as a suitable means of achieving an increase in part-time employment. Similar considerations apply to legislation which reduces the indirect cost of employing part-time labour. Then as to the threshold provisions being requisite to achieve the stated aim, the question is whether on the evidence before the Divisional Court they have been proved actually to result in greater availability of part-time work than would be the case without them. In my opinion that question must be answered in the negative. The evidence for the Secretary of State consisted principally of an affidavit by an official in the Department of Employment which set out the views of the Department but did not contain anything capable of being regarded as factual evidence demonstrating the correctness of these views. One of the exhibits to the affidavit was a report with draft Directives prepared by the Social Affairs Commissioner of the European Commission in 1990 (COM(90) 228 final — SYN 280 and SYN 281, Brussels, 13 August 1990; Official Journal 1990 No. C 224, pp. 4–8). This covered a wide range of employment benefits and advantages, including redundancy pay and compensation for unfair dismissal, but proposed a qualifying threshold for those benefits of eight hours of work per week. The basis for that was stated to be the elimination of disproportionate administrative costs and regard to employers' economic needs. These are not the grounds of justification relied on by the Secretary of State. The evidence put in by the E.O.C. consisted in large measure in a report of the House of Commons Employment Committee, "Park-Time Work," vol. 1 in 1990 (H.C. 122-I, 10 January 1990) and a report of the House of Lords Select Committee on the European Communities, "Part-Time and Temporary Employment," in 1990 (H.L. Paper 7, 4 December 1990). These revealed a diversity of views upon the effect of the threshold provisions on part-time work, employers' organisations being of the opinion that their removal would reduce the amount available with trade union representatives and some employers and academics in the industrial relations field taking the opposite view. It also appeared that no other member state of the European Community, apart from the Republic of Ireland, had legislation providing for similar thresholds. The Republic of Ireland, where statute at one time provided for an 18-hour-per-week threshold, had recently introduced legislation reducing this to eight hours. In the Netherlands the proportion of the workforce in part-time employment was in 1988 29.4 per cent. and in Denmark 25.5 per cent., neither country having any thresholds similar to those in the Act of 1978. In France legislation was introduced in 1982 providing for part-time workers to have the same rights as full-time, yet between 1983 and 1988 part-time work in that country increased by 36.6 per cent., compared with an increase of 26.1 per cent. over the same period in the United Kingdom. While various explanations were suggested on behalf of the Secretary of State for these statistics, there is no means of ascertaining whether these explanations have any validity. The fact is, however, that the proportion of part-time employees in the national workforce is much less than the proportion of full-time employees, their weekly remuneration is necessarily much lower, and the number of them made redundant or unfairly dismissed in any year is not likely to be unduly large. The conclusion must be that no objective justification for the thresholds in the Act of 1978 has been established.

A subsidiary issue of substance in the appeal is whether or not compensation for unfair dismissal is "pay" within the meaning of article 119 of the Treaty and the Equal Pay Directive. The definition of "pay" in article 119 has been set out above. In *Arbeiterwohlfahrt der Stadt Berlin e.V. v. Bötel* (Case C-360/90) [1992] I.R.L.R. 423, 425, the European Court of Justice said:

> "12. According to the case law of the court . . . the concept of 'pay' within the meaning of article 119 of the Treaty comprises any consideration whether in cash or in kind, whether immediate or future, provided that the employee receives it, albeit indirectly, in respect of his employment from his employer, whether under a contract of employment, legislative provisions or made ex gratia by the employer."

In *Barber v. Guardian Royal Exchange Assurance Group* (Case C 262/88) [1991] 1 Q.B. 344 the court held that reduncancy pay was pay within the meaning of article 119 on the ground (paragraph 18 of the judgment, at p. 400) that receipt of it arose "by reason of the existence of the employment relationship." There is much to be said in favour of the view that compensation for unfair dismissal is of a comparable nature, but the European Court of Justice has not yet pronounced upon this issue, and there may be a question whether the answer to it can properly be held to be acte clair, or whether resolution of it would require a reference to the European Court under article 177 of the Treaty.

Such a reference is in any event, however, unnecessary for the disposal of the present appeal. Discrimination as regards the right to compensation for unfair dismissal, if not objectively justified, is clearly in contravention of the Equal Treatment Directive.

In the light of the foregoing I am of the opinion that the appeal by the E.O.C. should be allowed and that declarations should be made in the following terms: (1)

that the provisions of the Employment Protection (Consolidation) Act 1978 whereby employees who work for fewer than 16 hours per week are subject to different conditions in respect of qualification for redundancy pay from those which apply to employees who work for 16 hours per week or more are incompatible with article 119 of the E.E.C. Treaty and the Council Directive of 10 February 1975 (75/117/E.E.C.); (2) that the provisions of the Employment Protection (Consolidation) Act 1978 whereby employees who work for fewer than 16 hours per week are subject to different conditions in respect of the right to compensation for unfair dismissal from those which apply to employees who work for 16 hours per week or more are incompatible with the Council Directive of 9 February 1976 (76/207/E.E.C.).

It remains to note that the E.O.C. proposed that the House should grant a declaration to the effect that the Secretary of State is in breach of those provisions of the Equal Treatment Directive which require member states to introduce measures to abolish any laws contrary to the principle of equal treatment. The purpose of such a declaration was said to be to enable part-time workers who were employed otherwise than by the state or an emanation of the state, and who had been deprived of the right to obtain compensation for unfair dismissal by the restrictive thresholds in the Act of 1978, to take proceedings against the United Kingdom for compensation, founding upon the decision of the European Court of Justice in *Francovich v. Italian Republic* (Cases C-6/90, C-9/90) [1991] E.C.R. I-5357. In my opinion it would be quite inappropriate to make any such declaration. If there is any individual who believes that he or she has a good claim to compensation under the *Francovich* principle, it is the Attorney-General who would be defendant in any proceedings directed to enforcing it, and the issues raised would not necessarily be identical with any of those which arise in the present appeal.

G. BRAZIL

1. Introduction

Brazil is a federal union composed of 26 states, the Federal District and the territories of which only one remains. It is governed by the Constitution of 1988 which went into effect on May 10 of that year. Although the Constitution vests the Union with exclusive jurisdiction to legislate with respect to civil, commercial, penal, procedural, electoral, agrarian, maritime, aeronautical, space and labor law (Const. Art. 22 I), the lower courts for civil, commercial and criminal matters are primarily the state courts.

Lower federal courts having jurisdiction in these fields are created for the Federal District in which the capital is located. (Const. Art. 92 VII, Law nr. 8.185/91. Law on the Judicial Organization of the Federal District.)

In addition, the Constitution creates a federal judiciary exercising jurisdiction of the first and second instance, operating nationwide. It is constituted by the *federal courts* and the *regional federal tribunals.* (Const., Arts. 106-109.) Their jurisdiction, however, is not as broad *ratione materiae* as that of the U.S. District Courts and U.S. Courts of Appeal. Furthermore, there are separate federal tribunals and courts for labor, electoral and military matters. (Const. Arts. 111-122.)

The Constitution of 1988 created a new *Superior Tribunal of Justice* (S.T.J.) with nationwide jurisdiction to be exercised by way of original, ordinary appellate or extraordinary appellate jurisdiction, Const. Arts. 104 and 105. The extraordinary appellate jurisdiction is invoked by a new procedure, called *special recourse* (*recurso special*). It serves to preserve by integrity and unity of the federal system.

On the top of the heap is the *Supreme Federal Tribunal* (S.F.T.), a judicial body composed of 11 justices, called ministers. It sits either in one of its two sections of 5 justices each, or as full court. Its jurisdiction is defined by the Constitution, Arts. 102 and 103. It comprises original and appellate jurisdiction. The latter in turn may be invoked either by an ordinary recourse or an extraordinary recourse (*recurso extraordinario*: *RE,* Const. Art. 102 II and III.)

As an important innovation, the Constitution vested the S.F.T. with new original jurisdiction over a direct action aimed at the declaration of the unconstitutionality of a federal or state statute or other normative act. (Const. Art.102 I a.) Standing to bring such action is given to specifically listed public officials and bodies or labor organization and entities of national scope (Const. Art. 103).

The extraordinary recourse (*RE*) interposed in judicial controversies is likewise a remedy to test the constitutionality of a decision or for the declaration of the unconstitutionality of a federal statute or to uphold the validity of a law or act of the local government against constitutional attack (Const. Art. 102 III). As a result, the Supreme Federal Tribunal is now to a large extent a constitutional court, vested with the 'abstract' and 'concrete' control of norms, comparable to the German Federal Constitutional Court. Judicial review of the constitutionality of legislation by way of the extraordinary recourse is not a change of the prior law. It was exercised by the S.F.T. since 1891, and governed by its internal regulation. The judgments of the Supreme Federal Tribunal are reported in the *Revista Trimestral de Jurisprudência* (*RTJ*) which now counts over 150 volumes.

The new Superior Tribunal of Justice (S.T.J.) which was established to reduce the caseload of the Supreme Federal Tribunal commenced its judicial business in 1989. Its jurisdiction and procedure under the special recourse have been much discussed in the Brazilian literature.[102] The S.T.J. was established on April 7, 1989. Its decisions are published in the Revista Forense.

The extraordinary or special recurso to the S.F.T. or the S.T.J. are now governed by the Law 8.038 of May 28, 1990.[103]

---

102. See e.g. P. R. Saraiva Da Costa Leite, *Recurso especial: admissibilidade e procedimento,* 305 *Revista Forense* (*R.F.*) 95 (1989); A. de Mendonça Lima, *Recurso extraordinario e recurso especial,* 306 *R.F.* 3 (1989); S. Teixeira, *O recurso especial e o Superior Tribunal de Justiça,* 307 *R.F.* 57 (1989).

103. Cf. S. Teixeira, Código de Processo Civil Annotado (5th ed. 1993) 325–327.

2. Direct Action for Declaration of Unconstitutionality of Normative Acts (*Açao Direta de Inconstitucionalidade* [ADIn]).

Preliminary Notes

One of the most important innovations of the Constitution of 1988 was the establishment of original jurisdiction of the Supreme Federal Tribunal over direct actions for the declaration *erga omnes* of the unconstitutionality of federal or state normative acts (ADIn). The scope of this 'abstract control of norms' has confronted the STF with many new and troublesome questions.

1. One of the hotly debated issues concerned the availability of the new remedy in regard to state or federal laws antedating the new Magna Carta of October 5, 1988. The matter was debated by the justices since 1989, but it was not settled until February 6, 1992 when the court rendered a 8:3 judgment in the case designated as *ADIn 2,* denying the applicability of the new remedy to pre-constitutional legislation because of *legal impossibility*. The victorious theory was deceptively simple. The established principle that a subsequent law inconsistent with a prior law supersedes the same to the extent of the inconsistency applies also to prior normative acts inconsistent with the new constitution (so-called supervenient unconstitutionality).

ADIn 2 was used the following day (February 7, 1992) as precedent for denying jurisdiction over an accumulated series of such actions, especially ADIn. 7 (another leading precedent) and a host of other cases (ADIn nrs. 74, 85, 381, 385, 389, 415, 438, 450, 454, 464, 503, 569 and 606). ADIn 7, which is often cited as precedent in lieu of ADIn nr. 2, is reported in 145 RTJ 339 (1993). Despite the unanimous action of the S.T.F. in the 14 cases following ADIn 2, disputes on the same issue flared up in some later cases, as is illustrated by direct action for the invalidation of a state statute enacted shortly prior to the entry into force of the Constitution in violation of the supremacy clause (ADIn. 75, 143 RTJ 4). In that case, the original reporting judge proposed, during a lengthy debate, that the action should lie in cases where a state legislature intruded into an exclusively federal subject. He did not prevail.

2. The scope of the new remedy has also created disputes in two other areas, viz. standing to bring the action and the type of normative act subject to invalidation because of unconstitutionality.

3. *Review of Constitutionality of Norms.*

By way of constitutional amendment nr. 3, of 1993, Art. 103 § 4 of the Constitution of 1988 was revised so as to provide for a declaratory action of constitutionality (*açao declaratoria de constitucionalidade)* with the effect specified in art. 102 par. 2 of the Constitution as revised by amendment nr. 3 of 1993 (leg. fed. 1993) p. 183). This was done to suppress an existing lacuna and to provide a judicial determination with binding force erga omnes establishing the constitutional validity of a statute.

The first case of that kind instituted in the Supreme Federal Tribunal was an action by the President of the Republic, Half of the Senate and Half of the House of Representatives for the Declaration of the Constitutionality of Articles 1, 2, 9, 10 and 13 of the Lei Complementar nr. 70 of December 30, 1991 on the financing of social security by means of contributions. The Supreme Federal Tribunal rendered judgment on December 1, 1993, 156 R.T.J. 721, holding the action to be admissible and declaring Arts. 1,2 and 10 of the Lei Complementar nr. 70 of December 30, 1991 *in toto* and Arts. 9 and 13 thereof in their relevant part to be constitutional.

Judgment of April 14, 1993. A judgment involving a direct action for declaration of unconstitutionality of a normative act is ADIn Nr. 829, *Party for Restoration of the National Order (PRONA) c. National Congress* (158 R.T.J. 451), Judgment of April 14, 1993. In that case, a political party sought abstract norm control with respect to a constitutional amendment, EC 2 of August 25, 1992. This amendment provided:

> "Single Article: The plebiscite referred to in Article 2 of the Act of Transitory Constitutional Provisions shall take place on April 21, 1993.
>
> §1. The form and structure of the government as defined by the plebiscite will enter into force on January 1, 1995.
>
> §2. A law may determine the holding of the plebiscite including the gratuitous information about forms and structures of government by way of mass media of communication, licenses or permission holders of public services, under assurance of equal time and parity of scheduling.
>
> § 3. The provision conforming to the preceding paragraph does not exclude the competence of the Superior Electoral Tribunal to promulgate necessary instructions for the holding of the plebiscite."

The complainant contended that the constitutional amendment was invalid because it scheduled the plebiscite at an earlier date than that specified in Article 2 of the Act of Transitory Constitutional Provisions (ADCT) and because it was incompatible with the so-called petrification clauses which limited the possibilities of amendments of the Constitution pursuant to Article 60 of the Constitution of 1988.

The Supreme Federal Tribunal, sitting as a full bench, under the presidency of Justice Sydney Sanches and with Justice Moreira Alvez as reporting judge, held by unanimous vote that the action was admissible but decided on the merits, by a vote 8:3, that it should be dismissed. Two of the dissenting justices, Marco Aurélio and Carlos Velloso, voted that the action should succeed, while the third dissenter, Sepúlveda Pertence, voted for partial unconstitutionality of the amendment.

The difficulties faced by the Supreme Federal Tribunal consisted in the fact that the Constitution of 1988 and the ADCT were adopted by the Constituent National Assembly as separate documents and that the ADCT did not provide for amendments, while the permanent Constitution did not authorize amendments of the democratic form of government. The majority based its holding on the fact that the substance of the plebiscite was determined by the ADCT (and not by the EC nr. 2) and that the EC nr.2 changed only the date of the holding of the plebiscite to an earlier day.

3. Cases and Notes

a. National Federation of Teaching Establishments

Supreme Federal Tribunal, National Federation of Teaching Establishments
v.
President of the Republic.
Judgment of February 6, 1992 (ADIn 2)

(Not reported in RTJ.)

Opinion by Mr. Justice Brossard (not yet reported).

* * *

Opinion by Mr. Justice Sepúlveda Pertence, dissenting and concurring in the result, published as part of ADIn 7, 145 RTJ 351 (1993).

I

I observe, to begin with, in order to document the congestion in the work of the sessions of the full court, that this opinion waited to be called for since the beginning of 1990. Since that time, I am not responsible for the delay which existed in the arrival at the final judgment.

As a matter of introduction, the issue involved is the non-availability of the direct action of unconstitutionality aimed at two decree-laws and one decree issued under the past constitutional regime.

The eminent Reporting Judge, Minister Paul Brossard propounds the thesis: an alleged discrepancy between the new constitution and normative acts anterior to its promulgation is tantamount, according to his Excellency, to their repeal, one effect to a declaration of which the direct action is not appropriate.

It is not possible to deny great persuasive force to the lengthy opinion of Minister Brossard, in part owing to the consistency of the case-law relied upon, in part owing to the authority of the scholars cited and in part owing to the brilliance, so characteristic of his works, bestowed upon the arguments for his puzzling thesis: so much as to permit his Excellency to label a contrary position as absurd.

Emphatic and erudite in turn is also the concurring opinion of the eminent Minister Celso de Mello.

Nevertheless, I have the audacity to dissent, due to a firm conviction that to bar the expurgation of old laws incompatible with the new constitutional order by way of a direct action of unconstitutionality would deprive the Supreme Federal Tribunal of a mission and responsibility which properly belongs to it. Intransferably to it!

Let me now summarize my position.

I do not deny the parity of the substantive effects between the concept of supervening unconstitutionality and the repeal by the Constitution of ordinary pre-constitutional law incompatible with it.

* * *

Nevertheless, all these are merely theoretical controversies despite of which one still could arrive at the solution, which appears to me to be the appropriate one and to affirm the applicability of the direct action for the declaration of unconstitutionality. Therefore, what is most important to emphasize is that the qualification of the phenomenon in question as repeal does not exclude, according to my thinking, that the antinomy between an anterior law and the supervening Constitution is primarily a relation of unconstitutionality.

* * *

I do not preoccupy myself to demonstrate with pretensions of pure legal logic that there exists only one correct legal solution; and even much less to develop a blame of absurdity against the thesis of my adversaries.

For myself, the conviction suffices that the thesis of supervenient unconstitutionality — in whichever of its forms, and far from being absurd — resists, and resists well, criticisms more ferocious than those leveled against it.

And that being so, I prefer it to that of a simple repeal, because I take the position that the basic consequence of its adoption — the availability of the direct action — is able to better serve the basic ideas of the Brazilian system of the control of constitutionality.

To reduce the problem to the dimensions of a simple repeal of the ordinary norm by the subsequent constitutional norm — a suggestion of seductive simplicity — results in a bar of the direct action. That, in consequence, leaves it open to the result that the settlement of arising controversies floats for 20 years with the disagreements between judges and courts of the entire country until the arrival, if there be an arrival, at a decision of the High Court at the end of a long journey through the often tortuous path of the system of recourses. In addition even a decision of the Supreme Tribunal lacking binding force *erga omnes* would not foreclose contradictions. * * * Conversely, if one takes the position that the conflict in issue translates into a supervening unconstitutionality — call it if you wish a repeal with a legal effect of its own — the door to the direct action is opened, generously amplified by the deconcentrated control of active legality.

Certainly, in contrast to the European Constitutional Courts, the Federal Supreme Tribunal possesses, under certain circumstances, the alternative possibility of dealing *incidenter* with the antimony, if and when it is submitted to it by way of the extraordinary recourse.

II

That it is not absurd to find unconstitutionality in a substantive conflict between an anterior law and a supervenient constitution is proven, with your permission, by the dominant understanding in comparative law.

The question arises in the European countries which have adopted the 'concentrated' system of control when it is to be decided whether or not the monopoly of the respective constitutional courts extend to an examination of the compatibility with their constitutions of prior ordinary legislation: an inquiry which obviously calls for an affirmative answer if the solution of the antinomy is qualified as supervenient or subsequent unconstitutionality, and for a negative response if it is deemed to be merely a repeal, the verification of which entails the diffused jurisdiction of the ordinary judiciary.

In Italy the solution was radical: It is well-known that after an initial academic controversy, the first judgment of the Constitutional Court sided with the hypothesis of constitutional illegality and not with a repeal. 'It is undeniable that the relation between ordinary laws and constitutional laws and the rank which belongs to them respectively in the hierarchy of sources' — announced the celebrated judgment nr. 1 of 1956 — 'does not change indeed, whether laws anterior or laws subsequent to the constitution are involved. The two judicial institutions of abrogation and constitutional illegality of laws are not identical with one another and belong to different levels with different effects and subject to different jurisdictions. The field of abrogation, in addition, is more restricted than that of constitutional illegality and the requisites that pursuant to general principles must be met to find abrogation because of incompatibility are rather more limited than those which may authorize a declaration of constitutional illegality of a statute.' (Cf. *Giurisprudenza della Corte Costitutionale* 1985 p. 3).[104]

Thus — the doctrine prevailed which was preeminently represented by the great *Calamandrei* in his article Corte Constitucional y Autoridad Judicial (reproduced in *Estudios sobre el Proceso Civil,* translation, Buenos Aires 1973, III/121).

The celebrated judgment, which was greeted with enthusiasm by Calamandrei (La Primera Sentencia de la Corte Constitucional, op. cit. III/185) has since then been sustained with refinements and advances in its basis by the major names in Italian public law, names such as * * *.

For a view contrasting with that of Italy is cited the case of the Federal Republic of Germany where the opposite doctrine is dominant, i.e. that of a mere repeal (cf. Jorge Miranda, *Manual de Direito Constitucional,* 2d ed. 1982, p. 249; G. Zagrebelsky, *Giustizia Costituzionale,* 1988 p. 142).

Nevertheless, *est modus in rebus.*

---

104. Quotation in the Italian original.

More detailed information available to me is to the effect that the Federal Constitutional Court actually holds that it has no jurisdiction if the issue of incompatibility of anterior law with the Constitution arises *incidenter* and that in that case it can be decided by the judge seized with controversy without raising the constitutional question. The Court nevertheless takes the view that an adjudication of the same issue is within its exclusive jurisdiction when it is requested by means of the direct way of abstract control of norms. 'Object of the "abstract control" of norms' — writes Ernst Friesenhahn (*La Giurisdizione Costituzionale della Repubblica Federale Tedesca,* translation 1973 p. 64 — 'are all legal norms, regardless of the moment of their enactment or their character, including therefore regulations and provisions of laws enacted before the entry into force of the Basic Law.'

In the same sense is the exposition by Garcia de Enterria (La Constitucion como Norma Jurídica, in El Tribunal Constitucional, Madrid, 1981, p. 85. And also de Gilmar Ferreira Mendes (*Controle de Constitucionalidade,* Mimeo, UNB, 1987 p. 61) with minute reference to the German bibliography.

The reasons for the apparently strange distinction — to which already Ernst Friesenhahn (op. cit. supra, p. 63) refers — are analyzed with precision by Odim Brandao Ferreira in an unpublished work based on *leading cases* of the German Court relating to that topic.

The young scholar demonstrates that the difference, in reality, is based on the different roles which the Court performs in the concrete and abstract control of norms.

In fact, in the concrete control — which according to Art. 100 of the Basic Law is prompted by the judge with suspension of the proceedings, provided that *incidenter* he considers the applicable law to be unconstitutional — the Court takes the view that its role as guardian of the Constitution is narrow and has the purpose of 'preventing that any tribunal thwarts the will of the ordinary federal or state legislators and fails to apply the laws promulgated by them by interpreting them as contrary to the Constitution.' (Judgment of March 20, 1952.) Therefore, the basic judgment on the issue of February 24, 1953 concluded that it was unnecessary to bring before the Court incidenter questions relating to the subsistence of laws anterior to the Constitution: 'The decision about the compatibility of prior law with the Basic Law' — explains the judgment — 'leaves the authority of the legislator untouched. (* * *) The examination of the compatibility of a law with a Constitution promulgated subsequently presupposes justly the original validity of the contested norm. Only if the normative act of the older legislator is considered to be effective, surfaces a question of the compatibility with a subsequent Constitution. If that is denied, the authority of the legislator is not reduced, but it is merely established that the will of the subsequent legislator must prevail over the prior one. For a response to the question of compatibility between the older and the younger norm, it is without significance that it comes into play by reason of a norm of higher rank. In this respect, the question of the jurisdiction of the courts to examine the compatibility of the anterior norm with the Basic Law is a problem of the collision between prior and new law.' (Odim B. Ferreira, op. cit.)

Conversely, the German Court takes the position that in the abstract control (corresponding to our direct action) its 'function * * * to be the guardian of the Constitution stands on the primary plane' and therefore that 'it is charged with the assessment of the compatibility between preconstitutional law and the Basic Law.' This conclusion, as the same work shows, does not fail to regard the security of law in view of the fact that the judgment operates *erga omnes.*

It should be noted that in the Judgment of October 2, 1968, the German Court retained its approach of 1952 by considering that in the context of the direct control 'the question whether the contested norm is anterior or subsequent to the Constitution is without significance' and by reaffirming that 'In contrast to the concrete control, the object of the abstract control may nevertheless also consist of law anterior to the Constitution.' * * *

Curious, in turn, is the markedly pragmatic solution by the Spanish constitutional court.

In the systems of exclusively concentrated control there may be distinguished with respect to successive unconstitutionality, the frequent cases of patent and indubitable incompatibility between the old law and the new constitutional order. In order to obviate in such cases the lengthy suspension of the proceedings, the Spanish Court leaves it to the ordinary judge seized with the case to decide the question instantly and incidently and requires the submission of the question of supervenient unconstitutionality only in the case of doubt (García de Enterría, *La Constitucíon como Norma Jurídica,* op. cit. pp. 88, A. Cano Mata, *Cuestiones de Inconstitucionalidad — Doctrína del Tribunal Constitucional,* 1986 p. 60).

Without importance here are the systematic criticisms which may be aimed against this approach and which are deduced already by García de Enterría. What *is* of interest is to emphasize its premise — correct according to my view — that, ultimately there is no true difference between the problem of validity v. repeal, and the problem of constitutionality v. unconstitutionality.' (Judgment of February 2, 1981, cit. in Enterría, op. cit. 90).

In Portugal, as is well known, the question merited an express solution in the constitutional revision of 1982 in which Art. 282(2) specified that in the case of unconstitutionality by way of infringement of a subsequent constitutional norm, 'the declaration produces effects only from the date of its entry into force.'

The positive rule was no innovation. It confirmed a doctrine which united the most authoritative Portuguese text-writers (cf. Jorge Miranda * * * *Manual de Direito Constitucional,* 2d ed. 1983 II/248; J.J. Gomes Canotilho, *Direito Constitucional,* 4th ed. 1986, p. 837;)' * * *

III

The perfunctory journey into comparative law, particularly into the jurisprudence and the doctrine of the countries which most recently had to confront that problem, assures me, with due respect to the reporting judge, that I do not propose to the Tribunal anything 'completely absurd'.

In addition, it is well to remember that also in the Brazilian doctrine the question is far from being settled. * * *

IV — VI * * *

VII

The two opinions and votes submitted, especially that of Minister Brossard, raise an additional objection against the idea of supervenient unconstitutionality.

In reference to that, the eminent Reporting Judge inquires with the eloquence so characteristic of him 'how can the legislator observe a constitution that does not exist at the time of the legislation, how can he infringe constitutional norms which only much later attain promulgation.'

'Even if the legislator were a prophet' — responds his Excellency — 'and could predict future events and in advance envision the promulgation of a constitution with such and such provisions, even then he could not obey them because he would be bound by the precepts and terms of the constitution in force.'

With all due respect, I am not convinced that that argument with all its fascinating rhetorical sparkle carries major juridicial weight. * * *

VIII

Finally, I do not overlook the pragmatic weight of an ultimate objection to which the opinion of the eminent Reporting Judge attributes particular relevancy: which argument proceeds from the requirement specified in the successive constitutions since 1934, of a *quorum* of the absolute majority of the Tribunals, for the declaration of the unconstitutionality of laws and other normative acts of the Public Authority, today Art. 97 of the current Constitution.

Since the same requirement is not posed when the problem is reduced to a declaration that the law or normative act are simply abrogated upon which the argument of Minister Brossard is based, according to him, the thesis of supervening unconstitutionality would have the result that the major law, the Constitution, would have less force with respect to a pre-constitutional ordinary law than a minor later law.

My disagreement, as I have already said, rests on the fact that, on the contrary, it is only the declaration of unconstitutionality upon which the Brazilian system confers, by way of a direct action, general efficacy: and this is a major proof of the force of its supreme efficacy.

It is my conviction nevertheless that the brilliant opinion of Minister Brossard supplies itself the data which permit to get around the apparent complication.

His Excellency showed that the qualified quorum referred to is tied to the presumption of the constitutionality of the laws. He also showed with unexcelled accuracy, that a law antecedent to the Constitution is not benefitted by a presumption of constitutionality, as his Excellency says, for the most obvious reasons. When it was elaborated within the legislative power and received the sanction of the executive power, none of the two powers did or could check against a constitution which did not exist and only was promulgated after that law.

Hence when thus there is — and I think there is — the objection of the quorum, with due respect, it can be obviated by itself or at any rate because of the absence of the reasons for its existence, reasons which explain and condition the requirement.

* * *

IX

Mr. President, I believe that I have given a sufficient — and certainly lengthier than excusable — account of the reasons for which I maintain the conviction of the complete technical viability of the doctrine of supervening unconstitutionality, whether as a matter opposed to and excluding the repeal of a law by a subsequent constitutional norm or as a basis of a qualified category of repeal.

Conviction, that certainly does not deny respect to the opposite notion of those who refuse to differentiate the phenomenon in question from the simple repeal of an ordinary norm by another subsequent one of the same level. * * *

Moreover, it is not novel to clearly recognize that the resolution of the question cannot disregard the consequences of each alternative with respect to the efficacy and control of the legitimacy of the laws. * * *

After recognizing that the arguments of either side, as much those invoked in favor of the thesis of unconstitutionality as those in favor of repeal, Zagrebelski (op. cit. p. 42) concludes that option of the Italian Constitutional Court depended more on its preoccupations of a politico-institutional nature and with the historical setting in which the constitutional adjudication was established than on the strict reasons of juristic logic. * * *

To be sure, the authorities discussed above wrote under systems with exclusive concentrated control.

Nevertheless, I do not believe that the institutional symbiosis of the Brazilian constitutionalism — which ended up by coupling the method of the incidental and diffuse control prevailing in the U.S.A., with the European method of the direct and concentrated control of the constitutionality of laws, — overcomes the preoccupation with legal security which elsewhere lead to the rejection of the thesis of a simple repeal of the pre-existing laws by the constitution. To the contrary!

To give maximum effectivity on all levels of the legal system to the outburst of values, principles and rules of the new constitution is a mission from which in my view the Supreme Tribunal cannot abstain.

Therefore, with homage for the brilliance of the opinions of and all due respect for the eminent colleagues which preceded me, and in testimony of my respect for the precedents of the Court invoked by them, I reject the jurisdictional ruling.

Nevertheless, I cannot for that reason vote for the continuation of the direct action, in view of the firmly established case-law of the Tribunal which denies *standing* to federations of labor unions, such as plaintiff — the National Federation of Teaching Establishments.

For that reason, I myself also vote for a dismissal.

NOTES

1. The opinion of Minister Celso de Mello rejecting the applicability of the direct action of unconstitutionality to laws enacted prior to the entry into force of the 1988 Constitution is reproduced in ADIn 7 of February 7, 1992, (145 RTJ 339, at 340-350) in the case of *Brazilian Chamber of the Construction Industry (CBIC) c. President of the Republic*. In that case Minister Sepúlveda Pertence voted with the other judges, but only because he considered further dissent useless and obstructionistic.

2. The Brazilian constitution does not provide for a parallel to the German 'constitutional complaint.' It grants, however, the right to abstract control of norms to a broader range of constitutional officials, political parties and 'labor organizations and entities of particular classes of members with national scope.' The meaning of that phrase has been the subject of a case by case determination by the STF. The leading precedent is the case of *Brazilian Association of Independent Teleproducers and Interamerican Council of Commerce and Production v. President of the Republic and National Congress,* (ADIn 79 of April 13, 1992, 147 RTJ 3 (1994).) In that case, upon the report of Minister Celso de Mello, the Court unanimously held that the associations entitled to institute a direct action of unconstitutionality must have a membership of natural persons belonging to specific occupational categories and cannot be associations of associations or of a hybrid type. Minister Celso de Mello took the position that the plaintiff in the case at bar (*ABTI*) possessed too diversified a membership to qualify as an association entitled to institute a direct action of unconstitutionality.

3. Legal norms and normative acts subject to the direct action do not include acts which are materially of an administrative character. (ADIn 834 of February 11, 1993, 147 RTJ 82 (1994).)

b. Party for the Brazilian Democratic Movement

Federal Supreme Tribunal, 1992
February 19, 1992.
Direct Action of Unconstitutionality Nr. 594
Party for the Brazilian Democratic Movement (PMDB) v. Superior Tribunal of Justice.
151 RTJ 20 (1995)
(Full Tribunal Justice Sydney Sanches, President.
Justice Carlos Velloso, Reporting Judge.)

Report. The Brazilian Democratic Movement Party (PMDB), on the basis of arts. 102 Ia and 103 VIII of the Federal Constitution, institutes an action for the declaration of the unconstitutionality of the Summary [*Súmula*] nr. 16 of the Superior Tribunal of Justice, coupled with a petition for preliminary suspension.

The plaintiff contends that the legislature, when it created the agricultural credit by way of Law nr. 4829 of November 5, 1965, excluded monetary adjustments of rural loans since it remained silent about a correction. On their part, articles 947 and 1061 of the Civil Code, reinforced by art. 1 of the Law nr. 5670/71, provide for the illegality of monetary corrections of debts expressed in money in the absence of a legal provision which is indispensable in each case in which a correction is involved.

According to the allegation of the plaintiff, the jurisprudence of the Supreme Court, in conformity with its holdings in RE 80.596-PR (RTJ 74/594) and in Ag. 73.855-RJ (Ag Rg RTJ 90/855) is settled in the sense of the necessity of the existence of a law of authorization in these cases. Nevertheless, — plaintiff continues — Summary nr. 16 of the STJ, reversing these notions, requires the existence of a prohibitory law using the following terms:

> 'Ordinary legislation concerning rural credit does not bar the incident of monetary correction.'

Plaintiff asserts that in addition to being directly contrary to article 5 nr. II of the Federal Constitution, the document under attack is also obliquely violative of section XXXV of art. 5, because it impedes the exhaustion of judicial appraisal, thereby inducing the judiciary to contravene equally arts. 2; 5, XXXV and LV; 48, XIII; and 93 IX, all of the Magna Carta.

It is evident initially that the Summary in question, based on four judgments that negate constitutional principle, instead of constituting mere paradigms, in reality are transformed into 'a federal normative act' the application of which transgresses the legal order by invading the province of the legislature.

Plaintiff continues to stress the following points:

a) The effects of the Summary nr. 16-STJ can be shown not only in judgments of the Superior Tribunal, but also in judgments of the lower courts where they are generally adopted in lieu of legal norms;

b)–e) * * *

f) By reason of Brazilian peculiarities, the Summaries are seldom used as doctrinal models. Rather in the majority of cases they are adopted as juridical models with binding force;

g) * * *

h) In the case at bar, there exists a legal system which bars the incidence of monetary correction in rural financing because of the inexistence of an authorizing law.

i) Summary nr. 16-STJ, on the other hand, inverting the quaestio juris governing the matter, rules that the rural credit legislation does not bar the incidence of monetary correction;

j) By reason of the pretorian practice, the questioned summary is applied in the way of a 'normative federal act' as binding, thereby affecting the establishment of the State of Law, thus causing irreparable injury to the rural development and social well-being.

The grant of a suspension is warranted, according to the plaintiff, because of the threat of irreparable injury and massive losses, coupled with an unjustified favoring of the Financial System to the detriment of socio-economic development of the country.

This is the report.

VOTUM.

Justice Carlos Velloso (Reporting Judge).

The concentrated abstract norms control, exercised by the Federal Supreme Tribunal, has as object a federal or state statute or normative act (Fed. Const. art. 102, I, a). This signifies that only a federal or state law or normative act may constitute the object of a direct action of unconstitutionality. It is consequently important to inquire first of all in the case at hand whether a provision of a Summary of the Jurisprudence of the Superior Tribunal of Justice can constitute the object of a direct action of constitutionality; in other words, whether a Summary presents the characteristics of a normative act, i.e. abstract nature, generality, impersonality and binding force, since these are the characteristic features of a law in the substantive sense.

The 'summary of the jurisprudence' originated within the Supreme Federal Tribunal owing to the inspiration of Justice Victor Nunes, and it has been affirmed since then that it gave birth to the new term 'summary law' created by the Judge and Professor José Pereira Lira and used as title for his work by Dr. Roberto Rosas, Victor Nunes Leal, Past and Future of the Summary of the STF, 145 RDA pp. 1-20. A Summary, notes its creator, is a work method 'instituted by the Supreme Tribunal by way of an amendment of its Internal Regulation, promulgated on August 30, 1963', which entered into force 'at the commencement of the judicial year 1964 with its first 370 amendments, approved in the plenary session of December 13, 1963.' Thus, as a work method, — still in the words of Victor Nunes — 'designed to organize better and to facilitate the judicial task, the Summary was successively adopted by [other tribunals] and is to be extended to the Tribunals of Justice (at least as a mandate of the Code of Civil Procedure). * * *

In the Supreme Federal Tribunal the subject of the Summary is governed by articles 102 §§ 1-4 and 103 of the Internal Regulation: Art. 102. The jurisprudence issued by the Tribunal is summed up in the Summary of the STF.

'§ 1. The inclusion of the holdings in the Summary as well as its modification or withdrawal is deliberated by the full bench and approved by the absolute majority.

§ 2. The Summaries which are withdrawn or modified retain their respective number with their corresponding annotation, giving new numbers to those which are modified.

§ 3. The additions and amendments to a Summary, dated and numbered in separate and successive series, are published three consecutive times in the Diário da Justiça.

§ 4. The citation of the Summary by its number, dispenses, before the Tribunal, with a reference to other judgments in the same sense.

Art. 103 — Any of the Justices may propose a revision of the jurisprudence issued in a constitutional question and reduced to a Summary, proceeding to a factual condensation if necessary.'

* * *

In the Superior Tribunal of Justice the matter is regulated in its Internal Regulation, approved on June 22, 1989, arts. 122-127.

* * *

Art. 34 of the RISTJ[105] provides that the Reporting Judge may refuse to accept a recourse which conflicts with a Summary of the Tribunal (Law nr. 8-038 of 1990, art. 38). Art. 136, conversely, provides:

'Art. 136. A declaration of the constitutionality or unconstitutionality of a law or act affirmed by the Special Court and the jurisprudence condensed in a Summary applies to disputes submitted to Panels, Sections or the Special Court, unless a proposal for the revision of the jurisprudence condensed in a Summary is accepted.'

* * *

As José de Moura Rocha teaches in that respect: 'With reference to that issue * * * we attribute to the Summaries a pre-dominant, not a binding force.' (José de Moura Rocha, *A importância da Súmula,* 257 Revista Forense, 91-98).

The conclusion of the eminent Professor from Pernambuco seems to me correct. The Summaries are not binding. They are merely predominant. Victor Nunes Leal, himself, has affirmed that the Summary does not entail 'effects which could be com-

105. Regimento Interno do Superior Tribunal de Justiçia (Internal Regulation of the Superior Court of Justice.)

pared with those of a law', rather that its effects 'restricted to judicial proceedings are rather modest,' suitable to emphasize its flexibility, since it is subject to modification as Justice Seabra Fagundes underscored in his opinion which he delivered on October 20, 1963 to the Federal Council of the Brazilian Order of Attorneys: a fortunate formulation. * * *

On that view of the question, it can be affirmed that a Summary of the predominant jurisprudence does not possess the attributes of a normative act. It simply imparts greater stability to the jurisprudence and gives greater security to the judgments because it leads to uniform decisions in similar cases in addition to accelerating the progress of the proceedings, according to the conclusions of Justice Aliomar Baleiro in his work written about the Supreme Federal Tribunal (*O Supremo Tribunal Federal,* in 34 Revista Brasileira de Estudios Politicos July 1972, pp. 9-47 at 30.)

* * *

It is certain that the Summaries, because they are affirmed by the dominant jurisprudence, possess a certain normativity, possess quasi-normative significance, but are nevertheless, deprived of a binding force, as noted by Professor José de Moura Rocha (op. cit. at 94 and 95). This quasi-normative significance nevertheless does not impart to them the character of a normative act subject to concentrated constitutional review. This, it is worth repeating, can have as an object only a true normative act with the attributes of a law within the substantive sense: abstractness, generality, impersonality and binding force.

* * *

In the case at bar, according to what we have seen, there is no norm which attributes to a Summary the character of bindingness, the character of pure normative act. If it existed it would lack constitutional validity, according to what we have already discussed and according to the emphasis of E. D. Moniz de Aragao in *Estudios sobre reforma processual* p. 66.

In order to conclude this votum, it is worthwhile to recall the lecture of the creator of the Summary, the learned and esteemed Justice Victor Nunes Leal in the conference at Belo Horizonte on August 12, 1964 and referred to in this Court by Justice Prado Kelly in the of Habeas Corpus nr. 42-958 SP on March 21, 1966 (37 RTJ 159).

* * *

A Summary which is not obligatory and which therefore constitutes no normative act realizes the ideal half-way solution, the best one, as its creator imagined.

On that exposition, I do not admit the action and at the same time reject the petition for preliminary relief.

VOTUM.

Justice Marco Aurelio.

Mr. President, the Summary emerged on the judicial scenario as a convenient method to preserve the unity of the law and to achieve a certain judicial policy, thus avoiding so far as possible a major discrepancy of judgments involving the same norm and the consequent rupture of the unity of the law. * * * Nevertheless, certain facts occurred subsequently and among them one which speaks to the binding force on the judge: the judge becomes bound by the declaration of the Summary, by its provisions. I don't refer to a major evolution, amounting to an enlargement of the organs vested with judicial powers that are not integrated into the tribunal, author and holder of the summary. I refer to organs of the very tribunal that holds the Summary. Art. 38 of the Law nr. 8038/90 does not in my view confer to the provisions quasi-normativity as mentioned by the Reporting Judge, but a veritable normativity to the provisions only of the Summaries of the Supreme Federal Tribunal and, specifically, the Superior Tribunal of Justice. This article employs the word deny (*negar*), in providing that if the Reporting Judge in the Superior Tribunal is confronted with a recourse the reasons of which conflict with the provisions of a Summary, he must — so the mandate of art. 38 — deny the processing of the lodged petition, i.e. the progress of the recourse.'

[At that point in the proceedings which occurred on October 24, 1991, an argument arose between the Justices Carlos Velloso, Marco Aurelio, and Moreira Alves and it was decided to postpone the decision until further study in particular by Justice Sepúlveda Pertence. After two further sessions, the Court held that the Summaries did not constitute normative acts.]

DECISION

Pursuant to the majority of votes: the Tribunal does not admit the direct action of unconstitutionality to invalidate the jurisprudential Summary (legal impossibility of relief) and, therefore, adjudicates the request for provisional relief as barred. Dissenting: Justice Marco Aurélia. The president cast a vote. Justice Célio Borja did not vote because he could not attend the whole proceedings. Absent, justifiedly, Justice Moseira Alves.

NOTE

The text case involved a direct action for the declaration of the unconstitutionality of *Súmula* nr. 16 of the Superior Tribunal of Justice stating that 'the ordinary legislation on rural credit does not bar the application of monetary adjustment.' The action required a decision of the issue whether the constitutionality of a súmula of the Superior Court of Justice could be challenged by means of a Direct Action for Declaration of Unconstitutionality of Normative Acts [*ADIn*]. This decision in turn depended on a solution of three problems:

1. Whether the Súmula of the Superior Court of Justice, as originally authorized by the Court's internal regulation constituted a normative act;
2. Whether, if the answer to 1. was no, the nature was transformed into a normative act by art. 38 of law 8-038 of 1990; and
3. Whether, if the answer to 2 was yes, the statute was unconstitutional. The preponderant majority of the court (8:1) held that the Súmula in question was not subject to review by means of an ADIn. (Sydney Sanches, Néri da Silveíra, Octavio Gallotti, Paolo Brossard, Sepúlveda Pertence, Celso de Mello, Carlos Velloso, Ilmar Galvao, diss. Marco Aurelio).

The Internal Regulation of the STJ provides for the composition and amendment of súmulas in arts. 122-127 and 136. Art. 34 of the RISTJ provides that the Reporting Judge 'could' (*poderá*) refuse the prosecution of a recourse which contradicts a súmula, while Art. 38 of the Law nr. 8-038 uses the expression 'will' refuse the prosecution. The majority, following a lengthy opinion of Justice Sepúlveda Pertence, concluded that this change in terminology was either irrelevant, or, if relevant, did not bind the Court. Only Justice Marco Aurelio held that it was relevant and effective.

SEQUELS

1. Constitutional Amendment 3/93 of March 17, 1993, Art. 1 introduced an additional method of concentrated abstract norms control — the action for the declaration of the constitutionality of a federal law or normative act, to be instituted in the Supreme Federal Tribunal, by the President of the Republic, the executive committees of the Senate or the Chamber of Deputies or the Procurator-General of the Republic. A decision on the merits was to be effective *erga omnes* and binding on the other organs of the judiciary and the executive, Fed. Const. Art. 102 and 103 as amended.

The constitutionality of the amendment was questioned by a number of officials and scholars. As a result the issue formed the topic of a symposium under the auspices of the Association of Brazilian Judges, published by its coordinators in 1994, I. Martins and G. Mendes, Açao Declaratória de Constitucionalidad, (Sao Paulo 1994).

The first case utilizing the new action was initiated by the President of the Republic and the Executive Committees of the Senate and the Chamber of Deputies for the declaration of the constitutionality of the complementary law nr. 70 of Dec. 30. 1991, which introduced contributions for the financing of social security. In the course of deciding that action (ADC nr. 1-1) the Court had to pass on the constitutionality of the part of the Amendment 3/93 which created the new method of norms control. The justices, with one dissent, upheld the constitutionality of the new remedy, declining to find a material constitutional difference between an action for the declaration of unconstitutionality (norm discarding) and an action for the declaration of constitutionality (norm retention). The opinion of the justices are remarkable for their attention to comparative law.

H. SPAIN

1. The Spanish Judicial System

The organization of the administration of justice in Spain is governed by the Constitution Arts. 117-127, and a number of organic and ordinary laws. The Constitution provides for the establishment of a Supreme Court which is the highest judicial organ in all branches of justice, except for the enforcement of constitutional guarantees for which the Constitution establishes a separate Constitutional Court (*Tribunal Constitucional*), Articles 159-165. The Constitution also provides for the Office of the Public Attorney (*Ministerio Fiscal*), headed by an Attorney General (*Fiscal General del Estado*), as part of the judiciary. The office is charged with the enforcement of the legality of governmental action and the function of the public prosecutor, without prejudice to the functions entrusted to other organs.

The details of the organization of the administration of justice are governed by the *Organic Law on the Judicial Power* of July 1, 1985 which establishes a hierarchy of national, regional, provincial and local courts. The Supreme Court is composed of 5 divisions (*sala*) for civil, penal, administrative, social and military controversies. In difference to Italy and France the Spanish *Council of State* has no adjudicatory functions and is merely a consultative body. Administrative disputes are handled by special divisions of the ordinary courts.

There are 17 *Superior Tribunals of Justice*, one for each of the autonomous regions, and 50 *Provincial Courts* (*Audiencias Provinciales*). The first instance courts consist of a variety of judges or tribunals, the most important ones being the *Courts of First Instance*.

The Supreme Court is relieved of some of its burden by the creations of an additional judicial body with state-wide jurisdiction, designated as *Audiencia Nacional* which has original and appellate jurisdiction over enumerated criminal, administrative and labor matters.[106]

The organization and jurisdiction of the Constitutional Tribunal is governed, in addition to the articles in the Constitution, by the *Organic Law on the Constitutional Court* of October 5, 1979, as amended in 1985 and 1988. The Office of the Public Attorney has its legal basis, in addition to the articles in the Constitution, in the *Law on*

106. Ley del Poder Judicial Art. 62 et s.

the Organization of the Public Attorney's Office of December 30, 1981, as amended. Its functions as defender of the Constitution are supplemented by the *Defender of the People* (equivalent to an ombudsman), established by Article 54 of the Constitution and an organic law of April 6, 1981.

In proceedings against the state the government is represented by an *Abogado del Estado* (State Attorney), belonging to a separate organization.

2. Texts

a. CONSTITUTION OF SPAIN OF DECEMBER 27, 1978

Art. 53(2)

Any citizen may secure the protection of the liberties and rights recognized in Article 14 and the first section of Chapter 2 in the ordinary tribunals by means of a procedure based on the principles of priority and summariness and, where specified, by means of the *recurso de amparo* before the Constitutional Tribunal. The latter recourse shall be open for the conscientious objection recognized in Art. 30.

Title IX: *The Constitutional Tribunal*
Art. 159

(1) The Constitutional Tribunal consists of 12 members appointed by the King; of them, four, upon the proposal of the House of Deputies, approved by 3/5 of its members, four upon proposal by the Senate, approved by the same majority, two upon proposal by the government and two upon proposal of General Council of the Judiciary.

2-5. * * *

Art. 160

The President of the Constitutional Tribunal is appointed by the King from its members for a period of three years upon proposal of the full Tribunal.

Art. 161

1. The Constitutional Court exercises nationwide jurisdiction in Spain and has jurisdiction:

a) Over the recourse for unconstitutionality (*recurso de inconstitucionalidad*) against laws and normative provisions with the force of laws. The declaration of the unconstitutionality of a legal norm with the rank of a law, interpreted by the jurisprudence, shall affect the same, but a judgment or judgments rendered shall not lose their res judicata effect.

b) Over the recourse of amparo or for violations of the rights and liberties referred to in Art. 53(2) of this Constitution in the cases and forms as the law establishes.

c) Over conflicts of jurisdiction between the state and the autonomous communities or between the autonomous communities inter se.

d) Over other controversies which the Constitution or organic laws attribute to it.

2. The Government can contest before the Constitutional Tribunal the provisions and resolutions adopted by the organs of the autonomous communities. * * *

Art. 162

1. Entitled to invoke the Constitutional Tribunal are:

a) To interpose the recourse of unconstitutionality: the President of the Government, the Defender of the People, 50 deputies, 50 senators, the executive collegial organs of the autonomous communities and, in the proper cases, the assemblies of them.

b) To interpose the recourse of amparo: any natural or juristic person which relies on a legitimate interest as well as the Defender of the People and the Ministry of Justice.

2. In the other cases, an organic law shall determine the persons and organs [entitled to invoke the Constitutional Tribunal].

Art. 163

If a judicial organ considers in any proceeding, that a norm with the rank of a law, applicable in the controversy, upon the validity of which the judgment depends, may be contrary to the Constitution, it shall submit the question to the Constitutional Tribunal in the manner, the form, and with the effects which shall be determined by the law, which shall in no case be suspensive.

Art. 164

1. The judgments of the Constitutional Tribunal are to be published in the Official Bulletin of the State (*B.O.E.*) with the particular votes, if any. They have res judicata effect on the day following the publication and there is no recourse against them. Those which declare the unconstitutionality of a law or a norm with the force of a law and all which do not limit themselves to the establishment of a subjective right have full effect against anyone.

2. Except that, unless the judgment declares otherwise, the portion of a law which is not affected by unconstitutionality remains in force.

Art. 165

* * *

b. ORGANIC LAW ON THE CONSTITUTIONAL TRIBUNAL.

(October 3, 1979, as amended by L.O. 4/1985 and 6/1988).

Art. 1

The Constitutional Tribunal, as supreme interpreter of the Constitution, is independent of the other constitutional organs and is subject only to the Constitution and this Organic Law.

It is unique in its position and extends its jurisdiction throughout the national territory.

Art. 2

1. The Constitutional Tribunal exercises jurisdiction in the cases and the form which this law specifies

a) Over the recourse and the question of unconstitutionality with respect to laws or normative provisions or acts with the force of a law;

b) Over the recourse of amparo for violation of the rights and public liberties enumerated in Art. 53(2) of the Constitution;

c) Over the constitutional conflicts of jurisdiction between the state and the autonomous communities and between the autonomous communities inter se;

d) Over conflicts between the constitutional organs of the state;

e) Over the constitutionality of international agreements;

f) Over the contests provided in Art. 167(2) of the Constitution;

g) Over the verification of the nominations of the judges of the Constitutional Tribunal to establish whether they meet the requirements established by the Constitution and this Law;

h) Over others matters assigned to them by the Constitution or organic laws.

2. The Constitutional Tribunal may adopt regulations for its functioning and organization. * * *

Art. 3

The jurisdiction of the Constitutional Tribunal extends to the cognizance and decision with regard to prejudicial and incidental questions not of constitutional character which are directly related to the matter in issue to the extent that they are relevant for the constitutional adjudication. * * *

Title II

Proceedings for the Declaration of Unconstitutionality

Chapter I

General Provisions

* * *

Chapter II

The Recourse of Unconstitutionality

* * *

Chapter III

The Question of Unconstitutionality Submitted by Courts and Tribunals

Chapter IV

The Judgment in Proceedings of Unconstitutionality and Its Effects.

Title III

The Constitutional Recourse of Amparo

Art. 41

1. The rights and liberties recognized in Articles 14-29 of the Constitution are susceptible to the constitutional amparo in the cases and forms established by this law, without prejudice to their general protection entrusted to the ordinary courts of justice. Equal protection is accorded to the right of conscientious objection, recognized in Art. 30 of the Constitution.

2. The constitutional recourse of amparo protects all citizens in the terms which this Law establishes with respect to violations of the rights and liberties referred to in the preceding paragraph caused by provisions, legal acts or simple actions of legal authorities of the State, autonomous communities and the other public entities of territorial, corporative or institutional character, as well as their officials and agents.

3. In the constitutional amparo, no other claims may be asserted than those aimed at the reestablishment or preservation of the rights and liberties, which were sought to be vindicated by the recourse.

Art. 42

The decisions and acts without the rank of a law, emanating from the Parliament or any of its organs or from the legislative assemblies of the autonomous communities or their organs, which violate the rights and liberties susceptible of the constitutional amparo may be vindicated by the recourse within the period of three months. * * *

Art. 43

The violations of the rights and liberties referred to above, originating in provisions, legal acts or mere factual actions of the Government or its authorities and functionaries, or of the collegiate executive organs of the autonomous communities or their authorities, functionaries or agents, may give rise to a recourse of amparo, provided that the legal remedies are exhausted in accordance with Art. 53(2) of the Constitution. * * *

Art. 44

1. Violations of rights and liberties susceptible to the constitutional amparo which originate immediately and directly in the act or omission of a judicial organ, may give rise to this recourse provided that the following requisites are met:

a) that all the remedies available by way of judicial proceedings are exhausted;

b) that the violation of the right of remedy is immediately and directly attributable to an act or omission of the judicial organ independently from the facts that gave rise to the proceedings in which they were produced, in regard to which the Tribunal in no case shall take cognizance;

c) that in the proceedings the infringed constitutional right has been invoked as promptly as, once the violation has been known, could take place.

2. The period to interpose the recourse of amparo is 20 days after the notification of the order rendered in the judicial proceedings.

* * *

Chapter III

The Adjudication of the Constitutional Recourses of Amparo and its Effect.

Art. 53

The Chamber, in adjudicating the merits of the issue, renders in its decision the following judgments:

a) Award of the amparo;
b) Rejection of the amparo.

Art. 54

* * *

Art. 55

1. The decision which awards the amparo pronounces one or several of the following rulings:

a) Declaration of the nullity of the decision, act or resolution which have impeded the full exercise of the protected rights or liberties, determining if proper the extent of its effects;

b) Recognition of the public right or liberty with its constitutionally declared content;

c) Reinstatement of the complainant to the integrity of his right or liberty with the means, appropriate in the case, for the preservation thereof.

2. In the case that the amparo is granted because the applicable law infringes fundamental rights and public liberties, the Chamber submits the question to the full bench which may declare the unconstitutionality of that law in a new judgment with the ordinary effects provided in Articles 38 and seq. The question is substantiated according to the procedure in Articles 37 and like ones.

NOTES

1. The result of the *Ley Organica del Tribunal Constitucional* Arts. 42 and 55(2) is that the constitutional *amparo* cannot be based solely on the unconstitutionality of a law, but that when it is concluded in proceedings allowing the amparo, that the violation of constitutional rights and liberties is caused by a law, that issue is submitted to the full bench by the way provided for the concrete control of norms. For comments (in Spanish) on that situation, see F. Cordon Moreno, *El Proceso de Amparo Constitucional* (1987) p. 113 and 153, 154; A. Moya Garrido, *El Recurso de Amparo Según La Doctrina del Tribunal Constitucional* (1983) nrs. 29, 182, 183, 184.

2. *Courts of First Instance:* The Law 1/2000 of January 7, 2000 of Civil Trials effects important reforms in the civil law and complements the Organic Law on the Judicial Power of 1985 (supra 149).

3. In the *Recurso de Amparo* nr. 1145/93, Judgment of May 31, 1993 (RA 1993 nr. 180) a recourse was sought against the decision of the Social Chamber of the Superior Tribunal of Justice of Madrid which, upon insolvency of the employer, held that the petitioners, as managerial employees, were not entitled to receive their salary from the Salary Guarantee Fund established pursuant to the Community Directive 80/987/CEE of October 20, 1980.

The petitioners based their recourse to the Constitutional Tribunal on the ground that the Social Chamber of the Superior Tribunal of Justice of Madrid had, in an unreasoned, arbitrary and notoriously erroneous manner, failed to apply Community Law and had neglected to submit a preliminary question to the ECJ. The Constitutional Tribunal rejected the recourse of amparo because the failure to submit a preliminary question did not constitute a violation of Art. 24.1 of the Constitution and because in the case at bar, it could not be said that the choice of the applicable law was arbitrary or manifestly unreasonable or patently erroneous.

4. An interesting illustration of the procedure of constitutional questions pursuant to Title II Chap. III of the *Ley Organica del Tribunal Constitucional* [*LOTC*] is furnished by the consolidated proceedings in the cases 1001/1988; 291/1990; 669/1990; 1629/1990 and 2151/1990, Judgment of the full court of February 14, 1991

(AR Nr. 36.) In these proceedings, judges in several courts for the protection of juveniles questioned the constitutionality of the whole legislation for the protection of minors or several articles thereof with respect to various articles of the Spanish Constitution. The purpose of the Law (*Ley de Tribunales Tutelares de Menores* [*LTTM*] of June 11, 1948 was to free the proceedings thereunder from the stigma of judicial proceedings and to dress up sanctions against juvenile offenders as education measures.

For that reason, it was provided in Art. 15:

> 'In the proceedings to correct and protect minors, the sessions of the Juvenile Tribunals shall not be public and the Tribunal shall not be subject to the procedural rules governing other courts. * * *'

Art. 16 of the Law added:

> 'Acts which are specified as crimes or misdemeanors in the Penal Code or special statutes which are attributable to minors of less than 16 years are evaluated by the Juvenile Court with reasonable freedom of judgment, taking into account the nature of the respective acts in direct relation to the moral and social conditions under which the minors have committed them and disregarding totally the legal character and severity of these acts if, with respect to the respective responsibility, they constitute crimes or misdemeanors under the Penal Code or special statutes.'

The Court decided to:

1. declare Art. 15 of the *LTTM* to be unconstitutional to the extent that it regulates the proceedings applicable to the exercise of the power of correction and reform;
2. declare that Art. 16 of the above mentioned law is not unconstitutional if interpreted within the meaning and scope set forth in this opinion;
3. reject all other questions.

The court reached its conclusion that Art. 15 is unconstitutional to the extent that it applied to the exercise of the power of correction and reform on the ground that Art. 24 of the Constitution required certain procedural safeguards for the imposition of measures of correction and reform. Although these measures do not constitute penalties, nevertheless, they are coercive and therefore Art. 24, by virtue of Art. 10.2 of the Constitution, must be construed in the light of the Human Rights Conventions ratified by Spain, such as the European Convention for the Protection of Human Rights and Fundamental Freedoms, the Covenant on Civil and Political Rights, The Convention on the Rights of the Child and others.

While Art. 10.2 is not capable of being autonomously infringed by a statute, it requires that the constitutional rights and liberties must be construed in accord with these commitments. Art. 16, on the other hand, does not imply that the correcting power of the Juvenile Court is not subject to some important limitations, especially The United Nations Standard Minimum Rules for the Administration of Juvenile Justice (The Beijing Rules, GA 40/33), Art. 17.1, providing that the competent authorities shall be guided by the following principles:

a) The reaction taken shall always be in proportion not only to the circumstances and gravity of the offence, but also to the circumstances and needs of the juvenile as well as the needs of society.
b) Restrictions on the personal liberty of the juvenile shall be imposed only after careful consideration and shall be limited to the minimum possible.
c) Deprivations of personal liberty shall not be imposed, unless the juvenile is adjudicated of a serious act or of persistence in committing other serious offenses or unless there is no other appropriate response.

The Court stated that it was aware of the fact that it created a serious normative gap which only the legislature, or, in the case that it failed to do so, the judges could fill.

I. CHILE

1. Introduction

The Chilean Constitution (*Constitucion Politica de la Republica de Chile*), establishes a bi-cameral form of government under a strong executive. The present Constitution was adopted by Decree Law 3.464 of 1980, ratified by plebiscite and promulgated by Decree 1.150 of October 21, 1980. It was extensively revised by Law 25 of August 17, 1989, ratified by plebescite, and promulgated by Decree 1.225 of October 27, 1989. Since that time, it has been amended several times, (e.g. by Law 19.055 of March 26, 1991, Law 19.097 of November 11, 1991 and Law 19.124 of January 30, 1992).

The court system is composed of a Supreme Court consisting of 17 justices, 17 courts of appeal and various courts of first instance. The Constitution provides for the Judicial Power in Chapter VI, (Arts. 73-80), but also deals with judicial matters in other articles, e.g. Art. 20, creating a recourse for protection (*recurso de protección*) to remedy infringements of constitutional rights.

The Constitution leaves the details of the organization and jurisdiction of the courts to an organic constitutional law. (Const. Art. 74) The present provisions, called *Código Organico de Tribunales,* were originally enacted in 1943, but have been amended frequently since that time. The *Código,* subject to subsequent amendments, was kept in force by Transitional Provision Nr. 5 of the Constitution. Apart from Arts. 80 and 83(3) of the Constitution, which confirm the Supreme Court's jurisdiction over the so-called recourse of inapplicability (*recurso de inaplicabilidad*) to declare the inapplicability of laws in pending proceedings because of inconsistency with the Constitution, the jurisdiction of the Supreme Court is governed by the *Código Organico de Tribunales*, as amended by Law 18.969 of March 7, 1990, Art. 95 *et s.*

The Supreme Court transacts its business either sitting as a full bench or in chambers (*sala*). The full bench must hear and adjudicate recourses of inapplicability, while chambers may hear and adjudicate recourses of cassation, recourses of grievance (*queja*) and appeals from Courts of Appeals in recourses of *amparo* or for protection pursuant to Art. 20 of the Constitution. The proper scope of these remedies has produced a number of controversies and debates among the judges.

The Constitution of 1980 created a separate Constitutional Tribunal, consisting of seven judges. (Const. Art. 81). The jurisdiction of the Tribunal is defined in Art. 82 of the Constitution. It does not include review of the constitutionality of organic constitutional or ordinary laws after their promulgation. The details regarding the organization and functioning of the Tribunal are established by an organic constitutional law, the *Ley Organica Constitucional del Tribunal Constitucional* of May 19, 1981, Law 17.997, as amended by Law 18.930 of February 17, 1990.

2. Texts

POLITICAL CONSTITUTION OF THE REPUBLIC OF CHILE

Chapter III: *On Constitutional Rights and Duties*

Art. 19

The Constitution assures to all persons:

1. The right to life and to physical and psychic integrity of the person.
2. Equality before the law.
3. Equal protection of the law in the exercise of their rights.
4. Respect for and protection of private and public life and the honor of the person and his or her family. * * *
5. The inviolability of the home and all forms of private communication.
6. Freedom of conscience. * * *
7. * * *
8. The right to live in an environment free of pollution.* **

9.–22. * * *

23. The freedom to acquire property in every type of asset except those which by their nature are common to all men or which should appertain to the whole nation and which are declared by statute to do so. * * *

24. The right of property in its different kinds in any type of corporeal and incorporeal goods. * * *

Art. 20

Anyone who, through arbitrary and illegal acts or omissions, suffers deprivation, disturbance or threats in the legitimate exercise of the rights and guarantees established in Art. 19, nrs. 1, 2, 3 subpar.(4), 4, 5, 6, 9 final subpar., 11, 12, 13, 15, 16, * * * 19, 21, 22, 23, 24 and 25, may resort for himself or for anyone else in his name to the competent Court of Appeals, which shall promptly adopt the measure which it judges to be necessary to reestablish the reign of the law and to assure the due protection of the affected person, without prejudice of the other rights she may assert before the respective authorities or tribunals.

The recourse of protection is also available in the case of Article 19, nr. 8 if the right to live in a pollution free environment is affected by an arbitrary and illegal act imputable to a particular authority or person.

Chapter V

* * *

Matters to Be Governed by Statute

Art. 60

Enactment of a law is required only for those subjects

1. which by virtue of the Constitution must be the object of constitutional organic laws;
2. which the Constitution requires to be regulated by statute;
3. which are the object of codification, whether civil, commercial, procedural, penal, or otherwise;
4. which concern basic aspects of the legal regime of labor, union assistance, or social security matters;

5.–19. * * *

20. Any other norm of general and binding character which establishes the essential basis for a legal order.

Enactment of Statutes

Art. 62.

* * *

Art. 63.

* * *

Legal norms which interpret constitutional provisions require for their approval, modification or derogation, a majority of 3/5 of the deputies and senators in service.

* * *

Legal norms which require a qualified quorum are adopted, modified or derogated by the absolute majority of the deputies or senators in service.

The other legal norms require an affirmative vote of the majority of the members of each House present or the majority which are applicable pursuant to Articles 65 et seq.

Chapter VI

Judicial Power

Art. 73

The authority to hear civil and criminal cases, to resolve them and to provide the enforcement of the judgments belongs exclusively to the tribunals. Neither the President, nor the Congress may in any case exercise judicial functions, arrogate to themselves pending cases, revise the bases or contents of their resolutions or revive terminated proceedings. * * *

Art. 74

An organic constitutional law determines the organization and functions of the courts that are necessary to the prompt and full administration of justice in the entire territory of the Republic. The same law fixes the qualifications which the judges must possess and the number of years during which persons must have practiced the profession to be nominated as justices of a Court or legal judges. * * *

Art. 80

The Supreme Court, either ex officio or upon petition by a party, in the matters over which it has cognizance or which were submitted to it by way of recourse in the conduct of litigation before any other tribunal, may declare as inapplicable in these particular cases any legal prescription that is contrary to the Constitution. This recourse may be taken at any stage of the litigation, the Court having the power to stay the proceedings.

Chapter VII

The Constitutional Tribunal

Art. 81

There shall be established a Constitutional Tribunal composed of 7 members, designated as follows:

a) 3 members of the Supreme Court, elected by it;
b) one attorney nominated by the President of the Republic;
c) two attorneys elected by the National Security Council;

d) one attorney elected by the Senate with an absolute majority of the Senators in service.

An organic constitutional law shall determine. * * * the organization and functioning of the Tribunal.

Art. 82

The Constitutional Tribunal has the following functions:

1. To exercise control of the constitutionality of the organic constitutional law before their promulgation and of the laws that interpret any prescription of the Constitution.
2. Resolve the questions about their constitutionality that arise during the deliberations of legislative proposals or constitutional reforms and of treaties submitted for Congressional approval.
3. Resolves questions that arise regarding the constitutionality of decrees with the force of law.

   * * *

12. Resolve the constitutionality of the decrees of supreme character issued in the exercise of regulatory power by the President of the Republic if they relate to matters which could be reserved to a law by virtue of the mandate of Art. 60.

    In the case of para. 1, the House where the measure originated transmits to the Court the bill within five days after its deliberations have been completed.

    In the case of par. 2, the Tribunal can only take cognizance of the matter on request by the President of the Republic or of either House or by a fourth of its members in service so long as it takes place before promulgation.

Art. 83

If the Constitutional Tribunal determines that a particular legal provision is constitutional, the Supreme Court may not declare it to be inapplicable because of the same defect which was the subject of the Tribunal's decision.

NOTE

As the texts indicate, the new Constitution of Chile, as revised in 1989 and twice amended in 1991, shows that its framers relied heavily on the French Constitution of 1958 as a model. Nevertheless, there are important differences. Like the French model, the Chilean Constitution differentiates between organic constitutional laws, and ordinary laws, adding however, still other categories. (Const. Art. 63).

Constitutional organic laws are envisaged for the organization and jurisdiction of the courts (Const. Art. 74) and for the organization and functioning of the Constitutional Tribunal (Const. Art. 81, last para.)

The organization and functioning of the judiciary is governed by the *Código Organico de Tribunales,* first enacted by Law no. 7.421 of June 15, 1943 (30 RECOPILACION DE LEYES 10 (1945)) and officially republished several times with intervening amendments. The last time, following extensive amendments by the Law 18.969 of March 7, 1990 (96 RECOPILACION DE LEYES Y REGLAMENTOS [Rec.L.R.] 442 (1991)) by decree 1.456 of November 19, 1990. (97 Rec.L.R. 1032 (1992)). The *Código* was retained pursuant to transitional provisions Nr. 5.

The organization and functioning of the *Constitutional Tribunal,* in addition to the constitutional provisions, is governed by the *Ley Organica Constitucional del Tribunal Constitucional* of May 19, 1981, Law 17.997 (79 Rec.L.R. 52 (1982)) as amended by Law 18.930 of February 17, 1990.

In addition, the *Supreme Court*'s practice in *recursos de inaplicabilidad* is governed by a Court rule of March 20, 1932 and the Supreme Court's practice on appeal in a recourse for the protection of constitutional guarantees by a Court rule of March 29, 1977.

3. Cases

a. In the Matter of Cortés Heyermann, M.

Supreme Court of Chile, 1986
Judgment of January 31, 1986
In the Matter of Cortés Heyermann, M.
(Recourse of Inapplicability)
83 Revista de Derecho y Jurisprudencia y
Gaceta de los Tribunales V, 7 (1986).

The Court,

after review of the following facts:

Don Luis Ortiz Quiroga, representing Mauricio Cortés Heyermann, has filed a recourse in this Court to have declared inapplicable in the case nr. 114.260 in the Fifth Criminal Court of Santiago the provision of Art. 163(f) of the Tax Code in the version enacted by Art. 1 Nr. 7(a) of Decree-Law 3.443 of 1980, on the ground that it violates Art. 19 Nr. 7(e) in conjunction with Nr. 26 of that article of the Political Constitution of 1980. The petitioner states that in the proceedings which prompted the recourse, his client and other officers of El Tattersall were accused of tax fraud under Art. 97(4) of the Tax Code and that his client Mr. Cortés was deprived of his liberty from September 15, 1980 to March 25, 1981; that on that date the Investigating Magistrate modified the original charge against his client to the charge of having committed the offense of fraud as specified and penalized in Art. 473 of the Criminal Code, granting provisional liberty upon posting bail fixed at 200,000 pesos. He stated additionally, that the Council of Defense of the State interposed an appeal from and objection to the order of the Magistrate and that in the judgment upon these remedies the contentions of the Fisc were accepted with the consequence that the accused were to be charged with the crime defined in the Tax Code, Art. 97 nr. 4 and not with that specified in Art. 473 of the Criminal Code, and that with respect to the provisional liberty of the accused, the relevant part of the order of the Investigating Magistrate which granted it in conformity with Art. 359 of the Code of Criminal Procedure was set aside and it was declared that it had to remain by the provision in Art. 163(f) of the Tax Code. He pointed out that in the case of his client Mauricio Cortés, this decision required the posting of bail in the amount of 164,179,590 pesos, corresponding to 30% of the taxes allegedly evaded as based on the provisional estimate given by the Internal Revenue Service in the criminal proceeding, thus compelling his client to deposit this exorbitant sum with the public treasury.

In support of his recourse, the petitioner makes an extensive analysis of provisional liberty as a constitutional guarantee, specifying that in respect to the case of his client, the issue does not relate to the continuation of his personal freedom, but to the mode of its restoration, because the Constitution provides specifically in the last sentence of Nr. 7(e) of Art. 19 that 'a law establishes the requisites and conditions for its obtainment', a provision which is identical with one which was contained with respect to that subject in the Constitutional Act Nr. 3, and which prompted the holding of this Court pronounced in recourses of the inapplicability of Art. 45 of the Law on Checks, Decree-Law 2.622, which were rejected because of the view that the cited phrase of the Constitutional Act accorded to the legislator full freedom to fix the amount of bail * * * all of which moved the Constitution-makers to establish the last of the guarantees which are set forth in Nr. 26 of Art. 19.

He asserts that the legal precept whose inapplicability is sought imposes an exaction which impedes the free exercise of the right to provisional freedom, whenever in the determination of the bail as condition of a release from prison is fixed at an amount not less than 30% of the evaded and readjusted taxes.

The Council for the Defense of the State, as representative of the Fisc in discharge of its duties, prayed for the rejection of the recourse, contending in essence that the Decree-Law nr. 3443 which established the current text of Art. 163(f) of the Tax Code has determined the conditions under which a person prosecuted for tax offenses may obtain his liberty in a fashion that the article in issue not only does not violate the Constitution, but to the contrary, found its origin in the Basic Charter. It added that in order to find a legal precept to be violative of the constitutional norm of Art. 19 it is necessary that it infringes the rights in their essence or that it imposes conditions, exactions or requisites that impede their exercise without, however, relating to factual situations.

Manuel Vergara Salinas, the defendant in the case of that name, joins the recourse, praying that it be granted.

Upon referral of the papers to the Fiscal [Official Amicus], he expressed the opinion that the issues raised in the recourse are such that are within the cognizance of the judges on the merits who must decide whether a legal rule is still in effect or has been abrogated at the date of the adjudication of the case before them. Wherefore he concludes that the interposed recourse of inapplicability be rejected;

In consideration:

1. That in the recourse of inapplicability which is interposed, the actual prayer requests the declaration of the inapplicability, of the provision contained in Art. 163(f) of the Tax Code, with the text fixed by Decree-Law 3.443, in the proceedings having the file number 11.260 pending before the Fifth Criminal Court of Santiago because of its conflict with the clauses Nr. 7(e) and Nr. 26 of Art. 19 of the Political Constitution of 1980;
2. That the recourse of inapplicability has as its object the resolution of a conflict or antinomy between a general law and a constitutional norm or precept that are in force at the time when the recourse is interposed and when it is decided. That therefore it presupposes that the law which is challenged was enacted when the Constitution, whose precepts are violated or infringed by it and to which it must conform in order to be qualified as constitutional, was in force;
3. That the text of Art. 163(f) of the Tax Code which the recourse challenges as unconstitutional was fixed by the above-mentioned Decree-Law 3.443 which entered into force upon its publication in the Official Gazette on July 2, 1980, i.e., when the Constitution of 1925 was still in force under the regime of which it was enacted.

   The present Political Constitution of 1980 entered into force on 11.3.1981, six months after its approval by a plebiscite, as provided in its final article;
4. That under the indicated facts, there is no possibility that the legal provision cited above which is challenged as unconstitutional be declared as inapplicable because the challenge made raises an issue foreign to that of the recourse interposed, viz. the issue whether the legal norm in question was still in force or abrogated by the new constitutional provisions which entered into force on 11.3.1981 and which are claimed to be breached by that norm;
5. That on the other hand it must be taken into account what this Court has resolved about the scope of the recourse of inapplicability by announcing that the recourse excludes any consideration or determination of questions of fact or matters of law not related to what is properly the subject of the recourse;
6. That, consequently, the question that is posed by the recourse interposed, is within the cognizance of, and must be decided by, the judges on the merits who must determine whether the legal provision which is attacked by petitioner is or is not in force for the purpose of setting the amount of the bail in a criminal prosecution for tax fraud, such as is pending against petitioner be-

fore Fifth Criminal Court in Santiago and, moreover, could reach the Supreme Court by means of the legal recourses;

7. That, because of the reasons given in the preceding considerations, the recourse of inapplicability must be rejected,

Therefore, in conformity with the opinion of the Official Amicus (*Fiscal*), the provision of Art. 80 of the Political Constitution and the Rule of the Court issued on 22.3 1932 about the treatment and adjudication of the recourse of inapplicability, it is declared that the recourse interposed by Don Ortiz Quiroga as representative of Mauricio Cortés Heyermann and which is joined by the accused Manuél Vergara Salinas is not admissible.

So held against the votes of the President Mr. Retamal and the councillors Messrs. Erbetta, Meersohn, Jordán and Zurita, who do not accept the reasons given in nrs. 4 *et seq.* of the judgment and insisted on giving their opinion relating to the recourse of inapplicability to the extent that it relates to a possible inconsistency between Art. 163(f) of the Tax Code, with the text fixed by Decree-Law 3.443 and Art. 19 Nr. 7(e) and Nr. 26 of the Political Constitution of 1980.

They render the following opinion:

Although the judges below may examine and pass on the possible abrogation of a prior law by the subsequent constitution if the latter is in conflict with the former, this authority of the judges does not prevent the Supreme Court from declaring the inapplicability of the prior law if it contravenes the subsequent Constitution.

In effect, Art. 80 of the Basic Charter of 1980 does not make any distinction between prior and subsequent statutes and it empowers the Supreme Court to declare inapplicable as unconstitutional any law that is found to be inconsistent with that Charter. Consequently if this Court under the pretext of a possible abrogation of that prior law by the Constitution hands over to the lower courts the decision to declare this possible abrogation and abstains from passing on the inapplicability, it shirks a constitutional duty and makes an exclusive transfer to the judges of a power which is naturally its own, provided that there is no doubt that the judges below, after being instructed on the conflict between the statute and the Political Charter, necessarily are bound to pass on the predominance of either the prior law or the subsequent Constitution.

To what is said, one may add that a possible conflict between a general statute of specific nature and the general Constitution might not be resolved by the judges below in view of their different hierarchical position, since the control of the law with superior rank over the ordinary law belongs exclusively to the Supreme Court. * * *

For the reasons given the dissenters rectify their former opinion which was in agreement with that of the majority on the issue relating to a decision by the judges on a possible abrogation by the Fundamental Charter of a prior law conflicting with it and to the abstention by this Court or the impropriety of rendering a declaration with respect to inapplicability properly so-called.

The dissenters, by virtue of these reasons, give the following opinion on the merits of the claimed inapplicability.

The recourse maintains that Art. 163(f) of the Tax Code is in conflict with Art. 19 Nr. 7(e) and Nr. 26 of the Political Constitution of the State.

The former provision says that when the release from prison is decided the judge must fix bail at an amount not less than 30% of the taxes evaded after readjustment in the form provided in Art. 53 and on the basis of the estimate given by the Internal Revenue Service. The constitutional precepts which are claimed to be infringed establish:

a) Art. 19 Nr. 7(e), that the provisional liberty continues unless that preventive detention or imprisonment is deemed to be necessary for the summary investigations or the security of the victim or society; and that a law will determine the requisites or modes to obtain it, and b) Art. 19 Nr. 26 guarantees the assurance that the legal precepts which by virtue of the mandate of the Constitution regulate and implement the guarantees which it confers or which limit the same in the cases where that is authorized cannot affect these rights in their essence or impose conditions, exactions or requisites that impede their free exercise.

Thus the task is to ascertain whether Art. 163(f) of the Tax Code does or does not conflict with any of these constitutional provisions which the recourse contends are infringed.

In order to resolve that problem it is necessary to determine at the outset the meaning of the constitutional provision which says that provisional liberty is the general rule with only two limitations: necessity of investigating conduct or security of the victim or society.

Consequently saying that provisional liberty shall continue means that it shall be available in all cases in which none of these exceptions are present, which signifies that it must be possible to obtain provisional liberty not only on a theoretical-legal level, but in the reality of practical experience. If the requisites or modalities which the law requires for the restoration of the provisional liberty are such that in the procedural and practical moment when it is sought, they render that attainment impossible, the legal provision results in its being violative of the constitutional rule of continued personal liberty. * * *

For the reasons set forth it is declared that Art. 163(f) of the Tax Code is inapplicable as unconstitutional in the respective case.

Announced by the President Don Rafael Retamal and by the councillors Messrs. José Maria Eyzaguirre, Israel Bórquez, Luis Maldonado, Octavio Ramirez, Victor Manual Rivas del C., Osvaldo Erbetta, Emilio Ulloa, Marcos Aburto, Estanislao Zúñiga, Abraham Meersohn, Hernán Cereceda, Servando Jordán and Enrique Zurita.

NOTES

1. As *Heyermann* and the following case (*Sociedad Benefactora*) indicate, the problem of 'intervening unconstitutionality' has posed a perennial problem for courts

charged with the review of the unconstitutionality of laws which are invoked as governing the outcome of controversies pending in other courts. In *Cortés Heyermann,* the majority held 10:4 that the recourse of inapplicability because of unconstitutionality applied only to laws passed under the regime of the Constitution with provisions of which they were claimed to conflict. The dissenters, who formerly agreed with the view of the majority, had changed their view. The minority became the majority in 1990. (See Note to *Sociedad Benefactora, infra.*)

2. In *Bunster Iñiguez, Jaime y otros c. Fisco y Servicio Agricola* (Supreme Court of Chile, January 29, 1987, 84 *Revista de Derecho y Jurisprudencia y Gaceta de los Tribunales,* V, 23 (1987)), the applicants in a recourse of inapplicability challenged the constitutionality of Law 17.988, enacted after the entry into force of the Political Constitution of 1980. Applicant's land had been expropriated in 1972 in the course of an ongoing land reform. After the change in government, most of the expropriated lands were restored to the former owners, on the condition that they transfer 5-10% of it and renounce any right to compensation. This happened also in the *Bunster* case.

Nevertheless, the petitioners then brought an action in the court of first instance in Santiago on November 5, 1984 to recover compensation for the portion of their agricultural holdings actually expropriated, claiming the coerced renunciation to be null and void. Defendant, the Chilean Fisc, interposed the defense that actions of the type brought by plaintiffs were extinguished by virtue of Decree-Laws 754 and 1.283 of 1974 and 1975, as interpreted by Law 17.988 of May 20, Law 17.988 provided that the Decree Laws of 1974 and 1975, although applying according to their wording, only to pending compensation claims, were meant also to bar future claims. (79 Rec. de Leyes 69 (1981).) The court of first instance, relying on Law Nr 17.988, dismissed the complaint.

Plaintiffs appealed and instituted a recourse for the declaration of the inapplicability of Law 17.988 in their lawsuit. They claimed the inapplicability of that Law for a variety of reasons, *inter alia,* because Law 17.988 was not a law within the meaning of Art. 60 Nr. 20 of the Constitution, and because it infringed Art. 73 of the Constitution, since the purported interpretation of Decrees 754 and 1.283 amounted to the enactment of a resolution of concrete cases, belonging to the prerogative of the courts.

While the Court rejected the contention that Law 17.988 was not within the provisions of the recourse of unconstitutionality because it was not a norm of general and binding character, it still held it to be inapplicable in the pending litigation because of its infringement of the powers of the judiciary.

b. Sociedad Benefactora y Educacional Dignidad

Supreme Court of Chile
Judgment of November 16, 1992
Sociedad Benefactora y Educacional Dignidad

(*Recourse of Inapplicability*)

89 *Revista de Derecho y Jurisprudencia y Gaceta de los Tribunales* II V 270 (1992).

The Court,
Having seen:

Mr Hermann Max Georgi, in his capacity as president and as representative of a corporation named Sociedad Benefactora y Educacional Dignidad, both domiciled for this effect in Santiago, Ñuñoa * * * in conformity with the provisions of Art. 80 of the Political Constitution of the State, interposes a recourse of inapplicability with the Supreme Court, the particulars of which are detailed in the files, for the purpose of having declared inapplicable as unconstitutional in a recourse of protection filed by the corporation with the Court of Appeals of Santiago, certain provisions of the Civil Code. The recourse of protection pending in the Court of Appeals in Santiago is directed against the Minister of Justice, Mr Francisco Cumplido Cereceda, and petitions that the Decree 143 of February 16, 1991, issued upon order of the President, be deemed without effect and annulled. Said Decree canceled the legal personality of the corporation and disposed of its assets. The Decree was based on Articles 559.2 and 561 of the Civil Code which are sought to be declared to be legal provisions contrary to the Political Constitution: Article 559.2 to the extent that it authorizes the President of the Republic to dissolve a juristic person; Art. 561, to the extent that it provides that if the charter of a dissolved corporation has not regulated the way in which its assets are disposed of, they will become the property of the State and to the extent that it authorizes the President of the Republic to indicate the objects to which these goods and properties are allocated.

The pertinent files were transmitted to the President of the Defense Council for the Minister of Justice who communicated his arguments and the Public Attorney of the Supreme Court who submitted his opinion.

Considering:

1. That it is the function of this Supreme Court, by virtue of the power vested in it by Art. 80 of the Political Constitution of the Republic to declare whether, in the aforementioned recourse for protection in the Court of Appeals of Santiago, the following are unconstitutional: Articles 559.2 Civil Code to the extent that it authorizes the President of the Republic to dissolve a juristic person and Art. 561 of the same Code, to the extent that it establishes that if the charter of a dissolved corporation has not regulated the way its assets are to be disposed of, they will belong to the State and to the extent that it authorizes the President of the Republic to indicate the objects to which these goods and properties are to be allocated. In the above mentioned recourse for protection, interposed before the Court of Appeals of Santiago, it is petitioned that the Decree 143, published in the Official Journal of February 16, 1991, which canceled the juristic personality of this corporation and disposed of its assets, be deemed to be without effect and annulled.

2. The Minister of Justice in his defense arguments and the Public Attorney in his opinion submit 'that the recourse before the Court must be scrutinized as to its possible dismissal because Art. 80 of the Fundamental Charter permits the Most Honorable Court to declare inapplicable only provisions in force which conflict with the Fundamental Charter and which have not been abrogated by it;' and that 'The situation where a prior law is claimed to be contrary to a subsequent constitution is not a proper subject of the recourse of inapplicability, but constitutes a problem of abrogation of statutes which must be examined by the judges with jurisdiction over the controversy.' In support of their thesis they rely upon the opinion of a professor of Constitutional Law and member of the Commission for the Draft of the Constitution of 1980, Mr Alejandro Silva Bascuñán, who expressed the view that the question of the subsistence or abrogation of the provision in issue 'is not comprised in the exclusive competency of the Supreme Court.'

3. That, as can observed from the mere reading of the quotation, its author does not exclude the competency of the Supreme Court in the case of the abrogation of a prior provision which is deemed to be contrary to a subsequent Constitution; the author states merely that the matter is not within the 'exclusive competence' of the Supreme Court; but he does not deny its existence.

4. That, obviously, it is possible that there appear contrary to the Constitutional, legal provisions which are prior or subsequent to its coming into force. The determination whether these provisions really do or do not possess this character requires an interpretative process which because of the nature and purpose is immersed in the power of the Supreme Court to declare the inapplicability, constituting therefore a function comprised in the power which Article 80 vests in it, given the clear sense of the literal wording of the norm which states:

> 'The Supreme Court, ex officio or on the motion of a party, in the subjects which are within its original cognizance or which are submitted to it by way of a recourse interposed at any stage of proceedings before another tribunal, may declare to be inapplicable in these particular cases, every legal provision contrary to the Constitution.'

5. That, likewise, the decision of the Supreme Court, because it emanates from the Tribunal with the highest rank in the hierarchy of the Judicial Power, has to be of special significance and serve for the orientation of the other tribunals of the Republic — besides being binding on those which have cognizance of the particular case in which the inapplicability is declared — a factor which contributes to the judicial functions and to the justicity.

6. That it is an axiom that from the date of the entry into force of a new political constitution in a country, the totality of the other legal norms existing therein at that date remain in force, except, obviously, those that are abrogated because they are in conflict with it. It is well-known that the abrogation may be expressed 'if the new

law provides expressly that it abrogates the old one,' as is provided in Art. 52(2) of the Civil Code, and implied 'if the new law contains provisions which cannot be reconciled with the prior one.' (Art. 52(2) Civil Code). The provision which can be deemed to be impliedly abrogated by the Constitution remains literally in force so long as it is not expressed that it is contrary to the Constitution. At that time, a question of the subsistence of the provision originates. And it is precisely the recourse of inapplicability which has as its object, as Art. 80 of the Fundamental Charter provides, to declare inapplicable any provision contrary to the Constitution.

7. That the Constitutional Tribunal, passing on the request formulated by various senators for a declaration of the unconstitutionality of the Supreme Decree Nr. 143 of the Ministry of Justice which decreed the dissolution and cancellation of the juristic personality of the Corporation 'Sociedad Benefactora y Educacional Dignidad' by way of a Judgement of 10.6.1991, attached in copy to these files, denied to accord this declaration of unconstitutionality.

8. That although the last paragraph of Art. 83 of the Political Constitution prescribes that if the Constitutional Tribunal concludes that a particular legal provision is constitutional, the Supreme Court cannot declare it to be inapplicable by reason of the same defect which was the substance of the decision, it is clear that in the case under consideration, the provision is not applicable and that therefore this decision does not prevent this Court from declaring the inapplicability due to unconstitutionality of the legal provisions which served as the basis for the enactment of the Supreme Decree referred to, namely for the following reasons:

a) Because the Constitutional Tribunal in the above-mentioned decision could only limit itself, which it appears to have done, to ascertain that the provisions of the Civil Code, which govern the granting and the termination of the juristic personality of corporations and foundations, were still in force and in this function to conclude that the President of the Republic was authorized to enact decrees like the one which was challenged, thus exercising his regulatory powers;

b) In effect that Tribunal could only limit itself to ascertaining the objective existence or force of Articles 559 and 561 Civil Code because it lacks the power to exercise constitutional control of these legal provisions, which, because it is expressly so provided by Art. 80 of the Constitution, is expressly entrusted to this Supreme Court.

9. That, as was expressly stated at the beginning, in the recourse for inapplicability, the challenge of unconstitutionality is directed against Art. 559(2) Civil Code, to the extent that it grants power to dissolve corporations to the authority which legitimized their existence, and against Art. 561 to the extent that it establishes as a result of the foregoing that 'upon a dissolution of a corporation — if in its charter it is not provided in which way its assets are to be disposed — its properties shall belong to the State with the duty to employ them for purposes analogous to those of the institution. It is the function of the President to indicate the same.'

10. That it results therefrom that is necessary to examine whether in the light of the present Constitution, the law has preserved these powers in the hands of the Republic or a Minister of the Government or whether these provisions are contrary to the Fundamental Charter.

11. That in order to analyze the constitutionality of the aforementioned provisions and therefore, to determine whether they are or are not applicable in the recourse for protection in the Court of Appeals of Santiago, it is necessary to emphasize that the Civil Code of which they form a part was promulgated on 14.12.1855, an epoch at which these provisions had to be in conformity with the Constitution of 1833 which, originating under the influence of the individualistic thought of the 18th Century and the principles of the French Revolution, which suppressed all corporations existing at that time, did not envisage a right of association.

* * *

16. That, finally, continuing in the historical evolution of strengthening the Right of Association, the Political Constitution of 1980, together with maintaining in Art. 19 Nr. 15 the right of association without prior permission, elevated to constitutional rank the compliance with the legal prerequisites for the enjoyment of juristic personality by providing in its subpar. 2 that 'in order to enjoy juristic personality, the associations must be constituted in conformity with the law.'

* * *

29. That, moreover, the aforementioned Art. 561 is contrary to and in breach of another constitutional guaranty which is also a basis for its unconstitutionality: 'The Constitution assures to all persons — provides Art. 19, Nr. 24 — the right of property in its various categories in any class of corporeal and incorporeal assets.' 'Nobody, in any case, can be deprived of his property, its proceeds or the attributes and powers essential to its exercise, except by virtue of a general or special law which authorizes the expropriation for the public benefit or in the national interest as defined by the legislator. The owner of the expropriated property — in addition — may contest the legality of the expropriatory act in the ordinary courts and assert a right to compensation of the financial loss sustained which is fixed either by agreement or by the judgment of said tribunals according to law.'

30. That said Art. 561 in disposing of the properties of a dissolved juristic person and indicating the objects in which they must be employed, is manifestly contrary to the aforementioned guaranty, given that it provides: 'Upon dissolution of a corporation * * * its properties belong to the state with the sole duty to employ them in objects analogous to those of the institution. It is the function of the President to designate the same.' But this provision neither envisions nor does there exist a law, general or special, which authorizes expropriation for the public benefit or in the national interest as defined by the legislator as the above-mentioned constitutional guaranty requires.

31. That it is obvious that the wide range of the constitutional protection of the right of property which is accorded to all persons and all assets protects also juristic persons and their assets. The cogent consequence of this protection is that, in providing that upon the dissolution of a corporation, unless there is a stipulation in what manner its assets shall be distributed, its properties belong to the state, Art. 561 disposes of the assets of a corporation without respecting the guaranty of the right of property.

32. That it has been argued, in opposition, that in this case the properties pass to the state because in virtue of the dissolution of the corporation, its properties cease to belong to it and not because of an expropriation.

33. That the foregoing argument is a sophistry and ethically it is not possible to accept it since in that way one could arrive at the deprivation of a corporation of its property by a simple administrative decree making thus tabula rasa both of the guaranties which the Constitution assures to all persons and all goods, as a basic tenet of the rule of law such as the separation of powers, and of the jurisdictional function solemnly accorded to the Judicial Power in its Art. 73 and casuistically in the abovementioned Article 19, Nr. 24(3).

34. That consequently, it follows ineluctably that Art. 561 of the Civil Code is inapplicable. * * *

35. That the judicial function which Art. 73, par. 1 of the Constitution vests exclusively in courts established by law — which constitute the Judicial Power pursuant to its par. 3 — is a mandate itself, contradicting, because of its clear sense and wording, the contention of respondent that this article 'does not establish in any of its parts that the Judicial Power is invested with the power envisaged in Art. 559 of the Civil Code.'

36. That to the respondent's question, whether Art. 559 of the Civil Code was unconsti tutional during the time when the Constitution of 1833 was in force, because this provision originated when that Constitution was in force, one needs to respond: first, that at that time no recourse of the inapplicability of laws contrary to the Constitution existed, since it was established only in the Constitution of 1925; and that even at that time it could not be contended that the President lacked the power to cancel the juristic personality of a corporation, since it was granted expressly in Art. 72, Nr. 11, in these terms: 'The President is especially vested with the power: (11) To grant juristic personality to corporations and to cancel it.'

37. That respondent presses the contention that Art. 559 of the Civil Code does not contradict in any way any of the provisions mentioned by the petitioner because this article -which regulates the dissolution of a juristic person governed by Title XXXIII of Book I of the Civil Code — is in harmony with Art. 60, Nr. 3 of the Constitution of 1980 which provides: 'Matters for legislation are only those which are objects of codification, whether civil, commercial, procedural, penal or other.'

38. That nevertheless, the unconstitutionality attributed to Art. 559 is not based on the reason that it does not belong in a code, but that it violates the provisions of the Constitution already mentioned.

39. That the respondent emphasizes that 'the great innovation of the Constitution of 1980 consists in the rule that the act, regulated by law, of canceling the juristic personality of a corporation or foundation is subject to judicial review, if it is arbitrary or illegal, in conformity with Art. 20 of the Fundamental Charter', whereas 'in the Constitution of 1925 the act of cancellation was not reviewable'.

40. That while the constitutional innovation referred to is beyond doubt, it does not exclude the recourse of inapplicability for unconstitutionality, because when in it the inapplicability of a provision is declared, the illegality of which serves as basis for an interposed recourse of protection, it necessarily and mandatorily must be entertained provided the other prerequisites are met.

41. That, likewise the declaration of inapplicability is not valid — pursuant to the mandate of Art. 80 of the Constitution — in any proceeding, separate from the recourse of protection, which is pending in any other tribunal with respect to its adjudication.

* * *

43. That Art. 23 of the Chilean Political Code [i.e. The Political Constitution] provides that 'the intermediate community groups and their directors which have misused the autonomy which the Constitution accords them by unduly intervening in activities outside their particular purposes, are subject to sanction in accordance with law.'

* * *

45. That it is obvious that in order to determine the constitutionality of the law which determines the authority which imposes the sanction mentioned in this provision, that law must be in conformity with the guiding principles of the rule of law [*Estado de Derecho*] to which in this case Art. 23 of the Fundamental Charter belongs, which, as has been pointed out, peremptorily, provides that the power to hear civil and criminal cases, to adjudicate them and to have the judgments executed, belongs exclusively to the courts established by law.

46. That the power to impose sanctions which is vested in the Public Administration is only legal provided no constitutional provision makes another grant and in no case, even under the pretext of extraordinary circumstances, can it extend to 'the power to hear civil and criminal cases, to adjudicate them and have the judgment executed' which 'belongs exclusively to the courts established by law.' Any act contravening the exclusivity solemnly established by Art. 73 of the Constitution is void. Thus is provided, in addition to other provisions in the chapter on the Institutional Bases, by its Art. 7. The general and special powers which Art. 24 and Art. 32 of the Fundamental Charter grant to the President of the Republic do not — and cannot — confer to him a judicial power which would invest him with the authority to cancel a juristic personality and to dissolve a corporation, which because of its judicial nature is not comprised in the governmental and administrative powers of the Executive

which must be exercised according to the Constitution and the laws as Art. 24 of the National Political Code mandates.

47. That the foregoing reflections force us to conclude that in the recourse of protection, interposed by the Corporation 'Sociedad Benefactora y Educacional Dignidad' before the Court of Appeals of Santiago against the Minister of Justice Mr Francisco Cumplido Cereceda and in which it is petitioned that the Decree of the Minister of Justice Nr. 143 of January 31, 1991 be deemed to be without effect and annulled, the following provisions are inapplicable because they are contrary to the Constitution: Art. 559(2) of the Civil Code to the extent that it prescribes that corporations may be dissolved by the authority which legitimized their existence; together with Art. 546 of the same body of laws to the extent that it prescribes, in the opposite sense, that juristic persons are the corporations which have been approved by the President of the Republic, and Art. 561 of that Code, to the extent that it is within the power of the President to indicate the objects in which the properties must be employed which, because of the dissolution of a corporation belonging to the state if in their charter there is no provision for the manner of their disposition.

* * *

So decided against the votes of Justices Dávila, Toro, Perales and Carrasco who were of the opinion that the recourse of inapplicability should be rejected.

[Seven justices voted for the grant: Justices Retamal, Jordán, Zurita, Béraud, Araya, Valenzuela and Alvarez.]

NOTES

1. The decision was greeted with enthusiasm by Professor Soto, who compared its authors with the legendary Prussian judges who defended the property rights of the owner of a windmill at Potsdam against King Frederick II, who wished to destroy it because it disturbed the view from his castle at Potsdam. (Eduardo Soto Kloss, 'Comentario' in 89 *Rev. de Der. y Jurispr. y Gac. Trib.* 284 (1992).)

The actual Miller Arnold case involved another mill in Prussia and culminated in the King's interference with the administration of justice by ordering the imprisonment of the judges on the highest court who had considered it their duty to rule against Arnold and in favor of the owner of the water supply. See M. Diesselhorst, *Die Prozesse des Müllers Arnold und das Eingreifen Friedrichs des Grossen* (1984) and infra p. 183.

2. The text case constitutes one of the recent judgments which illustrate that the change in the membership of the Court resulted in an extension of the recourse of inapplicability because of unconstitutionality to cases of 'supervening unconstitutionality.' Actually this switch originated in the 8:4 Judgment of June 8, 1990, in the Case of *Mrs. N. Campos Canales*, challenging the constitutionality of Decree Law 2.695 of 1979 (87 *Rev. de Der. y Jurispr. y Gac. Trib.* V 86 (1990)) and was confirmed

by the Supreme Court by a vote of 9:4 in the case of *Insunza Bascuñán*, Corte Suprema Judgment of August 24, 1990, involving the unconstitutionality of D.L. 2191 of 1977, granting amnesty. (87 *Rev. de Der. y Jurispr. y Gac. Trib.* IV 64 (1990).)

Other cases endorsing the new rule are e.g. *Puga González*, Corte Suprema Judgment of April 10, 1992 (11:4) (89 *Rev. de Der. y Jurispr. y Gac. Trib.* V 35 (1992)); *Vera Bascur*, Corte Suprema Judgment of October 31, 1991 (vote 10:3) (88 *Rev. de Der. y Jurispr. y Gac. Trib.* V 263 (1992).)

3. Another bone of contention among the judges of the Chilean Supreme Court involves the question whether a law can be declared to be inapplicable in toto or whether the declaration of inapplicability must be confined to specific provisions. *Vargas Figueroa*, Corte Suprema Judgment of July 26, 1992, held that the Court cannot declare globally that a law is inapplicable. (89 *Rev. de Der. y Jurispr. y Gac. Trib.* V 169 (1992).)

Contra, Puga González, Corte Suprema Judgment of April 10, 1992 (10:5) (89 *Rev. de Der. y Jurispr. y Gac. Trib.* V 35 (1992)) and *Cardone La Rosa*, Corte Suprema Judgment of April 24, 1992. (89 *Rev. de Der. y Jurispr. y Gac. Trib.* V 36 (1992) note.)

2/Sources of Law

A. LEGISLATIVE AND EXECUTIVE SOURCES OF LAW

Under most constitutions, not all generally applicable rules of law emanate solely from the legislature, i.e. the body charged principally with the law-making function. Rule-making power may also be vested in the executive by the constitution itself or by statute. Such non-legislative rules are usually designated by a special name.

1. In the *United States,* rule-making powers may be exercised in the form of regulations either by the executive departments or by independent regulatory agencies such as the Interstate Commerce Commission, the Federal Trade Commission or the International Trade Commission. The regulations are published in the Federal Register and collected in the Code of Federal Regulations.

2. In *England and Wales* statutes frequently delegate rule-making powers to the crown to be exercised by Orders-in-Council. They are promulgated in a separate official collection, called Statutory Instruments (S.I.) as orders by the Crown with advice from the Privy Council, which is composed of members of the House of Lords.

3. In *France* the Constitution fixes a number of subjects that require a parliamentary act (Art. 34 Const.). Other matters can be regulated by government regulation in form of decrees to be promulgated upon advice of one of the administrative sections of the Council of State (Art. 37 Const.). In addition, the legislature can delegate to the government the power and duty to implement a statute by decree upon advice of the Council of State (Art. 21 Const.). Finally the government, upon authorization by the Parliament, might provisionally enact rules of general application in form of acts called *ordinances.* These enactments take the place of measures that formerly were called decree-laws. Decrees, deliberated by the Council of Ministers, and ordinances require the signature of the President (Art. 13 Const.).

4. In *Italy,* the Constitution distinguishes between parliamentary laws, decrees having the force of laws, and other normative acts, called *regolamenti,* (Const. Art. 87 (5). Decrees having the force of laws are either decree-laws (*decreti legge*) or legislative decrees (*decreti legislativi*). Legislative decrees are issued by the Government upon

delegation to it of legislative power by the Parliament, subject to specific indication of the governing principles and criteria (Const., Art. 76). Decree-laws can be issued in emergencies without delegation. They lose their validity unless they are converted into law within 60 days.

As a consequence of this arrangement, there exist in Italy several types of normative acts called decrees, i.e. two types of decrees having the force of law and other types without such force, in particular decrees of the President of the Republic, decrees of the President of the Council of Ministers and ministerial decrees (*decreti del Presidente delle Republica, decreti del Presidente del Consiglio dei Ministri,* and *decreti ministeriali*). All five types are published in the *Gazetta ufficiale.* They are abreviated (i) D.L., (ii) D. Leg., (iii) D.P.R., (iv) D.P.C.M. and (v) D.M.

Details are regulated by the law of August 23, 1988 n. 400, governing the activity of the Government and providing the rules of the presidency of the Council of Ministers, Arts. 14, 15 and 17 (*Le Leggi,* 1988 p. 1942) and (by the decree of the President of the Republic of December 28, 1985 n. 1092) approving the consolidated text of the provisions governing the promulgation of statutes, and the issuance of decrees of the President of the Republic and the official publications of the Italian Republic (*Le Leggi,* 1986, p. 1981).

5. *Germany* likewise distinguishes between parliamentary and governmental rule-making. Normative acts of general applicability emanating from the government are called *Rechtsverordnungen* (legal ordinances). They require authorization by law which defines the content, purpose and scope of the delegation. The federal council (*Bundesrat*) must give its consent in the cases where a law would require such consent. The addressee of the delegation may either be the federal government or a particular minister. (Basic Law [GG] Art. 80.)

B. LAWS OF DIFFERENT STATUS

A number of constitutions provide for the possibility of amending them by legislation, adopted by a special majority or procedure and subject to specified limitations. Such provisions exist, e.g., in the German Basic Law (Art. 79), the French Constitution (Art. 89), and the Italian Constitution (Art. 138). Sometimes such amending laws are called constitutional laws.

A number of constitutions, in addition, distinguish between ordinary laws and laws of higher rank. The French Constitution, which apparently initiated that distinction, identified a number of subjects which must be governed by so-called organic laws (*loi organique*). Usually that is the case when the organization and functioning of governmental authorities, like the judiciary or branches of the legislature are concerned, (see e.g. Constitution, Arts. 25, 27, 63, 64, 65 and 71.) In adopting organic law, the legislative procedure must follow particular safeguards. (Const. Art. 46.)

Constitutional amendments made by a constitutional law may require implementation by one or more organic laws. A good example is furnished by the recent amendments of the French Constitution in 1993. The constitutional law nr. 93-952 of July 22, 1993 amended title VIII and titles IX-XV of the Constitution by revising Art. 65 and inserting a new title X, consisting of Arts. 68-1 and 68-2 in the text. Article 65 improved the independence of the judiciary, Art. 68-1 and 68-2 imposed criminal responsibility on the members of the government and established a new Court of Justice of the Republic for that purpose. Both sections of the law required implementation by an organic law. For the text of the constitutional law see *Actualité Législatif Dalloz* (ALD), 1993, 442.

The organic law on the Court of Justice of the Republic was adopted on 23.11.1993. See organic law 93-1252, ALD 1993, 542. Organic laws required by Const. Art. 65 as amended were adopted as Organic laws nrs. 94-100 and 94-101 of 5.2.1994, ALD 1994, 177 and 178. Organic law nr. 94-100 in turn was implemented by a decree upon advice by the Council of State, Decree 94-199 of 9.3.1994, ALD 1994 p. 224.

Other recent constitutions in Latin-American countries followed the French example and envisage laws of different rank.

C. CODES AND CODIFICATION

A code may be defined as a comprehensive systematic arrangement of the legal rules governing a major branch of the law as contrasted with a legal order consisting of judicial or customary rules, interspersed with occasional legal enactments with limited scope. If that view is accepted, the practice of enacting codes must be deemed to have a rather recent date of origin.

Actually, the practice of reducing customary rules to writing and in the process thereof of modernizing them reaches back to the end of the fifteenth century. Thus, King Charles VII of France ordered the written redaction of all territorial customs of France in Art. 125 of the *Ordonnance de Montil-les-Tours* of 1454 and Emperor Charles V took a similar step with respect to the seventeen provinces of the Netherlands in the so-called *Perpetual Edict* of 1531, a measure which was repeated by his successors, Isabella and Albert, in 1611.

The German cities which had acquired the power of self-government compiled and modernized their ordinances and customs beginning with the end of the fifteenth century, see especially the *Reformation of Nuremberg* of 1479/1484 and the *Renewed Reformation* of 1564 and the redaction of the laws of the City of Lubeck of 1586.

In Spain official compilations of the laws were likewise undertaken during the sixteenth century such as the '*recopilaciónes*' of the laws of the United Kingdoms of Aragon and Castilia, e.g. the *Recopilación* of 1567 and the *Nueva Recopilación* of 1775.

In Italy the division into city-states, such as Venice and Genova, and a number of kingdoms and duchies, i.e. Naples and Sicily, Sardinia, Milan, Toscany, Parma, Piedmont and Savoy, Modena, and the Church-State, caused the redaction of official or private compilations of the existing laws or even codification, as e.g. the *Code of the Duchy of Modena* of 1771.

During the reign of Louis XIV of France important subjects of commercial and maritime law were codified in the Ordonnances of 1673 and 1681 (*Ordonnance du Commerce and Ordonnance de la Marine*).

In the American colonies and early states, the local laws were subject to frequent revisions, starting with the Book of the *General Laws and Liberties of the Massachusetts Bay Colony* of 1648 and culminating in the New York, *Revised Statutes* of 1829.

One of the early comprehensive codifications in Europe (following the codes of Bavaria of 1756 and of Modena of 1771) was the *General Code of Laws for the Prussian States* of 1794. It was the fruit of an effort to regulate all fields of law, except procedure, in great detail and was primarily the work of a public official, named Carl Gottlieb Suarez. Because it reflected the social order of the absolute monarchy many parts of it were rather short-lived.

As the result of the French revolution, it was in France where codes of a general and succinct character were framed on the basis of notions developed by scholars before that time during the Consulate and the early Empire. They were the *Code Civil* of 21 March 1804, the *Code de Procédure Civile* of April 1806, the *Code de Commerce* of September 1807, the *Code d'instruction criminelle* of November 1808 and the *Code pénal* of February 1810. The *Code Civil* was the most famous among them. Its preparation reached back to the year 1790 and was in its final form the work of a committee of three (consisting of Misters Tronchet, Bigot and Portalis) under personal participation of the First Consul N. Bonaparte.

The *Code Civil* and the *Code de Commerce* became applicable in countries other than France, in part because they were enacted by France under the rule of Napoleon and in part because they were placed under the rule of members of Napoleon's family. The codes, however, inspired codification elsewhere, in other European countries as well as in South America.

Without retracing the spread of codification in detail, it should be noted that Austria in 1811, i.e. soon after the Napoleonic Codes, enacted a Civil Code of its own, the *General Civil Code* (*ABGB*) for the Austrian Empire. It was much more concise and limited in scope than its older Prussian counterpart.

Spain, after the end of the reign of Joseph Bonaparte, retained the idea of modern codes applicable throughout the country. In contrast to the Napoleonic legislation, Spain codified its commercial laws, relying on the *Ordenanzas de Bilbao* of 1737 (an important Spanish compilation of commercial laws) as well as on the French Code of Commerce as models, as early as 1829, whereas the promulgation of a Civil Code had to wait until 1889. The enactment of the *Código mercantil* of 1829 was accompanied by the law on mercantile proceedings of 1830 which was followed considerably later by the law on civil proceedings in 1855. In 1881 a unified code of civil procedure replaced both prior procedural enactments. In 1885 a new commercial code was enacted to dove-tail with the contemporary civil code.

In Germany, where, in addition to Prussia, the Grand Duchy of Bavaria had enacted a triad of codes between 1751 and 1756 (the *Codices Maximilianei*), efforts to enact modern codes remained for the most part unsuccessful, although practically all major states, especially Bavaria and Württemberg produced interesting drafts which attracted attention even abroad. (Bavarian project of 1861/1864; Württemberg, 1847). Only Saxony succeeded in enacting a new civil code in 1863.

The first German Code, adopted by nearly all German states, including Austria and Prussia, was the *General German Commercial Code* of 1861. It was the work of a commission that had been appointed in 1857 by the German Confederation (*Deutscher Bund*) which was the successor of the Holy Roman Empire after its dissolution in 1803. It took the establishment of the German Empire in 1871 to render it possible to enact codes applicable in the whole of Germany. Codes governing criminal law, criminal procedure, commercial law and civil procedure were adopted in due course. The crowning achievement was the creation of the *Civil Code* (*BGB*) which entered into force on January 1, 1900.

Switzerland codified the law of obligations in 1881 and adopted a civil code in 1907, followed by a revision of the Code of Obligations in 1911. Italy adopted four codes of 1942, consolidating civil and commercial law. The most recent European civil code is that of the Netherlands. It was enacted in 3 installments and is still incomplete. The most important portion entered into force on January 1, 1992.

The quest for codes spread to Latin America after its independence from Portugal and Spain. The South American codes are to a large extent the work of famous native jurists who used contemporary European codes and drafts as models, but also relied on the works of European academic writers. In Brazil codification is tied to the names of Augusto Teixeira de Freitas and Clóvis Beviláqua, in Argentina and Uruguay to those of Dalmacio Vélez Sársfield and Eduardo Acevedo, and in Chile to the famous jurist Andrés Bello. Thus Brazil adopted a commercial code in 1850, long before the end of the imperial government in 1889, but had to delay the enactment of a civil code (the work of Clovis Beviláqua) until 1916. In Argentina the commercial code, drafted by Acevedo and Vélez Sársfield, was promulgated as national law in 1862, while the adoption of the civil code, the work of Vélez Sársfield alone, occurred in 1869.

The Chilean civil code, the opus magnum of Bello, dated from 1855, the commercial code from 1865. The other states of Latin America (Bolivia, Colombia, Equador, Paraguay, Peru and Venezuela) adopted codes either borrowed or based on those of Argentina and Chile. Since the civil code of Brazil was adopted after the German Civil Code, it was influenced heavily by the latter, in addition to that of Portugal. Peru's civil code of 1936 likewise showed Swiss and German influences.

In Mexico commercial codes of nationwide application were enacted in 1854 (the so-called *Código Lares* 1885 and 1889.) The latter, although superseded by many special laws, is still in force. Mexico also enacted civil codes in 1870, in 1884 and in 1928. These codes applied proprio vigore; however, only in areas under federal jurisdiction. Thus, the code of 1928, in force since 1932, applies only in the Federal District and Territories and nationwide to the extent that federal questions are involved.

The codification movement, stimulated by the English philosopher Jeremy Bentham and the Italian author Count Filangieri, was itself a product of comparative law and, in turn, stimulated further studies in comparative law and legislation.

Experience has shown that the lifespan of comprehensive codes is limited and that they necessitate either constant tampering by the legislature or active judicial legislation (*Rechtsfortbildung*) by the courts. Nevertheless, the codification ardor in many countries has not subsided. Apart from extensive amendments of the respective codes, total revisions are still undertaken. Thus, Paraguay in 1985 completed and enacted a brand new *Código Civil* which, following the Italian model, consolidated civil and commercial law and repealed both the previous Civil Code and the Commercial Code, except its last book dealing with maritime commerce.

The Netherlands. The prime example of a recent comprehensive codification of private law is the new Civil Code of the Netherlands. It consists of nine books, numbered 1-7, 7A and 8. Instead of having a separate book called 'General Part', as in the German Civil Code, it distributes the subject matter as follows: Book 1: Law of Persons and Family Law; Book 2: Juristic Persons; Book 3: Property Rights in General (Patrimonial Law); Book 4: Inheritance Law; Book 5: Law of Things (Law of Property); Book 6: General Part of the Law of Obligations; Book 7: Special Contracts; Book 7A: Special Contracts; Book 8: Means of Transportation. The Code was enacted successively, commencing in 1958 with Book 1 (in force on 1.1.1970). A revised text of Books 3, 5 and 6 was published in 1991 and is governing in that form as of 1.1.1992 (Stb. 1991 No. 600). The original author of the project of the Code was the celebrated Dutch jurist E.M. Meijers, but in the course of the legislative debates many of his views were either not adopted or greatly modified.

Finally, it should be noted that the establishment of a single European Market and the resulting harmonization efforts of the European Community has caused a renewed invigoration of comparative legal studies.

NOTES

1. The most important presentation of the codifications in Europe are the articles on *Kodifikation* and *Gesetzgebung* by Ranieri, Scholz, Holthöfer, Döllmeyer and others in H. Coing, ed. *Handbuch der Quellen und Literatur der Neuen Europäischen Privatrechtsgeschichte* Vol. III, Parts 1 and 2 (1982). G. Drago, *Lois: de la codification à l'évolution: Premiers commentaires de la circulaire de 30 mai 1996 et de la loi no. 96-516 du 14 juin 1996* 70 J.C.P. 3953 (1996) discusses recent attempts to codify the increasing volume of French legislation.

For the codification in Latin America, see H. Valladao, *Historia do Direito, Especialmente do Direito Brasileiro* (1972), and R. Segal, M. Pinto and C.E. Colautti, 'Aperçu sur les systèmes juridiques de l'Amérique du Sud', 65 *Revue de Droit International et de Droit Comparé* 105 (1988).

2. In Prussia, codification culminated in the enactment of the Prussian Allgemeine Landrecht (ALR) of 1794. G. Dilcher, 'Die janusköpfige Kodifikation — Das preussische ALR 1794', 3 ZEITSCHRIFT FÜR EUROPÄISCHES PRIVATRECHT [EuP] 446 (1994) discusses its social and intellectual background, the Miller Arnold

'catastrophe of justice' (discussed *supra* p. 174) and its impetus to the Royal Order of 1780 establishing the codification commission consisting of von Carmer, Suarez and Klein, its structure and effect as a code and, last but not least, its impact on the emerging discipline of comparative law.

3. The central figures in the codification movement in America were Joseph Story and David Dudley Field, discussed in Charles M. Cook, The American Codification Movement, A study of Antebellum Legal Reform (1981). Story publicly dealt with the feasibility and possible advantages of a codification of law in the United States on at least two occasions. Around 1830, Story contributed an unsigned article on 'Law, Legislation and Codes' to Francis Lieber's *Encyclopedia Americana,* in which he expressed an opinion favoring 'judicious codification' of some branches of the common law such as commercial law. His article is reprinted in J. McClellan, *Joseph Story and the American Constitution* (1971) 356-72.

In 1836, Massachusetts appointed a Commission to Consider and Report upon the Practicability and Expediency of Reducing to a Written and Systematic Code the Common Law of Massachusetts, consisting of Story, Greenleaf, Metcalf, Forbes and Cushing, all outstanding lawyers of the Commonwealth. The Commission submitted its report, authored by Story, early in 1837 again favoring codification of limited areas of the common law. The report is reprinted in *Miscellaneous Writings of Joseph Story,* ed. William W. Story 698-734 (1852). For the role of Story in the codification debate, see also McClellan *op. cit.* 89-98.

On David Dudley Field and his codification achievements, see Cook *op. cit.* 185-200. On February 29, 1948, the Commissioners on Practice and Pleadings, Loomis, Grasham and Field, submitted the Draft of a Code of Procedure, which was enacted with certain amendments on April 12, 1848 as An Act to Simplify and Abridge the Practice, Pleadings and Proceedings of the Courts of the State. It was amended on April 11, 1848, after having been officially designated as the Code of Procedure. Although other codes drafted by Field failed in his home state, California adopted both the Code of Procedure and the Civil Code in 1872.

3/Applicability of Foreign Law

A. GERMANY

1. Pledge under English law:

Court of Appeal Koblenz
Judgment of February 5, 1993
The Emerald Necklace Case
Recht der Internationalen Wirtschaft [RIW] 502 (1993)

Plaintiff, an English national, sues the German defendant for the return of an emerald necklace. He claims to have a security interest in the necklace which he left with the defendant to be sold for his account, but which or the proceeds of which he did not receive back. The underlying facts are as follows: Defendant maintained business relations with C., a jeweller who operated the C. Ltd. in London. Plaintiff also was acquainted with C. and an occasional customer of C. In September 1982 C. deposited the contested necklace which belonged to C. as well as other jewelry, among it a YGG set which defendant had sold to C. with a retention of title clause, with T. Bank as security for a loan. In October 1982 defendant held claims against C. in the amount of DM 536, 599.77. Early in 1983 plaintiff made a loan to C. totalling £150,000 of which the amount of £100,000 was to be used to obtain the release of the deposited pieces of jewelry. C. obtained the release of the jewelry and handed it soon thereafter over to plaintiff who brought it to his house. Shortly prior thereto the property of the firm C. Ltd. was placed under voluntary liquidation. The defendant filed his claim for DM 536,599.77. On February 16, 1993 defendant dispatched his manager Sch. and an employee T. to London in order to collect his claim from C. and to secure the goods which he had delivered with a reservation of title. C. induced Sch. and T. to visit plaintiff together with him in plaintiff's house that was one hour distant from London. There Sch. and T., in the presence of C.'s wife, obtained not only the YGG set in which defendant had reserved title, but also the set belonging to C. which is the object of this litigation. The reason for that transaction and the negotiations accompanying it are disputed. The parties agreed upon an alteration of the necklace to facilitate its sale. Towards the end of 1983 defendant gave the jewelry to C. to take it to London to show it to customers. Since it was not sold, C. returned it to defendant. In November 1983 plaintiff demanded return of the set. Defendant refused, claiming that he had acquired property thereon as security for his claim against C.

The district court dismissed the complaint. On appeal plaintiff prevailed.

REASONS

The complaint, international jurisdiction over which is vested in the seized district court Bad K., is well founded. Plaintiff has a security interest in the jewelry. The defendant is obliged to release the property. He did not acquire ownership.

Plaintiff, pursuant to the applicable English law became a pledgee of the jewelry after its release by the bank and its surrender to him, a right which he did not lose either by virtue of the transfer to the witnesses Sch. and T. on February 16, 1983 or pursuant to bona fide acquisition of ownership by defendant. Rather, the evidence shows that plaintiff surrendered the jewels to Sch. and T. to have them sold and to use the proceeds to pay off the £150,000 loan of plaintiff to C. By not accounting for the proceeds from a sale or returning the objects to plaintiff, defendant impaired plaintiff's rights under the pledge. Defendant therefore is obliged, pursuant to German law which in that respect, by virtue of a change in applicable law, governs, to return the jewels to plaintiff (BGB §§ 1227, 985 BGB).

I.

1. Whether plaintiff towards the end of January 1983, when inter alia the jewelry in issue was turned over to him by C. after its release by the Bank, acquired the right of a pledge, is to be decided according to English law.

According to German conflicts rules (International Private Law) which determine the applicable law, the creation of rights in things depends on the law of the place where the thing is located (*lex rei sitae*). That place was England where the jewelry in issue was located when it was turned over to plaintiff, i.e. London. Therefore, the law of England governs, whereas other laws of Great Britain are inapplicable as the Max-Planck-Institute explains in its legal expert opinion.

2. According to English common law — statutory provisions of England applicable to pledges are not relevant to this case according to the opinion of the Max-Planck-Institute — the effective grant of a pledge depends on two factors, viz. an agreement between pledgor and pledgee, that a chattel shall be pledged to secure an

obligation and, additionally, a transfer of possession of the chattel to the pledgee. This too is convincingly shown with authorities by the legal opinion of the Max-Planck-Institute. (Cf. Kessel, RIW 1991, 812, 813).

In this case witness C. handed, inter alia, the jewelry in issue over to plaintiff after its release by the Bank and thus vested its possession in plaintiff. Plaintiff thereafter took the jewelry to his home. No longer controverted but substantiated and proven is also that plaintiff, in connection with the turnover of the jewelry, granted C. a loan of £150,000, £100,000 of which were used for the release of these and other pieces of jewelry by the Bank.

Whether — moreover — witness C. transferred the jewelry which had been deposited to plaintiff as security for the loan and whether there was an agreement to that effect between C. and plaintiff is to be proven by plaintiff.

The allocation of the burden of proof, according to established jurisprudence of the English courts and text writings, is determined by the substantive law which applies pursuant to the rules of international private law, consequently in this case the English law. This flows from the close connection between the allocation of proof and the substantive law (3 BGHZ 342 (1951); BGH 13 NJW 1960, 774, 775 (1960); 42 BGHZ 385 (1965); Celle RIW 1988, 137). As the legal opinion of the Max-Planck-Institute shows and substantiates, English law imposes on plaintiff the burden of proof that he obtained possession of the jewelry as security for the loan granted to C. The question whether plaintiff has met the burden of proof, i.e. the question of the quantum of proof, however, is determined by the lex fori, i.e. German law (§ 286 Z.P.O.), see Schack, Internationales Zivilverfahrensrecht, 1991, par. 694 ff.).

This proof has been made by plaintiff. * * *

II.

This right as pledgee — and therefore the right to sell the chattel — has not been lost by plaintiff when he permitted handing the jewelry to witness Sch. and T.

The question whether plaintiff lost his right as pledgee by reason of the turnover of the jewelry to Sch. and T. is likewise to be determined by the law of the place where the chattel is located at that time. At that time the jewelry was still in England. The conflict rules of England subject the totality of the rights in a chattel, i.e. also their loss, to the law of the place of location. Hence no question of renvoi arises, as the opinion of the Max-Planck-Institute shows. Accordingly, English law controls.

According to English law a pledge is normally extinguished if the object is returned to the pledgor. But under English law the pledge is not extinguished if the chattel is returned for a purpose which is compatible with the pledge. Moreover, a pledge is not extinguished when the pledgor obtains return of the pledged chattel by means of fraud, as the opinion of the Max-Planck-Institute demonstrates by reference to the case-law of the English courts and the uniform opinion of the literature. In the case at bar the view of C. who was subject to the pledge is controlling, as the Max-Planck-Institute's expert opinion demonstrates.

Consequently, not the restoration of the possession per se, but its purpose controls. Even if plaintiff was deceived by C. about the purpose of the release of the jewelry, he did not lose his pledgee's rights merely by reason of the return of the chattel without the need of an avoidance of the act of the return.

* * *

The Senate deems it to be proven (Z.P.O. § 286) that witness C. deceived plaintiff about the purpose of the return of the jewelry. Hence plaintiff did not lose his rights in the jewelry according to English law.

III

Defendant did not acquire unencumbered ownership in the set as a bona fide purchaser because Sch. and T. informed him that he was free to sell the jewelry in issue to recover his claims against the Firm C.

1. Whether plaintiff lost his pledgee's interests because defendant acquired bona fide unencumbered ownership of the set, depends on the location where the jewelry was located at the time when a bona fide acquisition free of encumbrance was possible (law of the location).

For that question it is material whether the acquisition transaction relating to the set which might have entailed a change in the legal relations was or was not perfected in England (cf. Palandt/Heldrich, BGB 52 ed. 1993, Appendix II to Art. 38 EGBGB, Note 7; Ferid, IPR 3d ed. 1986 notes 7-55 and 7-61). If the possible acquisition was completed in England on February 16, 1983, then it is only the English law which governs the question whether defendant acquired bona fide unencumbered ownership in the set and is permitted to keep it. On the other hand, if the acquisition transaction was only perfected in Germany — by delivery of the jewelry to the plaintiff — then a so-called change of applicable law (status-change) occurs and the decision whether defendant acquired bona fide unencumbered ownership of the set must be made on the exclusive basis of the law of the Federal Republic.

Whether the witnesses Sch. and T. received the jewelry in the capacity as messengers — as the district court thinks — or as representatives of defendant, is determined by English law. Decisive in that respect is the law of the place where the individual is to act (law governing powers of attorney). This, from defendant's perspective, was London. There the two witnesses were to collect money for defendant or to retrieve the merchandise.

According to English law, the witnesses Sch. and T. acted as representatives of the defendant, as the Max-Planck-Institute and Barrister Russell both explain in agreement. They carried the defendant's firm stamp along with them and Sch. receipted for the defendant the surrender of the pieces of jewelry.

At any rate they acquired the possession of the set with the consent and on account of the defendant when already in England. Accordingly, a bona fide unencumbered acquisition of the property by the defendant would have been perfected in

England, with the result that the question of such an acquisition is likewise to be decided according to English law. The fact that the final delivery to defendant occurred only in Germany is therefore in that respect without significance.

2. According to English law defendant did not acquire bona fide unencumbered ownership in the jewelry, despite the fact that witnesses Sch. and T. when delivering the jewelry told him that he was free to utilize the jewelry to recover his claims against Firm C. — which must be accepted as true as has been shown before.

As has been discussed and substantiated in the legal opinion of the Max-Planck-Institute, English law, on principle, does not enable anyone to transfer more rights than he has. C., therefore, when he handed over the jewelry to witnesses Sch. and T. on February 16, 1983 could only transfer ownership subject to the pledge to plaintiff.

This principle, to be sure, is subject to exceptions, the prerequisites of which, however, in the case at bar are not met.

A bona fide purchase of defendant, pursuant to the Sale of Goods Act 1979, is not involved, above all because C. from his and defendant's perspective wished to take care not of his own debts, but the debts of the Firm C. with the result that English law qualifies the surrender of his set as a gift. English law, however, does not recognize a bona fide acquisition by a donee, as the Max-Planck-Institute's legal opinion discusses in detail.

A bona fide acquisition by defendant pursuant to s. 2 of the Factors Act, which protects the good faith in the power of representation and disposition of a commercial agent, likewise is not in question because C. acted vis-à-vis the witnesses Sch. and T. in his own name and not as agent of the co-proprietor plaintiff.

Finally, as the Institute explains, the instant case does not indicate any reasons for a good faith acquisition according to the principles of estoppel, which permit a party to rely on a situation similar to notions derived under § 242 BGB with respect to security of transactions. * * *

This signifies in the result that plaintiff has not lost his rights as pledgee of the jewelry and therefore his rights to dispose of them due to a bona fide unencumbered acquisition of ownership by defendant.

IV

This leads to the result that according to the applicable German law the defendant is obliged to relinquish the jewelry in issue to plaintiff.

The bringing of the jewelry to J. in Germany caused the plaintiff's claim for restoration to be subject to German law as the law of location. German law takes over the rights in a chattel in the form in which they are created by the foreign law. (Cf. Palandt/Heldrich, op. cit. Appendix II to Art. 38 EGBGB, note 6). That means that the jewelry remains encumbered by the pledge to the plaintiff and his right to realization.

Defendant therefore is obliged to restore the jewelry pursuant to §§ 1227, 985 BGB.

NOTE

BGH, Judgment of May 9, 1996. Another example of a change in the applicable law governing transfer of title resulting from a trans-border transport of movables is a case adjudicated by the BGH in its Judgment of May 9, 1996.[1] In that case, plaintiff, an English corporation, brought an action for conversion against a German trustee in bankruptcy, alleging that the trustee had sold and transferred certain property belonging to it, situated in the bankrupt's warehouse as a result of a complex sequence of events.

The property consisted of two not yet fully completed, reconditioned bottling machines. These reconditioned machines were composed of parts of two bottling machines which originally had been purchased by the plaintiff from the bankrupt on account of U.D., an English end-user. The machines did not function properly and plaintiff and debtor agreed to substitute two other properly functioning machines. U.D. returned the malfunctioning machines to the debtor who disassembled them and stored the parts in its warehouse. In 1991 plaintiff and debtor agreed that the parts should be reassembled and resold to plaintiff as reconditioned machines for the price of DM 110,000 each. This agreement was reduced to a memorandum which specified the terms of the agreement, inter alia that certain specifications would be supplied subsequently and that the reconditioned machines should be kept in the storage of the debtor. Plaintiff paid an advance of DM 55,000 for each machine. The memo was confirmed by a letter of November 26, 1991 by debtor. On November 2, 1992, debtor was adjudicated bankrupt and the trustee sold the machines to a third party which took possession on December 31, 1992, after plaintiff had claimed possession of the machines on December 8, 1992.

The court of first instance and the court of appeal rendered judgment for the plaintiff, but on petition for review the Supreme Court of Germany (BGH) reversed and remanded. Defendant argued that the debtor had reacquired the property in the parts and not retransferred it to the plaintiff, while the appellate court concluded that plaintiff was owner of the re-conditioned machines at the time when they were delivered to the third party purchaser.

The Supreme Court held that the appellate court had failed to analyze the sequence of events without contradictions. According to the opinion of the Supreme Court, the court of appeal had correctly concluded that the various transactions should be evaluated on the basis of German law, which differs from English law in the definition of property.

But it criticized the court below because its opinion had left it unclear whether plaintiff had acquired the property in the defective machines from its customer U.D. and retained it thereafter, or whether the ownership had reverted to the bankrupt and

1. 50 WM 1242 (1996).

thereafter been retransferred to plaintiff or remained the in the ownership of the debtor.

Moreover, the appellate court had failed to clarify where and in what way plaintiff reacquired possession of the machines before their delivery to the third party. Finally, the court below had failed to justify its conclusion that the trustee had acted negligently, since it had not discussed the possibility that plaintiff was only a purchaser under a condition precedent, i.e. full payment of the price.

2. Right to Indemnification for Reclaimed Stolen Property

BGH VIII. Senate
Judgment of April 8, 1987
Firm M.-Z. GmbH v. Land Schleswig — Holstein
100 BGHZ 321 (1987).

Plaintiff, with headquarters in Kiel, is engaged in the trade with collectors' coins. The defendant *Land* is owner of a coin collection from which numerous coins were stolen between 1976 and 1978 and resold. A number of them, by way of intermediate traders, came into the possession of the Schweizerische Bankverein in Zurich. On October 17, 1978 it held an auction (Auction Nr. 4) at which plaintiff, pursuant to an order of its customers, acquired the coins at the highest bid of Sfr. 7150.

Plaintiff received the coins after the fall of the hammer at the end of the auction but returned them to the auctioneer for mailing to the Federal Republic of Germany where they were delivered to plaintiff and transmitted by it to its customers.

By writing of May 11, 1981 defendant *Land* demanded the surrender of the coins from the plaintiff, alternatively information of their whereabouts. Additionally the writing stated under IV, inter alia;

> 'The law governing the legal situation is principally the same both in Germany and Switzerland: Regardless of whether German or Swiss law applies to the acquisition of ownership, even a bona fide purchaser is not able to acquire ownership on the lost coins. However, to the extent that Swiss law applies — and this is true for all coins acquired at Auction 4 of the Schweizerische Bankverein — all successors have acquired a right to indemnification (the so-called *Lösungsrecht*) for the purchaser's price paid according to Art. 934 par. 2 of the Swiss Civil Code [ZGB]. This means that you too are obligated to return the coins only upon reimbursement of the purchase money paid by yourself. Since the *Land* is primarily interested in the restitution of the coins to the collection, the *Land* is also prepared in principle to redeem the coins which were acquired by you and are subject to a right to indemnification. According to our information, the auction price paid by you to the Schweizerische Bankverein amounted to Sfr. 7150. Of course, the *Land*

will pay that sum to you as soon as you have mailed the coins acquired by you at Auction 4 of the Schweizerische Bankverein to the Bundesbank in Frankfurt a/M in trust for examination and we have received the respective confirmation from the bank.'

Plaintiff replied that it had already resold the coins and that it would endeavor either to disclose the names of the purchasers or to reacquire the coins and deliver them to the defendant. It was, however, necessary to insist on the repayment of the Sfr. 7150 for the 2 pieces acquired in Switzerland. After further correspondence between the parties, which concerned also the duty of defendant *Land* to indemnify plaintiff, the latter reacquired the coins from its customers and mailed them to the Coin Museum of the German Bundesbank for examination. The result confirmed that in all likelihood the coins had been part of defendant's collection. Thereupon they were handed over to the defendant *Land*.

Plaintiff demanded from defendant *Land* payment of Sfr. 7150. The district court rendered judgment against defendant *Land* as requested. The appellate court dismissed the complaint. Plaintiff's petition for revision which was admitted was unsuccessful.

REASONS

According to the stipulation between the parties, as interpreted by the appellate court without legal error, defendant's duty to pay depends on the question of whether plaintiff was entitled to claim a right to indemnification pursuant to Art. 934 par. 2 of the Swiss Civil Code (ZGB) at the time when it returned the coins.

Article 934 of the Swiss Civil Code provides:

1. A possessor from whom a chattel is stolen or who loses it or otherwise is deprived of it against his will may demand its return within five years from any recipient.
2. If a chattel is sold at a public auction or in a market or by a merchant who deals in merchandise of the same kind, it can be demanded from the first or any subsequent bona fide purchaser only upon reimbursement of the price paid by him.

The court of appeal set forth that the acquisition of the coins at the auction in Zurich gave rise to a right of indemnification. According to the principles of private international law, transactions relating to the status of chattels are governed by the lex rei sitae, i.e. by the law of that country in which the facts of the acquisition occur. This happened in Switzerland in the case at bar. There plaintiff, following the acceptance of the bid, also obtained possession of the coins. According to the prevailing doctrine which in the opinion of the court of appeal was to be followed, the right to indemnification was discharged if the chattel, after its being brought to another country which does not recognize such a right, is sold there. The rule of international private law that upon a change of the applicable local law (by reason of the transfer of the chattel to the forum) the rights in the chattel continue in their prior form was applicable only to the extent that the pre-existing rights are not in conflict with new legal order. The recognition of a right to indemnity, however, as a type of limited bona fide acquisition of a chattel could not be harmonized with the principles of German law. This mandates as the result of the bona fide purchase from a non-user either the absolute acquisition of title or no acquisition, and thus protects either the property of the owner or the reliance of the purchaser in either case in its totality, a solution which would be circumvented by the recognition of a right to indemnity. In addition, it would conflict with the principle of the *Numerus Clausus* of German property law.

In the present case the point of departure had to be that a disposition of the coins in the Federal Republic of Germany, causing the extinction of the right to the indemnity had taken place. * * *

2. These arguments withstand, in their result, scrutiny by the court of revision. They are binding on this court to the extent that they declare the content of Swiss law (§§549 par.1 and 562 ZPO), but not, however, to the extent that they relate to German private international law.

a. According to German private international law, transactions and relations concerning property are, according to customary law, governed by the lex rei sitae, the law of the location of the property. This signifies that events affecting the legal status of property are adjudged pursuant to the law governing things in the jurisdictions where they are located at the time the event occurs (Judgments of the Senate, March 20, 1963, 39 BGHZ 173, 174 (1963); February 2, 1966, 45 BGHZ 95, 99 (1966), Münch. Komm./Kreuzer, EGBGB App. I, following Article 12 Marg.N.12 ff). According to the findings of the appellate court, which to that extent have not been challenged in the instance of revision, the relevant transfer within the meaning of Art. 934 par. 2 ZGB occurred in Switzerland and therefore resulted initially in the creation of a right to indemnification pursuant to this provision of Swiss law.

b. To be sure, the Supreme Court of the German Empire in a Judgment of March 3, 1898 (41 RGZ 152 (1898)), involving a similar case respecting the right to reimbursement pursuant to Art. 2280 of the French Code Civil, expressed the view that the right to reimbursement arises in all legal systems conferring such a right, arises only upon the claim for the return of the property by the owner. This, standing alone, would have had the consequence that the same local law which governs the right to restoration of the property also decides whether and to what extent a right of retention based on the right of indemnification could be asserted. Therefore, in the case at bar, in which the claim for restoration of the coins was only made subsequent to their transportation to the domain of the German law, the right to reimbursement would not yet have been created and could not arise subsequently, since the German law governing the right of restoration does not accord such a right.

c. The question, whether this court despite §562 ZPO could negate the appellate court's finding that pursuant to Art. 934 par. 2 ZGB, which it correctly held to apply, a right of indemnity had arisen because of the acquisition in Switzerland, need not be resolved. Because even if the appellate court's position that the right to indemnity was acquired when possession of the coins was obtained in Switzerland were accepted, plaintiff nevertheless could no longer claim the right to indemnification at the decisive moment, i.e. the return of the coins.

d. To begin with, it is questionable whether the right to reimbursement — which the appellate court found to have arisen — was extinguished when the coins were brought into the Federal Republic of Germany and, accordingly, under the dominion of German law which does not recognize this kind of right to indemnification. The prevailing view of the literature takes the position that a right to indemnity once it has arisen is not extinguished by a simple change of the applicable lex loci. (Cf. * * * Karrer, Der Fahrniserwerb kraft guten Glaubens im Internationalen Privatrecht, Zurich 1968, p. 84) * * * and Siehr, Das Lösungsrecht des gutgläubigen Käufers im Internationalen Privatrecht, 83 ZVglRW 108 (1984) with further references).

According to the Judgment of this Senate of 20 March 1963 (39 BGHZ 173 (1963)), the legal relations pertaining to a chattel after its removal to the Federal Republic of Germany are, in principle, subject to the provisions of German property law. This, however, accepts the chattel in that legal status that has been attributed to it by the prior law applicable to it, except where this would be totally irreconcilable with the applicable German property law (cf. also Judgment of this Senate 45 BGHZ 95, 97 (1966)).

e. The questions with respect to the right of reimbursement that result from a mere change of the applicable legal order need, however, not be resolved, because the right to reimbursement was at any rate extinguished by the resale of the coins within the territory of the F.R.G.

The question of the survival of the right to indemnification after an alienation of the chattel is to be distinguished from that of its survival after a mere change of the applicable law. According to German international private law, the property law effects of an alienation of a chattel are determined by the lex rei sitae governing the transfer (cf. cases cited above and 45 BGHZ 99 et. seq. (1966)). If, as must be assumed, the coins were resold by plaintiff to its customers after their removal to the Federal Republic, this transfer is subject to German property law as the applicable legal order. Since the possession of the coins had been lost and plaintiff had not acquired title thereto even according to Swiss law governing acquisition of title in Switzerland — §935 par. 2 BGB, which would apply as a matter of private international law, was not complied with because of the lack of a German public auction within the meaning of BGB §383 — the subsequent resale in the F.R.G. is governed by BGB §935 par. 1.

Conversely, this transfer, which occurred in Germany, is not subject to Art. 934 par. 2 ZGB, under which a bona fide recipient of a lost chattel, which one of his predecessors had acquired under the privileged conditions of Art. 934 par. 2 ZGB, obtains in each instance a right to reimbursement of his own, as measured by the price paid by him to his predecessor. (Cf. Staudinger/Stoll EGBGB, Internationales Sachenrecht, 12 ed., Marg. Note 240). Consequently, plaintiff's customers at any rate, could not, have acquired a right to indemnification by reason of the here applicable Art. 934 par. 2 ZGB (Cf Kreuser, loc. cit, Marginal N. 79. * * *)

To be sure, in the literature it is sometimes asserted (following Zitelmann, Internationales Privatrecht, 1912, Vol. 2 p. 251) that a right to indemnification, once acquired, rests on the chattel like an encumbrance, survives as a vested right a change of applicable law, and in the event of a resale passes to the purchaser, even if the law governing the transfer does not recognize the right to indemnification (cf. Siehr, loc. cit. at 113, 118). The comparison with an encumbrance or another right in the chattel which passes to the successor, however, is mistaken, especially with respect to the right of reimbursement according to Swiss law, because that law does not provide for a passage of the right to reimbursement from a prior holder, but for a *new* creation of such right in the person of the successor provided he is bona fide and only in the amount of the price paid by him to his predecessor (cf. Swiss BGE 103 II 186, 189; Karrer, op. cit. p. 85). If thus a derivative acquisition of the right to indemnification is not possible pursuant to the legal system which accords the same, a fortiori it cannot occur under the dominion of the German law to which it is unknown. The creation of a *new* right of indemnification in the person of the purchaser such is provided by Art. 934 par. 2 ZGB is impossible without the cooperation of the legal order which governs the resale. Since plaintiff lost its right to reimbursement which rested on its possession of the coins with the resale to its customers and the latter could not acquire a right to reimbursement under the applicable German law, it follows that the right to reimbursement was extinguished by reason of the resale. To the extent that this result may create a claim of damage reaching back to a foreign seller it must be accepted (Cf Karrer, loc. cit.) * * *

B. FRANCE

1. Cases

a. Société Heinrich Otto v. Mme Guyon

Court of Cassation (Civ.)
Société Heinrich Otto v. Mme Guyon
(*trustee in bankruptcy of Société Carlos Dorget*)
Judgment of January 8, 1991
Bull. Civ. I 6 (1991); D. Jur. 278 (1991).

The Court,

Considering that, according to the statement of the judges on the merits, the German firm Heinrich Otto sold on two occasions in 1985 polyester fibers to the French company Filature et tissage Carlos Dorget; that the sales contracts were subject to German law and reserved to the seller title to the merchandise until full payment of the price and even to the products manufactured after transformation of the materials delivered; that after insolvency proceedings were opened against the Société Carlos Dorget on May 16, 1986, the demand for reclamation by the seller was rejected by the judgment of affirmation under attack (Besançon, June 14, 1989) for the reason that French law does not authorize reclamation of merchandise which is not found in its original state at the debtors.

Upon the first assignment of error, submitted in its 5 branches:

Considering that the court of appeal is reproached for having violated the French rules governing the conflict of laws, Art. 121 of the Law of January 25, 1985 [the Insolvency Act] and the principles of *ordre public* within the meaning of private international law, by having applied, to the detriment of German law, the Law of January 25, 1985, Art. 121, which possesses neither the character of *ordre public,* nor of a rule of public safety, nor of immediate applicability; inasmuch as French law is not applicable whether as bankruptcy law in view of the fact that the requirement of identity in the original state is not an essential aspect of the reclamation against the mass of the creditors [i.e. the bankrupt estate], or as the lex loci of the merchandise in issue, since its whereabouts was not specified;

But considering that the conditions under which merchandise sold under reservation of title may be reclaimed in the case of insolvency proceedings against the buyer are determined by the law of the collective procedure, regardless of the law governing the validity and effectiveness of the reservation of title clause in general; that therefore the court of appeal with good reasons for the rejection of the demand of the Société Heinrich Otto, has applied Art. 121 par. 2 of the French Law of Jan. 2, 1985, relating to the reorganization and liquidation of enterprises; that thus the petition for review has no merit in any of its branches.

For these reasons rejects the petition.

[President: Massip, senior councilor, acting president; Reporting judge: Mr Lemontey; Advocat général: Mr Sadon]

NOTE

The holding that the law of the forum governs the validity of retention-of-title clauses is accepted in most nations. See comments by President Rémery, D. Jur. 277 (1991). He recalls that the reporting judge in the *Otto* case, Councilor Lemontey, when he was *sous-directeur* in the Department of Justice, commented on the excessive extent to which retention-of-title clauses had been expanded under German law, calling these forms '*tarabiscotées*' (over-refined) (D. Jur. 277 (1991) n. 4 citing 101 *Gaz. Palais* IV (Doctr.) 89 at 90 (1981)).

PART II

Constitutionalization and Internationalization of Private Rights

4/Dignity of Men and Women in the Workplace

INTRODUCTION

Legal protection of employees against sexual harassment in the workplace is a relatively recent example of the constitutionalization or internationalization of private rights which has gained world-wide acceptance. The right to freedom from indignities of a sexual nature in the workplace became recognized in the United States as an aspect of the legal prohibition of discrimination by an employer "against any individual with respect to * * * terms [or] conditions * * * of employment, because of such individual's race, color, religion, sex, or national origin", provided by Title VII of the Civil Rights Act of 1964 § 703(a)(1), 78 Stats. 253, 42 USC § 2000-2(a)(1).

In 1980, the Equal Employment Opportunity Commission (EEOC) issued guidelines specifying that "sexual harassment" as there defined is a form of sex discrimination prohibited by Section 703 of Title VII. The guidelines (29 CFR § 1604.11) distinguished between so-called "hostile environment" harassment and *quid pro quo* harassment, i.e. sex-related conduct submission to which is explicitly or implicitly a condition of an individual's employment or a decision affecting such individual's employment.

The courts soon followed and held that a plaintiff may establish a violation of Title VII by proving that discrimination based on sex had created a hostile or abusive work environment, e.g. *Bundy v. Jackson,* (D.C. Cir. 1981) 641 F. 2d 934.

The U.S. Supreme Court approved of this development and held "that a claim of 'hostile environment' sex discrimination is actionable under Title VII", but concluded that in the case at bar, further proceedings were necessary to determine whether the supervisor's sexual advances were "unwelcome" as evidenced by the employee's conduct, *Meritor Savings Bank v. Vinson,* 477 U.S. 57 (1986). Subsequently, the application of the rules against sexual harassment created many problems, among them the question as to the requisite severity or pervasiveness of the conduct creating a hostile or abusive work environment.

The U.S. Supreme Court, which ultimately had to pass on that issue, held "that the challenged conduct must be severe and pervasive enough to create an objectively hostile or abusive work environment, an environment that a reasonable person would find hostile and abusive." *Harris v. Forklift Systems, Inc.* 114 S.Ct. 367 (1993).

Other cases have discussed the issue whether Title VII or state law applies to sexual harassment of males by females, of homosexuals or transsexuals, of males by males, or females by females. *Mogilefsky v. Super Court,* 20 Cal.App.4th 1409 (1993), 26 Cal.Rptr. 2nd 116 (1993) (affirmative); *Oncle v. Sundowner Offshore Service,* (5th Cir. 1996) 83 F.3d 118 (negative); cert. granted No. 96-568, June 9, 1997, 1996 WL 605211. See also infra Note p. 12.

Since Title VII applies only to an employer engaged in an industry affecting [interstate] commerce which has at least 15 (formerly 20) employees, states have enacted legislation covering employees engaged in local trade or with fewer employees.

A. UNITED STATES

1. Legislation

a. U.S. Constitution, Amendment XIV (1865)

Sec. 1.

* * * No state shall make or enforce any law which shall abridge the privileges or immunities of citizens of the United States; * * * nor deny to any person within its jurisdiction the equal protection of the laws.

Sec. 5.

The Congress shall have power to enforce, by appropriate legislation, the provisions of this article.

b. 78 STAT. 255 (Civil Rights Act of 1964)

sec. 703 (42 U.S.C. § 2000e-2(a))

It shall be an unlawful employment practice for an employer —

(1) to fail or to refuse to hire or to discharge any individual, or otherwise to discriminate against any individual with respect to his compensation, terms, conditions, or privileges of employment, because of such individuals's race, color, religion, sex or national origins.

sec. 706g (105 Stat. 1075, 42 U.S.C. § 2000e-5(g)(1))

If the court finds that the respondent has intentionally engaged in or is intentionally engaging in an unlawful employment practice charged in the complaint, the court may enjoin the respondent from engaging in such unlawful employment practice, and order such affirmative action as may be appropriate, which may include, but is not limited to, reinstatement or hiring of employees, with or without back pay (payable by the employer, employment agency, or labor organization, as the case may be, responsible for the unlawful employment practice), or any other equitable relief as the court deems appropriate. Back pay liability shall not accrue from a date more than two years prior to the filing of a charge with the Commission.

CIVIL RIGHTS ACT 1991 (105 STAT. 1072)

Sec. 102. Damages in cases of intentional discrimination. The Revised Statutes are amended by inserting after section 1977 (42 USC 1981) the following new section:

s. 1977A; 42 U.S.C. § 1981a DAMAGES IN CASES OF INTENTIONAL DISCRIMINATION IN EMPLOYMENT

(a) RIGHT OF RECOVERY —

(1) CIVIL RIGHTS. — In an action brought by a complaining party under section 706 . . . of the Civil Rights Acts of 1964 (42 U.S.C. 2000e-5) against a respondent who engaged in unlawful intentional discrimination . . . the complaining party may recover compensatory and punitive damages as allow in subsection (b), in addition to any relief authorized by section 706(g) of the Civil Rights Act of 1964, from the respondent. * * *

(c) JURY TRIAL. — If a complaining party seeks compensatory or punitive damages under this section —

(1) any party may demand a trial by jury.

c. 29 Code of Federal Regulations Ch. XIV (Equal Employment Opportunity Commission)

§ 1604.11

(a) Harassment on the basis of sex is a violation of section 703 of title VII. Unwelcome sexual advances, requests for sexual favors, and other verbal or physical conduct of a sexual nature constitute sexual harassment when (1) submission to such conduct is made either explicitly or implicitly a term or condition of an individual's employment, (2) submission to or rejection of such conduct by an individual is used as the basis for employment decisions affecting such individual, or (3) such conduct has the purpose or effect of unreasonably interfering with an individual's work performance or creating an intimidating, hostile, or offensive working environment.

(b) In determining whether alleged conduct constitutes sexual harassment, the Commission will look at the record as a whole and at the totality of the circumstances, such as the nature of the sexual advances and the context in which the alleged incidents occurred. The determination of the legality of a particular action will be made from the facts, on a case by case basis.

(c) Applying general Title VII principles, an employer, employment agency, joint apprenticeship committee or labor organization (hereinafter collectively referred to as "employer") is responsible for its acts and those of its agents and supervisory employees with respect to sexual harassment regardless of whether the specific acts complained of were authorized or even forbidden by the employer and regardless of whether the employer knew or should have known of their occurrence. The Commission will examine the circumstances of the particular employment relationship and the job junctions performed by the individual in determining whether an individual acts in either a supervisory or agency capacity.

(d) With respect to conduct between fellow employees, an employer is responsible for acts of sexual harassment in the workplace where the employer (or its agents or supervisory employees) knows or should have known of the conduct, unless it can show that it took immediate and appropriate corrective action.

(e) An employer may also be responsible for the acts of non-employees, with respect to sexual harassment of employees in the workplace, where the employer (or its agents or supervisory employees) knows or should have known of the conduct and fails to take immediate and appropriate corrective action. In reviewing these cases the Commission will consider the extent of the employer's control and any other legal responsibility which the employer may have with respect to the conduct of such non-employees.

(f) Prevention is the best tool for the elimination of sexual harassment. An employer should take all steps necessary to prevent sexual harassment from occurring, such as affirmatively raising the subject, expressing strong disapproval, developing appropriate sanctions, informing employees of their right to raise and how to raise the issue of harassment under title VII, and developing methods to sensitize all concerned.

(g) Other related practices: Where employment opportunities or benefits are granted because of an individual's submission to the employer's sexual advances or requests for sexual favors, the employer may be held liable for unlawful sex discrimination against other persons who were qualified for but denied that opportunity or benefit.

d. California, Fair Employment and Housing Act (Government Code 12940)

It shall be an unlawful employment practice * * *

(h)(1) For an employer, * * * because of * * * sex * * * to harass an employee or applicant. * * *

(h)(3)(C) For purposes of this subdivision, "harassment" because of sex includes sexual harassment, gender harassment, and harassment based on pregnancy, childbirth, or related medical conditions.

2. Cases

a. Harris v. Forklift Systems, Inc.

United States Supreme Court, 1993
Harris v. Forklift Systems Inc.
114 S.Ct. 367

Justice O'CONNOR delivered the opinion of the Court.

In this case we consider the definition of a discriminatorily "abusive work environment" (also known as a "hostile work environment") under Title VII of the Civil Rights Act of 1964, 78 Stat. 253, as amended, 42 U.S.C. § 2000e *et seq.* (1988 ed., Supp. III).

I

Teresa Harris worked as a manager at Forklift Systems, Inc., an equipment rental company, from April 1985 until October 1987. Charles Hardy was Forklift's president.

The Magistrate found that, throughout Harris' time at Forklift, Hardy often insulted her because of her gender and often made her the target of unwanted sexual innuendos. Hardy told Harris on several occasions, in the presence of other employees, "You're a woman, what do you know" and "We need a man as the rental manager"; at least once, he told her she was "a dumb ass woman." App. to Pet. for Cert. A-13. Again in front of others, he suggested that the two of them "go to the Holiday Inn to negotiate [Harris'] raise." *Id.*, at A-14. Hardy occasionally asked Harris and other female employees to get coins from his front pants pocket. *Ibid.* He threw objects on the ground in front of Harris and other women, and asked them to pick the objects up. *Id.*, at A-14 to A-15. He made sexual innuendos about Harris' and other women's clothing. *Id.*, at A-15.

In mid-August 1987, Harris complained to Hardy about his conduct. Hardy said he was surprised that Harris was offended, claimed he was only joking, and apologized. *Id.*, at A-16. He also promised he would stop, and based on this assurance, Harris stayed on the job. *Ibid.* But in early September, Hardy began anew: While Harris was arranging a deal with one of Forklift's customers, he asked her, again in front of other employees, "What did you do, promise the guy . . . some [sex] Saturday night?" *Id.*, at A-17. On October 1, Harris collected her paycheck and quit.

Harris then sued Forklift, claiming that Hardy's conduct had created an abusive work environment for her because of her gender. The United States District Court for the Middle District of Tennessee, adopting the report and recommendation of the Magistrate, found this to be "a close case," *id.*, at A-31, but held that Hardy's conduct did not create an abusive environment. The court found that some of Hardy's comments "offended [Harris], and would offend the reasonable woman," *id.*, at A-33, but that they were not

> "so severe as to be expected to seriously affect [Harris'] psychological well-being. A reasonable woman manager under like circumstances would have been offended by Hardy, but his conduct would not have risen to the level of interfering with that person's work performance.
>
> "Neither do I believe that [Harris] was subjectively so offended that she suffered injury. . . . Although Hardy may at times have genuinely offended [Harris], I do not believe that he created a working environment so poisoned as to be intimidating or abusive to [Harris]." *Id.*, at A-34 to A-35.

In focusing on the employee's psychological well-being, the District Court was following Circuit precedent. See *Rabidue v. Osceola Refining Co.*, 805 F.2d 611, 620 (CA6 1986), cert. denied, 481 U.S. 1041, 107 S.Ct. 1983, 95 L.Ed.2d 823 (1987). The United States Court of Appeals for the Sixth Circuit affirmed in a brief unpublished decision, 976 F.2d 733. (CA6 1992)

We granted certiorari, 507 U.S. ———, 113 S.Ct. 1382, 122 L.Ed.2d 758 (1993), to resolve a conflict among the Circuits on whether conduct, to be actionable as "abusive work environment" harassment (no *quid pro quo* harassment issue is present here), must "seriously affect [an employee's] psychological well-being" or lead the plaintiff to "suffe[r] injury." Compare *Rabidue* (requiring serious effect on psychological well-being); *Vance v. Southern Bell Telephone & Telegraph Co.*, 863 F.2d 1503, 1510 (CA11 1989) (same); and *Downes v. FAA*, 775 F.2d 288, 292 (CA Fed.1985) (same), with *Ellison v. Brady*, 924 F.2d 872, 877–878 (CA9 1991) (rejecting such a requirement).

II

[1, 2] Title VII of the Civil Rights Act of 1964 makes it "unlawful employment practice for an employer . . . to discriminate against any individual with respect to his compensation, terms, conditions, or privileges of employment, because of such individual's race, color, religion, sex, or national origin." 42 U.S.C. § 2000e-2(a)(1). As we

made clear in *Meritor Savings Bank v. Vinson,* 477 U.S. 57, 106 S.Ct. 2399, 91 L.Ed.2d 49 (1986), this language "is not limited to 'economic' or 'tangible' discrimination. The phrase 'terms, conditions, or privileges of employment' evinces a congressional intent 'to strike at the entire spectrum of disparate treatment of men and women' in employment," which includes requiring people to work in a discriminatorily hostile or abusive environment. *Id.,* at 64, 106 S.Ct., at 2404, quoting *Los Angeles Dept. of Water and Power v. Manhart,* 435 U.S. 702, 707, n. 13, 98 S.Ct. 1370, 1374, 55 L.Ed.2d 657 (1978) (some internal quotation marks omitted). When the workplace is permeated with "discriminatory intimidation, ridicule, and insult," 477 U.S., at 65, 106 S.Ct., at 2405, that is "sufficiently severe or pervasive to alter the conditions of the victim's employment and create an abusive working environment," *id.,* at 67, 106 S.Ct., at 2405 (internal brackets and quotation marks omitted), Title VII is violated.

[3] This standard, which we reaffirm today, takes a middle path between making actionable any conduct that is merely offensive and requiring the conduct to cause a tangible psychological injury. As we pointed out in *Meritor,* "mere utterance of an . . . epithet which engenders offensive feelings in a employee," *ibid.* (internal quotation marks omitted) does not sufficiently affect the conditions of employment to implicate Title VII. Conduct that is not severe or pervasive enough to create an objectivity hostile or abusive work environment — an environment that a reasonable person would find hostile or abusive — is beyond Title VII's purview. Likewise, if the victim does not subjectively perceive the environment to be abusive, the conduct has not actually altered the conditions of the victim's employment, and there is no Title VII violation.

[4, 5] But Title VII comes into play before the harassing conduct leads to a nervous breakdown. A discriminatorily abusive work environment, even one that does not seriously affect employees' psychological well-being, can and often will detract from employees' job performance, discourage employees from remaining on the job, or keep them from advancing in their careers. Moreover, even without regard to these tangible effects, the very fact that the discriminatory conduct was so severe or pervasive that it created a work environment abusive to employees because of their race, gender, religion, or national origin offends Title VII's broad rule of workplace equality. The appalling conduct alleged in *Meritor,* and the reference in that case to environments "'so heavily polluted with discrimination as to destroy completely the emotional and psychological stability of minority group workers,'" *supra,* at 66, 106 S.Ct., at 2405, quoting *Rogers v. EEOC,* 454 F.2d 234, 238 (CA5 1971), cert. denied, 406 U.S. 957, 92 S.Ct. 2058, 32 L.Ed.2d 343 (1972), merely present some especially egregious examples of harassment. They do not mark the boundary of what is actionable.

[6] We therefore believe the District Court erred in relying on whether the conduct "seriously affect[ed] plaintiff's psychological well-being" or led her to "suffe[r] injury." Such an inquiry may needlessly focus the factfinder's attention on concrete psychological harm, an element Title VII does not require. Certainly Title VII bars conduct that would seriously affect a reasonable person's psychological well-being,

but the statute is not limited to such conduct. So long as the environment would reasonably be perceived, and is perceived, as hostile or abusive, *Meritor, supra,* 477 U.S., at 67, 106 S.Ct., at 2405, there is no need for it also to be psychologically injurious.

[7] This is not, and by its nature cannot be, a mathematically precise test. We need not answer today all the potential questions it raises, nor specifically address the EEOC's new regulations on this subject, see 58 Fed. Reg. 51266 (1993) (proposed 29 CFR §§ 1609.1, 1609.2); see also 29 CFR § 1604.11 (1993). But we can say that whether an environment is "hostile" or "abusive" can be determined only by looking at all the circumstances. These may include the frequency of the discriminatory conduct; its severity; whether it is physically threatening or humiliating, or a mere offensive utterance; and whether it unreasonably interferes with an employee's work performance. The effect on the employee's psychological well-being is, of course, relevant to determining whether the plaintiff actually found the environment abusive. But while psychological harm, like any other relevant factor, may be taken into account, no single factor is required.

III

[8] Forklift, while conceding that a requirement that the conduct seriously affect psychological well-being is unfounded, argues that the District Court nonetheless correctly applied the *Meritor* standard. We disagree. Though the District Court did conclude that the work environment was not "intimidating or abusive to [Harris]," App. to Pet. for Cert. A-35, it did so only after finding that the conduct was not "so severe as to be expected to seriously affect plaintiff's psychological well-being," *id.,* at A-34, and that Harris was not "subjectively so offended that she suffered injury," *ibid.* The District Court's application of these incorrect standards may well have influenced its ultimate conclusion, especially given that the court found this to be a "close case," *id.,* at A-31.

We therefore reverse the judgment of the Court of Appeals, and remand the case for further proceedings consistent with this opinion.

So ordered.

Justice SCALIA, concurring.

. . .

Justice GINSBURG, concurring.

. . .

NOTES

1. Courts uniformly recognize that actionable sexual harassment in the workplace can be committed by male supervisors or fellow employees against female em-

ployees or, less frequently, by female supervisors or coemployees against male employees.

2. More controversial is the question whether Title VII, § 703(a)(1) encompasses same-gender harassment, whether of the *quid pro quo* or hostile environment type. *Benekritis v. Johnson,* 882 F. Supp. 521, 525 (D.S.C. 1985), provides a survey of the early case law:

> "Several district courts and one circuit court of appeals have considered the issue of same-sex sexual harassment. Early district court opinions found that same-sex sexual harassment violated Title VII, *see Wright v. Methodist Youth Services, Inc.*, 511 F. Supp. 307 (N.D. Ill. 1981) (quid pro quo male- male harassment violates Title VII); and *Joyner v. AAA Cooper Transportation,* 597 F. Supp. 537 (M.D. Ala. 1983) (quid pro quo male-male harassment violates Title VII). Beginning, however, with the decisions in *Goluszek v. Smith,* 697 F.Supp.1452 (N.D.Ill. 1988) (male-male hostile environment sexual harassment not actionable under Title VII, but retaliatory discharge claim is), courts began considering the legislative history of Title VII for evidence of congressional intent to provide a Title VII remedy extended to same-sex sexual harassment. In concluding that no Title VII remedy extended to same-sex sexual harassment, *Goluszek* reasoned:
>
> [T]he defendant's conduct was not the type of conduct Congress intended to sanction when it enacted Title VII. * * *

The Fifth Circuit Court of Appeals relied on *Goluszek* in *Garcia v. Elf Atochem North America,* 28 F.3d 446 (5th Cir. 1994), concluding that harassment by male supervisor against male subordinate was not cognizable under Title VII, even if the alleged harassment had sexual overtones. Followed in *Vandeventer v. Wabash Nat'l Corporation,* 867 F. Supp. 790 (N.D. Ind. 1994) (male-male quid pro quo and hostile environment claims not cognizable); *Myers v. El Paso,* 874 F. Supp. 1546 (W.D. Texas 1995) (female-female hostile environment claim not actionable); *Hopkins v. Baltimore Gas and Elec. Co.,* 871 F. Supp 822 (D. Md. 1994) (male bisexual-male hostile environment claim not cognizable under Title VII, although retaliatory discharge claim is). **6.** * * * [T]he court accepts the reasoning of the district court in *Goluszek* and the Fifth Circuit Court of Appeals in *Garcia.*"

> "**6.** Two decisions that have rejected *Garcia* include *Prescott v. Independent Life and Accident Ins. Co.*, 878 F. Supp. 1545 (M.D. Ala. 1995) and *McCoy v. Johnson Controls World Serv., Inc.* 878 F.Supp. 229 (S.D. Ga. 1995)." [Note in original.]

The court in *Benekritis* was barely aware of the fact that the Eleventh Circuit Court of Appeals in *Henson v. Dundee,* 682 F. 2d 897 (11th Cir. 1982), also had held same-sex sexual harassment to be covered by Title § 703 (a)(1). *Raney v. District of Columbia,* 892 F. Supp. 283 (D.D.C. 1995) rejected *Garcia.*

In *Kelly v. City of Oakland* (9th Cir. 1999) 198 F.3d 779, 785, Circuit Judge John T. Noonan noted: "In distinction from cases of sexual harassment based on hostile environment where 'the state and federal courts have taken a bewildering variety of stances,' courts 'have had little trouble' in finding liability for quid pro quo harassment involving persons of the same gender."

2. Although the text case speaks of "actionable" abusive work environment, the relief to which the victim was entitled until the Civil Rights Act of 1991 did not include compensatory or punitive damages, unless the harassment amounted to a constructive discharge, *Konstantopoulos v. Westvaco Corp.* 893 F. Supp 1263 (D. Del. 1994) and authorities cited. The relief provided prior to 1991 included back pay, reinvestment or any other equitable relief as the court deems appropriate, 42 USC § 2000e-5(g).

In 1991 Congress enacted 42 USC § 1981a which entitles a complaining party under section 706 or 717 of the Civil Rights Act of 1964 (42 USC §§ 2000e-5 and 2000e-16) to recover compensatory and punitive damages, as allowed in subsection (b), in addition to any relief authorized by § 706 of the Civil Rights Act of 1964 (42 USC § 2000e-5(g). Applied in *Raney v. District of Columbia,* 892 F. Supp. 289 (D.D.C. 1995).

For the reasons and operation of the 1991 amendments see also *Landgraf v. USI Film Products,* 114 S.Ct. 1483 (U.S. Supr. Ct. 1994) (holding that § 1981a does not apply retroactively).

3. Title VII of the Civil Rights Act of 1964, 42 USC § 2000e-7 provides for states to maintain or enact supplementary legislation prohibiting discrimination based on sex, including sexual harassment in the workplace. Legislation of that type exists in many states. In California, sexual harassment in employment was first specifically prohibited in 1982 by an amendment in the Government Code, § 12940 contained in Cal. Stats. 1982 Ch. 1183 Sec. 2, adding subsection (i) — later renumbered (h) — to that section. The amendment stated specifically that it was declaratory of existing law. At that time the law applied only to employers of five or more, but an amendment of 1984 (Cal. Stats. 1984 ch. 1754) extended the coverage to employers of one or more.

In California, an employer is strictly liable for exemplary damages caused by sexual harassment perpetrated by a supervisor. Liability for punitive damages exists if the harassment was caused by a member of the managerial staff. Cal. Civ. Code § 3294. See also California *Kelly-Zurian v. Wohl Shoe Co. Inc.* (App. 2 Dist. 1994), 27 Cal. Rptr 2d 457, 22 Cal. App. 4th 397. In California the statute covers same-gender harassment, *Matthews v. Superior Court* 40 Cal. Rptr 2d 350.

See also California Code of Regulations 2 § 7287.6(b)(1)-(4).

4. In New York an employee who suffered harassment after a sex-change from female to male was held entitled to damages under the New York City law against discrimination based on gender. The court rejected the holding to the contrary under the Federal law in *Ulane v. Eastern Airlines Inc.* 742 F.2d 1081 (7th Cir. 1984), *Maffei v. Kolaeton Industry, Inc.* 626 N.Y.S.2d 391 (Sup. 1995).

5. American courts are split as to whether insurance coverage for sexual harassment is enforceable. In California, a court of appeal decided on public policy grounds that corporate employers cannot shift the costs of defending and settling claims for

sexual harassment to liability insurers. *Coit Drapery Cleaners, Inc. v. Sequoia Ins. Co.* (14 Cal. App. 4th 1595; 18 Cal. Rptr. 2d 692 (1992)).

Conversely, the U.S. Court of Appeals (5th Cir.) has held that Texas law does not prevent insurers from paying sexual harassment claims. *Western Heritage Insurance v. Magic Years Learning Centers* (45 F.3d 85 (5th Cir. 1995) (coverage was barred by a liability exclusion). Cf. G. Isaac & G. Brown, *Coverage for Sexual Misdeeds,* National Law Journal, May 22, 1995.

6. For alleviation of possible First Amendment concerns see J.M. Karner, *Political Speech, Sexual Harassment, and a Captive Workplace* 83 Cal.L.R. 637 (1995).

b. Collins v. Rizkana

Collins v. Rizkana
652 N.E.2d 653 (sct Ohio 1995)

ALICE ROBIE RESNICK, Justice.

The issue before the court is whether Ohio should recognize a common-law tort claim for wrongful discharge in violation of public policy based upon alleged sexual harassment/discrimination.

* * *

The traditional rule in Ohio and elsewhere is that a general or indefinite hiring is terminable at the will of either party, for any cause, no cause or even in gross or reckless disregard of any employee's rights, and a discharge without cause does not give rise to an action for damages. See *Phung v. Waste Mgt., Inc.* (1986), 23 Ohio St.3d 100, 102, 23 OBR 260, 261–262, 491 N.E.2d 1114, 1116; *Mers v. Dispatch Printing Co.* (1985), 19 Ohio St.3d 100, 19 OBR 261, 483 N.E.2d 150, paragraph one of the syllabus; *Henkel v. Educational Research Council of Am.* (1976), 45 Ohio St.2d 249, 255, 74 O.O.2d 415, 418, 344 N.E.2d 118, 121–122. See also *Wagenseller v. Scottsdale Mem. Hosp.* (1985), 147 Ariz. 370, 375–376, 710 P.2d 1025, 1030–1031. This has become known as the "employment-at-will" doctrine.

In the latter half of the twentieth century, an exception developed throughout the country which has come to be known as a cause of action for "wrongful discharge," "abusive discharge," "retaliatory discharge," or "discharge in derogation of public policy." Under this exception, an employer who wrongfully discharges an employee in violation of a clearly expressed public policy will be subject to an action for damages.

* * *

The origin of the public policy exception to the employment-at-will doctrine can be traced to the case of *Petermann v. Internatl. Bhd. of Teamsters, Chauffeurs, Warehousemen & Helpers of Am., Local 396* (1959), 174 Cal.App.2d 184, 344 P.2d 25.

In the approximately thirty-five years since the *Petermann* decision, an overwhelming majority of courts have recognized a cause of action for wrongful discharge in violation of public policy.

* * *

In *Greeley, supra,* 49 Ohio St.3d at 233–234, 551 N.E.2d at 986, the court stated that "the time has come for Ohio to join the great number of states which recognize a public policy exception to the employment-at-will doctrine." Allowing a cause of action for wrongful discharge violative of R.C. 3113.213(D), the court held as follows:

> "1. Public policy warrants an exception to the employment-at-will doctrine when an employee is discharged or disciplined for a reason which is prohibited by statute. (R.C. 3113.213[D], construed and applied.)
>
> "2. Henceforth, the right of employers to terminate employment at will for 'any cause' no longer includes the discharge of an employee where the discharge is in violation of a statute and thereby contravenes public policy. (*Fawcett v. G.C. Murphy & Co.* [1976], 46 Ohio St.2d 245, 75 O.O.2d 291, 348 N.E.2d 144, modified.)
>
> "3. In Ohio, a cause for action for wrongful discharge in violation of public policy may be brought in tort." *Id.* at syllabus.

Recently in *Painter v. Graley* (1994), 70 Ohio St.3d 377, 639 N.E.2d 51, at paragraph three of the syllabus, this court held further that:

> "'Clear public policy' sufficient to justify an exception to the employment-at-will doctrine is not limited to public policy expressed by the General Assembly in the form of statutory enactments, but may also be discerned as a matter of law based on other sources, such as the Constitutions of Ohio and the United States, administrative rules and regulations, and the common law."

In considering whether Collins has a viable cause of action in tort for wrongful discharge on the basis of alleged sexual harassment in accordance with the law as set forth in *Greeley* and *Painter,* we adopt the following suggested analysis in *Painter, supra,* 70 Ohio St.3d at 384, 639 N.E.2d at 57, fn. 8:

> "In reviewing future cases, Ohio courts may find useful the analysis of Villanova Law Professor H. Perritt, who, based on review of cases throughout the country, has described the elements of the tort as follows:
>
> "'1. That [a] clear public policy existed and was manifested in a state or federal constitution, statute or administrative regulation, or in the common law (the *clarity* element).
>
> "'2. That dismissing employees under circumstances like those involved in the plaintiff's dismissal would jeopardize the public policy (the *jeopardy* element).
>
> "'3. The plaintiff's dismissal was motivated by conduct related to the public policy (the *causation* element).

"'4. The employer lacked overriding legitimate business justification for the dismissal (the *overriding justification* element).' (Emphasis *sic.*)

"H. Perritt, The Future of Wrongful Dismissal Claims: Where Does Employer Self Interest Lie? (1989), 58 U.Cin.L.Rev. 397, 398–399."

The first task then is to identify whether a clear public policy exists in Ohio which this conduct violates (the clarity element). There are at least two sources of statutorily expressed public policy prohibiting the alleged sexual harassment/discrimination in this case, each independently sufficient to allow for the recognition of a cause of action for wrongful discharge in violation of public policy.

First, as pertinent to the allegations in this case, R.C. 2907.06,[1] prohibiting sexual imposition, expresses a public policy protecting sexual bodily security and integrity, and prohibiting offensive sexual contact.

* * *

Other courts have similarly found the sex offense statutes in their respective jurisdictions to embody sufficiently clear expressions of public policy to justify the public policy exception in cases of sexual harassment/discrimination. In *Watson v. Peoples Sec. Life Ins. Co.* (1991), 322 Md. 467, 588 A.2d 760, the plaintiff alleged that she was discharged in retaliation for having sued a coworker for sexual harassment. The harassment included two attempts by the coworker to bite the plaintiff's breast, the second attempt occurring even though the plaintiff had protested the first. The court noted that Md.Crim. Law Code Ann. 464C (1990) makes it a fourth degree sexual offense for a person to engage in sexual contact with another person against the will and without the consent of the other person. *Id.* at 482, 588 A.2d at 767. The court found that "[t]he clear mandate of public policy which Watson's discharge could be found to have violated was the individual's interest in preserving bodily integrity and personality, reinforced by the state's interest in preventing breaches of the peace, and re-

---

1. R.C. 2907.06 provides

"(A) No person shall have sexual conduct with another, not the spouse of the offender; cause another, not the spouse of the offender, to have sexual contact with the offender; or cause two or more other persons to have sexual contact when any of the following applies:

"(1) The offender knows that the sexual contact is offensive to the other person, or one of the other persons, or is reckless in that regard.

"(2) The offender knows that the other person's, or one of the other person's, ability to appraise the nature of or control the offender's or touching person's conduct is substantially impaired.

"(3) The offender knows that the other person, or one of the other persons, submits because of being unaware of the sexual contact.

"(4) The other person, or one of the other persons, is thirteen years of age or older but less than sixteen years of age, whether or not the offender knows the age of such person, and the offender is at least eighteen years of age and four or more years older than such other person.

"(B) No person shall be convicted of a violation of this section solely upon the victim's testimony unsupported by other evidence.

"(C) Whoever violates this section is guilty of sexual imposition, a misdemeanor of the third degree."

inforced by statutory policies intended to assure protection from workplace sexual harassment." *Id.* at 481, 588 A.2d at 767.

The second source of expressed public policy prohibiting sexual harassment/discrimination is R.C. 4112.02, which provides:

> "It shall be an unlawful discriminatory practice:
>
> "(A) For any employer, because of the race, color, religion, sex, national origin, handicap, age, or ancestry of any person, to discharge without just cause, to refuse to hire, or otherwise to discriminate against that person with respect to hire, tenure, terms, conditions, or privileges of employment, or any matter directly or indirectly related to employment."

Additionally, in *Kerans v. Porter Paint Co.* (1991), 51 Ohio St.3d 486, 495, 575 N.E.2d 428, 435, we commented that the adoption of Title VII, "Section 2000e *et seq.*, Title 42, U.S.Code, the enactment of R.C. Chapter 4112, and this court's recent decision in *Helmick v. Cincinnati Word Processing, Inc.* (1989), 45 Ohio St.3d 131, 543 N.E.2d 1212, reflect Ohio's strong public policy against workplace-based sexual harassment."

* * *

The foregoing establishes a clear public policy against workplace sexual harassment. Thus, having found clear public policy sufficient to justify an exception to the employment-at-will doctrine, we must now determine whether sexually motivated dismissals would jeopardize the public policy (the jeopardy element). The issue that most often arises under the jeopardy analysis, and upon which the courts are split, is whether the public policy tort should be rejected where the statute expressing the public policy already provides adequate remedies to protect the public interest.

* * *

In this case, however, there are two reasons why the availability to remedies under R.C. Chapter 4112 will not serve to defeat Collins's sexual harassment tort claim, irrespective of whether such statutory remedies would have a preclusive effect in other wrongful discharge cases.

[6] First, the issue of adequacy of remedies in confined to cases "[w]here right and remedy are part of the same statute which is the *sole source* of the public policy opposing the discharge." (Emphasis added.) *Watson, supra,* at 486, 588 A.2d at 769. In cases of *multiple*-source public policy, the statute containing the right and remedy will not foreclose recognition of the tort on the basis of some other source of public policy, unless it was the legislature's intent in enacting the statute to preempt common-law remedies.

* * *

In *Helmick, supra,* 45 Ohio St.3d 131, 543 N.E.2d 1212, at paragraphs one and two of the syllabus, we held that:

> "R.C. Chapter 4112 was intended to add protections for victims of sexual harassment rather than reduce the protections and remedies for such conduct.
>
> "Allowing a plaintiff to pursue common-law remedies in lieu of the relief provided under R.C. Chapter 4112 creates no conflict and serves to supplement the limited protection and coverage of that chapter."

In so holding, the court explained that "there is nothing in the language or legislative history of R.C. Chapter 4112 barring the pursuit of common-law remedies for injuries arising out of sexual misconduct." *Id.* at 133, 543 N.E.2d at 1215. The court concluded, "common-law tort actions are not preempted by R.C. Chapter 4112." *Id.* at 135, 543 N.E.2d at 1216.

Since Collins presents a viable wrongful discharge claim under *Greeley* independent of R.C. Chapter 4112, and since R.C. Chapter 4112 does not operate to preclude that claim, there is no need to consider whether the remedies contained in R.C. Chapter 4112 should serve as a basis to reject her claim.

Second, in the context of this case, the availability of remedies under R.C. Chapter 4112 cannot serve to defeat Collins's wrongful discharge claim because those remedies are simply not available to Collins. She is precluded from availing herself of those remedies by virtue of R.C. 4112.01(A)(2), which removes her employer from the scope of R.C. Chapter 4112 because he never employed "four or more persons within the state." Since R.C. Chapter 4112 does not preempt common-law claims, we cannot interpret R.C. 4112.01(A)(2) as an intent by the General Assembly to grant small businesses in Ohio a license to sexually harass/discriminate against their employees with impunity. Instead, we can only read R.C. 4112.01(A)(2) as evidencing an intention to exempt small businesses from the burdens of R.C. Chapter 4112, not from its antidiscrimination policy. See *Kerrigan, supra,* 804 F.Supp. at 736.

We do not mean to suggest that where a statute's coverage provisions form an essential part of its public policy, we may extract a policy from the statute and use it to nullify that statute's own coverage provisions. However, in the absence of legislative intent to preempt common-law remedies, we can perceive no basis upon which to find that R.C. 4112.01(A)(2) forms part of the public policy reflected in R.C. 4112.01(A). Therefore, we cannot find it to be Ohio's public policy that an employer with three employees may condition their employment upon the performance of sexual favors while an employer with four employees may not.

* * *

We hold, therefore, that in Ohio, a cause of action may be brought for wrongful discharge in violation of public policy based on sexual harassment/discrimination.

Accordingly, the decision of the court of appeals is reversed, and the cause is remanded to the trial court for further proceedings consistent with this opinion.

Judgment reversed and cause remanded.

B. European Union

The definition and response to sexual harassment in the EU Commission Recommendation of November 27, 1991 on the Protection of the dignity of women and men at work (92/131/EEC). O.J. No. L 49/1, ANNEX Protecting the Dignity of Women and Men at Work: a Code of Practice of Measures to Combat Sexual Harassment illustrates the influence of American law on European law.

II

(Acts whose publication is not obligatory)

COMMISSION

COMMISSION RECOMMENDATION

of 27 November 1991

on the protection of the dignity of women and men at work

(92/131/EEC)

THE COMMISSION OF THE EUROPEAN COMMUNITIES,

Having regard to the Treaty establishing the European Economic Community, and in particular the second indent of Article 155 thereof,

Whereas unwanted conduct of a sexual nature, or other conduct based on sex affecting the dignity of women and men at work, including the conduct of superiors and colleagues, is unacceptable and may, in certain circumstances, be contrary to the principle of equal treatment within the meaning of Articles 3, 4 and 5 of Council Directive 76/207/EEC of 9 February 1976 on the implementation of the principle of equal treatment for men and women as regards access to employment, vocational training and promotion, and working conditions,[2] a view supported by case-law in some Member States;

Whereas, in accordance with the Council recommendation of 13 December 1984 on the promotion of positive action for women,[3] many Member States have carried out a variety of positive action measures and actions having a bearing, *inter alia,* on respect for the dignity of women at the workplace;

Whereas the European Parliament, in its resolution of 11 June 1986 on violence against women,[4] has called upon national governments, equal opportunities committees and trade unions to carry out concerted information campaigns to create a proper awareness of the individual rights of all members of the labour force;

Whereas the Advisory Committee on Equal Opportunities for Women and Men,

2. OJ No L 39, 14. 2. 1976, p. 40.
3. OJ No L 331, 19. 12. 1984, p. 34.
4. OJ No C 176, 14. 7. 1986, p. 79

in its opinion of 20 June 1988, has unanimously recommended that there should be a recommendation and code of conduct on sexual harassment in the workplace covering harassment of both sexes;

Whereas the Commission in its action programme relating to the implementation of the Community Charter of Basic Social Rights for Workers undertook to examine the protection of workers and their dignity at work, having regard to the reports and recommendations prepared on various aspects of implementation of Community law;[5]

Whereas the Council, in its resolution of 29 May 1990 on the protection of the dignity of women and men at work,[6] affirms that conduct based on sex affecting the dignity of women and men at work, including conduct of superiors and colleagues, constitutes an intolerable violation of the dignity of workers or trainees, and calls on the Member States and the institutions and organs of the European Communities to develop positive measures designed to create a climate at work in which women and men respect one another's human integrity;

Whereas the Commission, in its third action programme on equal opportunities for women and men, 1991 to 1995, and pursuant to paragraph 3 (2) of the said Council resolution of 29 May 1990, resolved to draw up a code of conduct on the protection of the dignity of women and men at work,[7] based on experience and best practice in the Member States, to provide guidance on initiating and pursuing positive measures designed to create a climate at work in which women and men respect one another's human integrity;

Whereas the European Parliament, on 22 October 1991, adopted a resolution on the protection of the dignity of women and men at work;[8]

Whereas the Economic and Social Committee, on 30 October 1991, adopted an opinion on the protection of the dignity of women and men at work,[9]

RECOMMENDS AS FOLLOWS:

Article 1

It is recommended that the Member States take action to promote awareness that conduct of a sexual nature, or other conduct based on sex affecting the dignity of women and men at work, including conduct of superiors and colleagues, is unacceptable if:

(a) such conduct is unwanted, unreasonable and offensive to the recipient;
(b) a person's rejection of, or submission to, such conduct on the part of employers or workers (including superiors or colleagues) is used explicitly or

5. COM(89) 568 final, 29. 11. 1989. For example, 'The dignity of women at work: A report on the problem of sexual harassment in the Member States of the European Communities', October 1987, by Michael Rubenstein (ISBN 92-825-8764-9).

6. OJ No C 157, 27. 6. 1990, p. 3.

7. COM(90) 449 final, 6. 11. 1990.

8. OJ No C 305, 25. 11. 1991.

9. OJ No C 14, 20. 1. 1992.

implicitly as a basis for a decision which affects that person's access to vocational training, access to employment, continued employment, promotion, salary or any other employment decisions;
and/or

(c) such conduct creates an intimidating, hostile or humiliating work environment for the recipient;

and that such conduct may, in certain circumstances, be contrary to the principle of equal treatment within the meaning of Articles 3, 4 and 5 of Directive 76/207/EEC.

Article 2

It is recommended that Member States take action, in the public sector, to implement the Commission's code of practice on the protection of the dignity of women and men at work, annexed hereto. The action of the Member States, in thus initiating and pursuing positive measures designed to create a climate at work in which women and men respect one another's human integrity, should serve as an example to the private sector.

Article 3

It is recommended that Member States encourage employers and employee representatives to develop measures to implement the Commission's code of practice on the protection of the dignity of women and men at work.

Article 4

Member States shall inform the Commission within three years of the date of this recommendation of the measures taken to give effect to it, in order to allow the Commission to draw up a report on all such measures. The Commission shall, within this period, ensure the widest possible circulation of the code of practice. The report should examine the degree of awareness of the Code, its perceived effectiveness, its degree of application and the extent of its use in collective bargaining between the social partners.

Article 5

This recommendation is addressed to the Member States.

Done at Brussels, 27 November 1991.
For the Commission
Vasso PAPANDREOU
Member of the Commission

ANNEX

PROTECTING THE DIGNITY OF WOMEN AND MEN AT WORK
A code of practice on measures to combat sexual harassment

1. Introduction

This code of practice is issued in accordance with the resolution of the Council of Ministers on the protection of the dignity of women and men at work,[10] and to accompany the Commission's recommendation on this issue.

Its purpose is to give practical guidance to employers, trade unions, and employees on the protection of the dignity of women and men at work. The code is intended to be applicable in both the public and the private sector and employers are encouraged to follow the recommendations contained in the code in a way which is appropriate to the size and structure of their organization. It may be particularly relevant for small and medium-sized enterprises to adapt some of the practical steps to their specific needs.

The aim is to ensure that sexual harassment does not occur and, if it does occur, to ensure that adequate procedures are readily available to deal with the problem and prevent its recurrence. The code thus seeks to encourage the development and implementation of policies and practices which establish working environments free of sexual harassment and in which women and men respect one another's human integrity.

The expert report carried out on behalf of the Commission found that sexual harassment is a serious problem for many working women in the European Community[11] and research in Member States has proven beyond doubt that sexual harassment at work is not an isolated phenomenon. On the contrary, it is clear that for millions of women in the European Community, sexual harassment is an unpleasant and unavoidable part of their working lives. Men too may suffer sexual harassment and should, of course, have the same rights as women to the protection of their dignity.

Some specific groups are particularly vulnerable to sexual harassment. Research in several Member States, which documents the link between the risk of sexual harassment and the recipient's perceived vulnerability, suggests that divorced and separated women, young women and new entrants to the labour market and those with irregular or precarious employment contracts, women in non-traditional jobs, women with disabilities, lesbians and women from racial minorities are disproportionately at risk. Gay men and young men are also vulnerable to harassment. It is un-

10. OJ No C 157, 27. 6. 1990, p. 3.

11. 'The dignity of women at work: A report on the problem of sexual harassment in the Member States of the European Communities', October 1987, by Michael Rubenstein (ISBN 92-825-8764-9).

deniable that harassment on grounds of sexual orientation undermines the dignity at work of those affected and it is impossible to regard such harassment as appropriate workplace behaviour.

Sexual harassment pollutes the working environment and can have a devastating effect upon the health, confidence, morale and performance of those affected by it. The anxiety and stress produced by sexual harassment commonly leads to those subjected to it taking time off work due to sickness, being less efficient at work, or leaving their job to seek work elsewhere. Employees often suffer the adverse consequences of the harassment itself and short- and long-term damage to their employment prospects if they are forced to change jobs. Sexual harassment may also have a damaging impact on employees not themselves the object of unwanted behaviour but who are witness to it or have a knowledge of the unwanted behaviour.

There are also adverse consequences arising from sexual harassment for employers. It has a direct impact on the profitability of the enterprise where staff take sick leave or resign their posts because of sexual harassment, and on the economic efficiency of the enterprise where employees' productivity is reduced by having to work in a climate in which individuals' integrity is not respected.

In general terms, sexual harassment is an obstacle to the proper integration of women into the labour market and the Commission is committed to encouraging the development of comprehensive measures to improve such integration.[12]

2. Definition

Sexual harassment means unwanted conduct of a sexual nature, or other conduct based on sex affecting the dignity of women and men at work.[13] This can include unwelcome physical, verbal or non-verbal conduct.

Thus, a range of behaviour may be considered to constitute sexual harassment. It is unacceptable if such conduct is unwanted, unreasonable and offensive to the recipient; a person's rejection of or submission to such conduct on the part of employers or workers (including superiors or colleagues) is used explicitly or implicitly as a basis for a decision which affects that person's access to vocational training or to employment, continued employment, promotion, salary or any other employment decisions; and/or such conduct creates an intimidating, hostile or humiliating working environment for the recipient.[13]

The essential characteristic of sexual harassment is that it is unwanted by the recipient, that it is for each individual to determine what behaviour is acceptable to

12. Third action programme on equal opportunities for women and men, 1991 to 1995, COM(90) 449, 6. 11. 1990.

13. Council resolution on the protection of the dignity of women and men at work (OJ No C 157, 27. 6. 1990, p. 3, point 1).

them and what they regard as offensive. Sexual attention becomes sexual harassment if it is persisted in once it has been made clear that it is regarded by the recipient as offensive, although one incident of harassment may constitute sexual harassment if sufficiently serious. It is the unwanted nature of the conduct which distinguishes sexual harassment from friendly behaviour, which is welcome and mutual.

3. The Law and Employers' Responsibilities

Conduct of a sexual nature or other based on sex affecting the dignity of women and men at work may be contrary to the principle of equal treatment within the meaning of Articles 3, 4 and 5 of Council Directive 76/207/EEC of 9 February 1976 on the implementation of the principle of equal treatment for men and women as regards access to employment, vocational training and promotion, and working conditions.[14] This principle means that there shall be no discrimination whatsoever on grounds of sex either directly or indirectly by reference in particular to marital or family status.

In certain circumstances, and depending upon national law, sexual harassment may also be a criminal offence or may contravene other obligations imposed by the law, such as health and safety duties, or a duty, contractual or otherwise, to be a good employer. Since sexual harassment is a form of employee misconduct, employers have a responsibility to deal with it as they do with any other form of employee misconduct as well as to refrain from harassing employees themselves. Since sexual harassment is a risk to health and safety, employers have a responsibility to take steps to minimize the risk as they do with other hazards. Since sexual harassment often entails an abuse of power, employers may have a responsibility for the misuse of the authority they delegate.

This code, however, focuses on sexual harassment as a problem of sex discrimination. Sexual harassment is sex discrimination because the gender of the recipient is the determining factor in who is harassed. Conduct of a sexual nature or other conduct based on sex affecting the dignity of women and men at work in some Member States already has been found to contravene national equal treatment laws and employers have a responsibility to seek to ensure that the work environment is free from such conduct.[15]

As sexual harassment is often a function of women's status in the employment hierarchy, policies to deal with sexual harassment are likely to be most effective where they are linked to a broader policy to promote equal opportunities and to improve the

14. OJ No L 39, 14. 2. 1976, p. 40.

15. Council resolution on the protection of the dignity of women and men at work (OJ No C 157, 27. 6. 1990, p. 3, point 2 (3) (a)).

position of women. Advice on steps which can be taken generally to implement an equal opportunities policy is set out in the Commission's guide to positive action.[16]

Similarly, a procedure to deal with complaints of sexual harassment should be regarded as only one component of a strategy to deal with the problem. The prime objective should be to change behaviour and attitudes, to seek to ensure the prevention of sexual harassment.

4. Collective Bargaining

The majority of the recommendations contained in this code are for action by employers, since employers have clear responsibilities to ensure the protection of the dignity of women and men at work.

Trade unions also have responsibilities to their members and they can and should play an important role in the prevention of sexual harassment in the workplace. It is recommended that the question of including appropriate clauses in agreements be examined in the context of the collective bargaining process, with the aim of achieving a work environment free from unwanted conduct of a sexual nature or other conduct based on sex affecting the dignity of women and men at work and free from victimization of a complainant or of a person wishing to give, or giving, evidence in the event of a complaint.

5. Recommendations to Employers

The policies and procedures recommended below should be adopted, where appropriate, after consultation or negotiation with trade unions or employee representatives. Experience suggests that strategies to create and maintain a working environment in which the dignity of employees is respected are most likely to be effective where they are jointly agreed.

It should be emphasized that a distinguishing characteristic of sexual harassment is that employees subjected to it often will be reluctant to complain. An absence of complaints about sexual harassment in a particular organization, therefore, does not necessarily mean an absence of sexual harassment. It may mean that the recipients of sexual harassment think that there is no point in complaining because nothing will be done about it, or because it will be trivialized or the complainant subjected to ridicule, or because they fear reprisals. Implementing the preventative and procedural recommendations outlined below should facilitate the creation of a climate at work in which such concerns have no place.

---

16. Positive action: Equal opportunities for women in employment — a guide, Office for Official Publications of the European Communities, 1988.

A. Prevention

(i) Policy statements

As a first step in showing senior management's concern and their commitment to dealing with the problem of sexual harassment, employers should issue a policy statement which expressly states that all employers have a right to be treated with dignity, that sexual harassment at work will not be permitted or condoned and that employers have a right to complain about it should it occur.

It is recommended that the policy statement make clear what is considered inappropriate behaviour at work, and explain that such behaviour, in certain circumstances, may be unlawful. It is advisable for the statement to set out a positive duty on managers and supervisors to implement the policy and to take corrective action to ensure compliance with it. It should also place a positive duty on all employees to comply with the policy and to ensure that their colleagues are treated with respect and dignity.

In addition, it is recommended that the statement explain the procedure which should be followed by employees subjected to sexual harassment at work in order to obtain assistance and to whom they should complain; that it contain an undertaking that allegations of sexual harassment will be dealt with seriously, expeditiously and confidentially, and that employees will be protected against victimization or retaliation for bringing a complaint of sexual harassment. It should also specify that appropriate disciplinary measures will be taken against employees found guilty of sexual harassment.

(ii) Communicating the policy

Once the policy has been developed, it is important to ensure that it is communicated effectively to all employees, so that they are aware that they have a right to complain and to whom they should complain; that their complaint will be dealt with promptly and fairly; and that employees are made aware of the likely consequences of engaging in sexual harassment. Such communication will highlight management's commitment to eliminating sexual harassment, thus enhancing a climate in which it will not occur.

(iii) Responsibility

All employees have a responsibility to help to ensure a working environment in which the dignity of employees is respected and managers (including supervisors) have a particular duty to ensure that sexual harassment does not occur in work areas for which they are responsible. It is recommended that managers explain the organization's policy to their staff and take steps to positively promote the policy. Managers should also be responsive and supportive to any member of staff who complains about sexual harassment, provide full and clear advice on the procedure to be adopted, maintain confidentiality in any cases of sexual harassment and ensure that there is no further problem of sexual harassment or any victimization after a complaint has been resolved.

(iv) Training

An important means of ensuring that sexual harassment does not occur and that, if it does occur, the problem is resolved efficiently is through the provision of training for managers and supervisors. Such training should aim to identify the factors which contribute to a working environment free of sexual harassment and to familiarize participants with their responsibilities under the employer's policy and any problems they are likely to encounter.

In addition, those playing an official role in any formal complaints procedure in respect of sexual harassment should receive specialist training, such as that outlined above.

It is also good practice to include information as to the organization's policy on sexual harassment and procedures for dealing with it as part of appropriate induction and training programmes.

B. Procedures

The development of clear and precise procedures to deal with sexual harassment once it has occurred is of great importance. The procedures should ensure the resolution of problems in an efficient and effective manner. Practical guidance for employees on how to deal with sexual harassment when it occurs and with its aftermath will make it more likely that it will be dealt with at an early stage. Such guidance should of course draw attention to an employee's legal rights and to any time limits within which they must be exercised.

(i) Resolving problems informally

Most recipients of harassment simply want the harassment to stop. Both informal and formal methods of resolving problems should be available.

Employees should be advised that, if possible, they should attempt to resolve the problem informally in the first instance. In some cases, it may be possible and sufficient for the employee to explain clearly to the person engaging in the unwanted conduct that the behaviour in question is not welcome, that it offends them or makes them uncomfortable, and that it interferes with their work.

In circumstances where it is too difficult or embarrassing for an individual to do this on their own behalf, an alternative approach would be to seek support from, or for an initial approach to be made by, a sympathetic friend or confidential counsellor.

If the conduct continues or if it is not appropriate to resolve the problem informally, it should be raised through the formal complaints procedure.

(ii) Advice and assistance

It is recommended that employers designate someone to provide advice and assistance to employees subjected to sexual harassment, where possible with responsibilities to assist in the resolution of any problems, whether through informal or formal means. It may be helpful if the officer is designated with the agreement of the trade unions or employees, as this is likely to enhance their acceptability. Such officers could be selected from personnel departments or equal opportunities departments for example. In some organizations they are designated as 'confidential counsellors' or 'sympathetic friends'. Often such a role may be played by someone from the employee's trade union or women's support groups.

Whatever the location of this responsibility in the organization, it is recommended that the designated officer receives approprate training in the best means of resolving problems and in the detail of the organization's policy and procedures, so that they can perform their role effectively. It is also important that they are given adequate resources to carry out their function, and protection against victimization for assisting any recipient of sexual harassment.

(iii) Complaints procedure

It is recommended that, where the complainant regards attempts at informal resolution as inappropriate, where informal attempts at resolution have been refused, or where the outcome has been unsatisfactory, a formal procedure for resolving the complaint be provided. The procedure should give employees confidence that the organization will take allegations of sexual harassment seriously.

By its nature sexual harassment may make the normal channels of complaint difficult to use because of embarrassment, fears of not being taken seriously, fears of damage to reputation, fears of reprisal or the prospect of damaging the working environment. Therefore, a formal procedure should specify to whom the employee should bring a complaint, and it should also provide an alternative if in the particular circumstances the normal grievance procedure may not be suitable, for example because the alleged harasser is the employee's line manager. It is also advisable to make provision for employees to bring a complaint in the first instance to someone of their own sex, should they so choose.

It is good practice for employers to monitor and review complaints of sexual harassment and how they have been resolved, in order to ensure that their procedures are working effectively.

(iv) Investigations

It is important to ensure that internal investigations of any complaints are handled with sensitivity and with due respect for the rights of both the complainant and the alleged harasser. The investigation should be seen to be independent and objective. Those carrying out the investigation should not be connected with the allegation in any way, and every effort should be made to resolve complaints speedily — grievances should be handled promptly and the procedure should set a time limit within which complaints will be processed, with due regard for any time limits set by national legislation for initiating a complaint through the legal system.

It is recommended as good practice that both the complainant and the alleged harasser have the right to be accompanied and/or represented, perhaps by a representative of their trade union or a friend or colleague; that the alleged harasser be given full details of the nature of the complaint and the opportunity to respond, and that strict confidentiality be maintained throughout any investigation into an allegation. Where it is necessary to interview witnesses, the importance of confidentiality should be emphasized.

It must be recognized that recounting the experience of sexual harassment is difficult and can damage the employee's dignity. Therefore, a complainant should not be required repeatedly to recount the events complained of where this is unnecessary.

The investigation should focus on the facts of the complaint and it is advisable for the employer to keep a complete record of all meetings and investigations.

(v) Disciplinary offence

It is recommended that violations of the organization's policy protecting the dignity of employees at work should be treated as a disciplinary offence and the disciplinary rules should make clear what is regarded as inappropriate behaviour at work. It is also good practice to ensure that the range of penalties to which offenders will be liable for violating the rule is clearly stated and also to make it clear that it will be considered a disciplinary offence to victimize or retaliate against an employee for bringing a complaint of sexual harassment in good faith.

Where a complaint is upheld and it is determined that it is necessary to relocate or transfer one party, consideration should be given, wherever practicable, to allowing the complainant to choose whether he or she wishes to remain in their post or be transferred to another location. No element of penalty should be seen to attach to a complainant whose complaint is upheld and in addition, where a complaint is upheld, the employer should monitor the situation to ensure that the harassment has stopped.

Even where a complaint is not upheld, for example because the evidence is regarded as inconclusive, consideration should be given to transferring or rescheduling the work of one of the employees concerned rather than requiring them to continue to work together against the wishes of either party.

6. *Recommendations to Trade Unions*

Sexual harassment is a trade union issue as well as an issue for employers. It is recommended as good practice that trade unions formulate and issue clear policy statements on sexual harassment and take steps to raise awareness of the problem of sexual harassment in the workplace, in order to help create a climate in which it is neither condoned or ignored. For example, trade unions could aim to give all officers and representatives training on equality issues, including dealing with sexual harassment, and include such information in union-sponsored or approved training courses, as well as information on the union's policy. Trade unions should consider declaring that sexual harassment is inappropriate behaviour and educating members and officials about its consequences is recommended as good practice.

Trade unions should also raise the issue of sexual harassment with employers and encourage the adoption of adequate policies and procedures to protect the dignity of women and men at work in the organization. It is advisable for trade unions to inform members of their right not to be sexually harassed at work and provide members with clear guidance as to what to do if they are sexually harassed, including guidance on any relevant legal rights.

Where complaints arise, it is important for trade unions to treat them seriously and sympathetically and ensure that the complainant has an opportunity of representation if a complaint is to be pursued. It is important to create an environment in which members feel able to raise such complaints knowing they will receive a sympathetic and supportive response from local union representatives. Trade unions could consider designating specially trained officials to advise and counsel members with complaints of sexual harassment and act on their behalf if required. This will provide a focal point for support. It is also a good idea to ensure that there are sufficient female representatives to support women subjected to sexual harassment.

It is recommended too, where the trade union is representing both the complainant and the alleged harasser for the purpose of the complaints procedure, that it be made clear that the union is not condoning offensive behaviour by providing representation. In any event, the same official should not represent both parties.

It is good practice to advise members that keeping a record of incidents by the harassed worker will assist in bringing any formal or informal action to a more effective conclusion, that the union wishes to be informed of any incident of sexual harassment and that such information will be kept confidential. It is also good practice for the union to monitor and review the union's record in responding to complaints and in representing alleged harassers and the harassed, in order to ensure its responses are effective.

7. *Employees' Responsibilities*

Employees have a clear role to play in helping to create a climate at work in which sexual harassment is unacceptable. They can contribute to preventing sexual harassment through an awareness and sensitivity towards the issue and by ensuring that standards of conduct for themselves and for colleagues do not cause offence.

Employees can do much to discourage sexual harassment by making it clear that they find such behaviour unacceptable and by supporting colleagues who suffer such treatment and are considering making a complaint.

Employees who are themselves recipients of harassment should, where practicable, tell the harasser that the behaviour is unwanted and unacceptable. Once the offender understands clearly that the behaviour is unwelcome, this may be enough to put an end to it. If the behaviour is persisted in, employees should inform management and/or their employee respresentative through the appropriate channels and request assistance in stopping the harassment, whether through informal or formal means.

NOTES

1. *Effect of Recommendations.* The European Court of Justice [ECJ] has held that Community recommendations "cannot in themselves confer rights on individuals upon which the latter may rely before national courts. However, national courts are bound to take these recommendations into consideration in order to decide disputes submitted to them, in particular where they are capable of casting light on the interpretation of other provisions of national or Community law." ECJ C-322/88, Judgment of December 13, 1989, *Salvatore Grimaldi v. Fonds de maladies professionnelles.* [1989] ECJ Reports 4417.

The instant recommendation was published in the "L series" because of article 4, containing a mandate to the Member States. It is cited by national courts (see infra p. 232).

2. For the implications, legal and extra-legal of the Code of Practice in the U.K. see H. Houghton-James, Sexual Harassment (London 1995) 69 et s.; C. McCrudden, *The Effectiveness of European Equality Law,* 13 Oxford Journal of Legal Studies 357 (1993); M. Rubenstein, *Sexual Harassment: European Commission Recommendation and Code of Practice,* 21 Industrial Law Journal 70 (1992).

C. UNITED KINGDOM

1. Legislation

a. Sex Discrimination Act 1975 (c65)

s1(1) A person discriminates against a woman in any circumstances relevant for the purposes of any provision of this Act if —

(a) on the ground of her sex he treats her less favourably than he treats or would treat a man * * *.

s6(2) It is unlawful for a person, in the case of a woman employed by him at an establishment in Great Britain, to discriminate against her —

(a) * * *
(b) by dismissing her, or subjecting her to any other detriment.

s41 *Liability of employers and principals.*

(1) Anything done by a person in the course of his employment shall be treated for the purposes of this Act as done by his employer as well as by him, whether or not it was done with the employer's knowledge or approval.

2. Caselaw

a. Wadman v. Carpenter Farrer Partnership

Wadman v. Carpenter Farrer Partnership
Employment Appeals Tribunal
[1993] IRLR 374, [1993] C.M.L.R. 93

WOOD (P): By an originating application dated 19 May 1992 Miss Wadman alleged unfair dismissal by her employers, who are Carpenter Farrer Partnership, a partnership of architects.

Her dismissal in effect, because she did not have the two years' qualification, was an allegation of sexual discrimination. * * *

The [Industrial] Tribunal reserved its decision which was promulgated on 27 November 1992. Her application failed and she now appeals. * * * The evidence covers numerous complaints which Miss Wadman was making. They have been grouped under various headings by Miss Purkiss, her counsel: personal insults, pressure to change her appearance; rude remarks; pin-up pictures on the wall; leering at her legs; and some general sexist remarks denigrating women. It is also right to note that towards the end of her period of employment she was suffering, as the medical report shows, from clinical depression. The reasoning is contained in three paragraph towards the end of the decision: * * *

> "31. In particular we are mind that despite all the applicant tells us happened she still wished to retain her job, and in fact sought help from her mother in persuading Mr. Farrer not to dismiss her."

* * *

The relevant statutory provisions are those contained in s6(2)(b) and s1(1)(a) of the Sex Discrimination Act 1975. Section 6(2) reads:

> It is unlawful for a person, in the case of a woman employed by him at an establishment in Great Britain, to discriminate against her —
>
> (a) . . .
>
> (b) by dismissing her, or subjecting her to any other detriment.

* * *

The leading case of *Strathclyde Regional Council v. Porcelli* [1986] I.C.R. 564 ([1986] IRLR 134) was cited to the Industrial Tribunal, although not mentioned in their decision. * * *

Those passages [from *Strathclyde Regional Council*], in our judgment, are most helpful guides for Industrial Tribunals, who, as we know, are being faced quite often, with allegations of what has been called "sexual harassment." Bearing in mind the accuracy with which the correct question must be answered, it is nevertheless of assistance to see how the phrase "sexual harassment" is being understood in the present state of the law. "Sexual harassment" is not a definitive phrase in law, and it may be helpful to note recent moves within Europe. There have been Recommendations which the European Commission have adopted. We have been helpfully referred not only to the Recommendation but also to the Code of Practice on measures to combat sexual harassment which is attached to it. Article 1 of the Recommendations read as follows:

> "It is recommended that the Member States take action to promote awareness that conduct of a sexual nature or other conduct based on sex affecting the dignity of women and men at work, including conduct of superiors and colleagues, is unacceptable if:
>
> (a) such conduct is unwanted, unreasonable and offensive to the recipient;

(b) a person's rejection of or submission to such conduct on the part of employers or workers (including superiors or colleagues) is used explicitly or implicitly as a basis for a decision which affects that persons' access to vocational training, access to employment, continued employment, promotion, salary or other employment decisions; and/or

(c) such conduct creates an intimidating, hostile or humiliating work environment for the recipient;

and that such conduct may, in certain circumstances, be contrary to the principle of equal treatment within the meaning of Articles 3, 4 and 5 of Directive 76/207 EEC.

That is more commonly known as "Equal Treatment Directive."
In the Code of Practice there is a definition, it reads thus:

"Sexual harassment means 'unwanted conduct of a sexual nature, or other conduct based on sex affecting the dignity of women and men at work.' This can include unwelcome physical, verbal or non-verbal conduct."

That definition may also be of some assistance to Tribunals in considering these matters. However, it is perhaps important, and we would comment, that harassment indicates a degree of repetition rather than a single act, although every case will depend upon its own facts, and that stress has been laid under Article 1 on the working environment.

However, provided that a Tribunal has directed itself accurately on the law, to put to itself the correct question in UK law then the issue is one of fact. The Tribunal sees and hears the witnesses; the importance of that was stressed in the decision of this Tribunal, *Wileman v Minilec Engineering Ltd* [1988] IRLR 144. The Tribunal will look at all the surrounding circumstances; the personalities, the vulnerability of the personalities and indeed, the degree of severity of the incidents complained of, bearing in mind the phrase of Lord Grieve about "mere scratches."

* * *

DISPOSITION: Allowed the appeal and remitted the case to a differently constituted Industrial Tribunal.

NOTES

1. The Employment Appeals Tribunal [EAT] has since held that a single sexual remark could amount to sexual harassment where it caused humiliation and genuine embarrassment. *Insitu Cleaning Co Ltd. and Another v Heads,* (1995) 513 IRLB 10; *Legal Action* (May 1995) 21.
2. Numerous sexual harassment cases have been brought under the Sex Dis-

crimination Act 1975. (i) *Stewart v Cleveland Guest (Engineering) Ltd.* [1994] Industrial Relations Law Reports [IRLR] 440, noted A. McColgan, *Sexual Harassment, Sex Discrimination and Unfair Dismissal,* 24 Industrial Law Journal [I.L.J.] 181 (1995); (ii) *Bracebridge Engineering Limited v Darby* [1990] I.R.L.R. 3, noted V. Gay 19 I.L.J. 35 (1990); (iii) *Balgobin and Another v Tower Hamlets London Borough Council* [1987] Industrial Cases Reports [I.C.R.] 829; (iv) *Strathclyde Regional Council v Porcelli,* [1986] I.C.R. 564.

3. The Sex Discrimination and Equal Pay (Remedies) Regulations 1993, SI 1993 No. 2798 removed the prior £11,000 cap on awards.

4. For sexual harassment of lawyers see Barbara Hewson, *Sexual Harassment at the Bar,* New Law Journal May 5, 1995 p. 626; unreported case in LEGAL ACTION, July 1995 p. 5 *"Sex discrimination win against solicitor."* (Damages of £8000 awarded for abusive language and physical contact.)

5. *Confidentiality.* English law, like the EU Commission Recommendation of November 27, 1991 on the Protection of the dignity of women and men at work (92/131/EEC). O.J. No. L 49/7 and 49/8 promotes confidentiality. Since 1993, an order may be entered restricting publication of "any matter likely to lead members of the public to identify him as a person affected by the allegation" of sexual harassment. Employment Protection (Consolidation) Act [EP(C)A] 1978 c44, Schedule 9, para 5A. Para 5A was introduced by the Trade Union Reform and Employment Rights Acts (TURERA) 1993 c. 19.

6. CANADA. The Canadian Supreme Court describes anti-discrimination rights protected by the *Canadian Human Rights Act* as "almost constitutional." (*Robichaud v. Canada (Treasury Board)* ([1987] 2 S.C.R. 84, 92.) In *Robichaud,* decided under the Canadian Human Rights Act S.C. 1976-77 c33, the Court interpreted the phrase *"in the course of employment"* (*Human Rights Act* s7(b)) vis-à-vis a government employee, rejecting traditional tort notions of vicarious liability (p. 91) and concluding that:

> "the statute contemplates the imposition of liability on employers for all acts of their employees "in the course of employment", interpreted in the purposive fashion outlined earlier as being in some way related or associated with employment. It is unnecessary to attach any label to this type of liability; it is purely statutory. However, it serves a purpose somewhat similar to that of vicarious liability in tort by placing responsibility for an organization on those who control it and are in a position to take effective remedial action to remove undesirable conditions." (Citing Justice Marshall's concurrence in *Meritor Savings Bank v. Vinson* 106 S.Ct. 2399 (1986, at pp. 2410-11 concerning sexual discrimination by supervisory personnel.)

In *Jansen v. Platy Enterprises Ltd.* (59 D.L.R.(4th) 352), decided under the 1976–7 Manitoba Human Rights Act, (now superseded by the Manitoba Human Rights

Code), the Canadian Supreme Court reinstated a judgment by a lower court against a corporate employer for a cook's sexual harassment of waitresses "*in the course of employment*" because "his actions were clearly work-related", "related to his employment position as the next in line in authority." (*Ibid.* 382).

The court cited English and American cases. In lieu of the American "*quid pro quo*/hostile work environment dichotomy" the court preferred a broad definition of sexual harassment in the working place "as unwelcome conduct of a sexual nature that detrimentally affects the work environment or leads to adverse job-related consequences for the victims of harassment." (*Ibid.* p.375)

7. AUSTRALIA. In Australia, sexual harassment is covered by the Sex Discrimination Act 1984. For cases see *Hill v. Water Resources Commission* (1984); *Wacyk v. Australian Stock Exchange,* 61 SAIR 217 (1994) (Commission for Industrial Relations held to lack jurisdiction.) S.S. Berns, *A tort of Sexual Harassment for Tasmania* 13 U. Tasmania L.R. 412.

8. SOUTH AFRICA. Article 8 of the Interim Constitution of the Republic of South Africa, 1993 (Act 209 of 1993) provides:

> Art. 8 (1) Every person shall have the right to equality before the law and to equal protection of the law.
>
> (2) No person shall be unfairly discriminated against, directly or indirectly, and, without derogating from the generality of this provision, on one or more of the following grounds in particular: race, gender, sex, ethnic or social origin, colour, sexual orientation, age, disability, religion conscience, belief, culture or language.

Even prior to the enactment of this constitutional protection against discrimination on the ground of sex, it was suggested that the relief against "unfair labour practices" which an amendment of 1979 inserted into the Labour Relations Act (Act 28 of 1956) was available in case of sexual harassment. The statutory definition of "unfair labour practice" in sec. 1 of the Act was thought to be capable of accommodating conduct constituting sexual harassment, see J.G. Mowatt, *Sexual Harassment — New Remedy for an Old Wrong,* 7 Indus. L.J. (S.A.) 637 (1986). The idea was repeated in a more recent article, Lisa Dancaster, *Sexual Harassment in the Work-place: Should South Africa Adopt the American Approach?* 12 Indus. L.J. (S.A.) 449 (1991).

Although an amendment of 1988 which expressly included sex discrimination in the definition of unfair labor practice was repealed in 1991, the new definition which reverts to a general type still fits sexual harassment since it is an "act . . . that has or may have the effect that the labour relations between employer and employee is or may be detrimentally affected thereby."

So far there are no reported cases in which an employee claimed judicial relief from sexual harassment. However, it has been held that sexual harassment by a senior manager of members of the staff warranted dismissal, *J v M LTD* (1989), Industrial Court, 10 Indus.L.J. 755 (1989) (S. Afr.). In his opinion, the judge stated (757):

> "Sexual harassment, depending on the form it takes, will violate that right to integrity of the body and personality which belongs to every person and which is protected in our legal system both criminally and civilly."

See also P. Halfkenny, *Legal and Workplace Solutions to Sexual Harassment in South Africa (Part I): Lessons from Other Countries,* 16 Indus. L.J. 1 (1995) referring, inter alia, to the laws of Lesotho, Namibia and Zimbabwe.

D. FRANCE

1. Legislation

a. Labor Code

L. 122.46 (added by Law Nr. 92-1179 of Nov. 2, 1992 Art.1).

No employee may be punished or discharged for submitting or refusing to submit to the tactics of harassment of an employer, his representative or of any person who, abusing the authority conferred upon him by his office, gave orders, made threats, imposed restrictions or pressured the employee in any manner in order to obtain favors of a sexual nature for his or her own benefit or for a third party.

L. 122.48 (added by Law Nr. 92-1179 of Nov. 2, 1992 Art.1).

It is the responsibility of the head of a business to make all necessary arrangements required to prevent the acts envisaged in the 2 preceding articles.

b. Criminal Code of July 22, 1992

Art. 222-33. Of Sexual Harassment

Harassment of another by the use of orders, threats or compulsion for the purpose of obtaining favors of a sexual character by a person abusing his authority which his functions confer upon him is punishable with imprisonment of one year and a fine of 100,000 F.

2. Caselaw

Judgment of June 30, 1993

Versailles 11th Social Chamber
Judgment of June 30, 1993
D. IR 228 (1993).

A president-CEO is not liable for sexual harassment towards an employee for expressing amorous sentiments towards an employee through letters and poems without thereby abusing his authority by orders, threats, constraints or pressure in order to obtain sexual favors, as long as these poems and letters only convey the author's emotional feelings, without containing any indecent or obscene terms going beyond the simple expression of an amorous passion and being capable of affecting the dignity of the employee in her professional life, and even if, if the employee did not intend to react to the sentiments which her president expressed to her, she nevertheless maintained a certain intimacy with him in revealing certain aspects of her past private life;

The termination of the work contract is thus attributable to the employee's resignation.

NOTES

1. The appeal in the Versailles Judgment of June 30, 1993 concerns events which transpired prior to passage of the Sexual Harassment in the Workplace Act 1992.

2. Under American law, coworkers as well as employers may be liable for sexual harassment. By contrast, in France, Labor Code L. 122-46 only applies to sexual harassment by employers. The Court of Cassation, Social Chamber has interpreted L. 122-46 to mean that the harassing party must be superior to the victim in the labor hierarchy. (See Judgment of Oct. 2, 1997 *C . . . c. S.A. B. . . .* Cass.soc. 72 *Quotiedien Juridique* Feb. 1998 p. 7 with note.)

3. *Civil actions based on Criminal Code Art. 222-33.* In France, the victim of an infraction can seek damages in a civil suit brought before a criminal or a civil judge. Thus the victim of sexual harassment could seek damages (i) in a so-called "*action civile*" brought in an action ancillarily to the public prosecution (*action publique*

(Arts. 2, 5 and 464 C.P.P.)), (ii) by initiating her own criminal action (Art. 1 C.P.P.), or (iii) in a separate action before a civil judge (Art. 4 C.P.P.) In the Judgment of Jan. 4, 1995, *Sté Tempier Roustant c. Mme B . . .* Court of Appeals, Aix-en-Provence, 70 J.C.P. II 22624 (1998) affirmed a judgment for FF 20,000 after the employee's health suffered from an employer who abusively pressured an employee to quit when she refused his advances.

4. For a critical view of the situation in France see Claude Roy-Loustaunau, *La démission provoquée par le harcèlement sexuel* note on Judgment of Jan. 4, 1995 (CA Aix-en-Provence, 18th Ch.) 70 JCP I 3662 (p. 174) (1996). Françoise Dekeuwer-Defossez, *Le harcèlement sexuel en droit français: discrimination ou atteinte à la liberté?,* 67 JCP I 3662. C. Katz, *La dénonciation calomnieuse en matière de harcèlement sexuel,* 114 Gazette du Palais 1378 (1994). P. Acton & E. Delesseux, *De la nécessité de prévenir et de réprimer la discrimination ou le harcèlement psychologique dans la vie professionnelle,* 101 Petites Affiches 7 (1996).

E. GERMANY

1. Legislation

a. Basic Law (as amended 1994).

BASIC LAW (*Grundgesetz* [GG])
Article 3[17]

(1) All people are equal before the law.

(2) Men and women enjoy equal rights. The state shall promote the actual attainment of the equality of rights of women and men and aim at the elimination of existing detriments.

(3) Nobody may be disadvantaged or preferred because of sex, descent, race, language, homeland and provenance, faith, religious or political convictions. Nobody may be disadvantaged because of disabilities.

b. 2. GleiBG.

SECOND LAW FOR THE ACHIEVEMENT OF EQUAL RIGHTS FOR MEN AND WOMEN June 24, 1994 (2. GleiBG.)[18]
BGBl I 1994 p. 1406

Art. 10

Law for Protection of Employees against Sexual Harassment in the Workplace (Employee Protection Law)

17. Article 3 GG was amended by 42. ÄndG of Oct. 27, 1994 (BGBl I 3146).

18. Gesetz zur Durchsetzung der Gleichberechtigung von Frauen und Männern (Zweites Gleichberechtigungsgesetz [2. GleiBG].

§ 1

Aim and Scope of Application

(1) This law aims at the preservation of the dignity of women and men through protection against sexual harassment in the workplace.

(2) Employees within the Meaning of this Law are

1. Female and male employees in enterprises and administrative offices of private or public law (female and male workers, employees, persons employed for occupational training) as well as persons who, because of their economic dependence, are to be regarded as assimilated to employees. The latter include also home workers and persons of similar status; with respect to them the position of the employer is assumed by the person who ordered the work, or an intermediary;
2. female or male officials of the Federal Republic, the States, communities, association of communities as well as the other corporations, institutions or foundations of public law subject to the supervision of the Federal Republic or a State;
3. female or male judges of the Federal Republic or the States;
4. female or male judges of the Federal Republic or the States;
5. female or male soldiers (§ 6).

§ 2

Protection against Sexual Harassment

(1) Employers and superior officials are obligated to protect the employees against sexual harassment in the workplace. This protection also includes preventive measures.

(2) Sexual harassment in the workplace is any intentional sexually-determined conduct which violates the dignity of the employee in the workplace. To it belong:

1. sexual acts and types of conduct which are punishable according to the penal laws; as well as
2. other sexual acts or invitations to their commitment, sexually determined bodily touching, remarks with sexual content, as well as demonstrations or affixations of pornographic representations which are clearly rejected by the target;

(3) Sexual harassment in the workplace is a breach of the duties created by the labor contract or a service offence.

§ 3

Employees' Right to Lodge Grievances

(1) Aggrieved employees have the right to lodge complaints with the competent authorities in the enterprise or the office if they feel that they are sexually molested in the workplace within the meaning of §2(2) by the employer, superior, fellow employees or third persons. The provisions of §§ 84 and 85 of the Work Council Law remain unaffected.

(2) The employer or superior must examine the complaint and take the measures necessary to prevent the continuation of an ascertained harassment.

§ 4

Measures of the Employer or Superior, Right to Refuse Performance.

(1) In the case of sexual harassment

1. The employer has to take the disciplinary steps appropriate to the case, such as warning, relocation, transfer or dismissal. The rights of the work council according to §§ 87(1) Nr. 1,99 and 102 of the Work Council Law, and of the personal council, according to §§ 75(1) Nr. 2-4a and (3) Nr. 15, 77(2) and § 79 of the Federal Personnel Council Law and the correspondent provisions of the Personal Representation Law of the States remain unaffected.
2. The superior official has to take the necessary disciplinary and personnel-management measures. The rights of the Personnel Council of Public Officials according to §§ 76-78 of the Federal Officials' Representation Law and the correspondent Personnel Representation Laws of the States remain unaffected.

(2) If the employer or the supervisor fails to take, or resorts to obviously unsuited measures to stop the sexual harassment, the molested employees are entitled to discontinue their activity in the workplace without loss of wages or salary, to the extent that this is necessary to their protection.

(3) The employer or superior may not disadvantage the harassed employees because they have defended themselves against the sexual harassment, and exercised their rights in a permitted manner.

NOTES

1. For an example of a prosecution under the Employee Protection Law (*Beschäftigtenschutzgesetz)* see *Bundesverwaltungsgericht,* Order of November 15, 1996, 50 NJW 958 (1997) affirming temporary suspension and administrative penalties for a postal worker disciplined under Art. 10 § 2 (2)2 Employee Protection Law for violating the dignity of a fellow worker by sending obscene messages.

2. The enactment of this statute was followed by the 42nd amendment of the German Basic Law of October 27, 1994, BGBl I 1994 p. 3146, which, added the second sentence, to Art. 3 par. 2 GG. R. Sannwald, *Die Reform des Grundgesetzes* 47 NJW 3313, 3314 (1994).

3. The SPD party's proposals calling for penalties up to DM 100,000 were not adopted. A. Mittmann, *Das Zweite Gleichberechtigungsgesetz — eine Übersicht* 47 NJW 3048, 351 (at n. 47) (1994).

4. CZECH REPUBLIC. Sexual harassment of female employees is reportedly becoming a burning issue in post-Communist Central Europe. Cf. London Times September 6, 1996 p. 14 ("The sacking of Frantisek Batrla, a 57-year old Bank manager who was accused of making suggestive comments to women staff, has shocked Prague." "The case of Mr Batrla shows how quickly attitudes are shifting.")

5. JAPAN. Leon Wolff, *Eastern Twists on Western Concepts: Equality Jurisprudence and Sexual Harassment in Japan.* 5 Pacific Rim Law & Policy Journal 509.

F. ITALY

The basis for attacking sexual harassment (*molestie sessuali*) in Italy has been discussed in lower court decisions in Milan[19] and Trent.[20] In 1995, the Italian Court of Cassation (Sec. Labor Law) reversed a decision by the Prefect of Montepulciani serving as a labor court, which declared that the alleged acts were extra-contractual and therefore beyond its competence as a labor court.

In reversing, the Court of Cassation held that sexual harassment was a violation of obligations protected by Civil Code Art. 2087 requiring the protection of the physical and moral integrity of workers; it declared these are also Constitutionally protected values.[21] The Court referred to Community law:[22] The European Parliament's Resolution of June 11, 1986 on violence against women[23] and Council Resolution of May 29, 1990 on the protection of the dignity of women and men at work.[24]

---

19. Praetor Of Milan, Judgment of August 14, 1991 (*Neposteri v. Carbonstil et al.*) 11 Riv. It. Dir. Lav. [Revista Italiana di Diritto del Lavoro] 403 (1992).

20. Praetor of Trent, Judgment of February 22, 1993 (*Cardi v. Grassi*) 13 Riv. It. Dir. Lav. 172 (1994) (awarding contractual and extra-contractual damages).

21. Court of Cassation (Labor section) Judgment of July 17, 1995, 148 Giurisprudenza Italiana 1110 (1996). See Luca Iafisco, *Un'importante pronuncia della Suprema Corte in tema di responsabilità del datore di lavoro colpevole di molestie sessuali,* 148 Giurisprudenza Italiana 1109 (1996).

22. *Ibid.* 1114.

23. European Parliament Resolution of June 11, 1986, O.J. No C 176, July 14, 1986, p. 79 (cf. *supra* p. 214 n. 4).

24. O.J. No.C 157, June 27, 1990, p. 3 (Cf. *supra* p. 217 n. 10).

5/Privacy

INTRODUCTION

Modern emphasis on the so-called rule of law and the concomitant reliance on the judiciary as the guardian of constitutional government have exerted important repercussions on the power of legislatures over matters once thought to be within the autonomous province of private law. The evolution of judicial control over the constitutionality of legislation, whether in the centralized form via the creation of constitutional courts or in the de-centralized form of attribution of the power of review to any judicial tribunal,[1] the advent of modern constitutions with their growing catalogues of individual civil rights as well as the conclusion of international conventions protecting civil and political rights have given the problems a new aspect of great interest to the comparativist.

The materials included in this part of the readings are designed to convey a picture of the common or individual problems arising in different national settings. This includes not only various civil law countries, whether European or Latin American, but also common law countries, especially the United States and Canada. In the latter nation the relevant issues gained a new complexion as the result of the entrenchment of the Charter of Rights and Freedoms in the Canadian constitution in 1982.[2]

---

1. For a thoughtful criticism of the ever-increasing assertion of jurisdiction by the constitutional court, see B. Grossfeld, *Götterdämmerung*? [Twilight of the Gods.] 48 NJW 1719 (1995).

2. Can. Const. (Constitution Act, 1982) pt. I (Canadian Charter of Rights and Freedoms). See D. Beatty, Human Rights and Constitutional Review in Canada, 13 Human Rights L.J. 185 (1992).

A. GERMANY

1. Princess Soraya Case

Federal Constitutional Court
Resolution of February 14, 1973
Constitutional Complaint
Die Welt
v.
Judgment of the Federal Supreme Court of December 8, 1964
(*Princess Soraya*)
34 BVerfGE 269 (1973).

The complaint is dismissed.

The case-law of the civil courts which award monetary damages also for non-economic damages in case of grave violations of the general right of personality is compatible with the Basic Law.

REASONS
A.

1. According to the Civil Code [BGB] § 249, a person obliged to redress damages is under a duty to restore the condition which would exist if the event causing the duty of reparation had not occurred. This principle of restoration in kind (*restitutio in integrum*) applies also to the reparation of non-monetary "immaterial" damages. For instance, in the case of a defamation the impairment of the reputation of the offended person may be removed by a retraction or the publication of the judgment imposing a duty to retract.

A restoration in kind, however, presupposes that a restoration of the prior condition is possible. If for natural reasons damages are not capable of being repaired in this way, either not at all or only partially, the victim is entitled to monetary compensation, BGB § 251(1). For non-economic damages, however, this principle is limited by BGB § 253. Money damages, according to this provision, are available only in certain cases defined by statute. In these cases, compensation for pain and suffering is primarily involved, which pursuant to BGB § 847 is due to victims of personal injuries, unlawful deprivation of liberty, and sexual offenses. Apart from the Civil Code, non-economic damages must be compensated in a number of special instances * * *.

2. While the legal systems which applied in Germany during the middle of nineteenth century accorded a relatively broad protection to the personality, including compensation for pain and suffering, the framers of the projects of the Civil Code from the beginning rejected a general right of satisfaction in money for injuries to non-economic interests. Despite weighty objections by jurists (above all Otto von Gierke and Franz von Liszt), the legislator retained this view. It was primarily justified with the thesis that it was offensive to the popular opinion to put non-economic interests on the same level as economic interests and to compensate a non-economic injury with money; besides, the judge lacked a fixed standard for evaluation of the damage.

3. The case-law of the Supreme Court of the Empire on the protection of the personality kept until the very end within the confines of the written law of the Civil Code. Following the then prevailing doctrine, the Court rejected a general right of personality because it was foreign to the current private law and its recognition within the framework of BGB § 823(1) would entail an insecure limitation of that provision (113 RGZ 413 (1926)).

To remedy aggravated intrusions in the private sphere the Supreme Court of the Empire extended the scope of protection of existing special rights of personality such as the right to one's name and picture. In addition, in application by analogy with §§ 862 and 1004 BGB, the Court recognized claims for desisting from continued defamation and for retraction and correction. Monetary compensation for non-patrimonial damages was awarded, however, only if the defamation caused damages to the victim's health and therefore amounted to a personal injury (142 RGZ 116, 122 (1934)).

The deficiencies of the private law protection of the right of personality were felt particularly strongly after the Second World War, especially since National Socialism had narrowed the scope of personal freedom far more than it had been believed to be possible before. On the other hand, the forms of publicity and advertisement characteristic of modern life, the increased accent upon the right to information (of the individual as well as society at large), and the perfection of means of communication and other technical appliances created possibilities of the invasion of the personal sphere of the individual which were inconceivable for the legislator of the Civil Code.

For that reason, the Federal Supreme Court in 1954 met with general approval when for the first time, it expressed the existence of a general right of personality (13 BGHZ 334, 337 (1954)). It announced that the right to respect for personal dignity and to untrammeled development of personality, protected by the Basic Law, Arts. 1 and 2, also had private-law aspects, to be observed by everyone in everyday private law contacts. The general right of personality was within the protection of BGB § 823(1); the determination whether this right was infringed, however, required a careful and detailed balancing of values and interests. In subsequent judgments, the Court endeavored to concretize the scope of the general right of personality, thus defined in a manner resembling a general clause (cf. 15 BGHZ 249 (1955); 20 BGHZ 345 (1956); 26 BGHZ 52 (1958); 27 BGHZ 284 (1956); 31 BGHZ 308 (1960)).

4. Although the existence of a general right of personality was quickly accepted by courts and in the legal literature, the question whether an infringement of the right of personality was to be redressed by compensation for non-economic damages remained debated.

* * *

5. The courts did not await a statutory revision of the protection of the right of personality. In its so-called Equestrian (*Herrenreiter*)-Judgment the Federal Supreme Court in 1958 for the first time awarded to the victim of a violation of his right of personality an equitable monetary compensation for non-patrimonial damages (26 BGHZ 349 (1958)). In the reasons for the decision, the Court, relying on its Judgment of 1954 (13 BGHZ 134 (1954)), stated that Articles 1 and 2 of the Basic Law are not only the source of a duty to respect one's personality. The articles were also said to have the consequence that in the case of infringements of the private sphere, protection against injuries to the character of the personality must be awarded. The duty to compensate the damages rests on an analogous application of BGB § 847.

In numerous subsequent decisions the Federal Supreme Court reaffirmed and expanded the principles of that judgment. The right to damages for pain and suffering, however, is no longer based on an analogous application of BGB § 847. Rather, the decisions rest on the ground that the perfection of the private-law protection of the right of personality, which was accomplished under the impact of the value-judgments of the Basic Law, would remain full of gaps and unsatisfactory if a violation of the right of personality were not to entail a sanction commensurate to the non-economic injury. Just as the limitation of the law of torts to the invasion of certain specific legal interests of a person has proved to be too narrow to furnish the protection of the personality mandated by the Basic Law, the limitation of compensation for ideal damages to violations of single specified legal interests no longer corresponds to value system of the Basic Law. The exclusion of compensation for non-economic damages in the protection of the personality would signify that violations of human honor and dignity are left without a civil law sanction. The legal order thus would renounce the most effective and often sole means suitable for assuring the respect for the personal value of the individual.

* * *

6. The case-law of the courts in private law matters and the legal literature have followed the decision of the Federal Supreme Court to a prevailing extent. * * *

The criticism in the literature (e.g. of Larenz) * * * and in the decisions of a few appellate courts are directed less against the appropriateness of the result than against the method of the decision-making by the courts. It is argued that the claim could not be based on an analogous application of BGB § 847; that in the enactment of BGB § 253, the legislator provided an exhaustive regulation of the subject; that the prerequsites for a judicial development of the law is lacking. [According to this literature] [t]he argument that the private-law protection of the personality would remain full of gaps and unsatisfactory if the violations of the right of personality did not entail sanctions commensurate with the ideal injury does not have a legal character, but the character of legal policy. They say it is the task of the legislator and not of the courts to determine the consequences of the violation of a right and that the emphasis on the satisfaction function of the compensation for pain and suffering blurs the boundary with a penalty.

B.

1. The complainant publishing company Die Welt, a member of the Axel-Springer Group, formerly published a weekly called *Das Neue Blatt* * * *, which specialized in sensational reports regarding society. * * * On the front page of the edition of April 29, 1961 it published a so-called Special Report with the caption "Soraya: The Shah no longer wrote to me" in the form of an Exclusive Interview which Princess Soraya allegedly had granted to a journalist. In it, statements by the Princess about her private life were reproduced. The interview was sold to the journal by a free-lance reporter; it was totally invented. In the edition of July 1, 1961, *Das Neue Blatt,* inserted in a new report "Soraya-O'Brian: Examination of the Hearts," published a short counter-declaration of the Princess Soraya, stating that there had been no such interview.

The district court granted Princess Soraya's complaint demanding payment of damages for the violation of her right of personality and condemned complainant "to pay damages in the amount of DM 15,000." Appeal and petition for review had no success.

* * *

2. In its constitutional complaint, complainant charges a violation of Article 2, par. 1 in conjunction with Art. 20, par. 2 and 3, of Art. 5; par. 1, sentence 2 and par. 2, and of Art. 103, par. 2, GG, and, as a matter of precaution, of its fundamental rights flowing from Arts. 3, 12 and 14 GG.

They argue that the application of the rule according to which violations of the general right of personality, under certain conditions, calls for indemnification in money also in cases of non-economic injuries, does not remain within the framework of the constitutional order because this rule was established in violation of the principles of separation of powers fixed by the Basic Law, Art. 20 par. 2 & 3. The judgment under attack therefore infringes in an impermissible way on their freedom of action. The Supreme Court awards pain and suffering damages, so they claim, contra legem, because this result cannot be deduced either directly or by analogy from the provisions of the Civil Code. * * *

The judgement under attack, they contend, violates the basic right to freedom of opinion and of the press, because the rule developed by the Supreme Court upon which they are based represents an impermissible limitation of this basic right within the meaning of Art. 5 par. of the Basic Law. * * * In addition, the award of damages for pain and suffering for non-economic damages, according to complainants, violates the principle *nulla poena sine lege* (Art. 103 GG).

C.

The constitutional complaint is unfounded.

I.

1. The judicial proceedings in which the decision under attack was rendered was a private-law controversy which has to be decided pursuant to the provisions governing private law. The Federal Constitutional Court does not review the interpretation and application of private law as such. However, the value-system enshrined in the constitutional norms on fundamental rights also affects private law; it applies as a constitutional principle to all areas of the law. Assurance that this radiation-effect of the Constitution is observed is entrusted to the Federal Constitutional Court. It must therefore examine whether the decisions of the civil courts are based on a fundamentally erroneous view of the scope and force of a fundamental right or whether the result of a decision itself violates the fundamental rights of a party (cf. 7 BVerfGE 198, 205 (1958); 18 BVerfGE 85, 92f (1965); 30 BVerfGE 173, 183f, 196f (1971); 32 BVerfGE 311, 316 (1972)).

In the instant case the complainant challenges not only the result of the civil judgments; it objects above all to the method by which the courts have reached that result. Complainant disputes that the judge, in view of his being bound by the law, is permitted in these cases to impose monetary damages. This argument calls for a consideration of the essence and bounds of the judicial activity, as they are outlined in the Basic Law. It must be examined whether decision of this kind could be reached by way of judicial ascertainment of the law. The judge may not effectuate the value judgments of the Basic Law in any way he chooses. He would also violate the Constitution if he were to arrive at a result corresponding to the value system of the constitution by a methodological path which disregards the constitutional limits confining the judge in his ascertainment of the law. A decision arrived at in that way would be subject to censure by the Federal Constitutional Court.

2. The complaint in the instant civil litigation was based on BGB § 823, par. 1. The Federal Supreme Court includes in the circle of absolute rights there mentioned the so-called general right of personality, relying on its well-established jurisprudence, explained in detail in the Judgment of May 25, 1954 (13 BGHZ 334 (1954)); it considers complainant's conduct to constitute a violation of this right. It is not the function of the Federal Constitutional Court to pass on the "correctness" of this jurisprudence, to the extent that its foundation and evolution remains within the ambit of private law doctrine. It suffices to state that the notion of a general right of personality —

though originally rejected by the drafters of the Civil Code — was accepted in the literature after decades of debate and, after recognition by the Federal Supreme Court, now forms a firm component of our private law system. * * *

The Federal Constitutional Court sees no reason to oppose this jurisprudence on constitutional grounds. The value system of the fundamental rights has its center in the human personality freely developing within the social community, and its dignity (6 BVerfGE 32, 41 (1957); 7 BVerfGE 198, 205 (1958)). It is entitled to respect and protection by the entire power of the State (Arts. 1 and 2, par. 1 of the Basic Law). This protection, above all, is due to the private sphere of a human being, the ambit within which he wishes to be left alone, to make his own decisions with responsibility only to himself, and to be untrammeled by any type of interference (27 BVerfGE 1 (1970)). This protection is accomplished within the area of private law by means of the concept of the general right of personality; it fills the gap in the protection of personality that remained despite the recognition of special rights of personality and in the course of time were felt more and more. The Federal Constitutional Court therefore never objected to its judicial recognition by the civil courts (cf. 30 BVerfGE 173, 194ff (1971); 34 BVerfGE 118, 135f (1973); 34 BVerfGE 238 (1973)).

3. Section 823, par. 1, BGB, is a "general law" within the meaning of Art. 5, par. 2, of the Basic Law (7 BVerfGE 198, 211 (1958); 25 BVerfGE 256, 263 (1969)). If therefore the general right of personality belongs to the rights there listed, pursuant to an interpretation which is free from constitutional objections, it is capable, according to the constitutional wish, to limit the fundamental right of the Freedom of the Press, invoked by the complainant. This potential force of a general law is, as explained, reinforced by the mandate of protection specified in Arts. 1 and 2, par. 1 of the Basic Law. On the other hand, the fundamental importance of the Freedom of the Press in a free and democratic society must not be disregarded. It retains its weight in the necessary balancing that must be made if a conflict between the constitutionally protected interests of the parties to a private law controversy must be resolved (25 BVerfGE 256, 263 (1969); 30 BVerfGE 173, 196 (1971)). In the course of this balancing the general right of personality is not entitled to absolute priority; the Freedom of the Press may, according to the circumstances, effectuate a restriction of the claims derived from the right of personality (7 BVerfGE 198 (1959)).

4. The decision under attack accorded to the protection of plaintiff's private sphere priority over the Freedom of the Press. According to the facts found, this decision is free from constitutional objections. Complainant published in a journal belonging to the entertainment press a fictitious interview with plaintiff, describing events in her private in a fashion as if plaintiff herself had recounted them. The courts considered that as an unlawful invasion of the private sphere of plaintiff who alone is entitled to determine whether and in what way events of her private life should be made available to the public.

Indeed, under these circumstances complainant cannot invoke the Freedom of the Press to justify its conduct. To be sure, it would go too far to deny the protection of this fundamental right to the entertainment and sensational press in general, as was done by the trial court in reliance on some expressions in the literature. The concept of "press" must be interpreted in a broad and formal way; it cannot be made depending upon an evaluation — based on whatsoever criteria — of the particular printing products. The Freedom of the Press is not limited to the "serious" press (cf. 12 BVerfGE 205 (1962)). This does not mean, however, that the protection of the fundamental right must be accorded to every constituent of the press in every legal context and for every content of its expression in an equal manner. In balancing the Freedom of the Press against other constitutionally protected legal interests consideration may be given to the question whether the press, in the particular case discusses a matter of public interest in a serious and objective vein * * * or whether it merely satisfies the needs of a more or less extensive group of readers for superficial entertainment. * * *

In this case the need to protect the private sphere of plaintiff was not in opposition to a prevailing general interest in the public discussion of the matters treated in the interview. The readers have no right to be informed, by means of an invented interview, about the private life of a person temporarily within the light of public attention.

II.

If a general statute potentially limits the Freedom of the Press, the manner in which such limitation may be effected is likewise determined solely by the content of the statute. That means above all only the sanctions authorized by the statute may be imposed on the press and limit its freedom effectively. This is the basis for the challenge by the complainant. It contends that there exists no general statute which provides in the case of a violation of the general right of personality for the reparation of the non-economic injury by means of the payment of money; in fact BGB § 253 expressly excludes such claim. Accordingly, the courts, in awarding money damages, transgressed the boundaries within which the constitution permits a limitation of the Freedom of the Press. Moreover, the imposed sanction constituted a material violation of the press since it is specifically directed against the press and subjects it to an incalculable risk.

In addressing these contentions the Federal Constitutional Court must limit itself to the constitutional aspects of the judgments. This poses the questions: firstly, whether the substantive result of the decisions in itself violates the Freedom of the Press, and secondly, whether it is reconcilable with the Basic Law to arrive at that result despite the lack of a definite basis in the written law by means of judicial decision.

The examination of both questions results in the conclusion that the decisional law of the Supreme Court to the extent that it is the basis for the judgments under attack is free from constitutional objections.

III.

It is in the nature of things that violations of the general right of personality may primarily be perpetrated by constituents of the press, since they dispose of the technical means of information gathering and divulging and therefore are capable of relatively easy intrusion into the private sphere of the citizens. Examples of the case-law show, however, that the courts apply the rules developed for the protection of the general right of personality also outside activities of the press (cf. 26 BGHZ 349 (1958); 30 BGHZ 7 (1960); 35 BGHZ 363 1962)). Consequently no "special law against the press" is present. * * *

Reparation of non-economic damages by means of monetary payments is not a sanction which on principle is foreign to our legal system, as is shown by BGB § 253. It is provided in BGB § 847 for the violations of other rights listed in BGB § 847 and in a number of special laws. In the course of the evolution of the case-law the case groups in which non-economic damages must be compensated have gained clear contours. The right to monetary compensation has a subsidiary character. The courts award money damages only, if restoration in nature, e.g. by means of retraction or cessation, is impossible or, in view of the circumstances, insufficient. "Commercialization of honor" is not a reproach to be taken seriously. Since a noticeable infringement of the personal sphere and grave culpability are required, care is taken that the standards of diligence demanded of a responsible press are not excessive and that there is no responsibility for merely any inaccuracy or objectively erroneous information. Finally, a review of cases shows that — like in the present case — the amounts of the damages awarded are kept in appropriate limits, especially if consideration is given to the fact that the injurious conduct of the organ of the press usually is prompted by economic interests. The risk to which the press is exposed therefore does not exceed the rationally expectable amount. The present case shows this with particular clarity. The amount of care that must be expended to avoid the publication of an invented interview is never excessive.

IV.

The traditional maxim that the judge is bound by legislation, an immanent component of the principle of the separation of powers and consequently of the rule of law, has been modified, at least literally, by the formulation that the judiciary is bound by "statute and law" (Art. 20, par. 3 GG). This rejects, as is generally recognized, a narrow legal positivism. This formulation maintains the reminder that legislation and law are usually but not always congruous. Law is not identical with the aggregate of written statutes. Beyond the written enactments by the state power there might in certain circumstances exist a "plus" of law which has its source in the constitutional legal order as a coherent aggregate and is capable of operating as a corrective of the written statutes; finding it and enforcing it in its decisions is the task of the judiciary. The Basic Law does not limit the judge to apply the legislative mandates within the limits of a possible meaning of the language to a particular case. * * * The task of judicial decision-making may, in particular, require that value notions, which are immanent in the existing constitutional legal system but not or only insufficiently expressed in the written statutes, be brought to light and effectuated in the decisions. This may necessitate a value-oriented appraisal which does not lack intentional elements. The judge therefore must refrain from arbitrariness; his decision must rest on rational reasoning. It must be made evident that the written law does not perform its function to resolve a legal problem in a just way. The judicial decision thus fills a gap pursuant to the standards of practical reason and to "the well-founded general notions of justice in the community." (9 BVerfGE 338 (1959)).

This task and power of the judge to engage in "creative decision-making" has never been denied, at least not under the sway of the Basic Law. * * * The Supreme Courts have invoked them from the beginning (cf. 3 BGHZ 308, 315 (1951); 4 BGHZ 153, 158 (1952); 1 BAG 279, 280 (1957).) The Federal Constitutional Court has always recognized them (3 BVerfGE 225, 243 (1954); 13 BVerfGE 153, 164 (1963); 18 BVerfGE 224, 237 (1965); 25 BVerfGE 167, 183 (1969)). The legislator himself has expressly bestowed upon the Enlarged Panels of the Federal Supreme Courts the task of "progressive development of the law" (see e.g. § 132 GVG). In certain areas of the law, such as the field of labor law, this task has become particularly important because of the failure of the legislation to keep pace with the flux of social development.

The only question that remains concerns the limits which must be fixed for such creative decision-making because of the principle that the judge is bound by the legislation, a principle which cannot be abandoned without disregard of the rule of law. They cannot be expressed in a single formula applicable in the same way to all branches of the law and to all legal relationships created or governed by them.

2. For the purpose of this decision the question posed may be limited to the area of private law. Here the judge faces the great codification of the Civil Code which has been in force for more than 70 years. This is significant in a two-fold sense: In the first place the increasing aging of the codification, the growing chronological distance between the enactment of a norm and its judicial application in a concrete case, entails an increase in the freedom of the judge to resort to a creative development of the law. * * * In the second place, as experience demonstrates, legislative reforms meet particular difficulties and obstacles when they involve modifications of the great codifications which place their imprint on the entire legal system to an extent as it was done by the codification of private law by the Civil Code.

3. The question which forms the object of the decisions under attack was, as has been discussed under A., already controversial when the Civil Code was drafted. The answer given by the legislator attracted immediate criticism, at first without reliance on constitutional aspects, a criticism which subsequently never subsided. This criticism could base itself on the legal development in other parts of the western world where the possibility of monetary redress of non-material damages was recognized to a much larger extent. * * * This criticism became exacerbated after the civil courts, under the influence of "the Constitution's force to shape private law" (L. Raiser) had taken the step of recognizing a general right of personality. The gap which existed in relation to the sanctions that could be imposed in the case of a violation of the right of personality became evident; a problem the importance of which could not be fully perceived when the Civil Code was drafted called urgently for a solution in tune with the change in the consciousness of legal rights and the value-system of the new constitution, a solution not capable of being predicated on the Civil Code because of the enumeration method adopted by BGB § 253.

The courts were confronted with the question whether they should fill the gap by means within their power or await legislative action. In choosing the first alternative the courts were supported by important voices in the literature. * * * Since their result was reached in a manner that was from the point of view of private law at least debatable and not manifestly in conflict with the rules of private law hermeneutics, no constitutional objections can be raised, inasmuch as it serves the enforcement and effective protection of a legal interest which the constitution itself regards as the center of its value-system. This result is "law" within the meaning of Art. 20 GG — not in opposition, but as supplement and expansion of the written law.

NOTES

1. Judgments of courts, even of the Supreme Courts, are subject to review as to their constitutionality by the Federal Constitutional Court by way of a constitutional complaint. The Constitutional Court reviews only the conformity of the judgment with constitutional principles, not their conformity with non-constitutional provisions. See Rennert, *Die Verfassungswidrigkeit "falscher" Gerichtsentscheidungen,* 44 NJW 12 (1991).

2. The effect of constitutional guarantees on legal relations governed by private law has been the subject of many judicial and doctrinal discussions. Usually the simile of radiation effect is employed. See G. Hermes, *Grundrechtsschutz durch Privatrecht auf neuer Grundlage? Das BVerfG zu Schutzpflicht und mittelbarer Drittwirkung der Berufsfreiheit,* 43 NJW 1764 (1990) commenting on the judgment of the Federal Constitutional Court Judgment of February 2, 1990, holding that private law must protect the freedom of professional activity, in the case at bar of a commercial agent (43 NJW 1469 (1990)).

2. *Mephisto*

Federal Constitutional Court
Resolution of February, 24, 1971
Nymphenburg Publishing Co.,
v.
Judgment of BGH, March 20, 1968
1 BvR 435/68
30 BVerfGE 173 (1971).

HOLDING

The Constitutional Complaint is rejected.

REASONS
A.
I.

The Constitutional Complaint concerns the injunction against the printing, publication and sale of Klaus Mann's novel Mephisto, the Story of a Career, issued against complainant upon request by the adopted son and sole heir of the late Gustaf Gründgens, actor and artistic director.

The author, who emigrated from Germany in 1933, published the novel in 1936 with the publishing house Querido in Amsterdam. After his death in 1949 the novel was published again by the publishing-house Aufbau in East Berlin.

The novel describes the ascent of the gifted actor Hendrik Höfgen, who betrays his political conviction and frees himself of all his human and ethical ties in order to pursue an artistic career in concert with national-socialistic dictators in Germany. The novel depicts the psychological, spiritual and sociological conditions that rendered this ascent possible.

The actor Gustaf Gründgens served as the model for the figure of Hendrik Höfgen. During the twenties Gründgens, who at that time was a member of the stage at Hamburg was a friend of Mann and married to his sister Erika, from whom he was divorced soon thereafter. Numerous details in the life of the figure Hendrik Höfgen — his outward appearance, the plays in which he acted, their chronological sequence, the promotion to the rank of Prussian state counselor and principal manager of the Prussian State Theater corresponded to the outward appearance and the life of Gründgens.* * *

II.

1. On August 1963 the complainant in this case announced a new publication of the Mephisto novel. A complaint seeking a prohibition of such publication was sought by the adopted son and sole heir of Gustaf Gründgens who had died on October 7, 1963. He claimed that any reader who had any, even only a superficial knowledge of the world of the German theater during the twenties and thirties, would identify Höfgen with the actor Gründgens. Since the novel intermixed recognizable true facts with numerous fictitious derogatory stories, he claimed that a falsified and dishonorable picture of Gründgens' personality was created. The novel was no work of art but merely a key-novel written by Klaus Mann as revenge on Gründgens, because he believed that his sister Erika was dishonored by her marriage to Gründgens. The plaintiff sought an injunction against the publishing house prohibiting the printing, distribution and publication of the novel under the threat of penalties for contempt.

The District Court of Hamburg dismissed the complaint. * * *

2. The Court of Appeals reversed the judgment below and granted the requested relief basing it both on the plaintiff's own right and the subsisting right of personality of the late Gustaf Gründgens. * * *

3. The petition for revision by the BGH, lodged by defendant, remained unsuccessful. The BGH rested its judgment on the subsisting right of personality of the deceased and left it open whether plaintiff's own rights gave him standing. * * *

B.
I.

In the Constitutional Complaint against the judgments of the BGH and the Hanseatic Court of Appeal complainant contends that these judgments violate Art. 1, Art. 2, par. 1, Art. 5, pars. 1 and 3, Art. 14 and Art. 103, par. 1 GG as well as the constitutional principles of proportionality and legal security. This contention is based on the reason that the judgments under attack violate the freedom of the arts. * * *

Complainant argues that the protection of the right of personality of an individual may exist only in the world of reality and in respect to that reality; that it does not extend to the world of fantasy of poetic creation; that in that respect there exist two separate non-comparable worlds. Further, the autonomy of the artistic presentation is guaranteed by Art. 5, par. 3 sentence 1 GG.

He contends that the assumption that the rights based on Art. 5, par. 3 GG are subject to an inherent limitation ignores that the fundamental right is accorded without limitation. * * *

C.

* * *

III.

Art. 5, par. 3 sentence 1 GG proclaims the freedom of the arts alongside science, research and opinion. This guarantee of freedom, according to its wording and meaning, constitutes in the first place an objective value-determining basic norm governing the relation between art and state. At the same time this provision assures anyone who is active in this field an individual right of freedom. * * *

3. Art. 5, par. 3, first sentence GG contains a comprehensive guarantee of the freedom of action in the field of art. To the extent that media are needed to create the rapport between artist and public, the protection extends to the persons who exercise an activity necessary for such communication. Because a work of the novelistic art could not reach the public without printing, distribution and publication, the publisher therefore exercises an indispensable function as intermediary and the guarantee of freedom extends also to his activities. The complainant as publisher of the novel is therefore entitled to invoke the protection of Art. 5, par. 3, first sentence GG.

4. The independence and autonomy of the arts are guaranteed without reservation. Attempts to limit the guarantee of the freedom of the arts by means of a value-oriented restriction of the concept of art, or by means of an expansive interpretation of, or analogy to, the limitations governing other constitutional provisions are doomed to failure in the face of the clear text of Art. 5, par. 3 sentence 1 GG.

Inapplicable in particular * * * is Art. 5, par. 2 GG, which limits the fundamental rights granted by Art. 5, par. 1 GG. The systematic separation of the spheres of protection accorded by Art. 5, par. 1 and Art. 5, par. 3 GG, makes par. 3 the *lex specialis* and thus prohibits the application of the limitations of par. 2 to the matters listed in par. 3. Equally inapposite is the view that the freedom of the arts, pursuant to Art. 2, par. 1, last part of sentence 2 GG is limited by the rights of others, by the general constitutional order and morals. This follows from the constant pronouncements of the Federal Constitutional Court that Art. 2, par. 1 GG is subsidiary to the individual fundamental rights and that this character prevents its extension to the spheres of life protected by special fundamental rights. * * *

5. On the other hand, the freedom of the arts is not guaranteed without any limits. The guarantee of freedom accorded in Art. 5, par. 3 sentence 1 GG results like all fundamental rights from the human image of the Basic Law, i.e., a human being with responsible personality developing within the social community. * * * As a part of the constitutional system of values the freedom of the arts is related in particular to the guarantee of human dignity anchored in Art. 1 GG which, as the supreme value, governs the entire value system of fundamental rights * * *. Nevertheless, conflicts may arise between the guarantee of the freedom of the arts and also the constitution-

ally guaranteed personal sphere, because a work of art may have effects on the social level. * * *

IV.

The Federal Constitutional Court therefore must decide whether the courts, in balancing the constitutional protection of the personal sphere of the late Gustaf Gründgens and his adopted son against the constitutional protection of the freedom of the arts guaranteed by Art. 5, par. 3, sent. 1 GG, have taken account of the governing principles. In deciding this problem, the Senate was split into equal votes. Therefore, pursuant to §15, par. 2 of the Law on the Constitutional Court [*BVerfGG*], it could not be held that the judgments under attack violated the Basic Law.* * *

2. The Appellate Court, as the last finder of facts, has determined that Gründgens represents a person belonging to recent history and that his memory in the general public is still alive. For those reasons the Court of Appeals and the Federal Supreme Court have concluded that the protection of the right to respect of the late Gustaf Gründgens still continues in the social sphere. The Supreme Court has correctly considered that the need for and the duty of protection diminish as the memory of the deceased fades and that in the course of time the interest in the non-falsification of his image disappears. This application of Art. 1, par. 1 GG is free from error. On the other hand, the courts have recognized that the novel of the late Klaus Mann is a work of art within the meaning of Art. 5, par. 3 GG, and that the complainant is entitled to its protection. Accordingly the courts have correctly perceived the tension between the spheres protected by Art. 1, par. 1 and by Art. 5, par. 3 sent. 1 GG. They have endeavored to resolve it by balancing the conflicting interests.

The Federal Constitutional Court has consistently held that judicial decisions attacked by a Constitutional complaint are subject only to a limited review (22 BVerfGE 93, 97 (1957)), that in particular the determination and assessment of facts, the interpretation of ordinary statutes and their application to the particular case is within the exclusive competence of the courts and not subject to the scrutiny by the Federal Constitutional Court (18 BVerfGE 85, 92 (1956)). These principles govern also the scrutiny of the balancing of the spheres protected by Art. 1, par. 2 GG and Art. 5, par. 3 sent. 1 GG of two parties to a relation governed by private law. The Court of Appeals — without objection by the Supreme Court — has called the novel a libel in form of a novel. There are no reasons to contradict the Court's assessment that the author has drawn a portrait of the actual image of Gründgens with negative and falsifying features. * * *

[Two of the three dissenting judges appended blistering dissents.]

NOTES

1. As the controlling opinion of the Court indicates, the Senate in the text case was evenly divided. Of the 6 judges, 3 voted for the dismissal of the constitutional complaint, the other 3 for its grant. Two of the dissenting judges wrote dissenting opinions. The author of one of them, Judge Mrs. Rupp v. Brünneck, criticized the prevailing opinion for its undue restriction of the effect of the basic rights of one of the private parties on the rights of the other, in other words, for a disregard of or departure from the principles governing the effect of the constitutionally granted basic rights in the legal relations of citizens inter se. The pioneering judgment in this respect was the *Lüth* case, 7 BVerfGE 198 (1958).

In *Lüth,* the director of the press-office of Free and Hanser City of Hamburg called for the boycott of a recent movie produced by an author and director, who during the Nazi era, had gained a national predominance by his collaboration in a vehemently antisemitic film requested by the minister of propaganda Goebbels. The director had been acquitted in a denazification process.

The producer and the distributor of the new film brought an action for a cease and desist order and the Hamburg Court of First Instance granted the injunction. The judgment was affirmed by the Court of Appeals and Mr Lüth filed a constitutional complaint. The Federal Constitutional Court vacated the judgment below on the ground that it violated complainant's basic right to express his opinion guaranteed by Basic Law, Art 5(1) sent. 1.

In the reasons for its holding, the Constitutional Court emphasized that under the German Basic Law, the basic rights protect the private individual not only against public authorities, but operate also in private law relations between private individuals. They have not only vertical, but also horizontal effects (*Drittwirkung*) or radiation effects (*Ausstrahlungswirkung*). In particular, the basic right to a free expression of opinion is -citing Cardozo- "the matrix, the indispensable condition of nearly every other form of freedom." Therefore, the complainant's battle against the reappearance of the former Nazi artist as representative of contemporary German art was constitutionally protected.

2. For the development of the Federal Constitutional Court decisions on freedom of the press since *Lüth* see D. Grimm, *Die Meinungsfreiheit in der Rechtssprechung des Bundesverfassungsgerichts,* 48 NJW 1697 (1995).

3. Publication of Decree Declaring Person Incompetent Due to Alcoholism (ZPO § 687) Incompatible with Right of Personality.

Federal Constitutional Court, First Sen.
Resolution of March 9, 1988.
78 BVerfGE 77 (1989) = 41 NJW 2031 (1988)
1 BvL 49/86.

Upon certification of question submitted by the District Court. (Art. 2I GG in conjunction with Art. 1I GG)

HOLDING

§ 687 of the Code of Civil Procedure [ZPO] is incompatible with Basic Law Art. 2.1 in conjunction with Basic Law Art. 1 para. 1 and null and void.

This does not apply to revocation of the Declaration of Incompetency which has already been published if the person declared to be incompetent has consented to the publication.

REASONS

A.

Object of the reference is the question whether § 687 ZPO which mandates the publication of a declaration of incompetence of a person because of extravagance of alcoholism is compatible with the Basic Law. * * *

B.

The reference is admissible. * * * It is not excepted from being passed upon by this Court because § 687 ZPO as pre-constitutional law is withdrawn from norm-control pursuant to Art. 100 par. 1 of the Basic Law. The provisions of the Code of Civil Procedure are post-constitutional law even when they coincide verbatim with the wording existing before the entry into force of the Basic Law. (Cf. 8 BVerfGE 210, 215 (1959); 10 BVerfGE 185, 191 (1960), 35 BVerfGE 41, 45 (1973).

1. The general right of personality, guaranteed by Art. 2I in conjunction with Art. 1I GG comprises the power of every individual to determine by himself the disclosure and use of his personal data (Right to informational Self-determination, cf. 65 BVerfGE 1 [41 ff] (1984), 37 NJW 419 (1984).) The protected data include also the act and status of the deprivation of competency as well as the personal circumstances which have caused the loss of legal competence.

This right is infringed not only if the state requires an individual to communicate personal data or transmits the same for automatic processing. Although the possibilities and dangers of automatic data processing have heightened the need for a protection of personal data they are not reason or cause of the necessity of their protection; rather, the right to informational self-determination, because it rests on the right of personality, grants general protection against official collection and processing of personal data and is not limited to the scope of the applicability accorded by current federal or state laws on data protection or special laws bearing on data protection. A publication such as provided by § 687 ZPO for certain cases of judicial declarations of incompetency constitutes only a special form of public transmittal of data. It effectuates the communication of personal data to an uncertain and undefined group of recipients, within and without public authorities and other public agencies in the presumed interest of them, free from limitations on their use and without supplementary procedural protective measures.

Conversely, the publication of the restoration of legal competence represents in some sense the elimination of the interference. Since, however, under present conditions of communication and mobility, there is little likelihood that the group of recipients of the two communications is the same, the public communication of restoration of legal competency constitutes a renewed infringement since it reiterates the publicity of the loss of competency.

2. The right of informational self-determination is not guaranteed without limits. The individual is obliged to tolerate limitations in the paramount public interest. But limitations of that kind require a legal basis, in accord with Art. 2I GG and must satisfy the principle of proportionality. This requires that a limitation of fundamental rights be justified by sufficient reasons of general welfare, that the selected measure is apt and necessary to achieve its purpose, and that in balancing the gravity of the interference with the weight of the justifying reasons the limit of the tolerable is not exceeded. (71 BVerfGE 183 (1986) 39 NJW 1536 (1986)). These requirements are not satisfied by § 687 ZPO. * * *

The balancing of the gravity of the interference and the weight of the justifying reasons results in the conclusion that the limits of what can be expected of the individual are exceeded. On the one hand, it must be considered that the publication has no legal effect as such, but accomplishes merely a widely dispersed warning without fixed purpose. In addition, the legislator has dispensed with the publication requirement in the greatest number of deprivations of legal competency (less than 10% of them are for extravagance, alcoholism or drug addiction). On the other hand, the publication of the deprivation of legal competence by reason of alcoholism or extravagance signifies an extensive interference with the fundamental right of the individual to determine by himself the disclosure and use of his personal data. The gravity of the infringement flows from the content of the publication. It does not merely say something about the possession of legal capacity, a quality important for the conduct of legal transactions, but it concerns the person as a whole. It conjures the risk of social typification and may make it harder to take remedial measures for overcoming the addiction and rehabilitation, based on the idea of the welfare state. The public announcement to an indefinite and unascertainable group of persons reaches not only those persons in whose interests it is made but also an unquantifiable multitude of other persons. Under these circumstances, the use of the data therefore is not capable of being limited to the examination of legal capacity. Moreover, the publication diminishes the possibility of an eradication of the imparted information in the case of a restoration of the legal capacity.

To be sure, § 687 ZPO envisages the publication of a restoration of legal capacity. However, as was pointed out before, this constitutes a new infringement. This hits the individual whose legal capacity is restored at a phase that is particularly critical and important for the societal rehabilitation. It produces the likelihood of significant effects on the resocialization of the formerly incapacitated individual and impairs the same in an intolerable manner. To be sure, in cases where publication of the declaration of incompetency has already occurred, the person involved must remain entitled to obtain the publication of the restoration of his legal capacity. However, but for this limitation with respect to these past publications, § 687 ZPO conflicts with the Basic law.

4. Notable German Cases on the Right of Personality

The notion of a general right of personality protected by § 823 I BGB was recognized by the BGH as a result of the constitutional guarantees of Art. 1 and Art. 2 of the Basic Law. Sanctions for its protection were damages, retractions etc. For other notable BGH or Federal Constitutional Court decisions involving the protection of the right to privacy see the following:

(1) ***Dr. M. (pl.) v D.W. Verlags GmbH (def.),*** Judgment of May 25, 1954, 13 BGHZ 334 (1954) (involving Dr. Schacht and his new banking venture.) Defendant's failure to print a correction of the original article by including excerpts of the Nuremberg judgment concerning Dr. Schacht and, as requested by Dr. Schacht's attorney Dr. M. the publication of the attorney's letter as a "Letter from Readers" constitutes a violation of the right of personality of the author of the letter.

(2) ***W.W. (pl.) v R.B. (def.),*** Judgment of November 26, 1954 15 BGHZ 49 (1955) (involving the diaries of Cosima Wagner). Cosima Wagner had given her diaries to her daughter Eva and entrusted her with their custody. Eva delivered them to the mayor of the City of Bayreuth for the benefit of the Richard Wagner Memorial but prohibited their publication until 30 years after her death. She also bequeathed the diaries to the City of Bayreuth.

The Plaintiff was Winifred Wagner, the widow of Siegfried Wagner, the sole heir of Richard and Cosima; defendant B. was the executor of Eva. The Court held that Cosima's diaries belonged to her private sphere and that she had the power to entrust her daughter with its protection. As a result, the heiress of the author did not have the right to compel an earlier publication against the wishes of Eva, who, pursuant to the intentions of the author, had the sole right to determine that date.

(3) ***S.H. KG (pl.) v. S (def.),*** Judgment of February 14, 1958, 16 BGHZ 349 (1958) (so-called *Equestrian Case*). Plaintiff is the co-proprietor of a brewery, who participates in amateur equestrian contests. Defendant is a manufacturer of pharmaceutical products, including a product believed to increase potency. Defendant, without consent of plaintiff, published a slightly retouched picture of plaintiff. The Court held that the publication was an invasion of plaintiff's general right of personality and that the appellate court could award monetary damages.

(4) ***S.F. KG (def.) v. B (pl.),*** Judgment of September 19, 1961 (so-called *Ginseng-Roots* case) 35 BGHZ 363 (1962). Plaintiff is the Extraordinary Professor of International and Canon Law at the University G.; defendant is the manufacturer of a medicinal preparation containing ginseng sold to increase or restore potency. The advertising pamphlet named plaintiff as an expert on the beneficial effects of ginseng. The Court held that the publication of the pamphlet constituted a culpable invasion of plaintiff's right of personality and entitled him to an award of damages based on the enhanced constitutional protection of the dignity of human personality.

(5) ***Tape Recorder Case.*** Worth mentioning also is a decision of the Federal Constitutional Court of January 31, 1973, 34 BVerfGE 239 (1973) (*Tape Recorder case*) on a constitutional complaint against the admission into evidence of a secret and private taping of the negotiations between private parties. The Court held that admission of the tapes constituted an unjustified invasion of the basic right of personality guaranteed by Art. 2 par. 1 GG.

For discussion *see* Claus Roxin *Strafverfahrensrecht* 25th ed. (1998) 191 (§42); W. Pakter, *Exclusionary Rules in France, Germany and Italy,* 9 HAST. I'l & Comp. L.R. 1, 43. (1985).

(6) ***The Princess Caroline Cases.***

The rules governing the amount of compensation due to the victim of a violation of her right of personality, in particular of her right to her picture, have been redefined by the BGH starting with a decision of the VI. Senate in Civil Matters of November 15, 1994 in the case of *B. GmbH (Bekl.) v. C.v.M. (Kl.),* 128 BGHZ 1 (1996).

In that case, Princess Caroline of Monaco demanded the defendant publisher of the Journals B. and G., publish of a revocation, and two corrections as well as pay compensation for the non-economic damages suffered by violation of her right of personality from publications in both journals. The publications consisted of an allegedly fictitious interview, the untrue report of an announcement of the plaintiff regarding her relationship with the actor Lindon and the report of an imminent marriage accompanied by the publication of unauthorized paparazzi photos.

The Court of Appeal at Hamburg upheld the Judgment of the trial court ordering defendant to publish a revocation and correction, although in a smaller type size than that demanded by plaintiff, and confirmed the award of compensation for pain and suffering in the amount of 30,000 DM. Both parties petitioned for revision.

The BGH rejected the petition of defendant and granted plaintiff's petition. It held that the compensation in the amount of 30,000 DM was based on an erroneous assessment of its purpose and legal basis. Compensation for infringement of the general right of personality is not based on BGH § 847, but is a remedy resulting from Article 1 and 2(1) of the Basic Law. Hence its main purpose is to impart satisfaction to the victim. The view of the court below that the profit-motive of defendant's violation or the purpose of prevention is irrelevant for the amount of the compensation, was not shared by the Senate of the Supreme Court. Both profit-motive and intensity of the violation are proper assessment factors. Since the measure of compensation is primarily a function of the trier of facts, the Court remanded the case to the Court of Appeal.

On remand, the Appellate Court of Hamburg, after detailed analysis of the rule of the case, recognized that the attainment of an adequate prevention effect required a substantial increase of the award of compensation and fixed the total amount at 180,000 DM.[3]

(7) ***BGH, Judgment of December 5, 1995***

The BGH reiterated the principle governing the determination of the compensation for serious violations of the right of personality in another case involving Princess Caroline of Monaco and reaching the Supreme Court on petition for review of a Judgment of the Court of Appeal of Hamburg, Judgment of December 5, 1995, 48 NJW 984 (1996). In that case, defendant was the publisher of two weeklies, F. And N., in which two articles appeared relating to Caroline's battle against breast cancer, the title of which was apt to cause the reader to think erroneously that Caroline suffered from that disease. Plaintiff asked damages in the amount of 50,000 DM for each of the two articles. The trial court granted only 20,000 DM and the Court of Appeal Hamburg affirmed.

On petition for review, the Supreme Court reversed and remanded relying on its decision in the Judgment of November 15, 1994 and noting that plaintiff's claims did not tear the frame of the amount required for an effective prevention.

(8) ***BGH, Judgment of December 19, 1995***

Two cases dealt with the right of the Princess Caroline and of her oldest son to prevent the unauthorized publications of their pictures. In the first case, decided by BGH on December 19, 1995, 59 NJW 1128 (1996), Princess Caroline brought an action to prevent further publication of five so-called paparazzi pictures of her showing

3. Hamburg, Court of Appeal, Judgment of July 25, 1996. (50 WERTPAPIER- MITTEILUNGEN [WM] 2033 (1996)).

her in a variety of situations. The Court of Appeal dismissed her complaint on the merits and plaintiff sought review. The BGH affirmed in part and reversed in part. It held that the controversy was to be decided on the basis of German law, especially §§ 22 and 23 of the Law on Copyright of Artistic Works and Photography [KUG].[4]

In principle, pictures of persons belonging to contemporary history, including plaintiff, may be published without their consent, unless such publication infringes a special interest of the persons shown. (KUG § 23 I and II). Such special interest may not rest on the protection of the private sphere, a constitutionally protected fundamental right which extends to the right to one's picture. The private sphere is not restricted to one's home, but may include localities where the pictured person has intended to be unobserved and secluded. As a result, the plaintiff could not prohibit the publication of the pictures taken of her in public places.

Conversely, some of the pictures showing her and the actor Vincent Lindon in a two-some in a garden restaurant were subject to a prohibition of further publication. The court pointed out that the strict protection under French law was not available against a German defendant.

(9) *BGH, Judgment of December 12, 1995*

In contrast to his mother, his oldest son, a boy 8 years old, was no person belonging to contemporary history and therefore he was entitled to prohibit the publication of any pictures of himself without his consent. Defendant, publisher of the journals N. and E., repeatedly published pictures of the boy without his consent showing him in ordinary activity.

The Supreme Court accepted a petition of review with respect to a Judgment of the Hamburg Court of Appeal to the extent that it affirmed the denial of compensation. The Supreme Court by Judgment of December 12, 1995, 49 NJW 985 (1996), held that under the circumstances of the case, the repeated publication of pictures without consent, constituted a serious violation of his right of personality entitling plaintiff to satisfaction by means of compensation. Accordingly, the Court reversed the Judgment of the court below and remanded the case for the award of proper compensation.

For a discussion of the Judgments of November 15, 1994, 128 BGHZ 1 (1996), and of December 12, 1995, 49 NJW 985 (1996), see M. Prinz, *Geldenstschädigung bei Persönlichkeitsverletzungen durch Medien,* 49 NJW 953-57 (1996). See also J. Rosengarten, *Der Präventionsgedanke in deutschen Zivilrecht,* 49 NJW 1935 (1996). The author notes that the emphasis on prevention and satisfaction coincides with the purpose of exemplary damages.

---

4. Gesetz betreffend das Urheberrecht an Werken der bildenden Künste und der Photographie, January 9, 1907, [=KUG], [1907] Reichsgesetzblatt 7.

B. UNITED STATES

1. Introduction

1. The United States is the cradle of recognition and protection of the right of privacy. In 1890, S. Warren and L. Brandeis (later Justice Brandeis) published an article in the Harvard Law Review under the title *The Right to Privacy*.[5] In their article the authors argued that a group of cases granting relief on a variety of grounds were in reality based on a common principle calling for protection for a right to privacy. Gradually most U.S. jurisdictions accepted that view. Invasion of the right of privacy is held to be perpetrated by four types of conduct:

(i) appropriation of another's name or likeness,
(ii) unreasonable intrusion on the seclusion of another,
(iii) unreasonable publicity given to another's private life,
(iv) publicity that unreasonably places another in a false light in the public eye. See Prosser and Keaton on Torts (§ 117) (5th ed. 1984).

Although originating as the object of protection by a common law tort — the right to privacy, it was subsequently recognized in legislative enactments and became elevated to a constitutional right, both under the U.S. Constitution and under state constitutions.[6] The State of California, in contrast to the U.S. Constitution, explicitly guarantees the right to privacy without imiting protection to invasion by state action. Thus the California Constitution § 1 Sec. 1 provides:

> **§ 1.1** "All people are by nature free and independent and have inalienable rights. Among these are enjoying and defending life and liberty, acquiring, possessing and protecting property, and pursuing and obtaining safety, happiness and privacy."

Privacy was added in 1972 and retained in 1974.

2. Apart from "constitutionalization" the right of privacy has also been "internationalized" and recognized as a basic human right. Thus the Universal Declaration of Human Rights (1948) Art. 12 provides:

> "No one shall be subjected to arbitrary interference with his privacy, family, home or correspondence, nor to attacks upon his honour and reputation.

5. 4 Harv. L. R. 193 (1890).

6 See authorities listed in Prosser & Keeton Torts 5th ed. 866, and in L. Tribe, American Constitutional Law (2nd ed. 1988) Ch. 15, entitled *Rights of Privacy and Personhood* (pp. 1302-1435). Jed Rubenfeld, The Right of Privacy, 102 Harv. L. Rev. 737 (1989).

Everyone has the right to the protection of the law against such interference or attacks."

Similar provisions protecting a person's privacy are included in (i) The International Covenant on Civil and Political Rights of Dec. 16, 1966, Art. 17, (ii) The European Convention for the Protection of Human Rights and Fundamental Freedoms of Nov. 4, 1950, Art. 8 and (iii) The American Convention on Human Rights of Nov. 22, 1969, Art. 11.

2. Cases

a. Diaz v. Oakland Tribune

Diaz v. Oakland Tribune
139 Cal. App 3d 118; 188 Cal. Rptr. 762
Court of Appeal, First District
Division 3.
Jan. 18, 1983

BARRY-DEAL, Associate Justice.

Plaintiff Toni Ann Diaz (Diaz) sued the Oakland Tribune, Inc., owners and publishers of the Oakland Tribune (the Tribune), and Sidney Jones (Jones), one of its columnists, for invasion of privacy. Diaz claimed that the publication of highly embarrassing private facts in Jones' March 26, 1978, newspaper column was unwarranted and malicious and caused her to suffer severe emotional distress. The jury awarded Diaz $250,000 in compensatory damages and $525,000 in punitive damages ($25,000 against Jones and $500,000 against the Tribune). Judgment was entered on February 14, 1980. Defendants' motion for a new trial based on insufficiency of the evidence, errors of law, and excessive damages was denied. This timely appeal followed. As discussed below, we reverse the judgment because of instructional errors.

The facts are for the most part undisputed. Diaz is a transsexual. She was born in Puerto Rico in 1942 as Antonio Diaz, a male. She moved to California from New York in 1964. Suffice it to say that for most of her life Diaz suffered from a gender identification problem and the anxiety and depression that accompanied it. She testified that since she was young she had had the feeling of being a woman. In 1968 Diaz began receiving psychological counseling and hormone therapy. In 1970 or 1971 Diaz embarked on the lengthy process of evaluation as a candidate for gender corrective surgery at the Stanford University Gender Dysphoria Clinic. She was untimately considered to be a good candidate for surgery. In 1975 gender corrective surgery was performed by the Stanford staff.

According to Diaz the surgery was a success. By all outward appearances she looked and behaved as a woman and was accepted by the public as a woman. According to her therapist, Dr. Sable, her physical and psychological identities were now in harmony.

Diaz scrupulously kept the surgery a secret from all but her immediate family and closest friends. She never sought to publicize the surgery. She changed her name to Toni Ann Diaz and made the necessary changes in her high school records, her social security records, and on her driver's license. She tried unsuccessfully to change her Puerto Rican birth certificate. She did not change the gender designation on her draft card, however, asserting that it would be a useless gesture, since she had previously been turned down for induction.

Following the surgery she no longer suffered from the psychological difficulties that had plagued her previously. In 1975 she enrolled in the College of Alameda (the College), a two-year college. The College was one of five colleges of the Peralta Community College District.

In spring 1977, she was elected student body president for the 1977–1978 academic year, the first woman to hold that office. Her election and an unsuccessful attempt to unseat her were reported in the College newspaper, the Reporter, in the May 17, June 1, and June 14, 1977, editions. At no time during the election did Diaz reveal any information about her sex-change operation.

In 1977 Diaz was also selected to be the student body representative to the Peralta Community College Board of Trustees (the Board). Diaz's selection as student body representative, together with her photograph, appeared in the June 1977 issue of the Peralta Colleges Bulletin.

Near the middle of her term as student body president, Diaz became embroiled in a controversy in which she charged the College administrators with misuse of student funds. The March 15, 1978, issue of the Tribune quoted Diaz's charge that her signature had improperly been "rubber stamped" on checks drawn from the associated students' account.

On March 24, 1978, an article in the Alameda Times-Star, a daily newspaper, mentioned Diaz in connection with the charge of misuse of student body funds.

Shortly after the controversy arose, Jones was informed by several confidential sources that Diaz was a man. Jones considered the matter newsworthy if he could verify the information. Jones testified that he inspected the Tribune's own files and spoke with an unidentified number of persons at the College to confirm this information. It was not until Richard Paoli, the city editor of the Tribune, checked Oakland city police records that the information that Diaz was born a man was verified. The evidence reveals that in 1970 or 1971, prior to the surgery, Diaz was arrested in Oakland for soliciting an undercover police officer, a misdemeanor.[7]

On March 26, 1978, the following item appeared in Jones' newspaper column: "More Education Stuff: The students at the College of Alameda will be surprised to learn their student body president, Toni Diaz, is no lady, but is in fact a man whose real name is Antonio.

"Now I realize, that in these times, such a matter is no big deal, but I suspect his female classmates in P.E. 97 may wish to make other showering arrangements."

---

7. The record reveals that pursuant to a plea bargain, Diaz entered a guilty plea to the charge. However, Diaz was later allowed to withdraw her guilty plea. Following a trial she was acquitted of the charge

Upon reading the article, Diaz became very depressed and was forced to reveal her status, which she had worked hard to conceal. Diaz testified that as a result of the article she suffered from insomnia, nightmares, and memory lapses. She alse delayed her enrollment in Mills College, scheduled for that fall.

In her complaint Diaz did not charge that any of the information was untrue, only that defendants invaded her privacy by the unwarranted publicity of intimate facts. Defendants defended on the ground that the matter was newsworthy and hence was constitutionally protected.

At trial the jury returned a special verdict and found that (1) defendants did publicly disclose a fact concerning Diaz; (2) the fact was private and not public; (3) the fact was *not* newsworthy; (4) the fact was highly offensive to a reasonable person of ordinary sensibilities; (5) defendants disclosed the fact with knowledge that it was highly offensive or with reckless disregard of whether it was highly offensive; and (6) the disclosure proximately caused injury or damage to Diaz.

In this appeal defendants challenge the jury's finding on issues Nos. (2) and (3) above. Defendants also urge instructional error and attack the awards of compensatory and punitive damages. Before we address these issues, it is useful briefly to discuss the competing rights involved herein: the right to privacy and the right to free speech and press.

Background

The concept of a common-law right to privacy was first developed in a landmark article by Warren and Brandeis, *The Right to Privacy* (1890) 4 Harv.L.Rev. 193, and has been adopted in virtually every state.[8] The specific privacy right with which we are concerned is the right to be free from public disclosure of private embarrassing facts, in short, "the right to be let alone." (*Melvin v. Reid* (1931) 112 Cal. App. 285, 289, 297 P. 91.)[9]

The development of the public disclosure tort in California is well documented. (See *Forsher v. Bugliosi* (1980) 26 Cal.3d 792, 163 Cal.Rptr. 628, 608, P.2d 716; *Briscoe v. Reader's Digest Association, Inc.* (1971) 4 Cal.3d 529, 93 Cal.Rptr. 866, 483 P.2d 34; *Kapellas v. Kofman* (1969) 1 Cal.3d 20, 81 Cal.Rptr. 360, 459 P.2d 912.) In fact, California has recognized this right for over 50 years. (See *Melvin v. Reid, supra,* 112 Cal. App. 285, 297 P. 91.)[10]

---

8. See Woito and McNulty, *The Privacy Disclosure Tort and the First Amendment: Should the Community Decide Newsworthiness?* (1979) 64 Iowa L.Rev. 185 (hereafter cited as *The Privacy Disclosure Tort*).

9. See Nimmer, *The Right to Speak from* Times *to* Time: *First Amendment Theory Applied to Libel and Misapplied to Privacy* (1968) 56 Cal. L.Rev. 935, 958–959, fn. 80 (hereafter cited as *The Right to Speak*).

10. It may be reasonably argued that this right is also recognized under the broad right to privacy granted under article I, section 1, of the California Constitution (adopted November 5, 1974). For a more complete discussion, see Gerstein, *California's Constitutional Right to Privacy: The Development of the Protection of Private Life* (1982) 9 Hastings Const.L.Q. 385, 402–411.

The public disclosure tort is one of four distinct torts which are actionable under the general rubric of invasion of privacy. The other three are: (1) intrustion upon plaintiff's solitude or into his or her private affairs; (2) "false light" publicity; and (3) appropriation of plaintiff's name or likeness to the defendant's advantage. (*Kapellas v. Kofman, supra,* 1 Cal.3d at p. 35, fn. 16, 81 Cal.Rptr 360, 459 P.2d 912; *Virgil v. Time, Inc.* (9th Cir.1975) 527 F.2d 1122, 1125.)

The public disclosure cause of action is distinct from a suit for libel or "false light," since the plaintiff herein does not challenge the accuracy of the information published, but asserts that the publicity is so intimate and unwarranted as to outrage the community's notion of decency. (*Briscoe v. Reader's Digest Association, Inc., supra,* 4 Cal.3d at p. 542, 93 Cal.Rptr. 866, 483 P.2d 34; *Sidis v. F–R Pub. Corporation* (2d Cir.1940) 113 F.2d 806, 809.) "'The gravamen of a defamation action is engendering a false opinion about a person, whether in the mind of one other person or many people. *The gravamen in the public disclosure [privacy] cases is degrading a person by laying his life open to public view.*'" (*The Right to Speak, supra,* at pp. 958–959, emphasis added.)

Of course, the right to privacy is not absolute and must be balanced against the often competing constitutional right of the press to publish newsworthy matters. (See *Cox Broadcasting Corp. v. Cohn* (1975) 420 U.S. 469, 489, 95 S.Ct. 1029, 1043, 43 L.Ed.2d 1122, 1127; *Forsher v. Bugliosi, supra,* 26 Cal.3d at p. 809, 163 Cal.Rptr. 628, 608 P.2d 716; *Briscoe v. Reader's Digest Association, Inc., supra,* 4 Cal.3d at p. 534, 93 Cal.Rptr. 866, 483 P.2d 34; *Kapellas v. Kofman, supra,* 1 Cal.3d at pp. 35–36, 81 Cal. Rptr. 360, 459 P.2d 912.)[11] The First Amendment protection from tort liability is necessary if the press is to carry out its constitutional obligation to keep the public informed so that they may make intelligent decisions on matters important to a self-governing people. (See *Cox Broadcasting Corp. v. Cohn, supra,* 420 U.S. at pp. 491–493, 95 S.Ct. at pp. 1044–45.)

However, the newsworthy privilege is not without limitation. Where the publicity is so offensive as to constitute a "'morbid and sensational prying into private lives for its own sake, . . .'" it serves no legitimate public interest and is not deserving of protection. (See *Virgil v. Time, Inc., supra,* 527 F2d at p. 1129; Rest.2d Torts, § 652D, com. h.)

As discerned from the decisions of our courts, the public disclosure tort contains the following elements: (1) public disclosure (2) of a private fact (3) which would be offensive and objectionable to the reasonable person and (4) which is not of legitimate public concern. (See *Forsher v. Bugliosi, supra,* 26 Cal.3d at pp. 808–809, 163 Cal.Rptr. 628, 608 P.2d 716; *Briscoe v. Reader's Digest Association, Inc., supra,* 4 Cal.3d at pp. 541–544, 93 Cal.Rptr. 866, 483 P.2d 34; *Kapellas v. Kofman, supra,* 1 Cal.3d at pp. 34–39, 81 Cal.Rptr, 360, 459 P.2d 912.)

---

11. See *The Privacy Disclosure Tort, supra,* at pages 194–197.

INSTRUCTIONAL ERROR

At the outset defendants urge that the trial court misinstructed the jury (1) on the right to privacy and (2) that defendants had the burden of proving newsworthiness. We agree and find that either of these errors was prejudicial and requires reversal.

1. The Right to Privacy

Plaintiff Diaz proffered a jury instruction properly defining the right to privacy.[12] However, the trial court, *sua sponte,* added the following language: "It prevents business or government interests from misusing information gathered for one purpose in order to serve other purposes, or to embarrass us. *This right should be abridged only when there is a compelling public need.*" (Emphasis added.)

The language contained in the last sentence was taken from *White v. Davis* (1975) 13 Cal.3d 757, 120 Cal.Rptr. 94, 533 P.2d 222. The trial court misplaced its reliance on that case. In *White, supra,* plaintiff challenged covert police surveillance of University of California at Los Angeles students in their classrooms. There, the court required the *government* to demonstrate a " 'compelling public need' " for the instrusion. (*Id.,* at p. 775, 120 Cal.Rptr. 94, 533 P.2d 222.) That case did not attempt to balance the competing rights of free speech and press against the right to privacy. Rather, it recognized the heavy burden on the government to justify interference with First Amendment freedoms. (*Id.,* at pp. 767–773. 120 Cal.Rptr. 94, 533 P.2d 222.)

Unlike the government's activity in *White,* defendants' publication of the article is a preferred right which is not encombered by the presumption of illegality. Defendants enjoy the right to publish information in which the public has a *legitimate interest.* (See *Briscoe v. Reader's Digest Association, Inc., supra,* 4 Cal.3d at p. 541, 93 Cal.Rptr. 866, 483 P.2d 34; *Virgil v. Time, Inc., supra,* 527 F.2d at pp. 1128–1129; Rest.2d Torts, *supra,* § 652D, com. d.) To require that the article meet the higher " 'compelling public need' " standard would severely abridge this constitutionally recognized right of free speech and press.

* * *

12. The complete instruction reads as follows: "The California Constitution provides that all persons have an inalienable right of privacy. It is the right to live one's life in seclusion, without being subjected to unwarranted or undesirable publicity. In short, it's the right to be left alone."

2. The Burden of Proving Newsworthiness

Next, defendants argue that the trial court improperly instructed the jury that the burden of proving newsworthiness was for the defendants. We agree.

* * *

Our research has discovered no published decision expressly allocating to one of the parties the burden of proving newsworthiness. While a publisher may *defend* itself against a public disclosure cause of action by proving that the matter was newsworthy, it is misleading to assert that said defendant has the burden of proving newsworthiness to be free from tort liability. As discussed below, the plaintiff has the burden of proving that the publication was not privileged, i.e., that it was *not* newsworthy. Of course, defendants may rebut plaintiff's showing with evidence that the matter was newsworthy. However, to assert, as plaintiff does, that defendants have the burden of proving newsworthiness is error.

* * *

The proof that defendants have published an article containing highly offensive private matters does not itself establish a claim for relief. It certainly must be recognized than an otherwise embarrassing article may be newsworthy, depending on the circumstances. Only when the embarrassing publicity is *not* newsworthy can plaintiff recover damages, consistent with defendants' rights of free speech and press. To hold otherwise would permit a plaintiff to obtain a default judgment against a media defendant without any showing that the defendant had exceeded its constitutional prerogative. The effect would be to read the rights of free speech and press out of the Constitution.

Of course, once plaintiff has established a prima facie case that the publicity is not constitutionally protected, i.e., not newsworthy, defendants can meet it with a showing that the information was newsworthy. However, to place the burden of proving newsworthiness on the defendants in order to defend against the action would have a chilling effect on their freedom of expression.

* * *

Although the judgment is reversed, it is in the interests of judicial administration to address the merits of defendants' remaining contentions.

THE PUBLIC DISCLOSURE TORT

1. Private Facts

Defendants next argue that the evidence establishes as a matter of law that the fact of Diaz's original gender was a matter of public record, and therefore its publicity was not actionable. In support of their contention defendants rely on *Cox Broadcasting Corp. v. Cohn, supra*, 420 U.S. 469, 95 S.Ct. 1029, 43 L.Ed.2d 328. That reliance is misplaced.

* * *

In *Cox Broadcasting Corp.*, the Supreme Court ruled that Cohn, the father of a deceased rape viction, could not maintain a disclosure action against media defendants who identified Cohn's daughter as the victim during the television coverage of the murder trial. (*Cox Broadcasting Corp. v. Cohn, supra,* 420 U.S. at pp. 496–497, 95 S.Ct. at 1046–47.) Central to the court's conclusion was the fact that the reporter obtained the victim's name from the indictment, which had been shown to him in open court. (*Id.,* at p. 496, 95 S.Ct. at 1046.)

* * *

Here there is no evidence to suggest that the fact of Diaz's gender-corrective surgery was part of the public record. To the contrary, the evidence reveals that Diaz took affirmative steps to conceal this fact by changing her driver's license, social security, and high school records, and by lawfully changing her name. The police records, upon which Jones relied, contained information concerning one Antonio Diaz. No mention was made of Diaz's new name or gender. In order to draw the connection, Jones relied upon unidentified confidential sources. Under these circumstances, we conclude that Diaz's sexual identity was a private matter.

* * *

Moreover, matter which was once of public record may be protected as private facts where disclosure of that information would not be newsworthy. (See *Briscoe v. Reader's Digest Association, Inc., supra,* 4 Cal.3d at pp. 537–538, 93 Cal.Rptr. 866, 483 P.2d 34 [publication of identity of ex-offender for past crime was held to be improper]; *Melvin v. Reid, supra,* 223 Cal.App. at pp. 290–291, 297 P. 91 [disclosure of plaintiff's past life as a prostitute, seven years after she reformed, was actionable].)

2. *Newsworthiness*

As discussed above, whether the fact of Diaz's sexual identity was newsworthy is measured along a sliding scale of competing interests; the individual's right to keep private facts from the public's gaze versus the public's right to know. (See *Kapellas v. Kofman, supra,* 1 Cal.3d at p. 36, 81 Cal.Rptr. 360, 459 P.2d 912.) In an effort to reconcile these competing interests, our courts have settled on a three-part test for determining whether matter published is newsworthy: "'[1] the social value of the facts published, [2] the depth of the article's intrusion into ostensibly private affairs, and [3] the extent to which the party voluntarily acceded to a position of public notoriety. [Citations.]' [Citation.]" (*Briscoe v. Reader's Digest Association, Inc., supra,* 4 Cal.3d at p. 541, 93 Cal.Rptr. 866, 483 P.2d 34.)

Defendants argue that in light of Diaz's position as the first female student body president of the College, her "questionable gender" was a newsworthy item. As a subsidiary contention, they assert that the issue of newsworthiness should not have been submitted to the jury. We address the latter contention first.

a. Newsworthiness as a Jury Question

Whether a publication is or is not newsworthy depends upon contemporary community mores and standards of decency. See *Briscoe v. Reader's Digest Association, Inc., supra,* at p. 541, 93 Cal.Rptr. 866, 483 P.2d 34; *Virgil v. Time, Inc., supra,* 527 F.2d at p. 1129; Rest.2d Torts, *supra,* § 652D, com. h.) This is largely a question of fact, which a jury is uniquely well-suited to decide. (*Virgil v. Time, Inc., supra,* 527 F.2d at p. 1129, fn. 12.)

* * *

b. Newsworthiness as a Matter of Law

Next, defendants urge that, as the first female student body president of the College, Diaz was a public figure, and the fact of her sexual identity was a newsworthy item as a matter of law. We disagree.

It is well settled that persons who voluntarily seek public office or willingly become involved in public affairs waive their right to privacy of matters connected with their public conduct. (*Kapellas v. Kofman, supra,* 1 Cal.3d at pp. 36–38, 81 Cal.Rptr. 360, 459 P.2d 912.) The reason behind this rule is that the public should be afforded every opportunity of learning about any facet which may affect that person's fitness for office. (See *Briscoe v. Reader's Digest Association, Inc., supra,* 4 Cal.3d at p. 535, fn. 5, 93 Cal.Rptr. 866, 483 P.2d 34; Rest.2d Torts, *supra,* § 652D, com. e.)

* * *

Contrary to defendants' claim, we find little if any connection between the information disclosed and Diaz's fitness for office. The fact that she is a transsexual does not adversely reflect on her honesty or judgment. (Cf. *Kapellas v. Kofman, supra,* 1 Cal.3d 20, 81 Cal.Rptr. 360, 459 P.2d 912 [plaintiff, a mother and candidate for Alameda City Council, who repeatedly left her minor children unsupervised, could not maintain an action against a newspaper for publishing information taken from police records of her children's criminal behavior]; *Beruan v. French* (1976) 56 Cal.App.3d 825, 128 Cal.Rptr. 869 [candidate for secretary-treasurer of union local could not maintain action based on publication of a letter disclosing his six prior criminal convictions].)

Nor does the fact that she was the first woman student body president, in itself, warrant that her entire private life be open to public inspection. The public arena entered by Diaz is concededly small. Public figures more celebrated than she are entitled to keep some information of their domestic activities and sexual relations private.

* * *

INSUFFICIENT EVIDENCE OF MALICE

Defendants next urge that the award of punitive damages was improper, since there was insuffcient evidence to support a finding of malice on the part of either defendant.

* * *

Viewing the article as a whole, as well as Jones' conduct in preparing the article, we cannot say as a matter of law that there was insufficient evidence to support a finding of malice.

* * *

The Oakland Tribune, Inc., was also liable for punitive damages since the newspaper publishing company reviewed and approved Jones' article for publication.

* * *

EXCESSIVE COMPENSATORY DAMAGE AWARD

Finally, defendants urge that the compensatory damage award was excessive. The jury awarded Diaz $250,000, largely for emotional and psychological injury caused by the article. Diaz's special damages for psychotherapy approximated $800.

* * *

The actual injury involved herein is not limited to out-of-pocket loss. It generally includes "impairment of reputation and standing in the community, personal humiliation, and mental anguish and suffering." (See *Gertz v. Robert Welch, Inc., supra,* 418 U.S. at p. 350, 94 S.Ct. at p. 3012.) The harm Diaz alleged to have suffered is not easily quantifiable, and the amount of damages must necessarily be left to the sound discretion of the jury. (See *Bertero v. National General Corp.* (1974) 13 Cal.3d 43, 64, 118 Cal.Rptr. 184, 529 P.2d 608.)

* * *

The judgment is reversed.

NOTE

Briscoe v. Reader's Digest Ass'n. The text case is an illustration of an invasion of the right of privacy by unreasonable publicity given to another's private life. In *Briscoe v. Reader's Digest Ass'n,* 4 Cal.3d 529 (1971), noted in the text case, the Briscoes brought an action against the defendant because of its publication on hijacking in which plaintiff was named as typifying an inexperienced beginner, without revealing the date of his crime. Actually, the event, while true, antedated the appearance of the article by more than a decade. Plaintiff alleged that since then, he had abandoned the life of crime and had become a respected member of society, but was now scorned and rejected by his family and friends due to the publication. The Superior Court sustained a general demurrer without leave to amend. Plaintiff appealed from the ensuing judgment.

The Supreme Court held that plaintiff had stated a valid cause of action, that sustaining a general demurrer was improper and that the judgment therefore had to be reversed. It remanded the case to determine whether the identification of defendant as a former criminal constituted an injurious and reckless invasion of his right to privacy, not covered by the freedom of the press.

b. Galella v. Onassis

Ronald E. GALELLA, Plaintiff-Appellant,
Jacqueline ONASSIS, Defendant-Appellee,
John Walsh et al., Defendants,
and United States of America, Intervenor-Appellee.
Nos. 260, 618 and 619, Dockets 71-1902, 72-1993 and 72-2312.
United States Court of Appeals, Second Circuit.

Rehearing and Rehearing En Banc
Denied Nov. 13, 1973.
487 F. 2d 986 (1983)

Before SMITH, HAYS and TIMBERS, Circuit Judges.

J. JOSEPH SMITH, Circuit Judge:

Donald Galella, a free-lance photographer, appeals from a summary judgement dismissing his complaint against three Secret Service agents for false arrest, malicious prosecution and interference with trade (S.D.N.Y., Edward C. McLean, Judge),[14] the dismissal after trial of his identical complaint against Jacqueline Onassis and the grant of injuctive relief to defendant Onassis on her counterclaim and to the intervenor, the United States, on its intervening complaint and a third judgment retaxing transcript costs to plaintiff (S.D.N.Y., Irving Ben Cooper, Judge), 353 F.Supp. 196 (1972). In addition to numerous alleged procedural errors, Galella raises the First Amendment as an absolute shield against liability to any sanctions. The judgments dismissing the complaints are affirmed; the grant of injunctive relief is affirmed as herein modified. Taxation of costs against the plaintiff is affirmed in part, reversed in part.

Galella is a free-lance photographer specializing in the making and sale of photographs of well-known persons. Defendant Onassis is the widow of the late President, John F. Kennedy, mother of the two Kennedy children, John and Caroline, and is the wife of Aristotle Onassis, widely known shipping figure and reputed multimillionaire. John Walsh, James Kalafatis and John Connelly are U.S. Secret Service agents assigned to the duty of protecting the Kennedy children under 18 U.S.C. § 3056, which provides for protection of the children of deceased presidents up to the age of 16.

Galella fancies himself as a "paparazzo" (literally a kind of annoying insect, perhaps roughly equivalent to the English "gadfly.") Paparazzi make themselves as visible to the public and obnoxious to their photographic subjects as possible to aid in the advertisement and wide sale of their works.[15]

Some examples of Galella's conduct brought out at trial are illustrative. Galella took pictures of John Kennedy riding his bicycle in Central Park across the way from his home. He jumped out into the boy's path, causing the agents concern for John's safety. The agents' reaction and interrogation of Galella led to Galella's arrest and his action against the agents; Galella on other occasions interrrupted Caroline at tennis, and invaded the children's private schools. At one time he came uncomfortably close in a power boat to Mrs. Onassis swimming. He often jumped and postured around while taking pictures of her party notably at a theater opening but also on numerous other occasions. He followed a practice of bribing apartment house, restaurant and nightclub doormen as well as romancing a family servant to keep him advised of the movements of the family.

After detention and arrest following complaint by the Secret Service agents protecting Mrs. Onassis' son and his acquittal in the state court, Galella filed suit in state court against the agents and Mrs. Onassis. Galella claimed that under orders from Mrs. Onassis, the three agents falsely arrested and maliciously prosecuted him, and that this incident in addition to several others described in the complaint constituted an unlawful interference with his trade.

Mrs.Onassis answered denying any role in the arrest or any part in the claimed interference with his attempts to photograph her, and counterclaimed for damages[16] and injunctive relief, charging that Galella had invaded her privacy, assaulted and battered her, intentionally inflicted emotional distress and engaged in a campaign of harassment.

The action was removed under 28 U.S.C. § 1442(a) to the United States District Court. On a motion for summary judgment, Galella's claim against the Secret Service agents was dismissed, the court finding that the agents were acting within the scope of their authority and thus were immune from prosecution. At the same time, the government intervened requesting injunctive relief from the activities of Galella which obstructed the Secret Service's ability to protect Mrs. Onassis' children.[17] Galella's motion to remand the case to state court, just prior to trial, was denied.

Certain incidents of photographic coverage by Galella, subsequent to an agreement among the parties for Galella not to so engage, resulted in the issuance of a temporary restraining order to prevent further harassment of Mrs. Onassis and the children. Galella was enjoined from "harassing, alarming, startling, tormenting, touching the person of the defendant . . . or her children . . . and from blocking their movements in the public places and thoroughfares, invading their immediate zone of privacy by means of physical movements, gestures or with photographic equipment and from performing any act reasonably calculated to place the lives and safety of the defendant . . . and her children in jeopardy." Within two months, Galella was charged with violation of the temporary restraining order; a new order was signed which required that the photographer keep 100 yards from the Onassis apartment and 50 yards from the person of the defendant and her children. Surveillance was also prohibited.

Upon notice of consolidation of the preliminary injunction hearing and trial for permanent injunction, plaintiff moved for a jury trial — nine months after answer was served, and to remand to state court. The first motion was denied as untimely, the second on grounds of judicial economy. Just prior to trial Galella deposed Mrs. Onassis. Under protective order of this court, the defendant was allowed to testify at the office of the U.S. Attorney and outside the presence of Galella.

After a six-week trial the court dismissed Galella's claim and granted relief to both the defendant and the intervenor. Galella was enjoined from (1) keeping the defendant and her children under surveillance or following any of them; (2) approaching within 100 yards of the home of defendant or her children, or within 100 yards of either child's school or within 75 yards of either child or 50 yards of defendant; (3) using the name, portrait or picture of defendant or her children for advertising; (4) attempting to communicate with defendant or her children except through her attorney.

We conclude that grant of summary judgment and dismissal of Galella's claim against the Secret Service agents was proper. Federal agents when charged with duties which require the exercise of discretion are immune from liability for actions within the scope of their authority. Ordinarily enforcement agents charged with the duty of arrest are not so immune. Bivens v. Six Unknown Named Agents of Fed. Bur. of Narc., 456 F.2d 1339 (2d Cir. 1972). The protective duties assigned the agents under this statute, however, require the instant exercise of judgment which should be protected. The agents saw Galella jump into the path of John Kennedy who was forced to swerve his bike dangerously as he left Central Park and was about to enter Fifth Avenue, whereupon the agents gave chase to the photographer. Galella indicated that he was a press photographer listed with the New York City Police; he and the agents went to the police station to check on the story, where one of the agents made the complaint on which the state court charges were based. Certainly it was reasonable that the agents "check out" an individual who has endangered their charge,[18] and seek prosecution for apparent violation of state law which interferes with them in the discharge of their duties.

Discrediting all of Galella's testimony[13] the court found the photographer guilty of harassment, intentional infliction of emotional distress, assault and battery, commercial exploitation of defendant's personality, and invasion of privacy. Fully crediting defendant's testimony, the court found no liability on Galella's claim. Evidence offered by the defense showed that Galella had on occasion intentionally physically touched Mrs. Onassis and her daughter, caused fear of physical contact in his frien-

13. The court's findings on credibility are indeed broad, but they are supported in the record. Galella demonstrated a galling lack of respect for the truth and gave no indication of any consciousness of the meaning of the oath he had taken. No only did he admit blatantly lying in his testimony, he admitted attempting to have other witnesses lie for him.

zied attempts to get their pictures, followed defendant and her children too closely in an automobile, endangered the safety of the children while they were swimming, water skiing and horseback riding. Galella cannot successfully challenge the court's finding of tortious conduct.[14]

Finding that Galella had "insinuated himself into the very fabric of Mrs. Onassis' life . . ." the court framed its relief in part on the need to prevent further invasion of the defendant's privacy. Whether or not this accords with present New York law, there is no doubt that it is sustainable under New York's proscription of harassment.[15]

Of course legitimate countervailing social needs may warrant some intrusion despite an individual's reasonable expectation of privacy and freedom from harassment. However the interference allowed may be no greater than that necessary to protect the

---

14. Harassment is a criminal violation under New York Penal Law § 240.25 (McKinney's Consol. Laws, c. 40, 1967) when with intent to harass a person follows another in a public place, inflicts physical contact or engages in any annoying conduct without legitimate cause. Galella was found to have engaged in this proscribed conduct. Conduct sufficient to invoke criminal liability for harassment may be the basis for private action. *Cf.* Long v. Beneficial Finance Co. of New York, 39 A.D.2d 11, 330 N.Y.S.2d 664 (1972).

15. *See* n. 11, [–14] *supra.*

Although the New York courts have not yet recognized a common law right of privacy, if we were required to reach the question, we would be inclined to agree with the court below that when again faced with the issue the Court of Appeals may well modify or distinguish its 1902 holding in Roberson v. Rochester Folding-Box Co., 171 N.Y. 538, 64 N.E. 442 (1902), that "The so-called right of privacy has not as yet found an abiding place in our jurisprudence." There is substantive support today for the proposition that privacy is a "basic right" entitled to legal protection, Time v. Hill, 385 U.S. 374, 415, 87 S.Ct. 534, 17 L.Ed.2d 456 (1967) (Fortas, J., dissenting), nor can the "power of a State to control and remedy such intrusion [even] for news gathering purposes . . . be denied." *Id.* at 404, 87 S.Ct. at 550 (Harlan J., concurring and dissenting). Privacy essential to individual dignity and personal liberty underlies the fundamental rights guaranteed in the Bill of Rights. *See* Katz v. United States, 389 U.S. 347, 350 n. 5, 88 S.Ct. 507, 19 L.Ed. 2d 576 (1967); Tehan v. U. S. ex rel. Shott, 382 U.S. 406, 416, 86 S.Ct. 459, 15 L.Ed.2d 453 (1966) (Fifth Amendment); Stanley v. Georgia, 304 U.S. 557, 564–566, 89 S.Ct. 1243, 22 L.Ed.2d 542 (1969) (First and Fourteenth Amendments). *See also* Time v. Hill, *supra,* 385 U.S. at 412–415, 87 S.Ct. 534; Bloustein, Privacy As An Aspect of Human Dignity: An Answer to Dean Prosser, 39 N.Y.U. L.Rev. 962, 971 (1964); Fried, Privacy, 77 Yale L.J. 475, 482ff (1968). There is an emerging recognition of privacy as a distinct, constitutionally protected right. Roe v. Ingraham, 480 F.2d 102 (2d Cir., 1973), (Friendly, J.)

While the Constitution provides protection for specific manifestations of privacy ". . . the protection of a person's general right to privacy — his right to be let alone by other people is like the protection of his property and his very life left largely to the law of the individual states. . . ." *Katz, supra,* 389 U.S. at 350–351, 88 S.Ct. at 511, citing Warren & Brandeis, Right to Privacy, 4 Harv. L.Rev. 193 (1890).

The vast majority of states have now recognized and protect a right to privacy. Restatement of Torts 2d § 652(a), comment a (Tent.Draft No. 13, 1967). Statutory protection has been afforded the right in New York through imposition of criminal sanctions for invasion of privacy through the use of mechanical devices for wiretap and eavesdropping and for tampering with certain private communications. New York Penal Code §§ 250.00–250.35 (McKinney, 1967).

Although not recognizing a right to privacy as such except as defined by statute, the New York courts have softened this rule in many cases by recognizing and liberally applying freedom from emotional distress as a protectable interest. *See* Long v. Beneficial Finance Co. of New York, 39 A.D.2d 11, 330 N.Y.S.2d 664, 667–668 (1972); Halio v. Lurie, 15 A.D.2d 62, 222 N.Y.S.2d 759, 763–764 (1961); Callarama v. Associated Discount Corp. of Delaware, 69 Misc.2d 287, 329 N.Y.S.2d 711 (1972); Ruiz v. Bertolotti, 37 Misc.2d 1067, 236 N.Y.S.2d 854 (1962), aff'd mem. 20 A.D.2d 628, 245 N.Y.S.2d 1003 (1963).

overriding public interest. Mrs. Onassis was properly found to be a public figure and thus subject to news coverage. *See* Sidis v. F. R. Publishing Corp., 113 F.2d 806 (2d Cir.), cert. denied, 311 U.S. 711, 61 S.Ct. 393, 85 L.Ed. 462 (1940). Nonetheless, Galella's action went far beyond the reasonable bounds of news gathering. When weighed against the *de minimis* public importance of the daily activities of the defendant, Galella's constant surveillance, his obtrusive and intruding presence, was unwarranted and unreasonable. If there were any doubt in our minds, Galella's inexcusable conduct toward defendant's minor children would resolve it.

Galella does not seriously dispute the court's finding of tortious conduct. Rather, he sets up the First Amendment as a wall of immunity protecting newsmen from any liability for their conduct while gathering news. There is no such scope to the First Amendment right. Crimes and torts committed in news gathering are not protected. *See* Branzburg v. Hayes, 408 U.S. 665, 92 S.Ct. 2646, 33 L.Ed.2d 626 (1972); Rosenbloom v. Metromedia, 403 U.S. 29, 91 S.Ct. 1811, 29 L.Ed.2d 296 (1971); Dietemann v. Time, Inc., 449 F.2d 245, 249–250 (9th Cir. 1971). *See* Restatement of Torts 2d § 652(f), comment k (Tent. Draft No. 13, 1967). There is no threat to a free press in requiring its agents to act within the law.

In addition to his substantive claims, Galella challenges the court's (a) refusal to remand the case; (b) refusal to allow a jury trial despite an untimely request; (c) exclusion of Galella from defendant's deposition; (d) failure to recuse himself; (e) consolidation of the temporary injunctive proceedings and trial on the merits. Numerous claims of error in evidentiary rulings are also raised. Little need be said about most of these evidentiary rulings;[22] the rulings were either clearly correct or if error, harmless.[23] Galella's procedural claims must fail.

Injunctive relief is appropriate. Galella has stated his intention to continue his coverage of defendant so long as she is newsworthy, and his continued harassment even while the temporary restraining orders were in effect indicate that no voluntary change in this technique can be expected. New York courts have found similar conduct sufficient to support a claim for injunctive relief. Flamm v. Van Nierop, 56 Misc.2d 1059, 291 N.Y.S.2d 189 (1968).[24]

[38] The injunction, however, is broader than is required to protect the defendant. Relief must be tailored to protect Mrs. Onassis from the "paparazzo" attack which distinguishes Galella's behavior from that of other photographers; it should not unnecessarily infringe on reasonable efforts to "cover" defendant. Therefore, we modify the court's order to prohibit only (1) any approach within twenty-five (25) feet of defendant or any touching of the person of the defendant Jacqueline Onassis; (2) any blocking of her movement in public places and thoroughfares; (3) any act foreseeably or reasonably calculated to place the life and safety of defendant in jeopardy; and (4) any conduct which would reasonably be foreseen to harass, alarm or frighten the defendant.

Any further restriction on Galella's taking and selling pictures of defendant for news coverage is, however, improper and unwarranted by the evidence. *See* Estate of Hemingway v. Random House, Inc., 49 Misc.2d 726, 268 N.Y.S.2d 531, 535, aff'd 25

A.D.2d 719, 269 N.Y.S.2d 366 (1966); Youssoupoff v. Columbia Broadcasting, 41 Misc.2d 42, 244 N.Y.S.2d 701, 704, aff'd 19 A.D. 2d 865, 244, N.Y.S. 2d 1 (1963); Thompson v. C. P. Putnam's Sons, 40 Misc.2d 608, 243 N.Y.S.2d 652, 654 (1965).

Likewise, we affirm the grant of injunctive relief to the government modified to prohibit any action interfering with Secret Service agents' protective duties. Galella thus may be enjoined from (a) entering the children's schools or play areas; (b) engaging in action calculated or reasonably foreseen to place the children's safety or well being in jeopardy, or which would threaten or create physical injury; (c) taking any action which could reasonably be foreseen to harass, alarm, or frighten the children; and (d) from approaching within thirty (30) feet of the children.

As modified, the relief granted fully allows Galella the opportunity to photograph and report on Mrs. Onassis' public activities. Any prior restraint on news gathering is miniscule and fully supported by the findings.

Affirmed in part, reversed in part and remanded for modification of the judgment in accordance with this opinion. Costs on appeal to be taxed in favor of appellees.

TIMBERS, Circuit Judge (concurring in part and dissenting in part):

With one exception, I concur in the judgment of the Court and in the able majority opinion of Judge Smith.

With utmost deference to and respect for my colleagues, however, I am constrained to dissent from the judgment of the Court and the majority opinion to the extent that they modify the injunctive relief found necessary by the district court to protect Jacqueline Onassis and her children, Caroline B. and John F. Kennedy, Jr., from the continued predatory conduct of the self-proclaimed paparazzo Galella.

ON PETITION FOR REHEARING EN BANC

Ordered that said petition be and it hereby is denied.

NOTES

British law, in contrast to American, German and French law, has no common law or statutory right to privacy, although Parliament has been investigating the question of a generalized remedy for invasion of privacy for a number of years.[16] English academics have favored creation of a tort of molestation or harassment[17] and some courts are slowly moving in that direction.

In *Khorasandjian v Bush* ([1993] 3 All ER 669), the Court of Appeal (Dillon J.) affirmed a preliminary injunction forbidding defendant, an unwelcome, over-ardent admirer of a young woman of 18 years, "from using violence to, harassing, pestering or communicating with the plaintiff" prior to trial. (p. 672). Gibson J. dissented from

16. Winfield & Jolowicz on Tort, 14th ed., W.V.H. Rogers (London 1994) 586.

the order granting the injunction on the grounds that "[t]here is no tort of harassment" at English law, and therefore the injunction could not issue to protect any legal right of the plaintiff (p. 683).

The late Princess Diana was all too frequently a target of paparazzi. In one widely-publicized case in 1993, London tabloids published photographs of Princess Diana exercising in a London health club. The Princess was only able to obtain an injunction against the newspaper and gym prohibiting publication of additional photos on the grounds of breach of confidence and breach of contract. New York Times, November 9, 1993 (International News).

The Court of Appeal has recently expanded potential privacy rights at common law on the basis of the European Convention of Human Rights Art. 8, even without a breach of confidence, in the case of *Michael Douglas, Catherine Zeta-Jones, and Northern Shell PLC v. Hello!* Ltd (Court of Appeal, December 21, 2000, London Times Dec. 21, 2000. — All English Reports —). Plaintiffs won an injunction barring unauthorized publication of nine photos taken at the N.Y. wedding of actors Douglas and Zeta-Jones.

Reversing, the Court of Appeal declared that English law does recognize a right of privacy in accordance with Art. 8 of the European Convention on Human Rights. However, because the European Court of Human Rights distinguishes different degrees of privacy, which interact with Convention Art. 12 concerning freedom of expression, the British Court held that serious triable issues remained as to whether the unauthorized photos violated those privacy rights; the couple had already marketed photo rights of the event to OK! Magazine. The Court discharged the lower court injunction against publication of the unauthorized photos based on a balance of convenience: it would be easier to quantify damages (based on profits earned) if publication of the photos were permitted and Plaintiffs later prevailed, than to assess damages if publication were enjoined and the defendant later prevailed.

C. ITALY

1. Caselaw

a. Princess Soraya Case

Corte di Cassazione, Sez. I,
Soraya Esfandiari c. S.p.a. Rusconi
Judgment of May 27, 1975
25 Giustizia Civile I 1686 (1975).

Recourse, seeking vacation of the judgment of the Court of Appeals of Milan of January 19, 1971. [The court had held that the former spouse of the then Emperor of

17. I. Mackey & J. Earnshaw, *Skirting around sexual harassment* 145 New Law Journal p. 338 (March 10, 1995).

Iran was liable in damages for having wrongfully obtained the sequestration of a weekly magazine that had published pictures of petitioner without her permission. Petitioner submitted eight grounds for cassation of the judgment below.]

The Court's First Section, under the presidency of Mr. Justice Rossi with counsellor Santosuosso as the reporting justice: * * *

[p. 1691]

II.

Before examining the third, fourth, fifth and sixth grounds of error submitted in the principal petition — which concern the injurious consequences of the illegal seizure of the edition and the publication of the judgment which recognized the violation of the right of Mrs. Esfandiari — the court must preliminarily confront the question of the thesis of recognition of an autonomous right to a reserved sphere (*riservatezza*) for personal affairs, which petitioner asserted in her eighth ground for vacating the judgment, for the purpose of strengthening demonstration of the asserted violation of her rights.

That question — which, as is well-known, has been debated countless times by scholars at several international congresses and has been the subject of numerous decisions of lower courts as well as of several pronouncements of this Supreme Court — requires a solution that in the natural evolution of decisional law, while remaining anchored in constitutional mandates and other provisions of our positive legal order, is sensitive to the mutual adjustment of the protection of diverse interests, in the light of a strong trend, also on the international legal level, towards the extension of the defense of human personality both against abuse by public authorities and in the private relations among individuals.

This exigency is felt all the more because of the dimensions and alarming aspects which the problem is progressively assuming by reason of the development of modern technology, which by means of perfected instruments for gathering information offers to public authorities and private persons immeasurable possibilities for exercising pervasive control of every aspect of life and for rapid general divulgence of the gathered data. This extraordinary development, especially with respect to its negative implications, while calling for assessment on other levels in respect to its management and restriction, can nevertheless not be ignored by the private law and in particular at the judicial level.

When the question of the existence and the limits of the right to a reserved sphere was subjected for the first time to an examination by the Supreme Court, that body observed that "no provision of the law authorizes the contention that absolute respect for the intimacy of private life is sanctioned as a matter of general principle." Rather only particular subjective personal rights are recognized and protected in various ways (Judgment nr. 4487 of 1956). This approach was confirmed by the same court in its Judgment nr. 3199 of 1960, according to which, nevertheless "disclosure of facts or thoughts belonging to another person encounters the double limitation of protection of the honor, decorum and reputation and of the proscription of distortion of the truth."

Furthermore, in its Judgment nr. 990 of 1963 this Court — while still adhering to its denial of the existence of a "right to a reserved sphere in the typical sense" — maintained that "nevertheless legal protection must be admitted in the case of a violation of the absolute right of personality, understood as a right vis-à-vis anybody (*erga omnes*) to a free self-determination of the development of one's human personality as an individual. This right is violated if somebody else divulges information about the private life of a person that by reason of its nature must be deemed to be reserved, at least if there is lacking consent, even though only implied, of the person, derived from the specific activity exercised, or if, given the nature of the activity or of the divulged fact, there is no prevalent public interest in the knowledge, considered with regard to duties of political and economic solidarity inherent in the position of the subject."

This substantial — though indirect — recognition of the right to a reserved sphere was followed by judgments which, incidentally, made formal reference to a right of that character (Constitutional Court, nrs. 34 and 38 of 1973, Court of Cassation nr. 868 of 1974).

The indicated directions of the case law did not remain free from criticism and it is therefore appropriate, within the limits to be observed by the Court, to delineate in greater depth the underlying notions, also in the light of intervening normative factors.

At the outset it must be clarified that the solution of the problem cannot disregard the technical instrument of a private subjective right based on a time-honored doctrinal notion.

Although theoretical efforts, directed to open broader vistas, particularly with respect to modern elaboration of the institute of a private wrong are not inconsiderable, it seems that the time has not yet come for maintaining that the traditional notion of a subjective right has lost its validity as a category that qualifies the relevant subjective legal situations which are directly protected in our legal system. * * *

The inquiry about the normative basis of the so-called right to a reserved sphere requires at least a quick survey of the definitions given to that right to the extent that it furthers the determination of its content and, accordingly, of its correspondence to the ambit of the individual norms which must be examined.

By the term "right to a reserved sphere" — one of the first and most used formulations of the phenomenon that cannot be discarded any more — are indicated diverse hypotheses which imply an issue not only of form but of substance. These can be synthesized at least under three aspects.

On one side there is a tendency to rigorously restrict the scope of this right to preservation of "domestic intimacy" by tying it to protection of the home. To this notion corresponds perhaps *the right to be alone* of the anglo-saxons.

On the opposite end, there are very generic formulations — immunity of "private life" from any intrusion or so-called privacy (*privatezza*) — which would correspond to a substantial and overbroad and undetermined sphere of protection.

An intermediate concept which keeps the scope of this right within reasonable limits may be identified with the formulae which refer to a certain sphere of the individual and family life, to the inviolate personal intimacies in certain manifestations of life in relation to all these vicissitudes, i.e. in which intimate character is given by the fact that they develop in an ideal domicile not bound by the traditional refuges of the human individual (like the walls of the home or correspondence).

Now, this Court maintains for the purpose of the investigation of the normative basis of the subjective right to a reserved sphere, that — beyond the ways pursued so far, i.e. that of legal analogy or of a recourse to the general principles of the legal order — it is possible to find a direct protection of such an interest not only with respect to the first restricted exception, but also for the scope indicated by the third exception.

The norms which form the basis of the right to a reserved sphere strictly restricted to the reserve of all those events that pertain to the intimacy of the home are too obvious to require an extensive demonstration. * * *

But the freedom of a person from intrusion of another into one's own sphere of intimacy finds valid normative anchors also in the third hypothesis indicated above, i.e. when the situations or events, personal or familial, take place outside the home and notice thereof is acquired by lawful means.* * *

[p.1695] A protection of the right to a reserved sphere of a larger scope than that circumscribed by the intimacy of the home not only does not conflict with constitutional principles but finds in them various grounds for confirmation.

This Court in the above mentioned judgment nr. 990 of 1963 saw in art. 2 of the Constitution the only basis of an absolute right of personality which is infringed by disclosure of information relating to private life. In view of the criticism according to which art. 2 enunciates only in a general fashion the protectability of inviolable rights which find their effective recognition in other specific norms, it must be clarified that this Court — deducing from the cited article the "right vis-à-vis anybody (*erga omnes*) to the freedom of self-determination," intended to place the accent — not so much on the reference to inviolable rights — but on the expression of the norm which accords to humans the respect of their personality, as individuals as well as in the social formations where such personality unfolds.

A double intimation of confirmation of the right to a reserved sphere can also be drawn from art. 3 of the Constitution in part because recognition of the social dignity of the citizen necessitates an autonomous sphere which guarantees such dignity, in part because within the factual limits on the freedom and equality of the citizens fall also those impairments caused by undue intrusions of others into the sphere of autonomy of any person. And under that aspect also the inviolability of the personal freedom (art. 13) must be recorded, understood in a broader sense than mere physical liberty. * * *

If the right to a reserved sphere is in harmony with constitutional principles, it is expressly recognized by diverse deliberations of international character. * * *

It is useful to refer to the Universal Declaration of Human Rights (approved by the United Nations on Dec. 10, 1948) and to the International Covenant on Civil and Political Rights of Dec. 16, 1966, approved by the General Assembly of the United Nation by the resolution nr. 2000 of December 1966, which result in the prohibition of any arbitrary interference with the "privacy" of an individual.

Likewise the European Convention for the Protection of Human Rights and Fundamental Freedoms, signed at Rome on Nov. 4, 1950 (rendered executed by the act of Aug. 4 nr. 848) has stipulated that everyone has the right to respect for his private and family life, his home and his correspondence (art. 8), establishing moreover that the freedom of thought encounters a limit in "the protection of the reputation or rights of others for preventing the disclosure of information received in confidence" (art. 10(2)).

The content of these provisions is incorporated and developed by Resolution nr. 428 of 1970 of the Assembly of the Council of Europe which has specified that the right to privacy "should not only protect an individual against interferences by public authorities but also against interference by private persons or institutions, including the mass media."

The same European Convention of 1950 furnishes a precise frame within which the right of privacy must be recognized by providing that an interference with the privacy may be permitted "if it is in accordance with the law and is necessary in a democratic society in the interest of national security, public safety or the economic well-being of the country, the prevention of disorder or crime, for the protection of health or morals or for the protection of rights and freedoms of others."

In accepting therefore the eighth ground of the principal recourse — although it is inopportune to give the right to a reserved sphere rigid analytical delineations which would impinge on the necessary adaptability to the exigencies of surroundings, place and times — it may be affirmed that such right consists in the protection of such purely personal or family situations and events which, although they occur outside the home do not possess a socially appreciable interest for third persons, against invasions which are not justified by overriding public interests even if they are committed by lawful means, for purposes that are not exclusively speculative, and without offense to the honor, reputation and decorum.

The right cannot be denied to any category of persons because of their notoriety unless it is required by a real social interest in the information or other public exigencies.

The court of remand will have to reevaluate all aspects of the case.

(Part III Omitted.)

NOTES

1. *Soc. Austria Tabakwerke GmbH c. Veronesi ed altri.*

In Italy, case law and doctrinal writings have come to recognize another subjective right of personality, designated as right to one's personal identity (*diritto all'identità personale*) which is entitled to judicial protection by way of various means of relief.

The Italian Supreme Court recognized the right to one's personal identity in the case of *Soc. Austria Tabakwerke GmbH c. Veronesi ed altri,* Corte di Cass., Sez. I, 22 June 1985 nr. 3769, 35 Giustizia Civile 3049 (1985). In that case a noted cancer specialist and director of the Institute for Tumor research brought an action against the Austria Tabakwerke GmbH because it had stated in a paid newspaper advertisement of its cigarette Milde Sorte "that according to Professor Umberto Veronesi this type of cigarette reduces the danger of cancer to about one half."

Actually Professor Veronesi, an ardent anti-smoking crusader, had stated, during an interview granted to the weekly *Oggi* in response to a question, "that not all cigarettes were equally harmful, but that all smoking created a risk which only total abstention from smoking could avoid." Because of the alleged misrepresentation of his views plaintiff asked for damages caused by the violation of his right to the untouchability (*intangibilità*) of his moral personality and to his name.

The tribunal of first instance decided in his favor and the court of appeal (Milan) affirmed on the ground that the right to one's name was violated if the use of that name had a negative impact on the personality of its bearer. Defendant sought "cassation" of the judgment below, among other grounds, because the judge below, holding defendant liable in damages for its advertising campaign, had exalted the concept of the name as symbol and ignored that there could be a lawful commercial use without distortion and without injury to the personality.

The Court rejected the petition for quashing the judgment below, holding the grounds assigned for the petition unfounded. With respect to the first ground the Court noted that everyone has an interest to be represented to others in his true identity. According to the Court the right to the personal identity (*diritto all'identità personale*) was distinguished from the right to a reserved sphere (*diritto alla riservatezza*). The former assured the faithful representation of one's proper social image, while the latter assured the non-display to others of one's private affairs that are without socially appreciable interest. Nevertheless the lower court's incorporation of the former right into the ambit of the right to the reserved sphere was harmless error since the court below considered the infringed subjective right correctly as the right to personal identity which is accorded judicial protection by virtue of analogous application of other private rights of personality, conceived within frame of article 2 of the Constitution, though not the subject of an express constitutional guaranty.

For a discussion of the Court's opinion, see Dogliotti, *Il diritto all'identità personale approda in Cassazione,* 35 Giustizia Civile 3059 (1985).

2. Compare the Italian right of personal development with the American protection against publicity that unreasonably places another in a false light in the public eye.

D. FRANCE

1. Legislation on the Right of Personality

Code Civil, Art. 9
(as amended by Law 70-643 of July 17, 1970)

Everyone has a right to the respect for his or her private life.

The judges may without prejudice to the compensation for the damages suffered, prescribe all measures, such as sequestration, seizure and others, appropriate to prevent or stop an infringement upon the intimacy of one's private life. In case of urgency, the measures may be ordered by the judge for emergency relief.

2. Cases

a. *Princess Caroline of Monaco*

Court of Cassation (Civ. Ch. I),
Judgment of November 5, 1996
SNC Prisma Presse c. Mme G.
71 JCP II 22805 (1997).

The Court:

Upon the second assignment of error, considered in its four branches:

Considering that the company Prisma Presse, publisher of the journal "*Voici*" challenges the Judgment in issue (Court of Appeal of Paris, Judgment of February 15, 1994) because it ordered petitioner to pay to Mrs. G. [Grimaldi, i.e. Princess Caroline of Monaco] damages and interest due to invasion of her right of privacy and her right to object to the publication of her picture; that the petition claims first that if Art. 9 of the Civil Code grants to the victim of an invasion of her privacy an action to prevent or discontinue this invasion, the compensation for the damages sustained is subject to the conditions for the application of Art. 1382 of the Civil Code with the result that the Court of Appeal of Paris has misapplied the necessary combination of the two texts in holding that Mrs. G. was not subject to Art. 1382 with respect to the proof of damages and a causal connection thereof with the fault committed; that furthermore the Court of Appeal of Paris is blamed for having awarded an indemnity in the nature of a civil penalty independent of any compensable harm, in violation of the principle that the damages awarded must equal the prejudice suffered and for not having justified its decision which is based on a simple assertion.

But considering that according to Article 9 of the Civil Code the mere finding of an invasion of the right of privacy confers the right to compensation; that the Court of Appeal, having established an invasion of Mrs. G.'s right of privacy by the publication disclosing her sentimental life, has determined in its own discretion the amount of the prejudice sustained; that therefore it has legally justified its decision;

Therefore,
Rejects the petition.

Messrs. Lemontey, Pres.; Ancel, Reporting Judge; Mme La Foyer de Costil, Gen. Av.

NOTE

In France, as in Germany, damages for invasion of the right of privacy, tend to be exemplary or punitive in character, cf. Note by Prof. J. Rawanas to the Judgment reported above.

b. Le Grand Secret

Court of Appeal, Paris, 1st Civil Ch.
Judgment of May 27, 1997
S.A. Éditions Plon et al. c. Parties Mitterrand
71 JCP 1997 (éd. G.) II 22894 (p. 370);
82 Petites Affiches (July 9, 1997) 26.

The Court, * * *

Regarding the admissibility of the action by the parties Mitterrand for the protection of the right of privacy of Mr. François Mitterrand:

Considering that if every person, without regard to his rank, his birth, his fortune, his present or future functions, has a right that his privacy be respected, the faculty open to each to prohibit any form of divulging features thereof belongs only to the living;

That accordingly, the parties Mitterrand who do not allege an infraction against the memory of Mr. Mitterrand by way of a report of distorted facts published in bad faith or due to blameworthy recklessness, have not interposed an admissible complaint in that respect;

Regarding the invasion of the right of privacy of the parties Mitterrand:

Considering that for good reasons the judges below held that certain passages of the book contain invasions of the privacy of the parties Mitterrand, for example, the desire of Mr. François Mitterrand to hide his illness from his spouse (p. 35), the story of the presence of the latter near one of his grand-daughters (p. 98), the assertion that Mr. Gubler was often sent to Miss Pingeot's (p. 65), the report of the conversations between the President and his daughter (p. 161), the report that the spouse of the late chief of state and his sons were not informed in 1981 of his cancer (pp. 166, 167);

Considering, however, that if these infringements of the privacy of another confer the right to reparation on the basis of Art. 9 of the Civil Code, they cannot, in the instant case, as regrettable as they may be, in particular because of their incidental character in the book, justify the prohibition against the publication thereof in its entirety;

Regarding the violation of medical secrecy:

Considering that it is established by the Judgment of July 5, 1996 which has become final and binding upon the civil courts, that Mr. Gubler violated the professional secrecy to which he was obligated;

That it has been justly recalled in this decision that the offense of the violation of professional secrecy has been established not only in the public interest in order to assure confidence in the exercise of certain professions, but also in the interest of the individual, in order to guarantee the security of confidences which they are compelled to communicate to certain persons in view of their status and their profession; that medical secrecy finds its basis in the confidential relationship indispensable to medical action which assures patients that that which they communicate to, or permit their physicians to see, hear or understand necessarily in confidence, will not be revealed by the latter;

Considering that according to Art. 4 par. 2 of the Code of Medical Ethics, that medical secrecy covers "everything that comes to the knowledge of the physician in the exercise of his profession, that is to say, not only what has been disclosed to him, but also what he has seen, heard or understood."

Considering that the presence of Mr. Gubler at Mr. François Mitterrand's had no other cause than his function of a treating physician, all the facts which he tells in his book and which were learned or found by reason of the exercise of his profession are covered by the medical secrecy to which he is bound towards his patient, even if they at the same time may likewise constitute an invasion of the right of privacy or intimacy of the latter.

Considering * * *

That the parties Mitterrand therefore, as successors of their decedent find, in addition to their right of reparation due to the violations of medical secrecy by communication of the secret to Mr. Gonod in May/June 1995, and subsequently to Mr. Orban during November 1995, as has been held by the penal jurisdiction, the right to obtain indemnification for the consequences of the publication decided on November 8, 1995, a possibility which was not excluded in the Judgment of July 17, 1995 and is not contrary to the res judicata effect of that decision;

Regarding the reparations:

Considering that the exercise of the freedom of expression, principle of constitutional value, reinforced by Art. 10 of the European Convention of Human Rights, implies duties and responsibilities; that it may be subjected to certain formalities, conditions, restrictions or sanctions established by law which consists of measures necessary in a democratic society, in particular for the protection of health, for the protection of the reputation or rights of another or to hinder the divulging of confidential information;

That in the case at bar the interdiction of the work in issue is necessary, because it constitutes the only means of permitting to stop the prejudice caused thereby and the penal offense which it constitutes;

Considering that the prejudice has been correctly assessed by the judges below in view of the circumstances of the case, more than 40,000 books having been sold, since destination of the indemnity which must be proportional to the damage proven, and its unrestricted use by the recipients are without relevance on its evaluation; (. . .)

Therefore,

Reverses the Judgment below;

Dismisses the action against Mr. Orban;

Declares that the action by the parties Mitterrand is inadmissible to the extent that it is based on violation of a right of privacy of Mr. François Mitterrand;

Condemns Mr. Claude Gubler and the Société des Éditions Plon jointly to pay as damages: to Mrs. Danielle Mitterrand the sum of 100,000 F.;

to each of the three other plaintiffs the sum of 80,000 F.;

Affirms the Judgment to the extent that it upheld the prohibition against the distribution of the book *Le grand secret* issued by Order of the President of TGI of Paris of January 8, 1996 and confirmed by the Judgment of March 13, 1996;

In addition;

It condemns Mr. Claude Gubler and the Société des Éditions Plon to pay plaintiffs the sum of 30,000 F. to defray the expenses incurred in the first instance and the appeal pursuant to Art. 700 of the NCPC;

Declares that nothing is due to appellants on the basis of Article 700 NCPC.

NOTES

1. The text case is the climax of a protracted litigation by which the family Mitterrand sought to stop the distribution of the book *Le Grand Secret,* written by the physician of the late President of France disclosing that the latter since 1981 suffered from prostate cancer and discussing the impact of that illness on his capacity to govern, and to recover damages for the violation of the decedent's and their right of privacy.

The preceding judicial pronouncements are (i) TGI Paris réf., Order of the President, January 18, 1996, 70 JCP (éd. G.) II 22589 (1996); (ii) Court of Appeal, Paris 1st

Ch. March 13, 1996, 70 JCP (éd. G.) II 22632 (1996); (iii) TGI Paris 1st Ch. Oct. 23, 1996, 70 JCP (éd. G.) II 22844 (1996). The last of these decisions was reversed by the text case.

2. In the case *Proc. République et consorts Mitterrand c. R. Théron et Cogedipresse,* TGI Paris, 17 ch., Judgment of January 13, 1997, 82 Petites Affiches 31 (1997), the family Mitterrand joined a criminal prosecution against the director of publications and the publisher of the *Paris-Match* because they published a picture of the late President on his deathbed without proper authority. The French Criminal Code includes provisions penalizing invasions of privacy (Arts. 226-1 to 226-7). Prosecutions require complaints by the victim, his legal representatives or his successors (Art. 226-6).

In the case noted, the TGI imposed a fine of 100,000 F. on the director of *Paris-Match,* because the family Mitterrand had not authorized publication of the picture, but it awarded only 1 F. symbolic damages to each of the five complainants, because they had not asked for more and apparently had forgiven the infraction, because Mitterrand's widow granted numerous interviews and supplied pictures to this Weekly. The court, however, ordered publication of the Judgment in the next issue of the paper.

It is noteworthy that the Judgment expressly rejected the argument of defendants that the right of privacy expires at the death of its holder, even if the picture of a deceased president is in issue.

c. *Case of Farah Diba*

Court of Cassation (1st Civil Chamber)
Judgment of April 13, 1988.
Société de press "Jours de France"
c.
Former Empress of Iran, Farah Diba, et al.
Bull. Cassation (Civil), 1 ch. (Nr. 95)
63 JCP II 21320 (1989); D. I.R. 120 (1989)

The Court,

Considering that, according to the Judgment under attack (Paris, May 12, 1986), the weekly newspaper *"Jours de France"*, in September 1983, published, accompanied by a short text, two photographs of the former empress of Iran, Mrs. Farah Diba, in a bathing suit, one of which showed her in conversation in a garden, and the other depicted her standing upon some rocks with a fishing rod in her hand; that the Court of Appeal condemned the Société *"Jours de France"* to pay 150,000 francs to Mrs. Farah Diba in damages because of the invasion of her private life and of the right which she possesses with respect to her picture; that the court, in addition, condemned the Société Gamma and the Agency Angeli which had sold the pictures in issue to the Société "*Jours de France*", to guaranty to that firm payment of one half of the damages imposed upon it.

Upon the first assignment of error, considered in its first branch:

Considering that the Société "*Jours de France*" faults the Judgment for having reached that result although according to the contention of petitioner the protection of the private life and the right to one's picture is governed by the personal law of the party in interest, i.e. by the national law or, for stateless persons, the law of their domicile, and that by failing to ascertain, despite the contentions contesting the applicability of French law, what the nationality or the domicile of Mrs. Farah Diba was and thus to determine the applicable law, the Court of Appeal deprived its decision of a proper basis pursuant to Code Civil, Article 3;

But considering that the consequences of an invasion of the private life of a person or of the right that such person possesses with respect to his picture flow from the law of the place where such acts have been committed;

Wherefrom it follows, that this assignment of error is without significance

Upon the first assignment of error, considered in its second branch,

Considering that the Société "*Jours de France*" likewise faults the Judgment below because, in violation of Article 9 of the Code Civil, it held that the negatives in issue "did not concern the public life" of Mrs. Farah Diba, since the public life of a person depends on the function which she assumes,

But considering that, after having held correctly that a monarch like every other person, is entitled to respect of his private life and may object to any publication of his picture so long as it does not represent him in the exercise of his public functions, the appellate court could conclude from the nature of the controversial pictures that they reproduced moments of the private life of Mrs. Farah Diba;

Wherefrom it follows that the first assignment of error, considered in its second branch, is not less unfounded.

Upon the second assignment of error:

Considering that the Société "*Jours de France*", additionally, faults the Judgment below for having limited the guaranty of the Société Gamma and Agence Angeli to one half of the damages awarded to Mrs. Farah Diba although, according to the assignment of error, the merchant who sells photographs to an enterprise of the press for publication, is under a duty of supplying negatives whose use is not unlawful and that, under these circumstances the Court of Appeal did not give a legal basis to its decision in respect to Article 1147 of the Code Civil when it divided the responsibility without specifying which contractual fault the Société "*Jours de France*" had committed against its suppliers by failing to make sure that the person pictured in the controversial photographs had given her consent;

But considering that the Court of Appeal legally justified its decision by holding, that, in view of the personality of the subject and the nature of the negatives, the Société "*Jours de France*", by publishing the same without ascertaining by itself the consent of Mrs. Farah Diba, was itself guilty of a personal fault which contributed to the origin of the liability to pay damages for which it claims indemnification,

For these reasons,

The Court rejects the petition.

Mr. Ponsard, president; reporting judge: Councillor Gregoire, avocat général: Mr. Charbonnier.

NOTES

1. Various aspects of the text case are discussed by P. Bourell, 77 Revue critique de droit international privé 548 (1988); B. Edelman, 115 Journal du droit international 754 (1988); E. Putman 63 JCP II 21320 (1989); and P. Kayser, *La Protection de la vie privée* 2nd ed. (Paris/Aix-en-Provence 1990) p. 403 (§ 316).

2. In France the primary normative bases for the protection of the right of privacy (*la vie privée*) are Art. 9 and Art. 1382 of the Civil Code and the European Convention on the Protection of Human Rights and Fundamental Freedoms. Discussion of French privacy law may be found in P. Kayser, *La Protection de la vie privée* 2nd ed. 9 (§ 9) *et seq.*; A. Lacabarats, *La protection judiciaire des atteintes à la réputation: La voie civile,* 114 Gazette du Palais 1003 (2e sem. 1994). See also communications by J.-P. Ancel, D. Bécourt, M. Domingo and G. Levasseur in the same volume.

d. Prince Karim Aga Khann

Cour de Cassation (première Ch. Civ.)
Soc. Mail Newspaper PLC et autre
c.
Prince Karim Aga Khan et autre
Judgment of October 22, 1990
Lexis

The Court,

Considering that, according to the findings of the judges on the merits, the British bi-monthly The Mail on Sunday published in its issues of September 7 and 21, which are distributed in France, two articles signed by Mr. Dempster, which were devoted to Prince Rahim, minor son of Prince Karim Aga Khan and that the Court of Appeals of Paris in its Judgment under attack (Paris, February 1, 1989) which was ordered to be published, condemned the company Mail Newspaper PLC, publisher of the bi-monthly, and Mr. Dempster to pay, jointly and severally, the sum of 50,000 F. to Prince Aga Khan and his spouse as damages for the injury caused to their son by way of an infringement of his right of privacy and an additional sum of 50,000 F. to Prince Aga Khan as damages for his own injury;

Upon the first assignment of error taken up in its three branches,

Considering that the company Newspaper PLC and Mr. Dempster, blame the Court of Appeals for having so held in violation of Art. 9 par. 1 of the Code Civil, because on the one hand the story in the first article reporting a trite incident did not constitute objectively an intrusion into the privacy of a minor and his family and because on the other hand, the education and schooling of a prince belong traditionally to the sphere of his public life, and because finally, the conduct of persons whom their birth, their public or moral responsibilities, or their wealth has placed in the first rank of newsworthiness may be disclosed to a greater extent than that of other persons, so that the educational methods employed by a head of a religion vis-à-vis his son called to succeed him and the behavior of the latter in society are not placed in the ambit of his private life.

But considering that, after having correctly held that every person, whatever his rank, his birth, his wealth or his present or future functions, has the right to have his private life respected, the Court of Appeal has found that the articles reported, without the authorization of the legal representatives of the person concerned, facts respecting the conduct of a minor of 14 years in a private island and divulged certain strictly private habits of him as well as the conditions of his schooling and education; that the court in addition found that the articles commented on "the educational methods of Prince Karim Aga Khan by presenting them as being the roots of the little commendable behavior of his son";

That the judges of the second instance could therefore conclude that these revelations infringed upon the privacy of the young prince and his father; that their decision is therefore legally justified;

Wherefrom it follows that the assignment of error is without foundation.

Upon the second assignment of error,

Considering that the Judgment under attack is also challenged because it reached its result although, according to the assignment of error, Article 10 of European Convention for the Protection of Human Rights and Fundamental Freedoms guarantees the freedom of expression; that the public has the right to be informed of the moral conduct of religious authorities outside the sphere of the intimacy of the private life understood strictly in a manner that the decision under attack which amounts to an interference of the judicial authority with the freedom of expression violates the aforementioned provision.

But considering that the Judgment under attack, after holding in a decision legally justified on the basis of Article 9 part 1 of the Civil Code that the publications constituted an infringement of the privacy of Prince Aga Khan and his son and without misapplication of article 10 of the European Convention for the Protection of Human Rights and Fundamental Freedoms, point 2 of which provides certain limitations on the Freedom of Expression, and by applying Article 8-1 of the same convention, has condemned Mr. Dempster and the Société Mail newspaper PLC to a reparation of the injury suffered by the parties in interest as a result of the publications.

Wherefrom it follows that the assignment of error cannot be accepted.
For these reasons,
Rejects the petition.

NOTES

1. As noted previously, the Court of Cassation relied not only on the amendment to the Civil Code of July 17, 1970, but also on the European Convention for the Protection of Human Rights and Fundamental Freedoms.

2. The Judgment February 1, 1989 of the Court of Appeal of Paris is published in D. Jur. 48 (1990) with a note by Agostini, discussing the conflicts aspects of the case. For a prior successful action based on Art. 9 C.C. by the Princess Yasmina Aga Khan against the publishing house Axel Springer, see Cour de Cassation, 2d Ch. Civ., Judgment of February, 9, 1980, Lexis.

3. **Droit à l'oubli.** As noted above, one aspect of privacy in American law is the right to be forgotten, see Prosser and Keeton on Torts (5 ed. 1984) 859. French lower courts also seem to recognize a right of a person to be forgotten (*droit à l'oubli*) if the publicity would endanger his social rehabilitation. See e.g. Paris, TGI Judgment of March 25, 1987, (*L. . . . c. Soc. anon. Kenner Parker France*), D. Somm. Comm. 198 (1988), dealing with the liability of the manufacturer of a question and answer game, one card of which exposed a present psychiatrist as a former bank robber. The court ordered withdrawal of the game from the market.

Nevertheless, in a Judgment of November 20, 1990 (*Dame M. . . . et K. . . . et autre,* Bull. Cass. No. 256 (p. 181); 111 Gazette du Palais. Panorama 80 (1991)), the Court of Cassation seems to have severely limited, if not totally eliminated such a right. In that case, which involved an action by a Mrs. Monanges against Mr. Paul Kern and his publisher Mr Marsue, because of an unflattering reference to her and a report of her indictment and conviction in a notorious trial in 1946, without mentioning that she soon thereafter received a presidential pardon and was later rehabilitated by a law of 1951. Mr Kern's book consisted of an autobiographical account of his activities during the period of the occupation. The Court of Appeal of Bensançon dismissed the action and plaintiff filed a petition for cassation, assigning as error that the Judgment under attack had violated her right to privacy under Art. 9 C.C. and her protection against tortious acts under Art. 1382 C.C.

The Court held that the facts recounted were well-known to contemporaries because they were reported by the local press and therefore did not belong to plaintiff's private life, justifying a right to be forgotten. Conversely, plaintiff's failure to mention the plaintiff's presidential pardon and rehabilitation under the law of 1951 constituted a misapplication of the general tort law and called for vacation of the Judgment below.

See, however, the comments of J.-P. Ancel, Councillor on the Court of Cassation, who questions whether it should be permissible to retell a forgotten event solely in pursuit of profit. *Protection de la personne: Image et vie privée* 114 Gazette du Palais (1994 2d sem.) 988, 991.

4. Public disclosure of financial success is not necessarily desirable in France. Nevertheless, following two cassations,[18] the Court of Appeals of Versailles ultimately held that publication of an individual's financial holdings (in this case the gathered from publicly available sources) does not constitute an invasion of privacy. Versailles Court of Appeal, Judgment of May 17, 1995 (*aud. sol.*) D. jur. 409 (1996) n. J. Ravannas. (The *audience solennelle* formation, comprising 5 judges — 1 president and 2 judges from 2 chambers — is required for deciding case on remand (*renvoi*) from the Court of Cassation. Code of Judicial Organization Art. R. 213-5 (1979).)

E. SWITZERLAND

1. Legislation

Civil Code
Article 28 — Article 28g

(as amended by Federal Law of December 16, 1983.)

Article 28

He who is illegally injured in his personality may ask for judicial protection against any person who cooperates in the injury.

An injury is illegal if it is not justified by the consent of the injured person, by a preponderant private or public interest or by a statute.

Article 28a

The plaintiff may ask the judge,

1. to prohibit an imminent injury,
2. to eliminate an existing injury,
3. to establish the illegality of an injury if it continues to have disturbing effects.

He may ask in particular that a correction or the Judgment be communicated to a third person or published.

Actions for payment of damages and satisfaction or restitution of gains pursuant to the provisions governing meddling in the affairs of a third person without request remain unaffected.

18. Cass. Civ. Judgment of May 31 1988 (Bull. civ. I. no. 167) and Cass. Civ. Judgment of October 20, 1993 (Bull. civ. I no. 295, D. jur. 594 (1994).)

Article 28b

Competency to adjudicate complaints for the protection of the personality is vested in the judge at the domicile of the plaintiff or defendant.

If the plaintiff asks simultaneously for the payment of damages, satisfaction or restitution of gains, he may assert these claims also at his domicile.

Article 28c

He who furnishes prima facie evidence that he is injured illegally in his right of personality or that there is a danger of such injury and that such injury threatens to inflict irreparable harm may request the imposition of protective remedies.

The judge, in particular may

1. provisionally enjoin or eliminate the violation;
2. take the necessary measures for the perpetuation of evidence.

The judge, however, may provisionally enjoin or eliminate a violation by periodic media only if it is apt to cause a particularly severe harm, is manifestly unjustified and if the measure does not appear to be disproportionate.

* * *

Article 28g

A person who is directly affected in his personality by presentations of facts in periodic media, in particular Press, Radio and Television, is entitled to a counter-presentation.

There exists no claim to a counter-representation in the case of a factually correct report of public transactions of a public authority and the participation of the affected person in these transactions.

2. Case

a. Case of the Swiss Journalists

Federal Tribunal of Switzerland
Association of Swiss Journalists (VSJ) and another
v.
Canton of Aargau
Constitutional Complaint of March 2, 1987
BGE 113 Ia 309 (Nr. 48)

By plebiscite of December 1, 1985 the voters of the Canton of Aargau approved the law on the Organization of the Ordinary Judicial Authorities [*GOG*[19]] of Decem-

19. Gesetz über die Organisation der ordentlichen richterlichen Behörden.

ber 11, 1984. Section 15 thereof includes, under the Title "Press, Radio and Television" the following provision:

"1. Reports of judicial hearings by Press, Radio or Television shall be objective and may not expose anybody unnecessarily.
2. Press, Radio and Television are obligated to publish a correction of their reports as ordered and formulated by the appropriate court.
3. Reporters of judicial proceedings who disobey the rules established for such reporting may be excluded from public hearings of the cantonal courts by order of the Superior Court.
4. The Government Council shall enact a regulation governing the reporting of court proceedings."

The Association of Swiss Journalists and one editor filed a constitutional complaint against §15 GOG claiming violation of the supremacy of Federal law and violation of the Freedom of Expression, Freedom of the Press, Freedom of Information, Equal Protection and the Principle of Public Judicial Proceedings.

The Federal Tribunal dismissed the constitutional complaint.

EXTRACT OF REASONS

3. The complainants charge a violation of the principle of the supremacy of the Federal law and thus claim a violation of Art. 2 of the transitional provisions of the Constitution. They argue that §15 of the Law on the Organization of the Ordinary Judicial Authorities has the sole purpose of protecting the personality of the participants in the proceedings. The protection of the right of personality according to them is guaranteed by the Federal Civil Law in an exclusive manner. Therefore, §15 GOG interferes in an illegal fashion with the Federal legislative power of private law.

[a.–c. omitted]

d. Complainants misunderstand the scope of Federal private law if they try to attribute to it an exclusive protection of personality. The protection of personality is a universal concern of the legal order in general. The dignity of mankind is not only an object of protection of private law but of the legal order at large. It is manifested also in the Guarantee of Fundamental Rights in the Federal Constitution (cf. Hans Huber, Discussion thesis for the Annual Meeting of Swiss Jurists 1960, 79 ZSR II p. 667a ff. (1960)). The protection of personality is a concern of private as well as public law. This applies in particular to the ambit of procedural law. [Citations omitted.] The participants in judicial proceedings have a right to the guarantee of their dignity in the proceedings flowing from the Mandate of Fairness. This purpose is served not only by the cantonal codes of civil procedure and the procedural guarantees of Art. 4 of the Federal Constitution, but also by the general right to be treated during the proceeding with the necessary respect for the personality. This holds true in particular for an accused in criminal proceedings. * * * The danger of a violation of human dignity and the right of personality, however, is not only inherent in an incorrect course of proceedings, but in the same measure in reporting of judicial proceedings in an unnecessarily offensive or exposing manner. The reports of trials therefore must respect the personality of the participants. The assurance of that obligation rests also with the cantonal procedural laws.

Public law and private law protections of the right of personality coexists in that sense. The fact that claims of a participant in judicial proceedings resulting from reporting of judicial proceedings in a manner violating his personality may be adjudged pursuant to private law and asserted according to Civil Code Art. 28 *et s.* does not exclude the authority of the cantons to safeguard the interests of the participants also within the framework of the provisions or the maintenance of discipline in the hearings.

* * *

4. a) Complainants additionally contend that § 15 GOG violates in various respects written and unwritten constitutional rights as well as guarantees of the European Convention on Human Rights [ECHR]. They rely in particular on Art. 55 Federal Constitution — the Freedom of Expression, and Art. 10 of the ECHR as well as the Freedom of Information and the Principle of Publicity of Judicial Proceedings.

* * * The Guarantees of the Convention * * * correspond to the written and unwritten law of the Federal Constitution. The challenge of the complainants may therefore be treated together under the aspects of Freedom of the Press, Freedom of Expression of opinion and Art. 10 of the European Convention on Human Rights as well as the Freedom of information flowing therefrom.

* * *

6. Because of all these reasons, the attacked provision of § 15 GOG does not succumb to the asserted challenges in the abstract norms control.

NOTES

For Swiss discussions see Pierre Tercier, *Erste Erfahrungen mit dem neuen Persönlichkeitsrecht,* 106 Zeitschrift für Schweizerisches Recht 187 (1987) and R. Zäch, *Der Einfluss von Verfassungsrecht auf das Privatrecht bei der Rechtsanwendung,* 85 Schweizerische Juristen-Zeitung at 1 *et seq.* and 25 *et seq.* (1989).

PART III
SECURITY FOR PERFORMANCE

A. ATYPICAL TRANSACTIONS SECURING PERFORMANCE STANDBY LETTERS OF CREDIT GUARANTEES ON FIRST DEMAND AND COGNATE INSTRUMENTS

B. TYPICAL TRANSACTIONS SECURING PERFORMANCE RETENTION OF TITLE TRANSFERS AS SECURITY FACTORING

INTRODUCTION

Credit transactions may be secured or unsecured. Secured credit transactions may involve either collateral belonging to the debtor, such as retention of titles clauses in sales, mortgages of land or chattels, fiduciary assignments of accounts or fiduciary transfers of present or future goods, or collateral belonging to third parties. Third parties may also obligate themselves to guarantee the performance of the debtor to the creditor. Modern international commercial practice has developed new instruments for securing the performance of a debtor by way of an undertaking of a third party, but comparative law demonstrates important difference in the details.

The main methods of securing performance by way of an undertaking by a third part are standby letters of credit, bank guaranties on first demand and (to a lesser degree) comfort letters. These instruments will be discussed in Chapters 6 and 7.

PART III/A:

ATYPICAL TRANSACTIONS SECURING PERFORMANCE

6/Standby Letters of Credit & Guarantees on First Demand

INTRODUCTION

In modern international trade each party to a transaction is desirous to be assured that the other party performs its obligations. These duties may involve a variety of actions, such as construction of plants designed to fulfil complex functions (airports, highways, hospitals, powerplants), delivery and installation of control systems, payments of advances, repayment of advances if performance becomes impossible, payment of installments of the price for the performance. In order to satisfy these needs, modern banking practice has developed two devices which have common features, viz., the standby letter of credit and the bank guaranty on first demand.

The *standby letter of credit* is mainly used in countries influenced by U.S. practice, while the bank guaranty on first demand is utilized in counties following the continental European model. The reason why U.S. banks developed the standby letter of credit, rather than using guaranties on first demand, was the accounting methods imposed by the supervisory authorities. Outstanding guaranties had to be debited in the balance sheet in their full amount, while this rule was not applied to letters of credit.

The standby letter of credit was an adaptation of the documentary letter of credit used traditionally in international sales to facilitate collection of the purchase price by the buyer. It permitted the buyer to receive payment upon the loading of the merchandise on the carrier's vessel, rather than only after arrival. The bank issuing the documentary letter of credit had to pay the exporter (called the '*beneficiary*') upon presentation of documents specified in the credit, usually a 'clean' bill of lading, a bill for the price and a certificate of origin. Often more than one bank was involved, one in the country of the buyer and one in the country of the seller.

Under the practice used in the common law countries, the buyer's bank is the '*is-*

suing bank' (or issuer). The seller's bank is either a *'confirming bank'* or an *'advising bank'*. The difference between these two types of functions consists in the liability to the beneficiary (seller). A *confirming bank* undertakes a duty to pay upon presentation of the requisite documents, while an *advising bank* is not bound to honor the credit.

The bank guaranty on first demand. Under the practice used in civil law countries, the two banks have a different arrangement: primary guaranty and counter-guaranty. The customer (buyer) requests a bank in the customer's own country to provide for the issuance of a documentary credit in the beneficiary's country upon furnishing a counterguaranty to the bank issuing the primary guaranty. The *bank guaranty on first demand* resembles the documentary credit situation, except that the documents to be presented usually consist in the written declaration by the beneficiary that the customer is in default.

The characteristic feature of documentary credits, standby letter of credits and bank guaranties on first demand is the so-called *'independence principle'*, i.e. the rule that the bank may and must pay if the beneficiary presents the requisite documents or declarations and need not and cannot raise defenses based on the underlying relation between the beneficiary and the customers. The ramifications of the independence principle have been subject to many disputes and uncertainties which are illustrated in the following materials.

The rules governing these types of instruments have been discussed in an ever-increasing body of case-law and a growing number of treatises and articles. Since the subject is of world-wide scope, international bodies have endeavored to codify it in transnational rules and to propose international agreements.

The International Chamber of Commerce published in 1993 a revision of the *Uniform Customs and Practice for Documentary Credits* (ICC Publication No. 500) which is incorporated in many credits of that type. Article 1 specified that the provisions

> 'shall apply to all Documentary Credit, (including to the extent to which they may be applicable, Standby Letter(s) of Credit) where they are incorporated into the text of the Credit.'

In addition, the ICC in 1992 issued the *Uniform Rules for Demand Guarantees* (ICC Publication No. 458). Publication No. 458 observes in the Introduction that standby letters of credit

> 'are used in a much wider range of financial and commercial activity than demand guarantees, and regularly involve practice and procedures * * * that are infrequently encountered in relation to demand guarantees and that ally standby credits more closely with documentary credits. Accordingly, while standby letters of credit are technically within the definition of a demand guarantee, it is expected that issuers of standby credit will continue to use the UCP. * * *'

In difference to the ICC, UNCITRAL (United Nations Commission on International Trade Law) is working on the preparation of a convention, focussing on independent guarantees, including standby letters of credit. In sharp contrast to the ICC, UNCITRAL concluded that bank guaranties on first demand and standby letters of credit performed equivalent functions and should be dealt with in the same convention. See Eric E. Bergsten, *A New Regime for International Independent Guarantees and Stand-by Letters of Credit: The UNCITRAL Draft Convention on Guaranty Letters*', 27 INTERNATIONAL LAWYER 859 (1993).

A. ENGLAND

1. Cases

a. Hongkong and Shanghai Banking Corp. v. Kloeckner & Co. A.G.

Queen's Bench Division (Commercial Court) 1989
Hongkong and Shanghai Banking Corp. v. Kloeckner & Co. A.G.
[1990] 2 QB 514; [1990] 3 WLR 634.

SUMMONSES

The plaintiffs, Hongkong and Shanghai Banking Corporation, issued a writ, dated 7 December 1988, claiming against the defendants, Kloeckner & Co. A.G., a West German company, (1) U.S.$7,972,779.81, pursuant to undertakings given to the plaintiffs by the defendants in connection with crude oil dealings between the Gatoil group of companies and the defendants; (2) damages; (3) interest pursuant to section 35 of the Supreme Court Act 1981; (4) a declaration that the defendants were not entitled to exercise any right of set-off against sums payable by the defendants to the plaintiffs in accordance with the terms of the defendants' undertakings. The defendants denied liability and sought to set off against the claim a counterclaim under a standby letter of credit given to them by the plaintiffs in respect of the liabilities of Gatoil to the defendants. By a summons dated 5 January 1989 and a cross-summons dated 20 February 1989 the plaintiffs and the defendants sought summary judgment under R.S.C., Ord. 14 on the claim and counterclaim respectively.

The summonses were heard, and judgment was given, in chambers. The case is reported by permission of Hirst J.

The facts are stated in the judgment.

21 March. HIRST J. read the following judgment.

Introduction

The two Order 14 summonses which are presently before the court arise out of a very substantial series of banking transactions between the plaintiffs, the Hongkong and Shanghai Banking Corporation ("the bank") and the defendants, Kloeckner &

Co. A.G. ("Kloeckner"), in connection with oil trading both in pre-sold physical cargoes of oil ("wet cargoes") and in relation to forward contracts ("dry cargoes").

The essential background is that the London branch of the bank provided certain facilities to the Gatoil group of companies, comprising a number of companies registered overseas linked by the common ownership and control of Mr. Ghattas, in connection with crude oil trading dealings between Gatoil and Kloeckner, under which Kloeckner would "front" Gatoil's contracts with the general market under an umbrella arrangement by means of back-to-back contracts.

The bank provided to Gatoil a facility used for dealings in wet cargoes, under which the bank paid Gatoil's suppliers, sometimes via letters of credit, and received a pledge of the relevant bill of lading. Kloeckner in their turn gave to the bank an undertaking to pay the bank against delivery to Kloeckner of the bill of lading, or, where the bill of lading was not yet available, against provision by the bank of an indemnity. The bank also advanced moneys to Gatoil against assignments by Gatoil of the proceeds of matched pairs of forward contracts in dry cargoes together with undertakings by Kloeckner to pay the difference debt to the bank. In the case of the dry cargo arrangements, identical procedures were entered into with other banks which are relevant in the present context for reasons which will shortly appear. The bank in addition provided a standby letter of credit in favour of Kloeckner in respect of the liabilities of Gatoil to Kloeckner on dry cargo transactions.

Kloeckner are a German company who carry on a substantial steel business, but who, as is readily apparent from the facts which I am about to recite, embarked recently on massive oil trading. By the early autumn of 1988 this trading got completely out of hand, and on 12 October 1988 Kloeckner announced losses of D.M. 600m. on forward oil contracts; there then followed a rescue operation by the Deutsche Bank who took over the company, which has since been re-structured so that its corporate status is that of an Aktiengesellschaft ("A.G.") and no longer that of a Kommanditgesellschaft auf Aktien ("K.G.a.A.")

The head of Kloeckner's crude oil trading department ("I.R.P.H.") and chief oil trader Mr. W. Zeschmar was dismissed, and he is now under arrest in Germany.

The claim by the bank in the present action is for approximately $8m. for the balance due under payment undertakings given by Kloeckner to the bank in respect of wet cargo contracts, and it is the bank's case that Kloeckner has no defence to this claim so that the bank are entitled to summary judgment. Kloeckner deny liability, contending that the relevant payment undertakings were entered into by Mr. Zeschmar in excess of his authority and by means of telexes purporting to bear not only his signature but also that of another employee who in fact played no part and had no knowledge of Mr. Zeschmar's activities. Kloeckner also raise two technical defences which I will describe shortly. In addition Kloeckner seek if necessary to set off against the bank's claim the sums claimed on their counterclaim which I am about to describe; in answer to the set-off the bank rely on a clause in the letter of undertaking debarring any set-off counterclaim or deduction whatsoever, but Kloeckner make rejoinder that as a matter of law a party cannot contract out of his right of set-off.

By their cross-summons under Order 14 Kloeckner seek summary judgment on their counterclaim for $10m. payable under the standby letter of credit. This was the subject matter of two successive demands by Kloeckner, the first of which for exactly $10m. was rejected by the bank, but the second for a slightly lower sum was accepted. The bank do not therefore dispute liability in principle for this lower sum, but assert a set-off in the sum of approximately $10.2m. under assignments or undertakings relating to dry cargo contracts; these are the subject matter of separate litigation in an action 1988 Folio No. 3262, in which both the bank and several of the other banks referred to above are also parties. Kloeckner concede that the dry cargo claims which the bank seek to set off are arguable, but contend that as a matter of first principle the court cannot as a matter of law entertain a set-off against a claim under a letter of credit.

The issues in the summons may therefore conveniently be grouped as follows, and I shall deal with them in this order following upon a brief narrative of the salient documents. (i) The two questions of pure law which arise in relation to set-off; first, whether it is open to a party to contract out of his right of set-off, and secondly, whether a set-off can be maintained in answer to a claim under a letter of credit. Both these are obviously questions of importance and the latter is devoid of any authority. (ii) The two other short technical defences raised by Kloeckner in answer to the bank's claim. (iii) The questions of fact which arise in connection with Mr. Zeschmar's alleged lack of authority. This will require a more detailed narrative of the background, which it is convenient to defer until that stage.

* * *

Main narrative of relevant documents

The relationship between the bank and Kloeckner began in November 1987, and until June 1988, when the wet cargo dealings began, was confined to dry cargo transactions. The typical documentation in a wet cargo transaction comprised a contract between a Gatoil company and Kloeckner for the sale of a physical cargo of oil, a letter in standard form from Gatoil to the bank pledging the shipping documents, i.e., the bills of lading, a request from Gatoil to Kloeckner seeking a purchase undertaking in favour of the bank, bills of lading to the order of the bank, the usual letter of indemnity to cover the situation where as so often happens the shipping documents are delayed, and an invoice from Gatoil to Kloeckner.

The critical document, which is the basis of the bank's claim is the purchase undertaking, and I quote a typical example in full:

> "We refer to the contract dated 6 September 1988 between Gatoil S.R.T. S.A. and Kloeckner and Co. K.G.a.A. Duisburg for the purchase by Kloeckner of:
>
> "Type of Product — Saharan Blend Crude Oil as usually made available for export.
>
> "Quantity — 600,000 barrels plus or minus five per cent.
>
> "Price — The simple average of the midpoints of daily spot quotations for dated Brent effectively published as quote

	Brent (DTD) unquote in the Platt's crude oil marketwire telex for the last two publications preceding B/L date, the publication of B/L date if it exists, plus the first two publications following the B/L date plus usd 0.25/BBL F.O.B. Bejaia.
"Parity	Latest 3 October 1988.
"Payment	30 days from bill of lading date additional 30 days at cost.

"We have duly noted that your bank possesses a security interest in this cargo and we, Kloeckner and CO. K.G.a.A., irrevocably undertake to make payment in full of Gatoil's invoice without any discount, deduction, offset, or counterclaim whatsoever on the due date, i.e., 60 days from bill of lading date directly to The Hong Kong and Shanghai Banking Corporation — London account with the Hong Kong and Shanghai Banking Corporation New York in favour of Gatoil S.R.T., S.A. Payment will be made directly by our bank on our behalf against presentation to us of below listed documents: seller's original commerical invoice signed by the seller's duly authorised signatory. Full set of 3/3 original clean on board ocean bills of lading issued or endorsed to the order of Kloeckner and Co. K.G.a.A. Duisburg and other usual shipping documents. In the event of non-availability of documents as specified above payment shall be made upon presentation of the following documents: seller's original commercial invoice signed by the seller's duly authorised signatory (telex acceptable with hard copy to follow). A letter of indemnity countersigned by Hong Kong and Shanghai Banking Corporation — London (telex letter of indemnity acceptable with hard copy to follow).

"Best regards
"Kloeckner and Co. K.G.a.A.
"W. Zeschmar/H. Escher."

It will be noted that the signatories or purported signatories are Mr. Zeschmar and Mr. H. Escher, who was an employee of Kloeckner's assigned to I.R.P.H. from another division. There were in all three purchase undertakings given by Kloeckner to the bank.

* * *

Issues of law on set-off
(a) Contracting out

It will have been noted that Kloeckner's letter of undertaking specified that Kloeckner "irrevocably undertake to make payment in full of Gatoil's invoice without any discount, deduction, offset, or counterclaim whatsoever on the due date." This very clear form of words is relied upon by Mr. Donaldson on behalf of the bank as precluding any right of set-off by Kloeckner against the claims under the letters of credit.

Mr. Havelock-Allen relies in answer on two old first instance authorities, namely *Lechmere v. Hawkins* (1798) 2 Esp. 626 and *Taylor v. Okey* (1806) 13 Ves. Jun. 180.

* * *

These two cases are cited as good authority for the proposition that a right of set-off "cannot be waived" in *Halsbury's Laws of England,* 4th ed., vol. 42 (1983), p. 252, para. 434, and though not strictly binding on me, are of course very highly persuasive.

However in *Halesowen Presswork & Assemblies Ltd., v. Westminster Bank Ltd.* [1971] 1 Q.B. 1 the Court of Appeal (Lord Denning M.R., Winn and Buckley L.JJ.) held that the right in law of a banker to combine the accounts of a customer and to set off debits on or against credits on the others could be excluded by an agreement, express or implied, to keep the accounts separate.

* * *

Manifestly, as Mr. Havelock-Allen recognised, the *Halesowen* case makes at the very least a major inroad into the suggested general principle stated by *Halsbury's Laws of England* in reliance on the two old cases. However he seeks to distinguish the Court of Appeal case on the footing that it enshrines some special rule relating to bank accounts. I am unable to see any sound foundation for this distinction. Nor was Mr. Havelock-Allen able to suggest any rational basis for such a rule. In my judgment the *Halesowen* case gives me very ample grounds for departing from the two old cases. In consequence, I hold that as a matter of law the bank are entitled to rely on the clause excluding any right of set-off against the letter of undertaking, and that this effectively debars the set-off which Kloeckner seek to maintain.

(b) Letters of Credit

Mr. Havelock-Allen submits that there can in law be no set-off by a bank against a beneficiary of a cross-claim in response to a claim by the latter under a letter of credit. He relies by analogy on the very well known line of cases which establish that the bank's obligation under a letter of credit or performance bond is quite independent of any disputes between the customer and the beneficiary, so that the bank must pay in full irrespective of any right of set-off being asserted between the parties to the underlying transaction. This rule is typified by the decision of the Court of Appeal in the leading case of *Edward Owen Engineering Ltd. v. Barclays Bank International Ltd.* [1978] Q.B. 159. This was of course a performance bond case, but the decision reflected the same rule which applies to letters of credit. In the leading judgment Lord Denning M.R. stated, at p. 169:

> "A performance bond is a new creature so far as we are concerned. It has many similarities to a letter of credit, with which of course we are very familiar. It has been long established that when a letter of credit is issued and

> confirmed by a bank, the bank must pay it if the documents are in order and the terms of the credit are satisfied. Any dispute between buyer and seller must be settled between themselves. The bank must honour the credit. That was clearly stated in *Hamzeh Malas & Sons v. British Imex Industries Ltd.* [1958] 2 Q.B. 127. Jenkins L.J. giving the judgment of this court, said, at p. 129: 'it seems to be plain enough that the opening of a confirmed letter of credit constitutes a bargain between the banker and the vendor of the goods, which imposes upon the banker an absolute obligation to pay, irrespective of any dispute there may be between the parties as to whether the goods are up to contract or not. An elaborate commercial system has been built up on the footing that bankers' confirmed credits are of that character, and, in my judgment, it would be wrong for this court in the present case to interfere with the established practice.' To this general principle there is an exception in the case of what is called established or obvious fraud to the knowledge of the bank."

Lord Denning M.R. then proceeded to identify the one well-established exception, namely where there is obvious fraud to the knowledge of the bank, and thereafter to discuss particular features of performance bonds both generally and in relation to that particular case. He then continued, at p. 171:

> "All this leads to the conclusion that the performance guarantee stands on a similar footing to a letter of credit. A bank which gives a performance guarantee must honour that guarantee according to its terms. It is not concerned in the least with the relations between the supplier and the customer; nor with the question whether the supplier has performed his contracted obligation or not; nor with the question whether the supplier is in default or not. The bank must pay according to its guarantee, on demand, if so stipulated, without proof or conditions. The only exception is when there is a clear fraud of which the bank has notice."

Browne and Geoffrey Lane L.JJ. delivered concurring judgments.

Mr. Havelock-Allen also placed particular reliance on the decision of the Court of Appeal in *Power Curber International Ltd. v. National Bank of Kuwait S.A.K.* [1981] 1 W.L.R. 1233 where it was held that the bank was obliged to honour a letter of credit notwithstanding a successful application by the buyers to the Kuwaiti court for an order of provisional attachment of the sums due payable by the defendant bank to the plaintiff sellers under the letter of credit. Lord Denning M.R., in considering whether the English court should recognise the order of the Kuwaiti court, stated, at p. 1241:

"On this question of recognition, I must draw attention to the importance of letters of credit in international trade. They are the means by which goods are supplied all the world over. It is vital that every bank which issues a letter of credit should honour its obligations. The bank is in no way concerned with any dispute that the buyer may have with the seller. The buyer may say that the goods are not up to contract. Nevertheless the bank must honour its obligations. The buyer may say that he has a cross-claim in a large amount. Still the bank must honour its obligations. A letter of credit is like a bill of exchange given for the price of goods. It ranks as cash and must be honoured. No set-off or counterclaim is allowed to detract from it: see *Nova (Jersey) Knit Ltd. v. Kammgarn Spinnerei G.m.b.H.* [1977] 1 W.L.R. 713. All the more so with a letter of credit. Whereas a bill of exchange is given by buyer to seller, a letter of credit is given by a bank to the seller with the very intention of avoiding anything in the nature of a set-off or counterclaim. This is borne out by the Uniform Customs and Practice for Documentary Credits which have been adopted by the banks in all, or practically all, the countries of the world — from China to Andorra — from Cuba to Nauru. All subscribe to the Uniform Customs and Practice which declare: 'Credits, by their nature, are separate transactions from the sales or other contracts on which they may be based and banks are in no way concerned with or bound by such contracts.' If the court of any of the countries should interfere with the obligations of one of its banks (by ordering it not to pay under a letter of credit) it would strike at the very heart of that country's international trade. No foreign seller would supply goods to that country on letters of credit — because he could no longer be confident of being paid. No trader would accept a letter of credit issued by a bank of that country if it might be ordered by its courts not to pay. So it is part of the law of international trade that letters of credit should be honoured — and not nullified by an attachment order at the suit of the buyer."

Griffiths L.J. and Waterhouse J. delivered concurring judgments.

Mr. Havelock-Allen also relied on the well-known passage in the judgment of Donaldson L.J. in *Intraco Ltd. v. Notis Shipping Corporation (The Bhoja Trader)* [1981] 2 Lloyd's Rep. 256, 257:

"In refusing to interfere with the sellers' right to call upon the bank to make payment under its guarantee, the . . . judge acted in conformity with the well-established principle that the court will not grant such an injunction unless fraud is involved (see *Richardson (Howe) Scale Co. Ltd. v. Polimex-Cekop and Another* [1978] 1 Lloyd's Rep. 161). We agree with him. Irrevocable letters of credit and bank guarantees given in circumstances such that they are the equivalent of an irrevocable letter of credit have been said to be

> the life blood of commerce. Thrombosis will occur if, unless fraud is involved, the courts intervene and thereby disturb the mercantile practice of treating rights thereunder as being the equivalent of cash in hand."

Mr. Havelock-Allen submitted that the rationale of the principle laid down in these cases is that the beneficiary should have the assurance of a certain paymaster, and should be able to treat the payment mechanism as an equivalent to cash in hand, free from the taint of any argument he may have with the bank's customer concerning some other transaction; that there is no reason why the rule of no set-off should not equally apply to the relationship between the bank and the beneficiary; and that as a matter of policy there is every reason why it should so apply.

Mr. Donaldson submitted that all these cases, and the dicta contained in them, must be interpreted by reference to their essential ratio decidendi, namely, that the relationship between the bank and the beneficiary is entirely independent of any differences which may arise between the buyers and the sellers in connection with the underlying contract. They are therefore no authority whatsoever in the present situation which relates to a cross-claim by the bank themselves against the beneficiary.

In the very rare cases, such as the present, where there was a claim as between the bank themselves as claimants and the beneficiary there was no good reason for extending the rule in the *Edward Owen Engineering Ltd. v. Barclays Bank International Ltd.* [1978] Q.B. 159 line of cases which arose from quite different circumstances.

Alternatively, Mr. Donaldson submitted that any restriction to a right of set-off by the banks themselves should be no greater than that in relation to bills of exchange which are also intended to be "equivalent to cash" i.e., that (as is well settled) a set-off is permissible where the cross-claim is liquidated, though not where it is unliquidated: see *Agra and Masterman's Bank v. Leighton* (1866) L.R. 2 Ex. 56 and *Nova (Jersey) Knit Ltd. v. Kammgarn Spinnerei G.m.b.H.* [1977] 1 W.L.R. 713.

Dealing now with the general point of principle, I do not think that the analogy with the *Edward Owen* line of cases is a sound one. The basis of those decisions is that the bank's obligation to the beneficiary under the letter of credit is wholly independent from any disputes between the buyer and the seller in relation to the underlying contract. The reason of policy on which this doctrine is based is that otherwise a letter of credit would be almost valueless, since, as the everyday experience of the Commercial Court and the City of London arbitration community shows such disputes (e.g. as to short delivery, damage in transit, defects of quality and the like) are commonplace; if, therefore every time such a dispute arose (or was even alleged by the buyer to arise), the buyer was free to stop payment under the letter of credit, the assurance given to the seller by a letter of credit would be severely undermined, and the lifeblood of international trade would truly be afflicted by a thrombosis.

The present situation is quite different; it is only on the rarest occasions, as Mr. Havelock-Allen recognised, that a separate dispute will arise between the bank and the beneficiary, since from the beneficiary's point of view the choice of paying bank is fortuitous, and it is only in the rarest cases that there will be any antecedent banking connection between them that could give rise to such a dispute.

There is thus nothing in the *Edward Owen* line of authorities which compels me to adopt the conclusion sought by Mrs. Havelock-Allen. I should add that the statement in Lord Denning M.R.'s judgment in *Power Curber International Ltd. v. National Bank of Kuwait S.A.K.* [1981] 1 W.L.R. 1233, 1241, that "No set-off or counterclaim is allowed to detract from [the letter of credit]" must be interpreted as meaning a set-off or counterclaim by the buyer against the seller and not one by the bank against the seller, the latter situation not being under consideration in that case.

There are two striking features of the present case; first the standby letter of credit was opened for the specific purpose of financing the liabilities on the dry cargo transactions, so that it would seem very unjust if the bank were precluded from enforcing a set-off in relation to the present claims which arise directly out of selfsame transactions. Second, this is a liquidated set-off, and it would seem to me anomalous that such a set-off should be unavailable in letters of credit cases, but available against bills of exchange which, as the judgments quoted above show, are closely analogous in that a bill of exchange is also virtually equivalent to cash.

Had it been necessary to decide the point I should have been prepared to hold that there is no principle equivalent to that laid down in the *Edward Owen* line of cases that debars a bank setting off against a beneficiary under a bill of exchange a claim by the bank themselves against that beneficiary. Given the additional circumstances present here, namely, that the bank's claim is liquidated and relates to the very banking transactions which gave rise to the letter of credit itself, the case in favour of a right of set-off seems to me overwhelming.

It therefore follows that in the present case it is open to the bank to set off their liquidated claims under the dry cargo transactions (which are admittedly arguable) against their admitted liability to Kloeckner on the counterclaim under the standby letter of credit.

[Hirst J. then considered questions of fact in the rest of his judgment, which was not released for publication.]

Application dismissed.

NOTE

The reported opinion involves motions for summary judgment on a claim and counterclaim. The claim involved an action by the Hong Kong and Shanghai Banking Corporation [HKSBC] against Kloeckner Co. (an oil trader) on an irrevocable undertaking by Kloeckner to pay plaintiff a specified sum upon presentation of certain documents 'without any discount, deduction, offset or counterclaim.' Kloeckner's counterclaim was based on a standby letter of credit, issued to it by HKSBC.

The court held that the counterclaim on the standby letter of credit was subject to a set-off based on the undertaking, but that the claim on the undertaking was not subject to a set-off based on the standby letter of credit. Accordingly, the court dismissed defendant's application for summary judgment and reserved judgment in the main action.

b. United City Merchants v. Royal Bank of Canada

House of Lords, 1982
United City Merchants v. Royal Bank of Canada
[1982] 2 WLR 1039

APPEAL from the Court of Appeal.

This was an appeal by the appellants, United City Merchants (Investments) Ltd. (first plaintiffs) and Glass Fibres and Equipments Ltd. (second plaintiffs) from a decision of the Court of Appeal (Stephenson, Ackner and Griffiths L.JJ.) [1982] Q.B. 208 given on March 13, 1981, affirming a decision of Mocatta J. given on March 12, 1979, rejecting their claim for U.S. $494,537.59 allegedly due to the appellants under a confirmed irrevocable letter of credit. The credit had been opened by the second third party, Banco Continental S.A., a Peruvian bank, and then confirmed at the request of the first third party, Vitrorefuerzos S.A., a Peruvian company ("the buyers") pursuant to the buyers' obligations under a contract made in October/November 1975, for the purchase from the second-named appellants, an English company ("the sellers") of a glass-fibre forming plant on f.o.b. United Kingdom port terms. Thereafter, and on the Peruvian bank's instructions, the credit had been confirmed by the London branch of the respondents, the Royal Bank of Canada (defendants), to the sellers on March 30, 1976. It provided for an advance of 20 per cent. to be drawn down by the sellers, 70 per cent. to be paid on presentation of shipping documents, and 10 per cent. on erection of the plant. The sellers assigned their rights under the credit to the first-named appellants in July 1976.

Their Lordships took time for consideration.

May 20. LORD DIPLOCK. My Lords, this appeal, which is the culmination of protracted litigation, raises two distinct questions of law which it is convenient to deal with separately. The first, which I will call the documentary credit point, relates to the mutual rights and obligations of the confirming bank and the beneficiary under a documentary credit. It is of general importance to all those engaged in the conduct and financing of international trade for it challenges the basic principle of documentary credit operations that banks that are parties to them deal in documents only, not in the goods to which those documents purport to relate. The second question, which I will call the Bretton Woods point, is of less general importance. It turns upon the construction of the Bretton Woods Agreements Order in Council 1946 and its application to the particular fact of the instant case.

A Peruvian company, Vitrorefuerzos S.A. ("the buyers") agreed to buy from the second appellants ("the sellers") plant for the manufacture of glass fibres ("the goods") at a price of $662,086 f.o.b. London for shipment to Callao. Payment was to be in London by confirmed irrevocable transferable letter of credit for the invoice price plus freight, payable as to 20 per cent. of the invoice price upon the opening of the credit, as to 70 per cent. of the invoice price and 100 per cent. of the freight on presentation of shipping documents and as to the balance of 10 per cent. of the invoice price on completion of erection of the plant in Peru.

The buyers arranged with their Peruvian bank, Banco Continental S.A. ("the issuing bank") to issue the necessary credit and the issuing bank appointed the respondents, Royal Bank of Canada ("the confirming bank") to advise and confirm upon its own behalf the credit to the sellers. The confirming bank duly notified the sellers on March 30, 1976, of the opening of the confirmed irrevocable transferable letter of credit. So far as concerned the 70 per cent. of the invoice price and 100 per cent. freight there was nothing that was unusual in its terms. It was expressed to be subject to the Uniform Customs and Practice for Documentary Credits (1974 revision) of the International Chamber of Commerce ("the Uniform Customs") and to be available by sight drafts on the issuing bank against delivery inter alia of a full set "on board" bills of lading evidencing receipt for shipment of the goods from London to Callao on or before a date in October 1976, which was subsequently extended to December 15, 1976.

The initial payment of 20 per cent. of the invoice price was duly made by the confirming bank to the sellers. Thereafter, in July 1976 the sellers transferred to their own merchant bankers, the first appellants, their interest under the credit as security for advances; but nothing turns on this so far as either the documentary credit point or the Bretton Woods point is concerned. In dealing with the relevant law on each of these points I shall accordingly treat the sellers as having continued throughout to be the beneficiaries of the confirmed credit.

The goods, which had to be manufactured by the sellers, were ready for shipment by the beginning of December 1976. It was intended by the loading brokers acting on behalf of Prudential Lines Inc. ("the carriers") that they should be shipped on a vessel belonging to the carriers (*American Legend*) due to arrive at Felixstowe on December 10, 1976. (The substitution of Felixstowe for London as the loading port is immaterial. It was acquiesced in by all parties to the transaction). The arrival of *American Legend* at Felixstowe was cancelled and another vessel, *American Accord*, was substituted by the loading brokers: but its date of arrival was scheduled for December 16, 1976, one day after the latest date of shipment required by the documentary credit. The goods were in fact loaded on *American Accord* on December 16, 1976; but the loading brokers, who also acted as agents for the carriers in issuing bills of lading, issued in the first instance a set of "received for shipment" bills of lading dated December 15, 1976, and handed them over to the sellers in return for payment of the freight. On presentation of the shipping documents to the confirming bank on the December 17, that bank raised various objections to their form, of which the only one that is relevant to the documentary credit point was that the bills of lading did not bear any dated "on board" notation. The bills of lading were returned to the carriers' freight brokers who issued a fresh set bearing the notation, which was untrue: "These goods are actually on board December 15, 1976. E. H. Munday and Co. (Freight Agents) Ltd. as agents." The amended bills of lading together with the other documents were re-presented to the confirming bank on December 22, 1976, but the confirming bank again refused to pay on the ground that they "had information in their possession which suggested that shipment was not effected as it appears in the bill of lading."

The learned judge after a careful hearing, lasting for no less than 30 days, held that Mr. Baker, the employee of the loading brokers to the carriers who was in charge of the transaction on their behalf, had acted fraudulently in issuing the bills of lading bearing what was to his knowledge a false statement as to the date on which the plant was actually on board *American Accord.* The judge held, however, that neither the sellers (nor their transferee) were parties or privies to any fraud by Mr. Baker; at the time of both presentations of the shipping documents to the confirming bank on December 17 and 22, 1976, they bona fide believed that the plant had in fact been loaded on *American Accord* on or before December 15, 1976, and that the annotation on the reissued bill of lading, stating the goods to be actually on board at that date, was true.

The additional facts that give rise to the Bretton Woods point may be stated even more concisely. The sellers' original quotation for the sale price of the glass fibre making plant was half the figure that ultimately became the invoice price for the purposes of the documentary credit. The buyers who were desirous of converting Peruvian currency into U.S. dollars available to them in the United States, a transaction which was contrary to Peruvian exchange control regulations, persuaded the sellers to invoice the plant to them at double the real sale price in U.S. dollars and to agree that they would within 10 days after drawing upon the documentary credit for each of the three instalments of the invoice price remit one half of the amount so drawn to the dollar account in Miami, Florida, of an American corporation controlled by the buyers. This the sellers agreed to do; and of the first instalment of 20 per cent. of the now doubled invoice price of $662,086, which was the only drawing that they succeeded in making under the credit, they transmitted one half, viz. $66,208 to the American corporation in Florida. They would have done the same with one half of the next drawing of 70 per cent. of the invoice price payable against shipping documents, if the confirming bank had paid this instalment.

The Documentary Credit Point

My Lords, for the proposition upon the documentary credit point, both in the broad form for which counsel for the confirming bank have strenuously argued at all stages of this appeal and in the narrower form or "halfway house" that commended itself to the Court of Appeal, there is no direct authority to be found either in English or Privy Council cases or among the numerous decisions of courts in the United States of America to which reference is made in the judgments of the Court of Appeal in the instant case. So the point falls to be decided by reference to first principles as to the legal nature of the contractual obligations assumed by the various parties to a transaction consisting of an international sale of goods to be financed by means of a confirmed irrevocable documentary credit. It is trite law that there are four autonomous though interconnected contractual relationships involved. (1) The underlying contract for the sale of goods, to which the only parties are the buyer and the seller; (2) the contract between the buyer and the issuing bank under which the latter agrees to issue the credit and either itself or through a confirming bank to notify the credit to the seller and to make payments to or to the order of the seller (or to pay, accept or negotiate bills of exchange drawn by the seller) against presentation of stipulated documents; and the buyer agrees to reimburse the issuing bank for payments made under the credit. For such reimbursement the stipulated documents, if they include a document of title such as a bill of lading, constitute a security available to the issuing bank; (3) if payment is to be made through a confirming bank the contract between the issuing bank and the confirming bank authorising and requiring the latter to make such payments and to remit the stipulated documents to the issuing bank when they are received, the issuing bank in turn agreeing to reimburse the confirming bank for payments made under the credit; (4) the contract between the confirming bank and the seller under which the confirming bank undertakes to pay to the seller (or to accept or negotiate without recourse to drawer bills of exchange drawn by him) up to the amount of the credit against presentation of the stipulated documents.

Again, it is trite law that in contract (4), with which alone the instant appeal is directly concerned, the parties to it, the seller and the confirming bank, "deal in documents and not in goods," as article 8 of the Uniform Customs puts it. If, on their face, the documents presented to the confirming bank by the seller conform with the requirements of the credit as notified to him by the confirming bank, that bank is under a contractual obligation to the seller to honour the credit, notwithstanding that the bank has knowledge that the seller at the time of presentation of the conforming documents is alleged by the buyer to have, and in fact has already, committed a breach of his contract with the buyer for the sale of the goods to which the documents appear on their face to relate, that would have entitled the buyer to treat the contract of sale as rescinded and to reject the goods and refuse to pay the seller the purchase price. The whole commercial purpose for which the system of confirmed irrevocable documentary credits has been developed in international trade is to give to the seller an assured right to be paid before he parts with control of the goods that does not permit of any dispute with buyer as to the performance of the contract of sale being used as a ground for non-payment or reduction or deferment of payment.

To this general statement of principle as to the contractual obligations of the confirming bank to the seller, there is one established exception: that is, where the seller, for the purpose of drawing on the credit, fraudulently presents to the confirming bank documents that contain, expressly or by implication, material representations of fact that to his knowledge are untrue. Although there does not appear among the English authorities any case in which this exception has been applied, it is well established in the American case of which the leading or "landmark" case is *Sztejn* v. *J. Henry Schroder Banking Corporation* (1941) 31 N.Y.S. 2d 631. This judgment of the New York Court of Appeals was referred to with approval by the English Court of Appeal in *Edward Owen Engineering Ltd.* v. *Barclays Bank International Ltd.* [1978] Q.B. 159, though this was actually a case about a performance bond under which a bank assumes obligations to a buyer analogous to those assumed by a confirming bank to the seller under a documentary credit. The exception for fraud on the part of the beneficiary seeking to avail himself of the credit is a clear application of the maxim ex turpi causa non oritur actio or, if plain English is to be preferred, "fraud unravels all." The courts will not allow their process to be used by a dishonest person to carry out a fraud.

The instant case, however, does not fall within the fraud exception. Mocatta J. found the sellers to have been unaware of the inaccuracy of Mr. Baker's notation of the date at which the goods were actually on board *American Accord.* They believed that it was true and that the goods had actually been loaded on or before December 15, 1976, as required by the documentary credit.

Faced by this finding, the argument for the confirming bank before Mocatta J. was directed to supporting the broad proposition: that a confirming bank is not under any obligation, legally enforceable against it by the seller/beneficiary of a documentary credit, to pay to him the sum stipulated in the credit against presentation of documents, if the documents presented, although conforming on their face with the terms of the credit, nevertheless contain some statement of material fact that is not accurate. This proposition which does not call for knowledge on the part of the seller/beneficiary of the existence of any inaccuracy would embrace the fraud exception and render it superfluous.

My Lords, the more closely this bold proposition is subjected to legal analysis, the more implausible it becomes; to assent to it would, in my view, undermine the whole system of financing international trade by means of documentary credits.

It has, so far as I know, never been disputed that as between confirming bank and issuing bank and as between issuing bank and the buyer the contractual duty of each bank under a confirmed irrevocable credit is to examine with reasonable care all documents presented in order to ascertain that they appear *on their face* to be in accordance with the terms and conditions of the credit, and, if they do so appear, to pay to the seller/beneficiary by whom the documents have been presented the sum stipulated by the credit, or to accept or negotiate without recourse to drawer drafts drawn by the seller/beneficiary if the credit so provides. It is so stated in the latest edition of the Uniform Customs. It is equally clear law, and is so provided by article 9 of the Uniform Customs, that confirming banks and issuing banks assume no liability or responsibility to one another or to the buyer "for the form, sufficiency, accuracy, genuineness, falsification or legal effect of any documents." This is well illustrated by the Privy Council case of *Gian Singh & Co. Ltd* v. *Banque de l'Indochine* [1974] 1

W.L.R. 1234, where the customer was held liable to reimburse the issuing bank for honouring a documentary credit upon presentation of an apparently conforming document which was an ingenious forgery, a fact that the bank had not been negligent in failing to detect upon examination of the document.

It would be strange from the commercial point of view, although not theoretically impossible in law, if the contractual duty owed by confirming and issuing banks to the buyer to honour the credit on presentation of apparently conforming documents despite the fact that they contain inaccuracies or even are forged, were not matched by a corresponding contractual liability of the confirming bank to the seller/beneficiary (in the absence, of course, of any fraud on his part) to pay the sum stipulated in the credit upon presentation of apparently confirming documents. Yet, as is conceded by counsel for the confirming bank in the instant case, if the broad proposition for which he argues is correct, the contractual duties do not match. As respects the confirming bank's contractual duty to the seller to honour the credit, the bank, it is submitted, is only bound to pay upon presentation of documents which not only appear on their face to be in accordance with the terms and conditions of the credit but also do not in fact contain any material statement that is inaccurate. If this submission be correct, the bank's contractual right to refuse to honour the documentary credit cannot, as a matter of legal analysis, depend upon whether *at the time of the refusal* the bank was virtually certain from information obtained by means other than reasonably careful examination of the documents themselves that they contained some material statement that was inaccurate or whether the bank merely suspected this or even had no suspicion that apparently conforming documents contained any inaccuracies at all. If there be any such right of refusal it must depend upon whether the bank, when sued by the seller/beneficiary for breach of its contract to honour the credit, is able to prove that one of the documents did in fact contain what was a material misstatement.

My Lords, in rejecting this broad proposition I have dealt with it at greater length than otherwise I would have done, because it formed the main plank of the confirming bank's argument on the documentary credit point before Mocatta J. — who, however, had no hesitation in rejecting it, but found for the confirming bank on the Bretton Woods point. It formed the main ground also in the confirming bank's notice of cross-appeal to the Court of Appeal upon which the confirming bank would seek to uphold the judgment in its favour if the sellers' appeal should succeed upon the Bretton Woods point. It was not until half-way through the actual hearing in the Court of Appeal that the notice of cross-appeal was amended to include a narrower proposition referred to as a "half-way house" which the Court of Appeal accepted as being decisive in the confirming bank's favour. This rendered it unnecessary for that court to rule upon the broad proposition that I have so far been discussing, although Stephenson L.J. indicated obiter that for his part he would have rejected it.

The half-way house is erected upon the narrower proposition that if any of the documents presented under the credit by the seller/beneficiary contain a material misrepresentation of fact that was *false to the knowledge of the person who issued the document* and intended by him to deceive persons into whose hands the document might come, the confirming bank is under no liability to honour the credit, even though, as in the instant case, the persons whom the issuer of the document intended to, and did, deceive included the seller/beneficiary himself.

My Lords, if the broad proposition for which the confirming bank has argued is unacceptable for the reasons that I have already discussed, what rational ground can there be for drawing any distinction between apparently conforming documents that, unknown to the seller, in fact contain a statement of fact that is inaccurate where the inaccuracy was due to inadvertence by the maker of the document, and the like documents where the same inaccuracy had been inserted by the maker of the document with intent to deceive, among others, the seller/beneficiary himself? Ex hypothesi we are dealing only with a case in which the seller/beneficiary claiming under the credit *has* been deceived, for if he presented documents to the conforming bank with knowledge that this apparent conformity with the terms and conditions of the credit was due to the fact that the documents told a lie, the seller/beneficiary would himself be a party to the misrepresentation made to the confirming bank by the lie in the documents and the case would come within the fraud exception, as did all the American cases referred to as persuasive authority in the judgments of the Court of Appeal in the instant case.

The American cases refer indifferently to documents that are "forged or fraudulent," as does the Uniform Commercial Code that has been adopted in nearly all states of the United States of America. The Court of Appeal reached their half-way house in the instant case by starting from the premiss that a confirming bank could refuse to pay against a document that it knew to be forged, even though the seller/beneficiary had no knowledge of that fact. From this premiss they reasoned that if forgery by a third party relieves the confirming bank of liability to pay the seller/beneficiary, fraud by a third party ought to have the same consequence.

I would not wish to be taken as accepting that the premiss as to forged documents is correct, even where the fact that the document is forged deprives it of all legal effect and makes it a nullity, and so worthless to the confirming bank as security for its advances to the buyer.

But even assuming the correctness of the Court of Appeal's premiss as respects forgery by a third party of a kind that makes a document a nullity for which at least a rational case can be made out, to say that this leads to the conclusion that fraud by a third party which does not render the document a nullity has the same consequence appears to me, with respect, to be a non-sequitur, and I am not persuaded by the reasoning in any of the judgments of the Court of Appeal that it is not.

Upon the documentary credit point I think that Mocatta J. was right in deciding it in favour of the sellers and that the Court of Appeal were wrong in reversing him on this point.

The Bretton Woods Point

The Bretton Woods point arises out of the agreement between the buyers and the seller collateral to the contract of sale of the goods between the same parties that out of the payments in U.S. dollars received by the sellers under the documentary credit in respect of each instalment of the invoice price of the goods, they would transmit to the account of the buyers in America one half of the U.S. dollars received.

The Bretton Woods Agreements Order in Council 1946, made under the Bretton Woods Agreements Act 1945, gives the force of law in England to article VIII section 2(*b*) of the Bretton Woods Agreement, which is in the following terms:

> "Exchange contracts which involve the currency of any member and which are contrary to the exchange control regulations of that member maintained or imposed consistently with this agreement shall be unenforceable in the territories of any member . . ."

Mocatta J., professing to follow the guidance given in the *Terruzzi* case [1976] Q.B. 683, took the view that the contract of sale between the buyers and the sellers at the inflated invoice price was a monetary transaction in disguise and that despite the autonomous character of the contract between the sellers and the confirming bank under the documentary credit, this too was tarred with the same brush and was a monetary transaction in disguise and therefore one which the court should not enforce. He rejected out of hand what he described as a "rather remarkable submission" that the sellers could recover that half of the invoice price which represented the true sale price of the goods, even if they could not recover that other half of the invoice price which they would receive as trustees for the buyers on trust to transmit it to the buyer's American company in Florida. He held that it was impossible to sever the contract constituted by the documentary credit; it was either enforceable in full or not at all.

In refusing to treat the seller's claim under the documentary credit for that part of the invoice price that they were to retain for themselves as the sale price of the goods in a different way from that in which he treated their claim to that part of the invoice price which they would receive as trustees for the buyers, I agree with all three members of the Court of Appeal the learned judge fell into error.

In the instant case there is no difficulty in identifying the monetary transaction that was sought to be concealed by the actual words used in the documentary credit and in the underlying contract of sale. It was to exchange Peruvian currency provided by the buyers in Peru for U.S. $331,043 to be made available to them in Florida; and to do this was contrary to the exchange control regulations of Peru. Payment under the documentary credit by the confirming bank to the sellers of that half of the invoice price (viz. $331,043) that the sellers would receive as trustees for the buyers on trust to remit it to the account of the buyer's American company in Florida, was an essential part of that monetary transaction and therefore unenforceable; but payment of the other half of the invoice price and of the freight was not; the sellers would receive that part of the payment under the documentary credit on their own behalf and retain it as the genuine purchase price of goods sold by them to the buyers.

Appeal allowed.

NOTES

1. *Defense of Fraud.* The text case deals with a documentary letter of credit and not with a standby letter of credit. It is, however, recognized that fraud by the beneficiary in collecting the amount of the instrument constitutes a defense of the confirming or issuing bank and entitles the person on whose order the letter of credit is issued to stop payment by injunction. Latin maxims regarding the nullifying effect of fraud are frequently cited in support of this result, e.g. '*ex turpi causa non oritur actio*' (supra p. 314) or '*fraus omnia corrumpit*' paraphrased here by Lord Diplock as 'fraud unravels all'. Cf Swiss Judgment of August 20, 1991 (Federal Tribunal of Switzerland, 1991) infra p. 381.

2. For *fraus omnia corrumpit* in France see e.g. *Kindig c. Crédit Lyonnaise,* (Cass. comm.) Judgment of May 6, 1969, Bull. Civ. 1969 IV Nr. 156; 44 J.C.P. Jur. 16216 (1970) with note by Stoufflet.

3. *Australia.* The leading case on standby letters of credit in Australia is *Commercial Banking Co. of Sydney Ltd. v. Patrick Intermarine Acceptances Ltd. (In Liq.) and Another,* Privy Council, 1978, 52 A.L.J.R. 404. See discussion in A. L. Tyree, *Banking Law in Australia,* Sec. 11.25 et seq. (1990).

B. GERMANY

1. Cases

a. Interpretation of the Scope of the Undertaking

BGH XI. Civil Senate
Judgment of April 26, 1994
15 ZIP 857 (1994) = 48 WM 1063 (1994).

A standby letter of credit, like a documentary letter of credit, is subject to an interpretation not only according to its wording, but also according to the sense and purpose, as ascertainable from the document, of the stipulations contained therein. Neither the inadmissibility of objections based on the underlying transaction, nor the principle of narrow construction of guarantees opposes this.

FACTS

The plaintiff demanded payment from the defendant as successor of A.- Bank AG on the basis of a Standby Letter of Credit issued by the latter. The factual situation was as follows:

On December 18, 1992, plaintiff obligated itself contractually to supply the B.-merchandising GmbH [limited liability corporation] with 30,000 blue jeans at DM 22. apiece, during the period from January 1992 until mid-February 1992. As a partial guarantee of the purchase price, on January 6, 1992, on behalf of B. GmbH, the A.-Bank issued an irrevocable Standby Letter of Credit, valid until September 20, 1992, for DM 330,000. The document, drafted in English, conditioned payment of the aforementioned sum upon presentation of a signed declaration by plaintiff asserting B.'s non-payment of bills due for ca. 30,000 blue jeans under the December 18, 1991 contract, as well as the inclusion of copies of the relevant bills and transport documents.

Under the heading 'Special Conditions', the Letter of Credit included a statement that it represented 50% of the total value of the contract, as well as the stipulation that upon each payment made by B. GmbH to plaintiff, the amount of the Letter of Credit should automatically be reduced by 50% of the amount paid.

With letters of September 9 and 15, at the request of plaintiff, N. Bank, submitted plaintiff's statement asserting nonpayment of 3 partial bills for a total of 9,809 blue jeans amounting to DM 215,798, appending copies of the relevant bills and transport documents, and demanded payment of an initial amount of DM 107,899. Later, by telex dated September 18, 1992, it demanded payment of an additional DM 107,899. Defendant only complied with the first payment request. With this action, plaintiff seeks payment of an additional DM 107,899 plus interest. In its view, it is entitled to the full amount on the basis of the Standby Letter of Credit, and not only to 50% of bills presented by it. The District Court dismissed this action. The appellate court allowed plaintiff's claims except for a part of the interest.

REASONS

I

Defendant's petition for revision results in the reinstatement of the District Court's judgment dismissing the complaint. The appellate court assumed that plaintiff, on the basis of the Standby Letter of Credit, was entitled to demand DM 107,899 in addition to the DM 107,899 already received. In justification of its decision it gave the following grounds:

The Standby Letter of Credit constituted a letter of credit, the conditions for the honoring of which plaintiff had satisfied in the amount of DM 215,798. According to its terms, a claim for its payment was conditioned upon the making of deliveries required by the underlying transaction and a corresponding declaration to that effect. In addition, the Letter of Credit was to be understood as meaning that defendant had to pay the presented partial bills up to the amount of DM 330,000 stipulated in the Letter of credit in full and not just 50%. A limitation of this kind could also not be derived from the content of the Letter of Credit by the way of interpretation. In particular, a restriction of that kind could also not be deduced from the 'particular circumstances' of the Letter of Credit. Defendant's argument that the assumption of a duty to a complete payment of the partial bills would render nugatory the agreement stipulated in the 'Special Conditions' regarding the credit to be given to payments made by B. GmbH and would entail a reward for a violation of the conduct of plaintiff, did not merit consideration. The Letter of Credit, as an independent promise of payment, did not permit defenses based on the underlying transaction, and was to be construed on the basis of its own terms.

II

This judgment does not withstand judicial scrutiny. In this respect, it may be left open whether the appellate court's assumption, which was shared by both parties in the prior instances, and was challenged by the defendant only in its petition for revision, was correct, viz. that payments on the Standby Letter of Credit had to be made upon presentation of partial bills and not only upon the settlement of the entire contract. The judgment of the appellate court is at any rate subject to reversal, because the interpretation of the Letter of Credit in the sense that the partial bills are to be paid in their full amount violates recognized principles of interpretation. It infringes on the principle of interpretation according to the proper balance of the interests in issue. (Cf in that respect 115 BGHZ 1,5 (1992) = 12 ZIP 1437 (1991) with further references and BGH Judgments of July 2, 1992, 46 WM 2026, 2028 (1992) and July 10, 1992, 47 WM 759, 760 (1993) both with additional references.)

1. In interpreting the Letter of Credit, the appellate court erroneously disregarded the stipulation in the Special Conditions concerning reduction of the total sum of DM 330,000 by 50% of each payment by the B. GmbH.

This arrangement had the result that in the event that plaintiff completely performed its duty to deliver, it could always only call the Letter of Credit in the amount of 50% of its outstanding claims. If in that case B. GmbH paid, for example, only DM 330,000 on plaintiff's claim for the purchase price of DM 660,000, plaintiff could seek satisfaction from the Letter of Credit not in the full amount of the still unpaid DM 330,000, but only in the amount of DM 165,000. The sense and purpose of this arrangement was obviously to grant plaintiff by means of a letter of credit a security always limited to 50% of its outstanding claims against B. GmbH. Consequently, for the not expressly covered case of merely partial performance of the delivery duties of plaintiff during the term of the Letter of Credit, it follows that plaintiff also in this case can call the Letter of Credit only in the amount of 50% of its outstanding claims. Another interpretation, as the petition for revision correctly asserts, would lead to the nonsensical result, that plaintiff would be better off by a merely partial performance of its delivery duty and non-payment by the B. GmbH, than it would be in the case of a full performance of its delivery duty and only partial payment by the B. GmbH.

2. The appellate court's disregard of these connections cannot be justified by the principle that letters of credit as independent promises of payment normally don't permit defenses based on the underlying transaction. (Cf BGH, Judgment of June 27, 1988, 9 ZIP 1102 (1988) = 42 WM 1298, 1299 *et seq.*, (1988) and 4 EWiR 1081 (1988) note by Schütze) and must be interpreted only by reference to their own terms. In this respect it is irrelevant whether the appellate court's equating, without giving reasons, a standby letter of credit, as involved here and serving as a security device (payment guarantee), with a documentary letter of credit, functioning predominantly as a means of payment (collection instrument) is correct in every respect. (Cf Canaris, *Bankvertragsrecht*, 3. ed. marginal number 1087. [additional citations]) The principle that defenses based on the underlying transaction normally are not admissible applies to both types of instruments. This principle, however, does not forbid, any more in the case of a standby letter of credit than in the case of a documentary credit, an interpretation of the instrument which relies not only on the wording, but also on the sense and purposes of the stipulations contained therein. In as much as the security for the performance of an underlying transaction constitutes the essence of the standby letter of credit, this sense and purpose must, if necessary, be ascertainable by taking account of the underlying transaction to the extent that it is mentioned in the instrument.

The so-called principle of strict interpretation of the instruments does not militate against this rule. This rule was developed originally with respect to the examination of the presented documents as to their conformity with the conditions of the documentary letter of credit (Canaris op. cit. marg. nr. 942). In the case of guarantees it is paralleled by the principle of strict construction of guarantees (90 BGHZ, 287, 291 (1984) = 5 ZIP 681, 685 (1984)) and prohibits neither here, nor in the case of a documentary letter of credit, an interpretation of unclear provisions, but opposes merely an interpretation 'which is not supported by anything in the text of the instrument and has to rely on circumstances extraneous to the instrument.' (To that effect 90 BGHZ 287 (1984) for bank guarantees on first demand. * * *)

III

Therefore, the judgment of the appellate court is to be vacated. Since further factual determinations are not necessary, the Senate is itself capable of interpreting the Standby Letter of Credit with the result that plaintiff may not demand more than the 50% of the bills which it presented during the life of the letter of credit and which it already received. It is irrelevant that plaintiff meanwhile performed fully its duty of delivery. Defendant was not required in good faith to honor such bills after the expiration of the guarantee period. Based on the conditions of the Standby Letter of Credit, there can be no question that the plaintiff could not require any payment for documents presented after September 20, 1992. Thus it was acting at its own risk if it failed to put forward a claim to the guarantee before that date.

NOTES
GUARANTEES ON FIRST DEMAND

1. In Germany the courts distinguish between a guarantee on first demand and a suretyship on first demand. In both cases the obligor has to pay upon a demand supported by the stipulated declarations, without being able to assert defenses based on the underlying transaction, Cf. Judgment of January 17, 1989 BGH (XI. Civil Sen.), 42 NJW 1480 (1989); Judgment of May 2, 1979, 74 BGHZ 244, 248 (1980) = 32 NJW 1500 (1979) = 33 WM 691 (1979); Judgment of March 3, 1976 (VIII. Civ. Sen.) 30 WM 422 (1976).

A surety who has paid on first demand, however, may recover for unjust enrichment under § 812 I(1) BGB, if the creditor was not entitled to the payment because of defenses based on the underlying transaction, while the guarantor on first demand has no such right because of the independence of his undertaking. In that case, the principal would be entitled to assert a right to reimbursement, if he has to indemnify the guarantor in the amount of his payment. In practice it is often difficult to distinguish between these two types of transactions, especially if the instrument itself uses both terms, cf Löwe/Graf von Westphalen/Trinker, *Grosskommentar zum ABG-Gesetz* Vol. III (22d ed. 1985) 36.2 marg. nt. 18.

2. According to the *ICC Uniform Customs and Practice for Documentary Credits* (ICC Publication No. 500), Art. 14d(1), an issuing bank which decides to refuse the presented documents

> 'must give notice to that effect by telecommunication or, if that is not possible, by other expeditious means, without delay but no later than the close of the seventh banking day following the day of receipt of the documents.'

A violation of this duty may obligate the issuer to pay damages.

3. *Judgment of July 21, 1992.* An interesting case calling for the application of the rule of 14d(1) (then numbered 16d) to standby letters of credit was decided by the Court of Appeal of Karlsruhe, Judgment of July 21, 1992 (46 WM 2095 (1992)). In that case, the defendant Savingsbank S. had issued four guaranties on first demand to secure plaintiff, a Swiss corporation, against losses caused by trading in oil futures with the F. Mineralölhandlung GmbH in F. (Germany). The guaranties specified that the Bank was liable on each guaranty in the maximum amount specified in the guaranty (DM 550,000, DM 150,000 and DM 500,000 respectively), and that each of them

was irrevocable, on first demand, and, irrespective of the validity of the underlying transaction, payable upon the written confirmation that the F. Mineralölhandlung GmbH had failed to pay the requested amount at maturity.

The four guaranties expired on April 22, 1991, April 29, 1991, and May 6, 1991 respectively. The guarantee expiring on April 22, 1991 was for the maximum amount of DM 500,000. On April 17, 1991 the Mineralölhandlung GmbH filed for bankruptcy and on the same day the bank faxed a notice of termination of the four guaranties to the plaintiff, the Swiss corporation. Plaintiff thereupon sent a fax to defendant demanding payment in the amount of DM 1,650,000, the maximum total of the four guaranties. On April 25, 1991, defendant by letter refused payment on the ground that plaintiff had failed to declare that the Mineralölhandlung GmbH had not paid the requested amounts when due. Thereupon, plaintiff presented the requisite declaration on April 26, 1991, i.e. before the expiration of the later three guaranties, but after the expiration on April 22, 1991 of the guaranty in a maximum amount of DM 500,000. Thereupon, the bank paid DM 1,150,000, but not the balance. The beneficiary brought an action against the bank claiming that defendant had violated its duty to promptly notify it of the lack of the requisite declaration and unduly delayed such notification until the expiration of the guaranty for a maximum of DM 500,000. The Court of Appeal agreed with plaintiff's contention and rendered judgment against the bank in the amount of DM 500,000 plus interest because of late payments, totalling DM 513,344.50.

b. Pleading Required for Claim on Suretyship Undertaking on First Demand

BGH IX. Civil Senate
Judgment of October 28, 1993
55 KTS 215 (1994).

By way of a construction contract of March 22/28, 1990, plaintiff was engaged as a general contractor by an entrepreneur, intervening as co-party of defendant bank, to undertake two construction jobs. It was stipulated that plaintiff should be compensated with a global amount. Payments were due according to the progress of the venture. The first partial payment was due upon the commencement of the actual construction. This was to occur on May 15, 1990 and May 16, 1990 respectively. To secure the performance of the owner's duties, on April 30, 1990 the bank executed a suretyship undertaking on first demand in the amount of DM 240,000. Commencement of the construction, however, was delayed for reasons which are in dispute between the parties. On February 13, 1992, plaintiff submitted a first bill to the owner, dated February 11, 1991, for DM 267,538.61 for work allegedly performed prior to that date.

On February 18, 1991, the owner canceled the construction contract and plaintiff demanded payment from the bank. In the Documentary Proceedings [summary proceedings based on submitted documents], plaintiff obtained a provisional judgment for DM 240,000 against defendant. In the Supplemental Proceedings, the trial court affirmed the judgement. The court of appeal sustained the supplemental judgment in the amount of DM 37,651.77 and dismissed the complaint with respect to the remainder of the claims. The petition for review resulted in reinstatement of the judgment of the trial court.

REASONS
I

The appellate court expresses the view that also in the case of a suretyship on first demand, the need for a conclusive allegation of the existence and scope of the principal claim could not be disregarded. Only a portion of items listed in the bill for the first partial payment were conclusively shown.

II

This position does not withstand scrutiny.

1. To be sure some of the text-writers express the opinion that even in the case of a suretyship (or guarantee) on first demand, the debtor does not need to pay upon a mere demand if it lacks conclusive allegations. Additionally, they say it was necessary to substantiate in a certain way the assertion that the condition stipulated in the suretyship (or guarantee) had occurred. This was the consequence of the fact that otherwise the Bank would be incapable of verifying the demand and would lack of any basis for the recognition of a misuse of the right of the beneficiary. Moreover, a substantiation were indispensable because otherwise the risk of a misuse would increase to a degree that the capability of the suretyship (or guarantee) on first demand to serve its institutional functions would become questionable and even its legality with reference to §138 BGB would appear to be problematic (Canaris, *Grosskommentar zu HGB* 4th ed. *Bankvertragsrecht* marg. n. 1130. [additional citations].)

2. This view should not be followed. The suretyship on first demand, which in the practice of the banks has largely replaced the formerly customary cash deposit, is designed to supply the creditor instantly with liquid funds, if he surmises that the condition of the suretyship has occurred. This purpose can only be achieved if the declaration which triggers the provisional duty to pay is strictly formalized, i.e. limited to that which is stated in the undertaking as prerequisite for payment and is recognizable for everyone. (BGH 37 NJW 923 (1984); 43 WM 1946, 1947 (1989).) The opposite opinion accepts that precisely the question whether the creditor has substantiated his claim conclusively may prompt a dispute. If it has to be resolved before the creditor may expect payment, a suretyship on first demand would be deprived of its function, (*accord*, Graf von Westphalen, *Die Bankgarantie im Internationalen Handelsverkehr*, 2d ed. p. 165; [additional citations]. The beneficiary must declare what is

stipulated in the suretyship contract as the condition for the payment on first demand. (BGH, 37 NJW 923 (1984).) Only with respect to the conformity of the demand of payment from the surety with the contractual terms and not with respect to the secured main claim is the surety obliged to examine the conclusiveness of the allegations (*accord,* Graf von Westphalen, *op. cit.* 164; * * *).

In the suretyship undertaking of defendant it is provided: 'We will pay upon the first written demand of the general contractor.' Defendant's obligation to pay therefore depended upon a communication by plaintiff that intervenor failed to make the payments demanded pursuant to the construction contract. This was done in plaintiff's letter of February 18, 1991. A further explanation or even evidence was not required by the suretyship agreement. In particular, plaintiff did not need to show that the principal claim existed. If the surety has defenses in that respect, he may assert them — including the allegation that the secured principal obligation is not conclusively shown — on principle, only after payment, by way of complaint for restitution against the beneficiary. (74 BGHZ 240, 248 (1980); 42 NJW 1480 (1989); 43 WM 1496 (1989).)

The right of the creditor to demand instant payment without substantiating and proving his actual right thereto is limited only in the case of abuse. If it is manifestly or incontestably proven that, despite compliance with the formal prerequisites, the conditions of the suretyship did not occur, the surety may raise the defense of an inadmissible exercise of a right (BGH 41 NJW 2610 (1988)). This defense, however, must be restricted to the cases in which the abusive exercise of a formal legal position is clearly recognizable by anybody. All factual or legal disputes for which the resolution is not self-evident, must be litigated in a proceeding for restitution. (90 BGHZ 287 (1984); BGH 41 NJW 2610 (1988); BGH 42 NJW 1480 (1989); 43 WM 1496, 1498 (1989).)

The appellate court is erroneously of the opinion that the manifest lack of a substantive claim against the principal debtor is equaled by the case that the creditor fails to show conclusively the existence or scope of such a claim. Whether a claim is shown conclusively can be determined only upon the basis of a legal subsumption. Certainly it cannot be said that anyone would come to the same conclusion — would on that basis recognize an abuse of right. On the other hand, in order to ascertain the abuse of a right, it is not sufficient to demand a conclusive allegation from the defendant. Whoever wants to cheat will have no difficulties in the presentation of conclusive allegations. The best way for the surety to obviate the risk of abuse is to inquire from the principal debtor whether the condition of the suretyship has occurred.

2. The assumption that the condition of the suretyship has manifestly not occurred is precluded in particular, if it is clear that the creditor is entitled to a secured claim against the principal debtor and only its amount is uncertain. This is the situation in the instant case. The appellate court itself proceeds on the basis that some of the items in the bills of February 11, 1991 are conclusively established. They consist in the expenditures of a geological opinion, the submission of which was requested

from the intervenor by the authority for building permits. The respective claims of plaintiff in the amount of DM 37,651.77 was indubitably covered by the suretyship undertaking. If, however, the occurrence of the condition for the liability of the surety is certain and only its scope is disputed, it is all the more not too burdensome for a surety who has obligated himself on first demand to litigate the matter in a proceeding for restitution. Even the items which the appellate court has not deemed to be conclusively demonstrated may constitute claims covered by the suretyship. In this case, plaintiff has billed alleged architect's services for bids and supervision (DM 37,146) and general expenditures (DM 180,000) which — if the construction contract had been performed, would have been compensated by the lump sum price. The appellate court, too, admits that 'in a construction job, especially in the case of a general contractor, it is possible that considerable expenses may be incurred prior to the actual construction by reason of costly preparatory measures.' Thus even the existence of the claims for these items is not a far cry. The petition for revision is correct when it observes in this connection that the suretyship on first demand would lose its purpose for plaintiff, if the latter — as the appellate court requires — would have to itemize and evaluate the performed preparatory measures in order to obtain payment from the defendant. To prepare a separate listing and billing of these expenditures, normally calculated as a lump sum, may in a particular case involve expenditures so costly that the aim of obtaining liquid sums by way of suretyship could hardly be achieved. * * *

4. The calling on the defendant's suretyship agreement does not constitute a misuse even if the construction contract was canceled by the intervenor. To be sure in that case the compensation for service performed is only due when the final accounting is submitted pursuant to VOB/B (General Conditions for Procurement of Construction Jobs) § 16 Nr. 3 I,1. (BGH, 40 NJW 382, 383 (1987).) After that, payments on account can no longer be demanded (BGH BGHR VOB/B § 16 Nr. 1 par. 3 'Cancellation'.) Whether the bill for payment on account can be considered as a final accounting is doubtful, because plaintiff reserved itself the right to demand compensation pursuant to BGB § 649, in addition to that for rendered services. The possible lack of the principal claim's maturity, however, is a defense which can be asserted only after payment, in restitution proceedings.

5. The legal situation is not changed by the fact that plaintiff has already secured a final preliminary judgment against defendant in the documentary proceedings. To be sure, Horn (*Bürgschaften und Garantien* 4th ed. p. 82) has * * * expressed the view that a surety by a preliminary judgment in a documentary proceeding should be entitled to assert defenses in the follow-up proceedings even if he has not yet rendered payment. This view, however, cannot be accepted. . . . The exclusion of defenses in the documentary proceedings (Cf § 598 ZPO) is based on procedural grounds. Conversely, the exclusion of defenses in the case of a suretyship on first demand has substantive reasons and another function. This can be epitomized by the formula: '*pay first, litigate later*' (Lieseke 22 WM 22, 26 (1968); Nielsen, *Bankgarantien bei*

Aussenhandelsgeschäften 107 (1986); Bydlinski 190 *Archiv für Civilistische Praxis* 165, 169 (1990); Heinsius in *Festschrift Merz* 177, 180 (1992).

The preliminary judgement does not supply the creditor with liquid funds which he may expect pursuant to the suretyship on first demand. So long as it is not yet res judicata, the debtor may avert execution by deposition of security. (§ 711 ZPO.) In addition, even in the case of preliminary judgments which are res judicata (cf BGH, 39 KTS 88 (1978)), execution may be temporarily suspended (§ 707 ZPO). This was done in the case at bar.

c. Restitution of Payments Made by a Bank as Surety on First Demand of Performance by Subcontractor

BGH X. Civil Senate
Judgment of March 9, 1989
42 NJW 1606 (1989); 43 WM 709 (1989).

FACTS

Plaintiff bank, after compliance with its duty of payment as surety on first demand, brought an action against defendant for restitution of the amount paid. Defendant was obligated to perform a construction job as general contractor. On July 4, 1983, by order Nr. 4.694 it engaged Heizungstechnik GmbH (hereafter called principal debtor) to supply and install the sanitary and air-conditioning systems at a lump sum price of DM 1,615,000 plus VAT, with the obligation to furnish a suretyship undertaking securing performance in the amount of DM 160,000 and not limited as to time. The order provides that its terms include 'The General Conditions for Deliveries and Services in Construction Jobs within the National Territory.' It stipulated in addition:

> 'Any supplemental claims for additions or diminutions, even in the case of extraordinary increases in the price of materials or labor costs, as well as the application of §2 VOB, Part B, Nr. 7 Par.1&2 sentences 2,3, and 4 are excluded. If the owner demands additional performances the demand is to be governed by agreement prior to the execution.'

The requisite suretyship undertaking, which was to be supplied by the principal debtor, was executed by plaintiff on November 17, 1983. Its typewritten suretyship declaration refers to Order Nr. 4,694 and the duty to furnish a suretyship undertaking for the performance 'of all duties resulting from this order' and contains an assumption of the obligations of a surety, waiving all suretyship defenses, with the duty to pay on first demand.

On February 12, 1985, the principal debtor transmitted to the defendant a bill in which it evaluated its performance rendered under the order of July 4, 1983 in the amount of DM 1,615,000, at DM 1,598,859, and the value of all performance including those under supplementary orders, at DM 1,937,761. Deducting a 10% security reserve and adding VAT, the total bill amounted to DM 1,988,142.79 which was paid by the principal debtor in the amount of DM 1,945,428. On April 15, 1985 bankruptcy proceedings were opened against the estate of the principal debtor. The trustee rejected the contract. Thereupon, defendant on August 6, 1985 submitted a final account and claimed, on the basis of savings and additions, a total DM 313,868.42. It demanded payment from the plaintiff. The latter paid DM 16,160, constituting the difference between the lump-sum price stipulated in Order 4,694 and the value of the performances of the principal debtor. Defendant obtained a judgment for DM 143,850 plus 5% interest since January 25, 1986, on the ground that plaintiff was obligated to pay on first demand and could raise defenses only in a proceeding for restitution. The plaintiff paid the judgement and now claims restitution of the paid amount, because defendant obtained it without legal cause. The courts below rendered judgment for plaintiff. Defendant's petition for revision results in vacation and remand.

REASONS

1. According to the findings of the appellate court, plaintiff, as a bank, entered into a suretyship contract with defendant, whereby it assumed responsibility for the performance by the principal up to the amount of DM 160,000, with the duty of making payment on first demand. The appellate court, as is not contested by petitioner, proceeded correctly on the theory that a surety on first demand is, at any rate on principle, deprived of the defense that the principal debt or the suretyship debt is extinguished and may assert such defenses only in an action for restitution. (74 BGHZ 244, 247 = 32 NJW 1500 (1979); Senate Judgment of November 24, 1983, 37 NJW 923 (1984) = 5 ZIP 32 (1984); Judgment of January 31, 1985, 38 NJW 1694 (1985); Judgment of April 21, 1988, 41 NJW 2610 (1988) with further references; constant jurisprudence.)

2. Plaintiff rests its demand for restitution on § 812 I, alt.1 BGB. According to this provision, anyone who has received a benefit by way of a performance by another, without legal cause, is bound to restore it to the latter. Plaintiff alleges that order Nr. 4,694 solely to which the performance suretyship related was performed by the principal debtor to the extent of 99%, with the result that the suretyship debt was extinguished upon payment of DM 16,150 (1% of the contract price of DM 1,615 million). Conversely, defendant contends that the principal rendered the performance owing under the main contract of July 4, 1983 only to the extent of approximately 85%, ar-

gues that the suretyship extended to the additional orders, and alleges that its claim against the principal totals DM 334,837.09.

a) The appellate court held for plaintiff, because defendant failed to show sufficiently that it received plaintiff's performance for legal cause. It stated that it was true that on principle in an action based on § 812 I(1) BGB, plaintiff must allege and prove that it rendered a performance without legal cause, a burden which was satisfied if he disproves the legal ground asserted by defendant. Defendant, however, bore the burden of asserting and proving the legal cause, if payment were made on account of a debt which was not acknowledged and was still to be ascertained. This was the case here. Plaintiff, who had obligated itself to pay 'on first demand', was compelled to pay despite the contested cause and was relegated to obtaining restitution of the excess payments pursuant to § 812 BGB.

The petition for revision reproaches the appellate court for having misconceived the burden of allegation and proof. In its view, the surety on first demand does not pay on a claim that has still to be ascertained, but performs an obligation which is fixed as to cause and amount at the time of such payment, with the result that in an action for restitution, the surety alone must allege the facts on which its claim is based and, if contested, prove them. That is not correct.

To be sure, on principle, the plaintiff must allege and prove the facts from which the desired legal consequences derive. (Cf. Senate, 39 NJW 2426 (1986).) This holds true also for a claim based on unjust enrichment. Already the Supreme Court of the German Empire held that a plaintiff who demanded restitution of payments had to prove the non-existence of the claim if it had been recognized by plaintiff either by virtue of the payment or prior thereto. If, however, the payment is made merely in expectation of the ascertainment of the claim, defendant has to prove that the ascertainment was made or should be made in its favor. This holding was followed by Civil Senate IVb of the BGH in its Judgment of June 8, 1988. (42 NJW 161 (1989).) The deciding Senate is in accord with that view.

A suretyship on first demand is a device to assure that the beneficiary obtains liquid funds without delay. (Senate, 37 NJW 923 (1984); 5 ZIP 32 (1984).) It is a particularly risky transaction, which is apt to be misused. It is therefore left to the agreement of the parties whether they wish to assume this risk for the better achievement of the purpose of a suretyship. (95 BGHZ 375 (1986) = 39 NJW 310 (1986).) Precisely because the surety is obliged to pay on first demand and, with respect to his objections against the existence of the principal obligation — which are essential for a surety pursuant to § 767 I BGB —, is relegated to an action for restitution, it cannot be said that his payment constitutes an acknowledgement of the principal obligation. Hence, so far as the burden of allegation and proof in the action for restitution is concerned, there is no difference from that existing in litigation arising from ordinary suretyships. This has the following consequence: In the action for restitution pursuant to § 812 BGB, the defendant must allege and prove the creation and maturity of the principal obligation secured by the suretyship, whereas the plaintiff, who alleges performances by the principal and deduces therefrom liberation from its obligation as surety, must allege and prove these performances. (Judgment of December 10, 1987, 42 WM 209 (1988), 41 NJW 906 (1988).)

b) The appellate court interprets the suretyship undertaking as covering only the performance of the Order Nr. 4,694 of July 4, 1983 but not the performance of numerous subsequent orders. This interpretation, which lies within the competence of the appellate court, is — especially in view of the express exclusion of subsequent demands and certain provisions of the VOB — not only possible, but plausible. The attack by the petition for revision is therefore unfounded. * * *

c) The principal debtor was adjudicated a bankrupt on April 15, 1985. At that time the mutually obligatory construction contract which existed between the bankrupt and defendant was still partially unperformed on both sides, as is conceded by plaintiff who alleges merely a 99% performance. Therefore, the rejection of further performance by the trustee transformed the nature of the legal relation. A claim for damages was substituted for the bilateral relation (§ 17 KO, 68 BGHZ 379, 380 (1977); 96 BGHZ 392, 394 (1986)). It is established by plaintiff's pleadings that defendant has a damage claim for the non-performance of the construction contract which is secured by plaintiff's suretyship agreement. Its amount, however, is not established and must be shown by defendant. This includes a showing of which performances owed under the original order of July 4, 1983 the principal debtor had failed to render prior to the bankruptcy, and which performances had been defective and required correction, as well as of the amounts spent for that purpose. Defendant alleged and offered evidence to the effect that it had expended DM 38,997.29 for equipment needed for installation of sanitary equipment in lieu of the principal debtor and, in addition, defrayed the costs for the repair of water-damages caused by principal's employees. Defendant complains justly that the appellate court should not have rejected the offer of proof and should not have concluded that such payments to suppliers of the principal debtor and subcontractors were outside the scope of the suretyship. (Cf this Senate, Judgment of December 17, 1987, 41 NJW 907 (1988); 7 ZIP 222 (1988).)

3. The remand will enable the appellate court to make the requisite findings without legal error.

NOTES

1. In the text-case, the BGH reaffirms its view that a 'suretyship on first demand' bars the surety from asserting defenses based on the extinction of the principal obligation in an action on the suretyship agreement, but permits a subsequent action for restitution of the amounts paid, if the promisee was not entitled to such

payments due to the absence of a claim in that amount against the principal. Such an action for restitution by a guarantor is denied by highly reputed text-writers, e.g. Canaris, *Handelsgesetzbuch, Grosskommentar,* Vol.3, Part 3 *Bankvertragsrecht* (1981) 571 *et s.*, at 591–592. Canaris adheres to his view even in the case of the bankruptcy of the customer, as in the instant case. (*Ibid.* 593–594.)

2. The text-case illustrates the division of the burden of proof in the case of a claim for restitution by the surety on first demand.

3. With respect to the allegations required to a valid guarantee on first demand see R. Rüssmann & J.W. Britz, *Die Auswirkungen des Grundsatzes der formellen Garantiestrenge* 48 WM 1825 (1995). With respect to the guarantor's right to subrogation see M.B. Castellvi, *Zum Übergang der gesicherten Forderung auf den zahlenden Garanten* 48 WM 868 (1995).

4. *Austria.* The view of the German Supreme Court was followed with qualifications by the Austrian Supreme Court in the Judgment of June 25, 1987, SZ 60/121 (1987). In that case, however, the bank which had entered into the suretyship on first demand had exceeded the request made to it by the customer.

5. The text case is criticized by P. Bydlinski, *Die Bürgschaft auf erstes Anfordern: Darlegungs-und Beweislast bei Rückforderung durch den Bürgen,* 44 WM 1401 (1990).

Professor Bydlinski emphasizes that German law distinguishes between suretyship on first demand and guaranty on first demand and that in the case of a guaranty on first demand, not the guarantor (the bank) but only the customer is entitled to restitution. The guarantor who has, as he had to, honored the guaranty is entitled to reimbursement from the customer (§§ 670, 675 BGB), who in turn may demand restitution from the beneficiary. The difference is particularly important in the case of a bankruptcy by the customer.

d. Prerequisites of an Injunction against Payment by the Bank of a Guaranty on First Demand.

Hanseatic Court of Appeal Bremen,
Judgment of June 14, 1990
44 WM 1369 (1990).

[Facts: Mauritania, a developing country in Africa and party to the Lomé Convention, decided in 1988 to construct a railway. It obtained financing from the European Development Fund. In pursuit of the project, the government agency in charge entered into a contract with a German exporter of industrial wood products for the delivery of 178,000 railroad ties of Azobé wood. The contract which was concluded on January 17, 1989, provided that the first deliveries of the ties should commence during the month of May of the same year. The supplier was to receive an advance of the purchase price, the repayment of which in the case of a rescission was to be secured by a bank guaranty on first demand to be issued by the B-Bank in Bremen. B-Bank issued the guaranty on February 20, 1989, stipulating that its obligations under the guaranty should be governed by German law.

Because of difficulties, the German firm did not commence its deliveries until November 1989, making the first shipment of 21,600 ties on November 5, 1989. The governmental agency and the German firm entered into negotiations with the participation of the Commission of the European Communities to resolve the difficulties. It was agreed to submit the controversy to an arbitral tribunal. Nevertheless, the Mauritanian agency notified the German firm by letter of November 13, 1989, that it rescinded the contract because of nonperformance. On February 8, 1990, it informed the bank that it demanded payment under its guaranty because of the termination of the contract.

Following that demand, the German firm initiated proceedings against the bank demanding the issuance of a preliminary injunction prohibiting the defendant bank to honor the guaranty prior to a decision of the arbitral tribunal. The Mauritanian agency intervened and asked for rejection of the demand for a preliminary injunction. Nevertheless, the court below issued the injunction and intervenor appealed.]

REASONS

The appeal of intervenor is admissible (§§ 66 and 70 ZPO) and justified on the merits. The injunction against payment of the bank guaranty of February 20, 1989, prior to a final award of the arbitral tribunal of the International Chamber of Commerce, without assent of plaintiff, is not supportable on appeal on the basis of the state of the controversy between the parties. Plaintiff has failed to demonstrate a ground calling for the issuance of a preliminary injunction (§ 935 ZPO).

It is doubtful whether the right and duty of the bank to refuse payment of the guaranty in the case of a misuse of right by the beneficiary is paralleled by a right of the customer to demand the dishonor of the guaranty. (Answered in the negative by the Court of Appeal of Frankfurt, 42 WM 1480, 1481 (1988), 34 NJW 1941 (1981), and the Court of Appeal of Stuttgart, 35 WM 621 (1981), 34 NJW 1913 (1981).) This issue does not need to be decided in this case. Even if one adheres to the prevailing view of doctrine and case law (references by Graf von Westphalen, *Die Bankgarantie im internationalen Handelsverkehr,* 2d ed. 1990, p. 259 et seq.), that the duty of the bank to protect the customer against damages, flowing from the contractual relation with the same, has crystallized into a legal duty and a corresponding right of the customer to resist an abusive demand for payment, plaintiff has failed to demonstrate that nonpayment is warranted. By undertaking the guaranty of February 20, 1989, and subjecting it to German law, defendant has obligated itself to pay on first demand (*de votre première demande*). In its demand, the intervenor has declared that the supplier-plaintiff has failed to deliver the 178,000 Azobé wood railway ties. By promising to pay on first demand, the defendant created an obligation which is independent of the relations between supplier and purchaser and between itself and its customer, and in that sense is an abstract obligation (cf. Canaris, *Grosskommentar HGB* 3d ed. — *Bankvertragsrecht,* 2 ed. — Marginal note 1134, Graf von Westphalen *op. cit.* pp. 78, 79). Therefore, the bank, upon a formally correct demand of the intervenor, is obliged to pay, without the defense that the principal obligation between the customer and the beneficiary has either not come into existence or has been extinguished. (BGH, Judgment of March 12, 1984, II. Civil Sen. 198/82, 38 WM 689 (1984), 37 NJW 2030 (1984).) This interpretation of the guaranty is not modified by the fact that the guaranty recited the occasion of the issuance thereof. * * *

The right of intervenor to draw on the guaranty immediately, without allegation and proof of substantive entitlement, is limited only by the prohibition against abusive exercise of rights. The defense of abuse of rights may be raised by defendant against the demand of payment by intervenor only if it is manifest or shown by uncontestable evidence that, despite compliance with the formal requirements, the substantive condition of the guaranty is not met. Accordingly, the defense of an abuse of right is limited to the case where everyone could discern the abusive exploitation of a formal entitlement. All controversies of a factual nature or of a legal character, the resolution of which is not self-evident, must be determined after payment by means of a demand for restitution. This is the established case-law of the Federal Supreme Court. (Judgment of March 12, 1984, cit. supra; Judgment of April 21, 1988, 41 NJW 2610 (1988), 42 WM 934 (1988); Judgment of January 17, 1989, 42 NJW 1480 (1989), 43 WM 443 (1989).) This Senate follows this view with the consequence that the sense and meaning of the guaranty-transaction calls for a narrow scope of the abuse-defense.

Accordingly, a demand of plaintiff against defendant that he refrain from paying the intervenor requires that plaintiff show the abusiveness of intervenor's demand for payment and adduce irrebuttable and convincing proof. (Canaris *op. cit.* marginal note 1017). The contention of plaintiff that the burden of demonstration and proof shifts in the case of a guaranty of the repayment of an advance which is drawn upon prior to the expiration of the time for performance with the result that intervenor has to show and prove the prerequisites for its demand of repayment is erroneous. Plaintiff overlooks that defendant made a promise of payment independent of the relation between plaintiff and intervenor and thereby relieved the intervenor of a duty to show and prove its substantive entitlement. This applies to the guaranty of repayment (*Garantie de restitution d'accompte*) the same way as to other guaranties on first demand. Therefore, it behooves plaintiff to demonstrate and prove with uncontestable evidence that the requirements of its claim are met. Plaintiff-appellee has not succeeded in doing so.

[The court explains, inter alia, that plaintiff's shipments of the ties on November 5 and December 12, 1989, did not constitute 'delivery' within the meaning of the ICC-Incoterms, C & F, B 2, since delivery requires the acceptance by purchaser which incontestably was refused by intervenor. Hence the validity of the right to repayment depended upon the validity of the rescission of November 13, 1989, a contention whose verity plaintiff had not conclusively disproved. Accordingly, the assertion of nonperformance constituted a proper basis for the draw on the guaranty.]

NOTES

1. It is generally recognized that in the case of a manifestly fraudulent attempt of a draw-down of a guaranty on first demand or standby letter of credit, the issuer may refuse to pay and the customer may get a judicial prohibition of such payment by the issuer. Except in the case of a manifest fraud, the issuer must pay and the customer may not obtain a judicial prohibition against the issuer.

2. For an Italian case to that effect, see *Allevamenti Toniatti s.a.s e La Bambolaccia s.r.l. c. Banca Friuladria, Jorgen jr. et Continental Farms*, Trib. Udine, June 22, 1995, Giurisprudenza Italiana, I,2, 428 (1996), with note by F. Tommaseo.

C. UNITED STATES

1. Cases

a. Rockwell International v. Citibank

Rockwell International Systems, Inc.,
Plaintiff-Appellee-Cross-Appellant,
v.
Citibank, N.A. and Bank Tejarat,
Defendants-Appellants-Cross-Appellees.
Nos. 1352, 1549, 1629, 1603, 1550,
Dockets 82-7864, 82-7866, 83-7216, 83-7228 and 83-7256
719 F.2d 583
United States Court of Appeals, Second Circuit.
Argued June 16, 1983.
Decided Oct. 11, 1983.

Before Friendly, Oakes and Cardamone, Circuit Judges.

Oakes, Circuit Judge:

Citibank, N.A. (Citibank), and Bank Tejarat (Tejarat) appeal from an order granting a preliminary injunction issued by the United States District Court for the

Sourthern District of New York, Vincent L. Broderick, Judge, on October 15, 1982, and from a second order, entered by Judge Broderick on March 1, 1983, denying appellants' motion to vacate the prior order. The October 15 order enjoined Tejarat from making, and Citibank from honoring, demands under two letters of credit issued by Citibank in favor of Tejarat to secure the performance of plaintiff Rockwell International Systems, Inc. (Rockwell), under a contract between Rockwell and the Ministry of War of the Imperial Government of Iran. The gist of Rockwell's case is that, as a result of the revolution in Iran and its aftermath, it was prevented by the new government in Iran from completing performance of the contract and that the subsequent calls by Iranian officials at Tejarat on the letters of credit were fraudulent. Judge Broderick denied the defendant-appellants' motion to vacate a temporary restraining order that had remained in effect by consent[1] of the parties since May 5, 1980, and, after finding that Rockwell's showing satisfied the requirements of probable success on the merits and irreparable harm, granted the preliminary injunction. Tejarat and Citibank appeal; Rockwell cross-appeals that portion of Judge Broderick's order requiring it to indemnify Citibank against any damages resulting from the injunction. We affirm.

Background

In September of 1977 Rockwell entered into Contract 120 (the contract) with the Ministry of War of the Imperial Government of Iran. Under the contract Rockwell was to provide engineering and advisory services and material in connection with the establishment of a communications system in Iran. Article 7.1 of the contract required that Rockwell

> submit to the [Ministry of War] one or several Bank Guarantee[s] issued by one of the Iranian Bank[s] accepted by the [Ministry], which [sic] the total amount of them to be equal to 10% of the total amount of the Contract . . . for the correct performance of the Contract. . . .

Accordingly Tejarat's prerevolutionary predecessor, Iranians' Bank, issued two guarantees totalling $2,364,782 in favor of the Imperial Government to secure Rockwell's performance. These guarantees were in turn backed up by two letters of credit in favor of Iranians' Bank issued by Citibank at Rockwell's behest, thus establishing the four-corner arrangement customary in international transactions of this sort, involving what are commonly referred to as "standby letters of credit." *See* Getz, Enjoining the International Standby Letter of Credit: The Iranian Letter of Credit Cases, 21 Harv.Int'l L.J. 189, 198–200 (1980).

1. Citibank now disputes that it ever consented to the continuation of the temporary restraining order.

The events surrounding the Shah's fall and the seizure of the American Embassy in Iran need not be recounted here; suffice it to say that Rockwell, in a letter dated February 11, 1979, invoked the *force majeure* clause of Contract 120, demanded an extension of completion time and offered to "discuss th[e] matter . . . by telephone . . . or . . . in Iran, as soon as circumstances permit." A meeting between Rockwell representatives and the Ministry of War, now called the Ministry of Defense, took place in Tehran on September 22, 1979, at which time Rockwell proposed that it be paid $3,159,400 for work to date and that the contract be terminated. This proposal was rejected, but neither Tejarat nor Citibank dispute Rockwell's contention that the Iranian representatives at the meeting "made it clear that they expected no further performance from [Rockwell] pending further negotiations, the termination of Contract 120, and the execution of new contracts." Although Rockwell arguably could have cancelled the contract, thus securing release of the letters of credit,[2] it instead indicated its willingness to complete performance.

By November of 1979 relations between Iran and the United States had become hostile; in response to the embassy seizure, President Carter froze all Iranian assets on November 14, 1979. Diplomatic relations with Iran were severed on April 7, 1980, and the Iranian Assets Control Regulations, 31 C.F.R. §§ 535.101–535.904 (1982), were broadened so as to prohibit virtually all transactions between Iranian and American nationals. On April 25, 1980, Rockwell was informed by Citibank that it had, on March 31 and April 22, received Tejarat's demands for payments under the letters of credit.[3] Rockwell immediately filed suit, and on May 5, 1980, obtained a temporary restraining order preventing Citibank from honoring the demands.

Discussion

As a threshold matter we emphasize that we deal here only with the propriety of interim, i.e., preliminary injunctive relief. Judge Broderick's order did not permanently enjoin Citibank from paying Tejarat's demands under the letters of credit and, except to the extent necessary to review the finding of probability of success on the

---

2. Article 6.2 of Contract 120 provides, in relevant part:

> In the event of Force Majeure when the performance of this Contract becomes impossible, the afflicted party must inform in writing to the other party of the occurrence [sic] of the said event or events, and also mention in his letter the estimated duration of time during which these circumstances will continue.
>
> Then, both parties of this Contract must consult and exchange views with each other to find ways to deal with such events.
>
> However, if within three (3) months from the date of requesting for negotiations by either party, a mutually agreeable solution is not found, each party can, on his opinion, cancel the Contract by giving a written notice to the other party.

3. The earlier demands were construed by Citibank as not conforming to the requirements of the letters of credit and were rejected.

merits, we do not address the merits of the issues involved in the contractual dispute or the continued validity of the letters of credit.

We reject at the outset Tejarat's argument that, by virtue of the January 19, 1981, "Hostage Agreement" establishing the Iran-United States Claim Tribunal (Tribunal), United States courts lack jurisdiction to grant preliminary injunctive relief. The Assets Control Regulations promulgated by the Executive Branch to implement the Tribunal Agreement prohibit only a "final judicial judgment or order (A) permanently enjoining, (B) terminating or nullifying, or (C) otherwise permanently disposing of any interest of Iran in any standby letter of credit. . . ." 31 C.F.R. § 535.504(b)(3)(i) (1983). As the "supplementary information" accompanying this regulation makes clear, the purpose of the regulation "is to preserve the status quo by continuing to allow U.S. account parties to obtain preliminary injunctions or other temporary relief to prevent payment on standby letters of credit. . . ." 47 Fed.Reg. 29,529 (1982).

Having determined that the district court had the authority to grant the preliminary injunction, we next address whether it properly did so in this case. In this circuit a movant must make a "showing of (a) irreparable harm and (b) either (1) likelihood of success on the merits or (2) sufficiently serious questions going to the merits to make them a fair ground for litigation and a balance of hardships tipping decidedly" in its favor. *Jackson Dairy, Inc. v. H.P. Hood & Sons, Inc.*, 596 F.2d 70, 72 (2d Cir. 1979) (per curiam). We turn first to the question of irreparable harm.

1. Irreparable Harm

Tejarat and Citibank argue that Rockwell has failed to show that in the absence of an injunction it would suffer irreparable harm because it could seek recovery either in a claim filed with the Tribunal or in a suit filed wherever Iran has assets subject to attachment.

Our assessment of irreparable harm in the context of this action thus necessitates an inquiry into whether Rockwell does indeed enjoy the prospect of a real, rather than merely speculative or illusory, opportunity to press its claims elsewhere.

Judge Broderick's decision to grant the preliminary injunction was based largely on his finding that it was "highly probable that the Hague Tribunal will refuse to accept jurisdiction over plaintiff's claims," a finding based on the fact that the agreement establishing the Tribunal expressly exludes from its jurisdiction claims under contracts — such as Rockwell's — that provide for resolution of disputes in Iranian courts. In response to this jurisdictional point, the appellants now point to *Ford Aerospace & Communications Corp. v. Air Force of the Islamic Republic of Iran* (Case No. 159) (Iran-United States Claims Tribunal, Nov. 5, 1982), *reprinted in* Iranian Assets Lit. Rep., Nov. 19, 1982 at 5,620, a Tribunal ruling handed down after Judge Broderick's first ruling. *Ford Aerospace* held that a forum selection clause almost identical to the one in Rockwell's contract did not divest the Tribunal of jurisdiction, and the defendants thus argue that the "linchpin to the District Court's opinion . . . has been removed." Tejarat Br. at 12. We disagree. The *Ford Aerospace* ruling is relevant only to Rockwell's claim against the Ministry of Defense for work performed under the underlying contract; the case does not speak to the Tribunal's jurisdiction over the secondary contracts — i.e., the letters of credit — securing the underlying contract. The letters of credit represent separate contractual undertakings that are, in legal contemplation, wholly distinct from whatever performance they ultimately secure. This is not merely an analytic nicety; the "independence" principle is an example of legal form following commercial function, and it is recognized in domestic as well as international law. *See* Getz, *supra,* at 203–04 and sources cited therein. Thus, although it does seem likely that the Tribunal has jursidiction over Rockwell's claim under the underlying contract, it is far from clear that it has jursidiction over Rockwell's claims against the defendants here, particularly those involving Citibank. *Cf. Harza Engineering Co. v. The Islamic Republic of Iran* (Case No. 98) (Iran-United States Claims Tribunal, Dec. 3, 1982), at 12–13, *reprinted in* Iranian Assets Lit. Rep., Jan. 21, 1983 at 5,952 (dismissing Iranian bank's counterclaim demanding payment under letters of credit because counterclaim was unrelated to claim that bank wrongfully blocked plaintiff's account, noting in dictum that "[a] letter of credit is a financial instrument embodying obligations which are autonomous and independent of the transaction to which it is a condition").

Neither Tejarat nor Citibank argues that the post-revolutionary Iranian judicial system is capable of affording an adequate remedy; courts that have passed on this contention have consistently rejected it. *See e.g., Harris Corp. v. National Iranian Radio and Television,* 691 F.2d 1344, 1356–57 (11th Cir.1982); *Itek Corp. v. First National Bank of Boston,* 511 F.Supp. 1341, 1349 (D.Mass.1981), *vacated and remanded on other grounds,* 704 F.2d 1 (1st Cir.1983); *American International Group, Inc. v. Islamic Republic of Iran,* 493 F.Supp. 522, 525 (D.D.C.1980); *Stromberg-Carlson Corp. v. Bank Melli Iran,* 467 F.Supp. 530, 532 n. 3 (S.D.N.Y.1979).

We have little difficulty in distinguishing this case from our decision in *KMW International v. Chase Manhattan Bank, N.A.,* 606 F.2d 10 (2d Cir.1979), a case in which we held preliminary injunctive relief inappropriate. In *KMW* the relief requested was essentially declaratory; no demands had been made on the letters of credit and any future damage was, at that time, "purely conjectural." *Id.* at 15. In the instant case, demands have, of course, been made, and the prospect of injury is immediate.[4]

4. In a memorial filed with the Iran-United States Claim Tribunal on April 18, 1983, the United States noted that Iran had outstanding 230 claims based on standby letters of credit and similar undertakings issued by United States banks. *Bank Mellat v. Manufacturers Hanover Trust Co.* (Case No. 582) (Iran-United States Claims Tribunal), Memorial of the United States Concerning the Tribunal's Jurisdiction over Iran's Standby Letter of Credit Claims (filed Apr. 18, 1983), at 1 n. 1. Of course, there may have been even more calls made than claims filed.

2. Success on the Merits

The letters of credit issued here were by their very terms subject to the Uniform Customs and Practice for Documentary Credits (UCP). Although the UCP does not explicitly provide for a "fraud in the transaction" defense, New York law — the defendants have not argued that New York law is inapplicable or directed us to any Iranian law on this point — recognizes the availability of this defense under the UCP. *See KMW International v. Chase Manhattan Bank, N.A.*, 606 F.2d 10, 15 n. 3 (2d Cir.1979) (citing *United Bank Ltd. v. Cambridge Sporting Goods Corp.*, 41 N.Y.2d 254, 258 n. 2, 392 N.Y.S.2d 265, 269 n. 2, 360 N.E.2d 943, 947 n. 2 (1976)).

The "fraud in the transaction" defense marks the limit of the generally accepted principle that a letter of credit is independent of whatever obligation it secures. No bright line separates the rule from the exception, to be sure, but we agree with Rockwell that "fraud" embraces more than mere forgery of documents supporting a call. *Cf. United Bank Ltd. v. Cambridge Sporting Goods Corp.*, 41 N.Y.2d at 260 & n. 5, 392 N.Y.S.2d at 271 & n. 5, 360 N.E.2d at 949 & n. 5 ("fraud in a required document" rejected in favor of "fraud in the transaction" by drafters of U.C.C. § 5-114(2)). The logic of the fraud exception necessarily entails looking beyond supporting documents, and this renders Tejarat's argument that the letters provide for unconditional payment unpersuasive, if not irrelevant. In this case, as in the leading case of *Sztejn v. J. Henry Schroder Banking Corp.*, 177 Misc. 719, 31 N.Y.S.2d 631 (Sup.Ct.1941), we must look to the circumstances surrounding the transaction and the call to determine whether Tejarat's call amounted to an "outright fradulent practice." *United Bank Ltd.*, 41 N.Y.2d at 261, 392 N.Y.S.2d at 271, 360 N.E.2d at 949.

In *Sztejn* and *United Bank Ltd.*, sellers called letters of credit after shipping goods — in the *Sztejn* case, garbage — that were clearly non-conforming, thus frustrating completion of the contract by non-performance. In the present case, the Iranian Ministry of Defense is in the position of a "buyer" and it has, for its own reasons, frustrated completion of the contract by suspending Rockwell's performance. We think that the essence of the fraud exception is that "the principle of the independence of [a] bank's obligation under the letter of credit should not be extended to protect" a party that behaves so as to prevent performance of the underlying obligation, *Sztejn*, 177 Misc. at 722, 31 N.Y.S.2d at 634; the "fraud" inheres in first causing the default and then attempting to reap the benefit of the guarantee. *See Dynamics Corp. of America v. Citizens & Southern National Savings Bank*, 356 F.Supp. 991, 999 (N.D.Ga.1973) (finding fraud and enjoining payment in order to prevent foreign sovereign from taking "advantage of [an unsettled political] situation and run off with [the] plaintiff's money on a *pro forma* declaration which has absolutely no basis in fact"). On this view of the fraud exception it is not necessary for Rockwell to demonstrate that either Tejarat or the Ministry of Defense acted deceitfully or with malicious intent.

In deciding that Rockwell will probably be able to demonstrate that the call in this particular case was fraudulent we are necessarily influenced by the fact that this demand is not an isolated occurrence. While we may agree in principle with Tejarat's contention that the economic or political motivations of a letter of credit beneficiary are irrelevant, as a practical matter the fact that calls have been issued wholesale tends to support Rockwell's contention that these letters — issued to secure its "good performance" — were called for reasons entirely unrelated to that performance and were therefore fraudulent. Accordingly, we agree with Judge Broderick's conclusion that there is sufficient probability of success on the merits of the fraud claim to justify injunctive relief, *see also Harris Corp. v. National Iranian Radio and Television,* 691 F.2d 1344, 1356 (11th Cir.1982); *Itek Corp. v. First National Bank of Boston,* 511 F.Supp. 1341, 1350–51 (D.Mass.1981), *vacated and remanded on other grounds,* 704 F.2d 1 (1st Cir.1983), although not necessarily because the guarantees were released under the contract when performance was suspended. Finally, we agree with Judge Broderick, for the reasons expressed below, that Tejerat was not a "holder in due course" of the letters and was therefore not entitled to avoid the fraud in the transaction defense. *See* UCC Section 5-114(2)(a).

3. Rockwell's Cross-Appeal

Judge Broderick's order of March 1, 1983, requires Rockwell to indemnify "Citibank and its affiliates against any and all consequential damages Citibank and its affiliates may suffer, directly or indirectly, as a result of Citibank's compliance with this court's preliminary injunction. . . ." Pursuant to the order, Citibank is required in any action or proceeding for payment under the letters either to "give Rockwell an opportunity to assume or participate in its defense or . . . conduct its own defense with due diligence and reasonable prudence, so that [the] court's interlocutory judgment" with respect to fraud will be "adequately represented." Rockwell argues on its cross-appeal that, as a condition of indemnification, Citibank should be ordered to turn over to Rockwell its defense against claims of non-payment made in the Tribunal or elsewhere. Rule 65(c) of the Federal Rules of Civil Procedure states that "[n]o restraining order or preliminary injunction shall issue except upon the giving of security by the applicant"; indemnification is, in short, a condition precedent to the grant of a preliminary injunction. The district court's order strikes us as eminently fair and we have no reason to believe that Citibank will shirk its obligation to present the fraud defense adequately, capably and with its its best efforts.

Orders affirmed.

NOTES

1. The treatment of standby letters of credit issued by U.S. banks for the benefit of Iranian banks which in turn issued standby letters of credit to secure the performance of U.S. contractors under contracts with Iranian authorities presented difficult legal problems both under the regime of the freezing orders and after the conclusion of the Algiers Accords. The text case dealt with the situation following the U.S. adherence to the Algiers Declarations.

The Claim Settlement Declaration, Art. II(1), vested the Tribunal with jurisdiction over 'claims by U.S. nationals against Iran and . . . any counterclaim which arises out of the same contract, transaction or occurrence that constitutes the subject matter of that national's claim if such claims and counterclaims are outstanding on the date of this Agreement . . . and arise out of debts, contracts (including transactions which are the subject of letters of credit or bank guaranties), . . .'

In consequence of this jurisdictional grant, the Tribunal held in the case No. A-16 that it did not have jurisdiction over direct claims by Iranian banks against U.S. financial institutions based on dishonor of back-to-back standby letters of credit, but left it to each chamber to decide whether such claim could be joined as a counterclaim against a U.S. contractor, where the contractor is the claimant, 5 Iran-US CTR 57 (1985).

Following that holding the Tribunal dealt in numerous cases with issues of wrongful draw-down, recovery of payment, cancellation and expiration of standby letters of credit bank guaranties. One of the most important cases of this type is *Harris International Telecommunications, Inc. v. Iran,* 17 Iran-US CTR 31 (1988). In that case, the Chamber concluded that Harris brought a claim against Iran for breach of a contract for work in connection with the modernization of Iran's military electronic intelligence gathering system and wrongful attempts to draw on bank guaranties and letters of credit issued in connection with the contract. Claimant joined two Iranian banks, Bank Markari and Bank Melli as defendants. Iran and Bank Melli filed a counterclaim against claimant and Chase Manhattan Bank which had issued letters of credit for the benefit of Bank Melli.

The tribunal (Ch. One) held that the two Iranian banks were proper respondents to the extent that the claimant asked for cancellation and release of the letters of credit and bank guaranties. It dismissed the counterclaim against Chase Manhattan Bank as untimely.

On the merits the tribunal held that Harris had duly terminated the contract because of *force majeure.* It further ruled that the bank guaranties and letters of credit issued in connection with the contract no longer served any purpose and ordered Iran to withdraw demands for payment of the guaranties and to refrain from any further demands. Moreover, Iran was obligated to have the bank guaranties canceled and to ensure that the corresponding letters of credit were released and that Bank Melli withdraw all demands for payment of them and refrain from further demands.

2. California state law — Cal. Commercial Code 5114, (diverging in that respect from the official version of the U.C.C.) does not authorize injunctions against the issuer prohibiting payment of a letter of credit. As a result, it has been held that a beneficiary may likewise not be enjoined from calling a letter of credit, unless the beneficiary acts with intent to defraud. *TMTI v. Empresa Nacional de Comercializacion,* 829 F.2d 949 (9th Cir. 1987).

b. Mellon Bank

Mellon Bank, N.A., a National Banking Association, Plaintiff,
v.
General Electric Credit Corporation, a New York Corporation, Defendant.
Civ. A. No. 87-1443.
United States District Court, W. D. Pennsylvania.
Oct. 27, 1989.
724 F. Supp. 360 (1989)

OPINION

COHILL, Chief Judge.

Plaintiff, Mellon Bank, N.A. ("Mellon"), sues to recover for defendant's allegedly improper draw on a standby letter of credit. The parties have filed cross motions for summary judgment with several briefs and a considerable amount of evidentiary material. The pertinent agreements are before us, and as to most of the issues raised by the parties there are no apparent disputed issues of material fact. Partial summary judgment on these matters is appropriate. However, the parties have failed to address defendant, General Electric Credit Corp.'s ("GECC") defense of anticipatory repudiation, and therefore the cross motions for summary judgment must be denied.

FACTS

The entity at the eye of this storm is not a party to this litigation. Woodings Consolidated Industries, Inc. ("Woodings") manufactured oil drilling equipment, and over the years Mellon had been Woodings' primary source for financing. By 1986, Woodings owed Mellon more than $5 million.

On April 23, 1985, Woodings entered into a leaseback arrangement with GECC. Under the terms of this agreement Woodings sold GECC a valuable machine (known as a sucker rod machine for reasons we do not care to fathom), and GECC then leased the machine back to Woodings for a specified monthly payment. This contract will be referred to here as the "Lease Agreement."

In conjunction with the Lease Agreement, and to better secure GECC's interest, Woodings and GECC executed a Letter of Credit Agreement. In accord with its terms, Woodings arranged a standby Letter of Credit with Mellon Bank in the amount of $600,000 with GECC as beneficiary. The Letter of Credit issued by Mellon permitted GECC to draw up to $600,000 upon submission of a sight draft by GECC and a typewritten statement that the sum demanded was due and owing.

From 1984 to 1986 Woodings experienced increasing financial losses as a result of a severe downturn in the oil industry. On January 23, 1987 Woodings failed to make its scheduled lease payment to GECC. Defendant also alleges that Woodings failed to present proof of liability insurance for 1987 as required by the Lease Agreement.

Based on these alleged defaults, GECC presented Mellon with a sight draft on the Letter of Credit in the amount of $600,000, and a typewritten statement asserting that Woodings was in default and that the full amount of the draft was due and owing. Mellon paid the full amount to GECC.

Mellon has now sued GECC to recover the $600,000 drawn on the Line of Credit, asserting that Woodings was *not* in default at the time of the draft, that the $600,000 was not due and owing, and therefore GECC could not properly draw on the Line of Credit. Both sides seek summary judgment, raising a host of intertwined issues which we now attempt to unravel.

DISCUSSION

I. *Default*

The Letter of Credit Agreement between Woodings and GECC provides in pertinent part:

> Under the terms hereof, upon the occurrence of any default under the Lease, or upon the filing of a petition by or against Lessee under Title XI of the United States Code or any successor or similar law, GECC shall have the right to present sight draft(s) and a properly-executed statement to the issuer for any amount not exceeding, in total, the sum of U.S. $600,000.00 and to receive said monies therefrom, at GECC's sole discretion, in lump sum, or in several sums from time to time.

The Letter of Credit issued by Mellon provides in pertinent part:

> We [Mellon] undertake to honor from time to time your draft or drafts at sight on us not exceeding in the aggregate U.S. $600,000.00 when accompanied by a signed typewritten statement by GECC stating either (i) that the

> amount of the accompanying draft is due and owing by Customer to GECC, or (ii) that a petition has been filed by or against Customer under Title XI of the United States Code or a similar or successor law.

On February 11, 1987, GECC presented Mellon with a sight draft for $600,000 and the following typewritten statement:

> This is to advise you that Woodings Consolidated Industries, Inc. ("Customer") is in breach of certain agreements with General Electric Credit Corporation ("GECC") and that, accordingly, the amount of SIX HUNDRED THOUSAND AND 00/100 U.S. ($600,000) DOLLARS drawn by GECC under Draft No. 0001 dated February 11, 1987 against Mellon Bank Letter of Credit No. 56540 is due and owing by Customer to GECC.

Mellon honored the draft on the following day.

Mellon describes its claim as a breach of warranty action. Under § 5-111 of the Uniform Commercial Code, a party drawing on a line of credit "warrants to all interested parties that the necessary conditions of the credit have been complied with." 13 Pa. C.S.A. § 5111. Thus a beneficiary warrants to the issuing bank the truth of the statements necessary to a draw on the credit. *Pubali Bank v. City National Bank,* 676 F.2d 1326 (9th Cir. 1982); *Brown v. United States Bank of Omaha,* 220 Neb. 684, 371 N.W.2d 692, 701 (1985).

Mellon contends that GECC was required to make two assertions to effect a draw on the Letter of Credit: 1) that Woodings was in default of the Lease Agreement, and 2) that the amount of the draft was due and owing by Woodings to GECC. In fact, GECC made these assertions in its statement accompanying the sight draft. Mellon argues that both of these assertions were false, that under the terms of the Lease Agreement Woodings was not in default, and the sum of $600,000 was not due and owing at the time of the draw. Therefore Mellon concludes that GECC breached its § 5-111 warranties, and Mellon is entitled to recover the amount of the draw.

The parties have focused most of their time and attention on the question of whether Woodings was in default at the time of the draw. It is admitted that Woodings had failed to make its rental payment for January 1985, and therefore was in breach of its contractual obligation. GECC argues that this is a default, and therefore its assertion in support of the draw is truthful. On the other hand, Mellon contends that the Lease Agreement required a formal declaration of default:

> XII. DEFAULT: (a) If Lessee breaches its obligation to pay rent when due and fails to cure said breach within ten (10) days, or if Lessee breaches any of the terms hereof or any of terms or any Schedule hereto . . . then in either such case, Lessor may declare this Agreement in default. Such declaration

> shall be by written notice to Lessee and shall apply to all Schedules hereunder except as specifically excepted by Lessor in such declaration . . .

GECC did not make a declaration of default prior to the draw. Thus, Mellon argues, under the terms of the Lease Agreement Woodings was *not* in default at the time of the draw even though it had failed to make a timely payment, and GECC has therefore breached its § 5-111 warranty.

The sad part of all of this is that the issue of Woodings' default is utterly irrelevant to analysis of the § 5-111 warranties. Although GECC represented in its statement to Mellon that Woodings was in default at the time of the draw, and though the Letter of Credit Agreement between Woodings and GECC permits a draw only upon a default by Woodings, the Letter of Credit itself *does not require* such an assertion prior to a draw. The Letter of Credit states:

> We [Mellon] undertake to honor from time to time your draft or drafts at sight on us not exceeding in the aggregate U.S. $600,000.00 when accompanied by a signed typewritten statement by GECC stating *either* (i) *that the amount of the accompanying draft is due and owing by Customer to GECC, or* (ii) that a petition has been filed by or against Customer under Title XI of the United States Code or a similar or successor law. (Emphasis added.)

There simply is no requirement that GECC make any representation of Woodings' status under the contract. Default is irrelevant. The only representation necessary to a draw on the Letter of Credit, in the absence of Woodings' bankruptcy, is that the amount of the draft be due and owing. Thus GECC's assertion that Woodings was in default was merely gratuitous under the Letter of Credit. Though the issue of default may be relevant as between Woodings and GECC under their Letter of Credit Agreement, Mellon was not a party to that agreement, and neither the agreement nor its terms were incorporated in the Letter of Credit issued by Mellon. If no assertion of default is required by the Letter of Credit, no warranties attach to such an assertion. Therefore, even if GECC's statement that Woodings was in default was false, GECC would not be liable for breach of a § 5-111 warranty.

We return then to a consideration of what the Letter of Credit *does* require. As seen above, absent Woodings' bankruptcy, GECC was required to state that the amount of the draft "is due and owing by [Woodings] to GECC." In fact GECC submitted a draft for $600,000 and stated that this sum was due and owing at the time of the draw. Therefore § 5-111 is applicable, and GECC warranted to Mellon the truth of this assertion.

It is admitted that Woodings was late in making one monthly lease payment of $15,011.40. But GECC has asserted that $600,000 was due and owing, apparently on the basis of provisions of the Lease Agreement for acceleration of payments and stipulated loss.

The pertinent provisions of the Lease Agreement are found in Section XII:

> XII. DEFAULT: (a) If Lessee breaches its obligation to pay rent when due and fails to cure said breach within ten (10) days, or if Lessee breaches any of the terms hereof or any of terms or any Schedule hereto . . . then in either such case, *Lessor may declare this Agreement in default.* Such declaration shall be by written notice to Lessee and shall apply to all Schedules hereunder except as specifically excepted by Lessor in such declaration. *Lessee hereby authorized Lessor at any time after such declaration* to enter, with or without legal process, any premises where any Equipment may be and take possession thereof. *Lessee shall, without further demand, forthwith pay to Lessor, as liquidated damages* for loss of a bargain and not as a penalty, *an amount equal to all rentals and other sums then due hereunder, together with the Stipulated Loss Value* of the Equipment, *calculated as of the date Lessor declared a default hereunder,* together with interest thereon at the highest rate allowed by law . . . (Emphasis added.)

From these provisions it is clear that acceleration of payments and liquidated damages are invoked *only* after a declaration of default. Indeed accelerated payments and the Stipulated Loss Value are to be calculated "as of the date Lessor declared a default hereunder."

GECC admits that it did not declare a default prior to the draw on the Letter of Credit. Without such a formal declaration, the acceleration of payments and liquidated damages provisions are not applicable. Thus, on the date of GECC's draw on the Line of Credit, Woodings owed GECC the amount of one tardy rental payment. GECC's assertion that $600,000 was due and owing was erroneous, and constitutes a breach of its warranty under § 5-111.

II. *Independence Principle*

However, GECC objects to Mellon's reliance on the terms of the underlying Lease Agreement. GECC refers to this portion of the Letter of Credit:

> We agree that we shall have no duty or right to inquire as to the basis upon which GECC has determined to present to us any draft under this Letter of Credit.

GECC also invokes the doctrine known as the "independence principle," which prohibits reference to underlying contracts to determine the validity of a draft on a letter of credit. Under this principle the issuing bank may only determine whether the appropriate documents have been presented. It may not contest the truth of the assertions in those documents. *Intraworld Industries Inc. v. Girard Trust Bank,* 461 Pa. 343, 359, 336 A.2d 316, 324 (1975).

Although GECC states the principle accurately, it does not apply it correctly in this case. The independence principle, and the above-quoted portion of the Letter of Credit, speak only to the bank's obligation to honor the sight draft *in the first instance.* They do not preclude subsequent investigation and efforts at recovery. *Pubali Bank v. City National Bank,* 676 F.2d 1326 (9th Cir.1982), appeal after remand, 777 F.2d 1340 (1985).

The purpose of the independence principle, and of the similar provision in Mellon's Letter of Credit, is to provide the beneficiary with an unfettered, immediate remedy upon occurrence of the triggering event on a standby letter of credit. The purpose is not to prevent any subsequent challenge to the validity of the beneficiary's claim, but to ensure that "contractual disputes wend their way towards resolution with money in the beneficiary's pocket rather than in the pocket of the contracting party." *Itek Corp. v. First National Bank of Boston,* 730 F.2d 19, 24 (1st Cir.1984); *C.K.B. & Associates v. Moore McCormick Petroleum,* 734 S.W.2d 653, 655 (Tex.1987).

Indeed, if interpreted in the manner GECC suggests, the independence principle would make a nullity of § 5-111. Little purpose would be served if § 5-111 created warranties as to the truth of the conditions necessary to a draw, while the independence principle precluded the bank from contesting the truth of those assertions.

For the reasons stated we conclude that the independence principle and the similar contract provision quoted above are inapplicable to an action for breach of § 5-111 warranties, and do not preclude reference to underlying contractual documents to determine the truth or falsity of the warrantied assertions.

III. *Satisfaction*

Having crossed these hurdles, Mellon faces another erected by GECC.

Following GECC's draw on the Line of Credit, Mellon and Woodings entered into a Debt Reduction Agreement. By its terms, Woodings liquidated its assets, with proceeds going to retire Woodings' various obligations to Mellon. According to the Agreement, proceeds were applied to satisfy various categories of indebtedness, ranked in descending order. For example, all obligations in Category 1 must be satisfied before proceeds were applied to Category 2 obligations, and so on. Repayment of the $600,000 draw on the Letter of Credit ranked third.

Woodings' assets brought proceeds of nearly $2 million, enough to satisfy in full the first several ranks of indebtedness, including the $600,000 draw by GECC. Thus, GECC argues, Mellon has been paid its $600,000 and it therefore has no claim against GECC for an improper draw.

GECC has taken an accounting mechanism and tried to turn it into a bar to recovery. GECC ignores the $1.6 million shortfall still due Mellon by Woodings. The simple fact is that GECC's actions increased Woodings' obligation to Mellon by $600,000, and if not for that draw the proceeds from Woodings' assets would have gone to satisfy a portion of the existing debt. The fact that the accountants have marked this obligation satisfied on the books does not alter the reality that Mellon is still out an additional $600,000 due to GECC's improper draw.

But this may all be academic. Mellon has established without contradiction from GECC that Woodings has assigned all its claims to Mellon. If Mellon has no claim, Woodings certainly does because it paid $600,000 to Mellon to satisfy its indebtedness for GECC's draw. Section 5-111 warranties extend to both the bank and the customer, so Mellon can assert a breach of warranty claim on Woodings' behalf as assignee of the claim.

GECC notes that Mellon did not plead rights by assignment. However, amendment of the pleadings may be permitted to conform to the evidence, and the undisputed evidence here establishes the existence of an assignment.

IV. *Anticipatory Repudiation*

There remains one fly in the ointment. In the very last paragraph of the reply brief GECC raises anticipatory repudiation as a defense. GECC contends that prior to GECC's draw on the Letter of Credit, Woodings made clear by word and deed that it would not and could not perform its obligations under the Lease Agreement. GECC argues that Woodings' words and deeds constitute anticipatory repudiation of the contract which excuses GECC from its obligations, including the requirements for formal declaration of default and notice. Without these safeguards Woodings was in immediate default, and GECC was entitled to draw on the Letter of Credit.

With the exception of this passing reference in defendant's brief, apparently tacked on as an afterthought, the issue has not been addressed by the parties. However, GECC has submitted some small quantum of evidentiary material which on its face appears to support GECC's argument. Therefore we cannot ignore it, but neither can we address it intelligently on the inadequate presentation of the issue on the present motions. It *does* prevent the entry of summary judgment in favor of plaintiff.

We also note that the anticipatory repudiation argument is the basis, at least in part, for GECC's counterclaim. Neither party has addressed the counterclaim on the present motions, and this too prevents entry of final judgment in favor of plaintiff.

CONCLUSION

For the reasons stated above, partial summary judgment will be granted in favor of Plaintiff Mellon in the following respects:

1) GECC failed to make a formal declaration of default as required by the Lease Agreement, and as a result acceleration of payments and liquidated damages provisions are inapplicable.

2) Absent anticipatory repudiation, GECC's assertion in support of its draw on the Letter of Credit, that $600,000 was due and owing, was erroneous and in breach of GECC's § 5-111 warranty.
3) The independence principle and the like provision in the Letter of Credit are inapplicable and do not preclude reference to the underlying contractual documents to determine the truth of the warrantied assertions.

Nonetheless, complete summary judgment may not be entered in favor of plaintiff because plaintiff has not addressed the defense of anticipatory repudiation. Furthermore, the parties have failed to address defendant's counterclaim.

We do not know if the matter of anticipatory repudiation is susceptible to treatment on summary judgment motion in this case. Therefore we will afford counsel an opportunity to review this Opinion and to file a supplemental summary judgment motion if desired.

An appropriate Order accompanies this Opinion.

ORDER

AND NOW, this 27th day of October, 1989, in accord with the accompanying Opinion, it is hereby ORDERED that the cross motions for summary judgment are DENIED, but partial summary judgment is GRANTED in favor of plaintiff as described in the Opinion.

Either party may file a Supplemental Motion for Summary Judgment on the defense of anticipatory repudiation and/or defendant's counterclaim, with supporting brief and evidentiary material, on or before November 13, 1989. Any response with brief and evidentiary material shall be filed on or before November 27, 1989.

If no motions are forthcoming, this matter will be scheduled at a later date for Pretrial Conference and Trial.

NOTES

1. As the text case indicates, in the United States a beneficiary who draws on a letter of credit, governed by Art. 5 of the U.C.C., 'warrants to all interested parties that the necessary conditions of the credit have been complied with.' (U.C.C. § 5-111(1).) Parties, other than beneficiaries when collecting the credit are not subject to the same warranties. In *Cenlin Taiwan LTD. v. Centon, LTD. and Bank of California,* 5 F.3d 354 (9th Cir. 1993), Cenlin, Ltd., a Taiwanese corporation purchased fruit from Centon LTD., a Washington Corporation. Cenlin arranged for letters of credit for the benefit of Centon, issued by certain banks. BankCal served as an advising bank. BankCal was a creditor of Centon and received a security interest in the proceeds of the credits. Upon default, Centon authorized BankCal to collect the credits. Cenlin informed BankCal that it had paid Centon by means other than the letters of credit. Neverthe-

less, BankCal collected some amounts from the issuing banks. Cenlin sued BankCal for breach of warranty and negligence. The court below rendered a summary judgment for the benefit of BankCal and Cenlin appealed.

The U.S. Court of Appeals (9th Cir.) affirmed. It held that the BankCal was not a beneficiary and not subject to the warranties pursuant to U.C.C. § 5-111(1). BankCal, in addition, was not liable under the warranty pursuant to U.C.C. § 4-207, as it read prior to 1990. Under that section, a person who obtains payment on an instrument warrants to the payor that he is entitled to payment. The court held that Cenlin, despite of its ultimate liability, was not a payor within the meaning of former U.C.C. § 4-207, and not benefitted by any other warranty on the part of BankCal. As a result, Cenlin has no remedy against BankCal.

2. As *Mellon* states, under UCC 5 (Letters of Credit), before its revision in 1995, 'Section 5-111 warranties extend to both the bank and the customer'. Accordingly, the bank, as issuer could recover amounts drawn on a letter of credit by the beneficiary in breach of the warranty. The 1995 revision of Art. 5 modified the warranties section, now § 5-110, by limiting the beneficiary's warranty to the issuer and the applicant to the absence of fraud or forgery and by providing an additional warranty to the applicant that the drawing does not violate any agreement between the applicant and the issuer. See Official Comment Nr. 2.

3. In *Confeccoes Texteis de Vouzela v. Riggs National Bank* 994 F.2d 851 (D.C. Cir. 1993), the court dealt with the liability of a confirming bank which had honored a letter of credit, although the documents presented did not conform to the conditions of the letter. The merchandise involved, a computer controlled production system, did not match the description on the documents and was worthless to the plaintiff- buyer Confeccoes Texteis de Vouzela (*CTV*) a Portuguese Corporation. CTV, as account party, had secured a letter of credit from the issuing bank, Caixa Geral de Depositos (*Depositos*) which in turn had contracted with the Riggs National Bank as confirming bank. Riggs debited Depositos with its payment to the U.S. sellers, and Depositos charged CTV. CTV brought an action against Riggs claiming breach of warranty, violation of duty under the U.C.C. and tort.

The U.S. District Court dismissed the action and the U.S. Court of Appeals D.C. Cir. affirmed. The court held that a confirming bank's 'customer', to which it owes the statutory duties under U.C.C. §§ 5-103(1) and 5-107(2), is solely the issuing bank itself, and not the issuing bank's customer. The confirmation stamped on the letter of credit did not amount to an express warranty. Plaintiff made no claim under U.C.C. § 111(2). The claim based on general tort law principles was likewise subject to rejection because acceptance 'would undermine the objectivity and predictability [characterizing the function of a letter of credit] and would therefore be inconsistent with the dictates of Article. 5.' (*Ib.* 854).

4. In *Amwest Surety Insurance Company v. Republic National Bank*, 977 F.2d 122 (4th Cir. 1992), Amwest had written a performance bond securing the performance of the Hardaway Company performing excavation and landgrading work as subcon-

tractors in a highway construction project. Amwest was to be secured by a standby letter of credit issued by Republican National Bank in the amount of $160,000 available if it was held liable on the bond. When Amwest's performance bond was drawn upon in the amount of $38,000, Amwest called the entire $160,000 of the standby letter of credit. Noticing its error, it subsequently returned a check for $122,000, which was cashed by the bank. The bank did not reinstate the letter of credit as requested, but applied the money to reduce the amount of the promissory note delivered to it by the prime contractors. On a second call on the standby letter of credit, the bank correctly refused payment, because the standby letter of credit was discharged.

Thereupon, Amwest brought an action against the bank, claiming restitution of the $122,000, *inter alia,* because of unjust enrichment. The bank counterclaimed alleging the beneficiary's breach of warranty. The court held that Amwest, when drawing the whole $122,000, had not breached the warranty under U.C.C. § 5-111(1), since the statutory warranty merely assured that the draft complied with the terms of the letter of credit. Hence the bank had no defense against the liability for unjust enrichment.

c. Compton

Matter of Compton Corp.
U.S. Court of Appeals
831 F.2d 586 (5th Cir. 1987)

JERRE S. WILLIAMS, Circuit Judge:

This is a bankruptcy preference case in which a bankruptcy trustee seeks to recover a transfer made via a letter of credit for the benefit of one of the debtor's unsecured creditors on the eve of bankruptcy. The bankruptcy court and the district court found there to be no voidable preference. We reverse.

I. *FACTUAL BACKGROUND*

In March 1982, Blue Quail Energy, Inc., delivered a shipment of oil to debtor Compton Corporation. Payment of $585,443.85 for this shipment of oil was due on or about April 20, 1982. Compton failed to make timely payment. Compton induced Abilene National Bank (now MBank–Abilene) to issue an irrevocable standby letter of credit in Blue Quail's favor on May 6, 1982. Under the terms of the letter of credit, payment of up to $585,443.85 was due Blue Quail if Compton failed to pay Blue Quail this amount by June 22, 1982. Compton paid MBank $1,463.61 to issue the letter of credit. MBank also received a promissory note payable on demand for $585,443.85. MBank did not need a security agreement to cover the letter of credit transaction because a prior 1980 security agreement between the bank and Compton had a future advances provision.[5] This 1980 security agreement had been perfected as to a variety of Compton's assets through the filing of several financing statements. The most recent financing statement had been filed a year before, May 7, 1981. The letter of credit on its face noted that it was for an antecedent debt due Blue Quail.

On May 7, 1982, the day after MBank issued the letter of credit in Blue Quail's favor, several of Compton's creditors filed an involuntary bankruptcy petition against Compton. On June 22, 1982, MBank paid Blue Quail $569,932.03 on the letter of credit after Compton failed to pay Blue Quail.

In the ensuing bankruptcy proceeding, MBank's aggregate secured claims against Compton, including the letter of credit payment to Blue Quail, were paid in full from the liquidation of Compton's assets which served as the bank's collateral. Walter Kellogg, bankruptcy trustee for Compton, did not contest the validity of MBank's secured claim against Compton's assets for the amount drawn under the letter of credit by Blue Quail. Instead, on June 14, 1983, trustee Kellogg filed a complaint in the bankruptcy court against Blue Quail asserting that Blue Quail had received a preferential transfer under 11 U.S.C. § 547 through the letter of credit transaction. The trustee sought to recover $585,443.85 from Blue Quail pursuant to 11 U.S.C. § 550.

Blue Quail answered and filed a third party complaint against MBank. On June 16, 1986, Blue Quail filed a motion for summary judgment asserting that the trustee could not recover any preference from Blue Quail because Blue Quail had been paid from MBank's funds under the letter of credit and therefore had not received any of Compton's property. On August 27, 1986, the bankruptcy court granted Blue Quail's motion, agreeing that the payment under the letter of credit did not constitute a transfer of debtor Compton's property but rather was a transfer of the bank's property. The bankruptcy court entered judgment on the motion on September 10, 1986. Trustee Kellogg appealed this decision to the district court. On December 11, 1986, the district court affirmed the bankruptcy court ruling, holding that the trustee did not establish two necessary elements of a voidable transfer under 11 U.S.C. § 547. The district court agreed with Blue Quail and the bankruptcy court that the trustee could not establish that the funds transferred to Blue Quail were ever property of Compton. Furthermore, the district court held that the transfer of the increased security interest to MBank was a transfer of the debtor's property for the sole benefit of the bank and in no way benefitted Blue Quail. The district court therefore found no voidable preference as to Blue Quail. The trustee is appealing the decision to this Court.

II. *The Letter of Credit*

It is well established that a letter of credit and the proceeds therefrom are not property of the debtor's estate under 11 U.S.C. § 541. *In re W.L. Mead, Inc.*, 42 B. R. 57

5. A future advances clause in a security agreement subjects the specified collateral to any future loan made by the creditor in addition to the current loans.

(Bankr.N.D.Ohio, W.D.1984); *In re Leisure Dynamics, Inc.*, 33 B.R. 171 (Bankr. Minn.1983); *In re North Shore & Central Illinois Freight Co.*, 30 B.R. 377 (Bankr.N.D. Ill., E.D.1983); *In re M.J. Sales & Distributing Co.*, 25 B.R. 608 (Bankr.S.D.N.Y.1982). When the issuer honors a proper draft under a letter of credit, it does so from its own assets and not from the assets of its customer who caused the letter of credit to be issued. *In re W.L. Mead; In re M.J. Sales.* As a result, a bankruptcy trustee is not entitled to enjoin a post petition payment of funds under a letter of credit from the issuer to the beneficiary, because such a payment is not a transfer of debtor's property (a threshold requirement under 11 U.S.C. § 547 (b)). A case apparently holding otherwise, *In re Twist Cap., Inc.*, 1 B.R. 284 (Bankr.Fla. 1979), has been roundly criticized and otherwise ignored by courts and commentators alike.

Recognizing these characteristics of a letter of credit in a bankruptcy case is necessary in order to maintain the independence principle, the cornerstone of letter of credit law. Under the independence principle, an issuer's obligation to the letter of credit's beneficiary is independent from any obligation between the beneficiary and the issuer's customer. All a beneficiary has to do to receive payment under a letter of credit is to show that it has performed all the duties required by the letter of credit. Any disputes between the beneficiary and the customer do not affect the issuer's obligation to the beneficiary to pay under the letter of credit.

Letters of credit are most commonly arranged by a party who benefits from the provision of goods or services. The party will request a bank to issue a letter of credit which names the provider of the goods or services as the beneficiary. Under a standby letter of credit, the bank becomes primarily liable to the beneficiary upon the default of the bank's customer to pay for the goods or services. The bank charges a fee to issue a letter of credit and to undertake this liability. The shifting of liability to the bank rather than to the services or goods provider is the main purpose of the letter of credit. After all, the bank is in a much better position to assess the risk of its customer's insolvency than is the service or goods provider. It should be noted, however, that it is the risk of the debtor's insolvency and not the risk of a preference attack that a bank assumes under a letter of credit transaction. Overall, the independence principle is necessary to insure "the certainty of payments for services or goods rendered regardless of any intervening misfortune which may befall the other contracting party." *In re North Shore*, 30 B.R. at 378.

The trustee in this case accepts this analysis and does not ask us to upset it. The trustee is not attempting to set aside the post petition payments by MBank to Blue Quail under the letter of credit as a preference; nor does the trustee claim the letter of credit itself constitutes debtor's property. The trustee is instead challenging the earlier transfer in which Compton granted MBank an increased security interest in its assets to obtain the letter of credit for the benefit of Blue Quail. Collateral which has been pledged by a debtor as security for a letter of credit is property of the debtor's estate. *In re W.L. Mead*, 42 B.R. at 59. The trustee claims that the direct transfer to MBank of the increased security interest on May 6, 1982, also constituted an indirect transfer to

Blue Quail which occurred one day prior to the filing of the involuntary bankruptcy petition and is voidable as a preference under 11 U.S.C. § 547. This assertion of a preferential transfer is evaluated in Parts III and IV of this opinion.

It is important to note that the irrevocable standby letter of credit in the case at bar was not arranged in connection with Blue Quail's initial decision to sell oil to Compton on credit. Compton arranged for the letter of credit after Blue Quail had shipped the oil and after Compton had defaulted in payment. The letter of credit in this case did not serve its usual function of backing up a contemporaneous credit decision,[6] but instead served as a back up payment guarantee on an extension of credit already in jeopardy. The letter of credit was issued to pay off an antecedent unsecured debt. This fact was clearly noted on the face of the letter of credit.[7] Blue Quail, the beneficiary of the letter of credit, did not give new value for the issuance of the letter of credit by MBank on May 6, 1982, or for the resulting increased security interest held by MBank. MBank, however, did give new value for the increased security interest it obtained in Compton's collateral: the bank issued the letter of credit.

When a debtor pledges its assets to secure a letter of credit, a transfer of debtor's property has occurred under the provisions of 11 U.S.C. § 547. By subjecting its assets to MBank's reimbursement claim in the event MBank had to pay on the letter of credit, Compton made a transfer of its property. The broad definition of "transfer" under 11 U.S.C. § 101(50) is clearly designed to cover such a transfer. Overall, the letter of credit itself and the payments thereunder may not be property of debtor, but the collateral pledged as a security interest for the letter of credit is.

Furthermore, in a secured letter of credit transaction, the transfer of debtor's property takes place at the time the letter of credit is issued (when the security interest is granted) and received by the beneficiary, not at the time the issuer pays on the letter of credit. *In re Briggs Transportation Co.*, 37 B.R. 76, 79 (Bankr.Minn.1984). *In re M.J. Sales, supra* (transfer of pledged collateral occurs not when bank forecloses on it, but when it is pledged.)

The transfer to MBank of the increased security interest was a direct transfer which occurred on May 6, 1982, when the bank issued the letter of credit. Under 11 U.S.C. § 547(e)(2)(A), however, such a transfer is deemed to have taken place for purposes of 11 U.S.C. § 547 at the time such transfer "takes effect" between the transferor and transferee if such transfer is perfected within 10 days. The phrase "takes effect" is undefined in the Bankruptcy Code, but under Uniform Commercial Code Article 9 law, a transfer of a security interest "takes effect" when the security interest attaches. Because of the future advances clause in MBank's 1980 security agreement with Compton, the attachment of the MBank's security interest relates back to May 9,

---

6. As was the case in *In re W.L. Mead, Inc., In re Leisure Dynamics, In re North Shore & Central Illinois Freight Co.,* and *In re M.J. Sales,* all *supra.*

7. The letter of credit was dated May 6, 1982, and noted that it covered delivery of Oklahoma Sweet crude oil during March 1982.

1980, the date the security agreement went into effect. The bottom line is that the direct transfer of the increased security interest to MBank is artificially deemed to have occurred at least by May 7, 1981, the date MBank filed its final financing statement, for purposes of a preference attack against the bank.[8] This date is well before the 90 day window of 11 U.S.C. § 547(b)(4)(A). This would protect the bank from a preference attack by the trustee even if the bank had not given new value at the time it received the increased security interest. MBank is therefore protected from a preference attack by the trustee for the increased security interest transfer under either of two theories: under 11 U.S.C. § 547(c)(1) because it gave new value and under the operation of the relation back provision of 11 U.S.C. § 547(e)(2)(A). The bank is also protected from any claims of reimbursement by Blue Quail because the bank received no voidable preference.

The relation back provision of 11 U.S.C. § 547(e)(2)(A), however, applies only to the direct transfer of the increased security interest to MBank. The indirect transfer to Blue Quail that allegedly resulted from the direct transfer to MBank occurred on May 6, 1982, the date of issuance of the letter of credit. The relation back principle of 11 U.S.C. § 547(e)(2)(A) does not apply to this indirect transfer to Blue Quail. Blue Quail was not a party to the security agreement between MBank and Compton. So it will not be able to utilize the relation back provision if it is deemed to have received an indirect transfer resulting from the direct transfer of the increased security interest to MBank. Blue Quail, therefore, cannot assert either of the two defenses to a preference attack which MBank can claim. Blue Quail did not give new value under § 547(c)(1), and it received a transfer within 90 days of the filing of Compton's bankruptcy petition.[9]

III. *Direct/Indirect Transfer Doctrine*

The federal courts have long recognized that "[t]o constitute a preference, it is not necessary that the transfer be made directly to the creditor." *National Bank of Newport v. National Herkimer County Bank*, 225 U.S. 178, 184, 32 S.Ct. 663, 635, 56 L.Ed. 1042 (1912). "If the bankrupt has made a transfer of his property, the *effect* of which is to enable one of his creditors to obtain a greater percentage of his debt than another creditor of the same class, circuity of arrangement will not avail to save it." *Id.* (Emphasis added). To combat such circuity, the courts have broken down certain transfers into two transfers, one direct and one indirect. The direct transfer to the third

8. Tex.Bus. & Com.Code Ann. § 9.312(g) specifies that for purposes of priority among competing secured parties, the security interest for a future advance has the same priority as the security interest for the first advance. Conflicting security interests rank according to priority in time of filing or perfection. Tex.Bus. & Com.Code Ann. § 9.312 (e)(1).

9. Nor does Blue Quail have the protection of the 11 U.S.C. § 547(c)(2) "ordinary course of business" preference exception. Getting a standby letter of credit issued to cover a debt several weeks past due does not constitute ordinary course of business.

party may be valid and not subject to a preference attack. The indirect transfer, arising from the same action by the debtor, however, may constitute a voidable preference as to the creditor who indirectly benefitted from the direct transfer to the third party.

This is the situation presented in the case before us. The term "transfer" as used in the various bankruptcy statutes through the years has always been broad enough to cover such indirect transfers and to catch various circuitous arrangements. *Katz v. First National Bank of Glen Head,* 568 F.2d 964, 969 n. 4, (2nd Cir.), *cert. denied,* 434 U.S. 1069, 98 S.Ct. 1250, 55 L.Ed.2d 771 (1978). The new Bankruptcy Code implicitly adopts this doctrine through its broad definition of "transfer."[10] Examining the case law that has developed since the *National Bank of Newport* case yields an understanding of what types of transfers the direct/indirect doctrine is meant to cover.

* * *

IV. *The Direct/Indirect Doctrine in the Context of a Letter of Credit Transaction*

In the letter of credit cases discussed in Part II *supra,* the letters of credit were issued contemporaneously with the initial extension of credit by the beneficiaries of the letters. In those cases the letters of credit effectively served as security devices for the benefit of the creditor beneficiaries and took the place of formal security interests. The courts in those cases properly found there had been no voidable transfers, direct or indirect, in the letter of credit transactions involved. New value was given contemporaneously with the issuance of the letters of credit in the form of the extensions of credit by the beneficiaries of the letters. As a result, the 11 U.S.C. § 547(c)(1) preference exception was applicable.

The case at bar differs from these other letter of credit cases by one very important fact: the letter of credit in this case was issued to secure an antecedent unsecured debt due the beneficiary of the letter of credit. The unsecured creditor beneficiary gave no new value upon the issuance of the letter of credit. When the issuer paid off the letter of credit and foreclosed on the collateral securing the letter of credit, a preferential transfer had occurred. An unsecured creditor was paid in full and a secured creditor was substituted in its place.

---

10. "Transfer" means every mode, direct or *indirect,* absolute or conditional, voluntary or involuntary, of disposing of or parting with property or with an interest in property, including retention of title as a security interest and foreclosure of the debtor's equity of redemption. 11 U.S.C. § 101(50) (emphasis added). *See also* the Notes of the Committee on the Judiciary under 11 U.S.C. 101 ("The definition of transfer is as broad as possible.")

The district court upheld the bankruptcy court in maintaining the validity of the letter of credit issued to cover the antecedent debt. The district court held that MBank, the issuer of the letter of credit, could pay off the letter of credit and foreclose on the collateral securing it. We are in full agreement. But we also look to the impact of the transaction as it affects the situation of Blue Quail in the bankrupt estate. We hold that the bankruptcy trustee can recover from Blue Quail, the beneficiary of the letter of credit, because Blue Quail received an indirect preference. This result preserves the sanctity of letter of credit and carries out the purposes of the Bankruptcy Code by avoiding a preferential transfer. MBank, the issuer of the letter of credit, being just the intermediary through which the preferential transfer was accomplished, completely falls out of the picture and is not involved in this particular legal proceeding.

MBank did not receive any preferential transfer—it gave new value for the security interest. Furthermore, because the direct and indirect transfers are separate and independent, the trustee does not even need to challenge the direct transfer of the increased security interest to MBank, or seek any relief at all from MBank, in order to attack the indirect transfer and recover under 11 U.S.C. § 550 from the indirect transferee Blue Quail.

We hold that a creditor cannot secure payment of an unsecured antecedent debt through a letter of credit transaction when it could not do so through any other type of transaction. The purpose of the letter of credit transaction in this case was to secure payment of an unsecured antecedent debt for the benefit of an unsecured creditor. This is the only proper way to look at such letters of credit in the bankruptcy context. The promised transfer of pledged collateral induced the bank to issue the letter of credit in favor of the creditor. The increased security interest held by the bank clearly benefitted the creditor because the bank would not have issued the letter of credit without this security. A secured creditor was substituted for an unsecured creditor to the detriment of the other unsecured creditors.

We also hold, therefore, that the trustee can recover under 11 U.S.C. § 550(a)(1) the value of the transferred property from "the entity for whose benefit such transfer was made." In the case at bar, this entity was the creditor beneficiary, not the issuer, of the letter of credit even though the issuer received the direct transfer from the debtor. The entire purpose of the direct/indirect doctrine is to look through the form of a transaction and determine which entity actually benefitted from the transfer.[11]

The fact that there was a prior security agreement between the issuing bank and the debtor containing the future advances clause does not alter this conclusion. As we

---

11. We have found only one prior case that has fully addressed the application of the direct/indirect doctrine in the context of a letter of credit transaction. *In re Air Conditioning, Inc. of Stuart,* 55 B.R. 157 (Bankr.S.D.Fla.1985), *affirmed in part, reversed in part* 72 B.R. 657 (S.D.Fla.1987) (currently on appeal to the Eleventh Circuit). In a carefully and thoroughly reasoned opinion, the court reached the same conclusion we reach in this case.

pointed out in Part II *supra,* this prior security agreement gave MBank an additional shield from preferential attack because of the relation back mechanism of 11 U.S.C. § 547(e)(2)(A). 11 U.S.C. § 547(e)(2)(A), however, does not avail Blue Quail to shield it from a preferential attack for the indirect transfer. The indirect transfer to Blue Quail occurred on May 6, 1982, when the letter of credit was issued and the increased security interest was pledged. This was the day before the involuntary bankruptcy petition was filed. For purposes of 11 U.S.C. § 547, a transfer of Compton's property for the benefit of Blue Quail did occur within 90 days of the bankruptcy filing. The bankruptcy and district courts erred in failing to analyze properly the transfer of debtor's property that occurred when Compton pledged its assets to obtain the letter of credit. This transfer consisted of two aspects: the direct transfer to MBank which is not a voidable preference for various reasons and the indirect transfer to Blue Quail which is a voidable preference.

All of the requirements of 11 U.S.C. § 547(b) have been satisfied in the trustee's preferential attack against Blue Quail. There was (1) a transfer of Compton's property for the benefit of Blue Quail (2) for an antecedent debt owed by Compton (3) made while Compton was insolvent[12] (4) within 90 days before the date of the filing of the petition (5) that enabled Blue Quail to receive more than it would receive under a Chapter 7 liquidation.[13] The net effect of the indirect transfer to Blue Quail was to remove $585,443.85 from the pool of assets available to Compton's unsecured creditors and substitute in its place a secured claim for the same amount.

The precise holding in this case needs to be emphasized. We do not hold that payment under a letter of credit, or even a letter of credit itself, constitute preferential transfers under 11 U.S.C. § 547(b) or property of a debtor under 11 U.S.C. § 541. The holding of this case fully allows the letter of credit to function. We preserve its sanctity and the underlying independence doctrine. We do not, however, allow an unsecured creditor to avoid a preference attack by utilizing a letter of credit to secure payment of an antecedent debt. Otherwise the unsecured creditor would receive an indirect preferential transfer from the granting of the security for the letter of credit to the extent of the value of that security. Our holding does not affect the strength of or the proper use of letters of credit. When a letter of credit is issued contemporaneously with a new extension of credit, the creditor beneficiary will not be subject to a preferential attack under the direct/indirect doctrine elaborated in this case because the creditor will have given new value in exchange for the indirect benefit of the secured letter of credit. Only when a creditor receives a secured letter of credit to cover an unsecured antecedent debt will it be subject to a preferential attack under 11 U.S.C. § 547(b).

---

12. There is a presumption that a debtor is insolvent at least 90 days prior to its bankruptcy filing. 11 U.S.C. § 547(f).

13. There was undisputed evidence below that the other unsecured creditors of Compton would receive less than fifty cents on the dollar for their unsecured claims.

V. *Liability of MBank for the Preferential Transfer*

Blue Quail has no valid claim against MBank for reimbursement for any amounts Blue Quail has to pay the trustee under the trustee's preference claim, just as the trustee has no preference challenge against MBank. Blue Quail received the preferential transfer, not MBank. MBank gave new value in exchange for the increased security interest in its favor. Thus, it is insulated from any assertion of a voidable preference. The bank in no way assumed the risk of a preference attack by issuing the letter of credit. For these reasons, we affirm the district court's dismissal of Blue Quail's request to proceed against MBank for reimbursement.

In addition, the trustee may not set aside the $1,463.61 fee Compton paid MBank to issue the letter of credit. This payment is not a preferential transfer. MBank has fully performed its duties under the terms of the letter of credit and has earned this fee. The services MBank rendered in issuing and executing the letter of credit constitute new value under the 11 U.S.C. § 547(c)(1) preference exception.

VI. *Conclusion*

Blue Quail Energy received an indirect preferential transfer from Compton Corporation on May 6, 1982, one day prior to the filing of Compton's bankruptcy petition. We reverse the district court and render judgment in favor of Trustee Kellogg against Blue Quail Energy, Inc. in the amount of $585,443.85 plus interest to be fixed by the district court pursuant to 11 U.S.C. § 547, 550. The district court's dismissal of Blue Quail's claim against MBank for reimbursement is affirmed.

REVERSED IN PART, AFFIRMED IN PART, AND REMANDED.

ON PETITION FOR REHEARING 835 F.2d 584

* * *

Our previous decision, *Matter of Compton Corp.*, 831 F.2d 586 (5th Cir.1987), remanded this case in order for the district court to determine the amount of interest due on the preference claim. We now hold that on remand the district court needs to make factual findings regarding the amount MBank actually foreclosed on and received from Compton Corp.'s trustee to cover the letter of credit transaction. In addition, the district court needs to determine the amount Blue Quail received from MBank under the letter of credit. The trustee states the amount paid to Blue Quail on June 22, 1982, by MBank totaled $569,932.03, rather than $585,443.85, the face amount of the letter of credit and the amount Compton owed Blue Quail. This is a difference of $15,511.82. Whether this amount was paid to Blue Quail on another occasion by MBank under the letter of credit, whether Blue Quail and MBank reached some kind of compromise on the amount, or whether Blue Quail received this amount directly from Compton Corp. are all factual issues that need to be resolved by the district court on remand.

Overall, the amount of the preference which Blue Quail has to pay over to the trustee, prior to interest adjustments, is limited to the value of the collateral MBank actually foreclosed on to cover the letter of credit transaction. This amount represents the dimunition of the assets in Compton's estate available to the unsecured creditors. This amount in turn is to be limited by the actual amount Blue Quail received from MBank under the letter of credit transaction.

REHEARING GRANTED.

ADDITIONAL REMAND TO DISTRICT COURT.

d. *In re Slamans*

IN RE SLAMANS
69 F.3d 468 (10th Cir. 1995)

Before BALDOCK, BRORBY, and LUCERO, Circuit Judges.
BALDOCK, Circuit Judge.

I.

The facts of this case are undisputed. Debtor operated gas stations. On December 4, 1990, First Capital loaned Debtor $750,000. In return, Debtor executed a revolving credit note and a security agreement granting First Capital a security interest in its accounts receivable. First Capital perfected its security interest in Debtor's accounts receivable by filing a financing statement on December 5, 1990. State of Oklahoma records reflect that First Capital holds a first priority perfected security interest in Debtor's accounts receivable.

On December 20, 1990, Debtor entered into a distributor agreement with Sun Company to purchase fuel for resale in Debtor's gas stations. As part of the agreement, Sun Company required Debtor to obtain a letter of credit. On February 6, 1991, First National issued an irrevocable standby letter of credit in favor of Sun Company in the amount of $200,000. The letter of credit provided that First National agreed to pay Sun Company for fuel that Debtor purchased under the distributor agreement. To secure its right to seek reimbursement from Debtor in the event Sun Company drew on the letter of credit, First National took a second priority security interest in Debtor's account receivables subordinate to First Capital's perfected security interest in the same collateral.

Under the distributor agreement with Sun Company, Debtor purchased fuel on credit and then resold it in Debtor's gas stations for cash or by credit card sales. Debtor sent the credit card charge slips to Sun Company who would in turn reimburse Debtor for the amount of the credit card purchases. If, however, Debtor owed Sun Company for fuel, the distributor agreement authorized Sun Company to setoff the amount it owed Debtor for credit card proceeds against the amount Debtor owed for fuel.

On February 28, 1992, Debtor filed for bankruptcy protection under Chapter 11 of the Bankruptcy Code.[14] Because Debtor had failed to pay Sun Company for fuel purchased under the distributor agreement, on March 9, 1992 Sun Company drew upon the letter of credit issued by First National in the amount of $192,433.15. On March 11, 1992, First National honored the letter of credit and paid Sun Company $192,433.15. At that time, Sun Company owed Debtor $111,053.41 from proceeds collected from credit card charge slips. That same day, First National demanded that Sun Company turn over the $111,053.41 in credit card sales proceeds in its possession. Debtor disputed First National's right to the credit card proceeds and asserted that it was entitled to the $111,053.41 in Sun Company's possession.

Sun Company did not release the money to either party. Instead, Sun Company filed an interpleader complaint with the bankruptcy court on May 8, 1992 to determine who was entitled to the $111,053.41 in credit card proceeds. CCF appeared in the case as successor-in-interest to First Capital and asserted an interest in the money. CCF and First National filed cross motions for summary judgment, each contending they had a superior right to the credit card proceeds. CCF argued that as holder of a first priority perfected security interest in Debtor's accounts receivable, its interest in the credit card proceeds was superior to all other claimants. First National asserted that it was entitled to the $111,053.41 under 11 U.S.C. § 509(a). Specifically, First National maintained that pursuant to § 509(a) of the Bankruptcy Code, it was subrogated to Sun Company's right under the distributor agreement to set-off the credit card proceeds in its possession against the $192,433.15 Debtor owed Sun Company for fuel.

The bankruptcy court entered summary judgment in favor of First National finding "that under the plain language of § 509(a), [First National] is entitled to be subrogated to the rights of Sun Company." *Sun Company, Inc. v. Slamans (In re Slamans)*, 148 B.R. 623, 625 (Bankr.N.D.Okla.1992). The bankruptcy court concluded "[b]ecause [First National] is subrogated to the rights of Sun Company, it is entitled to the full amount of the $111,053.41 Sun Company owes Debtor. Consequently none of the other claimants are entitled to the fund." *Id.* at 626. On December 16, 1992, the bankruptcy court ordered Sun Company to pay the $111,053.41 to First National.

14. On June 5, 1995, an involuntary bankruptcy petition was filed against Tom Slamans, Inc. The bankruptcy court consolidated the individual case and the corporate case for purposes of the instant controversy.

The district court affirmed the bankruptcy court's entry of summary judgment in favor of First National. *CCF, Inc. v. First Nat'l Bank & Trust Co. of Okmulgee (In re Slamans),* 175 B.R. 762, 765 (N.D.Okla.1994). The district court determined that because Debtor was liable to Sun Company under the distributor agreement, and First National was liable to Sun Company under the letter of credit, First National was "liable with" Debtor to Sun Company within the meaning of § 509(a). As a result, the district court determined that First National was subrogated to Sun Company's right under the distributor agreement. The district court therefore found that First National, pursuant to § 509(a), was entitled to the $111,053.41 because it had an interest in the credit card proceeds superior to CCF's first priority perfected security interest. *Id.* In so doing, the district court recognized that its ruling "is contra to what appears to be the majority position. . . . [that] an issuer of credit can *never* be eligible for Section 509 subrogation." *Id.* This appeal followed.

II.

CCF contends the district court erred in affirming the bankruptcy court's entry of summary judgment in favor of First National. CCF asserts that First National was not "liable with" Debtor on Sun Company's claim against Debtor for unpaid fuel under the distributor agreement because the obligations of Debtor and First National to Sun Company were wholly independent and separate. Specifically, CCF argues that First National's liability to Sun Company under the letter of credit was separate and distinct from Debtor's liability under the distributor agreement. Because First National and Debtor were separately liable to Sun Company, CCF contends First National was not "liable with the debtor" and therefore not eligible for subrogation under § 509(a).

* * *

A.

* * *

Section 509(a) of the Code governs subrogation in bankruptcy proceedings. Section 509(a) provides:

> **§ 509. Claims of codebtors**
> **(a)** Except as provided in subsection (b) or (c) of this section, an entity that is liable with the debtor on, or that has secured, a claim of a creditor against the debtor, and that pays such claim, is subrogated to the rights of such creditor to the extent of such payment.

11 U.S.C. § 509(a). Under the plain language of the Bankruptcy Code, an entity is subrogated to the rights of a creditor if it: (1) "is *liable with* the debtor on" (or has secured) (2) "a claim of a creditor against the debtor;" and (3) "pays such claim." *Id.* (emphasis added).

Section 509(a) refers to the entity that is eligible for subrogation "as a 'codebtor,' but includes entities that are jointly or secondarily liable, such as a surety, guarantor, or comaker." 3 *Collier on Bankruptcy* § 509.01 (Lawrence P. King ed., 15th ed. 1995). "Section 509 is based on the premise that the only rights available to a surety, guarantor, or comaker are contribution, reimbursement, and subrogation." *Id.*

B.

* * *

"'The essential function of [a letter of credit] is to assure a party to an agreement that he will receive the benefits of his performance.'" *Centrifugal Casting Mach. Co. v. American Bank & Trust Co.*, 966 F.2d 1348, 1350 n. 1 (10th Cir.1992) (quoting *Wood v. R.R. Donnelley & Sons Co.*, 888 F.2d 313, 317 (3d Cir.1989)). The Oklahoma Supreme Court recently ruled in *First State Bank v. Diamond Plastics Corp.*, 891 P.2d 1262, 1266 (Okla.1995), that "the Tenth Circuit properly construed the provisions of Article 5 of the Oklahoma version of the UCC" in *Arbest.* Consequently, we restate here a relevant portion of *Arbest* regarding letters of credit under Oklahoma law. Under the Oklahoma version of the UCC,

> a letter of credit involves three parties: (1) an issuer (generally a bank) who agrees to pay conforming drafts presented under the letter of credit; (2) a bank customer or "account party" who orders the letter of credit and dictates its terms; and (3) a beneficiary to whom the letter of credit is issued, who can collect monies under the letter of credit by presenting drafts and making proper demand on the issuer.

Arbest, 777 F.2d at 583 (citing Okla.Stat.Ann. tit. 12A, § 5-103(1))

* * *

"Once the letter of credit is issued, the issuer becomes statutorily obligated to honor drafts drawn by the beneficiary that comply with the terms of the credit." *First State Bank,* 891 P.2d at 1267 (quotations omitted). Title 12A, § 5-114(1) provides: "An issuer must honor a draft or demand for payment which complies with the terms of the relevant credit *regardless of whether the goods or documents conform to the underlying contract for sale or other contract between the customer and the beneficiary.*" Okla.Stat.Ann. tit. 12A, § 5-114(1) (emphasis added). As Professors White and Summers observe, the "bank's obligation to the beneficiary is *independent* of the beneficiary's performance on the underlying contract. Put another way, the issuer must pay on a proper demand from the beneficiary even though the beneficiary may have breached the underlying contract with the customer." White & Summers, *supra,* § 19-2, at 8; *see also Centrifugal Casting Mach. Co.,* 966 F.2d at 1352 ("[T]he issuer's obligation to pay on a letter of credit is completely independent from the underlying commercial transaction between the beneficiary and the account party."). "This has come to be known as the 'independence principle' because of the independence of the letter of credit from the underlying commercial transaction." *First State Bank,* 891 P.2d as 1267. Indeed, the independence principle is "the cornerstone of letter of credit law." *Kellogg v. Blue Quail Energy, Inc. (In re Compton Corp.),* 831 F.2d 586, 590 (5th Cir. 1987).

An issuer who honors a beneficiary's demand for payment on a letter of credit is entitled to the remedy of reimbursement from the account party. "Unless otherwise agreed an issuer which has duly honored a draft or demand for payment is entitled to immediate reimbursement of any payment made under the credit...." Okla.Stat.Ann. tit. 12A, § 5-114(3). However, "the issuer must honor a proper demand even though ... the insolvency of the account party renders reimbursement impossible." *Centrifugal Casting Mach. Co.,* 966 F.2d at 1352; *see also* White & Summers, *supra,* § 19-2, at 9 ("If ... the customer goes into bankruptcy after the letter has been issued, but before it has been drawn upon, the issuer must pay despite the fact that the customer will not be able to pay the issuer.").

C.

* * *

Although subrogation under § 509(a) of the Bankruptcy Code is clearly available to entities that are "liable with" the debtor such as sureties, guarantors, or comakers, *e.g.,* 3 *Collier on Bankruptcy* § 509.01 (Lawrence P. King ed., 15th ed. 1995), the bankruptcy courts disagree whether an issuer of a letter of credit is eligible for § 509 subrogation.[15] Under the plain language of § 509(a) of the Bankruptcy Code, an entity is

15. *Compare Beach v. First Union Nat'l Bank of North Carolina (In re Carley Capital Group),* 119 B.R. 646, 648 (W.D.Wis.1990) (holding that issuer of letter of credit was not eligible for subrogation under § 509(a) because it was not "liable with" the debtor but was independently liable to creditor) *and In the Matter of Agrownautics, Inc.,* 125 B.R. 350, 353 (Bankr.D.Conn.1991) (concluding that issuer of letter of credit is not entitled to subrogation under § 509(a) because "[i]ssuers are neither codebtors nor parties that have secured a creditor's claim") *and Berliner Handels–Und Frankfurter Bank v. East Texas Steel Facilities, Inc. (In re East Texas Steel Facilities, Inc.),* 117 B.R. 235, 240 (Bankr.N.D.Tex.1990) (holding that an issuer of a letter of credit may not be subrogated under § 509(a) because the issuer was not an entity "liable with" the debtor on a claim of a creditor against the debtor) *and Bank of America Nat'l Trust and Savings Ass'n v. Kaiser Steel Corp. (In re Kaiser Steel Corp.),* 89 B.R. 150, 154 (Bankr.D.Colo.1988) (holding that issuer of letter of credit was not entitled to § 509(a) subrogation because it "was the primary obligor [and therefore] was not liable 'with' [the debtor]") *with In re Valley Vue Joint Venture,* 123 B.R. 199, 204 (Bankr.E.D. Va.1991) ("We reject the *Kaiser* analysis and hold that where a standby letter of credit is used to support a loan from a beneficiary to the debtor, a confirming bank, by honoring the credit and thereby reducing the debtor's obligation to the beneficiary is 'an entity ... liable with the debtor' ... under 11 U.S.C. § 509(a) and has satisfied a debt for which it is not primarily liable under general equitable principles of subrogation.") *and In re Sensor Systems, Inc.,* 79 B.R. 623, 626 (Bankr.E.D.Pa.1987) ("[A] party issuing a letter of credit in favor of another is logically characterized as a 'guarantor' or 'codebtor' [and] ... [t]herefore ...

subrogated to the rights of a creditor if it "is liable with the debtor on . . . a claim of a creditor against the debtor, and that pays such claim." 11 U.S.C. § 509(a). First National's liability arose from the letter of credit, not from the distributor agreement between Debtor and Sun Company. Consequently, First National's independent obligation to honor Sun Company's demand for payment under the letter of credit did not render First National "liable with" Debtor on Sun Company's claim against Debtor under the distributor agreement within the meaning of § 509(a).

Further, when First National honored Sun Company's demand for payment under the letter of credit, First National did not "pay [ ] such claim" "of a creditor against the debtor" within the meaning of § 509(a). Specifically, First National did not pay Sun Company's claim against Debtor for unpaid fuel under the distributor agreement. Instead, First National fulfilled its own primary and independent obligation to honor Sun Company's demand for payment under the letter of credit.

* * *

Because First National did not satisfy the requirements of the plain language of the Bankruptcy Code, we hold First National was ineligible for subrogation under § 509(a). The district court erred, therefore, by affirming the bankruptcy court's summary judgment ruling that First National was eligible to be subrogated to Sun Company's right to setoff the credit card proceeds under the distributor agreement because it was "liable with" Debtor under § 509(a).[16]

We REVERSE the district court's order affirming the bankruptcy court's entry of summary judgment in favor of First National and REMAND to the district court with instructions to enter an order reversing the bankruptcy court's summary judgment ruling and remanding to the bankruptcy court for further proceedings.[17]

---

clearly within the scope of application of § 509(a). . . .)" *and In re Minnesota Kicks, Inc.*, 48 B.R. 93, 104–05 (Bankr.D.Minn.1985) ("[P]recluding the assertion of subrogation rights to issuers of standby letters of credit while allowing guarantors to assert them would be no more than an exercise in honoring form over substance.").

16. Our holding that First National is ineligible for subrogation under § 509(a) does not leave First National without a remedy. As an issuer of a letter of credit, First National has a statutory right to reimbursement from Debtor. *See* Okla.Stat.Ann. tit. 12A, § 5-114(3). We note that First National secured its right to reimbursement from Debtor by perfecting a second priority security interest in Debtor's account receivables.

17. As of the date of this opinion, the National Conference of Commissioners on Uniform State Laws and the American Law Institute have prepared a comprehensive revision to Article Five of the UCC that has not yet been adopted by any state. Section 5-117 of the revised Article Five grants issuers of letters of credit the remedy of subrogation. Section 5-117 provides in relevant part:

> (a) An issuer that honors a beneficiary's presentation is subrogated to the rights of the beneficiary to the same extent as if the issuer were a secondary obligor of the underlying obligation owed to the beneficiary and of the applicant to the same extent as if the issuer were the secondary obligor of the underlying obligation owed to the applicant.

U.C.C. § 5-117 (Proposed Official Draft 1995), *reprinted in* 3 James J. White & Robert S. Summers, *Uniform Commercial Code* § 26-15, at 213 (4th ed. 1995). Although the revised Article Five provides an issuer with the remedy of subrogation, the UCC does not determine the availability of subrogation in a bankruptcy proceedings. Rather, § 509 of the Bankruptcy Code governs an entity's eligibility for subrogation in

D. FRANCE

1. Cases

a. BFCE

Court of Cassation
Banque française du commerce extérieur (BFCE)
c. S.A. Rhône-Mérieux
Judgment of June 7, 1994
66 J.C.P. Jur. 22311. (1994).

The Court,

Considering that, according to the judgment under attack, the Banque Française pour le Commerce Extérieur (BFCE) issued a counterguaranty for the benefit of the Saudi bank Al Bank Al Saudi (Al Bank) which on the same day executed a guaranty on first demand to the Ministry of Agriculture and Waters of Saudi Arabia (MAW) to secure the bid of the Société Rhône-Mérieux for the procurement of a laboratory; that the undertaking of the BFCE, given originally until March 3, 1989, was extended upon request of the Al Bank until July 16, 1990; that at the beginning of June 1990, BFCE was called by Al Bank either to extend its guaranty or to pay the amount and received the instruction from the Société Rhône-Mérieux to reduce the amount of the guaranty; that on May 29, 1991 Al Bank notified BFCE of MAW's refusal to reduce the amount of the guaranty; that on June 4, 1991 the Société Rhône-Mérieux sued BFCE and Al Bank before the Judge for Emergency Matters for the issuance of an injunction against BFCE prohibiting it to pay the amount demanded; that on June 14 BFCE paid the amount of the counterguaranty and debited with it the account of the Société Rhône-Mérieux; that this company asked the Judge for Emergency Matters to condemn BFCE to restore this sum;

Upon the first assignment of error, taken in its first branch: In view of Article 873 of the New CCP:

Considering that in order to hold that the Judge for Emergency Matters has jurisdiction, the judgment below maintains that the deprivation of a sum of 500,000 francs constitutes an imminent peril;

Considering that by so holding, although the Judge for Emergency Matters cannot order the restoration of a sum to the account party who has been deprived of it due to the payment of a guaranty on first demand, except in the case of fraud or manifest abuse, the court of appeal has violated the above mentioned provision;

---

a bankruptcy proceeding. Thus, the effect of the revised § 5-117 on § 509 subrogation is presently undecided, and suitable for resolution by a future court.

Upon the first assignment of error, taken in its second branch: In view of Article 873 of the New C.C.P.;

Considering that in order to hold that the Judge for Emergency Matters has jurisdiction, the judgment holds that the bank's conduct was illegal when it made a payment of the counterguaranty during the pendency before the Judge of Emergency Matters of a demand to enjoin it;

Considering that by so deciding, although even after commencement of the suit before the Judge for Emergency Matters, the Bank remained obliged to pay the counterguaranty, the appellate court has violated the provision mentioned above;

And upon the second assignment of error, taken it first branch: In view of Article 1134 of the Civil Code;

Considering that in order to condemn BFCE to restore to the Société Rhône-Mérieux the sum charged to its account, the judgment held that the call on the guaranty had a manifestly abusive character because the initial offer of the Société Rhône-Mérieux had not been maintained and a new offer in a lower amount had not yet led to an acceptance and, therefore, the guaranty had become without object and no new guaranty had been issued to the Ministry of Agriculture and Water.

Considering that in relying exclusively on reasons inherent to the underlying contract without defining the manifest abuse or fraud that Al Bank committed by calling on the counterguaranty, the court of appeal did not give a legal basis to its decision with respect to Article 1134 of the Civil Code.

Therefore, and without need to pass on the second branch of the second assignment of error,

Sets aside and annuls in all of its provisions the judgment of the Court of Appeal of Lyon of March 23, 1992 . . . and remands the case to the Court of Appeal of Chambéry.

b. Billet

Court of Cassation (Com.)
Spouses Billet et al. c.
Caisse Régionale de Crédit Agricole du Gers.
Judgment of May 10, 1994.
Le Quotidien Juridique, July 19, 1994, p. 6.

Upon the single assignment of error taken in its second branch: Based on Articles 1134 and 2011 of the Civil Code:

Considering that, according to the judgment under attack, the spouses Billet and the Groupement Agricole d'Exploitation en Commun de Saint-Pierre sold real estate to the Société civile immobilière de Mazet; that they brought an action against the Caisse Régionale de Crédit Agricole du Gers (the bank) for payment of the balance of the purchase price, for which it had become a surety for the purchaser; that the judge for summary cases, before whom it was maintained that the purchaser had sued the sellers for annulment of the transfer, rendered judgment against the bank;

Considering that in order to affirm this decision, the judgment of the court of appeal stated: 'that the notarized document of February 15, 1990 (annexed to the authenticated sales contract of February 16, 1990) which provided the payment guaranty of the Crédit Agricole bears the caption "bank suretyship" but stipulates expressly: "the payment of the purchase price will be made upon the first demand by the creditor after the expiration of a period ending on December 16, 1990, upon default by the principal debtor on that date. After the expiration of a period of two months following that date, the present agreement shall terminate and lose its effect without cancellation or return of the document;" that the authenticated sales contract between the individuals, the G.A.E.C. and the S.C.I. provided in the paragraph on the "guaranty of the payment of the balance of purchase price", on the one hand that the spouses Billet have noted and accepted the conditions of the notarized document dated the day before; and on the other hand that the sellers, the spouses Billet, "in consequence of the bank suretyship supplied by the purchaser", expressly waive the vendor's lien and the right to rescission and declare in addition that they have been informed by the notaries that in the event of a failure to pay the balance of the purchase price, they can only sue the bank; "that the combination of these elements should by a simple reading thereof (the phrase "first demand", waiver of the other guaranties, designation of the bank as the only person subject to an action after December 16, 1990, etc.) reveal clearly the intent of the parties to consider the undertaking of the bank as an irrevocable guaranty during the time limits of its validity, independent of the underlying contract which offered the guaranties which the sellers waived by reason of the undertaking of a professional lender;'

Considering, that by so holding, although it did not result from its findings that the spouses Billet and the G.A.E.C. Saint Pierre on the one hand, and the bank on the other hand, agreed that the guaranty in issue should be autonomous in relation to the underlying sales contract, and that therefore, the bank could not raise against the beneficiary a defense based upon the nullity of the sales contract, the appellate court has violated the provisions cited above.

FOR THESE REASONS, and without passing on the ground asserted in the first branch: invalidates and annuls in all its provisions the judgment rendered on November 23, 1991 in the litigation between the parties by Court of Appeal of Agen.

NOTES

1. As in other countries, in France, too, the classification of a writing as an autonomous guaranty on first demand or as a guaranty permitting defenses based on the nullity of the underlying contract has created difficult questions of interpretation. See annotation to the text-case by J.P.D. in 57 *Le Quotidien Juridique* 6 (1994).

2. Guaranties on first demand may be written in various forms and with varying consequences, such as justified guaranties on first demand or conditional guar-

anties on first demand. Cf Thierry de Galard, *Comparison du crédit documentaire et de la garantie payable à première demande,* 89 *Les Petites Affiches* 17 (1994).

3. Likewise, as in other countries, in France, too, the account party may recover from the beneficiary, on the basis of unjust enrichment, amounts which the latter has collected from the guarantor without legal entitlement thereto and with which the account party was debited. Cf. e.g. Court of Cassation (Com.) Judgment of June 21, 1994, 68 *Le Quotidien Juridique* Nr. 80 p. 2.

c. Tengor

Court of Cassation (Com.)
Société de droit européen Tengor Inc. et al. c.
Société Melair Prestige et al.
Judgment of November 6, 1990
Bull. Civ. 1990 IV 258; 65 J.C.P. II 21630 p. 41 (1991).

Upon the sole assignment of error examined in its four branches,

Upon examination of Art. 1134 Civil Code,

Considering,

that the Société Tengor Inc. (*Société Tengor*), in charge of the distribution of the tickets for the Festival of Israel, awarded to the Société Melair Prestige (*Société Melair*) the exclusive right to sell tickets in France; that upon the order of the latter company the bank Leumi Le Israel (*Bank Leumi*) has obligated itself vis-à-vis the Société Tengor to pay to it upon first demand, formulated between March 1 and 10, 1988, a specified sum; that the Société Tengor, having procured a loan from the firm Société AWT Internationale Handels-und Finanzierungs AG (*Société AWT*), assigned to this bank as security its rights and claims derived from the guaranty on first demand, and obligated itself to supply to AWT a signed letter, addressed to the Bank Leumi and demanding payment of the guaranty; that the guaranty was drawn upon on March 1, 1988; that the assignment of the guaranty was notified to the Bank Leumi on March 15, 1988;

that meanwhile the Société Melair summoned the Société Tengor and the Bank Leumi to appear before the Judge for Urgent Matters with the request to suspend the effect of the guaranty;

that the Judge for Urgent Matters dismissed the request for suspension but enjoined the Bank Leumi from paying the guaranty except against delivery by the Société Tengor of a bank suretyship in the same amount; that the Société Tengor and the Société AWT summoned the Société Melair and the Bank Leumi before the Judge for Urgent Matters, requesting that the prior decision be rescinded and the Bank Leumi be ordered to pay the amount of the guaranty; that the Judge for Urgent Matters announced that he would not modify or rescind his prior order and not pass on the demands for payment made by the firms Tengor and AWT;

Considering,

that the court of appeal, although finding fraud, dismissed the demand of the companies Société Tengor and Société AWT for immediate payment of the guaranty and conditioned the payment on the delivery by the Société Tengor of a bank suretyship in the same amount;

Considering

that in so ruling, although it could only either suspend the payment of the guaranty because of the fraud or deny the suspension without attaching modalities to that decision, the court of appeal has violated the provision cited above;

For these reasons, the Court

Vacates and Annuls in all its dispositions the judgment rendered between the parties on September 23, 1988, by the Court of Appeal of Paris and remands the case to the Court of Appeal of Versailles.

Opinion of Mr. Michel Jéol, Advocate General

The 'guaranty on first demand' which prompted this litigation would have been quite unexciting, had the Judge for Urgent Matters not, in a quite unusual manner, conditioned its payment on the furnishing of a bank suretyship in the same amount by the beneficiary.

Within the framework of the preparations of the Festival of Israel — which was to take place in May-June, 1988 — the Société Tengor, in charge of the distribution of the tickets, awarded in October 1987 the exclusive sales rights for France to the firm Société Melair. On its part the Société Melair was obliged to sell a minimum number of tickets and to supply the Société Tengor, in payment of its obligation with a guaranty on first demand in the amount of $ 750,000 — which was issued by the Bank Leumi.

Even though the letter of the undertaking of the Bank Leumi stipulated that it was 'neither negotiable nor assignable' the Société Tengor in December 1987 assigned to the firm Société AWT, as security for a loan which it had taken out in order to finance the promotion of the festival, the claims and rights flowing from the guaranty on first demand of which it was the beneficiary and promised to remit to the lender a letter addressed to the bank and drawing down the guaranty.

As the Société Melair had not paid the sums stipulated in the original contract at their due date the bank guaranty was regularly drawn upon on March 1, 1988, by the Société Tengor — although it is not quite clear whether it utilized for that purpose the letter promised to the Société AWT. However that may have been, on March 15, 1988, the lender notified the bank of the assignment of the claims which was agreed upon by the Société Tengor.

In the meantime the Société Melair, fearing the cancellation of the Festival of Israel, went before the president of the commerce court as Judge of Urgent Matters, who, on March 4, 1988, rendered an order refusing to suspend the guaranty on first demand, but enjoining the bank from honoring it, except upon delivery by the Société Tengor of a suretyship in the same amount.

When the Société Tengor and the Société AWT addressed in turn the Judge of Urgent Matters, the latter issued a second order in which he refused to revoke the first order and stated that there was no urgency to pass on the demands of payment presented by the applicants.

With its judgment of September 23, 1988 the court of appeal, joining the two procedures, affirmed the two ordinances. * * *

As a bottle which is half filled may be viewed as being half full or half empty, according to the angle from which it is viewed, in just the same way, there exist two ways to read the judgment under attack: either one takes the view that the court of appeal by subordinating the honoring of the guaranty to the furnishing of a security in the same amount has in effect suspended de facto the normal operation of the guaranty; or, conversely, one estimates that the court has not suspended the guaranty, but has merely taken a protective measure in the interest of the debtor-customer in application of Art. 489 of the New Code of Civil Procedure. * * *

The first way of reading the order is evidently that of the petition presented to you jointly by the Société Tengor and Société AWT, which blames the judgment under attack for having refused the normal collection of a guaranty on first demand by reason of an imputation of fraud to the beneficiary.

In so doing, petitioners invoke principles which, despite certain fluctuations, are today admitted by your jurisprudence: Because the guaranty on first demand is largely independent of the underlying contract, the nullity or non-performance of the latter are without influence on its being drawn upon, except in strictly circumscribed cases of fraud and manifest abuse.

In order to show that in the instant case the court of appeal has mistakenly referred to the notion of fraud, the petition — borrowing the tactic of Horatius to triumph over the Curatii — cuts the reasons of the judgment in two, and attacks them separately.

It focuses to begin with — in the first three branches of their single assignment of error on a reason which appeared decisive in the mind of the judges on the merits: by assigning the guaranty of which it was the beneficiary, the Société Tengor violated the stipulations in the letter of undertaking by the Bank Leumi and 'such a modification of the conditions of the resort to the guaranty was made in fraud on the party who had ordered the issuance and which did not assent thereto.'

Like the authors of the petition for cassation, I do not believe that this reason is justified because one could reasonably think that the prohibition against transfer or negotiation contained in the letter of credit did not bar an assignment of the rights *acquired* by Tengor after March 1, 1988, when it drew upon the guaranty.

The brief of the petitioners observes, moreover, that this solution is already accepted in the closely related area of documentary letters of credit . . . At any rate, even if one considers the disputed assignment by the beneficiary of its claim to be violative of the provisions of the bank's letter of undertaking, it is hard to see in what respect it constitutes a fraud against rights of the party ordering the letter.

The petition finally — in the last branch of the assignment of error — criticizes the reasons drawn from quite different 'factual circumstances' which confirm, according to the court of appeal, the disloyal character of the draw on the guaranty: The Société Tengor, with its headquarters in Geneva, did not disclose that it was subject to Panamanian law; it has utilized erroneous information in its publicity campaigns; finally, it has not given sufficient detail to the Société Melair to permit it to deliver the tickets.

Besides that these circumstances relate to the performance of the underlying contract of which the guaranty is independent, here again it is hard to see in what respect they constitute a fraud against the party ordering the issue of the guaranty.

In sum, even if one — renouncing the tactic of Horatius — lumps all the arguments of the court of appeal together, it seems that the criticized reasons remain far below the standards which are required of the judge should he make the grave decision to block the normal operation of a guaranty on first demand because of fraud or manifest abuse.

Moreover, in the instant case, was there a veritable blocking? * * *

Turning to the second way of reading the order under attack, the way which is selected by the brief of the bank to avoid the grievances of the petitioners, although it also may result in a vacating of the judgment below: the Judge of Urgent Matters has limited himself, as Art. 489 of the New Code of Civil Procedure empowers him to do, to condition the payment of the guaranty on first demand — which he ordered — on the furnishing by the beneficiary of security, designed to protect the party, ordering the issuance, in the case that the judge on the merits finds that the guaranty was drawn upon without just cause.

Certainly, the Judge of Urgent Matters is vested by the law, and not only by Art. 489 of the New Code of Civil Procedure, with broad powers of prevention, precaution or relief which permit him, in a case of urgency, to take care of all kinds of situations. But his intervention, as useful as it may be, must not lead him to immerse himself too deeply in the mechanism, the institutions or the contracts which prompt the resort to him. Otherwise he would run the risk, in an untimely manner, to distort their nature, to overturn their economic operation or to modify their scope.

The controversy that is pending before you reveals perfectly this risk of 'tinkering;' to decide that a guaranty on first demand is not suspended but that it cannot be drawn upon except against the furnishing of a security in the same amount, is, as Professor Vasseur in his comment to the judgment under attack has noted (D. jur. 157 (1989)), to talk out of both corners of the mouth, but it is also to distort a practice widely used in the world of commerce to render relations of international character more secure, to breach a logic that was meant to be rigorous; to reduce an efficacy believed to be assured.

Such use of article 489 of the New Code of Civil Procedure ought to be prohibited — as were abandoned the attempts made by some jurisdictions to attach the amount of the guaranties on first demand out of the same concern for the protection of the rights of the party procuring the guaranty. * * *

In conclusion you have the choice between two ways of vacating the judgment under attack, corresponding to the two ways of reading it.

The first, based on the second and fourth branch of the petition, would censor the court of appeal for not having sufficiently characterized the manifest fraud which may, by way of exception, warrant the blockage of the guaranty;

The second would impose a sanction against the denaturation of the guaranty on first demand; it would be based on the assignment of error in toto — of which the different branches indirectly pose the question without formulating it explicitly.

I invite you to adopt the second solution because it would correspond exactly to what the judges have decided and because it would clearly prohibit that approach.

d. Konutbank

Court of Cassation (Com.)
Konutbank c. Banque Byblos-France
Judgment of February 19, 1991
65 J.C.P. II (Jur.) No. 21670, p. 161 (1991).

The Court;

Considering, that, according to the judgment under attack (Court of Appeal of Paris, January 27, 1989), Mr. Diab, when concluding a contract for supplies with a Turkish exporter, obtained from the latter the issuance of a bank guaranty characterized as 'irrevocable' and 'on first demand,' notwithstanding any denial on the part of the seller, in the case where 'the latter' did not comply with all the terms and conditions . . . ; that this guaranty was accorded to him by the Bank Byblos-France, which itself was the beneficiary of a counter-guaranty with identical stipulations by the Bank Anadolu which was succeeded by the Bank Turkiye Emlak Bankasi Anonim (*Konutbank*); that in January 1985, M. Diab called the guaranty, specifying that the supplier had failed to perform his obligations; that the Bank Byblos had paid him the stipulated amount; but that the counter-guarantor bank refused to reimburse that sum;

Upon the first assignment of error, examined in its two branches;

Considering that the Konutbank faults the judgment below because it condemned petitioner to pay the amount agreed upon in the counterguaranty, even though, according to the petition, on the one hand, it had imposed as a condition of its irrevocable guaranty that all the terms and conditions of the letter of credit were met and that all requisite documents were submitted; that it had, actually, written that it obligated itself 'to pay to you the amount on first demand not withstanding any denial by the seller in the case that our customer did not comply with all terms and conditions, as well as in the case that the documents required in your letter of credit were not presented by us to your bank in conformity with the terms of the letter of credit'; that by expressing the view that the clause, whereby payment would be forthcoming in the case that not all the terms and conditions stipulated in the letter of credit were satisfied, could not have the effect of suppressing the obligation to pay on first demand regardless of the denials by the seller, but was designed to require the beneficiary to rely on this non-performance in formulating its demand for honoring the guaranty, the court of appeal had distorted the clear and precise meaning of the guaranty and violated Art. 1134 C.C.; and, on the other hand, that after noting the inclusion in the contract of a clause to the effect that payment would be made in the case that not all clauses and conditions stipulated in the letter of guaranty are satisfied, by stating that this clause could not have the effect of suppressing the obligation to pay on first demand regardless of contestations by the seller but was designed to define its demand for the guaranty, and by deducing therefrom that an autonomous guaranty on first demand was in issue, the court of appeal failed to draw the proper legal consequences from its own findings and violated Art. 1134 C.C.; — but considering that in holding that the clause specifying that the counter-guaranty would be honored if not all clauses and conditions stipulated in the letter of credit, were satisfied did not have the effect to suppress the obligation to pay on first demand without regard to the denials of the seller, but had the sole purpose to obligate the beneficiary to invoke the non-performance of its obligations by its co-contracting party as grounds for calling the guaranty, the court of appeal has correctly applied the law of the parties: that the assignment of error is without merit in any of its branches;

Upon the second assignment of error, examined in its three branches —

Considering, that the Konutbank claims also to be aggrieved by the judgment because it ordered it to reimburse the Bank Byblos because the underlying contract could not be carried out due to the conduct of the Turkish exporter upon whose order it had obligated itself, although, according to the petition, on the one hand, because the sale was FOB, it was the duty of the buyer to take delivery of the goods on the specified date; that by declaring that Konutbank had not furnished any document showing that the exporter was able to dispose of a sufficient quantity of the merchandise on the specified date or that the exporter had made a genuine offer of delivery or had sent a notice of default in taking delivery before the expiration of letter of credit but had merely presented a certificate stating that the steamer Eighteen Venture, designated by Mr. Diab for the transportation was not in the port of Mersin between November 25 and 30, 1984, and by concluding therefrom that the delivery could not take place solely because of the exporter's conduct, the court of appeal has violated Arts. 1134 and 1147 et seq. C.C.; and although, on the other hand, the agreements legally concluded operate as law for those who have made them; that by noting that the furnisher of the vessel, designated by Mr. Diab for the carriage explained in a telex to the Konutbank the absence of the vessel with the refusal of the exporter to confirm the loading on the envisaged date if he did not receive a bill of lading dated the next day, the court of appeal, which had declared that the loading had to take place before November 30, 1984, and which concluded from the necessity of a bill of lading dated as of the same date that the delivery could not be made solely because of the conduct of the exporter, did not draw the legal consequences from its own findings and therefore violated Articles 1134 and 1147 et seq. C.C.; and although, finally, agreements legally concluded operate as law between those who have made them; that by having noted that the telex of the furnisher of the vessel also certified that the Turkish exporter refused to load the goods in containers, despite the consent of Mr. Diab, under the pretext that the documentary letter of credit did not contain a clause to that effect and by having concluded that the delivery did not take place because of the sole act of the exporter, the court of appeal, which in doing so, had indicated that the demand of the furnisher of the vessel with the consent of the buyer, was in contradiction to the documentary letter of credit and which nevertheless had deduced the sole responsibility of the Turkish exporter for the non-performance of the contract, has not drawn the legal consequences from its own findings and has violated Articles 1134 and 1147 et seq. C.C.;

But considering that, after having determined that the Turkish supplier of Mr. Diab had itself recognized that it was impossible for it to assure the delivery on the date agreed upon and that this omission was confirmed by the Société Générale de Surveillance, the judgment found that the non-performance of the contract was not imputable to Mr. Diab; that in this state of these findings the court of appeal could decide that the calling of the guaranty was neither abusive nor fraudulent; that the assignment of error is therefore without merit in any of its branches —

For these reasons dismisses the petition.

NOTES

1. *Konutbank v. Banque Byblos-France,* which involves the integration of a counter-guaranty, is commented upon by Professor Vasseur in 65 J.C.P. Jur. Nr. 21670 p. 161 (1991).

2. The case illustrates the frequent situation in which the principal bank issuing a standby letter of credit is secured by a counter-guaranty or back-to-back (back-up) standby letter of credit by a second bank, issuing the second letter upon the order of its customer.

3. In the instant case three instruments existed:

(i) A documentary letter of credit, issued for the benefit of the Turkish exporter of a cargo of red lentils;

(ii) A guarantee on first demand issued by Bank Byblos for the benefit of the purchaser (Mr. Diab), in French called '*guarantie de premier rang*' (principal standby letter of credit); and

(iii) A back-to-back or back-up standby letter of credit issued by Konutbank.

The counter-guarantor who has issued a guaranty on first demand must pay unless calling the counter-guaranty is in itself manifestly fraudulent or abusive, e.g. because of collusion between the beneficiary and the issuer of the *guarantie de premier rang*. Cf. Cour. Cass. (Ch. Com.), *Compagnie des signaux et équipements électroniques c. Banque nationale de Paris*, February 5, 1991. Bull. Civ. 1991 Part IV p. 33.

e. *Rafidain*

Court of Cassation (Com.)
Rafidain Bank c.
S.A. Crédit Industriel et Commercial (C.I.C.) et autre
Judgment of January 24, 1989
64 J.C.P. II Nr 21425 (1990).

The Court — Upon the sole assignment of error, considered in its two branches.

Considering that the findings of fact of the judgment under attack (Paris, April 2, 1987) show that the company 'Air Industrie' concluded with the government of Iraq a contract to furnish a bakery; that upon the order of Air Industrie, the Crédit industriel et commercial de Paris (*C.I.C.*) requested, upon its counterguaranty, the Rafidain Bank to issue a guaranty upon first demand in a specified amount for the benefit of the Iraqi customer; that the guaranty and the counterguaranty were extended several times, the last time until December 31, 1984; that on October 8, 1984, the Iraqi customer asked the Rafidain Bank to do what was necessary for a further extension; that on December 11, 1984, by a telex addressed to C.I.C., Rafidain Bank requested an extension of the guaranty until July 31, 1985 or payment; that on January 13 and February 27 it reiterated this request in identical terms; that Air Industrie brought a suit against C.I.C. and Rafidain Bank for a declaratory judgment stating that the guaranty and the counterguaranty lapsed on December 31, 1984 because they had not been extended or properly called on that date, and for an injunction prohibiting C.I.C. to debit Air Industrie's account with the amount of the counterguaranty and Rafidain Bank to pay the guaranty;

Considering that Rafidain Bank reproaches the court of appeal for having granted the complaint, although, according to the petitioner, on the one hand, the counterguaranty is an autonomous obligation both with respect to the primary guaranty and to the basic contract; that the court of appeal indicated that in the event of a call by the Rafidain Bank upon the counterguaranty, the latter, according to its text, would have to be paid by C.I.C. upon first demand; that by nevertheless deeming that C.I.C. was not obligated to Rafidain Bank except to provide reimbursement, conditioned upon a call upon the primary guaranty by the customer, the court of appeal has failed to draw the conclusions from its findings and thus has violated Art. 1134 of the Civil Code; and although on the other hand, the telex addressed by Rafidain Bank to C.I.C. on December 11, 1984 stated: 'we ask you to authorize an extension until July 31, 1985 or to pay the amount'; that C.I.C. thus was placed before a perfectly clear alternative: extend or pay; that by holding, nevertheless, that the telex of December 11, 1984 was only a demand for a preservation of the guaranties and not a firm and unequivocal call to honor them immediately, the court has distorted its clear and precise meaning and thus violated Art. 1134 C.C.;

But considering that it happened, because the court of appeal, relying on the letter of the customer and the telex sent by Rafidain Bank to C.I.C. which the court, in its free discretion, interpreted in a way that was necessary for their harmonization, that the court of appeal concluded that these documents constituted only a request for the preservation of the guaranties and not a firm and unequivocal call for their honor; that therefore the court for these reasons and without any distortion had justified its decision; that therefore the assignment of error is without foundation;

For these reasons rejects the petition.

NOTES

1. The text case illustrates the problems which arise if the issuer of a counter-guaranty is faced with a demand 'extend or pay' by the primary guarantor on first demand. See the commentary to the decision by Mattout and Prüm, 64 J.C.P. (éd. G.) II 21425 (1990).

2. Note that in this case the person obtaining the guaranties secured an injunction, although in cases where the guaranties have not expired injunctions against payment will only issue in cases of manifest abuse or fraud.

3. Professor Vasseur periodically publishes summaries with comments on cases (French and foreign) involving independent guaranties, see e.g. D. Somm. 233 (1992); D. Somm. 191 (1991); D. Somm. 195 (1990); D. Somm. 145 (1989).

4. A survey of the increasing use of guarantees on first demand may be found in Jean-Loup Courtier, *La Guarantie à première demande: une nouvelle sûreté pour les créanciers,* 61 *Les Petites Affiches* 4 (1994).

f. Le Couviour

Court of Cassation (Com.)
Société Le Couviour internationale c. Banque Indosuez
Judgment of February 19, 1991.
Bull. Civ. IV No. 76 (1991).

Upon the sole assignment of error:

Considering that, according to the judgment under attack (Rennes May 10, 1989), the Société *Bouygues* has concluded a deal with the Saudi company National Metal Industry (*NMI*) and required from the latter a guaranty of full performance (*garantie de bonne fin*) and a guaranty for the restitution of the advance, which were furnished by the Arab National Bank (ANB); that for the execution of this contract the Société NMI subcontracted with the Société Le Couviour internationale (*LCI*) and required from it the supply of a guaranty of full performance and a guaranty of the return of the advance; that upon the order of LCI the Banque Indosuez procured these guaranties from ANB which became the primary guarantor, the Banque Indosuez being the counter-guarantor; that upon the request of the Société NMI, ANB called the guaranties of Indosuez; that after the Banque Indosuez made the payment the Société LCI filed a complaint against it for annulment of the charge of its account, while the defendant in that action filed a counterclaim for payment directed also against the Société Le Couviour, which had become a surety for its subsidiary, that the judgment of the Tribunal de commerce which rejected the claim of the LCI and granted that of the Banque Indosuez was confirmed by the appellate court;

Considering that the judgment is under attack because it condemned the Société LCI and the Société Le Couviour as joint and several obligors to pay to the Banque Indosuez the sum demanded by it, although, according to the assignment of error, the court in discarding summarily the manifestly abusive and fraudulent call of the guaranties consisting of a guaranty of full performance and a guaranty of the return of the advance for the sole reason that the return of its guaranties by Bouygues did not prove that the Société LCI on its part had performed all of its obligation without examining whether this return did not furnish proof that the contract had not at least begun to be performed which demonstrated the manifestly fraudulent or abusive nature of the call of the guaranty of the return of the advance, the court's decision lacked the legal basis as required by Art. 1134 C.C.

But considering that by having held correctly that the undertaking of the Banque Indosuez, as counter-guarantor bank, was independent of the underlying contract, the court of appeal was not bound to engage in the examination invoked, since the claimed state of the performance of this contract even if established would not suffice to prove a fraud or manifest abuse in the calling of the counterguaranty; and that therefore the assignment of error is not well-founded.

For that reason,

Rejects the petition.

NOTE

This case and *Tengor* (*supra*) are commented upon by Professor Vasseur in D. Somm. Comm. 191, 199, 202 (1991). He explained that Société Bouyguies was engaged in the construction of 3 hospitals in Saudi Arabia and contracted with NMI to perform part of the work, furnishing guaranties on first demand for full performance and return of advances. The Arab National Bank (ANB) issued these guaranties. NMI in turn subcontracted with a French firm, Le Couviour International (ICI), furnishing a guaranty of first demand for full performance likewise by ANB, secured by a counterguaranty by Indosuez. NMI called the guarantee by ANB which in turn called the counterguaranty by Indosuez which paid.

A litigation between ICI and Indosuez ensues. ICI claims that Indosuez should not have paid because the calls on the guaranties were manifestly fraudulent as proved by Bouyguies' return to NMI of its guaranties. The Chambre Commercial of the Cour de Cassation sustains the rejection of this contention by the appellate court on the ground that the facts pleaded furnished no proof of any collusion between NMI and ANB in calling on Indosuez's counterguaranty.

E. SWITZERLAND

1. Caselaw

a. Federal Tribunal of Switzerland

Federal Tribunal of Switzerland
C.R. v. L.SA
Judgment of August 20, 1991
117 Arrêts du Tribunal Fédéral Suisse [ATF] III 76
(writ against illegal public action)

> [Facts not stated in the published part of the judgment: Respondent obtained an order attaching petitioner's rights under a bank guaranty on first demand. The Execution Office issued the attachment upon the request of respondent who was the customer upon whose demand the bank had issued the guaranty and who now claimed that petitioner had breached the contract which was the basis for the issuance of the guaranty. Petitioner sought relief in the Federal Tribunal by means of a writ against illegal public action (*recours de droit public*). The Court refused relief on the following grounds.]

5. The Court leaves undecided whether the beneficiary of a bank guaranty whose claim against the bank is attached upon the request of the customer who has ordered the issuance of the guaranty must institute an action denying the existence of a ground for the attachment (Art. 279 Execution Law) or proceed by means of a complaint to the cantonal Supervising Authority (Arts. 17 et seq. Execution Law) rather than by the writ against illegal public action.

6. *a*) The issuing bank has obligated itself in the case at bar 'within the meaning of the acceptance of a written order' (assignation) to make payment to the petitioner of the amount of the guaranty.

In the judgment Bank A. v. C-Bank of March 22, 1977 (cited by NOBEL, Praxis zum öffentlichen und privaten Bankenrecht der Schweiz, 387 et seq.) the Federal Tribunal has qualified a bank guaranty as acceptance of a written order to pay the named bearer of a writing within the meaning of Art. 468, par. 1 of the Code of Obligations [CO] although the text-writers are in their majority opposed to this kind of assimilation (cf. DOHM, Les garanties bancaires dans le commerce internationale, p. 65 nr. 98; GUGGENHEIM, Les contrats de la pratique bancaire suisse, 2d ed., p. 178/179;

KLEINER, Bankgarantie, 4th ed., p. 115 et seq.; SCYBOZ, Le contrat de garantie et le cautionnement, in Traité de droit privé suisse, A. VII/2, p. 29; but see SCHÖNLE, 'Missbrauch von Akkreditiven und Bankgarantien', in RSJ 79/1983, p. 57). The opinion expressed in that judgment must be harmonized with the cases which classify documentary letters of credit as a combination of accepted order to pay a named bearer of a writing and simple payment order (assignation and mandate), see ATF 114 II 48(a) and citations. With respect to an accepted order to pay the named bearer of a writing, which is the basis of a documentary credit (ATF 115 II 69), the bank which accords the credit accepts the order of a payment to a named recipient in a writing within the meaning of Art. 468 CO (KLEINER, 'Die Zahlungspflicht der Bank bei Garantien und unwiderruflichen Akkreditiven', RSJ 72/1976, p. 353; NOBEL, op. cit. 409; cf. ATF 114 II 49b). The terms utilized in the bank guaranty issued on August 27, 1990 are inconclusive; the text-writers actually subject the admissibility of protective measures to the same conditions for bank guaranties as well as for documentary letters of credit (cf. DOHM, op. cit. p. 150 nr. 329).

b) According to the petitioner, the parties in their basic agreement stipulated the issuance of a guaranty independent of the underlying transaction the payment of which could not be barred by any defense or objection. The respondent on the other hand contends that this was not the case. The guaranty was merely issued to de-block his goods detained in Spain. The parties therefore could not be considered as having agreed upon an independent guaranty.

It is necessary to examine the nature of the obligation undertaken by the guaranteeing bank. Indeed, if the guaranty is not independent but, to the contrary, accessory, the literature affirms that it would not be abusive to seek protective remedies affecting the amount of the security because the guaranty depends then upon the underlying relationship (GUGGENHEIM, op. cit. 2d ed. 191c; id. Die Verträge der schweizerischen Bankpraxis, 3d ed. p. 161). The dependent guaranty coalesces in that case with a suretyship within the meaning of Art. 492 CO (GUGGENHEIM, op. cit. 2d ed. p. 174, p. 5). In order to classify the undertaking in issue as independent guaranty or suretyship it is necessary to resort to interpretation (ATF 113 II 437c; ATF 111 II 279b), unless the text is completely clear (ATF 111 II 287) which is not the case at bar.

It must be noted at the outset that the guaranty was issued by a bank which constitutes an indicium of an autonomous undertaking (ATF 113 II 438c). The text of the guaranty refers 'to the performance of work for the rehabilitation of the shipyard of Alicante'. This reference to the underlying contract, however, standing alone does not always permit the conclusion that an accessory undertaking exists (DOHM, op. cit. p. 60 nr. 77). As Guggenheim (op. cit. 2d ed. p. 179) notes, even the independent guaranty is not always totally 'separate' from the underlying transaction. With respect to the phrase that the guarantor obligates itself 'irrevocably', it is not more determinative. Kleiner (op. cit. p. 51/52) remarks that this is a formula that is usual in bank practice and not always to be understood in the sense of a waiver to interpose defenses or objections flowing from the underlying relationship. The fact that the guaranteeing bank has obligated itself 'to pay on first demand' constitutes by itself only an indicium in favor of the existence of an independent guaranty that must be reinforced by other elements (VASSEUR, Garantie indépendente, in Rec. Dall./Sir. 1991 Somm. 191; see likewise KLEINER, op. cit. p. 46 et seq.). While the waiver of the guarantor to interpose 'any exception or objection whatsoever', according to the case-law (ATF 113 II 440d) does not necessarily constitute a reason to find an independent guaranty, the text-writers to the contrary attribute to that clause a decisive importance (DOHM, op. cit. p. 60 nr. 79; KLEINER, op. cit. 48/49; VASSEUR, op. cit. 191). Nevertheless it must be noted that in the case at bar the guaranteeing bank obligated itself 'in the sense of accepting a written order to pay the named bearer of a writing'. By virtue of the abstract character of an order to pay the named bearer of a writing (assignation) (cf. for the documentary letter of credit ATF 115 II 71a, 100 II 145, 4a) the acceptance within the meaning of CO Art. 468 has the effect of creating a new independent debt obligating the addressee of the order (ATF 92 II 338, 3). In the present case the guaranteeing bank obliged itself therefore to pay without ability to interpose defenses or objections based on the underlying contractual relation. Finally, securities furnished within the framework of an international contract, as in the instant case, are on principle contracts of guaranties rather than suretyship contracts (ATF 113 II 438, 2c).

Taken separately none of the elements of the guaranty in issue permits the Court to conclude that an independent guaranty exists. But their combination permits the Court to admit it at least prima facie.

7. The ability of the author of the order to request an attachment of the claims of the beneficiary to the payment of the amount of an independent guaranty with effect against the issuing bank is controversial.

a. The text-writers in their majority, though with different shades, express themselves against the admissibility of a request for attachment on the part of the party giving the order. They argue that, in stipulating the issuance such a bank guaranty or payment by means of an irrevocable documentary letter of credit, the parties to the underlying contract are bound by a *pactum de non petendo* prohibiting to impede in any fashion the payment to the beneficiary. The request of an attachment amounts therefore to a *venire contra factum proprium* [inconsistent conduct], in other words to an abuse of right (DALLÈVES, Exécution forcée dans les opérations d'accréditif in SAS 57/1985 p. 22; DOHM, op. cit. p. 153 nr. 340, [citations omitted]). Other authors, for whom the resort to a *pactum de non petendo* is not necessary, reach the same result on the basis of the purpose and the abstract nature of a bank guaranty. But among these authors, some do admit a request for attachment if the author of the order asserts a cause of action which is not rooted in the underlying contractual relation the performance of which the guaranty has the purpose of securing (DOHM, op. cit. p. 152 nr. 335; ROSSI, La garantie bancaire à premier demande, thesis Fribourg 1989 p. 139; . . .) * * * The rigor of the inadmissibility of protective measures requested by the author of the order is, however, tempered. By virtue of the principle *fraus omnia corrumpit* the author of the order is no longer bound by his anticipatory renunciation of his right to request such measures, if the beneficiary manifestly abuses the legal position which the guaranty confers upon him (DOHM, op. cit. p. 151, p. 330; cf. DALLÈVES, op. cit. p. 22).

The Federal Tribunal, until today, has not rendered a judgment on principle regarding that question. In its judgment in the *Finagrain* case of February 27, 1984 the Chamber for execution and insolvency took the view that the conduct of a buyer who, after having supplied a documentary letter of credit and caused the presentation of the documents to the confirming bank, obtains the attachment of the amounts which the latter must pay to the seller would run contra to the irrevocable order to pay which he gave (ATF 110 III 40 ab initio). It relied for that point on the opinions of GAUTSCHI, Berner Kommentar nr. 20 ad. Art. 407 CO and KLEINER, op. cit. RSJ 72/1976 p. 354. In its judgment *Union de Banques Suisses c. Finagrain* of March 24, 1986 (S.J. 108/1986, p. 529 et seq.) the First Civil Court first expressed the opinion that the independent character of a documentary letter of credit did not deprive the parties of the ability either to assert, as between themselves, claims derived from other legal causes (p. 532, nr. 2) or to request attachment of the sold goods or the documents of title representing them obtained upon payment of the amount of the letters of credit upon asserting claims derived therefrom (p. 533s nr. e.). Next, it has affirmed that one could not reasonably assume that in an international sales transaction (on account or with payment by means of a documentary letter of credit) the seller has on the whole shown his willingness to waive his entitlement to obtain an attachment of the goods sold in the case where there is a reason to do so. This view militates against the admission of an implied agreement to that effect (p. 534). It appears doubtful to assert, as it is done by TEVINI DU PASQUIER (Le crédit documentaire en droit suisse, thesis Geneva, Bâle 1990) that the Federal Tribunal meant to limit the scope of the latter pronouncement to the case where the cause of action because of which the attachment is sought flows from a legal relation other than that upon which the attached claim is based. * * *

Several authors, at any rate, are opposed to the dominant theory and admit the possibility of an attachment, upon request by the author of the order, of the amount of the guaranty even by reason of a cause of action flowing from the underlying contract (GUGGENHEIM . . . , GANI . . . , TEVINI DU PASQUIER. . . .) These authors contest even the principle of a *pactum de non petendo* which could result neither from a hypothetical intent of the parties nor the implied manifestation of intent on the part of the author of the order [citations omitted].

> [The court then lists the various reasons given by the text-writers why there are no good reasons to deny the party ordering the issuance of a bank guaranty the power to attach the rights of the beneficiary in the case of a breach of contract.]

b) In his request for an attachment, respondent alleged that two representatives of petitioner came to his headquarters on February 20, 1991 and that an oral agreement was concluded whereby petitioner waived its right to call the guaranty. Nevertheless, on the following day the two representatives went to the headquarters of the guaranteeing bank in order to claim the amount of the security. In his brief to the Federal Tribunal respondent qualified this conduct as fraudulent. Nevertheless, he did not assert a claim for damages because of a fraudulent call of the guaranty but rather because of non-performance of the construction contract and the seizure of his primary material in Spain. His claims are based clearly on the underlying contract. True, certain authors maintain that the beneficiary who abusively calls a guaranty has no right to assert against the bank, and that in that case the author of the order requests the attachment of a nonexistent claim (DOHM op.cit. p.53/4; SCHÖNLE, op.cit. p.76/77; TEVINI DU PASQUIER, op.cit. p.299). But this argument, though subtle, is debated (GANI . . . ; ROSSI. . . .) Moreover, the author of the order, who invokes in support of his demand for attachment a claim derived from the underlying contract because of default, non-performance or mal-performance of the beneficiary requires protective measures precisely to prevent his co-contractant from calling the guaranty, when his conduct violates his contractual duties.

c) According to the case law, a decision is not arbitrary merely because a solution other than that by the cantonal authority appears conceivable or even preferable (ATF 116 Ia 104 nr. 4a; ATF 115 III 130; ATF 114 Ia 27 nr. 3b; ATF 114 III 70 nr. 3). This single consideration in the case at bar suffices to reject the complaint of petitioner. The order under attack which can rely on the opinion of 'some good authors' (AUBERT, *Traité de droit constitutionel suisse,* Vol. II, p. 662) is not unsustainable. Neither is it arbitrary merely because it departs from the jurisprudence of the Federal Tribunal to the extent that one would deduce from the judgment in Finagrain (ATF 110 II 40), an pronouncement on principle against the admissibility of an attachment requested by the author of the order.

NOTES

1. Most courts confronted with the issue have held that a customer cannot prevent payment of a guaranty on first demand by garnishing the beneficiary's claim against the issuer.

2. Remember that the denial of the Federal Court to quash the attachment was due to its view that sustaining the attachment would have been unsustainable or arbitrary.

F. ITALY

1. Caselaw

a. S.A. Unione di Banche Svizzere c. Maxfin spa e Banca d'America e d'Italia

COURT OF CASSATION (Sez. I)
S.A. Unione di Banche Svizzere c.
Maxfin spa e Banca d'America e d'Italia
Judgment of October 6, 1989
40 Giustizia Civile I 731 (1990); 13 Banca e Borsa II 5 (1990).

[The factual background is summarized in Note 1 following the textcase.]

It is correct that the fundamental notion of the autonomous guaranty contract according to the scheme that has been formulated in the international commercial practice (especially under the labels garantie vertrag, performance bond, or guarantee bond) is individualized in the independence of the relation from that which is guaranteed, in as much as the guarantor (normally a credit institution or insurance company) obliges itself to render the guaranteed performance 'on first demand', following a simple declaration of the creditor-beneficiary which affirms that the non-performance or incorrect performance of the principal obligation has been verified, and without the possibility to raise defenses relating to the validity, effectiveness or vicissitudes of the underlying relation, notwithstanding objections against payment interposed with respect thereto by the debtor-account party or controversies in that regard.

On that rests the difference from the suretyship, the characteristic feature of which is the strict tie to the principal obligation in the double sense that the surety's performance is equal to that of the principal obligation * * * and that the obligation of the guaranty is legally accessory to that which is guaranteed, by the content and modifications of which it is influenced at the moment of its creation and throughout the course of the relation.

In the autonomous guaranty contract the independence from the basic relation, by contrast, renders the performance of the principal debtor and that of the guarantor to be qualitatively different, the guarantor being obliged to assure in any case that the creditor obtains a performance that is equal or equivalent to that which he should have received by virtue of the basic relation, so as to avoid or eliminate the prejudice flowing from the lack or incorrectness of a performance.

This also implies a different function of the relation which aims not only to guarantee the punctual performance of the underlying obligation, but also to place the risk of the lack, or incorrect performance thereof, on the guaranteeing bank; and therefore, it does not deal with an abstract transaction, because its cause consists precisely in the covering of the risk connected with an objective non-performance of the underlying obligation, an event which justifies the attribution of the monetary advantages to the beneficiary.

But this particular causal aspect evidences the limits of the autonomy of the contract in the sense that it remains functionally tied to the basic contract, which constitutes the necessary point of reference, because it constitutes the basis and measure of the economic interest for the protection of which the guaranty is ordered. * * *

In the controversy under examination, where the bank rendered punctual performance of the contract of guaranty by making payment of the amount demanded, the (delicate) problematic of the defenses which may be interposed by the guarantor in order to reject the call on the guaranty does not arise. For the purposes which are here of interest, it is, however, apposite to observe that in the factual setting noted here, the defenses of the guarantor regarding the non-existence or lesser scope of the right, which according to the assertions of the beneficiary is unsatisfied in whole or in part, are not internal to the basic relation — which serves merely as objective parameter of reference for the definition of the interest of the beneficiary which is actually to be protected — but rather appertain to the guaranty relation itself, on equal footing with the defenses drawn from the wording of the respective contract (such as an irregular declaration of the non-performance by the debtor or of another condition of the guaranty, omission of the presentation of documents, untimely call on the guaranty, etc.). It must, therefore, be admitted that a guarantor may legitimately refuse to pay a beneficiary who in reality has already received the performance stipulated in the basic contract, or who, if that performance is less than his demand, has not suffered the alleged economic loss, and that, therefore, the prerequisite for calling the guaranty does not exist, provided always that objective non-existence of the injurious fact which must be shown by the guarantor becomes prima facie evident in a certain and indisputable way. In other words, it involves situations in which the jurisprudence, including foreign jurisprudence, considers the call on the guaranty to be deceptive, fraudulent and abusive and holds that the demand of the creditor may be rejected on the ground of fraud or lack of fair dealing and good faith.

This being established, the bank, which in such a situation, nevertheless for whatever reason (which may also consist in the actual unavailability of 'certain and ready' proof) renders the performance stipulated in the guaranty, makes a payment objectively not owed and has the right to resort to the action for restitution pursuant to Art. 2033 C.C. directly against the beneficiary, apart from the possibility, also, to proceed for reimbursement against the debtor-customer.

If the payment, which is not owed within the ambit of the relation which connects the principal debtor and the creditor, nonetheless must be deemed to be owed 'on first demand' by virtue of the guaranty contract, the autonomy of which renders defenses based on the former inadmissible (non-performance, set-off, prescription, etc.), then there exists no instance of a performance without cause on the part of payor and the action for restitution does not belong to the bank—which could not refuse to make the payment—but rather to the debtor against whom the bank itself has a right of reimbursement.

Conversely, if the bank makes a payment to which it was not obligated by reason of the guaranty contract and which was not justified by another suitable cause for payment, standing to bring an action for restitution belongs to the bank the same as in any other hypothesis where the lack of indebtedness is founded on the wording of the guaranty.

> [On the basis of this view of the law, the Corte di Cassazione upheld the court below, which had rendered judgment against U.B.S. because it determined that the scope of B.A.I.'s guaranty was measured by Max Mayer's actual liability, which in turn, was reduced by the statutory withholdings, concluding]

According to the principles set forth above, the guaranteeing bank could have victoriously interposed an immediate rejection of the demand, since it resulted from the declaration of the demand itself that the alleged objective non-performance did not exist since it had already received the performance to which it was entitled.

By having made the payment, the B.A.I. has well initiated the action for restitution, inasmuch — as the appellate judge has held — for the reasons set forth, there existed no legal duty to provide performance, and therefore, in the absence of a cause for the payment, it is clearly a situation of objective non-indebtedness.

NOTES

1. In the text case, the Corte di Cassazione, Sez. I had to pass on an action for the restitution of unjust enrichment instituted by the Banca d'America e d'Italia (B.A.I.) against the S.A. Unione Banche Swizzere (U.B.S.), a Swiss corporation. B.A.I. had guaranteed the performance owed by Max Mayer, subsequently renamed Maxfin S.p.A., by executing a guaranty 'on first demand' and 'without the possibility of interposing defenses based on the underlying legal relation.' The guaranty called for application of Swiss law. Max Mayer's performance consisted in the repayment to U.B.S. of 'capital, interest and cost' of a loan. Max Mayer paid U.B.S. the owed amounts, but deducted the statutory withholding taxes from the interest as required by Italian law. U.B.S., dissatisfied with Max Mayer's refusal to pay the total of the interest, called the guaranty. B.A.I. despite objections by Max Mayer, paid the amount demanded, in Switzerland. Subsequently, B.A.I. brought the present action for restitution in Italy.

The Court of Appeal of Milan rendered judgment against U.B.S., holding that B.A.I.'s guaranty extended only to Max Mayer's actual indebtedness which excluded the statutory withholdings. U.B.S. petitioned the Corte di Cassazione for reversal of the judgment, arguing that the court below had erred in applying Italian law to the controversy rather than Swiss law, and by declaring that B.A.I.'s payment was a 'payment not owed' within the meaning of Article 2033 of the Italian Civil Code, rather than a payment owing under the guaranty on first demand.

The Corte di Cassazione rejected both arguments and affirmed the judgment below. As to the applicability of Swiss law, it held that the Swiss law on restitution of unjust enrichment would have controlled had the issue of payment in Switzerland been raised and proven in the court below. On the merits the Corte di Cassazione held that the scope of B.A.I.'s undertaking was commensurate to Max Mayer's actual liability and that therefore the payment by B.A.I. was not owed and thus recoverable by the action for unjust enrichment.

2. For extensive notes on this case see M. Costanza, *Contratto automnomo di garanzie e ripetizione dell'indebito,* 40 Giustizia Civile I 736 (1990); F. Mastropaolo, 13 Banca e Borsa II 553 (1990); M. Rescigno, *Pagamento a prima richiesta, limiti alla inopponibilità delle eccezioni e problemi probatori.* For a comparison with Swiss law see G. Portale, *Il contratto autonomo di garanzia nel diritto svizzero,* 13 Banca e Borsa II 37 (1990).

BIBLIOGRAPHY

Standby Letters of Credit and Guarantees on First Demand

Bergsten, E., *A New Regime for International Independent Guarantees and Stand-by Letters of Credit: The UNCITRAL Draft Convention on Guaranty Letters,* 27 International Lawyer 859 (1993).

Bertrams, R., *Bank Guarantees in International Trade* (1990).

Bonelli, F., *Le garanzie bancarie a prima domando nel commercio internazionale* (Milan 1990).

Bydlinski, P., *Moderne Kreditsicherheiten und zwingendes Recht,* 190 Archiv für civilistische Praxis 165 (1990).

Cicala, R., *Sul contratto autonomo di garanzia,* 37 Rivista di diritto civile 143 (1991).

Courtier, J.L., *La Garantie à première demande: Attention messieurs les bénéficiaires,* 75 Les Petites Affiches 4 (1994).

Dohm, J., *Bankgarantien im internationalen Handel* (1985).

Ib. Mesures provisionnelles et séquestre pour empêcher l'appel abusif d'une garantie bancaire sur demande, [1992] RDAI/IBLJ 887.

Dolan, J.F., *The Law of Letters of Credit: Commercial and Standby Credits* 2nd ed. (1991). Cumulative Supp. 1994.

Ib., Weakening the Letter of Credit Product: The New Uniform Customs and Practice for Documentary Credits [1994] RDAI/IBLJ 149.

Egger, W., *Probleme des einstweiligen Rechtsschutzes bei auf erstes Verlangen zahlbaren Bankgarantien,* 62 Schweizerische Zeitschrift für Wirtschaftsrecht 12 (1990).

Galard, T. de, *Comparison du crédit documentaire et de la garantie payable à première demande,* 89 *Les Petites Affiches* 17 (1994).

Goode, R., *Guide to the ICC uniform rules for demand guarantees* (1992).

Graf v. Westphalen, F., *Die Bankguarantie im internationalen Handelsverkehr* 2d ed. (1990).

Graham, G. & Geva, B., *Standby Credits in Canada,* Canadian Business Law Journal 180 (1984).

Hardenberg, L., *First Demand Guarantees: Abuses and Remedies under Dutch Law,* Int'l Bus. Lawyer 241 (1991).

Harfield, H., *Guaranties, Standby Letters of Credit and Ugly Ducklings,* 26 Uniform Commercial Code L.J. 195 (1994).

Hoffmann, *Die Garantie auf erstes Anfordern (garantie à première demande) im belgischen Recht,* RECHT DER INTERNATIONALEN WIRTSCHAFT 389 (1996)

Horn, N., *Bürgschaften und Garantien zur Zahlung auf erstes Anfordern,* 33 NJW 2153 et seq. (1980).

Horn, N., *Bürgschaften und Garantien, Aktuelle Rechtsfragen in der Bank-, Unternehemens und Aussenwirtschaftspraxis* 5th ed. (1991).

Horn, N. & Wymeersch E., *Bank-Guarantees, Standby Letters of Credit and Performance Bonds in International Trade,* in Horn ed., The Law of International Trade Finance 455-529 (1989).

Kleiner, B., *Bankgarantie* 3rd ed. (1979) (Swiss law).

Klötzel, T. R., *Third Party Security in Financial Transactions in Germany* I'l Business Lawyer (May 1994) 230.

Kozolchyk, B., *Bank Guarantees and Letters of Credit,* 11 U.Pa. J. Int'l Bus. L. 7 (1989).

Lesguillons, H., *Les garanties bancaires dans les contrats internationaux,* Colloque de Tours (1980) (containing reports from Germany, the Netherlands, Switzerland, Belgium, France, Italy, Spain and the U.K., and a general report by Vasseur.)

Pleyer, K., *Die Bankgarantie im zwischenstaatlichen Handel,* 27 Wertpapier-Mitteilungen [WM], Sonderbeilage Nr. 2/1973 zu Heft 27 (1973). (The seminal study of the early German practice and problems.)

Riesenfeld, S., *Recent Developments in the Law Relating to Letters of Credit,* Festschrift für E. von Cammerer 997 (1978).

Rives-Lange, J.L. & Contamine-Raynaud, M., *Droit Bancaire,* Secs. 661-687 (1987).

Schütze, Rolf A., *Das Dokumentenakkreditiv im International Handelsverkehr* 5th ed. (1999).

Simler, Ph. & Delebeque, Ph., *Chronique: Droit des sûretés,* 66 J.C.P. (éd. G.) I 3583 p. 222 (1992).

Tyree, A.L., *Banking Law In Australian* 1990, Sec. 11.25 et seq. (Discussion of standby letters of credit.)

Vasseur, M., *Garantie indépendente,* (guaranties on First Demand) D. Sommaires commentés 95, 107 (1993); *Ib.* 233 (1992); *Ib.* 191 (1991); *Ib.* 195 (1990); *Ib.* 145 (1989). *Ib., Les nouvelles règles de la chambre de commerce internationale pour les 'garanties sur demande'* [1992] RDAI/IBLJ 239 (with Eng. trans.)

Viale, Mirella, *Le Garanzie bancarie* (Milan 1994).

Voskuil, C., Parac, Z., Wade, J.A., *Credit and Guarantee Financing, Hague-Zagreb Essays on the Law of International Trade* (1987) (with essays on Belgian, Dutch and Yugoslavian law in particular:)

Hanzekovic, M., *Contracts Involving Bank Guarantees, Particularly Abstract Guarantees* (p. 33)
Vukmir, B., *Contracts Involving (Abstract) Bank Guarantees* (p. 53)
Bannier, F.A.W., *Bank Guarantees and Documentary Credit* (p. 65)
Wijmeersch, E., *Bank Guarantees on First Demand under Belgian Law* (p. 91).

Wald, A., *Algunos aspectos da garantia à primeira demanda no direito comparado,* 303 Revista Forense 7 (Brazil 1988).

Zohrab, P., *Significant Developments in letter of credit law* [1994] New Zealand L.J. 170.

7/Security for Performance by Comfort Letters

INTRODUCTION

Comfort letters (*lettres de confort, Patronatserklärungen*) are instruments used in international and domestic trade to facilitate the opening of a line of credit for the benefit of a subsidiary of the corporation issuing the letter. The letters employ a variety of formulae to indicate that the parent pursues a policy and will use its best efforts to enable the subsidiary to meet its obligations. Some forms of letters have been held to create merely a moral obligation, while others have been considered to be legally binding, entitling the addressee to damages for the breach of a legal duty. Accordingly, case law distinguishes between 'hard' and 'soft' letters of patronage.

Comfort letters have occasionally been classified as a species of letters of intent, although the principal use of letters of intent is the reduction into writing of terms tentatively agreed upon during the negotiation of complex transactions. In most countries, the nature and effect of comfort letters have been the subject of a copious literature (See *infra*).

A. GERMANY

1. Case

a. Judgment of January 30, 1992

BGH IX. Senate
Judgment of January 30, 1992
13 ZIP 340 (1992); 53 KTS 275 (1992); 46 WM 501 (1992).

FACTS

Plaintiff, a Viennese Bank, maintained current business relations with the firm of SBMW.-GmbH in L. Austria. This company is a wholly-owned subsidiary of PHB Weserhütte GmbH Vienna, which in turn is a wholly-owned subsidiary of defendant — a corporation domiciled in Cologne. Plaintiff had accorded SBM a credit of 25 million Austrian shillings. In order to secure augmentations of the credit, plaintiff was to receive a comfort letter [*Patronatserklärung*] from defendant. In August 1986 defendant transmitted to plaintiff a letter of this type, which substantially contained the obligation of defendant, in the case of a credit exceeding Aust.S 30 million up to an additional sum of Aust.S 10 million, 'to impel the subsidiary . . . to meet its obligations'. After discussion between SBM and plaintiff, defendant supplied plaintiff with a second comfort letter, dated November 10, 1986 containing, by way of an excerpt, the following wording:

> 'We have learned with our approval, that PHB Vienna's subsidiary, the firm of SBM, maintains business relations with you. . . .
>
> The firm PHB Vienna is a wholly-owned subsidiary of our firm and in turn owns 100% of the stock of SBM. . . . So long as the above-mentioned business relation with you continues, or you have any claims arising out of that relation against our subsidiary, we will maintain our participation for the same amount without change. Should we consider a change, we will contact you promptly and proceed in accord with your consent.
>
> In addition, we assume vis-à-vis you, the irrevocable and unqualified obligation, as long as the credit extended by you . . . is not fully repaid, to exert our influence on our subsidiary and to supply it with the necessary finances so that it is always able to meet its present and future obligations to you on time. This declaration is subject to Austrian law.'

On December 28, 1987, SBM became subject to bankruptcy proceedings. Plaintiff terminated the credit and filed a claim for a balance of Aust.S 18,545,418.99. The proceedings ended with a compulsory composition, in which plaintiff received 25% of its claim.

On December 30, 1987 defendant likewise became subject to bankruptcy proceedings. Pursuant to a confirmed composition of October 6, 1989, the liquidation was terminated. The composition provided satisfaction in the amount of 35%, payable in 3 installments.

On the basis of the comfort letter of November 10, 1986, plaintiff filed a claim of DM 3,110,453.03, which was contested by the trustee. Plaintiff demands payment in the amount of 35% of its claim filed in the bankruptcy proceedings, payable at the dates specified in the composition. Plaintiff succeeded in the two courts below to a large extent — ultimately in the amount of Aust.S 6,490,896. Defendant's petition for revision was rejected.

REASONS
I.

The court of appeal has held correctly and without challenge by the petition for review, that defendant is the proper party upon the termination of the bankruptcy proceedings (cites omitted).

1. It has concluded: That defendant was liable, pursuant to the Austrian General Civil Code (*ABGB*) § 920, because it failed to perform its obligations undertaken in the comfort letter agreement. This agreement was contracted between the parties. According to its terms, defendant undertook to provide the necessary means to SBM for the satisfaction of plaintiff's claims. The respective offer by defendant was accepted by plaintiff pursuant to § 863 ABGB. According to this provision, an acceptance may also be declared by means of such acts 'which under consideration of all circumstances leave no reasonable grounds for doubt'. * * * At the appellate stage, plaintiff was contending that defendant, according to the text of its comfort letter, did not expect an express declaration of acceptance. Silence upon the receipt of a written contract which conforms with prior oral negotiations was sufficient as a declaration of acceptance. * * *

The arguments of the petition for review are unconvincing. * * * The appellate court could * * * base its conclusion on the consideration that from the beginning, plaintiff conditioned credit in excess of a stated limit on the receipt of a comfort letter and maintained the grant of credit after the respective letter was received. Pursuant to § 863 ABGB, it has been held that the unprotested execution of a transaction under the conditions stipulated in an offer can be deemed to be the conclusion of a contract (OGH, ÖJZ 1968, 349, 350). Also under Austrian law, silence may constitute an acceptance, provided the offeree is benefitted by the contract (cites omitted).

The appellate court, upon consideration of all facts, concluded that plaintiff was exclusively benefitted by the comfort letter. * * * A stronger comfort letter than that of November 1986 could hardly be expected either under Austrian law (citations omitted) or under German law (citations omitted). Therefore the acceptance of the second, 'hard' comfort letter by plaintiff was highly probable. * * *

2. The appellate court assumed that the parties were in agreement with respect to defendant's obligation to provide funds to SBM as defendant's 'granddaughter company', rather than to the daughter company PHB Vienna, and that this followed from the first paragraph of the declaration. Further, that plaintiff had contended without contradiction that it had no business relations with PHB Vienna; that the designation 'daughter company' was only used to disclose the possibilities of exerting influence and power, and hence also covered SBM indirectly. Therefore, it found no dissent within the meaning of § 869 par. 2 ABGB. * * *

II.

The appellate court — relying on Aichinger QuHGZ 85, 88 (1978 Issue 4) — established that 'hard' comfort letters under Austrian law have the same effects as under German law. If the debt secured thereby was uncollectible, the issuer is liable for damages resulting from the non-performance (as in Avancini, 38 ÖJZ 546 (1983)). Defendant was culpably violating its duty of supplying funds, because it is responsible for its own solvency. Its own financial difficulties, stemming from its own risk sphere, did not satisfy the prerequisites under Austrian law for a failure of the basic assumptions of the parties.

This is not disputed by the petition for revision. These conclusions are also in harmony with the preponderant view in the literature on the liability of the comfort letter issuer for damages due to a breach of contract. (Citations omitted.)

1. The appellate court further assumed that defendant, due to insufficient financing of SBM, had caused damages equal to the total unrepaid portion of the loan totalling Aust.S. 18,545,418.99. It concluded that pursuant to § 68 KO [the Bankruptcy Law],[1] plaintiff did not need to deduct from that claim the 25% received in the composition terminating SBM's bankruptcy. Until satisfied in full, plaintiff was entitled to assert the full claim in the bankruptcies of both debtors, that means the entire amount owed to it at the time of the opening of the bankruptcy proceedings. In its view, this result was not changed by the composition. Controlling was the amount owing at the time of the adjudication in bankruptcy. Of this amount, plaintiff was entitled to receive 35% by reason of the respective composition.

2. The petition for revision argues that § 68 KO is inapplicable because the debtor and the signer of the comfort letter are not co-debtors. The liability under the comfort letter is predicated on a deficiency in the payment of the subsidiary and is therefore subordinate. The percentage payable pursuant to the composition proceedings involving SBM diminishes the damage.

3. This argument is unsuccessful.

a. The appellate court has correctly ruled that the issue is determined by German law. This law governs the consequences of the bankruptcy proceedings conducted in Germany, involving the assets of residents of Germany (cf. Art. 4 in conjunction with Art. 2 par.1 of the German-Austrian Convention on Bankruptcy and Composition, May 25, 1979). In particular, foreign creditors pursuing their rights in domestic proceedings are subject to the limits of domestic compositions [citations omitted.]

---

1. KO § 68 provides: 'If the estate of several or one of several persons who are severally liable for the same obligation is subject to bankruptcy proceedings, the creditor may claim in each case the amount to which he was entitled at the time of the opening of the procedure until he is fully paid.'

b. The extent to which claims are extinguished pursuant to KO § 193(1) by a duly confirmed composition, depends on the content thereof (108 BGHZ 123 at 130 et seq. (1989). [Parallel citations omitted.] In the absence of a provision to the contrary, it may be assumed that the pertinent provisions of the Bankruptcy Law, including § 68 KO, and the corresponding provisions of the composition law are controlling. * * *

c. According to § 68 KO, a creditor to whom several debtors are liable side by side, may assert its claim in the full amount in the insolvency proceedings of each. Co-responsibility within the meaning of § 68 KO includes not only joint and several liability within the technical sense of § 421 BGB, but also obligations without internal connection [citations omitted], if the creditor may demand performance simultaneously from all debtors, but in the aggregate only once [citations omitted]. This corresponds to the purpose of § 68 KO, viz. to secure for the creditor the highest extent of satisfaction from the liability of several persons [citations omitted]. It does not matter that the claims connected in that fashion result from different legal transactions (BGH Sen. Resolution of October 10, 1991). In that way, in the case of a 'hard' comfort letter, the debtor and the issuer are liable to the creditor for the whole debt side by side and not only one after the other [citations omitted].

A comfort letter of the kind involved in this case is generally considered to be comparable to a suretyship or guaranty [citations omitted]. Both types of transactions create, in the debtor's bankruptcy, liability of equal rank. * * * An obligation to provide compensation for damages signifies, according to the general principles of damage law, not only indemnification for a deficiency remaining after payment by other debtors, but reparation of the entire damages, in appropriate circumstances, together with other debtors. If the defendant parent company had performed its obligation undertaken in the comfort letter to the plaintiff lender in a proper manner, the credit would have been fully repaid upon maturity. Whoever agrees to take care of the performance by another, incurs, in the event of a non-performance for which the other is responsible, even as joint obligor, liability in the full amount. (43 BGHZ 227 (1965); 59 BGHZ 97 (1973)).

Contrary to petitioner's contention, the obligation of the issuer of a comfort letter in the case of the debtor's bankruptcy is not merely that of a surety for the deficiency [citations omitted]. The text of the comfort letter in issue does not indicate that defendant wanted merely to assume liability for a deficiency. * * *

d. Application of § 68 KO has the result that the date of the adjudication is the controlling date for the extent of the claim during the whole procedure. Subsequent partial payments by a co-obligor are without relevance until the entire claim is paid. This has not occurred so far, if the two composition dividends are taken into account.

NOTE

A good illustration of a *soft comfort letter* is furnished by the Court of Appeal of Karlsruhe, Judgment of August 7, 1992, 46 WM, IV 2088 (1992) based on the following facts: Sch. GmbH was the personally liable partner of the defendant Sch. GmbH & Co. Defendant was represented by Sch. and L., the managers of the Sch. GmbH. Plaintiff was a bank entertaining business relations with defendant. L. informed the bank that it intended to develop a new process for the use of artificial fibers. For that purpose a new subsidiary (CPV) would be established. It needed credit in the amount of DM 1,000,000. In discussing the profitability, L. expressed the expectation that the new process would be used to glue the gravel between railroad tracks. Plaintiff was willing to extend the needed credit to CPV, provided that the defendant would deliver a 'Declaration of Loyalty to its future subsidiary' as negotiated between L. and the managers of a branch of plaintiff. The principal reasons for the choice of a loyalty declaration was the disclosed intent of the defendant to avoid the inclusion of conditional liabilities in the balance sheet pursuant to § 251(1) HGB [Commercial Code]. In a letter forwarding the requested Declaration to Plaintiff, defendant declared that it stood fully behind the engagement of the CPV.

The venture failed since the Federal Railroad lost interest in the project and CPV filed for bankruptcy. Plaintiff demanded that defendant pay it the amount of the defaulted loans, basing its claims (i) on the declaration of loyalty and the accompanying letter and (ii) factual domination by defendant over the affairs of its subsidiary by analogy to §§ 302 and 303 AG [Corporation Code]. The court of appeal held that the declaration and the letter of defendant created no legal obligation to provide for the repayment of the loan and that the defendant had not exercised any dominance over the affairs of its subsidiary.

B. ENGLAND

1. Case

a. Kleinwort Benson v. Malaysia Mining

QB Court of Appeal (1989)
Kleinwort Benson v. Malaysia Mining Corporation Berhad
[1989] 1 WLR 379 = [1988] All ER 714.

1988 Dec. 13, 14;
1989 Feb. 12 Fox, Ralph Gibson and Nicholls L.JJ.

APPEAL from Hirst J.

By a writ dated 3 September 1986 and points of claim served on 12 September 1986 the plaintiffs, Kleinwort Benson Ltd., claimed damages against the defendants,

Malaysia Mining Corporation Berhad, for breach of, inter alia, a warranty that in consideration of the plaintiffs granting to M.M.C. Metals Ltd. ("Metals") acceptance credit/multi-currency loan facilities the defendants would ensure that Metals was at all times capable of fulfilling its financial obligations to the plaintiffs under the terms and conditions on which the facilities were made available. Judgment was given for the plaintiffs.

The defendants appealed on the grounds, inter alia, that the judge erred in law in holding that the final paragraph of the letter of comfort dated 21 August 1984 and the penultimate paragraph of the letter of comfort dated 7 May 1985, which said that it was the defendants' policy to ensure that the business of Metals was at all times in a position to meet its liabilities to the plaintiffs constituted an undertaking that, now and at all times in the future, so long as Metals was under any liability to the plaintiffs under the facility arrangements, it was and would be the defendants' policy to ensure that Metals was in a position to meet those liabilities; and in holding that the defendants' indication at the end of 1985 that it was no longer their policy to ensure that Metals was able to meets its liabilities constituted a clear breach of contract.

The facts are stated in the judgment of Ralph Gibson L.J.

Ralph Gibson L.J. This is an appeal by the defendants, Malaysia Mining Corporation Berhad, from the decision of Hirst J. of 21 December 1987, by which the plaintiffs, Kleinwort Benson Ltd., obtained judgment for damages for breach of contract against the defendants for £12.26 million, including interest. The defendants ask that the judgment be set aside and that the plaintiffs' claim be dismissed on the ground that the defendants did not enter into any relevant contractual obligations to the plaintiffs.

The judgment of Hirst J. [1988] 1 W.L.R. 799 contains an account of the circumstances in which the defendants provided to the plaintiffs the "comfort letter" upon the terms of which the plaintiffs' claim is founded. The description of the document as a "comfort letter" is that used by the parties themselves in the negotiations which preceded the provision of it by the defendants.

The plaintiffs are merchant bankers of high reputation and long experience. The defendants are a public limited company incorporated under the laws of Malaysia in which the Republic of Malaysia has at all material times held a controlling interest. In 1983 the defendants caused to be incorporated under the laws of England a company, called M.M.C. Metals Ltd. ("Metals"), as a wholly owned but indirect subsidiary to operate as a ring dealing member of the London Metal Exchange. The paid up capital of Metals was £1.5 million. To carry out trading upon the London Metal Exchange much larger funds would be required. There were negotiations for the provision of funds by the plaintiffs to Metals. The plaintiffs sought from the defendants assurances as to the responsibility of the defendants for the repayment by Metals of any sums lent by the plaintiffs. A "comfort letter" dated 21 August 1984 was provided by the defendants as part of an acceptance credit/multicurrency cash loan facility granted by the plaintiffs to Metals to a maximum of £5 million. That letter contained, among other statements, the assertion by the defendants that "It is our policy to ensure that the business of [Metals] is at all times in a position to meet its liabilities to you under the above arrangements." This case turns upon the proper construction, in its context, of that assertion by the defendants. In 1985 the facility was increased by the plaintiffs to a maximum of £10 million in reliance upon a second comfort letter, dated 7 May 1985, which was in substantially identical terms.

In October 1985 the tin market collapsed when the International Tin Council ("I.T.C.") announced that it was unable to meet its liabilities, which ran to hundreds of millions of pounds. An account of those events and a list of the sovereign states (including the United Kingdom and Malaysia) which were members of the I.T.C. can be found in the judgment of Kerr L.J. in *J. H. Rayner (Mincing Lane) Ltd. v. Department of Trade and Industry* [1988] 3 W.L.R. 1033. When the tin market collapsed Metals ceased trading. The plaintiffs demanded repayment of all sums outstanding. Nothing was paid, and Metals went into liquidation. The plaintiffs called upon the defendants to ensure that the plaintiffs received payment of the sums due. The defendants refused to pay and said by telex of 3 December 1985:

> "We have been advised that the statements made in the letter of 7 May [1985] were not intended by either party to impose, and do not impose, any legally binding obligations on us to support M.M.C. Metals Ltd. You will appreciate that circumstances are now materially different from those existing at the date of that letter and that although the policy referred to was our policy at that time and in the light of the circumstances then prevailing, no assurance was given that such policy would not be reviewed in the light of changing circumstances. We therefore cannot accept, as you stated in your telex, that we have given any assurances to you that M.M.C. Metals Ltd. would at all times be kept in a position to meet its liability to you."

Hirst J. described in his judgment [1988] 1 W.L.R. 799 the course of the discussions between the defendants and the plaintiffs which led to the provision of the two comfort letters.

I will set out Hirst J.'s description, at pp. 802–803, of those events substantially in his words which have been accepted as full and accurate by the parties:

> "in the first instance, by letter dated 16 December 1983, the plaintiffs offered to both the defendants and M.M.C. Metals Ltd. jointly a facility totalling £5 million, on terms that, throughout the currency of the facility, both should be jointly and severally liable for all amounts due to the plaintiffs; on this basis an accepting commission/margin of 3/8 per cent. per annum was proposed.
>
> "On 9 February 1984 there was a meeting in Singapore, attended on the plaintiffs' side by Mr. Gordon Irwin, who was the sole witness at the trial. At this stage the plaintiffs were proposing a guarantee by the defendants rather

than joint and several liability, but one of the defendants' representatives at the meeting stated that it was the defendants' policy not to guarantee their subsidiary's borrowings. At a subsequent meeting in London on 21 June 1984, Mr. John Green, who had been newly appointed as the director in charge of M.M.C. Metals Ltd.'s operations, is recorded in the plaintiffs' meeting note as having stated: 'The original offer was outlined (£5 million u.f.n. @ 3/8 per cent. per annum margin guaranteed by [the defendants]). A facility of this sort appears to fit in with Green's requirements, with the exception of the guarantee. Green said that [the defendants were] now not so keen on issuing guarantees just to keep finance costs down by 1/8 per cent. per annum and Green himself would be recommending that all M.M.C. Metals bank lines should be covered by a letter of comfort, rather than by a guarantee. I said that a letter of comfort would not be a problem, but that we would probably have to charge a higher rate.' This was reported by Mr. Irwin in an internal memorandum dated 3 July 1984 as follows: 'Contrary to earlier reports, [the defendants] have now taken a decision not to issue guarantees to cover the banking facilities granted to M.M.C. Metals. As a result, we have been asked to consider a line which would be covered by a letter of comfort from [the defendants].' Mr. Irwin in evidence accepted that by this stage he realised that the plaintiffs would not be able to obtain either joint and several liability as originally proposed, or a guarantee from the defendants.

"Originally it was proposed that the defendants should draft the comfort letter, but eventually on 11 July 1984 the plaintiffs furnished to M.M.C. Metals Ltd. a revised facility letter addressed to them only, providing for 1/2 per cent. commission (i.e. an increase of 1/8) and accompanied by a draft of a proposed comfort letter, in which the crucial paragraph read: 'It is our policy to ensure that the business of M.M.C. Metals Ltd. is conducted in such a way that M.M.C. Metals Ltd. is at all times in a position to meet its liabilities to you under the above arrangements.' i.e., containing at this stage some extra words in the second line. On 10 August 1984 at a board meeting of the defendants the following directors' written resolution was passed: 'That M.M.C. Metals Ltd. be authorised to accept the above facility on terms and conditions contained in the letter from [the plaintiffs] dated 11 July 1984, and that the required letter of comfort in the form attached be issued to [the plaintiffs].' Eventually, on 17 September 1984, M.M.C. Metals Ltd. returned the formal facility letter to the plaintiffs, accompanied by the first comfort letter, dated 21 August 1984, with the crucial paragraph redrafted by the defendants. The full text of the letter is: 'We refer to your recent discussion with M.M.C. Metals Ltd. as a result of which you propose granting M.M.C. Metals Ltd.: (a) banking facilities of up to £5 million; and (b) spot and forward foreign exchange facilities with a limitation that total delivery in cash will

> not on any one day exceed £5 million. (1) We hereby confirm that we know and approve of these facilities and are aware of the fact that they have been granted to M.M.C. Metals Ltd. because we control directly or indirectly M.M.C. Metals Ltd. (2) We confirm that we will not reduce our current financial interest in M.M.C. Metals Ltd. until the above facilities have been repaid or until you have confirmed that you are prepared to continue the facilities with new shareholders. (3) It is our policy to ensure that the business of M.M.C. Metals Ltd. is at all times in a position to meet its liabilities to you under the above arrangements. Yours faithfully Malaysia Mining Corporation Berhad.' I have inserted numbers for the three main paragraphs for clarity of reference in this judgment. Paragraph (2) was, as is common ground, contractual."

* * *

The central question in this case, in my judgment, is that considered in *Esso Petroleum Co. Ltd. v. Mardon* [1976] Q.B. 801, upon which Mr. Waller relied in this court but which was not cited to Hirst J. That question is whether the words of paragraph 3, considered in their context, are to be treated as a warranty or contractual promise. Paragraph 3 contains no express words of promise. Paragraph 3 is in its terms a statement of present fact and not a promise as to future conduct. I agree with Mr. Stamler's submission that, in this regard, the words of paragraph 3 are in sharp contrast with the words of paragraph 2 of the letter: "We confirm that we will not [etc.]." The force of this point is not limited, as Hirst J. stated, to the absence from paragraph 3 of the words "We confirm." The real contrast is between the words of promise, namely, "we will not" in paragraph 2, and the words of statement of fact "it is our policy" in paragraph 3. Hirst J. held that, by the words of paragraph 3, the defendants gave an understanding that now and at all times in the future, so long as Metals should be under any liability to the plaintiffs under the facility arrangements, it is *and will be* the defendants' policy to ensure that Metals is in a position to meet its liabilities. To derive that meaning from the words it is necessary to add the words underlined, namely, "and will be," which do not appear in paragraph 3. In short, the words of promise as to the future conduct of the defendants were held by Hirst J. to be part of the necessary meaning of the words used in paragraph 3. The question is whether that view of the words can be upheld.

The absence of express words of warranty as to present facts or the absence of express words of promise as to future conduct does not conclusively exclude a statement from the status of warranty or promise. According to the well known dictum of Holt C.J., "an affirmation can only be a warranty provided it appear on evidence to have been so intended:" see *per* Ormrod L.J. in *Esso Petroleum Co. Ltd. v. Mardon* [1976] Q.B. 801, 824G, citing Viscount Haldane L.C. in *Heilbut, Symons & Co. v. Buckleton* [1913] A.C. 30, 38. Thus, in *Esso Petroleum Co. Ltd. v. Mardon*, the statement, at p. 815B, "'Esso estimated that the throughput of the . . . site, in its third year of operation, would amount to 200,000 gallons a year,'" which had been made as an expert estimate, which was of great commercial importance to a potential tenant of the site, and which induced Mr. Mardon to enter into the contract of lease, was held to be a warranty not that such a throughput would be achieved, but that, in effect, the estimate had been made with due care upon the basis of information in the possession of Esso: see *per* Lord Denning M.R. at p. 818E, Ormrod L.J. at p. 827A, and Shaw L.J. at p. 832B. Mr. Waller, in this court, placed reliance upon the decision in *Esso Petroleum Co. Ltd. v. Mardon.* It is, in my judgment, on the facts of this case of no assistance to the plaintiffs. The evidence does not show that the words used in paragraph 3 were intended to be a promise as to the future conduct of the defendants but, in my judgment, it shows the contrary.

The concept of a comfort letter was, as Mr. Stamler acknowledged, not shown to have acquired any particular meaning at the time of the negotiations in this case with reference to the limits of any legal liability to be assumed under its terms by a parent company. A letter, which the parties might have referred to at some stage as a letter of comfort, might, after negotiation, have emerged containing in paragraph 3 in express terms the word used by Hirst J. to state the meaning which he gave to paragraph 3. The court would not, merely because the parties had referred to the document as a comfort letter, refuse to give effect to the meaning of the words used. But in this case it is clear, in my judgment, that the concept of a comfort letter, to which the parties had resort when the defendants refused to assume joint and several liability or to give a guarantee, was known by both sides at least to extend to or to include a document under which the defendants would give comfort to the plaintiffs by assuming, not a legal liability to ensure repayment of the liabilities of their subsidiary, but a moral responsibility only. Thus, when the defendants by Mr. Green in June 1984 told the plaintiffs that Mr. Green would recommend that credit lines for Metals be covered by a letter of comfort rather than by guarantee, the response of Mr. Irwin, before any draft of a comfort letter had been prepared, was "that a letter of comfort would not be a problem, but that we would probably have to charge a higher rate." The comfort letter was drafted in terms which in paragraph 3 do not express any contractual promise and which are consistent with being no more than a representation of fact. If they are treated as no more than a representation of fact, they are in that meaning consistent with the comfort letter containing no more than the assumption of moral responsibility by the defendants in respect of the debts of Metals. There is nothing in the evidence to show that, as a matter of commercial probability or common sense, the parties must have intended paragraph 3 to be a contractual promise, which is not expressly stated, rather than a mere representation of fact, which is so stated.

Next, the first-draft of the comfort letter was produced by the plaintiffs. Paragraph 1 contained confirmation that the defendants knew of and approved of the granting of the facilities in question by the plaintiffs to Metals, and paragraph 2 contained the express confirmation that the defendants would not reduce their current financial interest in Metals until (in effect) the facilities had been paid or the plaintiffs consented. Both are relevant to the present and future moral responsibility of the defendants. If the words of paragraph 3 are to be treated as intended to express a contractual promise by the defendants as to their future policy, which Hirst J. held the words to contain, then the recitation of the plaintiffs' approval and the promise not to reduce their current financial interest in Metals, would be of no significance. If the defendants have promised that at all times in the future it will be the defendants' policy to ensure that Metals is in a position to meet its liabilities to the plaintiffs under the facility, it would not matter whether they had approved or disapproved, or whether they had disposed of their shares in Metals. Contracts may, of course, contain statements or promises which are caused to be of no separate commercial importance by the width of a later promise in the same document. Where, however, the court is examining a statement which is by its express words no more than a representation of fact, in order to consider whether it is shown to have been intended to be of the nature of a contractual promise or warranty, it seems to me to be a fact suggesting at least the absence of such intention if, as in this case, to read the statement as a contractual promise is to reduce to no significance two paragraphs included in the plaintiffs' draft, both of which have significance if the statement is read as a representation of fact only. That point can be made more plainly thus: if paragraph 3 in its original or in its final form was intended to contain a binding legal promise by the defendants to ensure the ability of Metals to pay the sums due under the facility, there was no apparent need or purpose for the plaintiffs, as bankers, to waste ink on paragraphs 1 and 2.

As I have said, the absence of express words of promise does not by itself prevent a statement from being treated as a contractual promise. The example given in argument by Mr. Waller, namely, of the shop stating by a notice that it is its policy to accept, within 14 days of purchase, the return in good condition of any goods bought, and to refund the price without question, seems to me to be a case in which a court would be likely to hold that the notice imported a promise that the policy would continue over the 14-day period. It would be difficult on those facts to find any sensible commercial explanation for the notice other than a contractual promise not to change the policy over the 14-day period. It would not be satisfactory or convincing to regard the notice as no more than the assumption of a moral responsibility by the shop giving such a notice to its customers. In such a case, and in the absence of any relevant factual context indicating otherwise, it seems to me that the court would probably hold that the statement was shown to have been intended to be a contractual promise.

In the present case, however, the opposite seems to me to be clear. The context in which the comfort letter was requested and given is before the court without dispute as to the relevance or admissibility of that context. That concession was, in my view, rightly made. The evidence showing the context in which the comfort letters were produced, as set out in the judgment of Hirst J., was evidence of the factual background known to the parties at or before the date of the contract and of the "genesis" and "aim" of the transaction (see *Prenn v. Simmonds* [1971] 1 W.L.R. 1381): in short the provision of a comfort letter by the defendants, as the parent company of Metals to which the plaintiffs were intending to provide finance, in circumstances in which the defendants had refused to assume legal liability for the repayment of money lent to Metals by the plaintiffs, whether in the form of joint and several liability or of guarantee. Those facts are not available to show merely that the defendants did not themselves subjectively intend to assume legal liability and that, therefore, the words eventually included in the comfort letter provided by the defendants should be construed so as to exclude such liability. That, as I understand it, would be misapplying the principles, stated in *Prenn v. Simmonds,* by which evidence of the factual background is admitted. But the evidence of the refusal by the defendants to assume legal responsibility for the liabilities of Metals to the plaintiffs in the normal form of joint and several liability or of guarantee, and the consequent resort by the parties to what they described as a comfort letter substantially in the terms submitted by the plaintiffs to the defendants, are, in my judgment, admissible on the question whether, for the purposes of the test applied by this court in *Esso Petroleum Co. Ltd. v. Mardon* [1976] Q.B. 801, the defendants' affirmation in paragraph 3 appears on the evidence to have been intended as a warranty or contractual promise.

With that evidence before the court I find it impossible to hold that the words in paragraph 3 were intended to have any effect between the parties other than in accordance with the express words used. For this purpose it seems to me that the onus of demonstrating that the affirmation appears on evidence to have been intended as a contractual promise must lie on the party asserting that it does, but I do not rest my conclusion upon failure by the plaintiffs to discharge any onus. I think it is clear that the words of paragraph 3 cannot be regarded as intended to contain a contractual promise as to the future policy of the defendants. If paragraph 3 had been drafted by the plaintiffs and submitted in the form in which Hirst J. formulated its meaning, namely, as "an undertaking, that now and at all times in the future, so long as [Metals is] under any liability to the plaintiffs under the facility arrangements, it is and will be the defendants' policy to ensure that [Metals] is in a position to meet those liabilities," it must have appeared to both parties, in the context proved in evidence, as a radically different term from that which was in fact submitted and accepted. Such an undertaking does not fit, as a matter of commercial probability, with the factual background. I do not suggest that people only act in accordance with apparent commercial probability; the plaintiffs might have submitted such an undertaking which, in the light of the prior refusal to give a guarantee, was likely to be rejected and the defendants, contrary to what seemed likely, might have accepted it, but the plaintiffs in fact submitted the words we see in paragraph 3. The plain meaning of those words, without the addition contained in Hirst J.'s formulation of its meaning, does fit the factual background. Most importantly, that factual background explains, notwithstanding the commercial importance to the plaintiffs of security against failure by Metals to pay and the plaintiffs' reliance upon the comfort letter, why the plaintiffs drafted and agreed to proceed upon a comfort letter which, on its plain meaning, provided to the plaintiffs no legally enforceable security for the repayment of the liabilities of Metals. I therefore find it impossible to hold that by the words of paragraph 3 the parties must be held to have intended that the plaintiffs be given that security.

I should mention briefly some other points which were argued. As is apparent from what I have said above, the plaintiffs are, in my judgment, to be regarded as the party putting forward the language contained in the comfort letters as a whole. The change in wording introduced by the defendants made no difference whatever to the meaning. It was not argued that it did. Hirst J. held that the principle of construction contra proferentem held no application because there was no ambiguity. I do not agree. The question was whether words, which are not in the form of a contractual promise, are on the evidence to be treated as intended to have been such a promise. Having regard to the defendants' prior refusal to assume joint and several liability or to give a guarantee, and to the resort by the parties to what was referred to as a comfort letter, it seems to me that the defendants are entitled to rely upon the fact that, if the plaintiffs required a promise as to the defendants' future policy, it was open to them as experienced bankers to draft paragraph 3 in those terms. I do not, however, regard the point as decisive. If the letter in its final form is to be regarded as the result of joint drafting, my conclusion would not be affected.

Submissions were made to Hirst J., and repeated in this court, as to the differences between the liability of the defendants upon a formal guarantee, and the ease of enforcement of that liability, on the one hand, and the liability and attendant problems of enforcement under paragraph 3, on the other hand, according to its meaning and effect as determined by the judge. I did not find these submissions to be of any assistance in the resolving of the main issue in this case, and I do not propose to deal with them in any detail. I agree with Hirst J. that the mere fact that the defendants had refused to give a formal guarantee did not mean that there was no further scope for the subsequent agreement by them to a term having the meaning and effect which Hirst J. gave in paragraph 3; but contemplation by either party of the alleged differences in certainty or of the availability of summary judgment seems to me to be wholly improbable.

If my view of this case is correct, the plaintiffs have suffered grave financial loss as a result of the collapse of the tin market and the following decision by the defendants not to honour a moral responsibility which they assumed in order to gain for their subsidiary the finance necessary for the trading operations which the defendants wished that subsidiary to pursue. The defendants have demonstrated, in my judgment, that they made no relevant contractual promise to the plaintiffs which could support the judgment in favour of the plaintiffs. The consequences of the decision of the defendants to repudiate their moral responsibility are not matters for this court. I would allow this appeal.

NICHOLAS L.J. I agree.

FOX L. J. I also agree.

Appeal allowed with costs in Court of Appeal and below.
Leave to appeal refused.

NOTE

For a discussion of *Kleinwort Benson* and English comfort letters see Philip R. Wood, *The uncomfortable comfort letter,* 5 *Int'l Financial L.R.* (April) 21 (1988) and M. Elland-Goldsmith, *Comfort Letters in English Law and Practice* RDAI/IBLJ No. 5 527 (1994).

C. FRANCE

1. Cases

a. Compagnie générale

Court of Cassation (com.)
Compagnie générale de travaux et d'installations électriques
c. Banque atlantique de Côte-d'Ivoire
Judgment of March 19, 1991
1991 Bull. IV, 77; D. Jur. 53, 54 (1992).

Upon the sole assignment of error, taken in its two branches: Considering that, according to the judgment below (Versailles, Feb. 9, 1989), on September 8, 1982 the Société compagnie générale de travaux et d'installations électriques (*GTIE*), at that time the sole owner of all shares of the capital of the Société L'Ivoirienne électrique (LIE) addressed to the Banque atlantique de Côte-d'Ivoire (the Bank) a letter, in which it declared in particular that it would watch 'very closely that the financial policy defined in a common agreement be observed and, especially, that the obligations of LIE vis-à-vis your enterprise be performed', that on the basis of the terms of this letter the bank brought an action against GTIE, which had transferred the essential portion of its participation in the capital of the LIE corporation in payment of the balance of a debt of its former subsidiary, now 'insolvent'.

Considering that GTIE challenges the judgment below for having sustained this demand although, according to the assignment of error, on the one hand, GTIE in its grounds for appeal, had asserted that it had intervened several times to support its subsidiary; that therefore the appellate court, when it concluded that GTIE had not afforded sufficient support by merely taking into account the payment by the latter of a liability as a surety in the amount of FF 209,011,980, CFA without taking also into account other interventions of the parent corporation (such as the pay-out of a running account indicating a positive balance of FF 1,700,000 in favor of LIE, resulting from a loan by GTIE to its subsidiary and the assistance agreement between the two corporations), had not legally justified its decision with regard to Art. 1142 C.C. and not responded to the arguments of GTIE, thereby violating Art. 455 of the New Code of Civil Procedure; and although, on the other hand, the obligation of furnishing means imposes upon the debtor the duty of providing means reasonably within its power;

that therefore by focusing merely on the needs of LIE without examining, as the grounds for appeal requested, whether GTIE possessed the means to go beyond the interventions made for the benefit of its subsidiary and thereby denying to the parent corporation the reliance on the impossibility of doing more for its subsidiary, the appellate court has not legally justified its decision with the respect to Art. 1142 C.C.;

But, considering that, after having pointed out that GTIE could not successfully rely upon the satisfaction of a suretyship agreement which had not been translated into a provision of funds for the benefit of its subsidiary, the judgment below also states that on November 28, 1985 GTIE reduced considerably its participation in LIE's capital without prior notice to the bank which it was obliged to give according to the terms of the '*lettre de confort*'; that this 'brutal disinvolvement' manifested its wish to limit for itself so far as possible the consequences of a management for which, however, it was responsible as a sole and later dominant majority stockholder of the LIE, whose financial situation was severely impaired at that time; that the judgment adds that this intentional violation of the agreement which linked it with the bank, proves that GTIE, by preventing the bank from taking the measures which it might have deemed to be appropriate in view of the new situation thus created, was conscious of the fact that it had not totally met its obligation to furnish its means, so as to be able to rely on the impossibility of doing more for the benefit of the bank; that by having thus examined whether GTIE had utilized the means at its disposal to satisfy its duty to the bank, and having concluded on the basis of considerations which respond to the arguments interposed that this was not the case, the appellate court has legally justified its decision; wherefore it follows that the assignment of error is not well-founded in any of its branches.

For these reasons: the court rejects the petition.

[President: M. Defontaine. Rapporteur: M. Le Dauphin. Avocat général: M. Curti.]

NOTES

1. The judgment of the text case is commented upon by Professor I. Najjar in D. Jur. 55 (1992).

2. French law considers 'comfort letters' to be a species of 'letters of intent'. In turn it distinguishes between comfort letters which — if legally binding at all — undertake the obligation of producing a result (*obligation de résultat*) and comfort letters which undertake the obligation to employ means (*obligation de moyens*). Whether a particular comfort letter obligates the author to achieve a *result* rather than to employ *means* often involves difficult questions of interpretation. A comfort letter by a parent corporation which promises the payment of the debts owed by the subsidiary to the addressee of the letter would be the promise of a result. It would amount to a guarantee and would not bind the corporation, unless authorized by the council of administration and annexed to the balance sheet. (Law of July 24, 1966. See following note.)

3. In a recent case decided by the Court of Cassation (Com.), Judgment of

March 29, 1994 (Le Quotidien Juridique July 7, 1994 p.2 with note), M. Charles Legorju, a President of the council of administration and majority stockholder of the Société Andax, sent a letter of intent to a group of banks stating that he would continue his policy of supporting Andax and see to it that no lender would sustain a loss. When Andax became insolvent the banks brought an action against M.Legorju for repayment of the loan. The Court of Appeal of Paris construed the letter as 'promising a result' and rendered judgment against petitioner.

In his petition for cassation, M. Legorju contended that individual non-merchants could not be held liable on a letter of intent and that even if they could be held liable, the letter in question was not sufficiently explicit and unambiguous to be construed as was done by the court below. The Court of Cassation dismissed the petition on the ground that the first contention was inadmissible, because it was not raised in the courts below and the second contention was unfounded because any ambiguity was due to petitioner.

4. The case-law has prompted a large number of studies and comments. See A. Schollen, *Do Letters of Intent Systematically Have good Intentions?* RDAI/IBLJ No. 7, 793 (1994); J. Devèze, *Aux frontières du cautionnement: Lettres d'intention et garanties indépendantes* 66 J.C.P. (éd. E.) Supp. 2, 26 (1992); J.-J. Daigre, *Les substituts de cautionnement: de la lettre à la garantie. La revanche de la liberté* 66 J.C.P. (éd. E.) Suppl. 6, 3 (1992); Ph. Simler & Ph. Delebeque, *Droit des sûretés,* 66 J.C.P. (éd. G.) I 3583, 222, 225 (1992).

5. See also the fictitious arbitration proceeding in the Matter of Banque de l'Orient et de l'Occident c. la Société Baby Boom by M. Antoine, Ph. Billot & J. Terray, [1990] RDAI/IBLJ 791.

b. Citibank

Court of Cassation (Com.)
Compagnie générale de banque Citibank c. S.A. Le Crédit d'équipement des petites et moyennes entreprises (C.E.P.M.E.) et autres
Judgment of October 23, 1990
Bull. civ. IV 256; 65 J.C.P. (éd. É.) 154 (p. 119) (1991) = 65 J.C.P. (éd. G.) II 21684 (p. 205) (1991).

The Court — Upon the sole assignment of error:

Considering that, according to the judgment under attack (Paris, Jan. 13, 1989), the Compagnie générale de banque Citibank (*Citibank*) in cooperation with the Société Crédit d'équipement des petites et moyennes entreprises (*C.E.P.M.E.*) . . . accorded a privileged line of credit (*crédit de mobilisation de créance*) to the Société Cooperative d'entreprise générale du midi (*C.E.G.M.*); that in order to enable the latter to obtain a renewal of the credit, the Société de pavage et des asphaltes de Paris (*S.P.A.P.A.*) addressed to the creditors of the C.E.G.M. a letter of intent; that when the latter declared the cessation of payments, Citibank and C.E.P.M.E. demanded the payment of certain amounts from S.P.A.P.A.; and,

Considering that Citibank attacks the judgment below for having rejected its demand for the reason that the letter of intent in issue was signed by the general director of S.P.A.P.A. without authorization by the administrative council, although, according to the assignment of error, the letter of intent which imposes on the signatory merely an obligation to bring about a result does not constitute an agreement of guarantee within the meaning of Art. 98 of the Law of July 24, 1966 whose provisions must be restrictively interpreted and that therefore this undertaking did not have to be authorized by the administrative council of the corporation; that this text envisages only guarantees which import the obligation of the obligor to substitute himself to a third person and constitute a necessary diminution of assets, that the letter of intent of April 1, 1981 which was signed by Mr. Gee, the director general of S.P.A.P.A. in the name of the latter, did not import either an obligation of substitution to a third person or a necessary diminution of assets of S.P.A.P.A. but stipulated that the latter would do 'everything necessary to enable C.E.G.M. to dispose of funds sufficient to meet its obligations', that therefore it did not constitute a guarantee agreement the validity of which is subjected by Art. 98 of the Law of July 24, 1966 to an authorization by the council of administration, and that the court below could not decide otherwise except on the basis of a misapplication of said article;

But considering that, by having found for reasons of its own and those of the court below that the letter in issue contained an obligation to achieve a result in a fashion to render its author liable for the consequences of a default of the debtor, it was on a good legal basis that the court below concluded that that letter constituted a guarantee and, after having established that the signing of the agreement was not authorized by the council of administration, held that it was not binding upon S.P.A.P.A.; and that therefore the assignment of error is therefore without foundation, for these reasons — Rejects the petition.

(Mr. Defontaine, pres.; Mrs. Loseau, reporting judge; Mr. Raynaud, adv. gen.)

NOTES

1. Comment by E. Dilger, *Patronatserklärung einer französischen Société anonyme*, 37 *Recht der internationalen Wirtschaft* [RIW] 342 (1991).

2. Since the Court of Cassation was bound by the finding of the Court of Appeal that the comfort letter in issue constituted an obligation to achieve a result and was tantamount to a guarantee, it had to be authorized by the council of administration. See the annotation to this case by Professor C. Larroumet, 65 J.C.P. (éd. G.) II, 21684 (p. 206) = J.C.P. (éd. E.) 154 (p.119).

c. SNE Sitraco

Court of Cassation (Com.)
SNE Sitraco c. Société Curtainwalls Unlimited Inc.
Judgment of July 16, 1991
D. Jur. 54 (1992); Petites Affiches, Issue 31, March 12, 1993 p.9.

The Court — Upon the only assignment of error considered in its two branches:

Considering that it results from the findings of the judgment under attack (Versailles, June 15, 1989) that the U.S. corporation Curtainwalls Unlimited Inc. (*Société Curtainwalls*), creditor of Société Sitraco-Curtainwalls (*Société Sitraco*), subsidiary of Société SNE Sitraco, brought an action against the latter relying on a letter of Aug. 26, 1982 in which it wants to see an agreement of the SNE Sitraco to substitute itself for the Société Sitraco if the latter defaults;

Considering that the SNE Sitraco challenges the judgment below because it held the defendant liable for the whole amount of the indebtedness of its subsidiary vis-à-vis the Société Curtainwalls although — so the petition contends — in the first place, according to its letter of Aug. 28, 1982, SNE Sitraco authorized its subsidiary to conclude the bargain with the Société Curtainwalls and granted it its 'support in all the obligations into which it entered' without ever declaring that it substituted itself for its subsidiary, to meet the financial obligations vis-à-vis the other party to the contract or that it obligated itself to satisfy its obligation in the case that the debtor defaulted; that in declaring nevertheless that the letter implied an undertaking of the SNE Sitraco to bear the financial charges upon its subsidiary the appellate court violated Arts. 1101, 1134 and 2011 et seq. C.C.; and in the second place, because by deducing an undertaking of the SNE Sitraco from the fact that the letter August 28, 1982 contained an 'allusion' to the financial conditions of the agreement concluded between the Société Curtainwalls and the Société Sitraco and from the fact that the SNE Sitraco had participated in the negotiation of this agreement, the appellate court did not rely upon an unequivocal and clear intent of the SNE Sitraco to be responsible for the debt of the debtor in the event that the latter failed to satisfy it herself, thus deprives its decision of a legal basis within the meaning of Arts. 1134, 2011 et seq. C.C.

But considering that the judgment shows that the SNE Sitraco did address to the Société Curtainwalls a letter in which it specified that Sitraco 'has and will have our total support in its engagements which it undertakes vis-à-vis you, according to the terms of the agreement mentioned below' and, upon a demand of supplementary services by the Société Curtainwalls, 'we confirm to you hereby the authorization of the Société Sitraco to obligate itself to incur this supplementary expenditure', that it has found in addition that the SNE Sitraco was closely implicated in the financial negotiations of its subsidiary with the Société Curtainwalls and that its director for finance personally participated therein; that in this state of its findings and conclusions the court of appeal merely applied the law of contract by holding that the SNE Sitraco had obligated itself to comply to all means for the purpose that the obligations entered into by its subsidiary vis-à-vis the Société Curtainwalls are satisfied and that because it failed to do so it had to be condemned to pay to the corporation the total claim owed to it; that the assignment of error is unfounded.

For this reason rejects the petition.

NOTE

Apparently no question existed whether the comfort letter addressed by SNE Sitraco to Société Curtainwalls was properly authorized. Cf. note on this case by O. Playoust in Les Petites Affiches, Issue 31, March 12, 1993 p.9, 12.

d. Viuda de José Tolra

Court of Cassation (Com.)
Société anon. Viuda de José Tolra c.
Société régionale de développement du Lanquedoc-Rousillon (SODLER)
Judgment of Dec. 21, 1987 D. Jur. 112 (1989).

Considering, that according to the findings of the judgment subject to the petition, (Montpellier, 2nd Ch., Jan. 10, 1985) the company Textiles du Vallespir (*Société T.V.*), subsidiary of the Spanish company Viuda de José Tolra (*Société Tolra*) obtained, according to three notarial documents of November 1973 and June and September, 1974, three loans from the Société régionale de développment (*SODLER*) for the purpose of constructing a factory, that, in addition to security given to secure repayment of the first loan, the Société Tolra signed a letter of May 29, 1974, addressed to SODLER in which it affirmed its intention to 'support its subsidiary in its financial needs and, in the event that it should be necessary, to substitute itself to meet all the commitments that it would make vis-à-vis SODLER', expressing at the same time its willingness to watch in a permanent fashion over its total solvency and confirming its 'intention, in the case of necessity, to take immediately the necessary steps with the Spanish authorities, in order to obtain permission for the transfer of funds', that this letter was mentioned in the notarial document of September 12 and 17, 1974, relating to the third loan, but that it envisaged also the second loan; that due to opening of reorganization proceedings against the Société T.V. and their conversion into liquidation, SODLER brought an action against the Société Tolra for the payment of principal and interest of the second and third loans based on the letter of intention.

With respect to the first assignment of error, taken in its first two branches: — Considering that Société Tolra on the one hand faults the appellate court on the ground that it held that the letter of intent bound it contractually and established an obligation on its part to produce a result, whereas, according to the contention of petitioner, a unilateral letter of intent, apart from certain exceptions, does not create a civil obligation; that, according to the findings of the judgment, the Société Tolra limited itself to expressing unilaterally its intent without the formation of a contract due to the lack of an agreement of the parties; that in holding that the letter of intent issued by the Société Tolra, could create a civil obligation engaging it, the appellate court violated Articles 1101 et seq. C.C.; that on the other hand, the obligation to substitute itself, if necessary, in place of the debtor in order to meet its obligation undertaken vis-à-vis a creditor, constitutes a contract of suretyship which must be express and have a determined or determinable object; that in considering that the letter of intent established an obligation to reach a result different from that of a suretyship the court of appeal violated Article 2011 et seq. C.C. But considering, on the one hand, that despite its unilateral character, a letter of intent may, according to its terms, if it has been accepted by the addressee and regarded to be the common intention of the parties, constitute a contractual engagement on the part of its issuer, to do or not to do something that may go as far as the obligation to produce a result, even if it does not constitute a suretyship; that it is for the judge to attribute or restore its exact qualification to an act of that kind without being tied to the designation which the parties propose,

— considering on the other hand, that the court of appeal noted that in its letter of May 29, 1974 the Société Tolra had indicated that it would, in the event that it was necessary, take the place of its subsidiary to meet the commitments undertaken vis-à-vis *Sodler* and added that this letter envisaged in a definite way the second and third loans, that although a suretyship is not presumed and must be express, a party who through an unambiguous and clear manifestation of its intent declares to engage itself vis-à-vis the creditor to satisfy the debtor's obligation, if the latter fails to do so himself, thereby renders itself surety for that obligation; that because of that purely legal reason, which is substituted to those that have been criticized, the decision of the Court of appeal is justified to the extent that it holds that the Société Tolra has obligated itself to pay *Sodler*, in the case of a default of the Société T.V., any balance remaining due on the stipulated loan; with the consequence that the assignment of error cannot be accepted in any of its branches.

* * *

But upon the second assignment of error, taken in its first branch: In view of Art. 3 C.C., in conjunction with Article 3 of the law of July 3, 1966 considering that, in order to reject the contentions of the Société Tolra, according to which even if the letter of intent contained an engagement to pay, the latter would be void because it failed to conform to the Spanish Companies Law, the court of appeal, limited itself to the statement that it was 'seized with a litigation based on acts and facts having taken place in France and to which French law applies'; and considering further that in so holding, after having noted that the Société Tolra was a Spanish corporation, because the determination of the powers of the managers of a company must be made on the basis of its national law, the court of appeal has violated, through misapplication, the texts cited above —

For these reasons the court vacates and annuls the judgment below in toto, but, within the limits of the second assignment of error, and remands the case to the Court of Appeal of Lyon.

NOTES

1. This case was the first occasion in which the Court of Cassation (Commercial Chamber) had to deal with a comfort letter and its effects. The opinion of the Avocat Général Michael Montainer is published in 62 J.C.P. Jur. 2113 (1988).

2. The French Civil Code, Art. 3 provides that the status and capacity of French nationals are governed by French law even if they reside abroad. Art. 3 of the Law of July 24, 1966 on commercial associations subjects the capacity of foreign corporations and their offices to the law of the location of their headquarters.

3. The text case is annotated by J. P. Brill, D. Jur. 113 (1989).

D. ITALY

1. Case

a. Italian Comfort Letters: Hard and Soft

Court of Cassation (Sect. I)
Cassa di Risparmio delle Province Lombarde
v. Selle Aquila and Rejna
Judgment of September 27, 1995, n. 10235
148 Giurisprudenza Italiana 738 (1996).

REASONS

3.1 Object of the scrutiny in this controversy is the legal effect of two comfort letters of varying content released to the Cassa di Risparmio delle Province Lombarde (Cariplo) by the Companies Selle Aquila, s.r.l. and Rejna, s.p.a. with respect to the grant of certain credit lines by that banking enterprise to a company (the Denver Italiana Sellerie Riunite s.p.a) whose capital is nearly totally owned by the two corporations.

3.2 It is today clarified that the specific functions performed by this type of declarations — which are normally issued for the benefit of banking institutions in connection with requests for the financing by entities upon which the declarant is able to exercise its influence — is not as much a guaranty of the performance by another in the sense in which that term is employed in the discipline of suretyship and other personal guarantees specifically provided by the legislator [in which the 'guarantor' assumes the obligation to render the (same) performance (as) owed by the obligor], as a reinforcement in the (future) creditor to whom the declaration is addressed, of the conviction that the comforter will meet his own undertakings.

Comfort letters, in fact, have come into wide use as substitutes for the typical personal guarantees. That, nevertheless, does not warrant depriving them of any legal effect, especially in view of the fact that they are often tied to operations of notable economic importance and therefore it is not reasonable to assume that with their issuance the parties intended to create merely obligations on the social level, the respect of which is merely left to the sense of honor and loyalty.

3.3 The legal significance of comfort letters, nevertheless is not always the same, but varies according to their content, excluding, as has been said, that they give rise to the veritable obligations of suretyship type.

If such declarations have merely an 'informational' content, (for instance about the existence of a position of influence and about the patrimonial, economical and financial conditions of that position) a possible liability of the issuer of the comfort letter may be predicated upon the principles sanctioned in Arts. 1337 and 1338 of the Civil Code. The author of the declaration of comfort in fact intervenes in the negotiations conducted between other parties precisely for the purpose of facilitating their successful conclusion, thus creating reasonable expectations of the happy ending of the venture: his position is therefore quite different from that of a third party who accidently interferes in a pre-contractual, for him extraneous, event and this difference is sufficient to justify the application of the rules of diligence, correctness and good faith dictated for the purpose of avoiding that the interest of the participants in the negotiations could be prejudiced by the conduct of another that is incorrect (Art. 1337 C.C.) or only negligent (Art. 1338 C.C.)

If on the other hand, the declarant does not limit himself to disclosing his position of influence, but assumes 'duties' (as e.g. the communication of his intention to transfer his participation or to terminate his continuing maintenance thereof or also to safeguard the solvency of the controlled entity) the problem arises to determine whether his responsibility may affirm, in addition to the aspect just mentioned, also under a transactional aspect.

The problem arises, as is well known, because our legal order includes a norm, Art. 1987 of the Civil Code, according to which 'the unilateral promise of a performance does not produce legal effect outside those cases admitted by the law.' The scope of the provision is, * * * however, less significant than could appear at first blush. * * * [B]ecause, in the Civil Code, there exists a provision * * * on the basis of which it is possible to argue that in our legal system legal relations with obligations burdening only one of the parties may be constituted by reason of the sole wish of the obligated party, subject to the power of rejection by the beneficiary (Art. 1333 C.C.)

In fact, the provision in its textual formulation refers to a '*contract, with obligations solely on the part of the proponent*' and establishes that it is concluded when the proposal '*has come to the knowledge of the party to which it is addressed,* unless it is rejected '*within the time required by the nature of the object or usage.*' The employment of these expressions could induce the assertion that the inaction by the offeree assumes, for the legislator, the significance of a tacit expression of intent (i.e. the acceptance of the proposal). But it is helpful to observe, in opposition, that it is possible to speak of a tacit intent (either by implication, or presumption) only when the law permits proof that, in the concrete case, such intent was lacking and not inferable from the conduct of the declarant (Art. 684, 686, 1237, par. 2 C.C.) If this proof is not permitted, because the law attaches a specified effect to a conduct (active or inactive) of a person (Arts. 476, 477, 1237(1), 1399(4), 1597, 1823(2) C.C.), it must be recognized that the actual intent plays, for that purpose, no part and that the effect therefore has no transactional effect.

* * *

The scheme of Art. 1333 C.C., as outlined, therefore is perfectly adapted to comfort letters, which have binding effect, and therefore there is no reason for any doubt as to their binding character, given that such declarations, even though they are instruments different from those proposed for personal guarantees of typical character, are always destined to reinforce the protection of the rights of the creditors and therefore to effectuate interests certainly '*meriting protection*' according to the legal order (Art. 1322 (2) C.C.).

* * *

[Since the Caripolo did not allege or prove a breach of the obligations assumed in the comfort letters, no reason for any liability of the authors of the comfort letters existed. The amounts of their investment in the subsidiary showed that they had full confidence in the success of the venture.]

NOTE

See Comment by G. Chinè, *La Cassazione sul* patronage: *una voce fuori dal coro,* 148 Giur. It. I, 738 (1996) with further references.

E. UNITED STATES

Case law indicates that issuance of comfort letters or letters of intent to guarantee are not unknown in United States practice. See e.g. *Hester Intern. Corporation v. Federal Republic of Nigeria,* 681 F. Supp. 371 (N.D. Miss. 1988) in which a Mississippi corporation brought an action against Nigeria, National Grains Production Company Ltd. (NGPC), a corporation wholly owned by Nigeria and the Government of Cross River, one of the nineteen states comprising the Federal Republic of Nigeria. The action was based on the alleged breach of a joint venture agreement between Hester, NGPC and Cross River, which provided for the issuance of a letter of intent to guarantee the financing of the project by Nigeria. The government of Nigeria refused to issue the contemplated letter of intent and the project collapsed. Since Nigeria was not a party to the joint venture agreement, Nigeria's motion to dismiss was granted.

Similarly, in *Barclay's Bank of New York v. Goldman,* 517 F. Supp. 403 (S.D.N.Y. 1981), Barclay's Bank had agreed with Dankers Diamonds (Israel) Ltd. (DDIL) that it would renew and increase a line of credit, inter alia, upon the condition that Gordon and Ruhame Goldman, officers of DDIL, would guarantee the repayment of the loan and that M. Daukner & Sons Ltd., the parent of DDIL, would provide a comfort letter, stating that should DDIL have financial difficulties and not be able to meet its liabilities, M. Daukner & Sons Ltd. would ensure that the Bank will be repaid. The Goldmans provided the guarantee and Barclay's renewed the increased line of credit, although M. Daukner and Sons did not issue the requested comfort letter.

In an action by Barclay's against the Goldmans on the guaranty, the court held that the Goldmans could not interpose a defense based on Barclay's failure to obtain the comfort letter, because the guarantee by the Goldmans was not conditioned on the Bank's also obtaining a comfort letter from M. Daukner & Sons Ltd.

F. BELGIUM

Belgium case law on comfort letters is reviewed in Chris Sunt, *Enforceability of comfort letters,* 6 International Financial L.R. (April) 44 (1987).

G. DENMARK

Although comfort letters are used increasingly in Denmark, their legal effect has not yet been defined by the courts. For a comparison with German law see Christian H. Wissum, *Comfort letters under Danish Law,* 6 International Financial L. R. (March) 23 (1987).

H. AUSTRALIA

For comfort letters in Australia see *Banque Brussels Lambert SA v. Australian National Industries Ltd.*[2] In that case, Australian National Industries Ltd. (*ANI*) had furnished a comfort letter to Banque Brussels Lambert SA (*BBL*) in connection with BBL supplying credit to Spedley Securities Ltd. (*Spedley*), (now in liquidation), owned by Spedley Holdings. ANI held a 45% participation in Spedley Holdings. The comfort letter contained assurances by ANI to the effect that:

(1) it would give 90 days notice to BBL of its intention to reduce its shares in Spedley Holdings, with the effect that BBL had the right to recall outstanding loans within 30 days;

---

2. Supreme Court of New South Wales Commercial Division, Chief Judge Rogers (Judgment of December 12, 1989), 21 N.S.W. Law Reports 502. Discussed in D.W. Greig & J.L.R. Davis, *The Law of Contract* 57 (5th Supp. 1993); M. Howard, *Interpreting Letters and Construing Statements: Banque Brussels Lambert SA v. Australian National Industries,* 18 Australian Bus. L.J. 188 (1990).

(2) it would continue its 'practice to ensure' that its associate, Spedley Securities, 'will at all times be in a position to meet its financial obligation as they fall due.' Despite its two reassurances, ANI failed to live up to them. Spedley became insolvent and BBL brought an action against ANI, alleging breach of its undertakings in the letter of comfort.

After a detailed review of the negotiations between the parties on the drafting of the letter, Chief Justice Rogers held that under Australian law, the letter of comfort constituted an enforceable contractual promise.

It is noteworthy that in his elaborate opinion, Chief Judge Rogers consulted the treatment of letters of comfort in other legal systems, approving in particular of the French approach (p. 521) referring specifically to *Société anon. Viuda de José Tolra*[3] and criticizing *Kleinwort Benson*[4] by implication (p. 525).[5]

I. IVORY COAST

For the Ivory Coast see *Société Africaine de plantations d'Hévéa (SAPH) c. Banque Internationale pour l'Afrique Occidentale Côte d'Ivoire (BIAO-CI),* Cour d'Appel d'Abidjan, Judgement March 30, 1990, RDAJ/IBLJ 431 (1991). Comments by H. François-Marsal and I. Dago Diatchi, *id.* 427.

BIBLIOGRAPHY

COMFORT LETTERS — 'HARD' AND 'SOFT'

Antoine, M.F., *Lettres de patronage,* 6 RDAI/IBLJ 771 (1990).

Avancini, P., *Rechtsprobleme bei Patronatserklärung* 38 *Österreichische Juristen-Zeitung* 546 (1983).

Barré, Xavier, La lettre d'intention (Paris 1995).

Brill, J.P., casenote on Judgment of Dec. 21, 1987 Cass. com. (*Société anon. Viuda de José Tolra*) D. Jur. 112, 113 (1989).

Chinè, G., *La Cassazione sul* patronage: *una voce fuori dal coro,* 148 Giur. It. I, 738 (1996) with further references.

Devèze, J., *Aux frontières du cautionnement: Lettres d'intention et garanties indépendantes* 66 J.C.P. Supp. 2/Cahiers de droit de l'entreprise 26 (1992).

3. Supra 410

4. Supra 396

5. In *Australian Bridal Centre, Pty. Ltd. v. Dawes Corporation Pty. Ltd. & Others* (Judgment of Oct. 5, 1990, Cole, J., Supreme Court of N.S.W., [1991] ATPR 52,095; Australian Digest, (1991) # 2256) Dawes Corporation was sued for rent. The holding company of the tenant was subsequently acquired by a takeover on the part of a wholly owned subsidiary of Hecron (*H*). During the takeover negotiations the Managing Director of *H* assured the shareholders of tenant's holding company who were guarantors of defendant's rental obligations that 'we will cover you' with respect to any liabilities as guarantors of defendant. The court held the managing director and *H* liable on the representation.

Dilger, E., *Patronatserklärung einer französischen Société anonyme,* 37 Recht der internationalen Wirtschaft [RIW] 342 (1991) (note on Judgment of October 23, 1994. Cass. com. (*Citibank*).

M. Elland-Goldsmith, *Comfort Letters in English Law and Practice* RDAI/IBLJ No. 5 527 (1994).

Gerth, A., *Atypische Kreditsicherheiten* (2d ed.) 1980.

Greig, D.W. & Davis J.L.R., *The Law of Contract,* 56 (5th Supp. 1993) (Australia).

Najjar, I., note on Judgment of March 19, 1991 *Compagnie générale de travaux et d'installations électriques* (Cass. com.) in D. Jur. 54, 55 (1992).

Schnyder, A., *Patronatserklärungen — Haftungsgrundlage für Konzernobergesellschaften,* 86 SJZ 57 (1990).

Seiler, I., *Die Patronatserklärung im internationlen Wirtschaftsverkehr* (1981).

Simler, Ph. & Delebeque Ph., *Chronique d'actualité: Droit des sûretés,* 66 J.C.P. (éd. G.) I 3583, 222 (1992).

Sunt, C., *Enforceability of Comfort Letters,* 6 RDAI/IBLJ (April) 44 (1987). (Belgian Law.)

Viale, Mirella, *Le Garanzie bancarie* (Milan 1994).

Wissum, C.H., *Comfort letters under Danish Law,* 6 RDAI/IBLJ (March) 23 (1987).

Wood, P.R., *Law and Practice of International Finance* (1980).

Id., The Uncomfortable Comfort Letter RDAI/IBLJ (March) 21 (1988).

PART III/B:

TYPICAL TRANSACTIONS SECURING PERFORMANCE

8/Retained and Granted Security Interests

A. GENERAL SURVEY: SECURITY INTERESTS IN TANGIBLE AND INTANGIBLE MOVABLE PROPERTY (CHATTELS AND CHOSES-IN-ACTION)

TRADITIONAL SECURITY INTERESTS

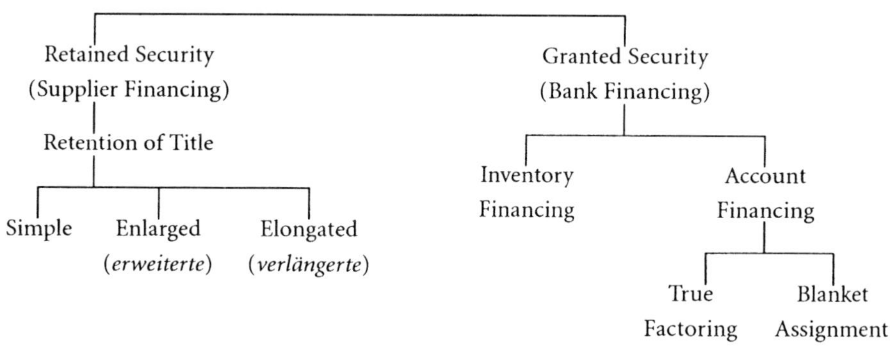

Movable (or personal) property, whether tangible (chattels) or intangible (choses-in-action or credits) is important 'collateral' in international trade and one of the chief objects of credit transactions. Generally speaking, in some legal systems non-possessory security interests may be valid without any forms of publicity, such as registration or notification (so-called latent security interests), while in others some publicity such as notification or registration is required for their validity, at least vis-à-vis third parties.

Representative of the recognition of latent security interests, even in the bankruptcy of the grantor of the security interest, is the law of Germany, whereas the opposite end of the spectrum is represented by the law of the United States, as incorporated in Art. 9 of the U.C.C. Other countries take intermediate positions, as e.g. France, the U.K., the Netherlands and the Scandinavian countries. The relevant issues are often complicated by the rules for the protection of bona fide purchasers or on the invalidation of oppressive transactions.

In addition, some legal systems distinguish between retained and granted security interests (as e.g. Germany, U.K. and numerous other countries),[1] while others like the U.S. (in the U.C.C.) have abolished that distinction and unified all forms of security interests.

Finally, the differences may raise important conflict-of-laws issues. The following materials are selected to illustrate the practical problems.

B. GERMANY

1. Introduction

German law is the prime example of a legal system that permits the creation of latent security interests in tangible moveable property (chattels) or intangible property (choses-in-action). A merchant needing credit, whether from a supplier of goods or services, or from a lending institution, may secure the creditor, — if a *supplier* — by deferring the passage of title until payment in full (*Kauf unter Eigentumsvorbehalt*), or — if a *credit institution* — by transferring as security property in goods at hand (inventory or equipment) or claims against third parties without registration, change of possession or notice to the third parties (*Sicherungsübereignung or Sicherungszession*). Moreover, by way of 'anticipatory transfer', it is possible to create security interests in future tangible personal property or monetary claims.

Retention-of-title clauses may take different forms. In addition to merely stipulating that title to the purchased goods shall pass upon full payment of the price (*simple retention of title clause*), they may validly provide (i) that the supplier shall retain title until all debts owed by the buyer to the supplier shall have been paid; (ii) that the supplier shall retain title, even if the goods have been processed into, or are affixed to, another class of merchandise (*processing clause*); or (iii) that, upon resale, the supplier

1. See Retention of Title, A Practical ICC Guice to Legislation in 35 Countries (2d ed. 1993). R. Welter, *Les sûretés réelles dans les relations juridiques entre l'Allemagne et la Belgique du point de vue du droit allemand*, 67 Revue de droit international et de droit comparé 158 (1990).

shall be entitled to the buyer's claim against the sub-purchaser. Usually all three stipulations are provided in a standard retention of title clause.

Customarily, a retention of title clause containing a stipulation of the type described above under (i) is called an enlarged (*erweiterte*) retention of title, while a reservation of title coupled with an anticipatory assignment of the claims against the subpurchasers, as described supra under (iii) is designated as an elongated or extended (*verlängerte*) reservation of title. A reservation of title containing a processing clause is often also classified as elongated (*verlängerte*) retention of title.

The terminology used above is that used by leading texts on the various types of retention of title clauses.[2] Unfortunately the terminology is not uniform and some authors classify the retention of title in processed goods as an *enlarged* (*erweiterte*) retention of title.[3]

The difference in terminology can be partially explained with the legal basis of the effectiveness of a processing clause. Some authors take the view that the buyer processes the merchandise for the benefit of the supplier, whereas others argue that the buyer acquires the property, but has transferred it anticipatorily to the supplier. The Federal Supreme Court does not follow a clear terminology. The translation of '*verlängert*' creates additional problems, since various English speaking authors use 'enlarged', 'prolonged', or 'extended' to translate this term.[4]

In Germany, special credit institutions often finance businesses by buying in advance claims of the borrower against future customers, so-called factoring. This type of financing originated in the United States, but took hold in Europe and other countries. It is practiced in two forms: *True factoring*, in which the factor assumes the del-credere risk of the solvency of the sub-buyers and *quasi-factoring* (or blanket assignment), which is merely an anticipatory assignment for security.

The collision between bank credit and supplier credit has presented important policy questions in many modern legal systems. In contrast to the preferred position of bank credit in the United States, as manifested by the amendments to Art. 9-312 of the U.C.C. in 1972, Germany has sided with the suppliers.[5]

---

2. F. Baur, Lehrbuch des Sachenrechts, 15 ed. 1989, § 53 b III 3 (p. 498); § 59 I 4 a)–c) (p. 589). Accord R. Serick, *Eigentumsvorbehalt und Sicherungsübertragung* Vol. IV pp. 9–13 (1976).

3. For references see R. Serick, *Eigentumsvorbehalt und Sicherungsübertragung* Vol. IV § 40 I 1 at n. 8 (p. 5) (1976).

4. Retention of Title, a Practical ICC Guide to Legislation in 35 Countries (2d ed. 1993) 52, translates *verlängerter Eigentumsvorbehalt* as 'prolonged (or continued) retention of title', whereas T. Weir, in his translation of R. Serick, Securities in Movables in German Law: an Outline (1990) renders *verlängert* as 'extended' and *erweitert* as 'expanded'.

5. See Baur, Lehrbuch des Sachenrechts, 15 ed. 1989 § 59 VI 2 p. 604.

2. Cases

a. Recognition of the enlarged and elongated retention-of-title clause.

BGH VII. Sen.
Firm W. (pl) v. Bank for W. & A. (def)
Judgment of December 16, 1957,
26 BGHZ 185 (1958).

In March 1955 plaintiff delivered to the Firm V. 15.5 meters of cloth for overcoats. In the General Terms for Delivery and Payment there was included as Nr. 13, a retention-of-title clause for plaintiff phrased as follows:

'a) The merchandise remains the property of the seller until full payment of all claims, including future claims of the seller against the buyer.
b) The buyer is entitled to process and sell the merchandise, provided the following conditions are complied with:
c) Pledge or transfer for security of the merchandise which is subject to the retention-of-title clause or of the assigned claims is prohibited.
d) The buyer does not acquire property, pursuant to § 950 BGB, of new merchandise manufactured from the merchandise subject to the retention-of-title clause. The manufacture is done by the buyer for the benefit of the seller.
If the merchandise subject to the retention-of-title clause is processed together with goods not belonging to the seller, the seller becomes co-owner of the new merchandise in proportion of the value of the merchandise subject to the retention-of-title clause to the other processed goods.
e) The buyer herewith assigns to the seller the claim resulting from a resale of the merchandise subject to the retention-of-title clause, even if and to the extent that the merchandise has been processed.
f) The seller will not collect the claims that have been assigned so long as the buyer complies with his payment obligations. The buyer, however, is obliged to inform the seller of the names of sub-buyers, and to notify them of the assignment if the seller so requests. The buyer may collect the claims against the sub-buyers, so long as the seller does not direct otherwise.
g) . . .
h) If the security derived from the retention-of-title clause exceeds the secured claim by 25%, the seller will release fully paid deliveries according to his choice.'

This clause is followed by other provisions relating to the duties of the buyer in the case of levies and in the case of cessation of payments, as well as the duties of safekeeping and insurance of the merchandise involved.

Firm V. processed the cloth delivered by plaintiff into twelve ladies' coats, which it sold to three customers together with other merchandise. Firm V. assigned its claims against these three customers to the defendant as security for a loan. The customers paid defendant, which credited the account of Firm V. with the respective amounts.

In September 1955 the assets of Firm V. became subject to composition proceedings to avert liquidation. Both parties participated as creditors in the proceedings.

Plaintiff sues defendant for surrender of the amounts obtained by collection of the purchase money claims. It contends that the purchase money claims passed to it pursuant to the anticipatory assignment stipulated by it in its general Sales and Delivery Terms and that therefore Firm V. was not capable of assigning these claims to defendant.

Defendant asserts the invalidity of the anticipatory assignment on the grounds that the assigned claims were not sufficiently determinable and that the anticipatory assignment unfairly restricted the economic freedom of the assignor.

The court of first instance rendered judgment for plaintiff; the court of appeal reversed the judgment.

The petition for revision was successful.

REASONS

The court of appeal assumed that the legal basis for plaintiff's claim for restitution of the proceeds of the coats which Firm V. manufactured out of the cloth delivered by plaintiff must rest on § 816 par. 2 BGB [unjust enrichment] (in conjunction with § 408 BGB). This is correct and the parties did not challenge it.

I

A claim based on § 816 par. 2 BGB requires that the rights to the purchase price of the coats, at the time of their payment, belonged to plaintiff due to the anticipatory assignment stipulated with Firm V. The court of appeal erred in denying that this prerequisite was met.

1. It is incontrovertible that the sale of the cloth for coats was validly concluded between plaintiff as seller and Firm V. as buyer, including the terms stipulated in the conditions governing delivery and payment and the retention-of-title clause. Pursuant to Nr.13e of these conditions, Firm V. assigned its claims arising from the resale of the merchandise subject to the retention of title to plaintiff and in particular also to the extent that this merchandise was processed. Fundamental doubts about the permissibility of such anticipatory assignment do not arise (cf. 7 BGHZ 365 (1953)). The purchase money claims coming into existence (§ 398 BGB) then pass to the assignee. Whether and to what extent this applies in the instant case depends on the question, which claims are encompassed by the assignment-clause. The conditions for delivery and payment are manifestly so-called typical contract clauses, i.e. conditions

aiming at a uniform regulation of the contractual relations with the customers to the greatest possible extent. They must therefore be interpreted on the basis of their content without regard to the individual circumstances (cf. 7 BGHZ 365, 368 (1953)). The court of revision therefore is not bound by the interpretation of the finders of fact. The applicability of the conditions of the plaintiff is not limited to the territorial district of the court of appeal.

2. According to plaintiff's delivery and payment terms, the wording of which is to that extent unambiguous, the anticipatory assignment comprises the claims of the Firm V. against its buyers flowing from the resale of the coats. The appellate court has correctly found that the purchase money claims of Firm V. were assigned to plaintiff in their full amount (reasons omitted).

3. The claims which Firm V. assigned to plaintiff anticipatorily are also clearly determinable. In contrast to the later holdings of the Supreme Court of the Empire (155 RGZ 26, 29 (1937); J.W. 563 (1939), D.R. 581 (1940)), it is not relevant, as the First Civil Senate in its Judgment of October 25, 1952 (7 BGHZ 365, 368 et seq. (1953)) has shown convincingly, that the claims which were assigned anticipatorily under a generic definition were determined with respect to all conceivable cases; rather it suffices if pursuant to the assignment clause, the debt which is claimed as assigned in a particular case is sufficiently determinable.

In this respect, there could have been doubts about the effectiveness of the anticipatory assignment stipulated by plaintiff and Firm V. in the case in which Firm V., in the manufacture of the coats, had utilized not only the cloth of plaintiff, but also materials bought from other suppliers likewise subject to a retention-of-title clause coupled with an anticipatory assignment. Defendant, however, according to the findings of the court of appeal, has not argued that other suppliers also asserted a retention-of-title clause. Moreover, it is irrelevant for the effectiveness of the anticipatory assignment to plaintiff, whether plaintiff was the sole proprietor or only co-owner with Firm V. of the resold coats. Subject to the limitations flowing from § 138 BGB [unconscionable transactions], plaintiff is free to accept assignments from its customers of claims which arise from the transfer of things which are owned by the customer in co-proprietorship or even in sole proprietorship.

Doubts about the determinability of the purchase price claims assigned by Firm V. to plaintiff relating to the coats manufactured from plaintiff's cloth, finally could arise by reason of the fact that Firm V. sold these coats together with other merchandise (cf. Court of Appeal Cologne, B.B. 1953, 898). These doubts, however, are also not well-founded. As the bills submitted by Firm V. to its customer show, there was no agreement of a lump-sum price, but separate prices were stipulated on the individual items, including the coats manufactured with plaintiff's cloth. It is therefore clearly ascertainable with respect to the date of the resale, which portion of the total price is attributable to the coats manufactured from plaintiff's cloth. Difficulties might only arise if the buyers had made only partial payments, without allocating them to the individual items. This contingency, however, did not occur.

4. The appellate court held that the anticipatory assignment of Firm V.'s purchase money claims was void pursuant to § 138 BGB, because it limited the economic freedom of Firm V. in a manner that violated standards of conscionability. We do not agree.

It is true that an elongated [*sic*] reservation of title, which shall remain in effect until all claims of the seller benefitted by that clause are satisfied, may result in an excessive over-security of the seller and an unbearable restraint on the economic liberty of the buyer. In the instant case, however, no such possibility exists. First of all, according to Nr. 13h of its Delivery and Payment Terms, plaintiff is obliged to waive its rights in the merchandise that is fully paid, whenever the security furnished by way of the retention of title exceeds the claim to be secured by an amount of 25%. It must be conceded to the appellate court that this clause does not assure absolutely the relinquishment of rights in all fully paid deliveries and that the buyer possibly may not obtain a waiver despite substantial payments in a case where none of the deliveries is fully paid. Nevertheless, this clause gives the customer at least a possibility of procuring free means for the satisfaction of its other obligations, with the result that already for this reason it appears doubtful that the anticipatory assignment tied to the reservation of title may be deemed to be an unreasonable and void restraint on the assignor. (Cf 7 BGHZ 365, 369 (1953).)

At any rate, it is impossible to speak of an invalid restraint on the economic freedom of movement of plaintiff's customers pursuant to § 138 BGB for the reason that under Nr.13f, sentence 3, of the general Conditions, the buyers are free to collect themselves the assigned claims, so long as plaintiff does not impart other directions. The appellate court committed error when it construed this clause as merely empowering the customers to collect the claims, but as obligating them to remit the proceeds to plaintiff. The wording of the provision as well as its connection with the preceding sentences and most of all its sense and purpose as an assignment for security militate against this construction. If the buyer is entitled to collect the assigned claims, so long as plaintiff does not direct otherwise without any hint of an obligation to remit the collected sums to plaintiff this must be understood only in the sense that the buyer may keep the amounts collected. This is in harmony with the first sentence of Term Nr.13f which provides that plaintiff will not collect the assigned claims so long as the buyer meets payment obligations. Accordingly, the provisions of Nr. 13f of the terms of contract have the sense that plaintiff, so long as its customers meet their obligations, will be satisfied with the security provided by the claims of its customers that are still extant and leaves it to them to collect the claims in the ordinary course of business and to utilize the proceeds. This corresponds to the ordinary economic purpose of an assignment for security, which is designed to provide the grantee of the security interest with a possible opportunity of satisfaction in the case that the grantor fails to meet its obligation. It amounts to a so-called silent assignment which vests the assignee with the status of a creditor, but according to its content and purpose is subject to the limitation that, until a different order by the assignee, i.e. so long as it takes care of its affairs in the normal way, the assignor shall be entitled to the management and utilization of the assigned claims. (RG, D.R. 1939, 865; 133 RGZ 234, 242 (1931); 136 RGZ, 100, 102 (1932).) The economic freedom of the assignor is not unduly impaired by reason of an assignment of this kind.

5. The court of appeal, however, considers the anticipatory assignment in this case to be void, even if Firm V. had the liberty to dispose freely of the proceeds obtained from the collection of the assigned claims. For it would then show that in reality plaintiff was only interested in obtaining unjustified advantages in the case of a default or insolvency of Firm V. These reasons misunderstand plaintiff's Delivery and Payment Terms and the essence of an assignment for security.

True, the Supreme Court of the Empire has held that an assignment for security which was to secure the assignee only in the case of an insolvency of the assignor was invalid (RG JW 1932, 1655 Nr.9). * * * In that case it could be concluded that the transfer of the claim was only intended if the assignor became insolvent. In the instant case, however, it follows from the text of plaintiff's Terms of Delivery and Payment that it possessed the right to collect the assigned claims from the very beginning. Although Nr.13f, sentence 1, provides that plaintiff will not collect the assigned claims so long as the customer meets its payment obligations, the customer is obliged to notify its own debtors of the assignment if plaintiff so requests. Accordingly, plaintiff shall have the full position of a creditor from the very beginning; it will only not exercise it vis-à-vis third parties, so long as the assignor does not create a cause therefore through neglect of its payment duties. This corresponds to the essential character of a security interest which is always only resorted to when the grantor thereof fails to perform his duties (cf. Flume, 3 NJW 841, 845 (1950).) * * * Only if the assignment is designed to give the assignee the position of a creditor solely in the case of a cessation of payments or insolvency of the assignor whereas the assignor prior to that event may freely dispose of the 'assigned' claims, is it possible to speak of an impermissible disadvantage of the other creditors. (Cf. 92 RGZ 105, 108 et seq. (1918); 138 RGZ 89, 94 1933).) This is not the case in this instance.

6. Since the purchase money claims for the coats were subject to a valid anticipatory assignment to plaintiff, defendant could not acquire the same claims by way of a subsequent contract with Firm V. Defendant obtained the payment of the purchase money without cause. Since the payment liberated the buyers of the coats (§ 408 par. 1, BGB; § 407 par. 1 BGB) the prerequisites of a claim of plaintiff against defendant according to § 816 par. 2 BGB are fulfilled.

II.

* * *

III.

[The Supreme Court discussed the question raised by the defendant whether, under the facts of the case, the unjust enrichment of defendant was diminished or eliminated because it credited the collected amounts to the account of Firm V. and therefore filed only a reduced claims in Firm V.'s composition proceedings. The Court concluded that certain facts required clarification by the court below.]

NOTES

1. The text case is the leading case on anticipatory assignments for security of claims against subpurchasers in a retention of title clause.

2. The recognition of elongated reservation of title clauses, which provide for the anticipatory assignment of claims arising from the resale of the goods delivered under reservation of title may result in a conflict between assignments under retention of title clauses and anticipatory global assignments to credit institutions. In other words, the recognition spawned a conflict between lenders of money (*Geldkreditgeber*) and suppliers of goods on credit (*Warenkreditgeber*).

As a result, the Supreme Federal Court of Germany (BGH) elaborated a complex network of rules for the protection of the 3 parties concerned: the borrower, the provider of money credit (credit institution), and the supplier of merchandise credit (seller under reservation of title.) The legislative basis of these judge-made rules is BGB § 138 (prohibition of immoral constraints) and AGBG § 9.[6] The provision of AGBG § 9(I) which 'invalidates provisions in general terms of trade if they subject the other party improperly to disadvantages in violation of the mandates of good faith,' has been construed to impose a stricter standard than § 138 BGB. It should be noted that the limitations on the validity of anticipatory assignments of accounts in the context of retention of title clauses vary from the limitations on the assignments of accounts agreed upon as security for loans by credit institutions.

3. Enlarged or elongated retention of title clauses must protect the buyer under such clauses against excessive security of the seller. Generally, the threshold of excessiveness is reached when the collateral exceeds 120% of the value of the outstanding indebtedness. Therefore, the respective retention clause must provide for a duty of the seller to release collateral in excess of that limit (so-called 'obligatory release stipulation'). The relevant decisions of the BGH (all VIII. Senate) are:

(i) Judgment of March 20, 1985 (94 BGHZ 105, 113 (1985));
(ii) Judgment of October 8, 1986 (98 BGHZ 303, 305 (1987));

6. Gesetz zur Regelung des Rechts der Allgemeinen Geschäftsbedingungen or *AGB-Gesetz* (Law governing General Terms of Trade) of December 9, 1976, as amended by the Laws of March 3, 1983, July 25, 1986 and July 24, 1996.

(iii) Judgment of November 29, 1989 (109 BGHZ 240, 246 (dictum) (1990));

(iv) Judgment of December 2, 1992 (120 BGHZ 300 (1993); release clause predicated upon excess security of 25% violates § 9(1) AGBG and invalidates the retention clause);

(v) Judgment of February 9, 1994 (48 WM 583 (1994)).

4. In cases dealing with the validity or effectiveness of lender-formulated global assignments as security of accounts receivable or transfers as security of inventory (stock-in-trade) with changing composition, the different senates of the BGH required the stipulation of a non-discretionary release clause providing for release of collateral exceeding a permissible coverage limit and a stipulation of such limit. This position was taken to protect the borrower against excessive security and to leave him the opportunity to acquire inventory subject to reservation of title clauses. BGH, VIIth Sen. Judgments of November 9, 1978, 72 BGHZ 308 (1970) and 72 BGHZ 316 (1970).)

Recently, on the initiative of the XIth Senate, the case lse has been modified and lender-formulated global assignments and transfers as security of revolving inventory have been held to be valid and effective without such clauses (see the following Note.)

Stipulations of maximum coverage ratios and release clauses which have the purpose of protecting the borrower have their counterpart in the so-called *'financial covenants'* which are found in international financing agreements and serve to protect the lender by imposing restrictions on the business conduct of the borrower, Cf Von Arne Wittig, *Financial Covenants im inländischen Kreditgeschäft*, 50 WM 1381 (1996).

5. *PROTECTION AGAINST EXCESSIVE SECURITY: Reorientation of BGH's Decisional Law.*

Under German law, bank-loans are frequently secured by a global assignment as security of present and future accounts receivable of the borrower or by a transfer as security of stock-in-trade (inventory) with changing composition. Usually the text of the respective agreements is prepared by the bank and printed on forms used in their deals. According to established case-law developed by the senates of the BGH having jurisdiction over transactions of this type — Senates VII, VIII, IX and XI, it was necessary for the validity of such transactions pursuant to BGB §§ 138 and 242 and their effectiveness under §9 of the Law on General Terms of Trade Contracts (*AGBG*) that they included stipulations fixing a limit on the amount by which the value of the collateral could exceed the unpaid balance of the secured claim (*konkrete Deckungsgrenze*) and providing for a mandatory non-discretionary release of collateral to the extent that it exceeded that limit for a substantial period of time. Generally it was held that a limit of 120% of the value of the collateral over the amount of the unpaid balance of the loan was not excessive. Beginning with 1994, the XIth Senate in Civil Matters expressed doubts on the appropriateness of these requirements.[7]

7. See e.g. BGH Judgment of December 12, 1995, 49 NJW 847 (1996) and authorities cited.

Early in 1996, the XIth Senate in Civil Matters was faced with cases which presented the questions whether the lack of a mandatory non-discretionary release clause or of a clause limiting excess security in a creditor-formulated agreement entailed the invalidity or ineffectiveness of the entire assignment as security of accounts receivable or the transfer of stock in trade with variable composition. Since the XIth Senate wished to give a definitive negative answer, it would have been obligated to refer the question to the Large Senate in Civil Matters pursuant to the Law on Organization of the Judiciary (*GVG*) § 132, unless the other interested Senates responded to a formal inquiry that they no longer maintained their former views. Accordingly, the XIth Senate issued two resolutions of inquiry, one relating to the need of a release clause[8], the other relating to the need for a concrete limit on excess collateral.[9]

The VIIth Senate replied informally that its judgments were not based on the position from which the XIth Senate wished to depart, while the VIIIth and IXth Senates replied that they no longer maintained the position that security agreements of the type in issue were invalid or ineffective without clauses limiting the excess collateral and requiring non-discretionary release of excess collateral. As a result, the XIth Senate in Civil Matters held in the respective case that a creditor-formulated global assignment of accounts receivable was neither invalid nor ineffective because it contained merely a limit on excessive security, but lacked a mandatory release clause.[10]

In its answer to the formal inquiry of April 16, 1996 by the XIth Senate, the IXth Senate gave the following reply:[11]

> 'The position that a global assignment of accounts receivable is not effective according to AGBG § 9(I) without an express fixation of a limit on the value of the collateral is not maintained; nevertheless, there is no assent to the reasons given in the order of inquiry submitted by the XIth Senate in Civil Matters of April 16, 1996 so far as essential issues are concerned.'

In the reasons appended to the reply, the IXth Senate in Civil Matters stated that it agreed with the XIth Senate that the grantor of the security in the case of a persistent excess of security is entitled to a release of the objectively determined excess of collateral independently of a stipulation to that effect. It disagreed, however, with the other Senate's position that the stipulation of a release obligation was not advantageous for the debtor. The fixation of a limit on excess of collateral in a creditor-formulated assignment as security for present and future accounts receivable dispensed with otherwise protracted litigation concerning the right to a release. Nevertheless, although the inclusion of a clause fixing an appropriate limit on excess se-

8. BGH, XI Sen., Resolution of January 23, 1996, 49 NJW 1213 (1996), 50 WM 476 (1996).

9. BGH, IX Sen., Resolution of April 16, 1996, 50 WM 902 (1996).

10. Judgment of May 14, 1996, 49 NJW 2092 (1996) = 50 WM 476 (1996).

11. BGH, IX. Sen. Resolution of July 11, 1996 (XI ZR 234/95, 50 WM 1436 (1996)) = 49 NJW 2790 (1996).

curity had definite advantages, the absence of such a clause should not result in the invalidity of the security agreement, since the right to a release could be determined by resort to rules immanent in security agreements of that type. The same principles should also govern the transfer as security of rotating stock-in-trade.

The IXth Senate concluded its reply by stating that despite its agreement with the result, the replying Senate felt that the disagreement of the two Senates was so fundamental that the XIth Senate should consider an invocation of the Large Senate for Civil Matters pursuant to the Law on the Organization of the Judiciary (*GVG)* *§ 132*IV.[12]

On the same day, the IXth Senate addressed the questions to the VIIth Senate:[13] 'Is the legal position maintained that:

a) the transfer as security of stock-in-trade with changing composition or the global assignment as security of accounts receivable without a non-discretionary release clause is invalid pursuant to BGB § 138(I) or ineffective pursuant to the AGBG § 9(I)?

b) the transfer as security of stock-in-trade with changing composition or the global assignment as security of accounts receivable without expressed fixation of a limit on excess security is invalid pursuant to BGB § 138(I) or ineffective pursuant to AGBG § 9(I)?

In its reasons the IXth Senate explained in detail its present position, viz. that the validity or effectiveness of a creditor-formulated transfer as security of stock-in-trade with changing composition or global assignment as security of present and future accounts receivable did not depend on the inclusion of a stipulation for the non-discretionary release of excess collateral and for the fixation of a limit on persistent excess collateral.

Even under the prior law the need for a qualified release clause existed only in the case of global assignments and transfer of stock-in-trade with changing composition and not in the case of individual assignments and transfers. Accordingly, the assignment of future rents as security for a loan which was also secured by a real estate security interest on the same premises did not constitute an unconscionable excessive security, in particular since the granted land security included as a matter of law the right to the rents.[14]

By resolution of October 10, 1996 (58 KTS 244 (1997), 51 WM 311 (1997), the VII. Senate for Civil Matters of the Federal Supreme Court gave its formal reply to the inquiries that the IX. and VI. Senates transmitted to it. The inquiry of the IX. Senate dated July 11, 1996, is printed in 51 WM 1439 (1996); the inquiry of the XI. Senate

---

12. For the full text of the BGH IXth Sen. Resolution of July 11, 1996 see 50 WM 1436 (1996) = 49 NJW 2790 (1996).

13. BGH, IXth Sen. Resolution of July 11, 1996 (IX ZR 74/95) 50 WM 1439 (1996) = 49 NJW 2788 (1996).

14. Court of Appeal, Cologne, Judgment of March 5, 1996, 17 ZIP 828 (1996).

dated April 16, 1996, is reprinted in 50 WM 902 (1996), 17 ZIP 957 (1996). In its reply, the VII. Senate stated as its guiding principle:

> 'If a coverage limit is neither fixed by agreement not determinable by means of interpretation, a global assignment for security violates § 138 BGB, if the context of the agreement impedes inequitably the claim for a release by the grantor of the security.'

The VII. Senate pointed out that it shared the view of the XI. Senate to a large extent, but disagreed with the view of the IX. Senate in cases where a fixed coverage ceiling cannot be expected.

Because of the remaining disagreements, both the IX. and the XI. Senates invoked the decision of the Large Senate: the IX. Senate by Order of March 16, 1997, 18 ZIP 632 (1997) = 51 WM 750 (1997) and the XI. Senate by Order of May 13, 1997, 50 NJW 1570 (1997), 51 WM 1197 (1997), 18 ZIP 1185 (1997).

In its reference to the Large Senate, the IX. Senate pointed out that the question it posed to the Large Senate required answers different from those given by the XI. Senate and advocated by the VII. Senate. Therefore a solution by the Large Senate was necessary for the development of the law. The IX. Senate was interested in a partial reorientation of the applicable law which had to be sanctioned by the authority of the Large Senate (Point III 5b of the *Reasons.*) In its subsequent reference, the XI. Senate — the driving force in the controversy — explained that it referred its question to the large Senate because of its continuing divergence from the position of the VII. Senate (Resolution of Reference, Point III 1 last par. and 2.)

Due to the practical importance of the controversy, it has generated extensive literature among text writers, see e.g.

C.W. Canaris, *Voraussetzung und Inhalt des Anspruchs auf Freigable von Globalsicherheiten,* 18 ZIP 813-36 (1997).

C.W. Canaris, *Die Problematik der Sicherheitenfreigabeklauseln im Hinblick auf § AGBG und § 138 BGB,* 17 ZIP 1109-23 (1996).

C.W. Canaris, Deckungsgrenze und Bewertungsmassstab beim Anspruch auf Freigabe von Sicherheiten gemäss § 242 BGB, 17 ZIP 1577-86 (1996).

Hans Gerhard Ganter, *Aktuelle Probleme der Kreditsicherheiten in der Rechtsprechung des Bundesgerichtshofes,* 50 WM 1705 (1996).

Thomas Pfeiffer, *Der gesetzliche Inhalt des allgemeine Freigabeanspruchs* 18 ZIP 49-59 (1997).

Martin Schwab, *Globalsicherheiten und Freigabeklauseln vor dem Grossen Senate,* 51 WM 1883-93 (1997).

Rolf Serick, *Das normative Leitbild der gewohnheitsrechtlichen Sicherungstreuhand und ihrer Haftobergrenze auf der Waage des Grossen Senats für Zivilsachen,* 51 WM 2053-75 (1997).

Rolf Serick, *Gewohnheitsrecht und fehlende vertraglich Deckungsgrenze bei fidiziarischen Kreditsichernehiten,* 51 WM 345-96 (1996).

Rolf Serick, *Freigabeklauseln, Deckungsgrenze und Haftobergrenze,* 50 NJW 1529-133 (1997).

b. Invalidity of anticipatory blanket assignment for security of all future claims against subpurchases under enlarged retention-of-title clauses.

BGH VIII. Sen.
Judgment of March 9, 1977
31 WM 480 (1977), 30 NJW 2261 (1977).

Plaintiff, in a current course of business, supplied the firm R, in the sole proprietorship of Hildegard D. [debtor], with cotton fabrics since 1970. According to Plaintiff's General Contract Terms governing the deliveries, the supplied merchandise was to remain the property of plaintiff until the full payment of all, including future claims of plaintiff against defendant based on this business relation. If the merchandise was processed, the reservation of title was to cover the newly created thing. Future claims resulting from the resale of the merchandise were to be considered as assigned to plaintiff. The retention of title was to remain operative if individual claims were to be included in a running account and the balance was fixed or acknowledged. Plaintiff was obligated to release security interests according to its choice if its claims were oversecured in excess of 20%. In addition, plaintiff, who was at that time still debtor's only supplier, concluded an assignment contract on November 25, 1970/ January 2, 1971 whereby debtor, for the purpose of securing all present and future claims of plaintiff, assigned to the latter without limitation all existing and future claims arising, until termination of the business relationship, against all third parties from deliveries of goods or rendition of services.

Furthermore, debtor assigned to plaintiff all claims to the balances of running accounts maintained by debtor with third parties, the right to determine the balances as well as the right to terminate the current account relationship. The assignment also included all security interests existing for the claims and the rights pertaining thereto. Moreover, on May 1, 1972 plaintiff and debtor concluded a space warehousing agreement whereby debtor transferred to plaintiff its present and future property rights in all textiles and jerseys, which were present in its storeroom on May 1, 1972 or would be brought there subsequently until termination of their business relationship. The warehousing agreement also comprised all objects processed from the collateral and all claims arising from a resale thereof. The assignment contract and the space warehousing contract provided for an oversecurity margin of 25% of the face amount of the secured aggregate claim of debtor.

Towards the end of February 1971 debtor, on the urging of plaintiff, approached defendant bank for a sizeable loan in order to be able to buy merchandise from foreign suppliers which insisted on cash. The bank accorded the credit, taking, in ignorance of the prior assignment of January 2, 1971, a blanket assignment by debtor, dated March 26, 1971, which included all present and future claims against third parties — excepting debtors whose name began with certain letters of the alphabet — as security. On September 1, 1972 debtor was adjudicated bankrupt in a proceeding following an unsuccessful attempt at composition. Defendant bank collected DM 58,145.98 on the basis of the blanket assignment of March 26, 1971. Plaintiff, whose claim was determined in the bankruptcy proceedings to amount to DM 184,218.67, brought an action against defendant for the amount collected by it, contending that it was entitled thereto by virtue of the assignment of January 2, 1971.

Both fact instances dismissed the complaint. The petition for review was unsuccessful.

REASONS
I

1. The court of appeal (Celle) considered the assignment of January 2, 1971 to be void as an unconscionable shackling agreement and endangering of creditors' rights pursuant to § 138(1) BGB, because it, together with the other security interests of plaintiff, deprived the debtor of its economic freedom to an impermissible extent, a factor of which plaintiff was aware because it knew debtor's financial situation.

2. The petition for revision argues that a supplier of materials such as plaintiff was not obliged to consider whether its customers may be compelled subsequently to seek a bank loan. It was not able, like a bank, to examine the existence of other collateral. If, in consideration of the grant of long-term credit terms, it requires security by way of a blanket assignment by its customers, it did not have to respect the interests of subsequent providers of credit.

II

The judgment of the court below resists this attack. We need not pass on the question, whether in a case like this in which plaintiff was debtor's sole supplier and already possessed ample security for its claims by virtue of its far reaching retention-of-title clause, an additional security by way of a comprehensive blanket assignment for security constitutes by itself an unconscionable shackling of debtor and therefore is void pursuant to BGB § 138(I). At any rate the objective endangering of the interests of other creditors which is achieved by this type of security renders the debtor's blanket assignment of January 2, 1971 violative of the standards of fairness in business and void according to that provision.

1. The case-law in the past had frequent occasions to pass on the efficacy of blanket assignments to banks — that is, to suppliers of money credit and their collision with an elongated retention-of-title clause for the benefit of providers of credit

in the form of goods. It has in general proceeded on the premise that a security agreement, which opens the possibility of deceiving future creditors about the credit risk involved and thereby injuring them, may be invalid, if this possibility under the particular circumstances of the case was so strong that the contracting parties had to reckon with that result of their security agreement for subsequent creditors but nevertheless accepted it (10 BGHZ 228, 232 et seq. (1953)). In this connection, a blanket assignment was always held to be violative of the standards of fair dealing and void (BGB § 138(I)) if it also included claims which the debtor would have subsequently to assign to its suppliers by virtue of a stipulated elongated retention-of-title clause (30 BGHZ 149, 153 (1930); 55 BGHZ 34, 35 (1971)); Judgments of this Senate of November 6, 1968, 51 WM 18 (1969) and of April 24, 1968, 21 WM 644 (1968). That this applies also to a case where the assignee of a blanket assignment is not a bank, but a supplier of merchandise, was decided already by the Supreme Court in its Judgment of March 7, 1974, 28 WM 368 (1974).

2. * * *

3. The Senate, following Serick concurs with the courts below and holds that in the instant case the blanket assignment between debtor and plaintiff of January 2, 1971 violates the standards of fair dealing because of its danger to the interests of creditors and therefore is void (BGB § 138(II).)

a) Even if one starts with the proposition, found by the appellate court, that at the date of the blanket assignment plaintiff was debtor's sole supplier and that the foreign creditors which were envisaged in the enlargement of debtor's business usually made no sales with retention-of-title clauses, with the result that debtor was not compelled to deceive them about the debtor's ability to comply with an elongated retention-of-title clause, there still remains the incontestable fact, that the debtor could no longer dispose of any extant claims because they belonged to plaintiff either by virtue of the elongated retention-of-title clause in the general terms of delivery or of the assignment of January 2, 1971.

According to its own pleadings, plaintiff knew the credit needs of the debtor, because the foreign suppliers which were contemplated in purchases by debtor would only sell against cash, as plaintiff stated itself in its arguments. Credit, therefore, was necessary under the circumstances of the case for the conduct of cash transactions with foreign suppliers as envisaged by debtor. At least this situation should have compelled plaintiff to refrain from tying debtor even tighter to itself by means of an unlimited blanket assignment, and thus to forestall a deception of other providers of credit in reference to the credit risk of debtor. The court of appeal is correct in stating that the interests of a bank as provider of credit in form of money deserves protection no less than those of a provider of credit in form of goods. The debtor no longer owned any extant claims of which it could lawfully dispose. It was fully dependant on plaintiff's behavior. The appellate court found that defendant showed without contradiction that no other collateral of the debtor was available. Plaintiff was vis-à-vis the debtor in the same position as that which the providers of money credit occupied in the cases cited above, vis-à-vis a debtor who had assigned to them all outstanding claims without exception or limitation. If the appellate court applied the principles which the case law developed for collisions between a blanket assignment and an elongated retention-of-title clause to this case of a collision between two blanket assignments, no reproach can be founded upon legal reasons.

b) If the court of appeal concluded on the basis of an evaluation of the totality of circumstances that plaintiff already at the time of the blanket assignment of January 2, 1971 had to reckon with a deception by the debtor of future creditors, but accepted that possibility, no legal error can be discerned. Plaintiff acted in this case vis-à-vis the debtor like a bank, without, however, supplying funds for the continuation of the business beyond the provision of credit by means of deliveries of goods. It was perfectly aware of the need for such funds as follows from the fact that it itself recommended to debtor to seek a loan from defendant. * * * In this situation the two courts below have correctly denied legal effect to the blanket assignment of January 2, 1971 invoked by plaintiff.

NOTE

This judgment of the BGH (VIII. Sen.) is one of the pioneer decisions subjecting elongated retention of title clauses to the limitations flowing from BGB § 138 and AGBG § 9(I) discussed in the preceding note.

c. *True factoring and elongated reservation of title.*

BGH VIII. Senate
U. GmbH (def) v. G. KG (pl)
Judgment of September 19, 1977
69 BGHZ 254 (1978).

On June 7, 1972 defendant entered into a factoring contract with the firm F. It required F to assign to it all future claims of F against its customers, derived from the delivery of merchandise or the rendition of services or performance of work, subject to the condition precedent that it, the defendant, would purchase the respective claim (§ 6a of the factoring agreement). Defendant assumed the del-credere risk (§ 7b of the agreement). The parties stipulated in addition that a special account would be formed to satisfy possible indemnity claims of defendant against F.

F had a contract with the Federal Postal Service to execute certain glass and light metal installations. With respect to the supply and installation of glass it entered into a subcontract with plaintiff. In that connection it agreed with plaintiff on an elongated reservation of title clause.

Plaintiff performed the subcontract and billed defendant for DM 21,371.02. F offered its claim against the Federal Postal Service to defendant for sale. Defendant purchased that claim. F was adjudicated bankrupt on March 13, 1974. The trustee in bankruptcy acknowledged the validity of the elongated reservation of title agreement. He directed plaintiff to seek payment from the Postal Service which retained the sum of DM 21,371.02 because it was also claimed by defendant.

Plaintiff seeks a declaratory judgment determining that defendant has no rights to the claim of F against the Postal Service. The district court and the court of appeal held for the plaintiff.

The admitted petition for review was successful.

REASONS

The decision of the controversy depends on the question whether the blanket-assignment pursuant to § 6a of the factoring agreement of June 7, 1972 is valid.

1. The court of appeal took the position that the assignment was invalid pursuant to § 138 BGB, because it constituted an inducement of F. to deceive its suppliers of credit and to breach its obligations, to the extent that it encompassed claims included in an elongated retention-of-title clause. According to the court of appeal, this follows from an analogous application of the principles developed by the Federal Supreme Court for the cases of a collision between a blanket assignment for security to grantors of money credits and rights flowing from an elongated reservation of title clause. The two groups of conflict were legally speaking similar. In its view, the factor, too, relies on the assigned claim as security, if purchased claims subsequently prove to be uncollectible. It was not evident to what extent in the case of a factoring transaction the risk that suppliers which made deliveries under a reservation of title clause might suffer damages would be less than in the case of a credit secured by an assignment. In both instances the customer was free to use the sums received for purposes other than payment of its obligation to the suppliers unless this was expressly prohibited by the agreement.

2. These reasons are controverted successfully in the petition for review.

a) The collaboration between the factoring-bank and its customer may, even in the optimal setting, not prevent that the customer fails to meet its obligations vis-à-vis its suppliers. If it becomes insolvent it is possible that in the relations between the factoring bank which is secured by an anticipatory assignment and the suppliers of the customers who delivered goods on credit subject to an elongated retention-of-title clause and received an assignment of claims resulting from resale or processing of those goods, the same conflict situation may arise as does in the relation between suppliers on credit of money and those of goods. This is the common problem of credit against assignment and of the factoring business * * *. (Cf. Glomb, *Finanzierung durch Factoring,* p. 124; Bette, *Das Factoring-Geschäft* 86 (1973). Controversial, however, is the question whether the principles which the Federal Supreme Court has developed for the resolution of the conflict between the providers of credit in form of money and the providers of credit in form of merchandise and which impose on the lender of money the duty to respect the interest of the sellers under a retention-of-title clause (51 BGHZ 113, 117 (1969)) also apply to the relation between the factoring bank and providers of credit by way of supplies. (Cf. the extensive survey of the different opinions, in Serick, *Eigentumsvorbehalt und Sicherungsübertragung*, Vol. IV § 52 III [1976]). The multiplicity of possibilities for the content of factoring transactions does not permit a generally applicable resolution of the controversy. It can be resolved only by a case-by-case approach.

b) The conditions which, according to the constant decisional law of the Federal Supreme Court, entail the nullity of an anticipatory blanket assignment to the provider of money credit (§ 138(1) BGB) to the extent that it also covers those claims which the debtor would have to assign to its suppliers in the future pursuant to an elongated retention-of-title clause, were laid down by this Senate in its most recent Judgment of March 9, 1977 (31 WM 480 (1977)). We adhere to this holding.

c) The question to be resolved, however is whether in the instant case the interests of the sellers under reservation of title that merit legal protection are safeguarded in a manner that, taking into account to the terms of the factoring contract of June 7, 1972, no reproach of unconscionable conduct can be made and therefore no nullity according to § 138 BGB ensues.

The defendant entered with F into a 'true factoring' relationship. Pursuant to § 7b of the factoring contract it assumed the risk of the debtor. The contract thus included the del-credere function (cf. Serick, op. cit. § 52 I1). Whereas the 'non-true factoring' which could have been selected in a particular case is to be classified as a credit transaction (Judgment of the Senate of May 3, 1972, 58 BGHZ 364 (1972) * * *), *true* factoring consists in a purchase of a claim (Serick, op. cit. § 52 II2b). It has the special feature that the customer is entitled to keep the purchase price which usually is paid by the factoring bank in advance before the maturity. Because of the fact that the buyer under a retention-of-title clause in the case of true factoring receives 'the full value of its claim' in a way 'that it is not obliged to a return thereof' the seller under a retention-of-title clause is placed exactly in the position, according to Serick, 'in which it would find itself, if in the case of an elongated retention-of-title clause, the buyer had extinguished the assigned claim by accepting — which it is entitled to do — its value' in cash 'either from the sub-buyer of the merchandise subject to the retention-of-title clause or from a third person' (Serick, op. cit. § 52 IV 3c; cf District Court Mainz, BB 1038 (1966)). Subject to the limitation, which is not material in this connection, that in practice the factoring bank because of its 'fee' never pays the full value of the claim, we agree with this analysis. Serick is also correct in asserting that no valid grounds exist against parallel treatment of the acceptance of the value of the claim from the factoring bank in the case of true factoring with the acceptance of cash from the sub-buyer, when the seller has permitted resale against cash by authorizing the buyer to make collections (Serick, op. cit. Vol. IV p. 575). As little as the buyer under an elongated retention-of-title clause can be charged with a breach of the contract with the supplier, because of a resale to a sub-buyer against cash, can he can be charged with such a breach in the case of true factoring when he is credited by the factoring bank with the value of the claim. The fact that the factoring customer retains the risk of the existence of the assigned claim does not justify a difference in treatment of the two case types because this arrangement corresponds to the usual legal situation pursuant to § 437 BGB. Possible claims of the factoring bank against its customer which might flow from this situation, apart from the rights as buyer, are satisfied, according to the governing stipulations (§ 9 of the factoring agreement), from the creation of a so-called cash deposit. Therefore, it cannot be said that the blanket anticipatory assignment serves as security for these claims.

True, plaintiff did not expressly authorize F to collect from its customers the claims that had been assigned anticipatorily to plaintiff. This authorization follows, however, from the unlimited power of disposition granted by plaintiff to F.

Consequently if the nature of true factoring precludes a breach of contract on the part of the buyer under a reservation of title clause to the extent that the loss of the effectiveness of the conditional anticipatory assignment to plainitff pursuant to § 161 par. 1 BGB is in issue, it is also impossible to charge defendant with participation in a breach of contract. The blanket anticipatory assignment by the customer to the factoring bank of all its future claims against all of its subpurchasers or contractors for work, under the condition precedent that the factoring bank buys the respective claims in the case of true factoring, does therefore not violate the mandates of fairness

3. Another question concerns the issue whether defendant may be guilty of a violation of good faith and therefore a misuse of rights when, in the case of a conflict, it invokes against plaintiff its priority based on the anticipatory assignment, without an express agreement in the factoring contract pursuant to which the customer is obliged to remit the factoring proceeds to the supplier under a retention-of-title clause (cf. Glomb, op. cit. p. 127).

A concrete duty to protect the interests of suppliers under retention-of-title clauses by way of corresponding contractual terms cannot be affirmed as a general rule. In principle the factoring bank must be able to rely on the assumption that its customer will use the proceeds from the factoring properly according to the rules of economic rationality (cf. Bette, op. cit. p. 86). This Senate has stated already in prior decisions that such clauses are not apt to influence the actual course of events and to prevent in serious cases conflicts between the providers of credit in form of money and the providers of credit in form of delivery of merchandise (cf. Judgments of April 24, 1968, 21 NJW 1516 (1968) and of November 6, 1968, 22 NJW 318 (1969).)

The factoring bank must take appropriate and reasonably expectable steps only at a time when it has grounds to assume that its customer does not meet its obligations vis-à-vis its suppliers under a retention-of-title clause. It might be necessary in such cases to institute blocked accounts for the benefit of the suppliers.

But in the instant case, no indication exists of such a situation.

NOTE

With reference to factoring as a special type of financing device See infra, Chap. 9.

C. UNITED KINGDOM

1. Statutes

a. The Companies Act 1989

Registration in the companies charges register

93 Charges requiring registration

The following sections are inserted in Part XII of the Companies Act 1985 —

'Registration in the company charges register

395 Introductory provisions

(1) The purpose of this Part is to secure the registration of charges on a company's property.

(2) In this Part —

'charge' means any form of security interest (fixed or floating) over property, other than an interest arising by operation of law; and

'property', in the context of what is the subject of a charge, includes future property.

(3) It is immaterial for the purposes of this Part where the property subject to a charge is situated.

(4) References in this Part to 'the registrar' are —

(*a*) in relation to a company registered in England and Wales, to the registrar of companies for England and Wales, and

(*b*) in relation to a company registered in Scotland, to the registrar of companies for Scotland;

and references to registration, in relation to a charge, are to registration in the register kept by him under this Part.

396 Charges requiring registration

(1) The charges requiring registration under this Part are —

(*a*) a charge on land or any interest in land, other than —

(i) in England and Wales, a charge for rent or any other periodical sum issuing out of the land,

   (ii) in Scotland, a charge for any rent, ground annual or other periodical sum payable in respect of the land;

(*b*) a charge on goods or any interest in goods, other than a charge under which the chargee is entitled to possession either of the goods or of a document of title to them;

(*c*) a charge on intangible movable property (in Scotland, incorporeal moveable property) of any of the following descriptions —

   (i) goodwill,

   (ii) intellectual property,

   (iii) book debts (whether book debts of the company or assigned to the company),

   (iv) uncalled share capital of the company or calls made but not paid;

(*d*) a charge for securing an issue of debentures; or

(*e*) a floating charge on the whole or part of the company's property.

(2) The descriptions of charge mentioned in subsection (1) shall be construed as follows —

(*a*) a charge on a debenture forming part of an issue or series shall not be treated as falling within paragraph (*a*) or (*b*) by reason of the fact that the debenture is secured by a charge on land or goods (or on an interest in land or goods);

(*b*) in paragraph (*b*) 'goods' means any tangible movable property (in Scotland, corporeal moveable property) other than money;

(*c*) a charge is not excluded from paragraph (*b*) because the chargee is entitled to take possession in case of default or on the occurrence of some other event;

(*d*) in paragraph (*c*)(ii) 'intellectual property' means —

   (i) any patent, trade mark, service mark, registered design, copyright or design right, or

   (ii) any license under or in respect of any such right;

(*e*) a debenture which is part of an issue or series shall not be treated as a book debt for the purposes of paragraph (*c*)(iii);

(*f*) the deposit by way of security of a negotiable instrument given to secure the payment of book debts shall not be treated for the purposes of paragraph (*c*)(iii) as a charge on book debts;

(*g*) a shipowner's lien on subfreights shall not be treated as a charge on book debts for the purposes of paragraph (*c*)(iii) or as a floating charge for the purposes of paragraph (*e*).

(3) Whether a charge is one requiring registration under this Part shall be determined —

(*a*) in the case of a charge created by a company, as at the date the charge is created, and

(*b*) in the case of a charge over property acquired by a company, as at the date of the acquisition.

(4) The Secretary of State may by regulations amend subsections (1) and (2) so as to add any description of charge to, or remove any description of charge from, the charges requiring registration under this Part.

(5) Regulations under this section shall be made by statutory instrument which shall be subject to annulment in pursuance of a resolution of either House or Parliament.

(6) In the following provisions of this Part references to a charge are, unless the context otherwise requires, to a charge requiring registration under this Part.

Where a charge not otherwise requiring registration relates to property by virtue of which it requires to be registered and to other property, the references are to the charge so far as it relates to property of the former description.'

b. Law of Property Act (1925) (c20) s136

136 Legal assignments of things in action

(1) Any absolute assignment by writing under the hand of the assignor (not purporting to be by way of charge only) of any debt or other legal thing in action, of which express notice in writing has been given to the debtor, trustee or other person from whom the assignor would have been entitled to claim such debt or thing in action, is effectual in law (subject to equities having priority over the right of the assignee) to pass and transfer from the date of such notice —

(*a*) the legal right to such debt or thing in action;

(*b*) all legal and other remedies for the same; and

(*c*) the power to give a good discharge for the same without the concurrence of the assignor:

c. Sale of Goods Act (1979) s19 (1)

Reservation of right of disposal

19. —(1) Where there is a contract for the sale of specific goods or where goods are subsequently appropriated to the contract, the seller may, by the terms of the contract or appropriation, reserve the right of disposal of the goods until certain conditions are fulfilled; and in such a case, notwithstanding the delivery of the goods to the buyer, or to a carrier or other bailee . . . for the purpose of transmission to the buyer, the property in the goods does not pass to the buyer until the conditions imposed by the seller are fulfilled.

(2) –(3) [*Subsections omitted.*]

2. Cases

[HOUSE OF LORDS]

a. ARMOUR AND ANOTHER .... RESPONDENTS

AND

THYSSEN EDELSTAHLWERKE A.G. .... APPELLANTS

1990 June 25, 26, 27, 28; Oct. 18

Lord Keith of Kinkel, Lord Griffiths, Lord Oliver of Aylmerton, Lord Goff of Chieveley and Lord Jauncey of Tullichettle

[1990] 3 WLR 810

Jonathan Mance Q. C. and *J.W. McNeill* (of the Scottish Bar) for the defenders.

J.E. Drummond-Young Q.C. and *N.F. Davidson* (both of the Scottish Bar) for the pursuers.

Their Lordships took time for consideration.

18 October. LORD KEITH OF KINKEL. My Lords, the appellants are a company carrying on business in West Germany as manufacturers and suppliers of steel. The respondents are the joint receivers on the assets of Carron Co. Ltd. ("Carron"), appointed on 3 August 1982 under powers contained in a floating charge in favour of two banks. Carron carried on business at Falkirk as manufacturers of metal, plastic and general engineering products.

For a considerable period prior to 3 August 1982 the appellants and Carron engaged in a course of dealing under which the appellants sold and supplied to Carron steel strip for use in its manufacturing processes. The contracts of sale between them were expressed as being subject to the appellants' General Conditions of Delivery and Payment. At the time of the respondents' appointment as receivers there were lying in Carron's works at Falkirk some 67,423 kilograms of steel strip which had been delivered in pursuance of such contracts. Part of the steel had been cut into sheets and a further part was in course of being so cut, but most of it was in the state in which it had been delivered. The invoice price of the 67,423 kilograms was £71,769, no part of which had been paid.

Clause I.3(1) of the appellants' General Conditions of Delivery and Payment provided, according to an agreed translation from the German:

> "All goods delivered by us remain our property (goods remaining in our ownership) until all debts owed to us including any balances existing at relevant times — due to us on any legal grounds — are settled. This also holds

good if payments are made for the purpose of settlement of specially designated claims. Debts owed to companies, being members of our combine, are deemed to be such debts."

Following the respondents' appointment as receivers, a dispute arose between them and the appellants as to whether the 67,423 kilograms of steel strip remained the property of the latter, by reason of clause I.3(1), or whether they formed part of the assets of Carron available to its preferred or other creditors. By telex dated 12 August 1982 the respondents informed the appellants that if they were able to prove retention of title the steel strip would be returned or paid for if used. In February 1983 the respondents raised an action against the appellants in the Court of Session claiming a number of declarators, the only one that remains relevant for purposes of this appeal being a declarator that Carron were the owners of all steel supplied to them by the appellants and delivered to Carron's premises. The appellants lodged a counterclaim concluding for payment by the respondents personally of the invoice price of 67,423 kilograms of steel strip, namely £71,769.

The case went to proof before Lord Mayfield, who on 4 February 1986 decided in favour of the respondents. A considerable amount of the proof was taken up with competing expert evidence about German law, which was claimed by the appellants to govern the contracts of sale. At the end of the day the Lord Ordinary was unable to reach any clear view about the nature and effect of the relevant German law, so he proceeded upon the presumption that it was the same as the applicable law of Scotland. He was further of the opinion that in any event Scots law, as the lex situs, governed the ownership of the goods. According to that law, clause I.3(1) amounted to an ineffective attempt to create a right of security over the steel strip without transfer of possession. The property in the steel strip passed to Carron on delivery. In reaching this conclusion the Lord Ordinary followed two decisions of Lord Ross in the Outer House, namely *Deutz Engines Ltd. v. Terex Ltd.*, 1984 S.L.T. 273, and *Emerald Stainless Steel Ltd. v. South Side Distribution Ltd.*, 1983 S.L.T. 162.

The appellants reclaimed, and the reclaiming action was heard by the Second Division (the Lord Justice-Clerk, Lord Ross, Lord McDonald and Lord Wylie). No attempt was made to found on the law of West Germany. On 6 July 1988 the Second Division found in favour of the respondents on substantially the same grounds as had the Lord Ordinary, namely that clause I.3(1) constituted an attempt, ineffective under the law of Scotland, to create a right of security over corporeal moveables without transfer of possession, and that the property in the steel strip had passed to Carron on delivery. The appellants now appeal to your Lordships' House.

It is well settled in the law of Scotland that a condition in a contract for the sale of corporeal movables which provides that, notwithstanding delivery, ownership of the goods shall not pass to the buyer until the price that has been paid is valid and effective. This was accepted in the opinion of the Lord Justice-Clerk, referring to *Stair's Institutions*, 5th ed. (1832) (More) I. XIV.4; *Gloag & Irvine on The Law of Rights in Se-*

curity (1897), p. 241; *Macartney v. Macredie's Creditors* (1799) Mor. App. s.v. Sale, No. 1; *Murdoch & Co. Ltd. v. Greig* (1889) 16 R. 396; and *Cowan v. Spence* (1824) 3 S. 42.

Cowan v. Spence was a case where the petitioner had granted to a partnership a sublease for a period of years of certain houses and lands and also of a paper mill situated on the lands. The petitioner was the owner of certain moveable machinery in the paper mill and elsewhere on the lands, and this was delivered to the partnership for their free use and benefit during the currency of the sublease, subject to a provision that at its expiry "at the term of Whitsunday 1828, and upon the rents or subtack duties hereby contracted to be paid, and which may then be due, being fully paid up and discharged the said . . . machinery shall be held to be the absolute and exclusive property" of the partnership. The latter was taken bound to pay, in addition to the rents, the further sum of £450 annually as remuneration for the use of the machinery during the currency of the sublease. The partnership was sequestrated under the Bankruptcy Act in 1822 and the respondent, having been appointed trustee, claimed the machinery for behoof of the creditors. The First Division decided that the petitioner was entitled to the machinery, on the ground that it was to belong to the partnership only in the event of the rents and other prestations being duly paid and on the expiration of the sublease, which period had not arrived. It is a feature of the case that the contract did not specifically fix any price for the machinery, though the provision for payment of the annual sums of £450 may perhaps warrant the case being regarded as an early instance of a hire purchase agreement. It is to be noted, however, that transfer of the property in the machinery was expressed as being conditional not only on payment of these sums but also on payment of all rents due under the sublease of the heritable property.

The Lord Justice-Clerk took the view that the validity of a provision in a contract for the sale of goods that the property in the goods should not pass until the price had been paid constituted a particular exception to the general rule that security over corporeal moveables is incapable of being created without transfer of possession. That rule is thus expressed in *Gloag & Irvine on The Law of Rights in Security*, p. 188:

> "It is a cardinal rule of the common law of Scotland that no real right to corporeal moveable subjects can be transmitted by a voluntary conveyance, assignation or other transfer, unless and until the transfer is completed by delivery of the subjects in question to the transferee."

and, at p. 189:

> "The rule that a security over moveables rententa possessione is of no effect is so well settled that the cases where it has been attempted to uphold an express security resting merely on a verbal or written assignation, have not been very numerous."

In the Lord Justice-Clerk's opinion an "all debts" provision such as clause I.3(1) is designed to provide security without possession and thus falls foul of the general rule. It is to be observed, however, that at the outset of the chapter in which the general rule is expressed *Gloag & Irvine* state, p. 187:

> "It is proposed in this and the succeeding chapters to consider by what method a party in possession of [corporeal moveable] property may convey or transfer it in security; that is, by what methods he may, while retaining the ownership in, or at least the ultimate right to, the subject, confer on a particular creditor a right over it, which will enable that creditor to vindicate that subordinate right in a question with the general creditors of his author, with particular creditors attaching the subject by diligence, or with a third party to whom it may have been transferred."

In the present case the appellants, the owners of the steel strip, transferred possession of it to Carron under what was unquestionably a contract of sale. There was no question of the appellants creating a right of security. They were not in the position of debtors seeking to give a right of security to a creditor. They were themselves creditors of Carron for the price of the steel strip and it may be for other debts also. Carron obtained possession of the steel strip upon delivery, subject to a condition that it should not obtain the property until it had paid all debts due to the appellants. Can it be said that Carron somehow attempted to create a security over the goods in favour of the appellants? In order that it might do so it would require to have both the ownership and the possession, actual or constructive, of the goods. The essence of a right in security is that the debtor retains at least what *Gloag & Irvine* call the ultimate right to the goods. Can it be said that Carron obtained anything which gave it the capacity to retain an ultimate right to the goods? That could be so only if the contract of sale gave it the property in the goods, but the contract of sale said that the property in the goods was not to pass until all debts due to the appellants had been paid. We are here very far removed from the situation where a party in possession of corporeal moveables is seeking to create a subordinate right in favour of a creditor while retaining the ultimate right to himself. It is true that by entering into the contract of sale Carron agreed that it should receive possession of the goods on delivery but should not acquire the property until all debts due to the appellants had been paid, and thus agreed that the appellants would in effect have security over the goods after they had come into Carron's possession. But at that stage Carron had no interest of any kind whatever in any particular goods. Carron was never in a position to confer upon the appellants any subordinate right over the steel strip, nor did it ever seek to do so.

Section 17 of the Sale of Goods Act 1979 provides:

> "(1) Where there is a contract for the sale of specific or ascertained goods the property in them is transferred to the buyer at such time as the parties to

> the contract intend it to be transferred. (2) For the purpose of ascertaining the intention of the parties regard shall be had to the terms of the contract, the conduct of the parties and the circumstances of the case."

In the present case the parties in the contract of sale clearly expressed their intention that the property in the steel strip should not pass to Carron until all debts due by it to the appellants had been paid. In my opinion there are no grounds for refusing to give effect to that intention.

Further, section 19(1) of the same Act provides:

> "Where there is a contract for the sale of specific goods or where goods are subsequently appropriated to the contract, the seller may, by the terms of the contract or appropriation, reserve the right of disposal of the goods until certain conditions are fulfilled; and in such a case, notwithstanding the delivery of the goods to the buyer, or to a carrier or other bailee or custodier for the purpose of transmission to the buyer, the property in the goods does not pass to the buyer until the conditions imposed by the seller are fulfilled."

Here the appellants, by the terms of the contract of sale, have in effect reserved the right of disposal of the steel strip until fulfilment of the condition that all debts due to them by Carron have been paid. By virtue of this enactment, that has the effect that the property in the goods did not pass to Carron until that condition had been fulfilled. Counsel for Carron argued that the word "conditions" in section 19(1) must be read as excluding any condition which has the effect of creating a right of security over the goods. I am, however, unable to regard a provision reserving title to the seller until payment of all debts due to him by the buyer as amounting to the creation by the buyer of a right of security in favour of the seller. Such a provision does in a sense give the seller security for the unpaid debts of the buyer. But it does so by way of a legitimate retention of title, not by virtue of any right over his own property conferred by the buyer.

In all cases where a right of security is conferred the debtor retains an ultimate right over the subject matter in question. The creditor, having realised out of that subject matter a sufficient sum to meet the debt, is obliged to account to the debtor for any surplus. Where, however, the seller of goods retains title until some condition has been satisfied, and on failure of such satisfaction repossesses them, then he is not obliged to account to the buyer for any part of the value of the goods. Where the condition is to the effect that the price of the goods shall have been paid and it has not been paid, then in the situation where the market price of the goods has risen, so that they are worth more than the contract price, the extra value belongs to the unpaid seller. That is clearly the position where the condition relates to payment of the price of the actual goods, and goes to show that the retention of title provision is not one creating a right of security forming an exception to the general rule requiring possession by the creditor. The same is true, in my opinion, where the provision covers not only the price of the very goods which are the subject of the particular contract of sale, but also debts due to the seller under other contracts.

In *Clough Mill Ltd. v. Martin* [1985] 1 W.L.R. 111 it was held that a retention of title provision in a contract for the sale of goods did not constitute the creation of a charge conferring a security over the property of the purchasing company such as required to be registered under what was then section 95 of the Companies Act 1948. The judgments of the Court of Appeal contain interesting discussions of the problems which might arise where the goods the subject matter of the contract of sale had been partially paid for before being repossessed by the seller. In that case the court did not find it necessary to form a concluded view as to the solution of these problems, nor is it necessary in this case.

The judges of the Second Division placed some reliance on section 62(4) of the Sale of Goods Act 1979, which provides:

> "The provisions of this Act about contracts of sale do not apply to a transaction in the form of a contract of sale which is intended to operate by way of mortgage, pledge, charge or other security."

The view seems to have been that the transaction here could be treated as being both a sale of goods and an attempt to create security without possession. In so far as the transaction was a contract of sale it was good but the provisions of clause I.3(1) were struck at by section 62(4). However, quite clearly clause I.3(1) in itself is not a transaction in the form of a contract of sale. It is simply one of the conditions of what is a genuine contract of sale. In my opinion section 62(4) has no application to this case.

My Lords, I am of opinion that the reasoning of the Lord Ordinary and of the judges of the Second Division was erroneous, as was that of Lord Ross in *Emerald Stainless Steel Ltd. v. Southside Distribution Ltd.*, 1983 S.L.T. 162 and in *Deutz Engines Ltd. v. Terex Ltd.*, 1984 S.L.T. 273. Clause I.3(1) is valid and effective.

I would therefore allow the appeal and recall the interlocutors of the Second Division and of the Lord Ordinary, and find that the respondents are not entitled to any of the declarators concluded for in their action, but that the appellants are entitled to decree for payment as concluded for in their counterclaim.

LORD GRIFFITHS. My Lords, I have had the advantage of reading in draft the speech of my noble and learned friend, Lord Keith of Kinkel and for the reasons he has given I would allow the appeal.

LORD OLIVER OF AYLMERTON. My Lords, I have had the opportunity of reading in draft the speech of Lord Keith of Kinkel. I agree with it and for the reasons he has given I would allow the appeal.

LORD GOFF OF CHIEVELEY. My Lords, I have had the opportunity of reading in draft the speech of my noble and learned friend, Lord Keith of Kinkel. I agree with it and for the reasons he has given, I would allow the appeal.

Lord Jauncey of Tullichettle. My Lords, I have had the advantage of reading in draft the speech prepared by my noble and learned friend, Lord Keith of Kinkel. I agree with it and for the reasons he has given and I would allow the appeal.

I consider that the courts below were in error in failing to appreciate the true nature of the transaction between the parties. A right in security is a right over property given by a debtor to a creditor whereby the latter in the event of the debtor's failure, acquires priority over the property against the general body of creditors of the debtor. It is of the essence of a right in security that the debtor possesses in relation to the property a right which he can transfer to the creditor, which right must be retransferred to him upon payment of the debt. The Second Division took the view that clause I.3(1) amounted to an ineffective attempt to create a right of security over moveables without the transfer of possession thereof. This conclusion presupposed that Carron were in a position to transfer the title to the steel to the appellants, this being the only right available to them to transfer so long as they retained possession.

My Lords, in terms of the contract of sale Carron never acquired title to the steel. They acquired possession thereof on delivery but would only have acquired dominium in and hence title to it upon fulfilment of the conditions in clause I.3(1). It follows that they never acquired any right under the contract, other than a right of possession, which they were in a position to transfer in security to the appellants. The contract of sale did not attempt to create a right in security in favour of the appellants, rather did it operate to transfer possession and dominium in two stages. Until the conditions of clause I.3(1). were satisfied dominium remained in the appellants.

Appeal allowed with costs.

Solicitors: Pritchard Englefield & Tobin for Bird Semple Fyfe Ireland W.S., Edinburgh; Masons for MacRoberts, Edinburgh.

NOTES

1. Cf M. N. Connock, *Retention of Title,* 22 Australian Bus. L.R. 37 (1994); G. McCormack, *Reservation of Title — The House of Lords speaks with a Scottish Accent,* [1991] Lloyd's Maritime and Commercial L.R. 154; G. McCormack, *Reservation of Title in England and New Zealand,* 12 Legal Studies 195 (1992); J. Mance, *The operation of an 'all debts' reservation of title clause* [1992] Lloyd's Maritime & Commercial L.R. 35. P. Rozenberg, *The Retention of Title Clause and Mixed Chattels,* 18 Australian Bus. L.J. 78 (1990) (surveying the common law doctrine of confusion of goods.)

2. The leading case on 'reservation of title' clauses in sales contracts in the U.K. is *Aluminium Industrie Vaasen BV v. Romalpa Aluminium Ltd.* ([1976] 2 All ER 552; [1976] 1 WLR 676.) In that case, the Court of Appeal had to pass on the effect of a rather elaborate elongated retention-of-title clause, included by a Dutch manufacturer in its general selling terms and conditions. The Dutch manufacturer (AIV) had supplied an English buyer, Romalpa, with aluminum foil. Romalpa became insolvent and was placed in receivership. At that time Romalpa owed more than £ 122,000 to AIV. A portion of the foil was still at hand; the remainder had been resold. The por-

tion still at hand was valued £ 50,235 and the receiver did not contest AIV's right thereto. Of the foil sold to sub-purchasers, the receiver had collected the price in the amount of £ 35,150 and deposited the same in a separate account. The remaining balance was unaccounted for. The controversy concerned AIV's right to the money in the separate account.

The main questions passed upon by the court below (Mocatta, J.) and the Court of Appeal (Megaw, L.J. and Roskill, L.J.) dealt with the question whether the clause was applicable between the parties and whether it entitled plaintiff to the deposited proceeds from the resale of the unprocessed foil. All three judges gave affirmative answers to both questions. The question whether the right to the proceeds was invalid as a charge under s. 95(1)(2)(e) of the Companies Act of 1948 was only raised in the court below and briefly denied by Mocatta, J. on the ground that the proceeds from the subsales belonged in equity to the plaintiff. It is that issue which has prompted different holdings in later cases.

See Iwan Davies, *Effective Retention of Title* 105 et s. (1991), and Davies, Textbook on Commercial Law (London 1992) 259 et s.

3. There seems to be a recent tendency to construe the reservation of rights to proceeds of a subsale of goods sold under a retention of title clause as a grant of a charge, subject to registration under the Companies Act, see *Re Weldtech Equipment Ltd*, Chancery Div. (Companies Court) October 29, 1990, [1992] BCC 18, discussed by Ian Smith, [1990] Insolvency Law & Practice 184, and *Compaq Computer Ltd v. Abercorn Group Ltd.* [1991] BCC 484, discussed in note following *E. Pfeiffer Weinkellerei-Weineinkauf GmbH & CO v. Arbuthnot Factors Ltd.* [1988] 3 WLR 150 (*infra*) G. McCormack *Reservation of Tile — An Overview* [1991] Insolvency Law and Practice 102.

b. E. Pfeiffer

QUEEN'S BENCH DIVISION

E. Pfeiffer Weinkellerei-Weineinkauf G.m.b.H. & CO. v. Arbuthnot Factors Ltd.

[1985 E. No. 184]

[1988] 3 WLR 150; [1987] BRITISH COMPANY LAW CASES 522.

1987 Jan. 19, 20, 21; Feb. 6 — Phillips J.

6 February. PHILLIPS J. read the following judgment. The parties have agreed that I should determine two preliminary issues of law which lie at the heart of the dispute between them. The plaintiff is a German company which carries on business as an exporter of wines. The plaintiff supplied the wine to an English importer, Springfield Wine Importers Ltd. ("Springfield") on terms that included a reservation of title

clause. Springfield sub-sold the wine to subpurchasers on credit terms. Springfield then entered into a factoring agreement pursuant to which Springfield assigned to the defendant debts owed to Springfield by sub-purchasers. In accordance with these assignments the sub-purchasers proceeded to pay the defendant. The plaintiff claims to enjoy a title to the moneys so paid superior to that of the defendant and, in these proceedings, calls upon the defendant to account for and pay over these moneys.

The facts

During 1983 and 1984 the plaintiff supplied wine to Springfield under contracts which were subject to the plaintiff's standard terms. These terms were expressly agreed between the plaintiff and Springfield in two versions, one the German original and the other an English translation. The English translation included the following clause:

"5. *Property Reservation*

The property reservation serves for the protection of all claims, which occur or which will occur in future from our business relation with our buyer, irrespective of there being a permanent payment account. The goods remain our property until payment has completely been effected for all obligations that occurred from the business relation with the buyer, including interests and costs and the like. The said payment shall be deemed to have been made when cheques and bills of exchange have been met and honoured in full. In case of mixing or production of a new good, we will become the owner, respectively the co-owner of the new product. Pledging or assignment by way of security of our goods before a complete payment has been effected, is not allowed. In case of pledging our goods by a third person or other prejudice of our rights, the buyer has to advise us immediately and has to protect our rights against the third person. The buyer is only allowed to dispose of the goods or to sell them in business operations carried out in due order and as long as there is no delay in payment. All claims that he gets from the sale or due to another legal reason regarding our goods, with all rights including his profit amounting to his obligations towards us, will be passed on to us. On demand the buyer is obliged to notify the assignment of the claim to give us in written all necessary information concerning the assertion of our claims and to deliver us all necessary documents. As long as he meets his obligations towards us, the buyer has the right with the expressively mentioned reserve of revocation at any time, to encash ceded obligations in his own name as our authorised agent and he may dispose of the ceded rights in the framework of business operations carried out in due order.

In case of an inefficacy of the cession, we must be regarded as authorized and allowed to encash the purchase price for the buyer and to make the necessary declaration for a legal business.

In case of cash sales, the money that has come from a third person immediately

27. becomes our own due to this, this money has to be separated from other money, it
28. must be booked correspondingly, and must be administered until called for.
29. If the buyer undertakes unusual dispositions, for example, selling-out assignment by
30. way of security or pledgings, when pledgings are made in his fortune, when he does
31. not honour bills of exchange or he stops payments, all our set terms for payment will
32. become due immediately. In this case the right for a sale of our goods and the above-
33. mentioned authorisation for disposal will be cancelled. If the buyer causes delays con-
34. cerning his obligations, we have the right to take goods that are still in his stocks for
35. our own without having to withdraw from the contract.
36. Cession according to § 46 Konkursordnung, is agreed."

I shall hereafter refer to this clause as clause 5. I have numbered each line of the clause for future reference in this judgment. Line 36 reflects the fact that the terms, and the contracts in which they were incorporated, are governed by German law. It is, however, accepted by the parties that I should proceed upon the basis that this does not differ from English law. The only other point to note about the terms upon which the plaintiff and Springfield dealt is that Springfield was entitled to 90 days' credit.

On 10 August 1984 Springfield entered into a factoring agreement with the defendant which replaced an earlier agreement with another factor. The agreement with the defendant provided for the purchase by the defendant of debts owed to Springfield by purchasers of wine from Springfield. It is not necessary to detail any of the terms of this lengthy agreement other than to observe that they included:

> "The company [i.e. Springfield] warrants to [the defendant] that no reservation of title by any third party will apply to all or any part of the goods sold by the company."

Counsel for the plaintiff, Mr. Hapgood, accepted that, having particular regard to this warranty, it could not be suggested that the defendant had constructive notice that wine sold by Springfield was governed by a reservation of title clause. Springfield was, of course, in flagrant breach of this warranty.

Pursuant to the factoring agreement, Springfield offered to sell and the defendant purchased a series of debts owed to Springfield in respect of wine purchased by Springfield from the plaintiff and sub-sold by Springfield to sub-purchasers. It is common ground that at the time of the purchase of these debts the defendant was unaware of any adverse rights or claim to the debts. It is also common ground that at all material times there were outstanding sums unpaid and due from Springfield to the plaintiff. Notice of assignment of the debts sold to the defendant was given to the sub-purchasers by both the defendant and Springfield. Mr. Hapgood accepted that all the requirements of section 136 of the Law of Property Act 1925 were satisfied so as to vest in the defendant a legal title to the debts.

Pursuant to the assignments of which they had been given notice, sub-purchasers paid to the defendant sums due in respect of wines supplied by Springfield. The moneys so received by the defendant form the subject matter of this action. It is possible that by the time that the defendant received these sums, or some of them, it had become aware of the plaintiff's adverse claim to the debts.

The issues

It is the plaintiff's case that it was, from the moment of each sub-sale of wine by Springfield, the beneficial owner of the proceeds of sale and that the title that the defendant received when it purchased the debts owed by the sub-purchasers was subordinate to the plaintiff's prior equitable title. Payment of the debts to the defendant was payment of moneys to which the plaintiff had superior title, and the plaintiff can trace the moneys into the hands of the defendant and recover them from it. To this claim the defendant raises, inter alia, the following defences: (1) In so far as the plaintiff had any beneficial interest in the proceeds of sale of the wine sub-sold by Springfield, that interest was in the nature of a charge created by Springfield on its property and was, by virtue of section 95 of the Companies Act 1948, void for want of registration as against the creditors of Springfield, of whom the defendant was one. (2) In any event the defendant's title to the payments received was superior to any equitable interest on the part of the plaintiff, regardless of the nature of that interest.

The preliminary issues which it has been agreed that I should try have been formulated as follows:

> "(a) Whether the plaintiff's alleged conditions of payment and delivery had the effect in law of creating a charge requiring registration under section 95 of the Companies Act 1948.
> "(b) Whether or not the defendant has priority over the alleged rights of the plaintiff by virtue of the factoring agreement made between the defendant and Springfield Wine Importers Ltd. and any assignments made pursuant thereto."

I turn to the first of these issues.

Did the plaintiff's alleged conditions of payment and delivery have the effect in law of creating a charge requiring registration under section 95 of the Companies Act 1948?

Mr. Hapgood contended that the correct legal analysis of the facts of this case is as follows. Under clause 5 the plaintiff, while unpaid, retained both legal and equitable title in the wine up to the moment that Springfield sold it to sub-purchasers. During this period Springfield held the wine as fiduciary for the plaintiff. In these circumstances, in the absence of any express agreement to the contrary, upon sub-sale by

Springfield of the plaintiff's wine, the plaintiff would automatically become beneficially entitled to the proceeds. Clause 5 did not constitute an agreement to the contrary, but on its true construction confirmed that the plaintiff was to be beneficially entitled to all proceeds of sub-sales. Section 95 of the Companies Act 1948 had no application for two reasons. First, the plaintiff's equitable interest did not constitute a charge over property owned by Springfield. It was an absolute beneficial interest in the proceeds of sale, albeit that the plaintiff would come under an implied contractual duty to account to Springfield to the extent that proceeds of sale ultimately recovered by the plaintiff exceeded the debts owed by Springfield to it. Secondly, the plaintiff's beneficial interest was not created by Springfield. It arose by operation of law as a consequence of sale by Springfield of property owned by the plaintiff. Clause 5 did not create the right — it merely recognised and confirmed its existence.

In support of his submissions, Mr. Hapgood relied on the decision of the Court of Appeal in *Aluminium Industrie Vaassen B.V. v. Romalpa Aluminium Ltd.* [1976] 1 W.L.R. 676. Because that decision formed the cornerstone of the plaintiff's case, I must examine it in a little detail. I have been assisted in so doing by the fact that there have been six subsequent reported cases to which I have been referred involving reservation of title clauses in which the *Romalpa* case has received detailed consideration.

In the *Romalpa* case the plaintiffs sold aluminium foil to the defendants under a contract which included the following reservation of title clause:

> "The ownership of the material to be delivered by A.I.V. [the plaintiffs] will only be transferred to purchaser when he has met all that is owing to A.I.V., no matter on what grounds. Until the date of payment, purchaser, if A.I.V. so desires, is required to store this material in such a way that it is clearly the property of A.I.V. A.I.V. and purchaser agree that, if purchaser should make (a) new objects(s) from the material, mixes this material with (an)other object(s) or if this material in any way whatsoever becomes a constituent of (an)other object(s) A.I.V. will be given the ownership this(these) new object(s) as surety of the full payment of what purchaser owes A.I.V. To this end A.I.V. and purchaser now agree that the ownership of the article(s) in question, whether finished or not, are to be transferred to A.I.V. and that this transfer of ownership will be considered to have taken place through and at the moment of the single operation or event by which the material is converted into (a) new object(s), or is mixed with or becomes a constituent of (an)other object(s). Until the moment of full payment of what purchaser owes A.I.V., purchaser shall keep the object(s) in question for A.I.V. in his capacity of fiduciary owner and, if required, shall store this(these) object(s) in such a way that it (they) can be recognised as such. Nevertheless, purchaser will be entitled to sell these objects to a third party within the framework of the normal carrying on of his business and to deliver them on condition that — if A.I.V. so requires — purchaser, as long as he has not fully dis-

> charged his debt to A.I.V. shall hand over to A.I.V. the claims he has against his buyer emanating from this transaction."

The defendants sold on some of the aluminium foil to third parties. The defendants were then placed in receivership by a debenture holder and the issue before the courts was whether the plaintiffs had a beneficial title to the proceeds of sale of the foil which entitled them to trace those proceeds into the hands of the receiver.

Both Mocatta J. and the Court of Appeal upheld the plaintiffs' claim that they enjoyed a beneficial title to the proceeds of sale of the foil which gave them a tracing remedy.

In *Borden (U.K.) Ltd v. Scottish Timber Products Ltd.* [1981] Ch. 25 Bridge L.J. made a detailed analysis of the *Romalpa* case. I respectfully concur with his view that the essence of the reasoning of the Court of Appeal in *Aluminium Industrie Vaassen B.V. v. Romalpa Aluminium Ltd.* [1976] 1 W.L.R. 676 can be collected from the following passages in the judgments of the court. First, in the leading judgment, Roskill L.J. said, at pp. 689–690:

> "Now, the crucial facts to my mind are two: first, that the defendants were selling goods which the plaintiffs owned at all material times; and secondly, that clause 13 as a whole is obviously designed to protect the plaintiffs, in the event of later insolvency, against the consequences of having parted with possession of, though not with legal title to, these goods before payment was received, 75 days' credit being allowed. When, therefore, one is considering what, if any, additional implication has to be made to the undoubted implied power of sale in the first part of clause 13, one must ask what, if any, additional implication is necessary to make effective the obvious purpose of giving the requisite security to the plaintiffs? One is, I think, entitled to look at the second part of clause 13 to answer this, for it would be strange if the first part were to afford no relevant security when the second part is (as I think) elaborately drawn to give such security in relation to manufactured or mixed goods. I see no difficulty in the contractual concept that, as between the defendants and their sub-purchasers, the defendants sold as principals, but that, as between themselves and the plaintiffs, those goods which they were selling as principals within their implied authority from the plaintiffs were the plaintiffs' goods which they were selling as agents for the plaintiffs to whom they remained fully accountable. If an agent lawfully sells his principal's goods he stands in a fiduciary relationship to his principal and remains accountable to his principal for those goods and their proceeds. A bailee is in like position in relation to his bailor's goods. What, then, is there here to relieve the defendants from their obligation to account to the plaintiffs for those goods of the plaintiffs which they lawfully sell to sub-purchasers?"

Then Roskill L.J., a little later, said, at p. 690:

> "It seems to me clear . . . that to give effect to what I regard as the obvious purpose of clause 13 one must imply into the first part of the clause not only the power to sell but also the obligation to account in accordance with the normal fiduciary relationship of principal and agent, bailor and bailee. Accordingly, like the judge I find no difficulty in holding that the principles in *Hallett's* case, 13 Ch.D. 696 are of immediate application, and I think that the plaintiffs are entitled to trace these proceeds of sale and to recover them, as Mocatta J. has held by his judgment."

Goff L.J. said at p. 691:

> "In my judgment the second part of the case comes down to a short question of construction. It is common ground that a power of sale during the period that any money remains owing to the plaintiffs must be implied; but the question is upon what terms."

Then, at the end of his judgment, Goff L.J. said, at p. 693:

> "In short, my conclusion is that the power of sale to be implied where none has been expressed must be so qualified as not to defeat the intention clearly shown by clause 13 as a whole, including the latter part, which only emphasises this. It follows that there was, as Roskill L.J. says, a sufficient fiduciary relationship between the parties, and this is indeed expressly contemplated in the reference to a fiduciary owner in the second part of clause 13. The implied power must, therefore, in my judgment be a power to sell, not for the defendants' own account, but for the account of the plaintiffs unless and until all moneys owing be paid."

Megaw L.J. said at p. 694:

> "The power of sale to be implied in the first part of clause 13, where none has been expressed, must be such as not to defeat the intention shown by clause 13. It is not a power to sell for the defendants' own account, but it is a power to sell for the account of the plaintiffs."

The first point to note about the passages I have just quoted is that the Court of Appeal in the *Romalpa* case were approaching the problem as essentially one of construction. The court held that, on the true construction of the contract between the plaintiffs and the defendants, the defendants were to hold the foil as fiduciaries and were to sell the foil as agents for the plaintiffs' account. In these circumstances the plaintiffs' beneficial interests in the proceeds of sale of the foil arose out of contractual agreement. It is right to note, however, that Roskill L.J. approached the question of construction on the basis that the relationship of the plaintiffs and the defendants prior to any sale of the foil by the defendants was such as to carry with it in the normal course a duty on the part of the defendants to account to the plaintiffs should they sell the foil.

In the *Romalpa* case there were special features that can explain the finding that the relationship of the plaintiffs and the defendants was fiduciary in nature, which is perhaps no more than another way of saying that the defendants were holding the plaintiffs' foil in circumstances where they had no right to deal with it for their own account but only for the account of the plaintiffs. Counsel for the defendants had conceded that the relationship of the plaintiffs and defendants was that of bailor/bailee — a concession described by Slade J. in *In re Bond Worth Ltd.* [1980] Ch. 228, 263, as "of crucial importance" — crucial no doubt, because it is an incident of the ordinary relationship of bailor/bailee that if the bailee sells the goods bailed he must account to the bailor for the proceeds. Furthermore the latter part of clause 13 in the *Romalpa* case expressly described the defendants as "fiduciary owner" of mixed goods of which foil formed part and the Court of Appeal considered that the express provisions in relation to mixed goods threw light upon what should properly be implied into the contract in respect of the foil itself.

In the majority of cases to which I have been referred in which the *Romalpa* case has been considered the courts have emphasised the influence that the special features of that case had upon its result — see for instance: *In re Bond Worth Ltd.* [1980] Ch. 228, 264; *Borden (U.K.) Ltd v. Scottish Timber Products Ltd.* [1981] Ch. 25, 38; *Hendy Lennox (Industrial Engines) Ltd. v. Grahame Puttick Ltd.* [1984] 1 W.L.R. 485, 499; *In re Andrabell Ltd.* [1984] 3 All E.R. 407, 415 and *Clough Mill Ltd. v. Martin* [1985] 1 W.L.R. 111, 115.

It seems to me inappropriate to describe the relationship of a seller and a buyer in possession to whom title has not yet passed as that of bailor/bailee, for it will not normally have the same incidents as the classic bailment relationship. The relationship of a buyer and a seller is inevitably the creature of contract. Where the seller retains title by way of security prior to sub-sale, but the contract expressly or impliedly authorises the buyer to effect sub-sales, I do not consider that any prima facie implication arises that sub-sales are to be effected by the buyer as agent for and for the account of the seller. On the contrary, I consider that the normal implication that arises from the relationship of buyer and seller is that if the buyer is permitted to sub-sell in the normal course of his business, he will do so for his own account. I consider that the conclusions of the Court of Appeal in *Aluminium Industrie Vaassen B.V. v. Romalpa Aluminium Ltd.* [1976] 1 W.L.R. 676 as to the fiduciary relationship of the plaintiffs and the defendants turned on the particular wording of clause 13 and on the concession that the relationship of the parties was that of bailor/bailee.

I turn then to the all-important matter, the wording of clause 5 in the present case. Mr. Hapgood, in the course of an attractive argument, submitted that the provisions of clause 5 are very similar to the provisions of clause 13 in the *Romalpa* case and that, if anything, clause 5 indicates more clearly than any sales made by Springfield were to be for the account of the plaintiff.

Lines 1 to 12 of clause 5 are undoubtedly similar in effect to the first part of clause 13 in the *Romalpa* case. The property in the wine, both legal and equitable, was to remain vested in the plaintiff until Springfield had made payment in full in respect of all obligations incurred to the plaintiff. Furthermore, Mr. Hapgood is plainly correct in submitting that the object of clause 5 is to provide the plaintiff with security.

Lines 12 to 13 of clause 5 grant to Springfield a right to sub-sell the wine "as long as there is no delay in payment." There was, of course, delay in payment by Springfield, but Mr. Hapgood conceded that this was waived by the plaintiff in so far as it consented to sub-sales by Springfield notwithstanding. In the *Romalpa* case there was no express right to sub-sell the foil itself but it was common ground that there was to be implied a right of sub-sale similar to the express right granted in respect of mixed goods incorporating foil, namely a right to sell in the normal course of business. So again Mr. Hapgood is justified in drawing a comparison between clause 5 and clause 13 in the *Romalpa* case.

Where the two clauses differ is in relation to what was to happen to proceeds of sale. Clause 13 in the *Romalpa* case made the following provision in relation to mixed goods. The right to sub-sell was

> "on condition that — if A.I.V. so requires — purchaser, as long as he has not fully discharged his debt to A.I.V. shall hand over to A.I.V. the claims he has against his buyer emanating from this transaction."

The Court of Appeal did not hold that the plaintiffs' sole security interest in mixed goods was conferred by this proviso, but that it was an ancillary right by way of additional security which entitled the plaintiffs to call for a formal assignment of what was beneficially already theirs. For the Court of Appeal held that, on true construction of clause 13, it created a fiduciary relationship such that, whether in the case of foil or mixed goods, there was an implied obligation on the part of the defendants to account to the plaintiffs for all the proceeds of sale.

Clause 5 in the present case makes express provisions in respect of the proceeds of sub-sale of wine, both in respect of credit sales and in respect of cash sales. The former provisions are the more important, although it is relevant also to consider the latter when examining the nature of the relationship between the plaintiff and Springfield. Lines 12 to 18 provide:

> "The buyer is only allowed to dispose of the goods or to sell them in business operations carried out in due order and as long as there is no delay in payment. All claims that he gets from the sale or due to another legal reason re-

> garding our goods, with all rights including his profit amounting to his obligations towards us, will be passed on to us. On demand the buyer is obliged to notify the assignment of the claim to give us in written [sic] all necessary information concerning the assertion of our claims and to deliver us all necessary documents."

In my view these provisions cannot properly be read as conferring mere ancillary security rights. They comprehensively set out the nature of such interest as the plaintiff is to have by way of security in respect of debts created by sub-sales. Mr. Potts, for the defendant, submitted that these provisions were, for a number of reasons, inconsistent with a fiduciary relationship of the kind contended for by the plaintiff. I agree with him in this.

First and foremost, the claims to be "passed on" are qualified by the words "amounting to his obligations towards us." This must mean that claims are to be passed on only up to the amount of Springfield's outstanding obligations to the plaintiff. This is not consistent with the proposition that Springfield was only authorised to sell wine for the account of the plaintiff, so as to vest the beneficial interest to *all* proceeds in the plaintiff. Mr. Hapgood contended that the plaintiff was beneficially entitled to all the proceeds and that, as Springfield "encashed" debts owed to it, Springfield was obliged to hold all the proceeds for the plaintiff in a separate account, regardless of the amount of Springfield's indebtedness to the plaintiff. The plaintiff was beneficially entitled to call for all the proceeds but would be under a contractual duty to repay any surplus to Springfield. I cannot accept this analysis. Not merely would such an arrangement be uncommercial, it is not one which can be reconciled with the express wording of the clause.

Secondly, the language used is essentially that of assignment or cession by Springfield of rights owned by Springfield. I have particularly in mind the reference to "claims . . . *he* gets . . . including *his* profit," the obligation on demand "to notify the *assignment*" and the right "to encash *ceded* obligations." I accept that provisions in relation to cash sales to be found in lines 26 to 28 of clause 5 are more consistent with the legal analysis for which Mr. Hapgood contends, but reading these provisions in the context of the clause as a whole I think that they do no more than provide that cash received is to be held for the plaintiff up to the amount of Springfield's outstanding indebtedness to it.

In summary I find that lines 12 to 18 of clause 5 constitute an agreement by Springfield to assign to the plaintiff future choses in action, namely future debts owed by sub-purchasers to Springfield up to the amount of any outstanding indebtedness on the part of Springfield to the plaintiff. In so far as debts came into existence falling within that agreement, the agreement created an equitable assignment of the debts. The agreement was plainly by way of security, and the assignments under it were capable of being redeemed by payment by Springfield of the outstanding indebtedness.

It follows that by agreeing to the provisions of clause 5 Springfield created a change by way of security over Springfield's property, namely book debts, which being unregistered was rendered void as against Springfield's creditors by section 95(1) and (2)(*e*) of the Companies Act 1948. The answer to the first preliminary issue is accordingly "Yes."

By way of completeness I should record that Mr. Potts expressly disavowed any right to rely upon the express authorisation granted by lines 21 and 22 of clause 5 having regard to the fact that this authorisation only applies so long as the buyer "meets his obligations towards us."

Does the defendant have priority over the alleged rights of the plaintiff by virtue of the factoring agreement made between the defendant and Springfield and any assignments made pursuant thereto?

Such equitable rights as the plaintiff enjoyed in the proceeds of sale of wine subsold by Springfield were acquired prior to the rights that the defendant acquired under the factoring agreement and the assignments pursuant thereto. Mr. Hapgood contended that on the facts of this case the plaintiff was entitled to invoke the rule "Qui prior est tempore potior est jure," which I shall call the "first in time rule," and thereby established a superior title to that of the defendant. To this Mr. Potts raised two alternative answers: (i) The rule does not apply where the competition is between the holder of an equitable title and the holder of a legal title who has purchased it bona fide for value without notice of the prior equitable title. The defendant was a bona fide purchaser of the legal title for value. (ii) Mr. Hapgood contended, for reasons I shall shortly explain, that the defendant must be treated for purposes of priorities as holders of equitable, not legal, title. In that event Mr. Potts submitted that the "first in time" rule gave way to the rule in *Dearle v. Hall* (1828) 3 Russ. 1 and that, in consequence, the defendant still had priority.

The defendant as bona fide purchaser for value

The debate between counsel proceeded on the premise that the competition was between the plaintiff's equitable rights in the debts owed to Springfield, whatsoever the true nature of those rights might be, and the defendant's rights as assignee of the legal title to those debts by virtue of a statutory assignment under the provisions of section 136(1) of the Law of Property Act 1925. That section provides:

> "(1) Any absolute assignment by writing under the hand of the assignor (not purporting to be by way of charge only) of any debt or other legal thing in action, of which express notice in writing has been given to the debtor, trustee or other person from whom the assignor would have been entitled to claim such debt or thing in action, is effectual in law (subject to equities having priority over the right of the assignee) to pass and transfer from the date

> of such notice — (*a*) the legal right to such debt or thing in action; (b) all legal and other remedies for the same; and (*c*) the power to give a good discharge for the same without the concurrence of the assignor: . . ."

Section 136 replaced section 25(6) of the Supreme Court of Judicature Act 1873 which provided:

> "Any absolute assignment, by writing under the hand of the assignor (not purporting to be by way of charge only), of any debt or other legal chose in action, of which express notice in writing shall have been given to the debtor, trustee, or other person from whom the assignor would have been entitled to receive or claim such debt or chose in action, shall be, and be deemed to have been effectual in law (subject to all equities which would have been entitled to priority over the right of the assignee if this Act had not passed), to pass and transfer the legal right to such debt or chose in action from the date of such notice, and all legal and other remedies for the same, and the power to give a good discharge for the same, without the concurrence of the assignor: . . ."

Mr. Hapgood submitted that the effect of section 136(1) of the Act of 1925 is clear and that of section 25(6) of the Act of 1873 even more clear. The section enables the assignee to acquire a title that has all the procedural advantages of legal title, but so far as priorities are concerned his position is no better than if the assignment had been effected prior to the Acts. It follows that, even if the assignment is effected for value without notice of a prior equity, priorities fall to be determined as if the assignment had been effected in equity, not in law.

Mr. Potts challenged this contention and referred me to *Stoddart v. Union Trust Ltd.* [1912] 1 K.B. 181 in support of the proposition that a bona fide purchaser of legal title to a chose in action under the statute acquires a title free of equities of which he has no notice. I do not think that *Stoddart v. Union Trust Ltd.* supports the proposition for which it was cited. In that case a debtor was seeking to raise by way of defence to an action by a statutory assignee of the debt a claim for damages for fraud on the part of the assignor which had induced the transaction out of which the debt arose. It is not easy to glean a common ratio decidendi from the judgments of the court but the case appears to me to have turned essentially upon a finding that a claim for damages for fraud by the assignor of a chose in action is not an equity which can be set up against an assignee: see, in particular, the judgment of Kennedy L.J. at p. 194.

Mr. Hapgood's submissions appear to me to be soundly based upon the natural meaning of the statutory wording. They gain support from a note in *Halsbury's Statutes of England*, 3rd ed., vol. 27 (1971), p. 549, and from a passage in *Snell's Principles of Equity*, 28th ed. (1982), p. 82. They also echo the view expressed by Channell J. in respect of section 25(6) of the Act of 1873 in *Marchant v. Morton, Down & Co.*

[1901] 2 K.B. 829, 832. I accept Mr. Hapgood's interpretation of section 136(1) and, accordingly, it is necessary to consider priorities as if the assignments of the debts to the defendant were no more than equitable assignments. It is at this point that Mr. Potts places reliance on the rule in *Dearle v. Hall,* 3 Russ. 1.

The rule in *Dearle v. Hall* is an exception to the general principle that equitable interests take priority in the order in which they are created. The rule applies to dealings with equitable interests in any property and, in particular, to equitable assignments of legal choses in action. Under the rule priority depends upon the order in which notice of the interest created by the dealing is given to the person affected by it, i.e., in the case of assignments of a debt, the debtor. Mr. Hapgood cited a number of authorities that were critical of the rule in support of his contention that the application of the rule should not be extended and, in particular, that the rule should not be applied to a competition between an equitable right to trace and an equitable assignment. He conceded, however, that if the rights asserted by the plaintiff were rights conferred by equitable assignment, the rule in *Dearle v. Hall* must apply. I have held that such security rights as were conferred upon the plaintiff by clause 5 were conferred by equitable assignment. Accordingly the rule in *Dearle v. Hall* governs and the defendant, which was the first to give notice of its right to the sub-purchasers, enjoys priority over the plaintiff. Thus the second preliminary issue falls to be answered "Yes."

This finding makes it unnecessary for me to determine a further point that arose late in argument. Assuming that the plaintiff's equitable interest in the debts owed by the sub-purchasers enjoyed priority to that of the defendant as statutory assignee, does the fact that the defendant has actually been paid the debts enable it to claim precedence as a bona fide purchaser for value of the legal title in the payments received? *Taylor v. Blakelock* (1886) 32 Ch.D. 560 would seem to favour the defendant in relation to this question, but the point is not an easy one and it is with some relief that I leave it to be determined on another occasion.

Judgment for defendant with costs.

Solicitors: Ward Bowie for Booth & Co. and Middletons, Leeds; Norton Rose Botterell & Roche.

[Reported by CLIVE SCOWEN ESQ., BARRISTER-AT-LAW]

NOTE

In *Compaq Computer Ltd v. Abercorn Group Ltd,* Ch. Div. May 10, 1991, [1991] BCC 484, the court had to deal with the conflict between the claim of a seller to the proceeds from the resale of goods sold under a reservation of title clause and the claim of an assignee of the buyer under an invoice discounting agreement. In analyzing in detail the powers and obligation of the buyer, who was a dealer in Compaq products and subject to a retention of title clause, the judge concluded that Compaq had merely a charge on the proceeds from the resale and that Abercorn's failure to register the charge rendered it void against the assignee under the invoice discounting agreement which had been registered as a charge on the accounts in issue.

Additionally, the judge indicated that he would follow the *Pfeiffer* case and apply the rule in *Dearle v. Hall* (1828) 3 Russ 1, unless he concluded that s136(1) of the Law of Property Act (1925) mandated a different allocation of priorities.

c. *Curtain Dream*

Chancery Division (Companies Court), 1990
Re Curtain Dream plc
[1990] BCLC 925

KNOX J. The applicants on the originating application before me are Mr Michael Joseph Moore and Mr David James Waterhouse, who are the joint receivers of a company called Curtain Dream plc (the company). They were appointed on 24 July 1989 under a debenture, which is held by the third applicant to the originating application, Barclays Bank plc. That debenture was duly registered under the Companies Act 1985 and its validity as such is not in issue. The respondent to that originating application is Churchill Merchanting Ltd (Churchill), which entered into transactions with the company in May 1989, which include an agreement for sale, with a retention of title clause incorporated in it.

The first and principal issue before the court on the originating application is whether that transaction conferred on Churchill a charge on the goods which were the subject matter of the transaction, some £430,000-worth or so of fabric, or whether all that the transaction effected was a sale of property followed very shortly by a resale, coupled with a retention of beneficial ownership in Churchill, which was the reselling party. It is common ground that if a charge was created in favour of Churchill, it was liable to be registered under s 395 of the 1985 Act. It is equally common ground that it was not registered, and on that footing, which of course is not accepted, it would be void as against the applicants.

I have also before me an originating summons, in which the plaintiff is Churchill and the defendants are the receivers and the company. That includes the same principal issue, in that it seeks a declaration that Churchill had retained title to the fabric in question and, secondly, an order for the return of the fabric or its value and damages for wrongful interference with it, and also a declaration that the defendants, that is to say the receivers and the company —

> 'hold on constructive trust all sums representing in whole or in part proceeds of sale of the fabric or part thereof whether it be the sale of the fabric itself or of goods manufactured from the fabric or part thereof . . .'

And further accounts and inquiries are asked for, and consequential relief.

The basic factual position is relatively simple and undisputed. The evidence before me is entirely on affidavit, and there has been no cross-examination on any of the affidavits, which are therefore not disputed as to veracity in any way. The company's business is described by Mr Moore in his first affidavit in the following terms:

> 'The Company carried on business and still carries on business manufacturing and selling, amongst other things, curtains. It accordingly maintains substantial stocks of fabric.'

He then continues:

> 'In May 1989 it appears that the Company desired to raise cash and entered into an arrangement with Churchill which is the subject of a facility letter from Churchill to the Company of the 15th May 1989.'

That is the first of the several critical documents in this matter. It is headed with Churchill's heading, dated 15 May 1989, addressed to the company, and it reads as follows:

> 'Dear Sirs
>
> Further to our recent discussions we, Churchill Merchanting Limited . . . write to confirm that we have established a supplier credit line of up to 90 days for you, CURTAIN DREAM PLC (The Company) which is subject to the following terms and conditions:

Credit Line:		£500,000 . . . by way of Bills of Exchange outstanding.		
Arrangement Fee:		*PERIOD IN DAYS*	*FEE*	
		0-90	1.25%	FLAT ON EACH BILL OF EXCHANGE
Interest:		Interest will be charged at a discount rate to yield LIBOR + 1% p.a.		
Conditions:	1	Completion by the Company of [Churchill's] standard form of Mandate and Contract of Trading.		
	2	All Bills of Exchange to be payable at the Company's principal Clearing Bank.		
	3	Approval by [Churchill] of a certified true copy of the Memorandum and Articles of Association of the Company and Certificate of Incorporation.		
Availability:		This credit line is available until further notice upon compliance with the terms contained		

herein. The line will be cancelled if undrawn within 30 days of the date hereof unless the arrangement fee is paid.

Procedure

(i) The Company (or its Supplier(s)) will invoice [Churchill] for merchandise as specified in the Contract of Trading. In cases where the merchandise already forms part of the Company's inventory the Company will, if requested, supply [Churchill] with evidence of the original purchase price(s).

(ii) [Churchill] will re-invoice the merchandise to the Company by return at a price which reflects cost to [Churchill] plus the transactional fee and interest referred to above. The company may specify any credit period it requires provided that it is not more than 90 days from date of [Churchill] payment.

(iii) [Churchill] will provide with its invoice a Bill of Exchange for acceptance by the Company in accordance with the Mandate provided by [Churchill].

(iv) Upon receipt of the accepted Bill of Exchange in order, [Churchill] will effect payment.

(v) Bills of Exchange will be presented for payment at the counters of the Company's bankers at maturity.

WARRANTY

The directors warrant when accepting the terms of this offer that all merchandise invoiced to [Churchill] as above will be invoiced at original cost to the Company or current market value whichever is the lowest and shall include no merchandise which is not readily saleable or which may be considered obsolete.

Then there is a request to sign and return the copy of the letter, if it is agreed. In fact the copy which is in evidence is only signed on behalf of Churchill, but there is no issue about that: the company accepted that facility letter.

There was a reference in that facility letter to a contract of trading. That is a separate document which in fact, on the copy which is in evidence, which is also dated 15 May 1989, was signed on behalf of both parties. It is not necessary to read the whole of that, but significant extracts do need to be read. It is headed 'CHURCHILL MERCHANTING LIMITED, GENERAL CONTRACT OF TRADING,' and it is made between

Churchill, which is described as the seller, and the company, which is described as the buyer. It starts by saying:

> 'This contract contains the entire bargain between the Seller and the Buyer. No variation of this contract shall bind either party unless such variation is made in writing and signed by the party to be bound.'

Pausing there for a moment, that plainly is not true, because the entire bargain was contained in the facility letter, which referred to this general contract.

Going on and passing over some less important parts of the general contract of trading, one finds an exclusion of any representation made by the seller and an indemnity by the buyer to the seller for infringement of registered designs, trade marks, copies, patents or the like. Then there are provisions with regard to delivery, which, however much they may have been of significance in relation to other transactions for which this form of general contract might have been used, were not at all appropriate for this particular transaction. A requirement is put on the buyer to obtain all necessary licences and exchange control consents. There is a provision that the seller is not to be liable for any loss of profit or for delay in delivery or for any direct or, as the contract actually says, 'inconsequential loss of any kind however caused and whether the same has been suffered by the Buyer of some third party' by reason of infringements of patent, copyright etc. More material, but equally inapposite to this particular transaction, is a provision headed 'RISK RE GOODS'. That reads as follows:

> 'All goods shall be at the Buyer's risk from the moment of delivery by the Seller to the Buyer. If on receipt any of the said goods are found to be damaged or any part missing, the Buyer must notify the Seller in writing within 3 days of such fact. All goods shall be thoroughly examined immediately on receipt and before they are cut up, treated, processed, resold, shipped or otherwise dealt with.'

There is more in the same vein, including a requirement that the buyer should be responsible for insuring the merchandise and for transportation and storage on it. There is an exclusion of any liability on the seller for —

> 'any liability in tort or for consequential loss or damage . . . for any defect in, or failure of or unsuitability for any purpose of the goods or any part thereof.'

That contains another misprint, but nothing much turns on that.

Then one comes to provisions which are much more significant and are directly applicable. They are headed 'PAYMENT' and they read as follows:

> 'The means of payment shall be by bill of exchange drawn by the Seller and accepted by the Buyer and time for payment shall be of the essence of this Contract. Interest (accruing daily) at the rate of 7% p.a. above Midland Bank Plc Base Rate shall be paid by the Buyer to the Seller on all sums at any time overdue and owing. The Buyer shall not be entitled to withhold or delay payment for any goods even though he may have a claim in respect of those goods or in respect of any other goods.'

I now come to the retention of title clause, which is the principal reason for this litigation. It reads:

> 'The goods shall remain the sole and absolute property of the Seller as legal and equitable owner until such time as the Buyer shall have paid in full the agreed price. Until such time as the Buyer becomes the owner of the goods he will keep the same separate from any other goods and readily identifiable as the goods of the Seller and will not enter into any contracts to sell them on whilst ownership remains with the Seller. In the event of the Buyer becoming bankrupt or a petition being presented for its winding up the Seller may for the purpose of recovery of its goods enter upon any premises where they are stored and may repossess them. In the event of the Buyer selling the goods, even though this is prohibited, then the Seller shall be entitled to the monies realised from the sale or if a Receiver has been appointed, he shall within seven days assign to the Seller all rights against persons to whom the goods have been supplied.'

Finally, there is a provision that the contract is to be treated as made in England and subject to English law.

There were two invoices raised a week and a week and a day after the date of the facility letter and the general contract. The first invoice was raised by the company and addressed to Churchill. It is dated 22 May and it merely reads:

> 'Fabric stock as per attached schedule.
>
> TOTAL GOODS 430153.84
>
> TOTAL V.A.T. 64523.08
>
> TOTAL INVOICE 494676.92 [that is the sum of the first two figures]
>
> PAYMENT DUE END OF MONTH FOLLOWING INVOICE DATE.'

That last rubric was, not surprisingly, not observed, because, as the facility letter indicated, that payment was to be made as soon as, but not before, there was receipt of the accepted bill of exchange, in the second transaction, the sale back. There was a covering letter, which was addressed of course to Churchill and written on behalf of the company, which enclosed the invoice and said that the company was —

> 'looking forward to receiving a Bill of Exchange in connection with our re-purchase of this stock together with your [that is Churchill's] cheque for £494,676.92.'

That expectation was satisfied, because that sum was paid by Churchill to the company.

The second half of the transaction is enshrined in the second invoice, which is on 'Churchill'-headed paper. It has 'CUSTOMER' and then the company's name is given. It is described as a sales invoice:

> 'DESCRIPTION OF GOODS
> To Fabric Stock as per attached Schedule.
> TERMS: 90 day Bill of Exchange.'

The amount is stated as 'TAX EXCLUSIVE VALUE £453,924.52' and with 15% value added tax, which is added on, that brings the total up to £522,013.20. At the bottom of the page there is inscribed:

> 'The title to each of the items or goods covered by this invoice is not legally transferred until complete payment of all amounts due from the customer has been received by Churchill Merchanting Limited. For general trading conditions see Contract.'

That of course is a reference to that general contract of trading, from which I have already read a number of excerpts.

The schedule of fabric was a very lengthy list of the fabric which the company had in stock in its warehouse in circumstances that I shall state in a moment. In fact the schedule contained a larger amount of fabric than the parties accept was the subject matter of this transaction. There was a deduction of over £542,000-worth and more. Nothing turns on that original inclusion of additional fabric, which it is now, although it was not at all material times, conceded was effectively excluded from the transaction.

The evidence before the court regarding what the physical circumstances were is contained partly in that affidavit from which I have already read an extract by Mr Moore, who, after stating his contention that only a mortgage or charge over the fabric was created in favour of Churchill and that the sole effect of the sale and sale back was that the company raised cash against the fabric (that is a matter of contention), says this, which is a matter of fact:

> 'I am informed by the company's warehouse manager and the Company's directors and believe that the fabric never left the Company's warehouse. So far as I am aware, Churchill does not carry on business and never has carried on business manufacturing curtains or dealing in fabric in any other way.'

Then there is a statement that there has been no registration under the 1985 Act, which is not an issue. The effect, therefore, is that the fabric in question remained stationary throughout, and it is for that reason that the provisions in the general contract of trading regarding the passing of risk and delivery are inappropriate to the transaction that the parties entered into in this particular case. I do not say that they might not have been appropriate in another case.

Before the 90 days were up and the acceptance of the bill of exchange became due to be honoured, the receivership occurred. As I have said, it occurred on 24 July 1989. It follows of course that Churchill had not by then been paid, and there is no doubt but that both the parties involved in this litigation substantially, that is to say the bank on the one side and Churchill on the other, are showing significant losses, because the bank is, I am told, although it is not strictly in evidence, not fully covered on its debenture, and it is self-evident that, if Churchill cannot recover in respect of this transaction, it will have lost what it paid. Even if it does recover, as it claims, in this transaction, it is fairly clear that it will still be showing a significant loss. Those facts merely show that all concerned are fellow parties in distress, and it does not in fact impinge on any question that I have to decide.

Mr Sayers, who is a director of Churchill, swore an affidavit, most of which is argumentative and does not advance matters significantly, but it does contain some statements of fact, of which I should take account. He says, for example in para 5:

> 'At the time of the sale of the fabric, I particularly emphasised to Stuart Pearson, Chairman of the Company that the Company must not deal with the fabric until payment had been made in full of the sums owed to [Churchill]. In these circumstances it cannot be said, as Mr. Moore has sought to allege in the Receivers' proceedings, that the parties agree that title passed to the Company and that [Churchill] would have a charge on the fabric.'

That really goes to this, that, because that statement is there and has not been cross-examined, there cannot in my view be any question of the term in the general contract that the buyer, 'will not enter into any contracts to sell them on whilst ownership remains with the Seller' being untrue, in the sense that it was a term that the parties entered into deliberately to cloak the truth, which on that footing would have been that the buyer was free to sell the property as and when it thought fit, and I do not approach this case on any such basis. I would only observe in passing that it is a remarkable transaction for a manufacturing company to enter into, where a substantial portion of its stock in trade is involved, that it would not enter into any contract to sell them on during a period effectively of 90 days. However, that is what is said was genuinely done and that is what the document provides, and I do not approach this question on the footing that that is in any way untrue or a sham.

After there was a failure at the end of the 90 days, due to the receivership and the events that had caused the receivership, to pay by way of honouring the accepted bill of exchange, a letter was sent on behalf of Churchill on 6 September 1989 to the receivers' solicitors:

> 'We hereby formally put you on notice on behalf of your Clients that [the company] is in fundamental repudiatory breach of the agreement for sale for the sale of the fabric copies of which are contained in Exhibit "MJM2" to the Affidavit of your Client Mr Moore as your Clients have not paid and cannot pay the sums that are due to Churchill Merchanting Limited. Please treat this letter as formal termination of the contract for sale and as a formal request for the immediate delivery up of the fabric which was the subject-matter of that sale.'

There have in fact been some dealings with the fabric, both before and after the receivership opened. There were, notwithstanding what was said in the contract, some sales of the fabric before the receivership and there have been some afterwards.

Mr Waterhouse has also sworn an affidavit, in the course of which he said:

> 'At all material times the bankers to [the company] were Barclays Bank Plc . . . The transactions upon which [the company] rely in respect of their claim took place on 22nd and 23rd May 1989. I have inspected the bank statements for the accounts with Barclays Bank Plc for the period between 22nd May and 24th July 1989. At all times the accounts were overdrawn in sums of not less than £434,027.97. At no time did any of the accounts into which customer remittances are lodged go into credit. Any money received by [the company] from purchasers of curtains or other items made from the fabric would have been paid into accounts with Barclays Bank Plc pursuant to the terms of the debenture.'

He then referred to the exhibits of Mr Moore's earlier affidavit that contained the schedule to the invoices that had passed between the two parties and said of that:

> 'Consequently, the transaction between [the company] and [Churchill] involved a significant proportion of [the company's] stock'

and he passed what I think must be an observation rather than evidence:

> 'It is difficult to envisage how [the company] could have continued the manufacture of curtains had it not been the intention of the directors of the company to use this stock in the production process.'

He then said the following in relation to what happened on the ground as regards retail sales:

'[The company] sold its products through 66 retail outlets of which 56 were operated by franchisees and 10 were owned by the company itself. Consequently, the purchasers of curtains manufactured from fabric were franchisees of [the company] or members of the public. The appointment of myself and Mr Moore had the effect of putting the company into a position where it breached its obligations to the franchisees under the relevant franchise agreements. Each of the franchisees has a claim against [the company] arising out of that breach. Consequently each franchisee has withheld the payment of money due to [the company] on the 24th July 1989 and has set off that debt against a claim for breach of contract. Since our appointment, only £9,695.75 has been received by myself and Mr Moore by way of debts recovered directly from franchisees and customers. Some portion of this sum relates to proceeds of sale of fabric sold by [the company] between 22nd May 1989 and 24th July 1989. I am unable to ascertain what part, if any, of the sum relates to fabric the subject-matter of this litigation.'

And he referred to the fact that Mr Moore had said in an earlier affidavit, as in fact he had, that the retail outlets of the company had been sold. That sale, he observed —

'also included an assignment of any debts due from the franchisees of those outlets.'

He finally pointed out that, of the fabric which was present at the premises of the company on 24 July 1989 and which is the subject of Churchill's claim, a small amount has been sold, and he exhibits a schedule which shows what that fabric was and says that the proceeds of sale amounting to just over £4,000 have been put in a separate account with the bank in his and Mr Moore's name. I was told, although it is not strictly in evidence, that there was an apportionment in relation to the sale of the retail outlets that were the subject of franchise arrangements of the proceeds of sale of fabric, but there are no details of that apportionment.

The only other fact that I need mention is that there is one slight complication, which I do not think affects what I have to decide, in that some of the fabric which had originally belonged to the company and was the subject of that transaction on 22 and 23 May with Churchill was itself supplied, or is claimed to have been supplied, on retention of title terms by the supplier. There is at least one such supplier who is still asserting the claims based on that retention of title clause in proceedings which will of course follow a quite independent course from these proceedings.

The question with which I am concerned is the nature of the transaction between the company and Churchill. The submission made on behalf of the receivers and the bank is that the transaction must be looked at as a whole and not as a series of independent transactions. That is the first and, in my judgment, a very important question. The facility letter was not suggested in evidence to be inadmissible or irrelevant in any way, and rightly so, because in my judgment it is quite impossible to arrive at a proper analysis of the nature of the transaction between the parties without having regard not only to the general contract of trading and the invoices but also the facility letter.

In my judgment the transaction was one global transaction and there was no moment of time at which, once the parties had embarked on implementing the facility letter, it was possible for one or the other to withdraw. I sought to test that by asking counsel for Churchill (Mr Gourgey) what the position would have been if, on the evening of the first day, that is to say 22 May, after the invoice from the company to Churchill had been passed, Churchill had turned up at the company's warehouse and demanded to take delivery of the fabric with a view to selling it on the open market the next day. He very properly, implicitly at least, accepted that it would not have been feasible for Churchill to take any such line. Once the company put in train the procedure, as it is called, in the facility letter by submitting its invoice in accordance with the facility letter, Churchill became bound, in my view, to reinvoice the merchandise to the company at the price that was specified by the combined effect of para (ii) in the procedure and the interest paragraph earlier in the facility letter.

There was an equally indissoluble link between the various parts of the transaction in the provision that it was on the receipt of the accepted bill of exchange in order (and, I interpose, not before) that Churchill would effect payment on the first limb, that is to say on the transfer of the title of the fabric from the company to Churchill. So there again the payment on the first limb of the transaction was held up until the machinery for securing payment on the second limb was in place. It is therefore, in my judgment, not possible to arrive at a correct overall appreciation of the effect of this transaction without looking at the whole of the transaction, and in particular that means that it is not possible to arrive at that correct appreciation by just looking at the second limb, which is the transfer back by Churchill to the company.

One effect of that, as a matter of law, is that Churchill, when it set about implementing the second half of the transaction by its invoice back to the company, subject to the general contract of trading, was not the sole absolute beneficial owner of the fabric. In my judgment what it was was the legal owner of the fabric at that stage, subject to the rights which the transaction as a whole conferred on the company, notably, of course, the entitlement of the company to recover the fabric back, which itself was subject to the obligation on the company to honour the bill of exchange, which it had accepted.

Counsel for the receivers and the bank (Mr Le Poidevin) accepted two propositions, first that, had the second limb, as I have called the sale back from Churchill to the company, stood alone and had Churchill been, as he put it, a genuine supplier of fabric, the retention of title clause would have been effective and would have entitled Churchill to bring the contract to an end by accepting the company's repudiatory breach in the letter which I have read, in such a way, it should I think be added, as to preclude any question of redemption by the company thereafter. That was the first proposition that he accepted.

The second was this, that, despite the absence of an express provision for sale by the company to Churchill, as opposed to a provision for an invoice, nevertheless the general title in the fabric did pass to Churchill. That counsel accepted but went on to qualify by saying that it did not pass to Churchill as an unfettered beneficial owner but only, in his submission, by way of security and subject to what he described as the redemption provisions in the resale, a formulation which goes some way towards begging the question in issue. But, as I have already held, Churchill, in his submission, was not the absolute beneficial owner as a result of the first leg of the transaction.

At the end of the day it was common ground between the parties that the issue that has to be addressed is what was the real intention of the parties. That has to be ascertained by a consideration of all the documents that I have either read or referred to, coupled with the evidence of the factual matrix, to which I have also referred.

On that material, the question is whether the transaction taken as a whole is one by way of mortgage or charge, with money being lent and the relationship between the parties being one of creditor and debtor, or whether, on the other hand, the transaction was one which consisted of a sale and a resale with a retention of title on the latter.

There are two ways in which this question can, in principle, be answered otherwise than by giving literal effect to the terms of the documents. One of them is described in *Re George Inglefield Ltd* [1933] Ch 1 at 17, [1932] All ER Rep 244 at 251 by Lord Hanworth MR in this way:

> 'It is old law, and plain law, that in transactions of this sort the Court must consider whether or not the documents really mask the true transaction. If they do merely mask the transaction, the Court must have regard to the true position, in substance and in fact, and for this purpose tear away the mask or cloak that has been put upon the real transaction.'

Such a cloak may be liable to be torn aside for one of two reasons. One may be that the documents are shams, in the sense that they are not genuine documents and they say things which the parties did not intend actually to govern their relationship. The other way is by analysing the effect of the totality of the transaction and seeing whether, on its true construction, the totality of the relationship between the parties was one which amounts to a creditor-debtor relationship or a vendor and purchaser and repurchase relationship. Those are of course quite separate and I am only concerned with the latter, but as regards the latter it is still true to say that it is the substance of the transaction that has to be looked at and not just the form. That is, I think, clear from a variety of judgments, notably in the judgment of Romer LJ in that same decision of *Re George Inglefield Ltd* [1933] Ch 1 at 27, [1932] All ER Rep 244 at 256 where he said:

> 'The only question that we have to determine is whether, looking at the matter as one of substance, and not of form, the discount company has financed the dealers in this case by means of a transaction of mortgage and charge, or by means of a transaction of sale; because, of course, financing can be done in either the one way or the other, and to point out that it is a transaction of financing throws no light upon the question that we have to determine.'

He then went on, in a very well known passage, to analyse the differences between a transaction of sale and a transaction of mortgage of charge, and he said ([1933] Ch 1 at 27–28 [1932] All ER Rep 244 at 256–257):

> 'It appears to me that the matter admits of a very short answer, if one bears in mind the essential differences that exist between a transaction of sale and a transaction of mortgage or charge. In a transaction of sale the vendor is not entitled to get back the subject-matter of the sale by returning to the purchaser the money that has passed between them. In the case of a mortgage or charge, the mortgagor is entitled, until he has been foreclosed, to get back the subject-matter of the mortgage or charge by returning to the mortgagee the money that has passed between them. The second essential difference is that if the mortgagee realizes the subject-matter of the mortgage for a sum more than sufficient to repay him, with interest and the costs, the money that has passed between him and the mortgagor he has to account to the mortgagor for the surplus. If the purchaser sells the subject-matter of the purchase, and realizes a profit, of course he has not got to account to the vendor for the profit. Thirdly, if the mortgagee realizes the mortgage property for a sum that is insufficient to repay him the money that he has paid to the mortgagor, together with interest and costs, then the mortgagee is entitled to recover from the mortgagor the balance of the money, either because there is a covenant by the mortgagor to repay the money advanced by the mortgagee, or because of the existence of the simple contract debt which is created by the mere fact of the advance having been made. If the purchaser were to resell the purchased property at a price which was insufficient to recoup him the money that he had paid to the vendor, of course he would not be entitled to recover the balance from the vendor.'

In that particular case it was found that there was a transaction of sale and not one of mortgage or charge.

There is also some guidance, in my judgment, to be found from old authorities which were concerned with the distinction between mortgage and sale coupled with a provision of one sort or another for a repurchase. The passage which has been referred to is taken from *Coote on the Law of Mortgage* (9th edn, 1927) p. 28. It reads as follows:

> 'It is not always easy to discriminate between a mortgage and a sale qualified by a power to repurchase. In determining questions of this nature, it must be borne in mind that a mortgage cannot be a mortgage on one side only; it must be mutual; that is, if it be a mortgage with one party, it must be a mortgage with both. But the rule only requires that it shall not be competent to one party alone to consider it a mortgage. In other respects the rights of the parties may be different, for it happens not unfrequently, that one party may not be able to foreclose at a time when the other may redeem. So in *Williams v. Owen* ((1840) 5 My & Cr 303, 41 ER 386) it was held that if the parties intended an absolute sale, a contemporaneous agreement for a repurchase not acted upon will not of itself entitle the vendor to redeem. The Lord Chancellor seemed to attach some weight to *Goodman v. Grierson* ((1813) 2 Ball & B 274), in which Lord Manners held, that the fair criterion to ascertain whether a transaction be a mortgage or not is, whether the remedies are mutual and reciprocal. The rule is that *prima facie* an absolute conveyance, containing nothing to show the relation of debtor and creditor, does not cease to be an absolute conveyance and become a mortgage merely because the vendor stipulates that he shall have a right to repurchase. In every case the question is what, upon a fair construction, is the meaning of the instruments, and the absolute conveyance will be turned into a mortgage if the real intention was that the estate should be held as a security for the money . . . The deed may be absolute in form but still a mortgage, and the absence of a proviso for redemption will not prevent its being a mortgage.'

A little further on it is said, 'The payment of interest will be evidence that the transaction was intended to be a mortgage.'

If one applies that (and part of that passage is lifted verbatim from earlier authorities, notably *Manchester Sheffield and Lincolnshire Rly Co v. North Central Wagon Co* (1888) 13 App Cas 554 at 568, where there is a quotation from *Alderson v. White* (1858) 2 De G & J 97 at 105, 44 ER 924 at 928, which is rehearsed almost verbatim in that passage I read from *Coote*), one looks to see what the indications are of the sort of transaction the parties were embarking on, and for that purpose one looks at all the documents.

I find, on balance, that this was intended to be a transaction of loan and that the technique of adopting a sale and resale was mere machinery or, to quote the facility letter, procedure. I say that for the following reasons.

First of all, we have the overall agreement to establish a supplier credit line of up to 90 days for the company. Secondly, we have a second reference to credit line. That, in my judgment, suggests the relationship of debtor and creditor rather than of vendor and purchaser. Thirdly, one has interest, which is one of the features which is identified in that passage I read from *Coote* as being *an* indication of a mortgage. Here it is interest at a discount rate to yield LIBOR plus 1% per annum, and it is significant to see on what the interest is to be payable. It is perfectly clear that the figure on which interest is chargeable is geared directly to the invoice price of the merchandise, so that the interest is interest on the value of the property which is the subject matter of the transaction. Next, one finds that there is a third reference to credit in the paragraph headed 'Availability': 'This credit line is available until further notice.' Finally, and by far and away, to my way of thinking, the most important, one finds that there was an exact degree of mutuality in both directions with regard to the passing of the title to the property in question. Just as the company was bound, once it had embarked on this transaction, to transfer the property to Churchill, so Churchill was bound to reconvey it, and in my judgment that fulfills the first and, to my way of thinking probably the most important, test of the three that Romer LJ identified in *Re George Inglefield Ltd,* the redemption requirement. In this case it was, so to speak, compulsory, but it was none the less a provision, in my judgment, for redemption by being one which was the subject matter of contractual obligation.

It was debated before me how far the other two items in Romer LJ's catalogue of the indications of mortgage as opposed to sale were satisfied, that is to say a liability to account for a surplus if the financier, to use an expression that does not prejudge the issue, sells and the extent to which there subsisted an obligation on the part of the trading company to pay, if there was a sale of the subject matter of the transaction and there was a shortfall in what was originally payable.

Counsel for Churchill sought to meet the analysis in this case as showing that Romer LJ's requirements were satisfied here in this way. He contended that there was in fact no power of sale in Churchill at any time while the contract was still on foot, and the effect of that was to render the question one which could not arise. He submitted, with some force, that during the 90-day period while the bill of exchange was awaiting its being honoured it would have been improper for Churchill to seek to sell the fabric, although it remained the proprietor of it under the retention of title clause. Once the 90 days had come to an end, either the company paid or it did not. If it paid, the transaction came to a natural conclusion, and on his analysis it made no difference whether it was a sale and a resale or a mortgage. On either view the result was the same. The company recovered its goods and Churchill got its money with its interest back. If, on the other hand, the company did not honour the bill of exchange, as in fact happened, then Churchill was at liberty, again as in fact happened, to treat the contract as repudiated by the company and recover the fabric. In those circumstances, he submitted, again as it seems to me with great force, Churchill at that stage would be entitled to sell its own property (the fabric) without any question of having to account to the company for any surplus over and above the amount of the bill of exchange.

Had the transaction been one which consisted only of the second part of the overall transaction (that is to say the sale back from Churchill to the company), those submissions would undoubtedly have been not only compelling but conclusive. But of course I have taken the view that that is not the proper analysis, that one has to have regard to the whole of the transaction. In itself that, I accept, is not necessarily conclusive on this aspect of the matter, because there is an element of circularity in deciding whether or not a surplus on a sale by Churchill, after there had been a fundamental breach by the company, allowed Churchill to retain any surplus that arose, because if the transaction was a mortgage, a mortgage is always a mortgage, in accordance with the well-known dictum, and the answer would have been that Churchill was not entitled to retain that surplus, but that of course is an answer that begs the question. If, on the other hand, the correct analysis was that there was only a sale by Churchill with a retention of title clause, equally, begging the question again, Churchill would have been entitled to retain the surplus. I do not, therefore, find a clear signpost in either direction in considering that aspect of the matter.

On the other hand, I do find an indication in favour of mortgage as opposed to sale in considering what was to happen if there was a sale in breach of the terms of the general letter trading, because in those circumstances there is a specific provision in that letter that the seller, that is to say Churchill, shall be entitled to the moneys realised from that sale. Accepting for the sake of argument that there was that entitlement, it seems to me clear enough that Churchill could not at one and the same time claim to retain those moneys and the whole of the moneys secured by the bill of exchange. Counsel for Churchill sought to meet that argument by saying that, in the circumstances contemplated, the payment by bill of exchange would pro tanto amount to a double payment and that therefore there would have to be a repayment on a basis which either was or was analogous to a total failure of consideration by Churchill of the surplus attributable to the goods which had been sub-sold and in respect of which Churchill had become entitled to the moneys realised by that sub-sale. I am not convinced that that would cover the situation and would obtain if there had been increase in value between the date of the original transaction in May and the sub-sale. In my judgment, there would have been an obligation on Churchill, on the transaction viewed as a whole, to account for any such increase in value that occurred while the transaction was still on foot. However that may be, in my judgment the critical indication in favour of mortgage is the compulsory redemption provision, which is the first and, as I see it, the most important of Romer LJ's indications.

I have not referred in my judgment to the several authorities in modern times to which I was referred on retention of title clauses, because the view that I take of this matter is one which is not affected by the many subtleties that surround that subject. None of those authorities was concerned with the situation with which I am faced of there being a transaction which is entirely circular and which starts with an absolute beneficial ownership in the company and was intended, had all gone well, to finish with exactly the same situation, coupled with a repayment of the money which

Churchill had paid, with some interest. Equally that is true of the earlier authorities to which I was referred, notably the *Manchester Sheffield and Lincolnshire Ely Co v. North Central Wagon Co*, where the original transaction was not one by an absolute owner but one by a company which had an interest in the property by way of hire-purchase agreement, on which in fact it had already defaulted, and the ownership of the property was in a third party, which received a lump sum on the first limb of the transactions involved in that case. This present case is unique, so far as authority that was shown to me, in having this circular nature, and it is that which makes it unnecessary for me, in my judgment, to analyse the retention of title cases in modern times.

It was accepted by counsel for Churchill, very rightly, that, if I was against him on the first point in relation to the nature of the transaction overall, the second separate point relating to the rights of Churchill in respect of proceeds of sale of fabric that had been sold did not arise, because, if there was a charge in relation to the first, there must necessarily equally be a charge in relation to the second category, and both are unprotected by registration.

In those circumstances I propose, subject to what counsel say on the form of the order, to make a declaration in the terms of para 1 of the amended originating application, but it may be that it would be better to make one on the third alternative basis.

Declaration in terms of paras 1 and 3 of originating application. Originating summons dismissed.

NOTE

H. N. Bennett, *Mortgage or Sale?: A problem of Circularity Highlighted,* [1991] Lloyd's Maritime and Commercial L.Q. 39.

D. FRANCE

1. Introduction

RETENTION OF TITLE CLAUSES

French law recognized non-possessory interests in tangible personal property and non-notification transfers of intangible personal property only at a relatively late date. Prior to 1980, the recognition of non-possessory security interests related only to particular types of assets, such as enterprises (*fonds de commerce*) (1909), professional equipment (1951) and automobiles (1953). Legislation (in 1966 and 1972) recognized the rights under financial leasing.

In 1980, an amendment to the Bankruptcy Act of 1967 accorded validity in bankruptcy to retention-of-title clauses (Arts. 65 and 66). The new Insolvency Act of 1985 (Law for the Rehabilitation and Judicial Liquidation of Enterprises[15]) retains the respective provisions in Arts. 121 and 122[16]. Although it is recognized that German law on reservation of title influenced the French legislation, the French law in many respects remains much more restrictive. Nevertheless, the French provisions automatically attribute to the beneficiary of a retention-of-title clause the right to a claim for the price from a resale and the courts have considered this substitution with some favor.[17]

In 1981 France enacted the so-called *Loi Dailly* 'to facilitate credit to enterprises'.[18] The Law provided a simplified method for assigning business claims to a credit institution either by way of sale or by way of security, permitting blanket transactions of that type. All that is needed is the manual tradition of an itemized statement, an example of which will be found infra (p. 483). This type of credit transaction may differ from true factoring (*affacturage*) which at that time had acquired a firm foothold in France.[19]

As was to be expected, conflicts between the holders of retention of title claims and the holders of claims under an assignment pursuant to the *Loi Dailly* have occupied the courts and prompted numerous debates. Cass. Comm., Judgment of June 20, 1989, (*BNP c. Société Micro-informatique et de télécommunications*) translated infra p. 492, favoring the retention-of-title seller over the assignee of business claims, is the leading case in that respect.[20]

The decisions of the Commercial Chamber of the Court of Cassation, written in its customary involved and cryptic style, illustrate some of the difficulties inherent in the French statute and their resolution by the high tribunal.

2. Statutes

a. BANKRUPTCY ACT — Law of January 25, 1985 nr. 85-98 for the Rehabilitation and Judicial Liquidation of Enterprises, as amended by The Reform

---

15. *Loi n° 85-98 du 25 janvier 1985 relative au redressement et à la liquidation judiciaires des entreprises,* reprinted in Dalloz, Code de Commerce (1994–95) *Appendice* pp. 1060 et s.

16. Amended by the Law on the Reform of the Prevention and Treatment of the Difficulties of Enterprises of June 10, 1994, which was belatedly implemented by a governmental decree. 68 J.C.P. *Actualités* (11/2/94).

17. E.g. Cass. Comm. Judgment of January 9, 1995 (*Soc. Soufflet c. Soc. Lesieur*) *infra* p. 491, and Cass. Comm. Judgment of June 20, 1989 (*BNP c. Société Micro-informatique*) infra p. 492.

18. Loi no. 81-1 du 2 Janvier 1981, *Facilitant le crédit aux entreprises.*

19. See infra Chapt. IX (p. 513).

20. Infra p. 492. A sequel case, *Société de micro-informatique c. BNP,* was decided by the Court of Cassation (Com.) in the Judgment of January 19, 1991, Bull. IV. 19.

Act of 1994, Title I, Ch. III, Section IV provided: Rights of the seller of movables and Restitutions

Art. 115[21]

An action for restitution of movables may be instituted only within 3 months of the publication of the judgment opening the procedure of judicial reorganization or immediate judicial liquidation.

(*Old version: Art.115. An action for the restitution of movables may be instituted only within 3 months of the announcement of the judgment opening the procedure of judicial reorganization.*)

Art. 115-1[22]

The owner of goods is dispensated from asserting his right of ownership if the contract relating to these goods has been the object of registration.

Art. 121

* * *

[2][23] Subject to an action of restitution are likewise goods which are present in their original state at the time of the opening of the procedure, that are sold with a clause subordinating the transfer of their ownership to the payment in full of their price. This clause, which may be included in a writing governing a combination of commercial operations agreed upon between the parties, must have been agreed upon between the parties in a writing executed, at the latest, at the moment of delivery.
[3] Restitution in their unprocessed state may also be demanded under the same conditions for movable goods incorporated in other movable goods, if their recovery can be achieved without damage to the goods themselves and the goods in which they are incorporated. Restitution in kind may also be demanded of fungible goods, if they are present in the hands of the buyer of goods of the same type and the same quality.
[4] In all cases, restitution cannot be demanded if the price is immediately paid. The delegate-judge, may with the consent of the demanding creditor, authorize a delay in the settlement. The payment of the price is then assimilated to that of a debt originating regularly after the judgment of opening.[24]

---

21. As amended by the Reform Act of 1994 Art. 57.
22. Inserted by the Reform Act of 1994 Art. 58.
23. As rephrased by the Reform Act of 1994 Art. 59.
24. (Old Version, Art. 121. (2) Merchandise may likewise be the subject of action for restitution if the goods are present in their original state, if they were sold with a clause subordinating the transfer of their ownership to payment in full of their price, agreed upon between the parties by way of a writing executed at the latest at the moment of delivery. Nevertheless, a claim of restitution cannot be interposed if the price has been paid immediately or, at the latest, at the time of the expiration of the initial observation period,

Art. 121-1[25]

The administrator, or in his absence, the creditors' representative, or the liquidator, may grant the demand for restitution or return of goods envisaged in the present section, with the consent of the debtor.

In the case of a lack of agreement or a contest, the demand is submitted to the judge-delegate who rules on the status of the contract in the light of the observations of the creditor, the debtor, and the administrator who are heard previously.

Art. 122[26]

Restitution may be demanded of the price or the portion of the price for the goods envisaged in Art. 121 which has not been paid, been the subject of an exchange or been set-off in a running account between the debtor and purchaser at the date of the judgment opening the judicial reorganization procedure.

NOTE

For comments on the new provisions, see J.-L. Courtier, *L'action en revendication de l'article 121, loi du 25 janvier, 1985 en cas de clause de réserve de propriété,* Petites Affiches, No. 84 (July 14, 1995) 15, 16; F. Pérochon, *La revendication favorisée (Loi 94-475 du 10 juin 1994),* D. Chron. 251 (1994).

b. The Loi Dailly (Assignments for security)

Law Nr. 81-1 of January 2, 1981, Facilitating Credit for Enterprises, (D. Lég. 40, 1981), the *Loi Dailly,* as amended by Law Nr. 84-96 of January 24, 1984 Relating to the Activity and Control of Credit Establishments, Art. 61. (Actualité Législative, D. lég. 148, 154 (1984)). Reproduced in Dalloz, Code de Commerce, *Appendice* 349 (1992–93).

Art. 1

Any credit which a credit establishment accords to a juristic person of private law or public law, or to an individual in the exercise by it of its professional activity, may

---

according to the waiting period set by the delegate-judge, the administrator being obliged to guarantee the payment of the price.)

25. Inserted by the Reform Act of 1994 Art. 60.

26. As rephrased by the Reform Act of 1994 Art. 61.

(Old Version Art. 122. Restitution may be demanded on the price or a part of the price for the goods envisaged by Art. 121 if it has not been paid, nor the subject of an exchange, nor been set-off in a running account between the debtor and the buyer.)

give rise to an assignment or pledge, merely by the delivery of a schedule, of any claim which the beneficiary of the credit may hold against a third party, whether that be a juristic person of public or private law, or an individual in the exercise of its professional activity.

Assigned or pledged may be liquidated and collectible claims even if subject to a waiting period. Assigned or pledged may be likewise claims resulting from an act which has already occurred or is going to occur, but for which the amount or collectibility are not yet determined.

The schedule must contain the following declarations:

1. The caption, as the case may be, 'Instrument of Assignment of professional claims' or 'Pledge of professional claims';
2. The notation that the assignment or pledge is subject to the provisions of the present law;
3. The name or firm name of the credit institution that is the beneficiary;
4. The designation or identification of claims assigned or pledged or the factors capable of effectuating such designation or identification, in particular the name of the debtor, place of payment, amount of the claims or their value and, if applicable, their due date.

Nevertheless, if transfer of the pledged or assigned claims is effected by electronic information procedures which permit their identification, the schedule needs only to indicate, in addition to notations referred to in nrs. 1, 2 and 3 above, the means by which they are transferred, their number and aggregate amount.

In the case of a dispute about the existence or transfer of one of these claims, the transferee may prove by any method that the claim which is in issue is included in the global amount reported on the schedule.

A document in which one of the notations listed above is lacking is invalid as an assignment or pledge of professional claims within the meaning of the present law.

Art. 1-1

Even if it is made for the purpose of a guaranty and without the stipulation of a price, the assignment transfers to the assignee the property of the assigned claim.

Absent an agreement to the contrary, the signatory of the act of assignment or pledge is a guarantor severally liable for the payment of the assigned or pledged claims.

Art. 2

The schedule is signed by the assignor. It may be made negotiable. The date is affixed by the assignee.

Art. 3

The schedule may only be transferred to another credit establishment.

Art. 4

The assignment or pledge takes effect between the parties and is effective against third parties from the date stated on the schedule.

From that date, the customer of the credit establishment which is the beneficiary of the schedule may not, without consent of that establishment, modify the scope of the rights attached to the claims represented by that schedule.

Absent agreement to the contrary, the delivery of the schedule entails, as a matter of law, the transfer of the securities guaranteeing each claim.

In the case of a dispute about the date indicated on the schedule, the credit establishment may demonstrate the correctness thereof by any means.

Art. 5

The credit establishment may at any time prohibit that the debtor in the assigned or pledged claim pay the signatory of the schedule. From the date of this notification, the forms of which will be established by decree of the Council of State as provided in Art. 13, the debtor may not validly discharge its obligation except at the credit establishment.

Art. 6

Upon request by the beneficiary of the schedule, the debtor may obligate himself to pay it directly. This obligation is established under the penalty of nullity by a writing with the caption, 'Act of acceptance of the assignment or pledge of a professional claim.'

In that case, the debtor may not interpose against the credit establishment any defenses based on his personal relations with the signatory of the schedule, unless the credit establishment, in acquiring or receiving the claim, had wittingly acted to the detriment of the debtor.

NOTES

1. The *Loi Dailly* was intended to modernize credit transactions by permitting the assignment or pledge of claims resulting from professional activities by means of entries in a schedule (*bordereau*).

2. A creditor cannot demand payment from a debtor if the Schedule does not contain all of the declarations required by Art. 1 of the *Loi Dailly.* Cass. Comm. Judg-

ment of April 9, 1991 (No. 121). *Société La Blanche Porte c. Banque française de l'agriculture.*

3. Document: Example of a Bordereau

INSTRUMENT OF ASSIGNMENT OF PROFESSIONAL CLAIMS
ASSIGNMENT FOR PURPOSES OF GUARANTEE

(*Law of January 2, 1981 — Decree of September 9, 1981 — Law of January 24, 1984*)

Between the undersigned:

— The BANQUE DE LA C., Société Anonyme [Stock Company] with a capital of 33 780 500 francs, registered seat at PARIS 75008, 12 avenue M., represented by A., Director and B. Legal Representative, by virtue of the authority conferred upon them by Mr. C., Director General by the resolution of June 3, 1991,

Hereinafter known as: THE BANK.

— The Société R., Stock Company with a capital of 610,000 francs, registered seat at Morangis (91420), 61 rue du G., represented by Mr. D., Director of Finances.

Hereinafter known as: THE ASSIGNOR.

It is decided and agreed as follows:

1) THE ASSIGNOR declares that he is the owner of the claims designated below.

2) For security of reimbursement and of payment of the ASSIGNOR's entire debt, with regard to THE BANK and in particular for the security of reimbursement of the possible negative balance of the account, the latter declares that he has assigned by way of guarantee under the terms of the law of January 2, 1981 as modified by the law of January 24, 1984, the claims listed below:

to LA BANQUE DE LA C., 12 avenue M., Paris, or to the Order of the said BANK. The execution of the Schedule of assignment, whether or not followed by a notification of the assigned debtor or his acceptance, shall at no time obligate the BANK to agree to the negotiation of the correspondent claims, such consent of the BANK having necessarily to be express and resulting only from written confirmation,

This assignment shall in no way constitute a novation of the ASSIGNOR's obligation or of any co-obligee vis-à-vis the BANK. It shall be purely and simply in addition to the real and personal sureties which could or shall be constituted for the benefit of the BANK by the ASSIGNOR or by a third party.

3) Pursuant to the assignment by way of guarantee made to the BANK, it shall be the only party entitled to receive the sum due.

As a consequence, the payment of the claims assigned shall be made to the BANQUE DE LA C. and for its account alone.

In addition, by the present instrument the ASSIGNOR transfers to the BANK all of his authority to create, draw, endorse or settle any bill of exchange, order paper or check which shall be issued by the assigned debtor in payment of these claims, it being understood that the settlement of the right to payment by the BANK by virtue of the agency thus conferred shall never constitute a novation of the assignor's obligations.

4) THE BANK is released from any obligation to recover the assigned claims and shall in no case be responsible for the omission or any possible delay, nor for the debtor's lack of assets for whatever reason.

5) THE ASSIGNOR expressly declares the guaranty of the existence and the total disposability of the claims designated above. It formally waives the right to alienate them, or to dispose of them or to modify their terms.

6) THE ASSIGNOR is jointly and severally liable for the payment at the dates or periods envisaged for the claims presently assigned.

7) The present assignment shall remain in effect until released by THE BANK.

8) THE BANK reserves to itself the right, if it thinks it advisable, to give notice by registered mail according to the terms of the Law of January 2, 1981, to the debtors of the assigned claims of the schedule. In addition, it shall undertake any formalities of publication or registration which may be necessary.

9) All costs, charges and fees shall be charged to the ASSIGNOR.

INVENTORY OF CLAIMS ASSIGNED

Debtor and basis of claim	Amount or estimated value	Place of payment	Contractual surety
Invoice no. 8143/1192	450.000	Paris	
Invoice no. 8143/1193	550.000	Paris	
Invoice no. 8143/1194	1.000.000	Paris	
	2.000.000		

Two copies drafted at Paris, June 8, 1995

THE ASSIGNOR THE BANK

/s/ /s/

4. Cases

a. Radiola

Court of Cassation (com.)
Société Radiola c.
Société Kerlann équipement et autre
Judgment of November 2, 1993,
Bull. civ. 1993 IV 273.

Considering that, according to the judgment under attack (Angers, April 3, 1991), the Société Meubles Lize (*Société Lize*) sold to the Société Kerlann équipement (*Société Kerlann*) three businesses, the delivery of which was set for March 16, 1987; that the price was to be paid, part in cash and part by bills of exchange falling due on May 31, June 30 and July 31, 1987; that the Société Lize was placed in reorganization on July 29, 1987 and subsequently in liquidation; that relying on a reservation of title clause covering part of the merchandise, the Société Radiola reclaimed the price from Société Kerlann and the judicial administrator, subsequently liquidator of the Société Lize;

Upon the first assignment of error, taken in its four branches:

Considering that the Société Radiola complains of the judgment because it rejected its demand to the extent that it was directed against Mr Martin, the judicial liquidator, even though, according to the petition — on the one hand, in accordance with Art. 26 of the Law of January 25, 1985 [the Bankruptcy Act] and Art. 51 of the Decree Nr. 85-1388 of December 27, 1987 [the Bankruptcy Rules], the administrator or else the liquidator is obliged to request from the chief of the enterprise, or to undertake himself, all acts necessary for the preservation of the rights of the enterprise and, in addition, he must also compile an inventory of the property of the debtor, one copy of which must be deposited with the clerk, it being specified that goods sold under reservation of title must be specially mentioned; that in declaring that not Mr Martin, the liquidator, but the Société Radiola, the original seller who remained owner of the unpaid goods, was obligated to establish that they existed without change on the day of the judgment opening the reorganization proceedings in the estate of Société Lize, the appellate court has reversed the burden of proof and violated the provisions mentioned above, together with Art. 1315 C.C.; and that even though, on the other hand, by virtue of Art. 1599 C.C., the sale of the property of another is void; the court of appeal, which in order to deny Société Radiola the payment of the price of the merchandise sold to the Société Lize under a reservation of title clause and resold by it before payment of the price, has pointed out, that the Société Kerlann, repurchaser of the merchandise, became their owner prior to the opening of the reorganization proceedings with respect to the Société Lize, has violated the provisions mentioned above; and even though, in addition, for the application of Art. 121 and 122 of the Law of January 25, 1985, the conditions required to enable the initial seller of goods sold under reservation of title and remained unpaid to reclaim either the goods or their price must be ascertained as of the date of the opening of the reorganization proceedings; that in declaring that the conditions must be ascertained as of the date of the reclamation of the merchandise and that this could not be exercised except by action for restitution instituted within three month from the judgment of opening, the court of appeal, by misapplication, has violated the provisions cited above; and that even though, finally, in application of Art. 121 of the Law of Jan. 25, 1985, the seller of merchandise delivered under reservation of title and not paid for, may reclaim the same if they are found without change in the localities of the debtor, in being satisfied with the fact that the Société Kerlann, transferee of the inventory of the insolvent, the Société Lize, had declared in the document of transfer to have entered into possession of the inventory prior to the opening of the reorganization proceedings, the court of appeal, neglecting to examine whether the entry into the possession of the inventory involved the removal of the merchandise which was stacked in the stores of the debtor, or whether the transferee took possession of the inventory without moving the merchandise, deprived its decision of its proper legal basis with respect to the provision cited above;

But, considering that, in reclaiming from the debtor, not the merchandise itself sold under reservation of property, but its price, the seller must prove that this price was paid by the sub-purchaser to the debtor after the judgment opening the collective proceedings; that having found for a reason not challenged, that the price had been paid prior to that judgment, the court of appeal, aside from other reasons, has justified its decision; that the assignment of error therefore cannot be sustained in any of it branches;

And on the second assignment of errors, taken in its two branches;

Considering that the Société Radiola also complains that the judgment below rejected its demand to the extent that it was directed against the subpurchaser, the Société Kerlann, even though, according to the petition, on the one hand, for the application of Art. 121 and 122 of the Law of January 25, 1985, the conditions required to enable the initial seller of merchandise sold under reservation of title to reclaim the merchandise or its price paid by the subpurchaser must be ascertained as of the date of the opening of the reorganization or liquidation proceedings; in declaring that these conditions must be ascertained as the date of the institution of the restitution action by Société Radiola, the unpaid original seller, in order to dismiss its action against the transferee of the stock-in-trade purchaser of the merchandise stacked in the stores of the insolvent debtor, the court of appeal has violated, because of misapplication, the above provisions; and even though, on the other hand, pursuant to Art. 3 of the Law of March 17, 1909, the transferee of a business, on whom an objection by a creditor of the transferor has been served, cannot be considered to have paid with liberating effect, unless he has followed the procedure provided by this text; that the court of appeal, which in order to dismiss the Société Radiola's action for payment of the merchandise, object of the transfer of the business, limited itself to declaring that the bad faith of the Société Kerlann, transferee of the business, had not been established and that the oppositions to the payment of the price served on the transferee were ineffective, in view of the lack of an action for restitution, but had not found that the transferee, once the objections had been received, had respected the 10 day waiting period prescribed by the above-mentioned provision for effectuating a payment with liberating effect, had deprived its decision of a legal basis with respect to the above-mentioned provision;

But considering that in the first place, that if the Société Radiola had indicated in its appellate brief that on June 17 and 24, prior to the judgment opening the collective procedure, it had lodged an objection with the notary sequester of the inventory, in accordance with the Law of March 17, 1909, in order to receive payment in the amount of FF 605,226.38 which remained due to it on its bills, it did not draw any legal consequences from that fact, by limiting itself to demanding from the Société Kerlann the payment of the merchandise sold under reservation of title listed in the inventory of the transfer, or FF 246,731.75;

Considering, in the second place, that if the claim must exist against the debtor on the day of the opening of the collective procedure, the price of the goods sold under reservation of title must not have been paid in money nor other value, nor off-set in a running account between the debtor and the subpurchaser prior to the exercise against the latter of the action of restitution; that by having found that the Société Kerlann, in payment of the unpaid balance of the price not paid in cash, had accepted three bills of exchange already prior to the opening of the procedure, the court of appeal has correctly concluded that in consequence of the satisfaction of the claim thus achieved and in accordance with Art. 122 of the Law of January 25, 1985, the Société Radiola could no longer exercise the action for restitution of the purchase price against the sub-purchaser of the merchandise.

Wherefore it follows, that the assignment of error is inadmissible in the second branch because it newly raised and mixed law and fact and as to the surplus, not found on the merits.

Wherefore the petition is dismissed.

NOTE

The case deals with the right of the seller under a reservation of title clause to receive the full price in the insolvency of the buyer. According to French law, the seller may recover the price from the estate only if it was paid after the opening of the proceedings and from the sub-purchaser only if the purchase debt has not been regulated by other arrangements.

b. Gallé

Court of Cassation, (com.)
Établissements Gallé c. Msrs. Pavec et Philippot, as trustees in bankruptcy of the Société des chargeurs agricoles Agroshipping, and another
Judgment of February 13, 1990,
Bull. civ IV 30 (No. 45) (1990).

Considering, according to the judgment under attack, that in November 1984, the Société Gallé sold sunflower seeds to the Société des Chargeurs Agricoles Agroshipping (Société Agroshipping) and that the seeds were placed in a shipping silo operated by the firm Sonastock; that by a document of December 4, 1984, the Société Agroshipping pledged to the Crédit Lyonnais (*bank*) a quantity of sunflower seeds stored in the silo of the firm Sonastock, among which were included in part those sold by the Société Gallé; that according to this document the Société Sonastock, which had accepted that, was designated as third party custodian for the benefit of the bank; that on January 10, 1985 the Société Agroshipping was placed in reorganization proceedings ultimately converted into liquidation; that the Société Gallé, not having been paid, brought an action for the return of the merchandise on the basis of Art. 62 of the Law of July 13, 1967 in conjunction with a reservation of ownership stipulated in the sales contract; that the court of appeal, considering that the bank was entitled to invoke the protection of the provisions of Art. 2279 C.C. held that the complaint was subject to dismissal to the extent that it concerned the merchandise which had been pledged to the bank;

Upon the sole assignment of error, taken in its first branch, on the basis of Art. 2279 C.C. together with Art. 92 of the Commercial Code;

Considering that in order to so decide and to hold that the merchandise in issue had been placed in the possession of the bank, the court of appeal stated that this merchandise had been transported from the place of production to the named silo by the Société Agroshipping which took possession thereof, according to the customs of the trade, with the help of the Société Sonastock which operated the silo as its agent and depositary and which subsequently held it as third party custodian for the benefit of the bank;

Considering finally that by so holding, despite its finding that the Société Gallé had placed the merchandise in issue into a compartment of the silo which had been rented to it by the Société Sonastock in a way that the seller preserved its control, the court of appeal did not draw the legal conclusions from its findings; For that reason, and without need to pass on the other branches of the petition,

The Court reverses and annuls, in all its dispositions, the judgment of the Court of Appeal of Paris, rendered between the parties on October 2, 1987, and, accordingly, remands the case and the parties to the Court of Appeal of Versailles.

c. Pogic

Court of Cassation (Com.)
Société Pogic et autre
c. Société Astral
Judgment of January 9, 1990
Bull. civ. IV Nr. 8 (1990).

Upon the only assignment of error, examined in its first branch;

Taking note of Art. 65 of the Law of July 13, 1967;

Considering that by virtue of this provision reclamation may be demanded of merchandise sold with a clause postponing the transfer of ownership until full payment of the price, provided that this clause was agreed upon by the parties in a writing executed at the latest at the time of the delivery and that the merchandise still exists in its original state at the debtor's on the day of the opening of the collective proceedings; that it follows that if successive sales of identical merchandise have been concluded between the same parties and the buyer is subjected to reorganization or liquidation without having paid the totality of the sums owed to the seller, reclamation may be demanded by the latter only if it is established that the deliveries found in the debtor's possession are those the price of which is still unpaid and not those which are already paid for; that the parties cannot derogate from this rule of public policy by inserting into their agreements a provision to the contrary;

Considering that according to the judgment under attack the Société Pogic was placed in insolvency proceeding without having paid for certain deliveries effected by the Société Astral; that the supplier, invoking a reservation of title clause, has reclaimed the merchandise bearing its trade mark listed in the schedule of assets compiled by the trustee in bankruptcy; that the Société Pogic and trustee have opposed that claim contending that it was impossible to know, due to the presence of merchandise with the same characteristics, whether the products reclaimed came from the unpaid deliveries; that for its part the Société Astral has relied on a contractual clause which provided that 'merchandise still in possession of the debtor is presumed at any time to be that which remained unpaid and that the seller may retake it in payment of the bills still unpaid';

Considering that to admit the reclamation by the Société Astral, the judgment below holds that the presumption of the identity of the merchandise still in stock with that unpaid established by agreement is not violative of the equality of creditors to the extent that it solely concerns the problem of proof of the identity of the merchandise. That by so holding, the court of appeal has violated the provisions referred to:

For that reason, and without need to pass on the second branch, the Court vacates and annuls, in all its dispositions, the judgment of the Court of Appeal of Montpellier of February 18, 1988 rendered in the litigation; reinstates the cause and the parties to the state in which they found themselves prior to the judgment and remands them for adjudication to the Court of Appeal of Toulouse.

NOTES

1. *Société Pogic et autre c. Astral* deals with the requirement that the retention of title clause permit reclamation only if the merchandise is 'in its original state' (*'en nature'*) in the possession of the buyer at the time of the opening of the insolvency proceedings. It must be the identical material that is reclaimed. See comments by Virassamy, D. Jur. 130 (1991) and J. Böckenhoff, *Der Begriff der Vorbehaltsware 'en nature' im französischen Insolvenzrecht,* 37 Recht der internationalen Wirtschaft 465, 466 (n.16) (1991).

2. *Incorporation*: Bankruptcy Act 1985, (as amended 1994) Art. 121 part 3 allows separation of movables '*if their recovery can be achieved without damage to the goods themselves and the goods in which they are incorporated.*' This confirms cases of the Court of Cassation holding that if the object sold under a retention-of-title clause were attached to another object, the reclamation would fail unless the attachment could be severed easily and without damage. Cass. Comm. Judgment of February 12, 1991, (*Sigma Prim et autres c. Société APV Baker Perkins),* Bull. Civ. 1991 IV 48 (N.69) (1991); Cass. Comm. Judgment of January 29, 1991, (*Établissements Oldham France c. M. Ameye ès qualités de syndic*), Bull. civ. IV 30 (N.47) (1991). (Easily identifiable and detachable batteries severable even if no longer new.)

3. In a case decided under the regime of the old law, but after the promulgation of the new law, the Court of Cassation (Comm. ch.) seems to have relaxed its prior strict standards as to the existence of the merchandise in its 'natural state' at the initiation of the collective proceedings. In the Judgment of January 3, 1995 the debtor (S.M.M.S.) had purchased a machine from the supplier (TCHR) and mounted the same upon an assembly line ordered by the Société D.C. Since TCHR had furnished the machine under a reservation of title and the Société D.C. had not paid the full price to the debtor, TCHR demanded the unpaid portion of the price from D.C. on the basis of Section 122 of the 1985 Bankruptcy Act. The Court of Appeal of Rennes granted the demand of plaintiff and the authorities in charge of the collective proceedings petitioned for review contending that the unpaid balance belonged to the estate because the incorporation of the machine in the assembly line barred the claims to the proceeds from its resale. The Court of Cassation rejected the petition on the grounds that the Court of Appeal had justified its opinion by finding that the removal of the machine did not impair its use without having to investigate whether the removal impaired the use of the assembly line. Cass. Comm. Judgment of January 3, 1995 (Petites Affiches, No. 84 (July 14, 1995) 15, 16, note J.-L. Courtier.)

d. Société Soufflet

Court of Cassation (Com.),
Société Soufflet et Cie c. Société Lesieur et autres
Judgment of January 9, 1990
Bull. Civ. 1, IV, Nr. 9 (1990).

Considering, *that,* according to the findings of the judgment under review (Versailles, March 17, 1988), in order to meet its obligations under a contract of sale of sunflower seeds concluded on October 17, 1984 with Lesieur Co., the Company Chargeurs Agricoles Agroshipping (*Société Agroshipping*) turned primarily to the Company J. Soufflet et Cie (*Société Soufflet*) which sold to it, by way of a contract of October 18, 1984, a part of the necessary quantity; *that* Lesieur Co. accepted several bills of exchange drawn upon it on November 20 and 23, 1984 by Agroshipping Co. and that Agroshipping discounted them with Crédit Lyonnaise and the Company Unicrédit (*the banks*); *that* Agroshipping was placed into insolvency proceedings on January 10, 1985 without having paid for the sunflower seeds delivered to it by Soufflet; *that* in view of an attachment levied by Soufflet on December 17, 1984 on the sums due from Lesieur to its supplier, the banks invoked the jurisdiction of the *juge des référés* [emergencies judge] and obtained payment of the bills of exchange by the acceptor; *that* relying on a reservation of title clause Soufflet brought suit against Lesieur reclaiming the price pursuant to Art. 66 of the Law of July 13, 1967[27] and joined the banks, contending that they were liable for the price of the merchandise in view of the circumstances in which the bills of exchange were discounted; *that,* secondarily, because the sales agreement between Agroshipping and Lesieur provided payment of a percentage of the price by acceptance of bills of exchange, while the balance was to be the subject of a final billing after determination of the quality of the merchandise, Soufflet has asked that Lesieur Co. be condemned to pay it the amount for which it is still liable and which is still subject to the levy of attachment;

Upon the sole assignment of error,

Considering *that* Soufflet complains that the judgment below has rejected its reclamation of the price, although, by virtue of the right of subrogation to the proceeds flowing from Art. 65 and 66 of the Law of July 13, 1967, the reservation of title clause from the time of the sales contract can be asserted directly against the sums owed by Lesieur to Agroshipping; *that* from that time on, the execution of accepted bills of exchange could not, any more than their discounting with the banks, transfer to them the property of the proceeds exclusively reserved to the sellers; *that* in holding to the contrary the court of appeal has misapplied the provisions of Art. 65 and 66 of the Law of July 13, 1967.

---

27. The predecessor of the Bankruptcy Act of 1985 Art. 121.

But considering *that* by recognizing that Lesieur, as payment of the price of the purchased merchandise to the company Agroshipping, has remitted to it accepted bills of exchange, the court of appeal has correctly concluded that, as a result of the settlement of the price thus achieved in accordance with the provisions of Art. 66 of the Law of July 13, 1967, Soufflet can no longer assert its action for reclamation of the price against the buyer on the resale of the merchandise; that therefore the petition for review has no merit,

For these reasons the Court dismisses the petition for cassation.

NOTE

Société Soufflet et Cie. v. Société Lesieur holds that a payment by the sub-purchaser by means of the acceptance of a bill of exchange drawn upon it extinguishes the supplier's rights to buyer's rights from a resale. See comments by Vasseur, D. Som. com. 121 (1990); and by Cabrillac and Teyssié, 43 Rev. Trim. Droit Commercial 436 (1990).

e. *Société Micro-informatique*

Court of Cassation (com.),
Banque Nationale de Paris c. Société Micro-informatique et de Télécommunications et autres
Judgment of June 20, 1989
Bull. civ. IV Nr. 197.

The Court:

Upon the sole assignment of error, taken in its three branches;

Having seen Art. 545 C.C. together with Arts. 65 and 66 of the Law of July 13, 1967.

Considering that, since merchandise sold under reservation of title serves as security for the claim of the seller, the latter exercises his right of reclamation against the merchandise itself so long as it exists in its original state in the possession of the debtor and that after its resale in its original state by the latter, since the price is substituted for the merchandise, the seller exercises his reclamation against the price;

Considering, on the basis of the judgement under attack (Paris, February 3, 1988), that the Société Microfrance was placed into insolvency proceedings which were subsequently converted into liquidation proceedings without having paid for deliveries of various materials by the Société Microinformatique et de Télévision (*SMT*); that before the opening of the collective proceedings the Société Microfrance had resold a portion of these materials and assigned its claim to the Banque Nationale de Paris (*BNP*), according to a schedule executed pursuant to the provisions of the Law of January 2, 1981 [*Loi Dailly*] facilitating credit for enterprises; that relying on a retention of title clause, SMT has reclaimed the price still owing to the Société Microfrance by the buyer on a resale, while for its part BNP has reclaimed that payment in its capacity as assignee of the claim of the Société Microfrance;

Considering that BNP blames the judgment below for having accepted the reclamation of SMT, even though, according to the petition, *on the one hand* reclamation may be had by the seller, at the opening of collective proceedings, of the price or a portion of the price of merchandise sold with a clause postponing the transfer until full payment if the price has neither been paid by regular means of payment, nor set-off by a running account between the debtor and the buyer; that it follows therefrom that the action for reclamation of the price can be exercised only if the claim for the price from the resale still belongs to the reseller at the time of the opening of the collective proceedings; that accordingly that action can no longer be exercised if the buyer-reseller has previously assigned its claim by way of a schedule pursuant to the law, to a credit institution, since such an assignment constitutes a normal way of payment; that therefore the appellate court has violated Art. 65 and 66 of the Law of July 13, 1967 and Article 29-4 of the same Law as amended by Art. 64 of the Law of January 21, 1984, in conjunction with Art. 4 of the Law of January 2, 1981, facilitating credit for enterprises; even though, *on the other hand,* the attacked judgment itself stated that the reselling company, prior to its subjection to insolvency proceedings, had assigned to its banks 'the claims to which it held title against its sub-purchasers' and the existence of which was threatened by the reclamation 'by the initial seller tied to the eventuality of an opening of a collective procedure' against that company; that it results from these statements that on the date at which it assigned these claims to the banks, the reseller did indeed hold 'title' to these claims and that if their existence was 'threatened' by the 'potential' reclamation, these claims at least 'existed' in its assets at the date of the assignment; that, accordingly, when at the opening of the collective proceedings the original vendor was able to exercise its right of reclamation, the claims had left the assets of the buyer which no longer held title to any right against the sub-purchaser; that as a result, by stating that the initial seller was 'owner of the claim for the resale price since its alienation of the merchandise,' the court of appeal contradicted its own statements and again violated the texts examined above; and even though, *finally* the reclamation of the price of merchandise 'envisaged in Art. 65' and encumbered by a reservation of title clause cannot be accorded — outside the particular situation specified in Art. 66 — except under the same conditions as the reclamation of the merchandise itself prior to their resale, and, in particular, to the extent that this merchandise was still existent in their original nature at the time of the opening of the collective proceedings; that in the instant case, it is unquestioned and it results from the respective findings of the judgment under attack itself that the materials were resold prior to the opening of the collective proceedings and thus no longer existent in its original form in the assets of the debtor at the time of the opening of the collective proceedings; that therefore in granting reclamation to the seller the court of appeal again violated the texts referred to above.

But considering that by holding that SMT was entitled to rely on its reservation of title clause with respect to the materials in issue and that the same were resold unchanged by the Société Microfrance in a way that the price owed to it was substituted for the merchandise of which SMT had remained the owner, it is with good reason that the court of appeal has decided that the assignment invoked by BNP could not bar the reclamation of SMT; that the petition for review is thus without merit in any of its branches.

For these reasons, Rejects the petition.

NOTE

On *BNP c. Soc. Micro-informatique et de télécommunications* see comment by Professor Françoise Pérochon, D. II 431 (1989). The Court of Cassation (Ch. Com.) held that the supplier under a reservation-of-title clause prevailed over a bank which prior to the opening of insolvency proceedings against the debtor had extended credit upon an assignment for security of debtor's business claims in conformity with the *Loi Dailly.* Professor Pérochon criticizes the holding as a 'brutal', 'cryptic', and 'unwelcome' solution. Pérochon pointed out that the bank could have protected itself by resorting to Art. 6 of the Loi Dailly (acceptance of assignment by debtor). See Pérochon, D. II 431 n. 33 (1989); Vasseur, D. Sommaires Commentés, 227, 235 (1990). Although it is standard practice for banks to seek such acceptance from the assignor's debtor, he is not obligated to formally accept the assignment of his debt.

In a subsequent judgment involving the same parties, the Commercial Chamber held that the subrogation did not include the margin of profit derived from the resale. *Société de micro-informatique et télécommunications c. BNP,* Judgment of January 19, 1991, (Bull. civ. IV 19 (1991)).

f. Société Heinrich Otto

Société Heinrich Otto c. Mme Guyon
(trustee in bankruptcy of Société Carlos Dorget)
Judgment of January 8, 1991
Bull. Civ. I 6; D. Jur. 278 (1991).

(Text and note are found *Supra* Chap. 3 p. 195.)

NOTE

The cases reproduced above illustrate the narrowness of the recognition of reservation of title clauses in France and the relative ease with which a financial institution may gain priority over the rights of the supplier to the claims against a buyer on a resale. Annotations to the cases reproduced can be found in various French legal periodicals.

E. SECURITY INTERESTS IN ITALY

1. Introduction

Security Interests in Personal Property

a. Reservation of Title

In Italy, the Civil Code Book IV (On Obligations), Title III (particular Contracts), Ch. I (Sales), Section II (Sale of Movables) § 3 (Sale with retention of title) contains four sections (§§ 1523-1526) dealing with validity and effects of sales with reservation of property clauses.

For a brief comparative survey, see C. Ducouloux-Favard, S. Kopp, & F. Pernazza, *La clause de réserve de propriété dans les systèmes de droit allemand, français et italien,* Les Petites Affiches, Nr. 110, p. 99 (1994).

b. Assignment of Enterprise Credits

Like France, Italy enacted a special statute facilitating the assignment of claims of enterprises resulting from their entrepreneurial activities to enterprises engaged in the acquisition of such credits. (Law of February 21, 1991, Nr. 52.)

2. Statutes

Law of February 21, 1991 nr. 52 governing the assignment of credits owed to enterprises. *Le Legge* 593 (1991).

Art. 1
Ambit of Application

1. The assignment of monetary claims for a consideration is governed by this law if the following conditions concur:
   a) the assignor conducts an enterprise;
   b) the assigned claims result from contracts concluded by the assignor in the conduct of his enterprise;
   c) the assignee is a society or a public or private enterprise with legal personality, provided that in any case the authorized purpose provides for the acquisition of claims of enterprises and that its stated capital or endowment is not less than ten times the minimum capital for stock corporations.

2. The application of the norms of the Civil Code for the assignment of private claims not meeting the conditions of subsection 1 remains unaffected.

Art. 2

Catalogue of Enterprises Practicing the Assignment of Claims

1. There is established at the Bank of Italy a catalogue of the enterprises which practice the assignment of claims of enterprises within the meaning of this statute. The Bank of Italy exercises surveillance over the correct development of this activity, also for the purpose of preventing the employment of money, goods or valuables of illegal origin.

2. Within six months after the entry into force of this statute, the Minister of the Treasury will by decree enact the rules for the inscription in the catalogue mentioned above, and for the cancellation of such inscription, the scope and form of the surveillance as well as the respective administrative sanctions.

3. The assignee of the enterprise claims subject to this statute is bound to observe the duty of certifying the annual balance sheet.

3.

Assignment of Future Claims and Claims in Bloc.

1. Claims may also be assigned before the contracts from which they originate are concluded.

2. Existent and future claims may be assigned also in bloc.

3. Bloc assignments of future claims may include only claims which originate from contracts which must be concluded within a period of time not exceeding twenty-four months.

4. A bloc assignment of claims is considered to have a determined object also with respect to future claims, if the obligor of the assigned debt is indicated, provided that the provisions of subsection 3) are observed.

4.

Guaranty of Solvency

1. The assignor guarantees, within the limits of the stipulated consideration, the solvency of the debtor, unless the assignee waives the guaranty in whole or in part.

5.

Effect of the Assignment Against Third Parties

1. When the assignee has paid in whole or in part the consideration for the assignment and the date of the payment is certain, the assignment is effective against:

a) others deriving rights from the assignor whose title of acquisition has not become effective against third parties prior to the date of payment;

b) the creditor of the assignor who has levied upon the claim after the date of the payment;

c) the bankrupt estate of the assignor if the bankruptcy was declared after the date of the payment, subject to the provisions of Art. 7, par. 1.

2. The above provision is subject to the power of the assignee to render the assignment opposable to third parties by the means provided by the Civil Code.

3. It is also subject to the liberating effect of payments made to third parties according to the norms of the Civil Code.

Art. 6

Avoidability in Bankruptcy of Payments by the Debtor of the Assigned Claim.

1. The payment made to the assignee of the debtor of the assigned claim is not recoverable pursuant to the avoidability of Art. 67 of the text of the provisions governing bankruptcy, preventive accords, supervised administration and compulsory administrative liquidation approved by the Royal Decree of March 16, 1942, nr. 267. Nevertheless, such action may be brought against the assignor if the trustee proves that he knew of the insolvency of the debtor of the assigned claim at the date of the payment to the assignee.

2. The above provision is subject to the recourse of the assignor against the assignee who has waived the guaranty provided in Art. 4.

7.

Bankruptcy of the Assignor

1. The effectiveness of the assignment against third parties provided in Art. 5, par. 1, may not be asserted against the bankrupt estate of the assignor if the trustee proves that the assignee knew of the status of insolvency of the assignor when he made the payment and always provided that the payment was made within the year prior to the judgment declaring the bankruptcy and before the extinction of the claim assigned.

2. The trustee in bankruptcy of the assignor may rescind the assignments stipulated by assignor limited to the claims not yet arisen at the date of the judgment declaring bankruptcy.

3. In the case of a rescission, the trustee must restore to the assignee the consideration paid by the assignee to the assignor for the assignments referred to in par. 2.

NOTES

1. The statute set forth in the text concerns primarily domestic factoring. For comments see M. Viale, *Le Garanzie Bancarie* (Vol. 18 in *Trattato di Diritto Commerciale e di Diritto Pubblico dell Economia*, ed. F. Galgano) 146-152 (1994). For Italian

law concerning international factoring, see, A. Panzera, *Brevi note in tema di 'factoring' internazionale,* 145 Giurisprudenza Italiana, IV, 345. (1993).

2. The statute of 1991 does not deal with the mutual rights and duties governing the relation between the assignee (factor) and the debtor of the assigned claim, see M. Berlandini, *In Tema di denuncia dei vizi al factor da parte del debitore ceduto,* 146 Giurisprudenza Italiana, I, 2, 511 (1994).

F. UNITED STATES

SECURITY INTERESTS IN PERSONAL PROPERTY

The Uniform Commercial Code

1. Introduction

a. In the United States the law governing security interests in personal property (movable tangible property and intangible property — except rights in land) is governed by the U.C.C., Article 9.

b. The U.S. system has the following characteristics:

(i) Consolidation of all types of security interests. § 1-201(37). Reservation of title is reservation of a security interest.
(ii) General recognition of non-possessory security interests. § 9-102(1) and (2).
(iii) Differentiation between attachment and perfection of security interests. § 9-203, § 9-302.
(iv) Filing of financing statement as principal form of perfection. § 9-302.
(v) Possibility of advance filing. § 9-303.
(vi) Security interests may be created on after-acquired property (anticipatory creation). Possibility of securing future debts. §§ 9-108 and 9-204. Validity of 'cross-collateralization.'
(vii) Extension of security interests to proceeds. §§ 9-203(3) and 9-306.
(viii) Priorities. §§ 9-301 and 9-312.
(ix) The notion of the purchase money security. § 9-107.

c. Resolution of the relative priority between accounts receivable financing and inventory financing in favor of accounts receivable financing. §§ 9-312(4), (5) and (6) adhere to the principle that an accounts receivable financer who files first prevails over an inventory financer who files subsequently, for the reasons stated in the Reasons for the 1972 Amendments.

The Official Comments to the new 1990 text suppress the old reasons given by the Review Committee for Art. 9 in 1972.

UNIFORM COMMERCIAL CODE

TWELFTH EDITION

OFFICIAL TEXT — 1990

With Comments

§ 1-201. General Definitions.

Subject to additional definitions contained in the subsequent Articles of this Act which are applicable to specific Articles or Parts thereof, and unless the context otherwise requires, in this Act:

(37) "Security interest" means an interest in personal property or fixtures which secures payment or performance of an obligation. The retention or reservation of title by a seller of goods notwithstanding shipment or delivery to the buyer (Section 2-401) is limited in effect to a reservation of a "security interest". The term also includes any interest of a buyer of accounts or chattel paper which is subject to Article 9. The special property interest of a buyer of goods on identification of those goods to a contract for sale under Section 2-401 is not a "security interest", but a buyer may also acquire a "security interest" by complying with Article 9. Unless a consignment is intended as security, reservation of title thereunder is not a "security interest", but a consignment in any event is subject to the provisions on consignment sales (Section 2-326).

Whether a transaction creates a lease or security interest is determined by the facts of each case; however, a transaction creates a security interest if the consideration the lessee is to pay the lessor for the right to possession and use of the goods is an obligation for the term of the lease not subject to termination by the lessee, and

(a) the original term of the lease is equal to or greater than the remaining economic life of the goods,
(b) the lessee is bound to renew the lease for the remaining economic life of the goods or is bound to become the owner of the goods,
(c) the lessee has an option to renew the lease for the remaining economic life of the goods for no additional consideration or nominal additional consideration upon compliance with the lease agreement, or
(d) the lessee has an option to become the owner of the goods for no additional consideration or nominal additional consideration upon compliance with the lease agreement.

A transaction does not create a security interest merely because it provides that

(a) the present value of the consideration the lessee is obligated to pay the lessor for the right to possession and use of the goods is substantially equal to or is greater than the fair market value of the goods at the time the lease is entered into,

(b) the lessee assumes risk of loss of the goods, or agrees to pay taxes, insurance, filing, recording, or registration fees, or service or maintenance costs with respect to the goods,

(c) the lessee has an option to renew the lease or to become the owner of the goods,

(d) the lessee has an option to renew the lease for a fixed rent that is equal to or greater than the reasonably predictable fair market rent for the use of the goods for the term of the renewal at the time the option is to be performed, or

(e) the lessee has an option to become the owner of the goods for a fixed price that is equal to or greater than the reasonably predictable fair market value of the goods at the time the option is to be performed.

For purposes of this subsection (37):

(x) Additional consideration is not nominal if (i) when the option to renew the lease is granted to the lessee the rent is stated to be the fair market rent for the use of the goods for the term of the renewal determined at the time the option is to be performed, or (ii) when the option to become the owner of the goods is granted to the lessee the price is stated to be the fair market value of the goods determined at the time the option is to be performed. Additional consideration is nominal if it is less than the lessee's reasonably predictable cost of performing under the lease agreement if the option is not exercised;

(y) "Reasonably predictable" and "remaining economic life of the goods" are to be determined with reference to the facts and circumstances at the time the transaction is entered into; and

(z) "Present value" means the amount as of a date certain of one or more sums payable in the future, discounted to the date certain. The discount is determined by the interest rate specified by the parties if the rate is not manifestly unreasonable at the time the transaction is entered into; otherwise, the discount is determined by a commercially reasonable rate that takes into account the facts and circumstances of each case at the time the transaction was entered into.

§ 9-102. Policy and Subject Matter of Article.

(1) Except as otherwise provided in Section 9-104 on excluded transactions, this Article applies

(a) to any transaction (regardless of its form) which is intended to create a security interest in personal property or fixtures including goods, documents, instruments, general intangibles, chattel paper or accounts; and also

(b) to any sale of accounts or chattel paper.

(2) This Article applies to security interests created by contract including pledge, assignment, chattel mortgage, chattel trust, trust deed, factor's lien, equipment trust, conditional sale, trust receipt, other lien or title retention contract and lease or consignment intended as security. This Article does not apply to statutory liens except as provided in Section 9-310.

(3) The application of this Article to a security interest in a secured obligation is not affected by the fact that the obligation is itself secured by a transaction or interest to which this Article does not apply.

Note: *The adoption of this Article should be accompanied by the repeal of existing statutes dealing with conditional sales, trust receipts, factor's liens where the factor is given a nonpossessory lien, chattel mortgages, crop mortgages, mortgages on railroad equipment, assignment of accounts and generally statutes regulating security interests in personal property.*

Where the state has a retail installment selling act or small loan act, that legislation should be carefully examined to determine what changes in those acts are needed to conform them to this Article. This Article primarily sets out rules defining rights of a secured party against persons dealing with the debtor; it does not prescribe regulations and controls which may be necessary to curb abuses arising in the small loan business or in the financing of a consumer purchase on credit. Accordingly there is no intention to repeal existing regulatory acts in those fields by enactment or re-enactment of Article 9. See Section 9-203(4) and the Note thereto.

§ 9-103. Perfection of Security Interest in Multiple State Transactions.

(1) Documents, instruments and ordinary goods.

(a) This subsection applies to documents and instruments and to goods other than those covered by a certificate of title described in subsection (2), mobile goods described in subsection (3), and minerals described in subsection (5).

(b) Except as otherwise provided in this subsection, perfection and the effect of perfection or non-perfection of a security interest in collateral are governed by the law of the jurisdiction where the collateral is when the last event occurs on which is based the assertion that the security interest is perfected or unperfected.

(c) If the parties to a transaction creating a purchase money security interest in goods in one jurisdiction understand at the time that the security interest attaches that the goods will be kept in another jurisdiction, then the law of the other jurisdiction governs the perfection and the effect of perfection or nonperfection of the security interest from the time it attaches until thirty days after the debtor receives possession of the goods and thereafter if the goods are taken to the other jurisdiction before the end of the thirty-day period.

(d) When collateral is brought into and kept in this state while subject to a security interest perfected under the law of the jurisdiction from which the collateral was removed, the security interest remains perfected, but if action is required by Part 3 of this Article to perfect the security interest,

(i) if the action is not taken before the expiration of the period of perfection in the other jurisdiction or the end of four months after the collateral is brought into this state, whichever period first expires, the security interest becomes unperfected at the end of that period and is thereafter deemed to have been unperfected as against a person who became a purchaser after removal;

(ii) if the action is taken before the expiration of the period specified in subparagraph (i), the security interest continues perfected thereafter;

(iii) for the purpose of priority over a buyer of consumer goods (subsection (2) of Section 9-307), the period of the effectiveness of a filing in the jurisdiction from which the collateral is removed is governed by the rules with respect to perfection in subparagraphs (i) and (ii).

(2) Certificate of title.

(a) This subsection applies to goods covered by a certificate of title issued under a statute of this state or of another jurisdiction under the law of which indication of a security interest on the certificate is required as a condition of perfection.

(b) Except as otherwise provided in this subsection, perfection and the effect of perfection or non-perfection of the security interest are governed by the law (including the conflict of laws rules) of the jurisdiction issuing the certificate until four months after the goods are removed from that jurisdiction and thereafter until the goods are registered in another jurisdiction, but in any event not beyond surrender of the certificate. After the expiration of that period, the goods are not covered by the certificate of title within the meaning of this section.

(c) Except with respect to the rights of a buyer described in the next paragraph, a security interest, perfected in another jurisdiction otherwise than by notation on a certificate of title, in goods brought into this state and thereafter covered by a certificate of title issued by this state is subject to the rules stated in paragraph (d) of subsection (1).

(d) If goods are brought into this state while a security interest therein is perfected in any manner under the law of the jurisdiction from which the goods are removed and a certificate of title is issued by this state and the certificate does not show that the goods are subject to the security interest or that they may be subject to security interests not shown on the certificate, the security interest is subordinate to the rights of a buyer of the goods who is not in the business of selling goods of that kind to the extent that he gives value and receives delivery of the goods after issuance of the certificate and without knowledge of the security interest.

(3) Accounts, general intangibles and mobile goods.

(a) This subsection applies to accounts (other than an account described in subsection (5) on minerals) and general intangibles (other than uncertificated securities) and to goods which are mobile and which are of a type normally used in more than one jurisdiction, such as motor vehicles, trailers, rolling stock, airplanes, shipping containers, road building and construction machinery and commercial harvesting machinery and the like, if the goods are equipment or are inventory leased or held for lease by the debtor to others, and are not covered by a certificate of title described in subsection (2).

(b) The law (including the conflict of laws rules) of the jurisdiction in which the debtor is located governs the perfection and the effect of perfection or non-perfection of the security interest.

(c) If, however, the debtor is located in a jurisdiction which is not a part of the United States, and which does not provide for perfection of the security interest by filing or recording in that jurisdiction, the law of the jurisdiction in the United States in which the debtor has its major executive office in the United States governs the perfection and the effect of perfection or non-perfection of the security interest through filing. In the alternative, if the debtor is located in a jurisdiction which is not a part of the United States or Canada and the collateral is accounts or general intangibles for money due or to become due, the security interest may be perfected by notification to the account debtor. As used in this paragraph, "United States" includes its territories and possessions and the Commonwealth of Puerto Rico.

(d) A debtor shall be deemed located at his place of business if he has one, at his chief executive office if he has more than one place of business, otherwise at his residence. If, however, the debtor is a foreign air carrier under the Federal Aviation Act of 1958, as amended, it shall be deemed located at the designated office of the agent upon whom service of process may be made on behalf of the foreign air carrier.

(e) A security interest perfected under the law of the jurisdiction of the location of the debtor is perfected until the expiration of four months after a change of the debtor's location to another jurisdiction, or until perfection would have ceased by the law of the first jurisdiction, whichever period first expires. Unless perfected in the new jurisdiction before the end of that period, it becomes unperfected thereafter and is deemed to have been unperfected as against a person who became a purchaser after the change.

(4) Chattel paper.

The rules stated for goods in subsection (1) apply to a possessory security interest in chattel paper. The rules stated for accounts in subsection (3) apply to a non-possessory security interest in chattel paper, but the security interest may not be perfected by notification to the account debtor.

(5) Minerals.

Perfection and the effect of perfection or non-perfection of a security interest which is created by a debtor who has an interest in minerals or the like (including oil and gas) before extraction and which attaches thereto as extracted, or which attaches to an account resulting from the sale thereof at the wellhead or minehead are governed by the law (including the conflict of laws rules) of the jurisdiction wherein the wellhead or minehead is located.

(6) Investment Property

As amended in 1972 and 1977.

See Appendices I and II for material relating to changes made in text in 1977 and 1972.

Official Comment

Prior Uniform Statutory Provisions: Paragraph 1(d): Section 14, Uniform Conditional Sales Act.
Purposes:

1. The general rules on choice of law between the original parties in Section 1-105 apply to this Article. However, when conflicting claims to collateral arise, the question depends on *perfection* of security interests, and thus on the effect of perfection or non-perfection. These problems are dealt with in this section. The general rule (paragraph (1)(b)) is that these questions are governed by the law of jurisdiction where the collateral is when the last event occurs on which is based the assertion that the security interest is perfected or unperfected. This event will frequently be the filling. If the last event is not filing and perfection is through filing, the filing required is in the jurisdiction where the collateral is when the last event occurs; prior filing in another jurisdiction is not effective and is not saved by the four-month rule discussed below, which applies only when the security interest was *perfected* in the jurisdiction from which the collateral was removed. If the security interest was perfected in one jurisdiction and then removed to another jurisdiction, maintenance of perfection in the latter jurisdiction or failure to do so is the "last event" to which the basic rule refers.

There are, however, exceptions to this basic rule:

2. If the parties to a transaction creating a purchase money security interest in goods understand when the security interest attaches that the collateral will be kept in another jurisdiction, the law of that jurisdiction governs perfection and the effect of perfection or non-perfection until 30 days after the debtor receives possession of the goods (paragraph (1)(c)). A filing in that jurisdiction perfects the security interest even before the goods are removed. The 30-day period is not a period of grace during which filing is unnecessary or has retroactive effect, but merely states the period during which the other jurisdiction is the place of filing. The effect of late filing is governed by other provisions, such as Section 9-301 and 9-312.

3. If the goods reach that jurisdiction within the 30 days, the effectiveness of the filing in that jurisdiction continues without interruption. If the collateral is not kept in that jurisdiction before the end of the 30-day period, paragraph (1)(c) ceases to be applicable and thereafter the law of the jurisdiction where the collateral is controls perfection. A failure of the collateral to reach the intended destination jurisdiction before the expiration of the 30-day period because of a conflicting claim or otherwise may cause disappointment of expectations that the law of the destination jurisdiction will govern continuously, and caution may dictate filing both in that jurisdiction and in the jurisdiction where the security interest attaches.

This section uses the concepts that goods are "kept" in a state or "brought" into a state, and related terms. These concepts imply a stopping place of a permanent nature in the state, not merely transit or storage intended to be transitory.

* * *

5. The general rules of the section based on location of the collateral could not be applied to certain types of intangible collateral which have no location in any realistic sense, or to certain movable chattels which have no permanent location.

(a) For accounts and general intangibles there is no indispensable or symbolic document which represents the underlying claim, whose endorsement or delivery is the one effectual means of transfer. There is a considerable body of case law dealing with the situs of choses in action such as these. This case law is in the highest degree confused, contradictory and uncertain: it affords no base on which to build a statutory rule.

An account arises typically out of a sale; the contract of sale may be executed in State A, the goods shipped from a warehouse in State B to buyer (account debtor) in State C. The account may then be assigned to an assignee in State D. The seller-assignor may keep his principal records in State E. Under the non-notification system of accounts financing, the seller-assignor, despite the assignment, bills and collects from the account debtor; under notification financing the account debtor makes payment to the assignee, but the bills may be prepared and sent out by either assignor or assignee. The contracts of the transaction are with many jurisdictions: to which one is it appropriate to look for the governing law? Even more complicated situations may be anticipated when the collateral consists of novel or uncommon types of personal property, which fall within the definition of general intangibles.

If we bear in mind that our principal question is where certain financing statements shall be filed, two things become clear. *First:* since the purpose of filing is to allow subsequent creditors of the *debtor-assignor* to determine the true status of his affairs, the place chosen must be one which such creditors would normally associate with the assignor; thus the place of business of the assignee and the places of business or residences of the various account debtors must be rejected in ordinary situations. *Second:* the place chosen must be one which can be determined with the least possible risk of error. The place chosen by subsection (3) is the debtor's location, which is ordinarily the location of its chief executive office. This concept is discussed below.

* * *

§ 9-109. Classification of Goods: "Consumer Goods"; Equipment"; "Farm Products"; "Inventory".

Goods are

1. "consumer goods" if they are used or bought for use primarily for personal, family or household purposes;

2. "equipment" if they are used or bought for use primarily in business (including farming or a profession) or by a debtor who is a non-profit organization or a governmental subdivision or agency or if the goods are not included in the definitions of inventory, farm products or consumer goods;

(3) "farm products" if they are crops or livestock or supplies used or produced in farming operations or if they are products of crops or livestock in their unmanufactured states (such as ginned cotton, wool-clip, maple syrup, milk and eggs), and if they are in the possession of a debtor engaged in raising, fattening, grazing or other

farming operations. If goods are farm products they are neither equipment nor inventory;

(4) "inventory" if they are held by a person who holds them for sale or lease or to be furnished under contracts of service or if he has so furnished them, or if they are raw materials, work in process or materials used or consumed in a business. Inventory of a person is not to be classified as his equipment.

VALIDITY OF SECURITY AGREEMENT AND RIGHTS OF PARTIES THERETO

§ 9-201. General Validity of Security Agreement.

Except as otherwise provided by this Act a security agreement is effective according to its terms between the parties, against purchasers of the collateral and against creditors. Nothing in this Article validates any charge or practice illegal under any statute or regulation thereunder governing usury, small loans, retail installment sales, or the like, or extends the application of any such statute or regulation to any transaction not otherwise subject thereto.

§ 9-203. Attachment and Enforceability of Security Interest; Proceeds; Formal Requisites.

(1) Subject to the provisions of Section 4-208 on the security interest of a collecting bank, Section 8-321 on security interests in securities and Section 9-113 on a security interest arising under the Article on Sales, a security interest is not enforceable against the debtor or third parties with respect to the collateral and does not attach unless:

(a) the collateral is in the possession of the security party pursuant to agreement, or the debtor has signed a security agreement which contains a description of the collateral and in addition, when the security interest covers crops growing or to be grown or timber to be cut, a description of the land concerned;

(b) value has been given; and

(c) the debtor has rights in the collateral.

2. A security interest attaches when it becomes enforceable against the debtor with respect to the collateral. Attachment occurs as soon as all of the events specified in subsection (1) have taken place unless explicit agreement postpones the time of attaching.

(3) Unless otherwise agreed a security agreement gives the secured party the rights to proceeds provided by Section 9-306.

§ 9-204. After-Acquired Property; Future Advances.

(1) Except as provided in subsection (2), a security agreement may provide that any or all obligations covered by the security agreement are to be secured by after-acquired collateral.

(2) No security interest attaches under an after-acquired property clause to consumer goods other than accessions (Section 9-314) when given as additional security unless the debtor acquires rights in them within ten days after the secured party gives value.

(3) Obligations covered by a security agreement may include future advances or other value whether or not the advances or value are given pursuant to commitment (subsection (1) of Section 9-105).

RIGHTS OF THIRD PARTIES; PERFECTED AND UNPERFECTED SECURITY INTERESTS; RULES OF PRIORITY

§ 9-301. Persons Who Take Priority Over Unperfected Security Interests; Rights of "Lien Creditor".

(1) Except as otherwise provided in subsection (2), an unperfected security interest is subordinate to the rights of

- (a) persons entitled to priority under Section 9-312;
- (b) a person who becomes a lien creditor before the security interest is perfected;
- (c) in the case of goods, instruments, documents, and chattel paper, a person who is not a secured party and who is a transferee in bulk or other buyer not in ordinary course of business or is a buyer of farm products in ordinary course of business, to the extent that he gives value and receives delivery of the collateral without knowledge of the security interest and before it is perfected;
- (d) in the case of accounts and general intangibles, a person who is not a secured party and who is a transferee to the extent that he gives value without knowledge of the security interest and before it is perfected.

(2) If the secured party files with respect to a purchase money security interest before or within ten days after the debtor receives possession of the collateral, he takes priority over the rights of a transferee in bulk or of a lien creditor which arise between the time the security interest attaches and the time of filing.

(3) A "lien creditor" means a creditor who has acquired a lien on the property involved by attachment, levy or the like and includes an assignee for benefit of creditors from the time of assignment, and a trustee in bankruptcy from the date of the filing of the petition or a receiver in equity from the time of appointment.

(4) A person who becomes a lien creditor while a security interest is perfected takes subject to the security interest only to the extent that it secures advances made before he becomes a lien creditor or within 45 days thereafter or made without knowledge of the lien or pursuant to a commitment entered into without knowledge of the lien.

§9-302. When Filing Is Required to Perfect Security Interest; Security Interests to Which Filing Provisions of This Article Do Not Apply.

(1) A financing statement must be filed to perfect all security interests except the following:

(a) a security interest in collateral in possession of the secured party under Section 9-305;
(b) a security interest temporarily perfected in instruments or documents without delivery under Section 9-304 or in proceeds for a 10 day period under Section 9-306;
(c) a security interest created by an assignment of a beneficial interest in a trust or a decedent's estate;
(d) a purchase money security interest in consumer goods; but filing is required for a motor vehicle required to be registered; and fixture filing is required for priority over conflicting interests in fixtures to the extent provided in Section 9-313;
(e) an assignment of accounts which does not alone or in conjunction with other assignments to the same assignee transfer a significant part of the outstanding accounts of the assignor;
(f) a security interest of a collecting bank (Section 4-208) or in securities (Section 8-321) or arising under the Article on Sales (see Section 9-113) or covered in subsection (3) of this section;
(g) an assignment for the benefit of all the creditors of the transferor, and subsequent transfers by the assignee thereunder.

(2) If a secured party assigns a perfected security interest, no filing under this Article is required in order to continue the perfected status of the security interest against creditors of and transferees from the original debtor.

(3) The filing of a financing statement otherwise required by this Article is not necessary or effective to perfect a security interest in property subject to

(a) a statute or treaty of the United States which provides for a national or international registration or a national or international certificate of title or which specifies a place of filing different from that specified in this Article for filing of the security interest; or
(b) the following statutes of this state; [list any certificate of title statute covering automobiles, trailers, mobile homes, boats, farm tractors, or the

like, and any central filing statute.]; but during any period in which collateral is inventory held for sale by a person who is in the business of selling goods of that kind, the filing provisions of this Article (Part 4) apply to a security interest in that collateral created by him as debtor; or

(c) a certificate of the title statute of another jurisdiction under the law of which indication of a security interest on the certificate is required as a condition of perfection (subsection (2) of Section 9-103).

§ 9-303. When Security Interest Is Perfected; Continuity of Perfection.

(1) A security interest is perfected when it has attached and when all of the applicable steps required for perfection have been taken. Such steps are specified in Sections 9-302, 9-304, 9-305 and 9-306. If such steps are taken before the security interest attaches, it is perfected at the time when it attaches.

(2) If a security interest is originally perfected in any way permitted under this Article and is subsequently perfected in some other way under this Article, without an intermediate period when it was unperfected, the security interest shall be deemed to be perfected continuously for the purposes of this Article.

§ 9-304. Perfection of Security Interest in Instruments, Documents, and Goods Covered by Documents; Perfection by Permissive Filing; Temporary Perfection Without Filing or Transfer of Possession.

(1) A security interest in chattel paper or negotiable documents may be perfected by filing. A security interest in money or instruments (other than certificated securities or instruments which constitute part of chattel paper) can be perfected only by the secured party's taking possession, except as provided in subsections (4) and (5) of this section and subsections (2) and (3) of Section 9-306 on proceeds.

§ 9–306. "Proceeds"; Secured Party's Rights on Disposition of Collateral.

(1) "Proceeds" includes whatever is received upon the sale, exchange, collection or other disposition of collateral or proceeds. Insurance payable by reason of loss or damage to the collateral is proceeds, except to the extent that it is payable to a person other than a party to the security agreement. Money, checks, deposit accounts, and the like are "cash proceeds". All other proceeds are "non-cash proceeds".

(2) Except where this Article otherwise provides, a security interest continues in collateral notwithstanding sale, exchange or other disposition thereof unless the disposition was authorized by the secured party in the security agreement or otherwise, and also continues in any identifiable proceeds including collections received by the debtor.

(3) The security interest in proceeds is a continuously perfected security interest if the interest in the original collateral was perfected but it ceases to be a perfected security interest and becomes unperfected ten days after receipt of the proceeds by the debtor unless

(a) a filed financing statement covers the original collateral and the proceeds are collateral in which a security interest may be perfected by filing in the office or offices where the financing statement has been filed and, if the proceeds are acquired with cash proceeds, the description of collateral in the financing statement indicates the types of property constituting the proceeds; or
(b) a filed financing statement covers the original collateral and the proceeds are identifiable cash proceeds; or
(c) the security interest in the proceeds is perfected before the expiration of the ten day period.

Except as provided in this section, a security interest in proceeds can be perfected only by the methods or under the circumstances permitted in this Article for original collateral of the same type.

§ 9-312. Priorities Among Conflicting Security Interests in the Same Collateral.

(1) The rules of priority stated in other sections of this Part and in the following sections shall govern when applicable: Section 4-208 with respect to the security interests of collecting banks in items being collected, accompanying documents and proceeds; Section 9-103 on security interests related to other jurisdictions; Section 9-114 on consignments.

(2) A perfected security interest in crops for new value given to enable the debtor to produce the crops during the production season and given not more than three months before the crops become growing crops by planting or otherwise takes priority over an earlier perfected security interest to the extent that such earlier interest secures obligations due more than six months before the crops become growing crops by planting or otherwise, even though the person giving new value had knowledge of the earlier security interest.

(3) A perfected purchase money security interest in inventory has priority over a conflicting security interest in the same inventory and also has priority in identifiable cash proceeds received on or before the delivery of the inventory to a buyer if

(a) the purchase money security interest is perfected at the time the debtor receives possession of the inventory; and
(b) the purchase money secured party gives notification in writing to the holder of the conflicting security interest if the holder had filed a financing statement covering the same types of inventory (i) before the date of the filing made by the purchase money secured party, or (ii) before the beginning of the 21 day period where the purchase money security interest is temporarily perfected without filing or possession (subsection (5) of Section 9-304); and

(c) the holder of the conflicting security interest receives the notification within five years before the debtor receives possession of the inventory; and

(d) the notification states that the person giving the notice has or expects to acquire a purchase money security interest in inventory of the debtor, describing such inventory by item or type.

(4) A purchase money security interest in collateral other than inventory has priority over a conflicting security interest in the same collateral or its proceeds if the purchase money security interest is perfected at the time the debtor receives possession of the collateral or within ten days thereafter.

(5) In all cases not governed by other rules stated in this section (including cases of purchase money security interests which do not qualify for the special priorities set forth in subsections (3) and (4) of this section), priority between conflicting security interests in the same collateral shall be determined according to the following rules:

(a) Conflicting security interests rank according to priority in time of filing or perfection. Priority dates from the time a filing is first made covering the collateral or the time the security interest is first perfected, whichever is earlier, provided that there is no period thereafter when there is neither filing nor perfection.

(b) So long as conflicting security interests are unperfected, the first to attach has priority.

(6) For the purposes of subsection (5) a date of filing or perfection as to collateral is also a date of filing or perfection as to proceeds.

(7) If future advances are made while a security interest is perfected by filing, the taking of possession, or under Section 8-321 on securities, the security interest has the same priority for the purpose of subsection (5) with respect to the future advances as it does with respect to the first advance. If a commitment is made before or while the security interest is so perfected, the security interest has the same priority with respect to advances made pursuant thereto. In other cases a perfected security interest has priority from the date the advance is made.

9/Factoring

Introduction

As was shown before, factoring enterprises are providers of credit, in the form of money, conducting a particular type of business, consisting of a purchase or payment in advance of future claims. German and English cases reveal special rules applying to factors either because they pay in lieu of the original debtor, or they are considered bona fide purchasers for value.

In France it has been held that their payments call for subrogation, rather than 'assignment', with the result that the articles of the C.C. on subrogation (Art. 1249-1252 C.C.) apply, rather than those on assignment (Art. 1689-1693 C.C.). Hence there is no need for notification of the debtor.

This form of business originated in the U.S. in the late twenties[1], and was later known in France as *affacturage* or *factoring.*[2] The basic analysis of factoring under French law is the notion that the factor, pursuant to its agreement with its customer (called *adhérent* in French, like *Anschlusskunde* in German) pays the debts which are owed to the customer by third-party debtors arising from goods or services supplied by the customer. Payment by a third party of debts owed to the creditor by its debtors, subrogates the third party to the rights of the creditor against the debtors. In the case of factoring the subrogation is a so-called contractual subrogation, which must be agreed upon at the time of the payment (Art. 1250 C.C.). Under French law the factor is not considered to be a 'purchaser' of the claims passing to it via subrogation.

While the customers' debtors are usually notified of the factoring, such notification is not required for the transfer of the claim. In the absence of notification, however, payment to the customer may discharge the debtor.

As in other cases of subrogation mere payment by the subrogee (the factor) subordinates the rights of the subrogee to that of the subrogor (the customer), Art. 1252 C.C.

1. R. Steffen and F. Danziger, The Rebirth of the Commercial Factor, 36 Columbia L. R. 745 (1936).
2. Gavalda & Stoufflet, *Le contrat dit de 'factoring'*, J.C.P. (éd. G.) Doctrine Nr. 2044 (1966); Rives-Lange & Contamine-Raynaud, *Droit bancaire* (4th ed. 1986) Sec. 481.

A. FRANCE

1. Cases

a. Sofinter

Court of Cassasation (Com.),
SOFINTER v. Latimier et M. Hadengue
Judgment of November 21, 1972
D. jur. 213 (1974).

The Court — Upon the only assignment of error: —

Considering, that according to the finding of the judgment of affirmation under attack (Paris, April 10, 1971) the Société Latimier and the Société Française pour le développement du commerce internationale (SOFINTER) concluded on June 8, 1967 a so-called contract of factoring, pursuant to which SOFINTER assumed the task of collecting the claims of the Société Latimier from its customers and guaranteed their solvency; that the Société Latimier was obliged to supply it with a duplicate of its bills and to subrogate it to its rights; that on March 31, 1969 the Société Latimier informed SOFINTER, which thereupon immediately terminated the contract, that since the end of 1967 in order to procure funds it had submitted to it, and received value for, bills which corresponded to orders not yet been filled; that the Société Latimier was declared to be insolvent on April 25, 1969; that it continued to do business and that the orders which had given rise to the bills had been executed and delivered; that SOFINTER contended to be entitled to receive the payment on its account; Considering that SOFINTER claims to be aggrieved by the judgment because it rejected this demand and decided that SOFINTER could only file a claim in bankruptcy for the amount of the advances made upon these bills, even though, according to its petition, the estate, by executing the bargains entered into by the debtor, merely substituted itself for the debtor in the preexisting legal relation flowing from the accepted orders and, moreover, the subrogation agreed upon by the debtor for the benefit of SOFINTER had to become effective at the moment when the germ of the claim transferred to the said company transformed itself into a complete and effective right by the very fact of the execution of the orders.

But considering that the court of appeal, finding that the claims which are the subject of the controversy originated by virtue of the execution of the orders only after the opening of the insolvency proceedings and holding specifically that the contracts between the Société Latimier and its clients were not continued except in the interest of the estate, has decided with good reason that SOFINTER could not rely on the subrogation agreement between it and the Société Latimier in order to claim the amount of the claims arising for the benefit of the estate after the institution of the insolvency proceedings; that therefore the assignment of error has no merit,

For these reasons rejects the petition.

b. Société Polysius Polygon

Court of Cassation (Com.),
Soçiété Française de Factoring International Factors France
v.
Société Polysius Polygon
Judgment of October 14, 1975
Bull. civ., IV, Nr. 232 (1975)

The Court;

Upon the sole assignment of error, examined in its three branches,

Considering that, according to the findings of fact of the judgment below (Paris, June 28, 1974), the company Études, Travaux industriels, Montage (SETIM) concluded a factoring agreement with the soçiété française de factoring international Factors France (SFF) which enabled the latter company, after having paid the billings issued by the SETIM, to benefit from the subrogation to the rights of the latter and to collect directly from SETIM's customers the amounts of said billings; that SFF, after payment of a bill for FF 60,457.14 of December 12, 1969 addressed to the Société Polysius Polygon (*Soçiété Polysius*), nevertheless was not able to collect from that firm which declared to have paid SETIM by means of a bill of exchange due on February 28, 1970; that SFF, contending that the payment made by the Soçiété Polysius had no liberating effect because its subrogation was mentioned on the bill, brought an action against it for the amount of the bill;

Considering that petitioner contends to be aggrieved by the judgment below because it dismissed its complaint by declaring that because the Soçiété Polysius was not informed of the subrogation 'in an acceptable manner' its payment to the SETIM did have liberating effect although, according to the petitioner, the contractual subrogation, agreed upon by the creditor within the terms of art. 1250-1 of the Civil Code, operates automatically as a transfer of the claim to the subrogee and that such transfer is effective against the debtor without further formality; that it is the burden of the subrogee to inform, if need be, the debtor of the subrogation in order to prevent that the latter, on the basis of Art. 1240 C.C., may attribute liberating effect to a payment made to the original creditor in ignorance where it was to be made in consequence of the subrogation, but that this information was not subject to any particular form and that the subrogee could establish by any means of proof that the debtor had notice of the subrogation; that by virtue of these rules which apply to 'factoring' the debtor cannot validly make a liberating payment to the original creditor itself from the moment that he is informed by appropriated means of the subrogation of the factor agreed upon by the creditor; that this occurred in the instant case, as it follows from the clear and precise notations affixed to the bill of December 4, 1969 that the Société Polysius was informed in a certain and unequivocal manner of the subrogation which was accorded to SFF by SETIM; but, that consequently, by declaring that the payment made on February 6, 1970 had liberating effect, the court of appeal, misconceived the nature of the notations that were affixed to the bill and that, moreover, the court, after it conceded in its opinion that the subrogated creditor was not obligated to give notice of the subrogation to make it effective against third parties and that it was sufficient that the debtor was informed in a sufficiently clear and precise manner of the subrogation, failed to draw from its own statements the legal consequences flowing therefrom; that, in addition, as the notice of the subrogation is not subject to any prescribed form, it follows in the instant case that the insertion could be validly made by an insertion into the bill by means of a stamp without the requirement that it be followed by the signature of a representative of SETIM or that otherwise it be accompanied by a particular notice by the subrogated creditor.

But considering that the court of appeal holds in a reason not criticized in the petition, that the notice of the subrogation was not affixed in a manner sufficiently manifest to attract the attention of the personnel of the Société Polysius and in particular of the employee in charge of the payment of bills; that, apart from the justly criticized reasons relating to the requirement that the notice of subrogation be signed by a representative of SETIM or, if not, that a special notification be sent to the Société Polysius which may be held to be superfluous, the court of appeal, which quoted the notice affixed to the bill exactly without distortion, has, in deciding as it did, exercised its sovereign power to appraise the value of the elements of proof submitted to it,

Wherefore the petition is without merit.

For these reasons,

Rejects the petition interposed against the Judgment of June 28, 1974 by the Court of Appeal of Paris.

c. Société des Transports Debeaux

Court of Cassation (Ch. Com.),
Société Française de Factoring International Factors France (SFF) v.
Société des Transports Debeaux
Judgment of April 3, 1990
Bull. civ. No. 4, Nr. 116 (1990).

Considering that, according to the judgment under attack, the Société Française de Factoring International Factors France (*SFF*) paid various billings of the Société STAIC in performance of a factoring agreement and demanded their payment from the company owing them, the Société des Transports Debeaux (*Société Debeaux*); that the latter asserted a set-off by reason of a counterclaim against the Société STAIC;

Upon the single assignment of error, second branch;

After examination of Arts. 1250-1 and 1252 C.C.;

Considering that a contractual subrogation, which is expressly agreed upon by a creditor and a third party from whom he receives payment at the time of such payment, transfer to the latter the rights and actions of the creditor against the debtor; that this transfer operates against the debtor from the date of the subrogatory payment;

Considering that after having held correctly that, on principle, a debtor can rely on a set-off against a company that is subrogated to its creditor pursuant to a factoring agreement only if the set-off took place before the subrogation and having found that this was not the case in the instant controversy, the judgment, in dismissing the complaint of SFF, nevertheless declares that this limitation on the right of the debtor to interpose a defense is not effective, unless the debtor was regularly informed of the transfer of the ownership of the claims to the factor; that, since it is not shown that the Société Debeaux was informed of the factoring contract, the transfer of accounts of the Société STAIC to the SFF cannot be asserted against the Société Debeaux,

Considering that by rendering judgment to that effect the Court of Appeal has violated the provisions referred to above.

Wherefore the Court

Vacates and annuls the judgment rendered by the Court of Appeal of Grenoble on Nov. 9, 1988 between the parties, reinstates them and the proceedings to the state in which they were before the judgment, and remands them for adjudication to the Court of Appeal of Lyon.

B. ITALY

Statutes

Law of February 21, 1991 nr. 52 governing the assignment of credits owed to enterprises. *Le Legge* 593 (1991). (printed supra p. 495)

PART IV

Acquisition of Property Rights In Movables Other Than By Transfer from the Owner: Bona Fide Purchase and Acquisitive Prescription

10/Protection of Bona Fide Purchasers of Tangible Personal Property

INTRODUCTION

Modern legal systems exhibit a marked difference in the rules protecting bona fide purchase of movable property, tangible or intangible, from a non-owner. Such a non-owner may be a person who betrayed the confidence of a person who entrusted the chattel in issue to him, a thief, a person who innocently bought from a thief, or from one who wrongly believed he possessed a power of sale. Generally speaking, the dilemma whether to protect the original owner or the bona fide purchaser is conceived as the result of the antinomy between the principle of *security of rights* and the principle of *security of transactions*.[1] Credit for having reduced the problem to that basic conflict of interest is due to Victor Ehrenberg.[2]

As a matter of history, Roman law, adhering to the maxim, 'no one can transfer a greater right than he possesses,'[3] entitled the original owner to rely on his ownership, unless he had voluntarily parted with it, and did not recognize the acquisition of title from a non-owner.[4] German law, by contrast, protected the bona fide purchaser who relied on 'legal appearance,'[5] expressed in the maxim '*Hand wahre Hand*.'[6] Roman law,

1. See Roscoe Pound, *Jurisprudence* III, 292, 293 (1959).

2. Victor Ehrenberg, *Rechtssicherheit und Verkehrssicherheit*, 47 Jherings Jahrbücher für die Dogmatik des Bürgerlichen Rechts 273 (1904).

3. '*nemo plus iuris transferre potest quam ipse habet*' based on Digest of Justinian 50. 17.54.

4. W. W. Buckland & A. D. McNair, Roman law and common law (2nd ed. Cambridge 1952) 130. Critical, historical analysis of the traditional contrast between the Roman and the German approaches in Ulrich von Lübtow, *Hand wahre Hand, Festschrift der Juristischen Fakultät Berlin zum 41. Deutschen Juristentag in Berlin 1955* (1955) 119, 121.

5. *Rechtsschein.* See Joachim Gernhuber, Bürgherliches Recht (3rd ed.) 67 (§ 8) (1991).

6. '*Hand wahre hand*' originally (in the 14th century) referred to the strict liability of the borrower towards his lender. However, it later came to mean that an owner who entrusted chattels to a bailee was re-

despite its rules against the protection of bona fide purchasers, recognized the usucaption of chattels. It required continuous bona fide possession for one year and excluded goods obtained by force or theft.[7]

While the problem of the protection of bona fide purchasers arises principally with respect to chattels, it may also be encountered with respect to land by reason of the recording acts and to choses-in-action. Some legal systems require notice to make assignments effective against third parties, with the result that a bona fide junior assignee will prevail over a senior assignee.

To the extent that bona fide purchasers are protected, their acquisition of title is instantaneous. This distinguishes this type of acquisition from acquisition by prescription or adverse possession. In civil law countries which, following Roman law, recognize a claim to the return of chattels by reason of ownership in itself (the so-called *rei vindicatio*), the problem arises whether only the claim or the old owner's property itself is extinguished by prescription. The practical importance of that distinction arises in the case of a theft from a thief against whom the statute of limitations has run. If one obtained title by prescription, one is entitled to return from the second thief, otherwise the old owner. The answer to that question is controversial.

The prevailing view in France seems to support the thesis that an adverse possessor for 30 years of land or chattels acquires title.[8] The argument is based on Arts. 2262 and 2265 of the Code Civil. In Germany the same question arises under §§ 195 and 985 BGB.[9] It has been held that the running of the prescriptive period of 30 years extinguishes only the claim.

In the United States, it has likewise been held that the law recognizes a prescriptive acquisition of ownership in chattels when the running of the limitation period bars the prosecution of a claim to a return against the possessor. Such claim, however, is based on tort or contract and not on ownership as such.[10] The possession must be adverse, continuous, and open and notorious during the prescriptive period.

---

quired to keep watch and bore the risk that his bailee might sell them. Erik Anners, *Hand wahre Hand, Studien zur Geschichte der germanischen Fahrnisverfolgung* (Stockholm 1952) 1. n. 1.

7. Buckland, Text-Book of Roman Law, (3d. ed. 1963) 241 *et seq.* For antiquity, David Daube, *Jewish Law in the Hellenistic World,* Jewish Law Annual, Suppl. 2, Jewish Law in Legal History and the Modern World 45, 56 (1980) contrasts Roman law (CJ 6.2.2) with Jewish law, which permitted redemption of stolen objects (*Lösungsrecht*).

8. H. Mazeaud, J. Mazeaud, L. Mazeaud and F. Chabas, Leçons de Droit Civil, T.II, 2d vol. 7th ed. (1989), sec. 1349 and 1481–1495.

9. For discussion of the problem see Quack in Münchener Kommentar zum Bürgerlichen Gesetzbuch, Vol. 4, 2d ed. (1986), § 985 nrs. 24 and 25.

10. See R. Brown and W. Raushenbush, The Law of Personal Property (3d ed. 1975), 33 at ftn. 4.

A. ENGLAND AND WALES

1. Statutes

a. FACTORS ACT 1889
(52 & 53 Vict. c 45)

s2 Powers of mercantile agent with respect to disposition of goods.

(1) Where a mercantile agent is, with the consent of the owner, in possession of goods or of the documents of title to goods, any sale, pledge or other disposition of the goods, made by him when acting in the ordinary course of business of a mercantile agent, shall, subject to the provisions of this Act, be as valid as if he were expressly authorised by the owner of the goods to make the same; provided that the person taking under the disposition acts in good faith, and has not at the time of the disposition notice that the person making the disposition has not authority make the same.

(2) Where a mercantile agent has, with the consent of the owner, been in possession of goods or of the documents of title to goods, any sale, pledge, or other disposition, which would have been valid if the consent had continued, shall be valid notwithstanding the determination of the consent: provided that the person taking under the disposition has not at the time thereof notice that the consent has been determined.

(3) Where a mercantile agent has obtained possession of any documents of title to goods by reason of his being or having been, with the consent of the owner, in possession of the goods represented thereby, or of any other documents of title to the goods, his possession of the first-mentioned documents shall, for the purposes of this Act, be deemed to be with the consent of the owner.

(4) For the purposes of this Act the consent of the owner shall be presumed in the absence of evidence to the contrary.

s8 Disposition by seller remaining in possession.[11]

Where a person, having sold goods, continues, or is, in possession of the goods or of the documents of title to the goods, the delivery or transfer by that person, or by a mercantile agent acting for him, of the goods or documents of title under any sale, pledge, or other disposition thereof, or under any agreement for sale, pledge, or other dispostion thereof, to any person receiving the same in good faith and without notice of the previous sale, shall have the same effect as if the person making the delivery or transfer were expressly authorised by the owner of the goods to make the same.

---

11. The origins of this section are discussed in *Pacific Motors Auctions v. Motor Credits* infra p. 525.

s9 Disposition by buyer obtaining possession.

Where a person, having bought or agreed to buy goods, obtains with the consent of the seller possession of the goods or the documents of title to the goods, the deliver or transfer, by that person or by a mercantile agent acting for him, of the goods or documents of title, under any sale, pledge, or other disposition thereof, or under any agreement for sale, pledge, or other disposition thereof, to any person receiving the same in good faith and without notice of any lien or other right of the original seller in respect of the goods, shall have the same effect as if the person making the delivery or transfer were a mercantile agent in possession of the goods or documents of title with the consent of the owner.

b. Sale of Goods Act 1979

(1979 c54)

s21 Sale by a person not the owner

(1) Subject to this Act, where goods are sold by a person who is not their owner, and who does not sell them under the authority or with the consent of the owner, the buyer acquires no better title to the goods than the seller had, unless the owner of the goods is by his conduct precluded from denying the seller's authority to sell.

(2) Nothing in this Act affects —

(*a*) the provisions of the Factors Acts or any enactment enabling the apparent owner of goods to dispose of them as if he were their true owner;

(*b*) the validity of any contract of sale under any special common law or statutory power of sale or under the order of a court of competent jurisdiction.

s22 Market overt.[12]

(1) Where goods are sold in market overt, according to the usage of the market, the buyer acquires a good title to the goods, provided he buys them in good faith and without notice of any defect or want of title on the part of the seller.

* * *

s24 Seller in possession after sale.

Where a person having sold goods continues or is in possession of the goods, or of the documents of title to the goods, the delivery or transfer by that person, or by a mercantile agent acting for him, of the goods or documents of title under any sale,

12. s22 was repealed November 3, 1994. (Halsbury's Statutes Service: Issue 61.)

pledge, or other disposition thereof, to any person receiving the same in good faith and without notice of the previous sale, has the same effect as if the person making the delivery or transfer were expressly authorised by the owner of the goods to make the same.

s25 Buyer in possession after sale

(1) Where a person having bought or agreed to buy goods obtains, with the consent of the seller, possession of the goods or the documents of title to the goods, the delivery or transfer by that person, or by a mercantile agent acting for him, of the goods or documents of title, under any sale, pledge, or other disposition thereof, to any person receiving the same in good faith and without notice of any lien or other right of the original seller in respect of the goods, has the same effect as if the person making the delivery or transfer were a mercantile agent in possession of the goods or documents of title with the consent of the owner.

* * *

NOTES

English courts have held that the Factors Act 1889 and Sale of Goods Act 1893 "must for many purposes be treated as one code." *Worcester Works Finance Ltd v Cooden Engineering Co Ltd* [1972] 1 Q.B. 210, [1971] 3 All ER 708, 713. The Factors Act and SGA 1979 are similarly treated as one Code. *Forsythe International (UK) Ltd v Silver Shipping (The Saetta)* [1994] 1 All ER 851, 862.

2. Cases

a. Pacific Motors Auctions

Privy Council
Pacific Motors Actions Pty Ltd
v
Motor Credits (Hire Finance) Ltd
[1965] AC 867, [1965] 2 WLR 881

[In this case, the Motordom company sold cars to plaintiff, Motor Credits. After taking title, plaintiff customarily allowed Motordom to maintain possession of its vehicles on a 'floor plan' for sale in Motordom's name, subject to owner-plaintiff's right to reimbursement out of the proceeds from this second sale of the vehicles to the public. Later, when Motordom fell into difficulties, plaintiff withdrew Motordom's authority to sell its (plaintiff's) cars. Nevertheless, the same day, Motordom sold 16 cars after hours to defendant Pacific Motors Auctions (owned by one Webb). Motordom now being insolvent, plaintiff sought repossession of its cars and damages from defendant.

The trial court awarded the cars to defendant. The Australian High Court reversed on the grounds that the sale was not in the ordinary course of business, but on appeal the Privy Council ruled this was not an issue and reinstated the judgment of the trial court.]

On Appeal from the High Court of Australia.

March 3. The judgment of their Lordships was delivered by Lord Pearce. The present case is concerned with the title to certain motor cars which were sold to each part in turn by a dealer [Motordom] who became insolvent. * * * At the trial there was much controversy over the details of the complicated events which led up to the situation in which one or other of the parties, by reason of Motordom's misbehaviour, must lose its money. It was clear that, unless the appellant could establish that it bought the cars on November 2 bona fide in the belief that the cars belonged to Motordom, it had no case. For bona fides and ignorance of the former sale to the respondent were essential to any defence which it could raise against the respondent, who was the true owner at the time of the transaction. * * *

[T]he judge did not deduce that the appellant knew that the particular cars in dispute were 'on floor plan': and he held that since the appellant's previous dealings with Motordom had been in the belief and on the basis that Motordom had the right to dispose of the cars in its own name * * * the transaction on the appellant's part was done in good faith. He also held that in spite of the unusual features of the transaction it must be regarded as one of the sale and purchase of the cars in question.

Further, the trial judge considered that it was not material if the transaction was not one 'in the ordinary course of business,' since 'that is a limitation applicable where the only basis of the apparent authority is the possession of the goods and where the Factors Act is applicable.' Had that question been relevant, their Lordships deduce that he would have held (and rightly held) that the transaction was not in the ordinary course of business.

The Sale of Goods Act, 1923, provides as follows:

> 's26(1). Subject to the provisions of this Act, where goods are sold by a person who is not the owner thereof and who does not sell them under the authority or with the consent of the owner, the buyer acquires no better title to the goods than the seller had, unless the owner of the goods is by his conduct precluded from denying the seller's authority to sell.'
> s28(1) 'Where a person having sold goods continues or is in possession of the goods or of the documents of title to the goods, the delivery or transfer by that person or by a mercantile agent acting for him of the goods or documents of title under any sale, pledge or other disposition thereof to any per-

> son receiving the same in good faith and without notice of the previous sale shall have the same effect as if the person making the delivery or transfer were expressly authorised by the owner of the goods to make the same.'

The appellant relied on each of these sections. His Honour, having considered s26(1) and the question of estoppel and the case of *Eastern Distributors Ltd, v Golding* came to the conclusion that the respondent was, by its conduct in clothing Motordom with apparent ownership or apparent authority to sell, precluded from denying Motordom's authority to sell. It was therefore not necessary for him to deal with the contention that the appellant had acquired a good title under s28(1). He accordingly dismissed the respondent's claim. On appeal to the High Court of Australia the respondent succeeded by a majority. * * *

The appellant contended before their Lordships both that the respondent was estopped or precluded from denying Motordom's authority as the trial judge had found, and also that the appellant obtained a good title under s28(1) of the Sale of Goods Act, 1923, of New South Wales. Owing to the view taken by their Lordships on the effect of s28(1), it became unnecessary to consider the difficult question of estoppel.

The point under s28(1) turns on the construction of the words 'where a person having sold goods continues or is in possession of the goods.' Are those words to be construed in their full sense so that wherever a person is found to be in possession of goods which he has previously sold he can, whatever be the capacity in which he has possession' pass a good title? Or is some, and if so, what limitation to be placed on them by considering the quality and title of the seller's possession at the time when he sells them again to an innocent purchaser?

Section 28(1) does not limit its effect to a sale 'made in the ordinary course of business' as does s5 of the Factors (Mercantile Agents) Act, 1923, and the corresponding English provision. * * * [I]t applies to a purchase from any kind of seller made in good faith and without notice of the previous sale.

The English statutory provision which was the origin of s28(1) was introduced in 1877 with the object of mitigating the asperity of the common law towards an innocent party purchasing goods from a person who has the trappings of ownership but in truth has no proper title to the goods. Nemo dat quod non habet. The purchaser had no defence at common law against the true owner, subject to certain exceptions which are set out by Willes J. in *Fuentes v Montis* (1868 L.R. 3 C.P. 268, 276–77).

In *Johnson v Credit Lyonnais Co.* ((1877) 2 C.P.D. 224) an innocent purchaser attempted to establish that the true owner had 'so conducted himself as to have lost the right to follow his own goods into the hands of the purchaser or pledgee.' The true owner had in that case left in the hands of the seller the documents of title to the goods which he had bought and had failed to have an entry made in the books of the dock company which had custody of the goods, thus facilitating the fraudulent second sale. Denman J. held that there was no estoppel. As a direct consequence statutory protection was given to purchasers by s3 of the Factors Act, 1877 (40 & 41 Vict. c 39).[13]

* * *

In 1934, however, Mackinnon J., * * * put a further gloss on the statutory provision in *Staffs Motor Guarantee Ltd. v. British Wagon Co.* ((1934] 2 K.B. 305). In April one Heap agreed with a finance company to sell his lorry to it and then to hire it from the company on hire-purchase terms. He filled up a proposal form which was accepted, and a hire-purchase agreement dated May 2 was signed. During the term of the hiring he sold it to an innocent purchaser. * * * Mackinnon J. held that (*Ibid.* 314) 'Heap's possession of the lorry' (at the time of the second sale) 'was not the possession of a seller who had not yet delivered the article sold to the buyer, but was the possession of a bailee under the hire-purchase agreement . . .' Although the sale had not been completed by physical delivery nor had there been interruption of the seller's physical possession, he held that the case was covered by the principle in *Mitchell v. Jones.* (24 N.Z.L.R. 932)

* * *

Finally a judgment of the Court of Appeal delivered by Devlin J. in *Eastern Distributors Ltd. v. Goldring* ([1957] 2 Q.B. 600) on one point in a complicated case accepted and followed the decision in *Staffs Motor Guarantee Ltd. v. British Wagon Co.* ((1934] 2 K.B. 305) without discussing it or questioning its validity.

There is thus no case which holds that the section does not apply where after the sale the seller simply attorns to the buyer and holds the goods as his bailee.

It is plainly right to read the section as inapplicable to cases where there has been a break in the continuity of the physical possession. On this point their Lordships accept the observations of the judges in *Mitchell v. Jones* ((1905) 24 N.Z.L.R. 932) as to the words 'or is' which are the sole grounds for any doubt on this point. But what is the justification for saying that a person does not continue in possession where his physical possession does continue although the title under or by virtue of which he is in possession has changed? The fact that a person having sold goods is described as *continuing* in possession would seem to indicate that the section is not contemplating as relevant a change in the legal title under which he possesses. For the legal title by which he is in possession *cannot* continue. Before the sale he is in possession as an owner, whereas after the sale he is in possession as a bailee holding goods for the new owner. The possession continues unchanged but the title under which he possesses has changed. One may, perhaps, say in loose terms that a person having sold goods continues in possession as long as he is holding because of and only because of the sale; but what justification is there for imposing such an elaborate and artificial construction on the natural meaning of the words? The object of the section is to protect an innocent purchaser who is deceived by the vendor's physical possession of goods

13. [= s8 Factors Act 1889. Text *supra* p. 523.]

or documents and who is inevitably unaware of legal rights which fetter the apparent power to dispose. Where a vendor retains uninterrupted physical possession of the goods why should an unknown arrangement, which substitutes a bailment for ownership, disentitle the innocent purchaser to protection from a danger which is just as great as that from which the section is admittedly intended to protect him?

* * *

The climate of legislative opinion was at the time of the passing of the Factors Acts of 1877 and 1889 favourable to legislation which would prevent the buyers or others from being misled by an apparent possession of goods which was belied by legal transactions which were unknown to the world at large. In 1878 the Bills of Sale Act destroyed the validity of assignments and the like without delivery unless registered, and in 1883 the Bills of Sale (Amendment) Act made similar provisions in respect of agreements to secure money on goods remaining in the apparent possession of the borrower.

The heredity of the section which their Lordships are now considering can therefore be summed up as follows. Its words are identical with those of 8 of the Factors Act, 1889, where they first appeared in this exact form. In that Act it was expressly deemed that 'actual custody' should constitute possession. In the Sale of Goods Act, 1893, s25, the same form of words was again enacted. Part of that section (namely, 25(2)) contains an implicit reference and part of it (namely, 25(3)) an explicit reference to the Factors Acts. There was strong authority for saying that in part of the section (namely, 25(2)) 'actual custody' constitutes possession. It had never been suggested by 1923, when the same form of words was first enacted in New South Wales, that there could be written into another part of s25 (namely, 25(1)) an implied proviso that actual custody should *not* constitute possession if the possession though continuous became attributable to a bailment-thus giving to possession a meaning different from that which it had under the rest of the section and different from that which it had under a previous and co-existing section in identical terms (Factors Act, 1889; s8).

There is therefore the strongest reason for supposing that the words 'continues in possession' were intended to refer to the continuity of physical possession regardless of any private transactions between the seller and purchaser which might alter the legal title under which the possession was held.

Their Lordships do not think that such a view of the law which they believe Parliament to have intended could in practice create any adverse effect. It would mean that when a person sells a car a finance house in order to take it back on hire-purchase the finance house must take physical delivery if it is to avoid the risk of an innocent purchaser acquiring title to it. But in any event such arrangements where there is no delivery are not without some jeopardy owing to the Bills of Sale Acts.

It seems to their Lordships that *Staffs Motor Guarantee Ltd. v. British Wagon Co* ((1934] 2 K.B. 305) and *Eastern Distributors Ltd. v. Goldring* ([1957] 2 Q.B. 600) in so far as it followed it), was wrongly decided. Even if it were rightly decided, it would not cover the facts of this case. For even assuming that a separate agreement of bailment, following a sale, without any break in the seller's physical possession, were sufficient to break its continuity for the purposes of the section, here there was no separate bailment. Motordom's continued physical possession was solely attributable to the arrangement which constituted the sale. It was a term of the sale by Motordom to the respondent that Motordom should be entitled to retain possession of the cars for the purpose of selling them to customers. Motordom only received 90 per cent. of the price on the sale to the respondent, and it cannot be argued that the sale ended at that stage. It would be absurd to suppose that either party intended Motordom to sell its stock for 90 per cent. of its value without getting a right to any further benefit. The transaction by which Motordom sold the cars to the respondent was inextricably mixed with Motordom's right to keep the cars for display at its premises. In their Lordships' opinion Motordom having sold the goods whose ownership is disputed, continued in possession of them.

In spite of Mr. Newton's arguments, their Lordships cannot question the trial judge's conclusions as to the bona fides of the appellant and its lack of notice of the previous sale. No doubt those arguments were put to him at the trial, but having heard and seen the witnesses he did not accept the arguments.

Their Lordships will therefore humbly advise Her Majesty that the appeal should be allowed, the order of the High Court dated August 28, 1963, set aside with costs and the order of the Supreme Court of New South Wales dated July 25, 1962, restored. The respondent must pay the costs of this appeal.

NOTES

1. The text case deals the effects of a sale by a 'seller in possession' i.e. a party remaining in possession after a sale. *Staffs Motor Guarantee v British Wagon Co. (1934)* ([1934] 2 K.B. 305 held that a seller in possession could not pass good title because technically he had become a bailee rather than a seller. In *Pacific Motors* the Privy Council interpreted s28(1) of the New South Wales (Australia) Sale of Goods Act 1923, a text identical to English Sale of Goods Act 1893 s25, the forerunner of s24 of the Sale of Goods Act [SGA] 1979. The Privy Council rejected the English rule of *Staffs Motors* holding that 'continues in possession' meant physical possession.

Although *Pacific Motors* has only persuasive authority in England, it has been followed by the Court of Appeal in *Worcester Works Finance Ltd. v Cooden Engineering Co. Ltd.* [1972] 1 Q.B. 210, [1971] 3 All ER 708. BENJAMIN'S SALE OF GOODS (4th ed.) 7-057 (London 1992).

2. As the text case indicates, English law only protects bona fide purchasers of chattels against claims of the true owner to a limited extent. The earliest exception, the medieval rule of market ouvert, embodied in s22(1) SGA 1979 until 1994, allowed bona fide purchasers in a few ancient traditional street markets to acquire good title even from thieves. See Holdsworth, *History of English Law*, Vol. 5 (1927), pp. 104–105,

110–111. Parliament abolished s22 as a crime prevention measure on November 3, 1994, recognizing that modern transportation methods had made the rule of market ouvert obsolete.[14] Section 21 SGA 1979 refers to various other exceptions to the *nemo dat* rule, including estoppel[15] and provisions of the Factors Act 1889.

3. With respect to a bona fide acquisition of choses-in-action, see *Pfeiffer G.m.b.H. v Arbuthnot Factors*, QBD 1987, [1988] 1 WLR 150. (Supra Chap 8 p. 449)

b. National Employers' Mutual

National Employers' Mutual Insurance Ltd (Respondent)
v
Jones (Appellant)
House of Lords
Appeal Cases. 1990, 24; [1988] 2 WLR 952.

LORD GOFF OF CHIEVELEY. My Lords, this appeal raises a short, but nevertheless important, point of construction of two parallel statutory provisions, s9 of the Factors Act 1889, and s25(1) of the Sale of Goods Act 1979 (formerly s25(2) of the Sale of Goods Act 1893).

The facts can be very briefly stated. The case is concerned with the title to a Ford Fiesta car. The car belonged to Miss Hopkin. On 3 February 1983 it was stolen. The thieves were later caught and convicted, but they had already sold the car, shortly after the theft, to a man called Lacey; the price is unknown. Lacey sold the car almost immediately to a man called Thomas; again the price is not known. On 7 February 1983 Thomas sold the car to Autochoice (Bridgend) Ltd. for £2,100. Five weeks later, on 14 March 1983, Autochoice (Bridgend) Ltd. sold the car to Mid-Glamorgan Motors Ltd. for £2,350; and on 17 March 1983 that company sold it on to the defendant, Mr. Jones, for £2,650. It is accepted that Mr. Jones acted in good faith in buying the car.

The plaintiffs, National Employers' Mutual General Insurance Association Ltd., were Miss Hopkin's insurers. They bought out her interest after the theft, for £2,750, and so acquired her rights to the car. By a letter dated 6 January 1984, they demanded the car back from Mr. Jones; he refused to return it to them. They then commenced proceedings against Mr. Jones in the Bridgend County Court on 27 September 1984, claiming damages from him representing the value of the car. They succeeded in their claim. Mr. Jones then appealed to the Court of Appeal. The Court of Appeal ante, p. 27F, by a majority (May and Croom-Johnson L.JJ., Sir Denys Buckley dissenting) dismissed the appeal. Mr. Jones now appeals to this House, by leave of the Court of Appeal.

---

14. Halsbury's Statutes Service: Issue 61.

15. 's21(1) SGA (1979) unless the owner is precluded. . . .' For discussion see P. S. Atiyah, *The Sale of Goods* (8th ed. 1990) Chap. 19.

Since the decision of the case turns on the construction of the two sections to which I have referred, I think it desirable first to set out the relevant statutory provisions. I take first the Factors Act 1889. The statute is expressed to be an Act to amend and consolidate the Factors Acts. For present purposes, the most relevant sections are s2, s8 and s9. Section 2 falls under the sub-heading 'Dispositions by mercantile agents;' s8 and s9 fall under the sub-heading 'Dispositions by sellers and buyers of goods.' The sections provide:

* * * [Factors Act 1889, s2, s8 and s9. omitted here are reprinted supra p. 000]

Turning next to the Sale of Goods Act 1979, the most relevant sections are s21, s22(1), s24 and s25(1). These all fall under the subheading 'Transfer of title,' and provide:

* * * [Sale of Goods Act 1979 s21(1), s22(1), s24 and s25(1), omitted here are reprinted supra p. 000]

For the purposes of the present case, the sections directly in point are, as I have indicated, s9 of the Factors Act 1889 and s25(1) of the Sale of Goods Act 1979. These are in almost identical terms; the difference is not relevant to the decision in the present case. The argument of the appellant has been founded upon these sections. I shall for convenience refer to s9 of the Factors Act 1889. — The submission was that Mid-Glamorgan Motors Ltd. bought the car from Autochoice (Bridgend) Ltd., who gave possession of the car to them; and that Mid-Glamorgan Motors Ltd. then delivered the car to the appellant under a sale, and the appellant received the same in good faith without notice of any lien or other right of the original seller in respect of the goods. Accordingly, by virtue of the section, such delivery shall have the same effect as if Mid-Glamorgan Motors Ltd. were a mercantile agent in possession of the goods with the consent of the owner, i.e. (see s2(1)) such sale shall be as valid as if Mid-Glamorgan Motors Ltd. were expressly authorised by the owner to make the sale. It followed, submitted the appellant, that he acquired a good title to the car. This was the argument which found favour with Sir Denys Buckley; but was rejected by the judge in the county court, and by the majority of the Court of Appeal.

In order to consider the validity of this argument, it is necessary first to place the relevant statutory provisions in their legislative context. There have been five Factors Acts in all. The first was the Factors Act

> 'An Act for the better protection of the property of merchants and others, who may hereafter enter into contracts or agreements in relation to goods, wares or merchandises intrusted to factors or agents.'

The broad effect of the Act was that a person so entrusted with goods for the purpose of sale, who shipped such goods in his own name, should be deemed to be the true owner of them, so far as to entitle a bona fide-consignee of the goods to a lien upon them in respect of money, etc., advanced to, or for the use of, the named shipper. The protection so conferred was, therefore, limited to the lien. But the whole basis of the protection was that the person adversely affected by the lien was a person who had entrusted the goods to the named shipper. It was this entrusting that constituted the named shipper a factor or agent; and it is no doubt because this constituted the basis of the legislation that it became known as the Factors Act 1823.

The next Act was the Factors Act 1825. This was entitled:

> 'An Act to alter and amend an Act for the better protection of the property of merchants and others, who may hereafter enter into contracts or agreements in relation to goods, wares or merchandise intrusted to factors or agents.'

By this Act, the protection conferred by the Factors Act 1823 was extended in two ways. First, it extended the protection conferred by the Factors Act 1823 to cases where it was not the goods, but the bills of lading or other documents of title, which had been entrusted to the factor or agent. Second, it conferred protection not only in the form of a lien in such cases and in the cases specified in the Factors Act 1823; it went further, and provided that contracts for the purchase of goods made with agents entrusted with those goods, should be 'binding upon and good against the owner of such goods.' This provision (to be found in s4) was expressed to be subject to the following proviso:

> 'provided such contract . . . be made in the usual and ordinary course of business, and that such person [the purchaser] . . . shall not, when such contract is entered into . . . have notice that such agent . . . is . . . not authorised to sell the said goods, wares and merchandise . . .'

Now there can, in my opinion, be no doubt that 'the owner of such goods,' upon whom the contract made by the agent was binding, can refer only to the owner who had entrusted the goods to the agent. This is evident from the statutory purpose as demonstrated in the title to the Act, and from the proviso to s4, quoted above, which focuses upon the requirement that the purchaser must not have notice that the agent was not *authorised* to sell the goods. It is evident that the whole Act, like its predecessor, was directed to giving protection to those who had dealt in good faith with factors or agents, to whom goods, or documents of title to goods, had been entrusted, to the extent that the rights of such persons should (so far as provided) override those of the owner who had so entrusted the goods or documents to the factor or agent. There is not the slightest indication in the statute that it was intended to take so radical a step as to depart (except in the limited circumstances I have indicated) from the cardinal principle of the law of property in chattels embodied in the Latin maxim nemo dat quod non habet, so as to enable a factor or agent, entrusted with goods by a thief or a purchaser from a thief, to give a good title to a bona fide purchaser from him, overriding the title of the true owner. Not surprisingly, it does not seem that any such argument was ever advanced under s4 of the Factors Act 1825; if it had been, I cannot help but think that it would have been given very short shrift indeed.

The next Act was the Factors Act 1842. * * * I come next to the Factors Act 1877, which is of some importance, for it legislated for the first time for the cases of vendors permitted to retain documents of title to goods, and vendees permitted to have such documents of title, after the sale. The Act was entitled simply 'An Act to amend the Factors' Acts,' and it was introduced by the following recital:

> 'Whereas doubts have arisen with respect to the true meaning of certain provisions of the Factors' Acts, and it is expedient to remove such doubts and otherwise to amend the said Acts, for the better security of persons buying or making advances on goods, or documents of title to goods, in the usual and ordinary course of mercantile business.'

For present purposes, the relevant sections are s3 and s4, which provide:

> s3. Where any goods have been sold, and the vendor or any person on his behalf continues or is in possession of the documents of title thereto, any sale, pledge, or other disposition of the goods or documents made by such vendor or any person or agent entrusted by the vendor with the goods or documents within the meaning of the principal Acts as amended by this Act so continuing or being in possession, shall be as valid and effectual as if such vendor or person were an agent or person entrusted by the vendee with the goods or documents within the meaning of the principal Acts as amended by this Act, provided the person to whom the sale, pledge, or other disposition is made has not notice that the goods have been previously sold.
>
> s4. Where any goods have been sold or contracted to be sold, and the vendee, or any person on his behalf, obtains the possession of the documents of title thereto from the vendor or his agents, any sale, pledge, or disposition of such goods or documents by such vendee so in possession or by any other person or agent entrusted by the vendee with the documents within the meaning of the principal Acts as amended by this Act shall be as valid and effectual as if such vendee or other person were an agent or person entrusted by the vendor with the documents within the meaning of the principal Acts as amended by this Act, provided the person to whom the sale, pledge, or other disposition is made has not notice of any lien or other right of the vendor in respect of the goods.

Taking first s3, it is, I think, of importance to observe that it provided that the 'sale, pledge, or other disposition of the goods or documents . . . shall be as valid and effectual as if such vendor or person were an agent or person entrusted *by the vendee* with the goods or documents within the meaning of the principal Acts as amended by this Act. . . .' This can, I suppose, be described as a statutory hypothesis: but for me the significance of the provision is that it presupposes an *entrusting* by the *vendee* and an intention (consistent with the previous Factors Acts) that, by virtue of such entrusting, the title of the vendee may be adversely affected. Likewise, in s4, we find a similar hypothesis as if such vendee or other person were an agent or person *entrusted* by the *vendor* with the documents' — plainly with the same policy in mind. Once again, it cannot sensibly be suggested that this Act, any more than the Factors Act 1825, was intended to affect adversely the title of a person from whom goods or documents of title had been stolen: the intention was only to affect adversely the title of one who had entrusted documents of title to another, though here the person so entrusted would not be a factor or agent, but a vendor or vendee entrusted with possession after a sale.

Such are the statutory precursors of the Factors Act 1889. This Act is, as I have already recorded, entitled simply 'An Act to amend and consolidate the Factors Acts.' There is no hint of any change of fundamental policy in the title; nor is there any preamble to the Act, in which any such change of policy would surely have been set out, had it been intended by Parliament to make such a change. As I have previously said, the relevant sections are s2, s8 and s9. Section 2 is concerned to provide for the validity of sales, pledges and other dispositions of goods by mercantile agents who are, 'with the consent of the owner,' in possession of the goods or of documents of title to the goods; such transactions, it is provided, shall be as valid as if the mercantile agents were expressly authorised 'by the owner of the goods. to make the same.' Plainly, the owner of the goods here referred to is the owner with whose consent the agent is in possession of them. The section cannot be read as having the effect of adversely affecting the title of any person, other than the person who had entrusted the goods or documents of title to the mercantile agents; it cannot adversely affect the title of one from whom the goods had been stolen, whose goods have come into possession of the mercantile agent from the thief, or from a person deriving title from the thief. The policy underlying this section is, therefore, wholly consistent with the policy underlying the earlier Factors Acts.

I come therefore to s8 and s9. I will, for the sake of clarity set out the two sections again, in order to identify with initials the relevant actors in the drama. In s8, I have identified the vendor as A; the first purchaser, who has allowed A to remain in possession of the goods or documents of title, I shall hereafter refer to as B1; and the second purchaser, to whom A has sold, pledged or otherwise disposed of the goods or documents of title, I have identified as B2. In s9, I have identified the seller referred to in line 2 of the section as A; the person who bought or agreed to buy the goods from A, and who obtained possession of the goods or documents of title with A's consent, I have identified as B; and the person to whom B delivers or transfers the goods or documents of title under a sale, pledge or other disposal, or an agreement for the same, I have identified as C. Interpolating these initials, the sections read:

> s8. Where a person (A), having sold goods, continues, or is, in possession of the goods or of the documents of title to the goods, the delivery or transfer by that person (A), or by a mercantile agent acting for him, of the goods or documents of title under any sale, pledge, or other disposition thereof, or under any agreement for sale, pledge, or other disposition thereof, to any person (B2) receiving the same in good faith and without notice of the previous sale, shall have the same effect as if the person making the delivery or transfer were expressly authorised by the owner of the goods to make the same.
>
> s9. Where a person (B), having bought or agreed to buy goods, obtains with the consent of the seller (A) possession of the goods or the documents of title to the goods, the delivery or transfer, by that person (B) or by a mercantile agent acting for him, of the goods or documents of title, under any sale, pledge, or other disposition thereof, or under any agreement for sale, pledge, or other disposition thereof, to any person (C) receiving the same in good faith and without notice of any lien or other right of the original seller (A) in respect of the goods, shall have the same effect as if the person (B) making the delivery or transfer were a mercantile agent in possession of the goods or documents of title with the consent of the owner.

These two sections, of course, go slightly further than s3 and s4 of the Factors Act 1877, in that they take effect not only when the relevant person ((A) in s8, and (B) in s9) is allowed to be in possession of the documents of title to the goods, but also when he is allowed to be in possession of the goods themselves. It is relevant to observe also that, whereas the statutory hypothesis at the end of s3 and s4 of the Factors Act 1877 refers to the transaction taking effect as if the person making the delivery or transfer was a person entrusted by the vendee with the goods or documents, or entrusted by the vendor with the documents, as the case may be, we now see, in s8 and s9 of the Factors Act 1889, a different phraseology, referring not to the vendee (B1) or the vendor (A), but just to the 'owner of the goods' or 'the owner.' It is upon the slender foundation of this change of phraseology that the appellant, in the present case, has sought to build his argument that s9 has the effect of adversely affecting the title, not only of a person (A) who has allowed another person (B) to be in possession of the relevant goods or documents, but also of anybody from whom the goods have been stolen, and whose goods have come into the possession of another who sells them.

For s9 to have any such effect would constitute a change in policy of a fundamental kind, of which there is no evidence whatsoever in the remainder of the Act of 1889. I add for good measure that when, in 1893, s9 was effectively incorporated (with changes which are immaterial for present purposes) as s25(2) of the Sale of Goods Act of that year, it was incorporated into an Act of Parliament which expressly maintained the fundamental principle nemo dat quod non habet, in s21(1) of the Act (now s21(1) of the Act of 1979, quoted above). The succeeding sections enact what appear to be minor exceptions to that fundamental principle: yet, if the appellant's contention were to be correct, s25(2) would have made not so much an exception to the principle, but would have substantially amounted to a reversal of it.

For the reasons I have set out, the statutory context provides overwhelming evidence that the legislature never intended, either in s9 of the Factors Act 1889, or in s25(2) of the Sale of Goods Act 1893 (or its successor, s25(1) of the Sale of Goods Act 1979) to achieve the result contended for by the appellant. But there is further internal evidence, in the Act of 1889, that such a result can never have been intended.

Let me concentrate for a moment, not on s9, but on s8, of the Factors Act 1889. The submission for the appellant has to be that, when A has sold goods to B1, and B1 allows A to remain in possession of the goods after the sale, a subsequent sale by A to B2 will be effective to divest the title of a person from whom the goods have previously been stolen before they came into the hands of A. It is obvious that this can never have been the intention of the legislature. If it was, what was the relevance of the sale to B1, and the fact that B1 has allowed A to remain in possession? Assuming B1 to have acted in good faith, why should not A, whom I will assume to be the thief, give as good a title to B1 as to B2? Each is relying equally upon the possession of A of the goods. In truth, the whole section proceeds upon the assumption that the relevant owner of the goods, who is deemed to have authorised their delivery and transfer, is B1 — the person to whom the goods have been sold by A, and who has allowed A to remain in possession of them. And exactly the same point can be made in relation to s9 itself. What is the relevance of the fact that B is in possession of the goods or documents of title with the permission of A? Again, there seems to be no good reason why C should get a good title, but that B (whom I assume to be acting in good faith) should not; each is simply relying, in good faith, upon the possession of his vendor.

Furthermore, if the construction of s9 (and, by implication, s8) urged by the appellant is correct, then we find a startling contrast between the policy underlying those two sections, and that underlying s2. For s2 goes no further than to divest the title of a person who has entrusted the mercantile agent with the possession of the relevant goods or documents of title; if s8 and s9 were to have the effect of divesting the title of a person from whom the goods have been stolen, and who has not entrusted them to the person who has purported to sell them to the purchaser, it is difficult to see why s2 should have been so limited in its effect. As a matter of construction of the relevant statutory provisions, therefore, I have reached the conclusion that the submission advanced by the appellant cannot be sustained. In my opinion, s9 of the Factors Act 1889 must be read as providing that the delivery or transfer given by the intermediate transferor (B) shall have the same effect as if he was a mercantile agent in possession of the goods or documents of title with the consent of the owner who entrusted them to him (A). Such a construction is, in my opinion, to be derived from the terms of s2(1) of the Act, to which s9 evidently refers, and also from the legislative context which I have already discussed. The same construction must, of course, be placed upon s25(1) of the Sale of Goods Act 1979.

I find myself fortified in this conclusion by a number of matters. First, so far as the researches of counsel have been able to ascertain, the suggestion that s9 of the Act of 1889 should have the far-reaching effect now contended for by the appellant, has never before been advanced in an English court; in other words, the present case is preceded by almost a century of silence. Next, such statements of law in the authorities as can be interpreted as bearing upon the point appear to be unanimously against the appellant. I refer in particular to *Cahn v. Pockett's Bristol Channel Steam Packet Co. Ltd.* [1899] 1 Q.B. 643, 658659, *per* Collins L.J., and *Folkes v. King* [1923] 1 K.B. 282, 305–306, *per* Scrutton L.J. I would, however, add that the decision of the Court of Appeal in *Central Newbury Car Auctions Ltd. v. Unity Finance Ltd.* [1957] 1 Q.B. 371 and that of Pearson J. in *Butterworth v. Kingsway Motors* [1954] 1 W.L.R. 1286, are both implicitly inconsistent with the appellant's submission. Third, there is Commonwealth authority directly in point. There is first the decision of Beattie J. in *Elwin v. O'Regan and Maxwell* [1971] N.Z.L.R. 1124. That case was concerned with s27(2) of the New Zealand Sale of Goods Act 1908, which is in the same terms as s25(2) of the Sale of Goods Act 1893. Beattie J. rejected an argument which was similar to that advanced by the appellant in the present case. There is also the decision of Moore J. in *Brandon v. Leckie* (1972) 29 D.L.R. (3d) 633, a decision of the Alberta Supreme Court. That case arose under s27(2) of the Alberta Sale of Goods Act 1970, which is in similar terms. He reached the same conclusion as Beattie J. Lastly, there is distinguished academic authority to the same effect. I refer in particular to *Atiyah, The Sale of Goods*, 7th ed. (1985), pp. 302-303, a passage relied upon both by Beattie J. and by Moore J. In truth, all authority on the point is unanimously adverse to the contention of the appellant in the present case.

For these reasons, I would dismiss the appeal.

Appeal dismissed with costs.

NOTES

1. Leave to appeal to the House of Lords was not granted by the House but by the Court of Appeal which had split 2:1 on the interpretation of s9 of the Factors Act 1889 and s25(1) SGA 1979, see the report of the case in [1988] 2 WLR 952.

2. *Pacific Motors* dealt with a resale 'with the consent of the seller' (s9 Factors Act 1889). In *National Employers Mutual* the defendant argued that the effect of '*with the consent of the seller*' in §9 Factors Act was to cover consent from a seller who had never been the owner or his agent. Despite academic suggestions that s9 Factors Act might permit a thief to pass good title (see I. Davies's survey in *Transferability and sales of goods* 7 Legal Studies 1, 32 n.223 (1987)), the House of Lords rejected this literal reading of the text in part on the basis of decisions elsewhere in the Commonwealth (New Zealand and Canada) and Professor Atiyah's authority.

B. FRANCE

1. Statutes

Civil Code

Art. 1141 CC

If a thing which the owner had contracted to give or deliver to two persons successively is movable property, the one who is put into actual possession has priority and remains its owner although his title is later in time, provided that the possession was acquired in good faith.

Art. 2279 CC

As far as moveable things are concerned, possession is equivalent to title.

Nevertheless, he who has lost or from whom a thing was stolen may demand its return for a period of three years, counted from the day of the loss or the theft, from the person in whose hands he finds it; saving to that person his recourse against the entity from whom he got it.

Art. 2280 CC

If the actual possessor of the lost or stolen thing had bought it at a fair or market or at a public sale or from a merchant dealing in similar goods, the original owner may demand its return only upon reimbursing the possessor the price which he paid for it.

2. Cases

a. Établissements Gallé

Court of Cassation, Ch. Comm.
Judgment of February 13, 1990
Établissements Gallé
c.
Msrs. Pavec et Philippot, as trustees in bankruptcy of the Société des Chargeurs Agricoles Agroshipping, and another.
Bull. IV 30 (No. 45)

For text see p. 492.

NOTES

1. The *Gallé* case is one in a series of cases growing out of the bankruptcy of the Société Agroshipping and its pledge of sunflower seeds, purchased under retention of title clauses, to the Crédit Lyonnais bank.

To understand the Court of Cassation's reliance on art. 2279 CC for the decision it should be noted that in the Judgment of May 19, 1987 *(Société des anciens établissements Paul Cultru et Fils (SEPAC) c. Société des établissements Michel Blanc et Fils)*,[16] the Chambre Commerciale held that the recognition of retention of title clauses did not derogate from the provisions of Art. 2279 CC protecting a possessor in good faith and that therefore in the case at bar the dispossessed owner could not reclaim the goods from the good faith possessor.

Applying these principles in the bankruptcy of the Société Agroshipping, in the Judgment of November 14, 1989, *Société Les Silos viçois c. M. Pavec in his capacity as trustee of the bankrupt estate of the Société Agroshipping and others,*[17] and in the Judgment of November 28, 1989, *Société Commerciale de Produits Agricoles c. Société Agroshipping and another,*[18] the Court of Cassation, Chambre Commerciale upheld judgments of the Court of the Appeal of Paris of October 2, 1987, which had held that the Crédit Lyonnais was entitled to invoke Art. 2279 CC because in these cases Agroshipping was deemed to have obtained possession from the seller and its pledgee was considered to be bona fide.

In the second of these cases (Judgment of November 28, 1989) the Court found that the Société Sonastock had possession of the oil seeds for the benefit of the Crédit Lyonnais manifested in a sufficiently apparent manner.

---

16. [1989] Bull. Civ. IV 91 Nr. 120.
17. [1989] Bull. Civ. IV 196 Nr. 290.
18. [1989] Bull. Civ. IV 201 Nr. 200.

2. The provisions of the Bankruptcy Act (*Redressement judiciaire*) of 1985 concerning retention of title, as revised in 1994 may be found supra p. 478.).

It would seem that the extension to the proceeds does not affect the operation of art. 2279 CC.

3. Art. 2279 II and Art. 2280 CC establish special rules for the right of the original owner to the return of a thing which she has lost or which has been stolen from her. For lost or stolen property in the hands of a finder or thief, the true owner can recover her property within 30 years without indemnifying the possessor. For lost or stolen property transferred directly to a good faith purchaser, the true owner can recover her property within 3 years, still without needing to indemnify the possessor (CC 2279).[19] However, to recover lost or stolen property purchased at a public market, fair or from a merchant in that type of goods, the true owner must first indemnify the present possessor (CC 2280).

4. The present possessor of a thing is presumed to have been bona fide. The presumption may be rebutted by the true owner. In the Court of Cassation, Judgment of March 1, 1988, *Société anonyme d'assurance Winterthur c. Mme Lombard,*[20] a Mrs. Lombardo bought a used Mercedes from a garage operator and insured it against theft with the Société Winterthur. The car was stolen on a trip to Italy. Winterthur refused to reimburse Mrs. Lombardo on the grounds that she was not the true owner because the car had been stolen previously from its true owner. The Court of Appeal of Aix-en-Provence held that Winterthur was liable, because the operator of the garage was in peaceful possession of the vehicle when Mrs. Lombardo acquired its possession as purchaser for a proper price and Winterthur had not shown that its prior owner had and could have successfully demanded its return.

5. It is now settled that art. 2279 CC applies to the purchaser of fungible goods, Court of Cassation, First Civ. Ch., February 7, 1989, *Vincent c. Société d'intérêt collectif France Luzerne et autre.*[21]

6. Article 2279 of the Code Civil applies only to movable tangible property. Sometimes the question arises whether an object which has been separated from real property has become a chattel, especially if the separation constituted a tort.

The Court of Cassation, Assemblée plénière, Judgment of April 15, 1988, *Fondation Abegg c. Ville de Genève et autres; Ville de Genève c. Mme veuve Ribes et autres*, published with the report of the reporting judge Councillor Grégoire[22] involved fresco paintings, separated from an abandoned medieval church in Casenoves. The building of the former church was owned by four coproprietors. Two of them, without the consent of the two others, agreed to a separation and sale of the frescoes, which ultimately

19. Court of Cassation, Judgment of February 7, 1989, Bull. civ. I No. 57.
20. Court of Cassation, First Ch. Civ., Bull Civ. I 39 No. 59.
21. [1989] Bull. Civ. I, Nr. 57.
22. 62 JCP Jur. II nr. 21066 (1988).

ended up in the hands of the Abegg Foundation, domiciled in Bern (Switzerland), and the City of Geneva. The two non-consenting coproprietors brought an action for return of the frescoes against the Abegg Foundation and the City of Geneva.

The Tribunal de grande instance of Perpignan dismissed the action on the ground that the frescoes had become movable personal property and therefore were subject to the jurisdiction of Swiss courts, pursuant to the Franco-Swiss Convention on jurisdiction of June 15, 1896. The court of appeal of Montpellier reversed on the ground that the frescoes, originally immovable property by their nature, had become fixtures and retained this character after their illegal separation.

The Assemblée plénière annulled the judgment and dismissed the action on the ground that the frescoes after their detachment were movables in fact and that therefore the French courts lacked jurisdiction over the action.

If this case were heard in Switzerland would the Swiss Courts apply French or Swiss law?

b. Ottiger

Court of Cassation, First Civil Chamber
Compagnie d'assurance Groupe Drouot
c. M. Ottiger et al.
Judgment of November 22, 1988
Bull. Civ. I 224 (Nr. 331)

The Court (President Mr. Ponsard; Reporting judge: Mrs. Gié; Adv. Gen. Mrs. Flipo).

Upon the first assignment of error, taken in its first branch:

Considering, pursuant to the judgment under attack by the Court of Appeal of Pau of June 30, 1986, that Mr. Ottiger and Mrs. Collet bought a motor vehicle from Mr. Bernes, operator of a garage; that a pending indictment against Mr. Bernes shows that the vehicle was registered in the name of the garage operator by means of forged documents; that the police had seized the vehicle and restored it to the insurance company 'Groupe Drouot', which was subrogated to the rights of the true owner who had been indemnified; that Mr. Ottiger and Mrs. Collet had sued the 'Group Drouot' for reimbursement of the price of the vehicle;

Considering that the 'Group Drouot' attacks the judgment for having sustained the complaint although, according to the assignment of error, on the one hand by having stated that at the time of the sale Mr. Bernes was struck from the commercial register as seller of vehicles and only exercised an activity as mechanic and repairman, the Court of Appeal violated articles 2279 and 2280 of the Code Civil by attributing to Mr. Bernes the character of 'a merchant selling similar goods' and although on the other hand the Court of Appeal had failed to react to the contention that by reason that the sale took place within the framework of amicable relations with payment in cash Mr. Bernes had sold the vehicle not as a professional but as occasional seller;

But considering that, after having stated that Mr. Ottiger who was not sufficiently acquainted with the garage operator to doubt his honesty had previously purchased another car from him, the Court of Appeal stated also with proper reasons that Mr. Bernes had kept his garage, that he utilized the stamps corresponding to his activity as a dealer in new and used cars and that in the present case the receipt of the price given to Mr. Ottiger bore the stamp 'Bernes, sales and purchaser of used cars'; that it could find that despite his being struck from the commercial register Mr. Bernes could be considered to be a merchant selling similar goods within the meaning of art. 2280 of the Code Civil; that it therefore responded to the party's contentions and that the assignment of error is unfounded;

Upon the second assignment of error:

Considering that the company 'Group Drouot' also attacks the judgment for having condemned it to reimburse the price, although according to the assignment of error, the demand for reimbursement of the price interposed by the purchaser of a stolen or lost thing pursuant to art. 2280 of the Code Civil supposes that the latter has remained in the possession of the thing; that because this condition was not met according to the judgment itself which establishes the seizure of the vehicle by the police and its surrender to the Groupe Drouot prior to the bringing of the action; the court violated the above-mentioned text;

But considering that the Court of Appeal finds sovereignly that the seizure of the vehicle by the police caused only the temporary displacement of its possession, since the Groupe Drouot received the vehicle only by means of a proceeding which remained unknown to them and one of pure fact without the consent of the spouses Ottiger; that the court therefore justly concluded that the latter had not lost their claim for reimbursement; that therefore the assignment of error is unfounded;

For these reasons

The petition is rejected.

NOTES

1. The case is noted by Professor Robert in D. Sommaires commentés 86 (1990), and by Professor Zénati, 89 Revue trimestielle de droit civil 521 (1990).

2. The application of arts. 2279 par. 1 and 2 and 2280 CC has produced a copious case law which illustrates also the difficulties arising from the burden of proof and the applicable rules of evidence with respect to the issues raised by these two articles. The French rules of evidence in civil cases are governed by the Civil Code, arts. 1316-1348. Most important is art. 1341 CC which requires written proof in controversies that exceed an amount fixed by decree. It may suffice that a writing signed by the ad-

dressee of the claim makes the alleged fact probable, so-called 'incipient written proof'. Art. 1347 CC.

These rules were involved in Court of Cassation, First Civ. Ch., Judgment of December 8, 1987, *Mme Porterie dite Patrick c. époux Lacrampe*, Bull. Civ. I 243 (No. 338). Evicted tenant of a furnished apartment alleged that he had bought the furniture from the landlady and received part of it from the sheriff.

The Court of Appeal of Versailles held for the defendant tenant on the basis of art. 2279 par. 1 CC, because he was in possession of the furniture and bona fide and the landlady, the plaintiff, had not shown that she still owned the furniture. The Court of Cassation sustained the Court of Appeal because the landlady as plaintiff had failed to show by incipient written proof that the tenant's possession was only temporary.

c. Blue Bay Steamship Corporation

Paris Court of Appeal Ch. 1,
Sté Blue Bay Steamship Corporation c. Galerie Schmit et autres
Judgment of May 3, 1993
D. Somm. Comm. 305 (1993).

In 1958, Mr. Théodore Teryazos acquired at the Galeries A . . . at New York for the account of Sté B . . . a painting by de Sisley which the author called 'Bank of the River' and which later was rechristened 'Castle of the White Cross at Saint Mammès'. The painting was subsequently hung in a house belonging to his spouse Marielle Gohier and upon Mr. Teryazos' death bequeathed to his daughter, Athina. It was transferred to the widow together with the house within the framework of a succession agreement and brought by her to the Sté C . . . which deposited it with the Galerie D . . . for the purpose of sale. The latter sold it for U.S. $1,350,000 to the Sté E . . . which left it with the Galerie D . . . for an exposition. The Sté B . . . which was wholly owned by Athina, caused a seizure thereof for the purpose of obtaining restitution. Mrs. Marielle Gohier, widow of Teryazos, in a proceeding passing on the validity of the seizure in which several people intervened, opposed the claim of restitution and demanded compensation for the damages incurred due to the fact that the value of the picture had decreased as a result of the recession in the art market during its indisposability.

Confirming the decision of the judges of first instance, the court of appeal held that Sté E . . . possessor in good faith of an item of movable property, was its owner even if acquired from a non-owner. The court stated that good faith is to be presumed and observed that the possession was 'peaceful, public and unequivocal' in view of the reputation of the Galerie D . . . the presentation of the work at a prestigious exposition and its mention in the catalogue thereof. The plaintiff company, which did not maintain that the painting was lost or stolen, would have had to prove the bad faith of the purchase of the painting, but no serious offer of proof was proposed. In addition, the court found various elements in support of the good faith of the defendant, such as its conviction of the regularity of the transactions with respect to the Sisley. Finally, an indemnity of FF 800,000 was awarded to compensate for the damages suffered from the attachment of the picture.

C. GERMANY

1. Statutes: The Civil Code (BGB)

§ 929 BGB

A transfer of the ownership of a movable thing requires that the owner deliver the thing to the transferor and that both agree that the ownership shall pass. If the transferee is in possession of the thing, agreement on the passage of ownership suffices.

§ 930 BGB

If the owner is in possession of the thing, delivery can be replaced by the agreement on a legal relationship by virtue of which the transferee obtained indirect (constructive) possession.

§ 931 BGB

If a third person is in possession of the thing, the delivery may be replaced by the assignment of the right to the return of the thing on the part of the owner to the transferee.

§ 932 BGB

(1) If an alienation is made pursuant to § 929, the transferee acquires ownership even though the thing is not owned by the transferor, unless he is not bona fide at the time at which he would acquire the ownership pursuant to these provisions. In the case of § 929 sentence 2 this applies only if the transferee obtained the possession from the transferor.

(2) The transferee is not bona fide if he knows, or because of gross negligence, does not know that the thing is not owned by the transferor.

§ 933 BGB

If a thing alienated pursuant to § 930 is not owned by the transferor, the transferee becomes the owner when the thing is delivered by the transferor, unless he is not bona fide at that time.

§ 934 BGB

In the case that a thing alienated pursuant to § 931 is not owned by the transferor, the transferee acquires ownership if the transferor is indirect possessor of the thing at the time of the assignment of the right to its return, otherwise at the time when he obtains possession from the third party, unless he is not bona fide at the time of the assignment or the acquisition of the possession.

§ 935 BGB

(1) Acquisition of ownership pursuant to §§ 932-934 is precluded if the thing was stolen from, lost by or otherwise withdrawn from the owner. This applies also in the case that the owner was only an indirect possessor, if the thing was lost by the possessor.

(2) This provision does not apply to money, bearer paper or things sold at a public auction.

§ 936 BGB

(1) If the thing transferred was encumbered by the right of a third person, such right is extinguished by virtue of the acquisition of ownership. * * *

2. Case

BGH (VIII. Senate)
Firm M.-Z. GmbH v.
Land Schleswig - Holstein
Judgment of April 8, 1987
100 BGHZ 321 (1987)
(For text see Part I Chapter III [p. 191])

D. ITALY

1. Statutes

The Italian Civil Code (Codice Civile)

Art. 1153 CC

He to whom movable goods are alienated by one who is not their owner, acquires their ownership by way of possession, provided he is bona fide (art. 1147) at the time of the delivery and that there exists an appropriate title for the transfer of the ownership. (art. 769, 1470, 1552).

The ownership is acquired free of rights of another in the property if they do not result from the title and the transferee is bona fide.

In the same manner rights of usufruct, use or pledge may be acquired.

Art. 1154 CC

He who acquires the goods with the knowledge of their illegal source is not aided by the belief that the transferror or prior possessor has become the owner.

Art. 1155 CC

If anyone by successive contracts conveys a movable thing to several persons, the one who has acquired its possession bona fide is preferred over the others, even if his title is of a later date.

2. Case: The French Tapestries

Tribunale Roma, Judgment of June 27, 1987
The French State v. the Minister for Cultural Property and the Environment and De Contessini; intervenor Pilone
71 Revista di Diritto Internazionale 920 (1988)

The tapestries which are the object of the present controversy were placed in the hands of a sequester within the framework of criminal proceedings against — among others — Livio De Contessini, which vis-à-vis him terminated with a judgment of October 2, 1979 by the investigation-judge of the Tribunale de Milano, which ruled that there should be no prosecution for the charged offense ('acquisition of goods of suspect origin,' art. 712 Penal code) for the reason that the facts did not constitute an offense. The same judge did not pass on the restitution of the tapestries, which was demanded by De Contessini as well as by the French authorities, but remanded it to the civil court having jurisdiction in the matter, which constitutes the issue to be examined.

Before this court the plaintiff has produced a series of documents from which it can be concluded that the tapestries were the property of the French State (decorating a judicial office) which were removed as the result of a theft. On the basis of its ownership the complaining French authorities demand restitution.

The defendant De Contessini, however, as well as the intervener Pilone contend that they have become the owners by virtue of art. 1153 of the Codice Civile, because they purchased the tapestries from a non-owner and assert, therefore, that they are entitled to the restitution. The plaintiff counters with the argument that the tapestries, being inalienable and indisposable goods according to French law, because they are listed among the historical monuments belonging to the State, could not have been sold commercially either in France or in Italy. In addition, plaintiff claims, that neither the defendant nor the intervener had proven either their good faith or their possession and title apt to transfer ownership [as required by art. 1153].

The panel does not find the thesis of plaintiff to be well-founded. First of all it is necessary to identify the national law applicable to the case under examination pursuant to the rules of private international law. The relevant provision is that contained in art. 22 of the General Rules on the Laws, according to which 'the possession and the ownership of, and other rights in movable and immovable property are governed by law of the place where the property is located.'

In fact, it is asked that the Tribunal determine who is the owner of the goods, since the restitution of them depends on that determination, as only the owner is the proper person to obtain possession of the goods.

Hence, since the goods are in the hands of a sequester in our country, Italian law applies. In the case at bar it is impossible to invoke the doctrinal position, confirmed also judicially, that in some cases the transfer of a chattel from one country to another country does not suffice to change the *lex loci* which remains that of the place where the chattels were originally located (Court of Cass., Judgment of July 12, 1952 nr. 2169, dealing with acquisition of stolen animals, bought in a public market in the Republic of San Marino and subsequently brought to Italy; Tribunal of Torino, Judgment of March 25, 1982 dealing with the bona fide acquisition of archeological goods which were not subject to commercial transactions in Ecuador and were subsequently brought to Italy). The situation in the instant case is in fact different from both cases mentioned above, since there the purported acquisition of the goods occurred in a foreign country and the removal to Italy was effectuated by the very party to the proceedings who claimed to have acquired the ownership abroad.

In essence, the two cited judgments interpreted the provision of art. 22 in the sense, that the law which must be applied for the purpose of identifying the owner, must be determined with reference to the place where the goods are found at the moment when the claimed acquisition takes place, whereas a subsequent relocation of the goods is deemed to be irrelevant.

In the case at bar, both De Contessini and Pilone were persons different from those who took possession of the chattels abroad and do not assert a title of acquisition effectuated in France, but claim to have acquired the tapestries in good faith in Italy. Therefore according to the principle just enunciated it must be concluded that Italian law applies as the *lex loci* where the goods were located at the time of their purported acquisition.

Since thus the law of France is inapplicable, it follows that the provisions of that country relating to the inalienability and unsalability of the tapestries, relied upon by plaintiff, are irrelevant. Equally inapplicable is the norm of Italian law (art. 826 of the Codice civile) which subjects to the regime of indisposable property all movables of historical and artistic interest belonging to the State or other public territorial entities, because, in the absence of a provision to that effect, it cannot be extended to a case where the ownership is not in the Italian State, but rather in a foreign state.

Support for a contrary opinion cannot be found on the level of international conventions to which our country is a party and in particular not in the Convention on the Means of Prohibiting and Preventing the Illicit Import, Export and Transfer of Ownership of Cultural Property, adopted at Paris by the general conference of UNESCO on November 14, 1970 (rendered executed in Italy by the statute of October 30, 1975 nr. 873). In it, in fact, no provision can be found that extends automatically, on the level of domestic law, the shackles of inalienability of cultural goods fixed by other states. And with specific reference to the case in issue, it is provided that 'The States Parties to the present convention *oblige themselves* . . . to take the appropriate measures to seize and return, at the request of the State Party of origin which is a party to the convention, any cultural property stolen and imported after the entry into force of the present convention with respect to both states concerned, on the condition that the requesting state pays an equitable indemnity to the person who is a bona fide purchaser or who lawfully is in possession of that property.' (art. 7, (b) II).

With that norm our legal system has assumed an obligation vis-à-vis the other states, but has not introduced internal norms which establish that a bona fide purchaser or lawful owner of cultural property which originated abroad is obliged to return it upon payment of an indemnity. Rather that norm itself furnishes further proof of the full efficacy of an acquisition from a non-owner.

It is necessary, however to ascertain whether in the case at bar the conditions, upon the fulfillment of which art. 1153 ordains the acquisition of the ownership of a chattel, are met, to wit bona fides, transfer and possession.

With respect to the tapestry showing Odysseus and the sorceress Circe there is in the files a writing signed by Teresa Miglio in which she declares to sell to the Gallery De Contessini a tapestry showing a scene from the Odyssey for the sum of L10,000,000 . . .

With respect to the tapestry showing a scene in which Odysseus pays homage to Elphenor, who died by suicide, there is in the files a writing dated December 16, 1975 and signed by Maria Luisa Mainardi (authenticated with a proof of identity) in which she declares that she sold to De Contessini a chattel owned by her for the sum of L6,000,000. It is uncontested by the latter and the intervener, that the tapestry was sold to Pilone but later redelivered solely for the purpose of the investigation by the criminal police. Both tapestries were placed in the hands of a sequester by the police on Oct. 26, 1977.

On the basis of these factors, it seems that there can be no doubt, that the prerequisites for the acquisition on the part of De Contessini of the ownership of both tapestries from a non-owner are present, i.e. a purchase and possession.

So far as bona fides is concerned, it is presumed to exist by virtue of art. 1147, with the consequence that the party who demands the return and wishes to negate the effects of art. 1153 for the benefit of the possessor must show bad faith or gross negligence of the transferee at the moment of delivery (Cass. Judgement of June 12, 1976 n. 2178).

[Plaintiff did not succeed in impugning the good faith or showing gross negligence on the part of De Contessini.]

The demands of the plaintiff are therefore to be rejected and it is to be declared that Livio Contessini and Giovanni Vittorio Pilone are entitled to the restitution, respectively, of the tapestries showing Odysseus and the sorceress Circe and Odysseus paying homage to Elphenor.

NOTES

1. The text case is discussed by Anna Lo Monaco, *Sulla Restituzione di beni culturali rubati all'estero secondo la convenzione dell'unesco* in 71 Revista di Diritto Internazionale 842 (1988).

2. The provisions on the General Rules on the Laws were enacted at the same time and by the same royal decree that enacted the Italian Civil Code (R.D., March 16, 1942 n. 262).

3. The Italian Civil Code of 1942 has adopted the most radical and simplified approach to good faith acquisition of movable property. For general discussion see Alberto Trabucchi, Istituzione di diritto civile (32 ed. Padova 1991) 414 (No. 177).

E. SWITZERLAND

1. Statutes

Swiss Civil Code (*Code Civil; Zivilgesetzbuch* [ZGB])

932 CC

The person in possession of a movable chattel can in every action brought against him plead the presumption that he has the better title; subject nevertheless to the provisions on wrongful dispossession and trespass.

933 CC

When a movable chattel is transferred with a view to passing ownership or some other real right to the transferee, and he takes possession in good faith, his right over the chattel must be protected, even where the transferor had himself no authority to alienate it.

934 CC

Where a person in possession of a movable chattel loses it or had it stolen from him or otherwise taken from him against his will, he can demand it back within a period of five years from any person who is detaining it.

Where the chattel has been brought at a public auction or in a market overt or from a dealer in property of the same kind, it cannot be recovered from the first purchaser or any subsequent bona fide purchaser, unless he is compensated for the purchase-money price paid.

The rules in regard to the restoration of the thing are in other respects the same as those governing the rights of a bona fide possessor.

935 CC

Cash and negotiable instruments to bearer cannot be recovered from the bona fide holder, even though the plaintiff was deprived of his possession in them against his will.

936 CC

A person who has obtained the possession of a movable thing not bona fide is liable to the former possessor at any time. If the prior possessor was also not bona fidei, he cannot claim the chattel from the later possessor.

F. UNITED STATES

1. Statutes

Uniform Commercial Code

Art. 2 SALES § 2-401

PART 4
TITLE, CREDITORS AND GOOD FAITH PURCHASERS

§ 2-401. Passing of Title; Reservation for Security; Limited Application of This Section.

Each provision of this Article with regard to the rights, obligations and remedies of the seller, the buyer, purchasers or other third parties applies irrespective of title to the goods except where the provision refers to such title. Insofar as situations are not covered by the other provisions of this Article and matters concerning title become material the following rules apply:

(1) Title to goods cannot pass under a contract for sale prior to their identification to the contract (Section 2-501), and unless otherwise explicitly agreed the buyer acquires by their identification a special property as limited by this Act. Any retention or reservation by the seller of the title (property) in goods shipped or delivered to the buyer is limited in effect to a reservation of a security interest. Subject to these provisions and to the provisions of the Article on Secured Transactions (Article 9), title to goods passes from the seller to the buyer in any manner and on any conditions explicitly agreed on by the parties.

(2) Unless otherwise explicitly agreed title passes to the buyer at the time and place at which the seller completes his performance with reference to the physical delivery of the goods, despite any reservation of a security interest and even though a document of title is to be delivered at a different time or place; and in particular and despite any reservation of a security interest by the bill of lading

(a) if the contract requires or authorizes the seller to send the goods to the buyer but does not require him to deliver them at destination, title passes to the buyer at the time and place of shipment; but

(b) if the contract requires delivery at destination, title passes on tender there.

(3) * * *

§ 2-402. Rights of Seller's Creditors Against Sold Goods.

(1) Except as provided in subsections (2) and (3), rights of unsecured creditors of the seller with respect to goods which have been identified to a contract for sale are subject to the buyer's rights to recover the goods under this Article (Sections 2-502 and 2-716).

(2) A creditor of the seller may treat a sale or an identification of goods to a contract for sale as void if as against him a retention of possession by the seller is fraudulent under any rule of law of the state where the goods are situated, except that retention of possession in good faith and current course of trade by a merchant-seller for a commercially reasonable time after a sale or identification is not fraudulent.

(3) Nothing in this Article shall be deemed to impair the rights of creditors of the seller

(a) under the provisions of the Article on Secured Transactions (Article 9); or

(b) * * *

§ 2-403. Power to Transfer; Good Faith Purchase of Goods; "Entrusting".

(1) A purchaser of goods acquires all title which his transferor had or had power to transfer except that a purchaser of a limited interest acquires rights only to the extent of the interest purchased. A person with voidable title has power to transfer a good title to a good faith purchaser for value. When goods have been delivered under a transaction of purchase the purchaser has such power even though

(a) the transferor was deceived as to the identity of the purchaser, or

(b) the delivery was in exchange for a check which is later dishonored, or

(c) it was agreed that the transaction was to be a "cash sale", or

(d) the delivery was procured through fraud punishable as larcenous under the criminal law.

(2) Any entrusting of possession of goods to a merchant who deals in goods of that kind gives him power to transfer all rights of the entruster to a buyer in ordinary course of business.

(3) "Entrusting" includes any delivery and any acquiescence in retention of possession regardless of any condition expressed between the parties to the delivery or acquiescence and regardless of whether the procurement of the entrusting or the possessor's disposition of the goods have been such as to be larcenous under the criminal law.

§ 9-307. Protection of Buyers of Goods.

(1) A buyer in ordinary course of business (subsection (9) of Section 1-201) other than a person buying farm products from a person engaged in farming operations takes free of a security interest created by his seller even though the security interest is perfected and even though the buyer knows of its existence.

(2) In the case of consumer goods, a buyer takes free of a security interest even

though perfected if he buys without knowledge of the security interest, for value and for his own personal, family or household purposes unless prior to the purchase the secured party has filed a financing statement covering such goods.

(3) A buyer other than a buyer in ordinary course of business (subsection (1) of this section) takes free of a security interest to the extent that it secures future advances made after the secured party acquires knowledge of the purchase, or more than 45 days after the purchase, whichever first occurs, unless made pursuant to a commitment entered into without knowledge of the purchase and before the expiration of the 45 day period.

As amended in 1972.

California Civil Code

§ 3440. Transfer without delivery void as to transferor's creditors

(a) Except as otherwise provided in this chapter, every transfer of personal property made by a person having at the time the possession of the property, and not accompanied by an immediate delivery followed by an actual and continued change of possession of the property, is void as against the transferor's creditors (secured or unsecured) at the time of the transfer and those who become creditors while the transferor remains in possession and the successors in interest of those creditors, and as against buyers from the transferor for value in good faith subsequent to the transfer.

(b) As used in this chapter, "creditor" means a person who has a claim, as defined in Section 3439.01, and includes an assignee of a general assignment for the benefit of creditors, as defined in Section 493.010 of the Code of Civil Procedure, of a debtor. "Creditor" also includes any person to whom the transferor's estate devolves in trust for the benefit of persons other than the transferor. Any such assignee or trustee may exercise any and all the rights and remedies specified in this chapter, if they are available to any one or more creditors of the assignor or transferor who are beneficiaries of the assignment of trust, and, in that event (1) only to the extent the rights or remedies are so available and (2) only for the benefit of those creditors whose rights are asserted by the assignee or trustee.

Amended Stats 1985 ch 1368 § 1. Amended Stats 1987 ch 40 § 3, effective June 8, 1987.

§ 3440.3. Specified transfers void as against buyer in ordinary course of business

A transfer of personal property, as to which the conditions set forth in subdivision (h) of Section 3440.1, Section 3440.2, or subdivision (b) of Section 3440.5 are satisfied, shall, nevertheless, be void under Section 3440 as against a person who has purchased the personal property from the transferor and who is a "buyer in the ordinary course of business," as defined in subdivision (9) of Section 1201 of the Commercial Code.

Added Stats 1985 ch 1368 § 3.

§ 3440.6 Time within which to bring action or make levy

No action shall be brought or levy made under this chapter more than one year after the earliest of the following dates:

(a) The date the person bringing the action or making the levy should have discovered the transfer in the exercise of reasonable diligence.

(b) The date the person bringing the action or making the levy obtained actual knowledge of the transfer.

(c) The date the delivery of, and actual and continued change of possession of, the property transferred occurred.

(d) If the financing statement filed pursuant to subdivision (h) of Section 3440.1 has not lapsed, the date the filing and publication requirements of subdivision (h) of Section 3440.1 were met, other than the requirement that the filing of the financing statement and publication of the notice referred to therein by completed prior to the transfer.

Added Stats 1985 ch 1368 § 5.

§ 3440.9. Commercial Code provisions

Subdivision (2) of Section 2402 and subdivision (1) of Section 10308 of the Commercial Code are not restricted by the provisions of this chapter.

Added Stats 1982 ch 517 § 92 as § 3443. Amended and renumbered Stats 1985 ch 1368 § 10. Amended Stats 1988 ch 1368 sec 4, operative January 1, 1990.

11/Bona Fide Acquisition of Ownership in Intangible Movable Property

A. UNITED KINGDOM

1. Statutes

LAW OF PROPERTY ACT 1925 (c 20) s136.
(Text reproduced supra, p. 441)

2. Cases

Pfeiffer Weinkellerei-Weineinkauf v Arbuthnot Factors [1988] 3 WLR 150 Please see supra Chapter 8 (p. 449).

NOTES

In *Pfeiffer Weinkellerei-Weineinkauf v Arbuthnot Factors*, Judge Phillips deals with two separate issues. The first of these concerns the applicability of the respective Companies Act to 'prolonged' reservation of title clauses in contracts with corporate purchases. The English cases on retention of title clauses show that the applicability of the Companies Act depends to a large extent on the actual wording of the clause.

The second question (p. 459) deals with the protection of a factor as a bona fide purchaser of future choses-in-action.

B. FRANCE

1. Statutes:

Code Civil

Art. 1689 CC

The transfer of a claim, a right or an action against a third person between the assignor and the assignee is accomplished by the delivery of the instrument of title.

Art. 1690 CC

The assignee is vested vis-à-vis a third party only by the notification of the transfer given to the debtor.

Nevertheless the assignee may likewise be vested by the acceptance of the transfer by the debtor made in a notarized document.

Loi Dailly

Law nr. 81-1 of Jan. 2, 1981, to facilitate credit to enterprises (*Loi Dailly*) Translated in Chapter 8 B (p. 480).

NOTES

In France it has been held that a junior assignee whose assignment is first notified to the debtor is not protected if the subsequent assignment is fraudulent on his part, G. Marty, P. Reynaud and P. Jestaz, Droit Civil, Les Obligations (2d ed.) T.2 (Le régime) Sec. 364 (1989).

C. GERMANY

1. Statutes

Civil Code

§ 398 BGB

A claim may be transferred to another by the creditor by way of a contract (Assignment [*Abtretung*]). Upon the conclusion of the contract the new creditor takes the place of the prior creditor.

§ 407 BGB

(1) The new creditor is bound by a performance which the debtor renders to the former creditor after the assignment and by any legal transaction which is concluded

with respect to the claim after the assignment between the debtor and the prior creditor, unless the debtor knows of the assignment at the time of the performance or conclusion of the legal transaction.

D. CALIFORNIA

Statutes:

CIVIL CODE, § 955.1 General Intangibles; assignments; priorities; notice to obligor. (Amended 1982)

(a) Except as provided in Sections 954.5 and 955 and subject to subdivisions (b) and (c), a transfer other than one intended to create a security interest (Section 9102(1)(a) of the Commercial Code) of any general intangible (Section 9106 of the Commercial Code) consisting of any right to payment and any transfer of accounts or chattel paper excluded from the coverage of Division 9 of the Commercial Code by Section 9104(f) thereof shall be deemed perfected as against third persons upon there being executed and delivered to the transferee an assignment thereof in writing.

(b) As between bona fide assignees of the same right for value without notice, the assignee first giving notice thereof to the obligor in writing has priority.

(c) Such an assignment is not, of itself, notice to the obligor so as to invalidate any payments made by the obligor to the transferor.

NOTES

A number of legal systems such as those of California, France and Italy require notification of the debtor for the effectiveness of an assignment not only against the debtor, but also against third parties, in particular junior assignees. Are such statutes '*pure race-statutes*' or is a junior assignee who accepts an assignment of a claim with knowledge of the prior assignment outside of the protection? In California the statute itself provides that the junior assignee prevails only if he is bona fide. In France and Italy the issue is more dubious.

E. ITALY

In Italy the situation seems to be more controversial. Art. 1265 CC does not require absence of knowledge or bona fides on the part of the junior assignee, assignment to whom is first notified to or accepted by the debtor. It seems to be recognized that a debtor who has made payment to the senior assignee before he has been notified of either of the assignments has paid with liberating effect. Apparently, however, a junior assignee whose assignment is first notified to or accepted by the debtor will prevail in any case; but the matter seems to be unsettled, see V. Panuccio, *Cessione dei Crediti* in 6 Enciclopedia del Diritto (1960) p. 846 et seq., 875; T. Mancini, *La Cessione dei Crediti*, 9 Trattato di Diritto Privato, p. 379 et seq. (1984), at 391-393.

12/Title by Adverse Possession; Effect of Prescription

A. UNITED KINGDOM

1. Statute

Limitation Act 1980
(1980 c58)
Part I

ORDINARY TIME LIMITS FOR DIFFERENT CLASSES OF ACTION

Time limits under Part I subject to extension or exclusion under Part II

1 Time limits under Part I subject to extension or exclusion under Part II

(1) This Part of this Act gives the ordinary time limits for bringing actions of the various classes mentioned in the following provisions of this Part.

(2) The ordinary time limits given in this Part of this Act are subject to extension or exclusion in accordance with the provisions of Part II of this Act.

2 Time limit for actions founded on tort

An action founded on tort shall not be brought after the expiration of six years from the date on which the cause of action accrued.

3 Time limit in case of successive conversions and extinction of title of owner of converted goods

(1) Where any cause of action in respect of the conversion of a chattel has accrued to any person and, before he recovers possession of the chattel, a further conversion takes place, no action shall be brought in respect of the further conversion after the expiration of six years from the accrual of the cause of action in respect of the original conversion.

(2) Where any such cause of action has accrued to any person and the period prescribed has expired and he has not during that period recovered possession of the chattel, the title of that person to the chattel shall be extinguished.

4 Special time limit in case of theft

(1) The right of any person from whom a chattel is stolen to bring an action in respect of the theft shall not be subject to the time limits under sections 2 and 3(1) of this Act, but if his title to the chattel is extinguished under section 3(2) of this Act he may not bring an action in respect of a theft preceding the loss of his title, unless the theft in question preceded the conversion from which time began to run for the purposes of section 3(2).

(2) Subsection (1) above shall apply to any conversion related to the theft of a chattel as it applies to the theft of a chattel; and, except as provided below, every conversion following the theft of a chattel before the person from whom it is stolen recovers possession of it shall be regarded for the purposes of this section as related to the theft.

If anyone purchases the stolen chattel in good faith neither the purchase nor any conversion following it shall be regarded as related to the theft.

(3) Any cause of action accruing in respect of the theft or any conversion related to the theft of a chattel to any person from whom the chattel is stolen shall be disregarded for the purpose of applying section 3(1) or (2) of this Act to his case.

(4) Where in any action brought in respect of the conversion of a chattel it is proved that the chattel was stolen from the plaintiff or anyone through whom he claims it shall be presumed that any conversion following the theft is related to the theft unless the contrary is shown.

(5) In this section "theft" includes —

(a) any conduct outside England and Wales which would be theft if committed in England and Wales; and

(b) obtaining any chattel (in England and Wales or elsewhere) in the circumstances described in section 15(1) of the Theft Act 1968 (obtaining by deception) or by blackmail within the meaning of section 21 of that Act;

and references in this section to a chattel being "stolen" shall be construed accordingly.

NOTES

1. Limitations Act 1980 (1980 c 58) s4 bars acquisition of title by or through the running of the statute on an action against a thief.

2. The Limitation Act does not create title in an adverse possessor, *Mulcahy v. Curramore Pty Ltd.* [1974] NSWLR 464, 476A; it extinguishes the title of the paper owner. For real property see Gray, Land Law 2nd ed. 1992 p. 289.

B. FRANCE

1. Statutes

Civil Code

Art. 711 CC

Ownership of goods is acquired and transferred by way of succession, intervivos and testamentary gifts or by way of obligations.

Art. 712 CC

Ownership is also acquired by way of accession or incorporation or by prescription.

Art. 716 CC

The ownership of a treasure belongs to the person who finds it in his own property; if the treasure is found in the property of another, one half of it belongs to the discoverer and the other to the owner of the property.

A treasure is any thing hidden or buried in which no one can prove ownership and which is discovered solely by accident.

Art. 2262 CC

All actions whether in rem or in personam are subject to a prescriptive period of 30 years; without the one who invokes this prescription being obliged to rely on a title or being subject to the exception of bad faith.

2. Cases

a. Miramon Fitz James

Court of Appeal of Paris
De Caissaigne de Beaufort de Miramon Fitz James
c. S.C.P. Daussy-Ricqles et autres
Judgment of March 30, 1990
64 JCP III 21584 p. 50 (1990)

The Court: On the action for the return of property

Considering that Mr. de Miramon Fitz James deposited two books, taken from his library, for the oral arguments, one a *History of French Literature* by Nisard (1844) with spine bound in red Moroccan leather, bearing two flower emblems overlaid in black and one gilded floral emblem, being the coat of arms of Aldenburg and the other Alexander Dumas Jr.'s *Impressions de Voyage*, with spine bound in red Moroccan leather but embellished differently, with three floral emblems overlaid in black, separated by four embossings with gold lines beneath and with two rows of gilded arabesques on the bottom — Considering that this second binding is identical to that found in a photograph submitted at the deliberations stage of Balzac's *Chouans*, and to those which are shown on the cover page of the catalogue put out by the auctioneers;

Considering that this exact similarity of the bindings establishes not only the identity of the binder but that of the collector; that according to a certificate of Dec. 18, 1989 from an expert, Mr. Claude Guérin, Mr. de Miramon Fitz James keeps in his library 140 volumes with 'the same binding, with or without the coat of arms, as the works of Balzac which had figured in the sale of March 8, 1988 at the Hotel Drouot';

Considering that the judges of first instance rightly called attention to the difference in the description of these works in the Declaration of looting losses of Dec. 11, 1948 and the works in issue themselves; considering, however, that Mr. de Miramon Fitz James cannot be blamed, after an absence of many years and by reason of the absence of an inventory which he had no duty to compile while his father was still alive, for having retained a relatively imprecise memory of the works of Balzac dedicated by him to Mme de Castries; that it is unlikely that this author would have dedicated several copies of the same works to the same woman who was his inspiration and who would have received them as family property; that it is appropriate therefore to admit that, despite the inaccuracy of the Looting Declaration, the works in question have belonged to the Aldenburg library.

Considering, however, on the one hand that Mr. Miramon Fitz James failed to show by any document other than his Looting Declaration that the works in issue were located at Neuilly, the home of his late father during the war; that subsequent bequests did not provide an inventory of movable property which was produced during the arguments;

Considering on the other hand, that Mr. Miramon Fitz James did not present any proof, as is his burden, of the temporary and ambivalent possession of the books on the part of Mrs. Delaveau;

that the alleged defect of the possession cannot be deduced either from the absence of a justification for the original acquisition of the works by the grandparents of the defendant which cannot be automatically excluded in this case, or from the keeping of the books, after the war, in a private library, access to which was prohibited to children and the contents of which did not call for any particular measure of publicity, or from the fact that their removal was deferred until 1986, or from their being wrapped up on that occasion;

that in view of a possession which is attested not only by the mother of the defendant but also by a friend, Mrs. Aline Laurent, and which continued peaceful beyond the period of acquisitive prescription (usucapion), whether this was 3 years or 30 years, the judges of the first instance decided correctly that the action for restitution could not succeed.

Upon the appeal of Mrs. Delaveau: Considering that under the particular circumstances of the case at bar the action for restitution brought by Mr. Miramon Fitz James cannot be deemed an abuse of process; that the financial loss alleged by Mrs. Delaveau on the basis of a deprivation of income remains hypothetical; that the Court finds in that cause of action elements permitting to assess a non-pecuniary loss valued at one franc;

Upon the appeal of the S.C.P. Daussy: Considering that it is established by the letter of October 7, 1988 from the Chambers Couturier-Nicolay to Mrs. Ricqles that the cancellation of the sale of the books in issue caused additional expenses of FF 23,418.78 to the S.C.P. Daussy which also incurred expenses for photography and advertising amounting to FF 6,865.22;

that, with respect to the surplus, the expenses incurred by the S.C.P. Daussy together with the Chambers Couturier were related to that portion of the sale which took place; that the auctioneers did not prove any special damages other than non-pecuniary damage which must be assessed at one franc; that it is therefore proper to award to them damages in the amount of FF 30,285, for all causes of action combined;

For these reasons . . . confirms the judgment appealed from to the extent that it dismisses the action of restitution by Mr. de Miramon Fitz James against Mrs. Delaveau and amends the remaining portion of the judgment and condemns Mr. de Miramon Fitz James to pay damages in the amount of one franc to Mrs. Delaveau and of FF 30,285 to the S.C.P. Daussy.

Dismisses all other claims of the parties and orders, to the extent necessary, the temporary sequestration to be lifted.

NOTES

1. The text case is of interest first because of the person of the plaintiff and the facts of the case and secondly because of the issues involved. Mr. Henri de Caissaigne de Beaufort de Miramon Fitz James, the universal legatee of the last Duke de Fitz James, was a descendant of King James, the last of the Stuart kings of Great Britain. The Baron of Aldenburg, original owner of the works of Balzac in issue, was the son out of the adulterous relationship between the Marquess of Castries, the benefactor of Balzac, and Victor Metternich. The set of the works of Balzac which were to be auctioned off for the account of Mrs. Delaveau had been kept in a private library belonging to the family of the defendant and subsequently stored in a basement. See the facts recounted in the report of the case as decided by the court below in 1988 by Professor Robert in D. Somm. Comm. 87 (1988).

2. Plaintiff who tried to obtain the books to be offered at the auction by sequestering them and suing Mrs. Delaveau for their return failed to prevail because of the inherent difficulties of the proof required. He was unable to show the defendant's possession was defective and to disprove the acquisition of title by adverse possession during the three (Art. 2279 par. 2 CC) or the thirty years (Art. 2262 CC) period. The

significant feature of the case is the recognition by the court of appeal that the action for restitution of property is subject to the limitation period of Art. 2262 CC as well as of Art. 2279 CC and that expiration of these periods results in the acquisition of ownership by the adverse possessor.

3. On protection of bona fide purchasers in France see H., L. & J. Mazeaud, F. Chabas, Leçons de droit civil, T. II.2 Les Biens (1994) 267-303.

b. Mr. Sébastien c. Mrs. Slomovic

Court of Cassation, (Civ. I) Judgment of June 2, 1993
Mr. Sébastien c. Mrs. Slomovic et al.
Consorts Goldfinger et al c. Mr. Sébastien et al.
Mrs. Slomovic c. Société Générale
Joint Cases
[1993] Bull. civ. I, p. 136, Nr. 197.

Considering that Erich Slomovic, a student of Yugoslavian nationality, was, during the year 1993, in possession of an important collection of valuable objects and pictures stemming from the Gallery Ambroise Vollard; that after the death of the latter which occurred on July 22, 1939, he deposited a portion of that collection in a strong-box at the Société Générale and transported the other portion to Yugoslavia where it was exhibited at Zagreb in November 1940; that Erich Slomovic disappeared during World War II; that the Société Générale on October 24, 1946 proceeded to an opening of the strong-box and thereafter kept its content in a branch bank at Nantes until 1977; that it then had an official appraiser make an inventory of the objects kept in that branch bank and thereafter secured an order of the judge for urgent matters appointing a receiver with the task of conducting a public auction of these objects; that two public appraisers ordered by the sequester to arrange the auction provided broad publicity of the sale set for March 19 and 20, 1981; that, thus learning of the prospective sale, Mrs. Assunta Bertozzi, the widow of Mr. Jonas, to whose rights presently Mr. Sébastien her nephew and heir has succeeded, instituted, as successor of Ambroise Vollard, proceedings for restitution of the major portion of the objects found in the strong-box of the Société Générale; that at that instance, in their capacity as heirs of Erich Slomovic on the one hand the spouses Goldfinger-Eshel, his cousins on the maternal side, and on the other Mrs. Zdenka-Slomovic, a relative on the paternal side intervened; that the Court of Appeal of Paris, in its first Judgment of February 26, 1987 recognized the widow Mrs. Jonas' capacity to bring the action, declared the action for restitution as not barred by prescription and ordered the production of an expert opinion; that upon the rendition of the expert opinion, the Court of Appeal of Paris, in its second Judgment of October 3, 1990, declared Mr. Sébastien to be the owner of certain items and stated that the others formed part of Mr. Slomovic's estate, which according to the French law of succession, belonged in equal parts to the spouses Goldfinger-Eshel and Mrs. Zdenka-Slomovic; that it condemned the spouses Goldfinger-Eshel and Mrs. Zdenka-Slomovic to pay to the Société Générale, in the proportion of the shares in the inheritance, the sums of FF 30,894 and FF 400,216.64; that it rejected the claims of all parties for interest and damages.

Upon the sole assignment of error, taken in its two branches, asserted in the petition for cassation of the Judgment of February 26, 1987 in the case of Consorts Goldfinger et al. c. Mr. Sébastien:

Considering that the Consorts Goldfinger attack the judgment because it declared the action for restitution, instituted by Mrs. Jonas and continued by Mr. Sébastien, to be maintainable because it was not barred by prescription since the statute had not begun to run against them until the public auction of 1981, although on the one hand it had not established that the ignorance of the existence of the disputed items in which Mrs. Jonas found herself until 1981, constituted for her an unavoidable character, and although on the other hand it results from the judgment's own findings that Lucien Vollard, the brother of Ambroise Vollard and informant of Mrs. Jonas knew of the existence of the objects and paintings in the possession of Erich Slomovic who had them exhibited at Zagreb in 1940, without Lucien Vollard ever seeking to recover possession of them;

But considering that, because ownership is never extinguished by reason of non-use, the action for restitution is not susceptible of prescriptive extinction; that after this purely legal reason is substituted for that of the court of appeal, the judgment is correctly justified;

Upon the petition for review interposed by Mr. Sébastien against the Judgment of October 3, 1980:

Upon the third assignment of error taken in its second branch:

Considering that in order to eliminate the equivocal character of Erich Slomovic's possession of these paintings, the court of appeal held that the documents submitted to its assessment did not furnish any proof that Slomovic served as broker for the account of Ambroise Vollard or was his employee; that by limiting its inquiry to only two hypotheses regarding the possible bases of the possession, omitting additionally that of an occasional order with respect to all or a part of the paintings which were entrusted to him, and without investigating whether, standing alone, the acts of the possessor manifested without ambiguity his intention to behave like an owner of these works and that under conditions which left no doubt on that character, the court of appeal has failed to give a legal base to its decision;

Considering that the setting aside of the Judgment of October 3, 1990, upon the petition of Mr. Sébastien renders the interest which is attacked to the grievances articulated by the consorts Goldfinger and Mrs. Zdenka Slomovic contingent,

For these reasons and without need to pass upon the other assignments of error in the petition of Mr. Sébastien or to decide the petitions of the Consorts Goldfinger-Eshel or Mrs. Zdenka Slomovic,

The Court

Rejects the petition interposed by the Consorts Goldfinger against the judgment of February 26, 1987;

Vacates and annuls, in all its provisions, except those relating to the damage claims of Mr. Sébastien against the heirs of Erich Slomovic on the one hand and the Société Générale on the other, the Judgment of October 3, 1990 and * * * remands the case to the Court of Appeal of Amiens.

C. GERMANY

1. Statutes

Civil Code

§ 195 BGB

The ordinary period of prescription amounts to thirty years.

§ 937 BGB

(1) A person who possesses a movable thing as an owner for ten years acquires the ownership (title by adverse possession).

(2) The acquisition of ownership is precluded if the person who acquired possession as an owner is not bona fide at that time or learns subsequently that he is not entitled to ownership.

NOTE

In Germany the acquisition of title to movable things by adverse possession is governed by BGB § 937. The prevailing view denies acquisition of title by the 30 years prescription.

D. ITALY

1. Statutes

Civil Code

Art. 932 CC

Treasure is any valuable movable thing, hidden or buried, of which nobody can be proven to be the owner.

The treasure belongs to the owner of the land where it is found. If the treasure is found in the land of another, provided that it is discovered solely by accident, it belongs to the extent of one half to the owner of the land and of the other half to the finder. The same rule applies when the treasure is discovered in a movable thing.

With respect to the finding of objects of historical, archeological, paleontological and artistic character, special laws apply.

Art. 1161 CC

In the absence of a suitable title the ownership of movable goods and other rights of enjoyment relating to such goods are acquired by virtue of continuous possession of ten years whenever the possession was acquired in good faith.

If the possessor is in bad faith, the acquisition of ownership is completed with the expiration of twenty years.

Art. 1163 CC

Possession acquired through violence or secrecy does not serve the acquisition of ownership by adverse possession except from the time when the violence or secrecy has ceased.

NOTE

Codice Civile, Art. 1161 recognizes acquisition of title to chattels by bona fide possession (10 years) and possession in bad faith (20 years).

E. UNITED STATES

1. Cases

a. DeWeerth v. Baldinger

Gerda Dorothea DeWeerth, Plaintiff-Appellee,
v.
Edith Marks Baldinger,
Defendant-Third-Party-Plaintiff-Appellant,
v.
Wildenstein & Co., Inc., Third-Party-Defendant-Appellant.
Nos. 165, 296, Dockets 87-7392, 87-7402.
United States Court of Appeals, Second Circuit.
836 F2d 103
Argued Oct. 26, 1987.
Decided Dec. 30, 1987.

JON O. NEWMAN, Circuit Judge:

This appeal concerns a dispute over ownership of a painting by Claude Monet that disappeared from Germany at the end of World War II and has been in the possession of a good-faith purchaser for the last 30 years. The appeal presents primarily the issue whether New York law, which governs this dispute, requires an individual claiming ownership of stolen personal property to use due diligence in trying to locate the property in order to postpone the running of the statute of limitations in a suit against a good-faith purchaser. The issue arises on an appeal from a judgment of the District

Court for the Southern District of New York (Vincent L. Broderick, Judge) ruling that plaintiff-appellee Gerda Dorothea DeWeerth, a citizen of West Germany who owned the Monet from 1922 until 1943, was entitled to recover it from defendant-appellant Edith Marks Baldinger, an American citizen who purchased the painting. In New York in 1957 and who has possessed it ever since. We conclude that New York law imposes a due diligence requirement, that the undisputed facts show that DeWeerth failed to exercise reasonable diligence in locating the painting after its disappearance, and that her action for recovery is untimely. We therefore reverse the judgment of the District Court.

Background

Claude Monet is, perhaps, the most well-known and widely admired member of the school of impressionist painters active in France in the late nineteenth and early twentieth centuries. It was his early work, "Impression: Sunrise, Le Havre" (1872) from which the term "impressionism" was coined. His later works, including the depictions of haystacks, poplars, and the gardens at Giverny remain paragons of the impressionist style and reflect Monet's unsurpassed ability to capture on canvas the dazzling and magical play of light on the natural world.

The painting in the pending case, Monet's "Champs de Blé à Vétheuil," is one of a series of similar impressionistic landscapes painted by the artist near the town of Vétheuil, located on the Seine in Northern France. The oil painting, measuring 65 by 81 centimeters, shows a wheat field, a village, and trees. It is signed and dated "Claude Monet '79." The painting is estimated to be worth in excess of $500,000.

Plaintiff Gerda Dorothea DeWeerth is a citizen of West Germany. Her father, Karl von der Heydt, the owner of a substantial art collection, purchased the Monet in 1908. DeWeerth inherited the painting in 1922 along with other works of art from her father's estate. She kept the painting in her home in Wuppertal-Elberfeld, Germany, from 1922 until 1943, except for the two-year period 1927–1929 when the Monet was in the possession of her mother. A photograph taken in 1943 shows the Monet hanging on a wall in DeWeerth's residence.

In August 1943, DeWeerth sent the Monet and other valuables to the home of her sister, Gisela von Palm, for safekeeping during World War II. Von Palm lived in a castle in Oberbalzheim, Southern Germany. Von Palm received the shipment, including the Monet, which she hung in the castle. In 1945, at the end of the war, American soldiers were quartered in von Palm's residence. Following the soldiers' departure, von Palm noticed that the Monet was missing. She informed her sister of the painting's disappearance in the fall of 1945.[1]

---

1. Von Palm died in June of 1983 without ever having given testimony in connection with this case. Her account of the Monet's disappearance was related in the District Court by Margaret Huber, von Palm's maid in 1945. The District Court admitted Huber's testimony under the excited utterance exception to the hearsay rule. *DeWeerth v. Baldinger,* 658 F.Supp. 688, 690, n. 2 (S.D.N.Y.1987). Our disposition of the appeal makes it unnecessary to decide whether this or some other exception to the hearsay rule applied to Huber's testimony.

DeWeerth contacted several authorities concerning the lost Monet. In 1946, she filed a report with the military government administering the Bonn-Cologne area after the war. The report is no longer extant, but DeWeerth testified that it was a standard government form in which she briefly described items she had lost during the war. In 1948, in a letter to her lawyer, Dr. Heinz Frowein, regarding insurance claims on property she had lost, DeWeerth expressed regret about the missing Monet and inquired whether it was "possible to do anything about it." Frowein wrote back that the Monet would not be covered by insurance; he did not initiate an investigation. In 1955, DeWeerth sent the 1943 photograph of the Monet to Dr. Alfred Stange, a former professor of art and an expert in medieval painting, and asked him to investigate the painting's whereabouts. Stange responded that the photo was insufficient evidence with which to begin a search, and DeWeerth did not pursue the matter with him further. Finally, in 1957 DeWeerth sent a list of art works she had lost during the war to the *Bundeskriminalamt,* the West German federal bureau of investigation. None of DeWeerth's efforts during the period 1945–1957 to locate the Monet was fruitful. DeWeerth made no further attempts to recover the painting after 1957.

In the meantime, the Monet had reappeared in the international art market by 1956. In December of that year, third-party defendant-appellant Wildenstein & Co., Inc., an art gallery in New York City, acquired the Monet on consignment from François Reichenbach, an art dealer in Geneva, Switzerland. From December 1956 until June 1957, the painting was in the possession of Wildenstein in New York, where it was shown to several prospective buyers. Defendant Edith Marks Baldinger eventually purchased the painting in June 1957 for $30,900. The parties have stipulated that Baldinger purchased for value, in good faith, and without knowledge of any adverse claim.

Since 1957, Baldinger has kept the Monet in her New York City apartment, except for two occasions when it was displayed at public exhibitions. From October 29 to November 1, 1957, it was shown at a benefit at the Waldorf-Astoria Hotel, and in 1970 it was loaned to Wildenstein for an exhibition in its New York gallery for approximately one month.

DeWeerth learned of Baldinger's possession of the Monet through the efforts of her nephew, Peter von der Heydt. In 1981, von der Heydt was told by a cousin that DeWeerth had owned a Monet that had disappeared during the war. Shortly thereafter, von der Heydt identified the painting in a published volume of Monet's works, *Claude Monet: Bibliographie et Catalogue Raisonné, Vol. I 1840–1881* (intro. by Daniel Wildenstein, La Bibliothèque des Arts, Lausanne and Paris, 1974), which he found at the Wallraf-Richartz Museum in Cologne, less than 20 miles from where DeWeerth has been living since 1957. The *Catalogue Raisonné* indicated that the painting had been sold by Wildenstein in 1957 and that Wildenstein had exhibited it in 1970. In 1982, DeWeerth retained counsel in New York and requested Wildenstein to identify the current owner. When Wildenstein refused, DeWeerth brought an action in New York Supreme Court under N.Y.Civ.Prac.L. & R. § 3102(c) (KcKinney 1970) for "disclosure to aid in bringing an action." In December 1982, the court ruled in favor of

DeWeerth, and Wildenstein was compelled to identify Baldinger. By letter dated December 27, 1982, DeWeerth demanded return of the Monet from Baldinger. By letter dated February 1, 1983, Baldinger rejected the demand.

DeWeerth instituted the present action to recover the Monet on February 16, 1983.[2] At the conclusion of discovery, the parties submitted the case to Judge Broderick for decision on the record. The District Court adjudged DeWeerth the owner of the painting and ordered Baldinger to return it. The District Judge found that DeWeerth had superior title and that the action was timely as she had exercised reasonable diligence in finding the painting. *DeWeerth v. Baldinger,* 658 F.Supp. 688 (S.D.N.Y. 1987).

Discussion

In this diversity action, we must apply the substantive law of New York, including the applicable New York choice of law rules. *Klaxon Co. v. Stentor Electric Mfg. Co.,* 313 U.S. 487, 61 S.Ct. 1020, 85 L.Ed. 1477 (1941). Under New York law, actions that accrue within the State are governed by the local statute of limitations, while actions that accrue outside the State may be subject, pursuant to New York's "borrowing" statute, to the foreign jurisdiction's limitations provisions. *See Martin v. Julius Dierck Equipment Co.,* 43 N.Y.2d 583, 588–89, 403 N.Y.S.2d 185, 187, 374 N.E.2d 97, 99 (1978); N.Y.Civ. Prac.L. & R. § 202 (McKinney 1972). However, actions that accrue outside the State are subject to a borrowed limitations period only if it is shorter than New York's. *See* N.Y.Civ.Prac.L. & R. § 202 & practice commentary 202:3 (McKinney 1972). In the present case, if DeWeerth's action is time-barred under New York's limitations law, then the action is untimely regardless of whether it accrued in New York or Germany.

The New York statute of limitations governing actions for recovery of stolen property requires that suit be brought within three years of the time the action accrued. N.Y.Civ.Prac.L. & R. § 214(3) (McKinney 1972). The date of accrual depends upon the identity of the party from whom recovery is sought. Where an owner pursues the party who took his property, the three-year period begins to run when the property was taken. *See Sporn v. M.C.A. Records, Inc.,* 58 N.Y.2d 482, 487–88, 462 N.Y.S.2d 413, 415–16, 448 N.E.2d 1324, 1326–27 (1983). This is so even where the property owner was unaware of the unlawful taking at the time it occurred. *See Varga v. Credit-Suisse,* 5 A.D.2d 289, 291–92, 171 N.Y.S.2d 674, 677–78 (1st Dep't), *aff'd,* 5 N.Y.2d 865, 182 N.Y.S.2d 17, 155 N.E.2d 865 (1958); *Two Clinton Square Corp. v. Friedler,* 91 A.D.2d 1193, 1194, 459 N.Y.S.2d 179, 181 (4th Dep't 1983). In contrast, where the owner proceeds against one who innocently purchases the property in good faith, the limitations period begins to run only when the owner demands return of the

---

2. Baldinger brought a third-party action against Wildenstein. That action has been severed pursuant to Fed.R.Civ.P. 42(b).

property and the purchaser refuses. *Menzel v. List,* 22 A.D.2d 647, 253 N.Y.S.2d 43, 44 (1st Dep't 1964), *on remand,* 49 Misc.2d 300, 267 N.Y.S.2d 804 (Sup.Ct.1966), *modified on other grounds,* 28 A.D.2d 516, 279 N.Y.S.2d 608 (1st Dep't 1967), *modification rev'd,* 24 N.Y.2d 91, 298 N.Y.S.2d 979, 246 N.E.2d 742 (1969); *Duryea v. Andrews,* 12 N.Y.S. 42 (2d Dep't 1890); *accord Kunstsammlungen Zu Weimar v. Elicofon,* 536 F.Supp. 829, 848–49 (E.D.N.Y.1981) (applying New York law), *aff'd,* 678 F.2d 1150, 1161 (2d Cir.1982). Until demand and refusal, the purchaser in good faith is not considered a wrongdoer, *Gillet v. Roberts,* 57 N.Y. 28 (1874), even though this rule somewhat anomalously affords the owner more time to sue a good-faith purchaser than a thief.[3]

In the present case, it is undisputed that DeWeerth initiated her suit within three years of the date her demand for return of the Monet was refused. However, the fact that her action was brought soon after refusal does not end the inquiry. Under New York law, even though the three-year limitations period begins to run only once a demand for return of the property is refused, a plaintiff may not delay the action simply by postponing his demand. Where demand and refusal are necessary to start a limitations period, the demand may not be unreasonably delayed.[4] *See Heide v. Glidden Buick Corp.,* 188 Misc. 198, 67 N.Y.S. 2d 905 (1st Dep't 1947) (contract action); *Austin v. Board of Higher Education,* 5 N.Y.2d 430, 442–43, 186 N.Y.S.2d 1, 10–11, 158 N.E.2d 681, 687–88 (1959) (mandamus proceeding); *Reid v. Board of Supervisors,* 128 N.Y. 364, 373, 28 N.E. 367, 369 (1891) (reimbursement for price of real estate pur-

---

3. N.Y.Civ.Prac.L. & R. § 206(a) (McKinney 1972) provides that when a demand is necessary to entitle a person to commence an action, the action accrues at "the time when the right to make the demand is complete. . . ." This section has been interpreted to mean that a right to demand converted property is complete when the defendant acquires the property, whether or not the plaintiff knows the facts that gave rise to the right. *See Federal Insurance Co. v. Fries,* 78 Misc.2d 805, 810, 355 N.Y.S.2d 741, 747 (Civ.Ct. 1974); N.Y.Civ.Prac.L. & R. practice commentary 206:1 (McKinney 1972). However, section 206(a) applies only where the demand requirement is a procedural as opposed to a substantive element of the cause of action. *Frigi-Griffin, Inc. v. Leeds,* 52 A.D.2d 805, 806, 383 N.Y.S.2d 339, 341 (1st Dep't 1976). In *Menzel v. List, supra,* a case involving stolen art, the New York Appellate Division held that "with respect to a bona fide purchaser of personal property a demand by the rightful owner is a substantive, rather than a procedural, prerequisite to the bringing of an action for conversion by the owner." 22 A.D.2d at 647, 253 N.Y.S.2d at 44. Since, in the pending case, the defendant is a good-faith purchaser, the statute of limitations does not begin to run until demand and refusal actually occur. *Id; see also Kunstammlungen Zu Weimar v. Elicofon, supra,* 678 F.2d at 1161–63 (section 206 does not apply to actions to recover property from a good-faith purchaser).

4. The proscription against unreasonably delaying a demand is distinct from N.Y.Civ.Prac.L. & R. § 206(a) governing the accrual of actions requiring a demand. Section 206 specifies that the statutory limitations period, *e.g.,* three years for conversion, starts as soon as the right to make a demand is complete, but this provision has been construed to apply only where the demand requirement is procedural. *See Frigi-Griffin, Inc. v. Leeds,* 52 A.D.2d 805, 806, 383 N.Y.S.2d 339, 341 (1st Dep't 1976). By contrast, the unreasonable delay rule, applicable to this case as a substantive requirement, specifies that whenever a demand would be required to start the limitations period, that demand may not be unreasonably delayed. This rule, focusing on the plaintiff's conduct, conceptually starts the limitations period at the point where the plaintiff has had an opportunity to use due diligence in locating the property and making a demand, and has failed to do so.

chased at tax sale); *Kunstsammlungen Zu Weimar v. Elicofon, supra,* 536 F.Supp. at 849 (recovery of stolen art). While this proscription against unreasonable delay has been referred to as "laches," the New York courts have explained that the doctrine refers solely to an unexcused lapse of time and not to the equitable principle of laches, which requires prejudice to the defendant as well as delay. *See Devens v. Gokey,* 12 A.D.2d 135, 137, 209 N.Y.S.2d 94, 97 (4th Dep't), *aff'd,* 10 N.Y.2d 898, 223 N.Y.S.2d 515, 179 N.E.2d 516 (1961); *Curtis v. Board of Education,* 107 A.D.2d 445, 448, 487 N.Y.S.2d 439, 441 (4th Dep't 1985).

Baldinger asserts that DeWeerth's action is untimely because the delay between the painting's disappearance in Europe in 1945 and DeWeerth's demand for its return in 1982 was unreasonable. DeWeerth responds that she cannot be charged with unreasonable delay before learning the identity of Baldinger in 1982 because she could not have known before that time to whom to make the demand. These contentions frame the precise issue presented by this appeal: Whether New York law imposes upon a person who claims ownership of stolen personal property an obligation to use due diligence in attempting to locate the property. DeWeerth points out that no New York court has ever held that the unreasonable delay rule applies *before* the plaintiff has learned the identity of the person to whom demand must be made. In *Glidden Buick, Reid,* and *Austin,* plaintiffs were barred for unreasonably delaying demands to known defendants. DeWeerth suggests that in the absence of New York authority directly on point, her actions before she discovered that Baldinger possessed the Monet cannot be subject to the unreasonable delay rule. Baldinger responds that New York courts, confronting the issue, would impose an obligation of due diligence to attempt to locate the person in possession of another's property. The District Court did not decide the issue, concluding that plaintiff had exercised due diligence in any event. 658 F.Supp. at 694.

This Court's role in exercising its diversity jurisdiction is to sit as another court of the state. *Guaranty Trust Co. v. York,* 326 U.S. 99, 108, 65 S.Ct. 1464, 1469, 89 L.Ed. 2079 (1945). When presented with an absence of controlling state authority, we must "make an estimate of what the state's highest court would rule to be its law." *Stafford v. International Harvester Co.,* 668 F.2d 142, 148 (2d Cir.1981) (quoting *Bailey Employment System, Inc. v. Hahn,* 655 F.2d 473, 477 (2d Cir.1981)). In making that determination, this Court may consider all of the resources that the New York Court of Appeals could use, *see Francis v. INA Life Insurance Co.,* 809 F.2d 183, 185 (2d Cir.1987), including New York's stated policies and the law of other jurisdictions. We determine that in an action for the recovery of stolen personal property, the New York Court of Appeals would not make an exception to the unreasonable delay rule for plaintiff's actions prior to learning the identity of the current possessor. Rather, we believe that the New York courts would impose a duty of reasonable diligence in at-

---

5. We have elected not to submit the unresolved state law issue in this appeal to the New York Court

tempting to locate stolen property, in addition to the undisputed duty to make a demand for return within a reasonable time after the current possessor is identified.[5]

An obligation to attempt to locate stolen property is consistent with New York's treatment of the good-faith purchaser. The purpose of the rule whereby demand and refusal are substantive elements of a conversion action against a good-faith purchaser is to protect the innocent party by assuring him notice before he is held liable in tort:

> The rule is a reasonable and just one, that an innocent purchaser of personal property from a wrong-doer shall first be informed of the defect in his title and have an opportunity to deliver the property to the true owner, before he shall be made liable as a tort-feasor for a wrongful conversion.

Gillet v. Roberts, supra, 57 N.Y. at 34; *accord Kunstsammlungen Zu Weimar v. Elicofon, supra,* 536 F.Supp. at 848. The rule may disadvantage the good-faith purchaser, however, if demand can be indefinitely postponed. For if demand is delayed, then so is accrual of the cause of action, and the good-faith purchaser will remain exposed to suit long after an action against a thief or even other innocent parties would be time-barred. *See, e.g., Varga v. Credit-Suisse, supra,* 5 A.D.2d at 291, 171 N.Y.S.2d at 677–78 (action against converter accrues when property is taken); *Federal Insurance Co. v. Fries,* 78 Misc.2d 805, 810, 355 N.Y.S.2d 741, 747 (Civ.Ct. 1974) (action against recipient of mistaken delivery accrues at time of delivery). As the court in *Elicofon* observed, the unreasonable delay rule serves to mitigate the inequity of favoring a thief over a good-faith purchaser. 536 F.Supp. at 849. In this case, plaintiff's proposed exception to the rule would rob it of all of its salutary effect: The thief would be immune from suit after three years, while the good-faith purchaser would remain exposed as long as his identity did not fortuitously come to the property owner's attention. A construction of the rule requiring due diligence in making a demand to include an obligation to make a reasonable effort to locate the property will prevent unnecessary hardship to the good-faith purchaser, the party intended to be protected.

New York law governing limitations of actions also weighs in favor of a duty to attempt to locate stolen property. The New York Court of Appeals has said that

> the primary purpose of a limitations period is fairness to a defendant (*Flanagan v. Mount Eden Gen. Hosp.,* 24 N.Y.2d 427, 429, 301 N.Y.S.2d 23, 248 N.E.2d 871). A defendant should "'be secure in his reasonable expectation that the slate has been wiped clean of ancient obligations, and he ought

of Appeals pursuant to the recently authorized procedure permitting that Court to answer questions certified to it by the United States Supreme Court, a United States Court of Appeals, or a court of last resort of any state. *See* N.Y.Rules of Court § 500.17 (N.Y.Ct.App.) (McKinney 1987). That valuable procedure should be confined to issues likely to recur with some frequency. *See Kidney v. Kolmar Laboratories, Inc.,* 808 F.2d 955, 957 (2d Cir.1987). Though the issue presented by this appeal is interesting, we do not think it will recur with sufficient frequency to warrant use of the certification procedure.

> not to be called on to resist a claim where the "evidence has been lost, memories have faded, and witnesses have disappeared"' " (*id.*, quoting *Developments in the Law: Statutes of Limitations,* 63 Harv.L.Rev. 1177, 1185). There is also the need to protect the judicial system from the burden of adjudicating stale and groundless claims.

Duffy v. Horton Memorial Hospital, 66 N.Y.2d 473, 476–77, 497 N.Y.S.2d 890, 892–98, 488 N.E.2d 820 822–23 (1985) (citation omitted). These policies would be frustrated if plaintiffs were free to delay actions for the return of stolen property until the property's location fortuitously came to their attention. Conceivably, those claiming to be owners, or their heirs, could wait idly for decades or even centuries before any legal obligation arose to pursue their claims. In such cases, all of the problems of lost evidence, faded memories, and unavailable witnesses would undoubtedly be exacerbated. Additionally, fraudulent and groundless claims would be encouraged as defendants would face a heavy burden of refuting proffered testimony related to events of the distant past.

A rule requiring reasonable diligence in attempting to locate stolen property is especially appropriate with respect to stolen art. Much art is kept in private collections, unadvertised and unavailable to the public. An owner seeking to recover such property will almost never learn of its whereabouts by chance. Yet the location of stolen art may frequently be discovered through investigation. *See* F. Feldman & B. Burnham, *An Art Archive: Principles and Realization,* 10 Conn.L.Rev. 702, 724 (1978) (French and Italian authorities credit stolen art registries and investigation efforts for recovery rates as high as 75%). Unlike many other items of stolen personal property, such as jewelry or automobiles, art loses its value if it is altered or disguised. Moreover, valuable works of art, unlike fungible items like stereo components, tend to be easily remembered by those who have seen them. Thus, the owner of stolen art has a better chance than most owners of stolen property in tracking down the item he has lost.

Other jurisdictions have adopted limitations rules that encourage property owners to search for their missing goods. In virtually every state except New York, an action for conversion accrues when a good-faith purchaser acquires stolen property; demand and refusal are unnecessary. *See Restatement (Second) of Torts* § 229 & comment h (1965); Prosser, *Law of Torts* 93–94 (5th ed. 1984); 51 Am.Jur.2d *Limitation of Actions* § 125; *Federal Insurance Co. v. Fries, supra,* 78 Misc.2d at 807, 355 N.Y.S.2d at 744. In these states, the owner must find the current possessor within the statutory period or his action is barred. Obviously, this creates an incentive to find one's stolen property. It is true that New York has chosen to depart from the majority view. Nevertheless, the fact that plaintiff's interpretation of New York law would exaggerate its inconsistency with the law of other jurisdictions weighs against adopting such a view. At least one other state has recently confronted the limitations problems in the context of stolen art and has imposed a duty of reasonable investigation. *See O'Keefe v.*

Snyder, 83 N.J. 478, 416 A.2d 862 (1980); *See also* Comment, *The Recovery of Stolen Art: Of Paintings, Statues and Statutes of Limitations,* 27 U.C.L.A.L.Rev. 1122 (1980).

In light of New York's policy of favoring the good faith purchaser and discouraging stale claims and the approach to actions to recover property in other jurisdictions, we hold that under New York law an owner's obligation to make a demand without unreasonable delay includes an obligation to use due diligence to locate stolen property.

The District Court found that DeWeerth undertook the following efforts to locate the Monet after she learned of its disappearance in 1945:

> In 1946 she reported the loss of the Monet to the military government then administering the Bonn-Cologne area after the end of the War. In 1948 she solicited the assistance of her lawyer, Dr. Heinz Frowein, in attempting to find and recover it. Plaintiff also made inquiries in 1955 of one Dr. Alfred Stange, known to Mrs. DeWeerth as an art expert. In 1957 she reported the Monet as missing to the *Bundeskriminalamt* (the West German federal bureau of investigation) in Bonn. All of these efforts to find the Monet were unsuccessful.

658 F.Supp. at 691. The District Court held that these efforts constituted due diligence and that DeWeerth's demand upon Baldinger in 1982 was not unreasonably delayed. *Id.* at 695.

Plaintiff asserts that the determination of the District Court may be reversed only if clearly erroneous. She bases this assertion on her characterization of the decision below as an application of the equitable defense of laches. *See Esso International, Inc. v. S.S. Captain John,* 443 F.2d 1144, 1150 (5th Cir.1971) (existence of laches is a question of fact subject to review under clearly erroneous standard); *DeSilvio v. Prudential Lines, Inc.,* 701 F.2d 13, 15 (2d Cir.1983) (ruling on laches may be overturned only where trial court abused its discretion). Although Judge Broderick subsumed the laches issue into his discussion of the statute of limitations, 658 F.Supp. at 693 n. 7, the two issues are distinct. Laches is an equitable defense that requires a showing of delay and prejudice to the defendant, whereas the reasonably prompt demand principle involved in this case is a legal doctrine based exclusively on an unexcused lapse of time. *See Devens v. Gokey, supra,* 12 A.D.2d at 137, 209 N.Y.S.2d at 97. Where, as here, the issue is the application of a legal standard — "reasonable diligence" — to a set of facts, review is *de novo. See Utica Mutual Ins. Co. v. Fireman's Fund Ins. Co.,* 748 F.2d 118, 122 & n. 3 (2d Cir. 1984) (whether plaintiff's failure to discover a fraud was reasonable is a question of law subject to plenary review); *Reid v. Board of Supervisors, supra,* 128 N.Y. at 373, 28 N.E. at 369 ("What is a reasonable time [to make a demand that starts the limitations period] is *a question of law. . . .*") (emphasis added).

The question of what constitutes unreasonable delay in making a demand that starts the statute of limitations depends upon the circumstances of the case. *Id.; Kun-*

stsammlungen Zu Weimer v. Elicofon, supra, 536 F.Supp. at 849. When the action is for the return of stolen property, one of the key circumstances is the nature and value of the property at issue. *See O'Keefe v. Snyder, supra,* 83 N.J. at 499, 416 A.2d at 873. It has been recognized that when the property is valuable art, the search efforts that may reasonably be expected of an owner may be more exacting than where the property is of a different kind or of a lesser value. *Id.*

In *Elicofon,* we considered the issue of what search efforts may reasonably be expected of a plaintiff seeking to recover stolen art. A German museum had sought the return of two paintings by Albrecht Dürer that had disappeared from Germany in 1945 and had been discovered in Brooklyn in 1966. Among the issues presented was whether the plaintiff had exercised reasonable diligence in finding the paintings. The District Court held that plaintiff's search was reasonable, and this Court affirmed. 536 F.Supp. at 852, *aff'd,* 678 F.2d at 1164 n. 25, 1165. As described in the opinion of the District Court, the plaintiff's investigation "followed many channels" and "reflect[ed] a continuous and diligent search." 536 F.Supp. at 852. Specifically, the museum director informed numerous art museums and military agencies of the facts surrounding the theft. He contacted two German art museums, two American colleagues including the curator of Harvard's Germanic Museum, American military authorities, the Allied Control Council, and the Soviet Military Administration. Additionally, the loss of the Dürers was made known to several organizations specifically set up to locate art stolen during the war. These included a program run by the United States Department of State as well as the Federal Republic of Germany Trust Administration, which had taken over a program begun in Europe by the allied forces. Finally, the loss of the Dürers was reported in two publications listing stolen works of art. The paintings were eventually discovered in Brooklyn because a visitor to Elicofon's home recognized the Dürers from one of these publications. 536 F.Supp. at 850–52.

In contrast with the "continuous and diligent search" following "many channels" in *Elicofon,* DeWeerth's investigation was minimal. The "reports" filed with the military government and the *Bundeskriminalamt* amounted to no more than a standard form listing personal items lost during the war and a one-sentence letter submitting a list of works "I lost during and after the war." Unlike the correspondence described in *Elicofon,* neither of these reports gave any details as to how, where, or when the Monet had disappeared, nor any other information that would be essential to a credible search. DeWeerth's contacts with the lawyer Frowein and the art expert Stange were no more meaningful. She wrote to Frowein regarding her insurance coverage. She mentioned that the Monet was among the art she had lost and inquired generally, "Is it possible to do anything about it?" It is not clear whether this was a request to find the painting or simply a question about insurance coverage. In any event, when Frowein wrote back that the Monet would not be covered by insurance, DeWeerth let the matter drop. DeWeerth did ask Stange to find the Monet. But, as with Frowein, the investigation never was started; Stange replied that he had insufficient information on which to proceed, and DeWeerth then abandoned the effort.

More revealing than the steps DeWeerth took to find the Monet are those she failed to take. Conspicuously absent from her attempts to locate the painting is any effort to take advantage of several mechanisms specifically set up to locate art lost during World War II. As described in *Elicofon,* one such mechanism was a program initiated by the allied forces in Europe to handle works of art looted during the war. Under this program, Central Collecting Points (CCPs) were established throughout Germany where works of art turned in to the occupying forces were catalogued and stored until claimed by their rightful owners. In 1949, administration of the program was transferred to the German government and the paintings then located in the CCPs were given to a Trust Administration of the Federal Republic of Germany. Another program was run by the United States Department of State, which engaged in its own independent effort to locate stolen art. *Kunstsammlungen Zu Weimar v. Elicofon, supra,* 536 F.Supp. at 850–51. In *Elicofon,* the plaintiff corresponded with the State Department and the Trust Administration and may have contacted the CCPs as well. DeWeerth, in contrast, informed none of these agencies about the Monet, although she was aware of the CCPs; her family had attempted to recover other art from them.[6]

Nor did DeWeerth publicize her loss of the Monet in any one of several available listings designed to keep museums, galleries, and collectors vigilant for stolen art. *See id.* at 851 (German publications); F. Feldman & B. Burnham, *An Art Theft Archive: Principles and Realization,* 10 Conn.L.Rev 702, 703 n. 5, 706 n. 12 (1978) (American publications). As illustrated by *Elicofon,* where the painting was discovered via such a publication, this was a potentially fruitful channel of search.

Most indicative of DeWeerth's lack of diligence is her failure to conduct any search for 24 years from 1957 until 1981. Significantly, if DeWeerth had undertaken even the most minimal investigation during this period, she would very likely have discovered the Monet, since there were several published references to it in the art world. First, the Monet was pictured in the catalogues of two public exhibitions at which the painting was shown, *One Hundred Years of Impressionism, A Tribute to Durand-Ruel, A Loan Exhibition,* published in connection with an exhibition held from April 2 to May 9, 1970, at the Wildenstein Gallery in New York, and *Festival of Art,* published in connection with an exhibition held from October 29 to November 1, 1957, at the Waldorf-Astoria Hotel in New York. Second, the Monet was illustrated in a book by Daniel Wildenstein, *Monet: Impressions,* published in New York in 1967. Finally, the Monet is included in the comprehensive *Catalogue Raisonné, supra.* Consultation of any of these publications would likely have led DeWeerth to the Monet as each one is connected to the Wildenstein Gallery in New York, which sold the painting to Baldinger.

---

6. DeWeerth asserts that the CCPs would not have been helpful in her search because, pursuant to the agreement of the allied forces, the collecting points were established to deal with property looted by the Germans in occupied territory and not with property lost in Germany. *See Kunstsammlungen Zu Weimar v. Elicofon, supra,* 536 F.Supp. at 852. Even if the CCPs were not specifically created to restore art stolen from Germans, they were a potentially fruitful subject of investigation and ought to have been contacted. DeWeerth acknowledged that a painting her family had lost prior to the war found its way to the CCPs and the family attempted to reclaim it.

DeWeerth's failure to consult the *Catalogue Raisonné* is particularly inexcusable. A catalogue raisonné is a definitive listing and accounting of the works of an artist. The Monet *Catalogue Raisonné* depicts each of Monet's works in chronological order and sets forth each work's provenance — a history of its ownership, exhibitions in which it has been shown, and published references to it. The entry for painting number 595, the one here at issue, indicates that Wildenstein sold the painting in the United States in 1957 and that it was exhibited by Wildenstein in 1970. This entry could have easily directed DeWeerth to Wildenstein. Indeed, when in 1981 DeWeerth's nephew learned from a cousin of the lost Monet, he was able to identify it in the *Catalogue Raisonné* within three days, which led to the identification of Baldinger shortly thereafter.

The District Court excused DeWeerth's failure to search for the Monet after 1957 on the grounds that she was elderly during this period, that published references to the Monet were not generally circulated, and that as an individual she could not be expected to mount the sort of investigation undertaken by the government-owned art museum in *Elicofon*. 658 F.Supp. at 694–95. But in 1957, when DeWeerth made her last attempt to locate the painting, she was only 63 years old. Moreover, though the published references may not have been generally circulated, they were accessible to anyone looking for them as Peter von der Heydt's quick discovery in the *Catalogue Raisonné* makes clear. Finally, although an individual, DeWeerth appears to be a wealthy and sophisticated art collector; even if she could not have mounted a more extensive investigation herself, she could have retained someone to do it for her.

This case illustrates the problems associated with the prosecution of sale claims. Gisela von Palm, the only witness who could verify what happened to the Monet in 1945 is dead. Key documents, including DeWeerth father's will and reports to the military authorities, are missing. DeWeerth's claim of superior title is supported largely by hearsay testimony of questionable value. Memories have faded. To require a good-faith purchaser who has owned a painting for 30 years to defend under these circumstances would be unjust. New York law avoids this injustice by requiring a property owner to use reasonable diligence in locating his property. In this case, DeWeerth failed to meet that burden. Accordingly, the judgment of the District Court is reversed.

NOTE

In most states in the United States it has been held that title to moveable things can be acquired by adverse possession, R. Brown and W. Raushenbush, Law of Personal Property (3d. ed. 1975), Ch. IV, especially p. 34 n.4.

b. Autocephalous

Autocephalous Greek-Orthodox Church of Cyprus and The Republic of Cyprus, Plaintiffs,
v.
Goldberg & Feldman Fine Arts, Inc., and Peg Goldberg, Defendants.
No. IP 89-304-C.
United States District Court, S.D. Indiana,
Indianapolis Division.
Aug. 3, 1989.

717 F. Supp. 1374

MEMORANDUM OF DECISION AND ORDER

NOLAND, District Judge.

Summary of Decision

In this case the Court is asked to decide the right of possession as between the plaintiffs, the Autocephalous Greek-Orthodox Church of Cyprus ("Church of Cyprus") and the Republic of Cyprus, and the defendants, Peg Goldberg ("Goldberg") and Goldberg & Feldman Fine Arts, Inc., of four Byzantine mosaics created in the early sixth century. The mosaics, made of small chips of colored glass, were originally affixed to and for centuries remained in a church in Cyprus, a small island in the Mediterranean. In 1974, Turkish military forces invaded Cyprus and seized control of northern Cyprus, including the region where the church is located. At some point in the latter 1970s, during the Turkish military occupation of northern Cyprus, the mosaics were removed from their hallowed sanctuary. The plaintiffs claim that the Church of Cyprus has never intended to relinquish ownership of the mosaics, that the mosaics were improperly removed without the authorization of the Church or the Republic of Cyprus, and that the mosaics should be returned to the Church. The defendants, on the other hand, claim that export of the mosaics was authorized by Turkish Cypriot officials, and that in any event Goldberg should be awarded the mosaics because she purchased them in good faith and without information or reasonable notice that they were stolen. Having heard and reviewed all the evidence in the case, the Court concludes that possession of the mosaics must be awarded to the plaintiff, the Autocephalous Greek-Orthodox Church of Cyprus.

The Court concludes that because the place where the mosaics were purchased, Switzerland, has an insignificant relationship to this suit, and because Indiana has greater contacts and a more significant relationship to this suit, the substantive law of the state of Indiana should apply to this case. Under Indiana law, a thief obtains no title to or right to possession of stolen items. Therefore, a thief cannot pass any right of ownership of stolen items to subsequent purchasers. Because the mosaics were stolen from the rightful owner, the Church of Cyprus, Goldberg never obtained title to or right to possession of the mosaics. Under this analysis of Indiana law, it is unnecessary to consider whether Goldberg exercised good faith or due diligence in obtaining possession of the mosaics.

In the alternative, the Court considers the issues under Swiss law. Under Swiss law, in certain situations a thief may sell and pass good title to stolen items to a good faith purchaser. Whether one qualifies as a good faith purchaser is determined by evaluating certain factors. These factors are evaluated to determine whether the purchaser knew that the seller lacked title, or whether an honest and careful purchaser would have had doubts with respect to the seller's capacity to transfer property rights, and if so, then whether the purchaser reasonably inquired about the seller's ability to pass good title. Evaluating those factors under the facts of this case, the Court concludes that Goldberg is not a good faith purchaser under Swiss law. This is so because suspicious circumstances surrounded the sale of the mosaics which should have caused an honest and reasonably prudent purchaser in Goldberg's position to doubt whether the seller had the capacity to convey property rights, and because she failed to conduct a reasonable inquiry to resolve that doubt.

Therefore, principally under Indiana law and alternatively under Swiss law, Goldberg never obtained good title to or the right to possession of the mosaics. The Church of Cyprus, the original and rightful owner of the mosaics, has requested and made a proper showing for the return of the mosaics. The mosaics are unique. The paramount significance of their existence is as part of the religious, artistic, and cultural heritage of the Church and the government of Cyprus, and as a part of the national unity of the Republic of Cyprus. Therefore, the Court orders that possession of the mosaics is awarded to the plaintiff, the Autocephalous Greek-Orthodox Church of Cyprus.

Historical Setting and Factual Background

The facts established by the evidence presented are as follows.

A. The Mosaics of the Church of the Panagia Kanakaria

This case involves a dispute as to the ownership of four Byzantine mosaics. These four mosaics were originally part of a larger mosaic ("the original mosaic"). The original mosaic was affixed to the apse of the Church of the Panagia Kanakaria ("Kanakaria Church") in the village of Lythrankomi, Cyprus, in 530 A.D. Except for a unique quirk of fate, the original mosaic would have ceased to exist a thousand or more years ago. During the period of Iconoclasm (roughly the 8th century), government edicts mandated the destruction of religious artifacts so that such religious "images" would not be the subject of veneration. These iconoclast edicts were responsible for the destruction of many significant religious artifacts. The original Kanakaria mosaic is one of only six or seven Byzantine mosaics to survive the ravages of Iconoclasm and the passage of time.

The original Kanakaria mosaic depicted Jesus as a young boy seated in the lap of his mother, the Virgin Mary, who sat on a throne surrounded by a mandorla of light. The figures of Jesus and the Virgin Mary were bordered on each side by depictions of two archangels. This central composition was in turn bordered by a frieze containing the busts of the twelve apostles. The original mosaic was made of small pieces of colored glass referred to in the art world as tesserae.

As stated previously, the original mosaic was affixed to the apse of the Kanakaria Church in the early sixth century. Over the centuries, the mosaic has deteriorated. By 1960, all that remained of the original Kanakaria mosaic was the figure of Jesus, the bust of the North Archangel, and nine of the twelve apostles. Between 1959 and 1967, the mosaic was cleaned and restored under the sponsorship of the Department of Antiquities of the Republic of Cyprus, the Church of Cyprus, and Harvard University's Dumbarton Oaks Center for Byzantine Studies. With the knowledge gained in its efforts to restore the mosaic, Dumbarton Oaks published an authoritative volume on the Kanakaria Church and its art: *The Church of the Panagia Kanakaria at Lythrankomi in Cyprus: Its Mosaics and Frescoes*, authored by A.H.S. Megaw and E.J.W. Hawkins (1977).

The four mosaics at issue in this case were once a part of the original Kanakaria mosaic. These four mosaics depict the figure of Jesus as a young boy and the busts of the North Archangel, the apostle Matthew, and the apostle James. Each of the four mosaics measures approximately two feet by two feet.

This brief background enables one to understand the origin of the four mosaics at issue in this case and the invaluable and irreplaceable significance to Cyprus's cultural, artistic, and religious heritage. Had it not been for an unusual series of events, these four mosaics would probably have remained in the Kanakaria Church to this day — undisturbed in their deteriorating but readily recognizable state.

B. The Partition of Cyprus

Cyprus is an island located in the Mediterranean. The island covers 3,572 square miles and is smaller than the state of Connecticut. The population of Cyprus is approximately 696,000. The Cypriot population is comprised mainly of persons of either Greek or Turkish descent. Today, approximately 79 percent of the population is made up of persons of Greek descent, and approximately 18 percent of the population is made up of persons of Turkish descent. Historically, Greek Cypriots follow the Greek Orthodox faith; Turkish Cypriots follow the Muslim faith.

Cyprus was a British colony from 1878 to 1960, at which time it became an independent republic. In 1963, civil disturbances broke out between Greek Cypriots and Turkish Cypriots. United Nations peacekeeping forces were sent to Cyprus to restore order in 1964. The U.N. forces have remained in Cyprus ever since.

On July 20, 1974, Turkish military forces invaded Cyprus. Turkish troops landed on the north coast of Cyprus and advanced to Nicosia. By late August, the Turkish forces had extended their control over the northern 37 percent of the island. This region has remained under Turkish military occupation since the invasion.

After the invasion, the Turkish military established in essence a puppet government in northern Cyprus called the "Autonomous Cyprus Turkish Administration." That government was succeeded in February 1975 by the "Turkish Federated State of Cyprus." In 1983, the Turkish Federated State of Cyprus was succeeded by the "Turkish Republic of Northern Cyprus." The Turkish Republic of Northern Cyprus is recognized as a legitimate government by only one nation in the world: Turkey. It is not recognized, nor has it ever been recognized, by the United States government. The United States government recognizes only the plaintiff Republic of Cyprus as the legitimate government of all the people of Cyprus.

The Kanakaria Church is located in the village of Lythrankomi, which is in an area of northern Cyprus now under Turkish military occupation.

C. The Theft of the Mosaics

Since the 1974 Turkish invasion, the government of the Republic of Cyprus and the Church of Cyprus have generally been denied access to occupied northern Cyprus.

Sometime between August 1976 and October 1979, the interior of the Kanakaria Church was vandalized and the mosaics were forcibly removed from the apse of the church. The mosaics were severely damaged during their removal. Neither the Republic of Cyprus nor the Church of Cyprus has ever authorized the removal or sale of the Kanakaria mosaics.[7]

D. Cyprus's Efforts to Recover the Mosaics

As previously noted, since the Turkish invasion in 1974, the Republic of Cyprus has learned of the theft or destruction of much cultural property in Cyprus. Many churches, museums, and private collections have been looted, and other property has suffered destruction or loss. In some instances visitors who were allowed access to the

---

7. In the early 1970s, the Sixteenth General Conference of UNESCO adopted "The Convention on the Means of Prohibiting and Preventing the Illicit Import, Export and Transfer of Ownership of Cultural Property" ("the UNESCO Convention"). To date, sixty-one nations have ratified the UNESCO Convention. In 1983, the United States ratified the UNESCO Convention with the passage of "The Convention on Cultural Property Implementation Act," 19 U.S.C. § 2601 *et seq. See also* Executive Order No. 12555 (1986). This act provides in part:

> No article of cultural property documented as appertaining to the inventory of a museum or religious or secular public monument or similar institution in any State Party which is stolen from such institution after the effective date of this chapter [January 12, 1983], or after the date of entry into force of the Convention for the Party State, whichever date is later, may be imported into the United States.

19 U.S.C. § 2607.

The Hague Convention and the UNESCO Convention are not controlling in this case; however, they emphasize the importance that the United States and other countries have placed on restricting international trafficking in stolen art.

occupied area would note such losses and report them to the Republic of Cyprus. It was through one such visitor that the Department of Antiquities first learned in November 1979 that the mosaics of the Kanakaria Church were missing. The Department is charged with the responsibility, among other things, of protecting church property which is either an antiquity or a national monument. The mosaics fall under this responsibility. Therefore, the Republic of Cyprus decided to seek recovery of the mosaics.

Immediately upon learning that the mosaics were missing, the Republic of Cyprus contacted UNESCO, informing it of the significance of the lost art and seeking its assistance. Thereafter, the Republic of Cyprus notified several people and entities whom it believed could assist it in disseminating information about the missing mosaics and in recovering them.

The Republic of Cyprus also contacted both European and American museums about the missing mosaics. It contacted Harvard University's Dumbarton Oaks Institute for Byzantine Studies, considered to be the leading center in the United States for the study of Byzantine art. Dr. Vassos Karageorghis, Cyprus's Director of the Department of Antiquities from 1964 to 1989, and Anthanasios Papageorghiou, Curator of Ancient Monuments in Cyprus since 1962 and currently Acting Director of the Department of Antiquities, disseminated information about the missing mosaics to their colleagues and scholars throughout the world by sending letters and by addressing symposia, congresses, and other such meetings.

E. The Mosaics Resurface

Goldberg is president and majority shareholder of Goldberg & Feldman Fine Arts, Inc. The co-owner of the company is George Feldman who serves as its vice president. Since becoming an art dealer in 1981, Goldberg has dealt almost exclusively in 19th and 20th century paintings, etchings, and sculptures. Goldberg is not, nor does she claim to be, an expert in Byzantine art.

On June 30, 1988, Goldberg flew to Amsterdam, The Netherlands, to inspect and possibly purchase for a client a painting by Amadeus Modigliani. The availability of a Modigliani painting for sale was brought to Goldberg's attention by Robert Fitzgerald, an art dealer from Indianapolis whom she "had known [ ] casually since 1980 or '81."

After inspecting the painting, Goldberg developed doubts "about being able to prove the authenticity of the painting." Tr. 438. At this point, the sale of the Modigliani painting fell through.

After the Modigliani sale fell through, Fitzgerald mentioned to Goldberg another deal. On July 1, 1988, Fitzgerald informed Goldberg that he was aware of four early Christian mosaics that were for sale. Later that day, Fitzgerald introduced Goldberg to Michel van Rijn, a Dutch art dealer, and Ronald Faulk, an attorney from California. Goldberg knew very little about van Rijn or Faulk. She was told, however, that van Rijn was once convicted in France for forging Marc Chagall's signature to prints of that artist's work and that he also had been sued by an art gallery "[f]or failure to pay money." Tr. 539.[8] She was also aware that Faulk was in Europe to act as attorney for Fitzgerald and van Rijn.

At this July 1st meeting, van Rijn showed Goldberg photographs of the four Byzantine mosaics, and she immediately "fell in love" with them. Tr. 447. van Rijn told her that the seller requested $3 million for the four mosaics. She was also told that the seller was interested in selling the mosaics quickly because he "had recently become quite ill and had [a] cash problem." Tr. 457.

Goldberg was not told the identity of the seller at the initial meeting on July 1st; however, two days later she was told that the seller was a man named Aydin Dikman.[9]

On July 3, 1988, while still in Amsterdam, Goldberg negotiated an agreement with van Rijn, Fitzgerald, and Faulk, whereby "the parties agree[d] to acquire the mosaics for their purchase price of $1,080,000 (U.S.)." Exhibit 700. The agreement also provided that the parties would split the profits made on any future resale of the mosaics as follows: Goldberg & Feldman 50 %; Fitzgerald 22.5 %; van Rijn 22.5 %; and Faulk 5 %. *Id.* This agreement was executed on July 4th in Amsterdam. *Id.*

Later, Goldberg and Fitzgerald traveled to Geneva, Switzerland, to investigate a lead on a second possible Modigliani and to examine the mosaics. On July 5th, Faulk and Dikman transported the mosaics by airplane from Munich to Geneva. The mosaics were stored in crates in the free port area of the Geneva airport. The mosaics never passed through Swiss Customs.

After arriving in Geneva, Faulk and Dikman met Goldberg in the free port area of the airport. This was the only time that Goldberg met Dikman. Dikman introduced himself to Goldberg and then left. In the presence of Faulk, Goldberg then inspected the four mosaics. Upon seeing the mosaics, she "was in awe" and wanted to buy them "more than ever." Tr. 486. She was concerned, however, about their deteriorating condition.

Goldberg testified that while she was in Geneva she inquired as to whether the mosaics had been reported as stolen or missing and whether any applicable treaties might prevent the mosaics from being imported into the United States. She testified that she contacted, by telephone, the International Foundation for Art Research ("IFAR") in New York and UNESCO's office in Geneva. In addition, Goldberg claims she telephoned customs offices in the United States, Germany, Switzerland, and Turkey.

G. Goldberg Purchases the Mosaics

The sale and transfer of the mosaics was originally scheduled for July 5th; however, a delay in securing financing prevented Goldberg from consummating the sale

8. Goldberg testified that van Rijn also told her that he was a descendant of Rembrandt on his father's side and of Rubins on his mother's side. Tr. 462. No other evidence supporting this claim was introduced, however.

9. In the record, the seller's surname is spelled as "Dikman," "Dikmen," and "Diekman." Throughout this memorandum entry, the Court will refer to the seller as "Dikman."

on that date. The $1.2 million from Merchants did not arrive at a bank in Geneva until July 7th.

On July 8, 1988, Goldberg returned with the mosaics to the United States. Goldburg insured the mosaics for $1.2 million and declared their value at U.S. Customs to be $1.2 million. As previously noted, Goldberg paid $1.08 million for the mosaics.

H. Significant Events in Indiana

Goldberg intended to sell the mosaics. Beginning in the fall of 1988, she contacted at least two people in an attempt to market and sell the mosaics. By October 1988 Goldberg had discussed the sale of the mosaics with Dr. Geza von Habsburg, an art dealer operating out of Geneva and New York. In October of 1988 von Habsburg contacted Dr. Marion True of the Getty Museum in California and discussed whether the Getty would be interested in purchasing the mosaics. Dr. True explained that the Getty does not collect Byzantine art and told von Habsburg that, because of her close working relationship with Cyprus, it would be necessary for her to contact her friend Dr. Vassos Karageorghis about the mosaics. Dr. True had developed a working relationship with Dr. Karageorghis, and he had often spoken to her of Cyprus's attempts to recover the mosaics. Dr. True then called Dr. Karageorghis, who told her that export of the mosaics was not authorized by Cyprus and that the mosaics she described were the mosaics which Cyprus had been so interested in recovering.

The plaintiffs and their attorneys eventually learned that the mosaics were in Goldberg's possession in Indianapolis. The plaintiffs wrote to Goldberg requesting the return of the mosaics. Upon the defendants' refusal, the plaintiffs instructed their attorneys to file suit to recover the mosaics.

Statute of Limitations

> The Indiana code provides in relevant part:
>
> The following actions shall be commenced within six [6] years after the cause of action has accrued and not afterwards.
>
> Third. For injuries to property other than personal property, damages for any detention thereof, and for recovering possession of personal property.

I.C. § 34-1-2-1 (Burns 1986). Particularly in light of the plaintiffs' claim that the mosaics should be returned to the Church of Cyprus, the Court concludes that the Indiana statute of limitations providing specifically "for recovering possession of personal property" governs the issue of possession of the mosaics. Therefore, the plaintiffs' action is governed by a six-year statute of limitations.

Sometime between August 1976, when military force and threat of harm had forced church officials to leave the church involuntarily, and November 1979, the mosaics were removed from the Kanakaria Church. In November 1979 church and government officials first learned that the mosaics were missing from the Kanakaria Church. Goldberg acquired the mosaics in July 1988. The plaintiffs first learned that the mosaics were in Goldberg's possession in late 1988. The plaintiffs filed this action against Goldberg in March 1989. The defendants argue that the plaintiffs' cause of action first accrued in 1979 and that, because the complaint was not filed within six years thereof, plaintiffs' cause of action is barred. The plaintiffs, however, argue that under the circumstances of this case, they are not barred from recovering the mosaics. Thus the issue is whether the plaintiffs have filed their complaint in a timely fashion.

Determination of the Timeliness and Accrual of a Cause of Action

The fact that statutes of limitations exist, however, does not mean that the timeliness of a claim is determined solely by the mechanical application of a period of months to a file-stamp date. Rather, under certain circumstances a court is required to evaluate the timeliness of a claim under rules and doctrines of law designed to ensure fairness and equity in the adjudication of claims. The facts of this case warrant that the Court evaluate the timeliness of the plaintiffs' claims under the following rules and doctrines.

First, the Indiana supreme court has held that the determination of when a cause accrues is the court's responsibility. *Burks v. Rushmore,* 534 N.E.2d 1101 (Ind. 1989). The applicable Indiana statute of limitations states that actions for the recovery of personal property "shall be commenced within six [6] years after the cause of action has accrued and not afterwards." I.C. § 34-1-2-1. Regarding the language "after the cause of action has accrued," the court has stated that "the legislature designated the reasonable time for bringing an action and left to the courts the responsibility of determining when the cause accrues." *Burks,* 534 N.E.2d at 1103 (citation omitted). *See also Barnes v. A.H. Robins Co., Inc.,* 476 N.E.2d 84, 85 (Ind. 1985) ("[i]t is clear this Court has the authority and responsibility to interpret the intentions of the legislature by deciding when a cause of action accrues.").

Second, Indiana recognizes a discovery rule as it may affect the running of a statute of limitations.

The Court holds that the plaintiffs' cause of action did not accrue in this case until the plaintiffs, using due diligence, knew or were on reasonable notice of the identity of the possessor of the mosaics. In this context a discovery rule should apply and prevent the statute from running until the plaintiffs knew or reasonably should have known who possessed the mosaics.

The Court concludes that a plaintiff who seeks protection under the discovery rule has a duty to use reasonable diligence to locate the stolen items. *See DeWeerth v. Baldinger,* 836 F.2d 103 (2d Cir.1987), *cert. denied,* — U.S. —, 108 S.Ct. 2823, 100 L.Ed.2d 924 (1988). Determination of due diligence is fact-sensitive and must be made on a case-by-case basis. *O'Keefe,* 416 A.2d at 873. Having reviewed the facts of this case, the Court is persuaded that the plaintiffs exercised due diligence in their search to locate and to recover the mosaics.

V. *Choice-of-Law*

A federal district court exercising diversity jurisdiction under 28 U.S.C. § 1332 must apply state substantive law. *Erie Railroad Co. v. Tompkins,* 304 U.S. 64, 58 S.Ct.

817, 82 L.Ed. 1188 (1938); *DeValk Lincoln Mercury, Inc. v. Ford Motor Co.,* 811 F.2d 326, 329 (7th Cir.1987). Moreover, a federal district court sitting in diversity must follow the choice-of-law rules of the state in which it sits to determine which state's substantive law to apply. *Klaxon Co. v. Stentor Elec. Mfg. Co.,* 313 U.S. 487, 61 S.Ct. 1020, 85 L.Ed. 1477 (1941); *DeValk,* 811 F.2d at 329. Therefore, this Court, exercising diversity jurisdiction over this suit, must apply the choice-of-law rules of the state in which it sits, namely, Indiana.

A. Indiana Law Analysis

Indiana's traditional choice-of-law doctrine was *lex loci delicti commissi,* which dictated that the place where the wrong was committed governed which state's substantive law to apply. *Hubbard Mfg. Co., Inc. v. Greeson,* 515 N.E.2d 1071, 1073 (Ind.1987). Today, *Hubbard* is the leading case to discuss Indiana's choice-of-law rules.

The place where the wrong was committed in the present case is Switzerland; it was there that Goldberg took possession of and control over the mosaics. Switzerland "bears little connection" to the plaintiffs' cause of action. Neither the plaintiffs nor the defendants are citizens of Switzerland. None of the other individuals involved in the sale of the mosaics, namely, Dikman, Fitzgerald, van Rijn, or Faulk is a citizen of Switzerland. No Swiss citizen earned a profit on the sale of the mosaics, nor does any Swiss citizen own any interest in the mosaics.

After a court has determined that the place where the wrong was committed bears little connection to the legal action, the second step in the *Hubbard* analysis is to apply additional factors to determine which state or jurisdiction has the more significant relationship or contracts. *Hubbard,* 515 N.E.2d at 1074. Among the factors a court may consider are:

(1) the place where the conduct causing the injury occurred;
(2) the residence or place of business of the parties; and
(3) the place where the relationship is centered.

Id. at 1073–74; *see also Gollnick v. Gollnick,* 517 N.E.2d 1257, 1058 (Ind.Ct.App. 1988). The Court concludes, after weighing these and other relevant factors, that Indiana has the most significant contacts to this suit. Therefore, Indiana law applies.

Indiana's contacts to this suit are more significant than those of any other jurisdiction. Defendant Peg Goldberg is a citizen of Indiana. Defendant Goldberg & Feldman Fine Arts, Inc. is an Indiana corporation with its principal place of business in Indiana. The purchase of the mosaics was effected largely through the efforts of an Indiana art dealer, Robert Fitzgerald. The purchase of the mosaics was financed by a loan obtained from an Indiana bank, Merchants; Merchants presently holds a security interest in the mosaics in the amount of $1,200,000. Several Indiana residents (Goldberg, Fitzgerald, Dr. Bick, Frenzel) and one Indiana corporation (Merchants) hold an interest in any profits realized on the resale of the mosaics. The original resale agreement among Goldberg, Fitzgerald, van Rijn, and Faulk stipulated that Indiana law would govern any disputes arising out of the agreement. This indicates Goldberg's belief that the laws of her home state, Indiana, were more significant to this transaction. Finally, the mosaics are presently in Indiana and have been in Indiana since they were transported from Geneva in July 1988. For these reasons, Indiana has a significant interest in the application of its law to this transaction. Therefore, the Court concludes that Indiana has the most significant contacts to this suit. Indiana law applies.

B. Swiss Law Analysis

The conclusion that Indiana substantive law applies in this case is bolstered by Swiss choice-of-law principles. As Professor Arthur von Mehren[10] testified at trial:

> The choice of law rules of another system may assist in certain cases of forum in determining its ultimate choice of the applicable law. . . . [I]t may be of interest to the forum and of help to the forum in reaching a conclusion to consider what view would be taken by the courts of another legal order if the matter were before those courts.

Tr. 9 (von Mehren). This Court will now examine Swiss choice-of-law principles for whatever light they may shed on the issue of which jurisdiction's substantive law should be applied under the facts of this case. Swiss choice-of-law rules also dictate that Indiana substantive law should control.

As a general rule, Swiss law applies the so-called *lex situs* principle in determining choice-of-law in cases where the ownership of tangible, movable property is disputed. *Id.* at 10. Under the *lex situs* rule, a forum court must apply the substantive law of the place where the tangible, movable property was physically located at the time of its sale. *Id.* If this general rule applies in the present case, then Swiss law governs because the mosaics were physically present in Switzerland when the sale was consummated. However, the general rule does not apply in this case.

Swiss law recognizes an exception to the general *lex situs* rule. As Professor von Mehren explained, under Swiss choice-of-law rules,

> an exception is made for situations in which the goods though physically present, have only a fortuitous and transitory or casual connection with the legal order in question. This is often expressed as the exception for goods in transit.

---

10. Arthur Taylor von Mehren is Story Professor of Law at Harvard Law School. Professor von Mehren testified at trial as an expert witness for the plaintiffs on the subject of Swiss law. In summarizing Swiss law, the Court will cite to the transcript of Professor von Mehren's testimony in lieu of citing directly to the Swiss statutes and treatises upon which Professor von Mehren based his conclusions. The Court is persuaded that Professor von Mehren's testimony is supported by applicable Swiss law.

Id. at 10, 11. If a transaction falls within this "in transit" exception, then the law of the situs does not apply; instead, the law of the place of destination applies.[11] *Id.* at 11. In the case *sub judice,* the place of destination is Indiana. Therefore, if the exception for property in transit applies, then Indiana substantive law governs.

The Court agrees with Professor von Mehren's opinion that the "in transit" exception applies in this case. Id. at 18. The mosaics were transported from Munich to Geneva. Upon their arrival in Geneva, the mosaics were placed in storage in the free port area of the Geneva airport; there they remained in storage for four days until being shipped to Indianapolis. The mosaics never passed through Swiss customs. The mosaics never entered the Swiss stream of commerce. Their presence in Switzerland was temporary, as was intended. Those involved with the transaction intended that if the sale were consummated, the mosaics were to be shipped to Indiana; if not, the mosaics were to be returned to Germany. For the foregoing reasons, the Court concludes that under Swiss law the "in transit" exception to the general *lex situs* rule would apply. Therefore, the law of the place of destination controls, which in this case is Indiana. Accordingly, Swiss choice-of-law rules would agree with this Court's earlier conclusion that Indiana substantive law controls under the facts of this case.

VI. *Substantive Law*

A. Indiana Substantive Law

In Indiana to prove a claim for replevin, a plaintiff must prove that he has title or right to ownership, that the property has been unlawfully detained, and that the defendant is in wrongful possession of the property. *Snyder v. International Harvester Credit Corp.,* 147 Ind.App. 364, 261 N.E.2d 71, 73 (1970) (citations omitted); I.L.E. Replevin § 42 (West 1960). The Court now applies the elements of replevin to the facts of this case.

First, the plaintiffs must prove ownership of title or the right to possession of the mosaics.

The Court concludes that the plaintiffs have presented credible and persuasive evidence that the right to ownership and possession of the mosaics rests with the plaintiff Church of Cyprus, for all times relevant to this litigation.

Second, the plaintiffs must show that the items to be replevied were unlawfully or wrongfully detained. The mosaics were removed from the Kanakaria Church at some point between 1976 and 1979, during the Turkish occupation of northern Cyprus. Father Maheriotis testified that the Church of Cyprus has never authorized anyone to remove the mosaics or to sell anything from the Kanakaria Church. Tr. 261–263.

---

11. Swiss law is unsettled in this area. The opinion that, under the "in transit" exception, the law of the place of destination controls is, according to Professor von Mehren, "[t]he prevailing rule today." Tr. 11 (von Mehren). Other authorities argue that the law of the place of origin would apply. The Court finds persuasive Professor von Mehren's conclusion that the law of the place of destination controls when the facts of a case fall within the "in transit" exception.

For purposes of this opinion, the mosaics were stolen from the church. For these reasons, the Court concludes that the mosaics were unlawfully detained or taken from the rightful possession of the Church of Cyprus.

Finally, to recover under replevin, the plaintiffs must prove that the defendants are in wrongful possession of the mosaics. The defendants concede that the mosaics are in their possession. Thus the issue is whether the defendants' possession of the mosaics is wrongful. As previously noted, the Court has concluded that the mosaics were stolen. There are long established rules of law in Indiana that a thief never obtains title to stolen items, and that one can pass no greater title than one has. *Torian v. McClure,* 83 Ind. 310 (1882); *Breckenridge v. McAfee,* 54 Ind. 141 (1876). Therefore, one who obtains stolen items from a thief never obtains title to or right to possession of the item. *Id.*

Under Indiana law, as outlined, a thief obtains no title to or right to possession of stolen items and can pass no title or right to possession to a subsequent purchaser. The mosaics were stolen. For purposes of this analysis, it is of no significance whether Aydin Dikman originally stole the mosaics, or who originally stole them. Further, it matters not whether Goldberg purchased the mosaics from Dikman alone, or from Dikman, van Rijn, and Fitzgerald, or from only van Rijn and Fitzgerald. The evidence of theft and chain of possession under the facts of this case lead only to the conclusion that Goldberg came into possession of stolen property. Under Indiana law, she never obtained any title or right to possession. Therefore, the Court concludes that the defendants are in wrongful possession of the mosaics.

B. Swiss Substantive Law

Assuming, *arguendo,* that Indiana substantive law does not apply in this case, the Court next considers the issues under Swiss law. Under Swiss law, a purchaser of stolen property acquires title superior to that of the original owner only if he purchases the property in good faith. Tr. 19 (von Mehren). A bad faith purchaser of stolen property never acquires title. *Id.* at 20. As Professor von Mehren explained at trial, to conclude that a purchaser did not act in good faith, a court must *either* find that the purchaser actually knew that the seller lacked title, *or* find that "an honest and careful purchaser in the particular circumstances would have [had] doubts with respect to the capacity of the seller to transfer property rights." *Id.* at 24.

Swiss law presumes that a purchaser acts in good faith. *Id.* at 26. However, a plaintiff seeking to reclaim stolen property may overcome this presumption. *Id.* To do so he must show that suspicious circumstances surrounded the transaction which should have caused an honest and reasonably prudent purchaser to doubt the seller's capacity to convey property rights. *Id.* If the plaintiff shows that the circumstances surrounding the transaction should have created such doubt, then the defendant purchaser has the burden of establishing his good faith. A purchaser establishes his good faith by showing that he took steps to inquire into the seller's capacity to convey property rights and that such steps reasonably resolved such doubt. *Id.*

1. *Suspicious Circumstances*

As previously set forth, under Swiss law, this Court must begin its analysis by presuming that Goldberg purchased the mosaics in good faith. The plaintiffs argue that they have overcome this presumption by showing that suspicious circumstances surrounded the sale of the mosaics sufficient to cause an honest and reasonably prudent purchaser in Goldberg's position to doubt whether Dikman had the capacity to convey property rights. Therefore, plaintiffs contend, Goldberg cannot rest on the presumption that she purchased the mosaics in good faith. The Court agrees.

Many suspicious circumstances surrounded the sale of the mosaics. First, Goldberg knew the mosaics came from an area occupied by foreign military forces.

Second, the very nature of the items for sale warranted that a potential purchaser should proceed with caution.

Third, a vast disparity existed between the appraised value of the mosaics and the price Goldberg paid for them. Goldberg paid $1.08 million, in cash, for the mosaics; six months later, she offered to sell them to the Getty Museum for $20 million.

Fourth, Goldberg knew very little about the seller, Aydin Dikman.[12] Everything she knew about Dikman she learned from middlemen: Fitzgerald, van Rijn, and Faulk. She was told that Dikman was a Moslem Turk attempting to sell Christian mosaics from northern Cyprus. She was also told that Dikman "found" the mosaics while he was employed as "an archaeologist from Turkey assigned to northern Cyprus." Tr. at 456. The Court believes that a reasonable purchaser would have found it peculiar that a Turkish archaeologist would be in the business of selling Cypriot antiquities.

Fifth, the case of characters acting as middlemen, namely, Michel van Rijn, Ronald Faulk, and Robert Fitzgerald, were themselves suspect. Goldberg knew very little about Michel van Rijn; she first met him on July 1, 1988, or six days before the sale was consummated. She did know, however, that he was a felon. Goldberg testified that at the time of the sale she knew van Rijn had been convicted in France for art forgery. She also knew that van Rijn was being sued by an art gallery for "[f]ailure to pay money." Next, Goldberg knew very little about Ronald Faulk. She knew only that he was an attorney from California and that he was representing Fitzgerald and van Rijn in this transaction.[13] Goldberg was, however, familiar with Robert Fitzgerald, the principal middleman. She "had known him casually for several years." Tr. 533. She knew, for example, that in the past Fitzgerald had used the names Robert Jones, Robert Jones-Fitzgerald, and Robert Fitzgerald-Jones. Tr. 533. She also knew that Fitzgerald had been sued for his involvement in a transaction involving a purported Michelangelo modello. Tr. 323–24, 433–35. In addition, Goldberg knew that all three middlemen were to profit financially from the sale of the mosaics.

---

12. Goldberg was not told the identity of the seller at her initial meeting with van Rijn and Fitzgerald on July 1, 1988. It was not until July 3rd that she was told the seller was a man named Aydin Dikman.

13. Attorney Faulk did not represent, nor claim to represent, Goldberg in this transaction.

Finally, the haste with which the transaction was carried out raises suspicions. Goldberg first learned of the mosaics on July 1, 1988. On July 4th, she signed a contract with the three middlemen to divide the mosaics' resale profits. Later on July 4th Goldberg traveled from Amsterdam to Geneva. There she inspected the mosaics on July 5th. The sale was consummated on July 7th. On July 8th, the mosaics were on an airplane to the United States. The rush with which this sale took place raises suspicions.

Goldberg made only a cursory inquiry into the suspicious circumstances surrounding the sale of the mosaics. Therefore, the Court concludes that Goldberg's inquiry was deficient in resolving doubts as to Dikman's capacity to convey property rights to the mosaics.

In summary, the Court concludes that suspicious circumstances surrounded the sale of the mosaics which should have caused an honest and reasonably prudent purchaser to doubt whether Dikman had the capacity to convey property rights. Further, the Court concludes that Goldberg, in making only a cursory inquiry into Dikman's capacity to convey property rights to the mosaics, failed to take reasonable steps to resolve that doubt. Goldberg did not purchase the mosaics in good faith.

ORDER

This case came before the Court for trial to determine possession of the mosaics at issue in this case. Whereupon the Court, having heard and reviewed the evidence and having reviewed the briefs and submissions of counsel, and being duly advised in the premises, hereby concludes that possession of the mosaics should be awarded to the plaintiff, the Autocephalous Greek-Orthodox Church of Cyprus.

THEREFORE, IT IS ORDERED, ADJUDGED, AND DECREED that possession of the mosaics at issue in this case is awarded to the plaintiff, the Autocephalous Greek-Orthodox Church of Cyprus.

IT IS SO ORDERED.

NOTE

See L. Pinkerton and N. E. Palmer, *Restitution of Looted Antiquities,* 15 INTERNATIONAL LEGAL PRACTITIONER 30 (1990).

13/Title by Discovery

A. GERMANY

1. Case: *The Lübeck Coins*

BGH Judgment of January 20, 1988
41 NJW 1204 (1988)
OWNERSHIP OF TREASURE TROVE

FACTS

On June 5, 1984, during demolition operations in the Old City of Lübeck, 23,200 gold and silver coins from the 14th and 15th century were discovered on the site of premises belonging to the defendant state (*Land*). The owners could not be located. The parties have a dispute regarding the ownership of the treasure. On May 10, 1984, the defendant state contracted with K Company for demolition of the buildings. The provisions of the demolition contract included among other terms the VOB/B,[1] as well as a List of Specifications which included the following terms in its introduction.

> 'The principal contractor reserves to itself the right to mark and appropriate all construction materials and objects which possess value as historical monuments or for future construction. These building materials or objects are to be declared and stored separately. All other building and scrap materials as well as junk found in the buildings become the property of the contractor and are to be removed immediately as he sees fit."

According to its demolition contract, K Company was obligated to incorporate the terms of the VOB/B in any contracts with its subcontractors. On May 10, 1984, K Company transferred demolition operations in turn to Plaintiff 3 as a subcontractor, of which Plaintiff 2 is the sole manager. Plaintiff 3 engaged Plaintiff 1 under a labor

---

1. Verdingungsordnung für Bauleistungen Teil B: Allgemeine Vertragsbedingungen für die Ausführung von Bauleistungen DIN 1961 (General Conditions for the Execution of Construction Contracts according to German Industrial Standards 1961).

contract from May 23 until late July 1984 as a dredger and front-loading truck driver. He was assigned with others to the demolition operations for the defendant state. As he was about to break up the floor-base and foundation with a crane shovel, to remove it and to load it for removal, he exposed part of the coins hidden there.

He left the crane shovel in order to examine them more closely and then communicated his observations by radio to his employer at her office. Plaintiff 2, having picked up the radio conversation in his car, appeared shortly thereafter at the construction site. He too viewed the coins and ordered work to be suspended at the site. Shortly afterwards, staff-workers from the Bureau for Pre- and Early History of the defendant state, who had been notified, secured the coins, which have since remained in the defendant state's possession.

Plaintiff 1 claims a half-interest in the treasure as discoverer, and demands information from the defendant concerning the value of the treasure as well as a declaration of his co-ownership. Plaintiffs 2 and 3 claim full ownership as the discoverers and the owners under BGB § 984. The district court granted Plaintiff l's complaint and dismissed the complaints by Plaintiffs 2 & 3.

The appellate court rejected the appeal of Plaintiffs 2 & 3 from the judgment in favor of Plaintiff 1 as inadmissible to the extent that it concerned the property in the coins in the value of DM 50,000 and additionally dismissed the appeals of Plaintiffs 2 & 3 — also limited to DM 50,000 — as well as the appeal of the defendant State. The petition for review by Plaintiffs 2 & 3 (limited to the values asserted in the appeals below) and by the defendant state were unsuccessful.

REASONS

A. According to § 984 BGB, upon discovery and seizure of a treasure, ownership of half belongs to the discoverer ('The Discoverer's Share'), while ownership of the other half belongs to the owner of the property where the treasure was hidden ('The Owner's Share').

1. In the principal proceedings, Plaintiff 1 and defendant state have a dispute relating to the discoverer's share. Count 2 of the complaint demanding a declaration of plaintiff's right to one-half of the treasure is based on the contention that he alone is the discoverer. Count 1 demanding information regarding the total treasure's value serves only as preparation of the demand for the desired declaratory judgment determining the relative rights of the parties.

The discoverer's share is also claimed by Plaintiffs 2 & 3; they assert their claims by way of principal intervention pursuant to § 64 Code of Civil Procedure [ZPO], interposing complaints against Plaintiff 1 (complaint for a negative declaratory judgment) and against defendant state (complaint for delivery and preparatory complaint for information).

2. The owner's share is in dispute only between Plaintiffs 2 & 3 and defendant state. These parties accordingly claim the entire treasure for themselves. Plaintiffs 2

and 3 join their additional claim against defendant state for delivery of the owner's share — after previous information — with their complaint in principal intervention, by way of objective cumulation of claims (according to § 260 ZPO).

B. The Discoverer's Share

The district court considered Plaintiff 1 the discoverer and accordingly granted his claims in his action against the defendant state in the principal proceedings, while dismissing the complaints of Plaintiffs 2 & 3 against Plaintiff 1 and the defendant state in the intervention proceedings.

I. The appellate court rejected Plaintiffs 2 & 3's appeals against the dismissal of their action against Plaintiff 1 in the (Intervention-) suit, as untimely. Review by this court reveals no error.

[A lengthy discussion of this procedural point follows]

II. The lower court justified its rejection of the defendant state's appeal and of Plaintiffs 2 & 3's appeal against it as follows: Plaintiff 1 is the only discoverer of the treasure (§ 984 BGB), because he uncovered it at least in part with his crane shovel and was the first to observe it. The court considered this sufficient, because the direct result of his activity was that staff-workers from the Bureau for Pre- and Early History recovered and took possession of the entire treasure.

By virtue of this taking into possession, resulting from his discovery, the court found that Plaintiff 1 became owner of the discoverer's share. Conversely, neither the defendant state, as contractor for the demolition, nor Plaintiffs 2 & 3 as Plaintiff 1's employers were to be considered the discoverers. The circumstance that the discovery of a treasure was more likely at any demolition in the Old Quarter than elsewhere was thought to be irrelevant. What took place here was not a planned and systematic treasure hunt in which the defendant state might be seen as the originator or the Plaintiffs 2 & 3 as the discoverers by virtue of their direction. Rather, Plaintiff 1 found the treasure only by accident, and on the occasion of work on the accomplishment of another objective, namely the demolition of a building. The lower court doubted whether Plaintiffs 2 & 3 would have been deemed to be discoverers of the treasure, on the basis of their and the defendant state's alleged instructions to all co-workers that they were to search for objects of value and therefore for treasure, or at least to see to it that the objects would be recovered and delivered to them. In any event, the court found that such instructions were not proved. Had they been issued, they would not have been directed to Plaintiff 1 and would not have referred to this type of work — removing the floor-base and the foundation with a loading truck, during which Plaintiff 1 unearthed the treasure. Actually, there was no evidence that Plaintiff 3's employees had been following such instructions.

Whether agreements had been concluded between Plaintiff 3 and the defendant state, on the basis of which the defendant state was to be considered the discoverer or which would require Plaintiff 3 to surrender any treasure found during demolition work, could remain open, because restrictions on the rights of, or imposition of duties on Plaintiff 1 could only be arrived at through agreements with him. Such arguments, however, were lacking. There were no contractual relationships between him and the defendant state. Similarly, a duty on the part of Plaintiff 1 to surrender the treasure to Plaintiff 3 resulted neither from his employment nor from existing usage.

The attacks against these determinations made in Plaintiffs 2 & 3's petition for revision interposed against the defendant state, as well as the defendant state's petition for revision, are without success.

1. Petition for revision interposed by Plaintiffs 2 & 3:

a) There was no legal error in the appellate court's holding that the coins discovered during demolition operations were indeed a treasure (BGB § 984), that was first unearthed and observed by Plaintiff 1 and in consequence thereof taken into possession by staff-workers from the Bureau for Pre- and Early History. In that respect the petition for revision raises no questions. Therefore, the legal prerequisites for acquisition of a half share of the property in the treasure (the Discoverer's share) per se are met. In that situation, Plaintiffs 2 & 3 could acquire ownership only under special circumstances, on the basis of which, according to business practice, not Plaintiff 1 but Plaintiffs 2 & 3 are to be considered as the discoverers.

b) This, the petition for revision contends, is the case here, because Plaintiff 1 exposed the treasure in the course of work within the scope of his employment relationship with Plaintiff 3, and therefore, according to the allegations of Plaintiffs 2 & 3, like the other employees assigned to the demolition work, had been instructed to watch for valuable objects, including treasures, and to recover and deliver them.

The petition for revision cannot succeed on this point. To be sure, as is correctly pointed out by petitioners, it is generally recognized, in accordance with the judgment of the Reichsgericht 70 RGZ, 308 (310) in that respect, in a planned and directed treasure hunt, according to general business practice, the 'discoverer' within the meaning of § 984 BGB is not the employee who actually finds the treasure, but the employer as manager and director of the venture. (Palandt-Bassenge, BGB, § 984 n.1; Erman-Hefermehl BGB § 984, marginal note 7; Staudinger-Gursky, BGB § 984, marginal note 2; Staudinger-Berg BGB § 984, marginal note 2; Pikart in RGRK, 12 ed. § 984 n. 2; Plank-Brodmann BGB 984 n. 2a; OH in AK, § 984, marginal note 1; Biermann, SachenR, 3 ed. § 984 n. 2a; Baur, SachenR § 53g VI 2 = S. 528; Westermann, SachenR, § 60, marginal note 2 = S. 298; Wolff-Raiser SachenR § 83 III lb = S. 317.) But this was not the case here. Plaintiff 3 is a demolition contractor and the purpose of the job in which Plaintiff 1 was also employed, was demolition of a building. This is not changed by Plaintiff 3's assertion that during demolition work, an eye is regularly kept out for reuseable wood, precious metals, old bricks and other things of value, that these things are segregated, because their sale constitutes a part of its revenue and that this was also true in this case. But consistently, this relates to things which belong to the owner of a house which is to be demolished and which the owner perhaps leaves to the demolition contractor to appropriate, and not to treasures, i.e. things which have been hidden for so long that their owner can no longer be identified (BGB § 984). According to the unchallenged findings of the appellate court, none of the parties involved even suspected that a treasure might be hidden in the house which was to be demolished. Rather, as the appellate court also found — likewise without challenge — the discovery of the treasure occurred only accidentally on the occasion of demolition activity.

The question who acquires the discoverer's share if the employee uncovers and observes a treasure not as part of a planned and directed treasure hunt but accidentally on the occasion of demolition operations has been the object of different answers.

Some text writers would assign discovery of the treasure to the employer even in this case (citations omitted). Conversely, a widely held view considers the employee as discoverer when the treasure is found in the course of a dependent activity (citations omitted). This view also forms the basis of two additional decisions of the Reichsgericht concerning treasure trove (RG SeuffA 51, 12 [14]; RG SoergelRspr 1913, BGB § 984 Nr. 1).

Apart from such clearly exceptional cases as the organized treasure hunt, it is the view of the Senate that ordinarily the employee who finds a treasure within the framework of activities undertaken for his employer is himself to be considered to be the discoverer within the meaning of § 984 BGB. Since discovery of treasures is extremely rare and therefore does not belong to the purposes of an enterprise with a division of labor, the unusual and accidental discovery by an employee, under a natural analysis, cannot be connected with his activities in the enterprise which his employment contract imposes upon him and therefore cannot be attributed to the employer.

This factor constitutes the difference from cases of processing by an employee of goods belonging to a third person, which cases are invoked by the petition for revision. In such cases property in the new product is acquired not by the employee, but by the employer (entrepreneur) according to § 950 BGB. The reason for this result is the fact that the processing of the goods of a third person is the object of the duties of the employee pursuant to his labor contract and that therefore, according to popular notions, the owner of the production process who manufactures new products by means of a labor force subject to his instruction is considered to be the 'manufacturer' within the meaning of BGB § 950 (BGH, NJW, 1952, 661 [662]; 20 BGHZ 159 [164]). These cases are at best comparable to an organized and directed treasure hunt with employment of an auxiliary labor force, which was not the situation in the case at bar.

2. *The Petition for Revision by the Defendant State*

In the view of the petitioner, the defendant state must be considered to be the discoverer of the treasure within the meaning of § 984 BGB, because it was discovered during the demolition operations and it was the defendant state that promoted the decisive cause by awarding the demolition contract. That this view is incorrect already follows in large measure from the exposition in B II 1. If, as was explained in detail in that portion of the opinion, the mere circumstances, that the treasure was found within the framework of an employment relation is insufficient to attribute the discovery to the employer, then a fortiori, the fact that the employer is a contractor and that the employment relation serves the performance of the contract with the person ordering the work, cannot suffice to consider the latter as the discoverer. With the award of a discoverer's share, § 984 intended, as the appellate court correctly explained, to reward that person whose activities rescued the treasure from concealment and restored it to human use. (RG, SeuffA 51, 12 [14]; RGZ 70, 308 [311]; the owner who awards a construction contract is still further removed from the discovery of a treasure by an employee than the contractor himself).

The specifications included in the demolition contract between the defendant state with Firm K providing that objects of historic or scientific value are to be delivered by the contractor to the owner and that the owner has the rights of a discoverer under § 984 do not alter this result. This holds true even if for the benefit of the defendant state it must be assumed that these provisions are also part of the contract between Firm K and Plaintiff 3 as the subcontractor. The attempt by petitioner to draw a parallel between these provisions and the situation under the processing agreement does not lead to a more favorable result. True, it is recognized especially in decisions of this Senate, that in such cases the person ordering the processing or the supplier of materials furnished under reservation of title may become the owner of the processed goods. But this is subject to the condition that the processing took place in a manner as was contemplated and provided in the processing agreement or in stipulation of the reservation of title, BGHZ 20, 159, 164. If this prerequisite is lacking, then no processing for the benefit of a third party is present, with the result that the product of the processing cannot be attributed to the employer or even less to the third party who had contracted with him with regard to the processing. This means in the case at bar: The Condition for the allocation of the Discoverer's share to the defendant state is that the treasure, although uncovered and first noted by Plaintiff 1, can be attributed to a third person as discoverer, such as Plaintiff 3 as his employer, or — by way of the employer — to the defendant state by reason of its agreements with Plaintiff 3. However, as discussed supra in Nr. 1 of this opinion, this would be conceivable only if agreements had been concluded with Plaintiff 1 regarding the discovery and delivery of a found treasure or if he had been subject to directions to that effect. This was not done — neither through Plaintiff 3, his employer, nor by the defendant state.

Therefore it is not possible to consider the defendant state as discoverer nor can it be a defense against the claim of Plaintiff 1 for information and declaration that Plaintiff 3 may have assumed a duty vis-à-vis the defendant state to deliver the treasure to it.

C. The Owner's Share

In the controversy about the owner's share, the appellate court gives the following reasons for rejecting the appeal by Plaintiffs 2 & 3 from the judgment for defendant state:

> "According to the arguments of Plaintiff 3, the treasure of coins was hidden in the floor-base and foundation of the building. Until the lifting of these parts by the crane-shovel, the floor-base and the foundation were essential components of the building and therefore within the ownership of the defendant state which was also owner of the premises. The title to the structure to be demolished did not pass to Plaintiff 3 by the delivery of the keys; this argument is precluded by §§ 93, 94 BGB. To be sure, upon the removal of the floor-base and foundation by the crane shovel, Plaintiff 3, by virtue of its power of appropriation included in the contractual specifications became the owner of the separated materials pursuant to § 956 BGB. Nevertheless, even if a portion of the coins were located in the removed parts of the floor-base and foundation, it cannot be said that these demolished pieces were a thing hiding a treasure, since at that time, the coins were no longer hidden. It was, as Plaintiff 3 argues, uncovered through the removal by means of the crane shovel, which 'opened up' the foundation. This follows also from the fact that the coins in the crane-shovel were noted by Plaintiff 1 and therefore were visible. The uncovering of the treasure or at least a portion of it was accomplished at the time of the separation of the building parts. It also would be unrealistic and artificial if, during the unitary and brief span of recovery and discovery, first the building parts which were firmly connected with the soil and subsequently the separated and loaded parts were to be considered as objects hiding the treasure. Under any natural analysis, the brief and temporary interval during which the separated parts rested in the crane shovel could hardly be compared with the original hiding place that concealed the treasure effectively for centuries from observation."

These statements likewise are attacked by the petition for revision without success. It claims that the appellate court overlooked that the treasure was not discovered at the time of the separation of the building parts. The appellate court had failed to ascertain exactly when Plaintiff 1 first noted the coins. According to the contentions of Plaintiffs 2 & 3 and of Plaintiff 1, which form the point of departure in the instance of revision, Plaintiff 1 noted the coins only after the turning of the shovel containing the previously separated and lifted building fragments. At that time, however, the fragments on the loader had passed into the ownership of Plaintiff 3. This is incorrect. The petition fails to recognize that in a dispute relating to the owner's share, the moment when the treasure was noted is irrelevant. The uncovering which terminates the state of concealment and the first observation of the treasure are not necessarily simultaneous. (Staudinger-Gursky, BGB § 984, marginal note 1 with further references.) The decisive criterion for the allocation of the owner's share is the ownership of the thing in which the treasury 'was' hidden (BGB § 984), i.e. in which the treasure was located until its exposure. In this case this is the defendant state as the owner of the not yet 'opened' foundation and the not yet lifted floor-base of the building. The finding of the appellate court that the opening of the foundation and the lifting of parts of the floor-base and the foundation terminated the concealment of the treasure and exposed the same is not attacked by the petition for review; nor does it reveal any error.

Table of Cases

Table of Statutes

E

F

M

N

O

P

Index

D

E

F

G

R

S